PUBLISHER COMMENTARY

The Economic Report of the President – 2019 Volume 2

The Economic Report of the President is an annual report written by the Chairman of the Council of Economic Advisers. It overviews the nation's economic progress using text and extensive data appendices.

In order to make this report easier to read, we enlarged the size to 8 ½ by 11 inches. To keep the cost down and make the weight a little more manageable, we put the References and Appendices in Volume 2. The ePub is complete and you get the ePub FREE when you purchase Volume 1 of this paperback through Amazon.com under the Matchbook Program.

We are releasing a print of this book because we feel this is a critically important discussion and want to make sure the report reaches the widest possible audience.

Why buy a book you can download for free? We print this book so you don't have to.

Some books are only available on line, so you gotta print your own if you want hard copy (paper). We look over each document carefully and replace poor quality images. We proof each document to make sure it's all there – including all changes. You could print it using a network printer you share with 100 other people (typically the network printer is jammed, its out of paper or out of toner). If it's just a 10-page document, no problem, but if it's 200+ pages, you will need to punch 3 holes in all those pages and put them in a 3-ring binder. Takes at least an hour.

It's much more cost-effective to just order the latest version from Amazon.com

This book includes original artwork and commentary which is the only copyright material. Note that government documents are in the public domain. We print these large documents <u>as a service</u> so you don't have to. Although originally intended to be 6 by 9 inches, we enlarged it to 8 ½ by 11 inches so it is easier to read and you can write notes in the margins.

Buy the paperback from Amazon and get Kindle eBook FREE using MATCHBOOK. Go to https://usgovpub.com to learn how.

Copyright © 2019 – 4th Watch Publishing Co. All Rights Reserved

Other books we print on Amazon.com:

Prosecuting Intellectual Property Crimes
Prosecuting Computer Crimes
Criminal Resource Manual (CRM) 2019
Civil Resource Manual (2019)
Justice Manual (JM) 2019
Treasury Antitrust Division Manual (2017)
Rules of the Supreme Court of the United States (Effective November 13, 2017)
Naval Legal Service Command Manual (2013)
Budget of the United States Government, Fiscal Year 2020
Federal Rules of Appellate Procedure (2017)
Federal Rules of Criminal Procedure (2017)
Federal Rules of Civil Procedure (2017)
Federal Rules of Bankruptcy Procedure (2017)
Benchbook for U.S. District Court Judges (2013)
Military Judges' Benchbook (2017)
Principles of Federal Appropriations Law 4th Edition
Immigration Court Practice Manual
DoD Law of War Manual (2016)
DoD Operational Law Handbook (2017)
DoD Domestic Operational Law Handbook (2015 DOPLAW)
DoD Rule of Law Handbook (2015)
Uniform Code of Military Justice (2018)
Manual for Courts-Martial (2019)
DoD Commander's Legal Handbook (2015)
The Military Commander and the Law (2017)
U.S. Courts Design Guide + Standard Level Features and Finishes
GSA Courtroom Technology Manual
Title 26 - Internal Revenue Code (Section 1 - 59) 2018 release
GAO Government Auditing Standards 2018 Final (Yellow Book)
GAO Standards for Internal Control in the Federal Government (Green Book)
United States Sentencing Commission Guidelines Manual
U.S. Senate Manual
Rules of the House of Representatives
U.S. House Practice
Criminal Law Deskbook
Law of Federal Employment
Fiscal Law Deskbook
Contract Attorneys Deskbook

Visit usgovpub.com

References

Chapter 1

Abel, A. 1983. "Optimal Investment under Uncertainty." *American Economic Review* 73, no. 1: 228–33.

Alstadsaeter, A., M. Jacob, and R. Michaely. 2017. "Do Dividend Taxes Affect Corporate Investment?" *Journal of Public Economics* 151: 74–83.

Arulampalam, W., M. Devereux, and G. Maffini. 2012. "The Direct Incidence of Corporate Income Tax on Wages." *European Economic Review* 56, no. 6: 1038–54.

Asness, C., T. Hazelkorn, and S. Richardson. 2018. "Buyback Derangement Syndrome." *Journal of Portfolio Management* 44, no. 5: 50–57.

Auerbach, A. 1979. "Wealth Maximization and the Cost of Capital." *Quarterly Journal of Economics* 93, no. 3: 433–46.

Auerbach, A., and K. Hassett. 1992. "Tax Policy and Business Fixed Investment in the United States." *Journal of Public Economics* 47, no. 2: 141–70.

———. 2002. "On the Marginal Source of Investment Funds." *Journal of Public Economics* 87, no. 1: 205–32.

Averett, S., H. Peters, and D. Waldman. 1997. "Tax Credits, Labor Supply, and Child Care." *Review of Economics and Statistics* 79, no. 1: 125–35.

Bar-Ilan, A., and W. Strange. 1996. "Investment Lags." *American Economic Review* 86, no. 3: 610–22.

Barro, R., and J. Furman. 2018. "Macroeconomic Effects of the 2017 Tax Reform." *Brookings Papers on Economic Activity*, Spring, 257–345.

Barro, R., and C. Redlick. 2011. "Macroeconomic Effects from Government Purchases and Taxes." *Quarterly Journal of Economics* 126, no.1: 51–102.

Barth, E., A. Bryson, J. Davis, and R. Freeman. 2016. "It's Where You Work: Increases in Earnings Dispersion across Establishments and Individuals in the U.S." *Journal of Labor Economics* 34, no. S2 (part 2): S67–S97.

BEA (Bureau of Economic Analysis). 2018. "U.S. Direct Investment Abroad (USDIA)." https://www.bea.gov/index.php/help/glossary/us-direct-investment-abroad-usdia.

Bilicka, K., and M. Devereux. 2012. *CBT Corporate Tax Ranking 2012*. Oxford: Oxford University Centre for Business Taxation.

Blanchard, O., and R. Perotti. 2002. "An Empirical Characterization of the Dynamic Effects of Changes in Government Spending and Taxes on Output." *Quarterly Journal of Economics* 117, no. 4: 1329–68.

Blau, D., and P. Robins. 1989. "Fertility, Employment, and Child-Care Costs." *Demography* 26, no. 2: 287–99.

Blouin, J., and L. Krull. 2009. "Bringing It Home: A Study of the Incentives Surrounding the Repatriation of Foreign Earnings under the American Jobs Creation Act of 2004." *Journal of Accounting Research* 47, no. 4: 1027–59.

Bradford, D. 1981. "The Incidence and Allocation Effects of a Tax on Corporate Distributions." *Journal of Public Economics* 15, no.1: 1–22.

Brav, A., J. Graham, C. Harvey, and R. Michaely. 2005. "Payout Policy in the 21st Century." *Journal of Financial Economics* 77, no. 3: 483–527.

Brennan, M., and A. Thakor. 1990. "Shareholder Preferences and Dividend Policy." *Journal of Finance* 45, no. 4: 993–1018.

Business Roundtable. 2018. "Business Roundtable CEO Economic Outlook Index Reaches Highest Level in Survey's 15-Year History." https://www.businessroundtable.org/about-us/ceo-economic-outlook-index/ceo-survey-q1-2018.

Caballero, R. 1991. "On the Sign of the Investment Uncertainty Relationship." *American Economic Review* 81, no. 1: 279–88.

Caballero, R., E. Engel, and J. Haltiwanger. 1995. "Plant-Level Adjustment and Aggregate Investment Dynamics." *Brookings Papers on Economic Activity* 26, no. 2: 1–54.

Caldara, D., and C. Kamps. 2017. "The Analytics of SVARs: A Unified Framework to Measure Fiscal Multipliers." *Review of Economic Studies* 84, no. 3: 1015–40.

Card, D., A. Cardoso, J. Heining, and P. Kline. 2018. "Firms and Labor Market Inequality: Evidence and Some Theory." *Journal of Labor Economics* 36, no. S1: S13–S70.

CEA (Council of Economic Advisers). 2017a. "Corporate Tax Reform and Wages: Theory and Evidence." https://www.whitehouse.gov/sites/whitehouse.gov/files/documents/Tax%20Reform%20and%20Wages.pdf.

———. 2017b. "Evaluating the Anticipated Effects of Changes to the Mortgage Interest Deduction." https://www.whitehouse.gov/sites/whitehouse.gov/files/images/Effects%20of%20Changes%20to%20the%20Mortgage%20Interest%20Deduction%20FINAL.pdf.

———. 2018. "Taxes and Growth." In *Economic Report of the President*. Washington: U.S. Government Publishing Office.

Chetty, R., and E. Saez. 2005. "Dividend Taxes and Corporate Behavior: Evidence from the 2003 Dividend Tax Cut." *Quarterly Journal of Economics* 120, no. 3: 791–833.

Clausing, K. 2018. "Profit Shifting Before and After the Tax Cuts and Jobs Act." Unpublished paper. https://papers.ssrn.com/sol3/papers.cfm?abstract_id=3274827.

Cochrane, J. 2018. "Stock Buybacks Are Proof of Tax Reform's Success." *Wall Street Journal*, March 5. https://www.wsj.com/articles/stock-buybacks-are-proof-of-tax-reforms-success-1520292384.

Cummins, J., and K. Hassett. 1992. "The Effects of Taxation on Investment: New Evidence from Firm Level Panel Data." *National Tax Journal* 45, no. 3: 243–51.

Cummins, J., K. Hassett, and R. Hubbard. 1996. "Tax Reforms and Investment: A Cross-Country Comparison." *Journal of Public Economics* 62, nos. 1–2: 237–73.

Cummins, J., K. Hassett, R. Hubbard, and R. Hall. 1994. "A Reconsideration of Investment Behavior Using Tax Reforms as Natural Experiments." *Brookings Papers on Economic Activity* 25, no. 2: 1–74.

Cummins, J., K. Hassett, and S. Oliner. 2006. "Investment Behavior, Observable Expectations, and Internal Funds." *American Economic Review* 96, no. 3: 796–810.

De Long, J., and L. Summers. 1992. "Macroeconomic Policy and Long-Run Growth." Paper presented at Symposium on Policies for Long-Run Growth, sponsored by Federal Reserve Bank of Kansas City, Jackson Hole, WY, August 27–29. https://www.kansascityfed.org/publicat/sympos/1992/s92long.pdf.

Desai, M., C. Foley, and J. Hines. 2016. "Trade Credit and Taxes." *Review of Economics and Statistics* 98, no. 1: 132–39.

Desai, M., and A. Goolsbee. 2004. "Investment, Overhang, and Tax Policy." *Brookings Papers on Economic Activity*, no. 2: 285–355.

Devereux, M., R. Griffith, and A. Klemm. 2002. "Corporate Income Tax: Reforms and Competition." *Economic Policy* 17, no. 35: 451–95.

Dharmapala, D., C. Foley, and K. Forbes. 2011. "Watch What I Do, Not What I Say: The Unintended Consequences of the Homeland Investment Act." *Journal of Finance* 66, no. 3: 753–87.

Dittmar, A. 2000. "Why Do Firms Repurchase Stock?" *Journal of Business* 73, no. 3: 331–55.

Dittmar, A., and J. Mahrt-Smith. 2007. "Corporate Governance and the Value of Cash Holdings." *Journal of Financial Economics* 83, no. 3: 599–634.

Djankov, S., T. Ganser, C. McLiesh, R. Ramalho, and A. Shleifer. 2010. "The Effect of Corporate Taxes on Investment and Entrepreneurship." *American Economic Journal: Macroeconomics* 2, no. 3: 31–64.

Dwenger, N. 2014. "User Cost of Capital Revisited." *Economica* 81, no. 321: 161–86.

Dyreng, S., and R. Hills. 2018. "Foreign Earnings Repatriations and Domestic Employment." Working paper, Duke University. http://tax.unc.edu/wp-content/uploads/2018/04/Foreign-Earnings-Repatriations-and-Domestic-Employment.pdf.

Eisner, R., and M. Nadiri. 1968. "Investment Behavior and Neo-classical Theory." *Review of Economics and Statistics* 50, no. 3: 369–82.

Faulkender, M., and M. Petersen. 2012. "Investment and Capital Constraints: Repatriations under the American Jobs Creation Act." *Review of Financial Studies* 25, no. 11: 3351–88.

Favero, C., and F. Giavazzi. 2012. "Measuring Tax Multipliers: The Narrative Method in Fiscal VARs." *American Economic Journal: Economic Policy* 4, no. 2: 69–94.

Feldman, R. 2002. "Mortgage Rates, Homeownership Rates, and Government-Sponsored Enterprises." *Federal Reserve Bank of Minneapolis: The Region* 16: 5–23.

Fernald, J., R. Hall, J. Stock, and M. Watson. 2017. "The Disappointing Recovery of Output after 2009." Working paper, Brookings Institution. https://www.brookings.edu/wp-content/uploads/2017/08/fernaldtextsp17bpea.pdf.

Fried, J., and C. Wang. 2018. "Are Buybacks Really Shortchanging Investment?" *Harvard Business Review*, March–April, 88–95.

Gale W., H. Gelfond, A. Krupkin, M. Mazur, and E. Toder. 2018. "Effects of the Tax Cuts and Jobs Act: A Preliminary Analysis." Working paper, Tax Policy Center, Urban Institute, and Brookings Institution. https://www.brookings.edu/wp-content/uploads/2018/06/ES_20180608_tcja_summary_paper_final.pdf.

Gale, W., and J. Scholz. 1994. *Intergenerational Transfers and the Accumulation of Wealth.* NBER Working Paper 1827. Cambridge, MA: National Bureau of Economic Research.

Giroud, X., and J. Rauh. 2018. *State Taxation and the Reallocation of Business Activity: Evidence from Establishment-Level Data.* NBER Working Paper 21534. Cambridge, MA: National Bureau of Economic Research.

Goolsbee, A. 1998. "Investment Tax Incentives, Prices, and the Supply of Capital Goods." *Quarterly Journal of Economics* 113, no.1: 121–48.

———. 2000. "The Importance of Measurement Error in the Cost of Capital." *National Tax Journal* 53, no. 2: 215–28.

———. 2004. "Taxes and the Quality of Capital." *Journal of Public Economics* 88, nos. 3–4: 519–43.

Graham, J., M. Hanlon, and T. Shevlin. 2010. "Barriers to Mobility: The Lockout Effect of U.S. Taxation of Worldwide Corporate Profits." *National Tax Journal* 63, no. 4: 1111–44.

Grullon, G., and R. Michaely. 2004. "The Information Content of Share Repurchase Programs." *Journal of Finance* 59, no. 2: 651–80.

Guay, W., and J. Harford. 2000. "The Cash-Flow Permanence and Information Content of Dividend Increases Versus Repurchases." *Journal of Financial Economics* 57, no. 3: 385–415.

Guvenen, F., R. Mataloni, D. Rassier, and K. Ruhl. 2017. *Offshore Profit Shifting and Domestic Productivity Measurement.* NBER Working Paper 23324. Cambridge, MA: National Bureau of Economic Research.

Haan, P., and K. Wrohlich. 2011. "Can Child Care Policy Encourage Employment and Fertility? Evidence from a Structural Model." *Labour Economics* 18, no. 4: 498–512.

Hall, R., and D. Jorgenson. 1967. "Tax Policy and Investment Behavior." *American Economic Review* 57: 391–414.

Hanlon, M., J. Hoopes, and J. Slemrod. 2018. *Tax Reform Made Me Do It!* NBER Working Paper 23324. Cambridge, MA: National Bureau of Economic Research.

Hartman, R. 1972. "The Effects of Price and Cost Uncertainty on Investment." *Journal of Economic Theory* 5, no. 2: 258–66.

Herrick, A. 2018. "Estimates of TCJA Repatriation of Foreign Earnings on Investment and GDP." Issues paper for Penn-Wharton Budget Model. http://budgetmodel.wharton.upenn.edu/issues/2018/8/29/estimates-of-tcja-repatriation-of-foreign-earnings-on-investment-and-gdp.

Hines, J. 2010. "Treasure Islands." *Journal of Economic Perspectives* 4, no. 24: 103-1–25.

Hines, J., and E. Rice. 1994. "Fiscal Paradise: Foreign Tax Havens and American Business." *Quarterly Journal of Economics* 109, no. 1: 149–82.

Jagannathan, M., C. Stephens, and M. Weisbach. 2000. "Financial Flexibility and the Choice Between Dividends and Stock Repurchases." *Journal of Financial Economics* 57, no. 3: 355–84.

JCT (Joint Committee on Taxation). 2017. "Macroeconomic Analysis of the Conference Agreement for H.R. 1, The 'Tax Cuts and Jobs Act.'" https://www.jct.gov/publications.html?func=startdown&id=5055.

Jensen, M. 1986. "Agency Costs of Free Cash Flow, Corporate Finance, and Takeovers." *American Economic Review* 76, no. 2: 323–29.

Jorgenson, D. 1963. "Capital Theory and Investment Behavior." *American Economic Review* 53, no. 2: 247–59.

Keane, M., and R. Rogerson. 2012. "Micro and Macro Labor Supply Elasticities: A Reassessment of Conventional Wisdom." *Journal of Economic Literature* 50, no. 2: 464–79.

———. 2015. "Reconciling Micro and Macro Labor Supply Elasticities: A Structural Perspective." *Annual Review of Economics* 7: 89–117.

King, M. 1977. *Public Policy and the Corporation*. London: Chapman & Hall.

Kotlikoff, L., and L. Summers. 1981. "The Role of Intergenerational Transfers in Aggregate Capital Accumulation." *Journal of Political Economy* 89, no. 4: 706–32.

———. 1988. "The Contribution of Intergenerational Transfers to Total Wealth: A Reply." *Journal of Economic Perspectives* 2, no. 2: 41–81.

Krueger, A., and L. Summers. 1986. *Reflections on the Inter-Industry Wage Structure*. NBER Working Paper 1968. Cambridge, MA: National Bureau of Economic Research

———. 1988. "Efficiency Wages and the Inter-industry Wage Structure." *Econometrica* 56, no. 2: 259–93.

Lieberknecht, P., and V. Wieland. 2018. "On the Macroeconomic and Fiscal Effects of the Tax Cuts and Jobs Act." Paper presented at Second Research Conference of Macroeconomic Modelling and Model Comparison Network, Stanford University, Stanford, CA, June 7–8.

Mertens, K. 2018. *The Near Term Growth Impact of the Tax Cuts and Jobs Act*. Research Department Working Paper 1803. Dallas: Federal Reserve Bank of Dallas.

Mertens, K., and J. Montiel Olea. 2018. "Marginal Tax Rates and Income: New Time Series Evidence." *Quarterly Journal of Economics* 133, no. 4: 1803–84.

Mertens, K., and M. Ravn. 2012. "Empirical Evidence on the Aggregate Effects of Anticipated and Unanticipated U.S. Tax Policy Shocks." *American Economic Journal: Economic Policy* 4, no. 2: 145–81.

———. 2013. "The Dynamic Effects of Personal and Corporate Income Tax Changes in the United States." *American Economic Review* 103, no. 4: 1212–47.

———. 2014. "A Reconciliation of SVAR and Narrative Estimates of Tax Multipliers." *Journal of Monetary Economics* 68:1–19.

NAR (National Association of Realtors). 2017. "NAR Statement on Tax Reform." https://www.nar.realtor/nar-statement-on-tax-reform.

National Association of Business Economists. 2018. "Sales Strong, with Costs and Wages Rising in Second Quarter of 2018; NABE Panel Expects Additional Investment and Job Gains." https://nabe.com/NABE/Surveys/Business_Conditions_Surveys/July_2018_Business_Conditions_Survey_Summary.aspx.

Passmore, W., S. Sherlund, and G. Burgess. 2005. "The Effect of Housing Government-Sponsored Enterprises on Mortgage Rates." *Real Estate Economics* 33, no. 3: 427–63. http://citeseerx.ist.psu.edu/viewdoc/download?doi=10.1.1.454.9940&rep=rep1&type=pdf.

Phillips, R., M. Gardner, A. Robins, and M. Surka. 2017. "Offshore Shell Games 2017: The Use of Offshore Tax Havens by *Fortune* 500 Companies." https://uspirg.org/sites/pirg/files/reports/USP%20ShellGames%20Oct17%201.2.pdf.

Pomerleau, K. 2018. "A Hybrid Approach: The Treatment of Foreign Profits under the Tax Cuts and Jobs Act." Tax Foundation. https://taxfoundation.org/treatment-foreign-profits-tax-cuts-jobs-act/.

Poterba, J. 1997. *The Estate Tax and After-Tax Investment Returns.* NBER Working Paper 6337. Cambridge, MA: National Bureau of Economic Research,

Poterba, J., and T. Sinai. 2008. "Tax Expenditures for Owner-Occupied Housing: Deductions for Property Taxes and Mortgage Interest and the Exclusion of Imputed Rental Income." *American Economic Review: Papers and Proceedings* 98, no. 2: 84–89.

PwC (PricewaterhouseCoopers). 2017. "Impact of Tax Reform Options on Owner-Occupied Housing, Prepared for the National Association of Realtors." https://narfocus.com/billdatabase/clientfiles/172/21/2888.pdf.

Redmiles, M. 2008. "The One-Time Received Dividend Deduction." *Statistics of Income Bulletin*, Spring, 102–14.

Romer, C., and D. Romer. 2010. "The Macroeconomic Effects of Tax Changes: Estimates Based on a New Measure of Fiscal Shocks." *American Economic Review* 100, no. 3: 763–801.

Singh, K., and A. Mathur. 2018. *The Impact of GILTI and FDII on the Investment Location Choice of U.S. Multinationals.* Working Paper 2018-05. Washington, DC: American Enterprise Institute.

Smolyansky, M., G. Suarez, and A. Tabova. 2018. *U.S. Corporations' Repatriation of Offshore Profits*. FEDS Note. Washington: Board of Governors of the Federal Reserve System.

Song, J., D. Price, F. Guvenen, N. Bloom, and T. Wachter. 2019. "Firming Up Inequality." *Quarterly Journal of Economics* 134, no. 1: 1–50.

Whittington, L. 1992. "Taxes and the Family: The Impact of the Tax Exemption for Dependents on Marital Fertility." *Demography* 29, no.2: 215–26.

Williamson, J., and S. Bawa. 2018. *Estimated Effects of the Tax Cuts and Jobs Act on Farms and Farm Households*. Economic Research Report 252. U.S. Department of Agriculture, Economic Research Service. Washington: U.S. Government Publishing Office.

Yagan, D. 2015. "Capital Tax Reform and the Real Economy: The Effects of the 2003 Dividend Tax Cut." *American Economic Review* 105, no. 12: 3531–63.

Zion, D., R. Gomatam, and R. Graziano. 2015. "Parking A-Lot Overseas." Credit Suisse Securities Research & Analytics. https://research-doc.credit-suisse.com/docView?language=ENG&format=PDF&source_id=em&document_id=1045617491&serialid=jHde13PmaivwZHRANjglDIKxoEiA4WVARdLQREk1A7g%3d.

Zucman, G., T. Torslov, and L. Wier. 2018. *The Missing Profits of Nations*. NBER Working Paper 24701. Cambridge, MA: National Bureau of Economic Research.

Zwick, E., and J. Mahon. 2017. "Tax Policy and Heterogenous Investment Behavior." *American Economic Review* 107, no. 1: 217–48.

Chapter 2

Aldy, J. 2014. "Learning from Experience: An Assessment of the Retrospective Reviews of Agency Rules and the Evidence for Improving the Design and Implementation of Regulatory Policy." http://nrs.harvard.edu/urn-3:HUL.InstRepos:23936082.

Allcott, H., and M. Greenstone. 2012. "Is There an Energy Efficiency Gap?" *Journal of Economic Perspectives* 26, no. 1: 3–28.

Allcott, H., and C. Knittel. 2019. "Are Consumers Poorly Informed about Fuel Economy? Evidence from Two Experiments." *American Economic Journal: Economic Policy* 11, no. 1: 1–37.

Allcott, H., and D. Taubinsky. 2015. "Evaluating Behaviorally Motivated Policy: Experimental Evidence from the Lightbulb Market." *American Economic Review* 105, no. 8: 2501–38.

Allcott, H., and N. Wozny. 2014. "Gasoline Prices, Fuel Economy, and the Energy Paradox." *Review of Economics and Statistics* 96, no. 5: 779–95.

Ashley, E., C. Nardinelli, and R. Lavaty. 2015. "Estimating the Benefits of Public Health Policies That Reduce Harmful Consumption." *Health Economics* 24: 617–24.

Auerbach, A., and J. Hines Jr. 2002. "Taxation and Economic Efficiency." *Handbook of Public Economics* 3: 1347–21.

Avalere. 2018. "Association Health Plans: Projecting the Impact of the Proposed Rule." Prepared for America's Health Insurance Plans.

Ballard, C., and D. Fullerton. 1992. "Distortionary Taxes and the Provision of Public Goods." *Journal of Economic Perspectives* 6, no. 3: 117–31.

Barkume, A. 2010. "The Structure of Labor Costs with Overtime Work in U.S. Jobs." *Industrial and Labor Relations Review* 64, no. 1: 128–42.

Bauer, D. 2015. "The Misclassification of Independent Contractors: The Fifty-Four-Billion-Dollar Problem." *Rutgers Journal of Law and Public Policy* 12, no. 2: 138–78.

Becker, G., and K. Murphy. 1992. "The Division of Labor, Coordination Costs, and Knowledge." *Quarterly Journal of Economics* 107, no. 4: 1137–60.

Becker, G., K. Murphy, and M. Grossman. 2006. "The Market for Illegal Goods: The Case of Drugs." *Journal of Political Economy* 114, no. 1: 38–60.

Belfield, C., A. Bowden, and V. Rodriguez. 2018. "Evaluating Regulatory Impact Assessments in Education Policy." *American Journal of Evaluation*, 1–19.

BLS (Bureau of Labor Statistics). 2018a. "Independent Contractors Made Up 6.9 Percent of Employment in May 2017." https://www.bls.gov/opub/ted/2018/independent-contractors-made-up-6-point-9-percent-of-employment-in-may-2017.htm.

———. 2018b. "Multifactor Productivity." https://www.bls.gov/mfp/home.htm.

Blumberg, L., M. Buettgens, and R. Wang. 2018. *Updated Estimates of the Potential Impact of Short-Term, Limited Duration Policies*. Washington: Urban Institute.

Borenstein, S., and N. Rose. 2014. "How Airline Markets Work . . . or Do They? Regulatory Reform in the Airline Industry." In *Economic Regulation and Its Reform*, edited by N. Rose. Chicago: University of Chicago Press.

Breyer, S. 1993. *Breaking the Vicious Circle: Toward Effective Risk Regulation*. Cambridge, MA: Harvard University Press.

British Columbia. 2017. "Achieving a Modern Regulatory Environment: B.C.'s Regulatory Reform Initiative." Government of British Columbia. https://www2.gov.bc.ca/assets/gov/government/about-the-bc-government/regulatory-reform/pdfs/5330_regreform_ar_2017_web.pdf.

Broughel, J. 2015. "What the United States Can Learn from the European Commission's Better Regulation Initiative." *European Journal of Risk Regulation* 3: 380–81.

Busse, M., C. Knittel, and F. Zettelmeyer. 2013. "Are Consumers Myopic? Evidence from New and Used Car Purchases." *American Economic Review* 103, no. 1: 220–56.

Carey, M. 2016. "Methods of Estimating the Total Cost of Federal Regulations." https://crsreports.congress.gov/product/pdf/R/R44348.

Caves, R. 1962. *Air Transport and Its Regulators: An Industry Study*. Cambridge, MA: Harvard University Press.

CBO (Congressional Budget Office). 2017. "Federal Subsidies for Health Insurance Coverage for People Under Age 65: 2017 to 2027." https://www.cbo.gov/

———. system/files/115th-congress-2017-2018/reports/53826-healthinsurancecoverage.pdf.

———. 2018. "Federal Subsidies for Health Insurance Coverage for People Under Age 65: 2018 to 2028." https://www.cbo.gov/system/files/115th-congress-2017-2018/reports/53826-healthinsurancecoverage.pdf.

CCIIO (Center for Consumer Information and Insurance Oversight). 2011. "Essential Health Benefits Bulletin." https://www.cms.gov/CCIIO/Resources/Files/Downloads/essential_health_benefits_bulletin.pdf.

CEA (Council of Economic Advisers). 1970. *Economic Report of the President*. Washington: U.S. Government Printing Office.

———. 1980. *Economic Report of the President*. Washington: U.S. Government Printing Office.

———. 2018. *Economic Report of the President*. Washington: U.S. Government Publishing Office.

———. 2019. "Deregulating Health Insurance Markets: Value to Market Participants." https://www.whitehouse.gov/wp-content/uploads/2019/02/Deregulating-Health-Insurance-Markets-FINAL.pdf.

Cetin, T., and E. Deakin. 2017. "Regulation of Taxis and the Rise of Ridesharing." *Transport Policy*, September, 1–10.

Chetty, R. 2015. "Behavioral Economics and Public Policy: A Pragmatic Perspective." *American Economic Review* 105, no. 5: 1–33.

CMS (Centers for Medicare & Medicaid Services). 2018. "Estimated Financial Effects of the Short-Term, Limited-Duration Policy Proposed Rule." https://www.cms.gov/Research-Statistics-Data-and-Systems/Research/ActuarialStudies/Downloads/STLD20180406.pdf.

Coase, R., 1960. "The Problem of Social Cost." *Journal of Law and Economics* 3: 1–44.

Coglianese, C. 2018. "Improving Regulatory Analysis at Independent Agencies." *American University Law Review* 67: 733–67.

Cohen, P., R. Hahn, J. Hall, S. Levitt, and R. Metcalfe. 2016. *Using Big Data to Estimate Consumer Surplus: The Case of Uber*. NBER Working Paper 22627. Cambridge, MA: National Bureau of Economic Research.

Crafts, N. 2006. "Regulation and Productivity Performance." *Oxford Review of Economic Policy* 22, no. 2: 186–202.

Crain, W., and N. Crain. 2014. *The Cost of Federal Regulation to the U.S. Economy, Manufacturing, and Small Businesses*. Report for the National Association of Manufacturers. https://www.nam.org/Data-and-Reports/Cost-of-Federal-Regulations/Federal-Regulation-Full-Study.pdf.

Crews, C. 2018. "Ten Thousand Commandments: An Annual Snapshot of the Federal Regulatory State." Competitive Enterprise Institute.

Dafny, L., K. Ho, and M. Varela. 2013. "Let Them Have Choice: Gains from Shifting Away from Employer-Sponsored Health Insurance and Toward an Individual Exchange." *American Economic Journal: Economic Policy* 5, no. 1: 32–58.

DeMenno, M. 2017. "Technocracy, Democracy, and Public Policy: An Evaluation of Public Participation in Retrospective Regulatory Review." *Regulation and Governance*, October.

Demski, J. 2008. *Managerial Uses of Accounting Information*. New York: Springer.

DOT (U.S. Department of Transportation). 2018. "Preparing for the Future of Transportation." https://www.transportation.gov/sites/dot.gov/files/docs/policy-initiatives/automated-vehicles/320711/preparing-future-transportation-automated-vehicle-30.pdf.

Dougan, W., and J. Snyder. 1993. "Are Rents Fully Dissipated?" *Public Choice* 77, no. 4: 793–813.

Douglas, G., and J. Miller. 1974. *Economic Regulation of Domestic Air Transport: Theory and Policy*. Washington: Brookings Institution.

Dudley, S., and B. Mannix. 2018. "Improving Regulatory Benefit-Cost Analysis." *Journal of Law & Politics* 34, no. 1: 1–20.

Eisenback, J. 2010. "The Role of Independent Contractors in the U.S. Economy." Navigant Economics.

Elejalde-Ruiz, A. 2016. "Is McDonald's Responsible for Franchise Workers? Labor Law Hearing Set to Begin." *Chicago Tribune*, March 9.

Farrell, J., and C. Shapiro. 1990. "Horizontal Mergers: An Equilibrium Analysis." *American Economic Review* 80, no. 1: 107–26.

FDA (U.S. Food and Drug Administration). 2014. "Food Labeling: Nutrition of Standard Menu Items in Restaurants and Similar Retail Food Establishments." https://www.fda.gov/downloads/AboutFDA/ReportsManualsForms/Reports/EconomicAnalyses/UCM426165.pdf.

Feldstein, M. 1999. "Tax Avoidance and the Deadweight Loss of the Income Tax." *Review of Economics and Statistics* 81, no. 4: 674-–680.

Fisher, I. 1930. *The Theory of Interest: As Determined by Impatience to Spend Income and Opportunity to Invest It*. Pacifica, CA: Kelley.

Fraas, A., and R. Morgenstern. 2014. "Identifying the Analytical Implications of Alternative Regulatory Philosophies." *Journal of Benefit-Cost Analysis* 5, no. 1: 137–71.

FRED. 2018. "Professional and Business Services: Temporary Help Services." FRED Economic Data, Federal Reserve Bank of Saint Louis. https://fred.stlouisfed.org/series/temphelpn.

Friedman, M. 1953. "The Effects of Full Employment Policy on Economic Stability: A Formal Analysis." In *Essays in Positive Economics*, edited by M. Friedman. Chicago: University of Chicago Press.

Furchtgott-Roth, D. 2018. "Executive Branch Overreach in Labor Regulation." Manhattan Institute, New York.

GAO (U.S. Government Accountability Office). 2007. "Reexamining Regulations: Opportunities Exist to Improve Effectiveness and Transparency of Retrospective Reviews." https://www.gao.gov/new.items/d07791.pdf.

———. 2014. "Reexamining Regulations: Agencies Often Made Regulatory Changes, but Could Strengthen Linkages to Performance Goals." https://www.gao.gov/products/GAO-14-268.

Garvey, T. 2017. "A Brief Overview of Rulemaking and Judicial Review." https://fas.org/sgp/crs/misc/R41546.pdf.

Gayer, T., and W. Viscusi. 2013. "Overriding Consumer Preferences with Energy Regulations." *Journal of Regulatory Economics* 43, no. 3: 248–64.

———. 2016. "Determining the Proper Scope of Climate Change Policy Benefits in U.S. Regulatory Analyses: Domestic verses Global Approaches." *Review of Environmental Economics and Policy* 10: 245–63.

Gayer, T., R. Litan, and P. Wallach. 2017. "Evaluating the Trump Administration's Regulatory Reform Program." Brookings Institution. https://www.brookings.edu/research/evaluating-the-trump-administrations-regulatory-reform-program/.

Gitis, B. 2017. "The NLRB's New Joint Employer Standard, Unions, and the Franchise Business Model." American Action Forum. https://www.americanactionforum.org/wp-content/uploads/2017/04/Joint-Employer-and-Franchises.pdf.

Glaeser, E. 2006. "Paternalism and Psychology." *University of Chicago Law Review* 73: 133–56.

Goulder, L., and R. Williams III. 2003. "The Substantial Bias from Ignoring General Equilibrium Effects in Estimating Excess Burden, and a Practical Solution." *Journal of Political Economy* 111, no. 4: 898–927.

Government of Canada. 2015. "Annual Report on the Application of the One-for-One Rule: 2014-15." https://www.canada.ca/en/treasury-board-secretariat/services/federal-regulatory-management/annual-report-application-one-for-one-rule-2014-2015.html.

Gray, W. 1987. "The Cost of Regulation: OSHA, EPA and the Productivity Slowdown." *American Economic Review* 77, no. 5: 998–1006.

Greenhouse, S. 2014. "McDonald's Ruling Could Open Door for Unions." *New York Times* July 30.

Hahn, R., and P. Dudley. 2007. "How Well Does the U.S. Government Do Benefit-Cost Analysis?" *Review of Environmental Economics and Policy* 1, no. 2: 192–211.

Hahn, R., and P. Tetlock. 2008. "Has Economic Analysis Improved Regulatory Decisions?" *Journal of Economic Perspectives* 22, no. 1: 67–84.

Hansen, L., and T. Sargent. 2008. *Robustness.* Princeton, N.J.: Princeton University Press.

Harberger, A. 1954. "Monopoly and Resource Allocation." *American Economic Review* 44, no. 2: 77–87.

———. 1964. "Taxation, Resource Allocation, and Welfare." In *The Role of Direct and Indirect Taxes in the Federal Reserve System: A Conference Report of the NBER and the Brookings Institution*, edited by National Bureau of Economic Research. Princeton, NJ: Princeton University Press.

Harrington, W., R. Morgenstern, and P. Nelson. 2000. "On the Accuracy of Regulatory Cost Estimates." *Journal of Policy Analysis and Management* 19, no. 2: 297–322.

Haveman, R., and B. Weisbrod. 1975. "Defining Benefits of Public Programs: Some Guidance for Policy Analysts." *Policy Analysis* 1, no. 1: 169–96.

Hayek, F. 1945. "The Use of Knowledge in Society." *American Economic Review* 35, no. 4: 519–30.

Hazilla, M., and R. Kopp. 1990. "Social Cost of Environmental Quality Regulations: A General Equilibrium Analysis." *Journal of Political Economy* 98, no. 4: 853–73.

Hendrikse, G., and T. Jiang. 2007. "Plural Form in Franchising: An Incomplete Contracting Approach." In *Economics and Management Networks: Franchising, Strategic Alliances, and Cooperatives*, edited by G. Cliquet et al. Heidelberg: Physica-Verlag.

Institute of Medicine. 2009. *Secondhand Smoke Exposure and Cardiovascular Effects: Making Sense of the Evidence*. Report from Institute of Medicine and Committee on Secondhand Smoke Exposure and Acute Coronary Events. Washington: National Academies Press.

Joskow, P., and N. Rose. 1989. "The Effects of Economic Regulation." *Handbook of Industrial Organization* 2: 1450–98.

Kahn, A. 1979. "Applications of Economics to an Imperfect World." *American Economic Review* 69, no. 2: 1–13.

———. 1988. "I Would Do It Again." *Regulation*, no. 2: 22–28.

Karaca-Mandic, P., J. Abraham, and C. Phelps. 2011. "How Do Health Insurance Loading Fees Vary by Group Size? Implications for Healthcare Reform." *International Journal of Healthcare Finance and Economics* 11: 181–207.

Krueger, A., and O. Ashenfelter. 2018. *Theory and Evidence on Employer Collusion in the Franchise Sector*. NBER Working Paper 24831. Cambridge, MA: National Bureau of Economic Research.

Levy, H., E. Norton, and J. Smith. 2018. "Tobacco Regulation and Cost-Benefit Analysis." *American Journal of Health Economics* 4, no. 1: 1–25.

Luna, N. 2018. "McDonald's and NLRB Reach Settlement in Joint-Employer Case." *Nation's Restaurant News*, March 19.

Madrian, B., and D. Shea. 2001. "The Power of Suggestion: Inertia in 401(k) Participation and Savings Behavior." *Quarterly Journal of Economics* 116, no. 4: 1149–87.

Malone, T., and J. Lusk. 2016. "Brewing Up Entrepreneurship: Government Intervention in Beer." *Journal of Entrepreneurship and Public Policy* 5, no. 3: 325–42.

Morgenstern, R. 2018. "Retrospective Analysis of U.S. Federal Environmental Regulation." *Journal of Benefit-Cost Analysis* 9, no. 2: 285–304.

Morrison, R. 2013. "Lester Jones on Beer Taxes." Tax Policy Podcast, Tax Foundation.

Morse, A. 2016. *The Business Impact Target: Cutting the Cost of Regulation*. London: National Audit Office.

Mulligan, C. 2015a. "Misallocations, Substitution, and the Robustness of Activist Public Policy." Manuscript, University of Chicago, January.

———. 2015b. *Side Effects and Complications: The Economic Consequences of Health Care Reform*. Chicago: University of Chicago Press.

Mulligan, C., and K. Tsui. 2016. *The Upside-Down Economics of Regulated and Otherwise Rigid Prices*. NBER Working Paper 22305. Cambridge, MA: National Bureau of Economic Research.

Murray, B., A. Keeler, and W. Thurman. 2005. "Tax Interaction Effects, Environmental Regulation, and 'Rule of Thumb' Adjustments to Social Cost." *Environmental and Resource Economics* 30: 73–92.

NFIB (National Federation of Independent Business). 2001. "The National Small Business Poll."

NHTSA (National Highway Traffic Safety Administration) and EPA (U.S. Environmental Protection Agency). 2018. "The Safer Affordable Fuel-Efficient (SAFE) Vehicles Rule for Model Year 2021–2026 Passenger Cars and Light Trucks." https://www.nhtsa.gov/sites/nhtsa.dot.gov/files/documents/ld-cafe-co2-nhtsa-2127-al76-epa-pria-180823.pdf.

Niskanen, W. 1971. *Bureaucracy and Representative Government*. Chicago: Aldine-Atherton.

NLRB (National Labor Relations Board). 2014. "NLRB Office of the General Counsel Authorizes Complaints Against McDonald's Franchisees and Determines McDonald's, USA, LLC Is a Joint Employer." https://www.nlrb.gov/news-outreach/news-story/nlrb-office-general-counsel-authorizes-complaints-against-mcdonalds.

Norton, S. 2004. "Towards a More General Theory of Franchise Governance." In *Economics and Management of Franchising Networks*, edited by J. Windsperger, G. Cliquet, G. Hendrikse, and M. Tuunanen. Heidelberg: Springer.

OECD (Organization for Economic Cooperation and Development). 2018. "Table I.7: Top Statutory Personal Tax Rate and Top Marginal Tax Rates for Employees." https://stats.oecd.org/index.aspx?DataSetCode=TABLE_I7.

OMB (Office of Management and Budget). 1997. "1997 Report to Congress on the Benefits and Costs of Federal Regulations." https://obamawhitehouse.archives.gov/omb/inforeg_chap2#t1.

———. 2000. "Report to Congress on the Benefits and Costs of Federal Regulations." https://www.whitehouse.gov/sites/whitehouse.gov/files/omb/assets/OMB/inforeg/2000fedreg-report.pdf.

———. 2002. "Stimulating Smarter Regulation: 2002 Report to Congress on the Costs and Benefits of Federal Regulations and Unfunded Mandates on State, Local, and Tribal Entities." https://www.whitehouse.gov/sites/whitehouse.gov/files/omb/assets/OMB/inforeg/2002_report_to_congress.pdf.

———. 2003. "Circular A-4: Regulatory Impact Analysis—A Primer." https://obamawhitehouse.archives.gov/omb/circulars_a004_a-4/.

———. 2005. "Validating Regulatory Analysis: 2005 Report to Congress on the Benefits and Costs of Federal Regulations and Unfunded Mandates on State, Local, and Tribal Entities." https://www.whitehouse.gov/sites/whitehouse.gov/files/omb/assets/OMB/inforeg/2005_cb/final_2005_cb_report.pdf.

———. 2006. "2006 Report to Congress on the Costs and Benefits of Federal Regulations and Unfunded Mandates on State, Local, and Tribal Entities." https://www.whitehouse.gov/sites/whitehouse.gov/files/omb/assets/OMB/inforeg/2006_cb/2006_cb_final_report.pdf.

———. 2013. "2013 Report to Congress on the Benefits and Costs of Federal Regulations and Unfunded Mandates on State, Local, and Tribal Entities." https://www.whitehouse.gov/sites/whitehouse.gov/files/omb/inforeg/inforeg/2013_cb/2013_cost_benefit_report-updated.pdf.

———. 2017a. "Regulatory Reform: Two-for-One Status Report and Regulatory Cost Caps." https://www.reginfo.gov/public/pdf/eo13771/FINAL_TOPLINE_All_20171207.pdf

———. 2017b. "2017 Draft Report to Congress on the Benefits and Costs of Federal Regulations and Agency Compliance with the Unfunded Mandates Reform Act." https://www.whitehouse.gov/wpcontent/uploads/2017/12/draft_2017_cost_benefit_report.pdf.

———. 2018. "Regulatory Reform under Executive Order 13771: Final Accounting for Fiscal Year 2018." https://www.reginfo.gov/public/pdf/eo13771/EO_13771_Final_Accounting_for_Fiscal_Year_2018.pdf.

Phillips, M. 2014. "Amicus Brief of the General Counsel." Case 32-RC-109684, National Labor Relations Board.

Pizer, W., M. Alder, J. Aldy, D. Anthoff, M. Cropper, et al. 2014. "Using and Improving the Social Cost of Carbon." *Science* 346, no. 6214: 1189–90.

Pollitz, K., M. Long, A. Semanskee, and R. Kamal. 2018. *Understanding Short-Term Limited Duration Health Insurance*. San Francisco: Kaiser Family Foundation. http://files.kff.org/attachment/Issue-Brief-Understanding-Short-Term-Limited-Duration-Health-Insurance.

Potter, R. 2017. "Why Trump Can't Undo the Regulatory State So Easily." Brookings Institution.

Rao, P., S. Nowak, and C. Eibner. 2018. "What Is the Impact on Enrollment and Premiums If the Duration of Short-Term Health Insurance Plans Is Increased?" Commonwealth Fund. https://www.commonwealthfund.org/publications/fund-reports/2018/jun/what-impact-enrollment-and-premiums-if-duration-short-term.

Raso, C. 2017. "Assessing Regulatory Retrospective Review under the Obama Administration." Brookings Institution. https://www.brookings.edu/research/assessing-regulatory-retrospective-review-under-the-obama-administration/.

Renda, A. 2017. "One Step Forward, Two Steps Back? The New U.S. Regulatory Budgeting Rules in Light of the International Experience." *Journal of Benefit-Cost Analysis* 8, no. 3: 291–304.

Romer, D. 2011. *Advanced Macroeconomics*. New York: McGraw-Hill.

Rose, N. 2012. "After Airline Deregulation and Alfred E. Kahn." *American Economic Review* 102, no. 3: 376–80.

Rosen, J. 2016. "Putting Regulators on a Budget." https://www.nationalaffairs.com/publications/detail/putting-regulators-on-a-budget.

Rosen, J., and B. Callanan. 2014. "The Regulatory Budget Revisited." *Administrative Law Review* 66, no. 4: 835–60.

Saez, E., J. Slemrod, and S. Giertz. 2012. "The Elasticity of Taxable Income with Respect to Marginal Tax Rates: A Critical Review." *Journal of Economic Literature* 50: 3–50.

Sallee, J., S. West, and W. Fan. 2016. "Do Consumers Recognize the Value of Fuel Economy? Evidence from Used Car Prices and Gasoline Price Fluctuations." *Journal of Public Economics* 135: 61–73.

Stigler, G. 1971. "The Theory of Economic Regulation." *Bell Journal of Economics and Management* Science 2, no. 1: 3–21.

Sunstein, C. 2014. "Opening Keynote Address: The Regulatory Lookback." *Boston University Law Review* 94: 579–602.

———. 2018. *The Cost-Benefit Revolution*. Cambridge, MA: MIT Press.

Thaler, R., and C. Sunstein. 2009. *Nudge: Improving Decisions about Health, Wealth, and Happiness*. New York: Penguin Books.

Tirole, J. 1988. *The Theory of Industrial Organization*. Cambridge, MA: MIT Press.

Trejo, S. 1991. "The Effects of Overtime Pay Regulation on Worker Compensation." *American Economic Review* 81, no. 4: 719–40.

Tullock, G. 1967. "The Welfare Costs of Tariffs, Monopolies and Theft." *Western Economic Journal* 5: 224–32.

U.S. Chamber of Commerce Foundation. 2014a. "Food Truck Nation: U.S. Chamber of Commerce Foundation Food Truck Index." https://www.foodtrucknation.us/wp-content/themes/food-truck-nation/Food-Truck-Nation-Full-Report.pdf.

———. 2014b. "Regulatory Climate Index 2014." https://www.uschamberfoundation.org/sites/default/files/CityReg%20Report_0.pdf.

U.S. Congress. 1985. "H.R. 3128 Consolidated Omnibus Budget Reconciliation Act of 1985." https://www.congress.gov/bill/99th-congress/house-bill/3128.

Weber, C. 2014. "Toward Obtaining a Consistent Estimate of the Elasticity of Taxable Income Using Difference-in-Differences." *Journal of Public Economics* 117: 90–103.

Whinston, M. 2006. *Lectures on Antitrust Economics*. Cambridge, MA: MIT Press.

White House. 1981. "Executive Order 12291 on Federal Regulation." https://www.archives.gov/federal-register/codification/executive-order/12291.html.

———. 2018. "Memorandum of Agreement: Review of Tax Regulations under Executive Order 12866." https://www.whitehouse.gov/wp-content/uploads/2018/04/OIRA-TreasuryMOA_4.11.18.pdf.

Williamson, O. 1968. "Economies as an Antitrust Defense: The Welfare Tradeoffs." *American Economic Review* 58, no. 1: 18–36.

World Bank. 2018. "Doing Business: Rankings & Ease of Doing Business Score— Economy Rankings." www.doingbusiness.org/en/rankings.

Zerbe, R., Jr., and H. McCurdy. 1999. "The Failure of Market Failure." *Journal of Policy Analysis and Management* 18, no. 4: 558–78.

Chapter 3

Akerlof, G. 1970. "The Market for Lemons: Quality Uncertainty and the Market Mechanism." *Quarterly Journal of Economics* 84, no. 3: 488–500.

Aliprantis, D., and M. Schweitzer. 2018. "Opioids and the Labor Market." Federal Reserve Bank of Cleveland. https://www.clevelandfed.org/newsroom-and-events/publications/working-papers/2018-working-papers/wp-1807-opioids-and-the-labor-market.aspx.

Ashenfelter, O., H. Farber, and M. Ransom. 2010. "Labor Market Monopsony." *Journal of Labor Economics* 28, no. 2: 203–10.

Baker, M., J. Gruber, and K. Milligan. 2008. "Universal Child Care, Maternal Labor Supply, and Family Well-Being." *Journal of Political Economy* 116, no. 4: 709–45.

Baughman, R., and S. Dickert-Conlin. 2009. "The Earned Income Tax Credit and Fertility." *Journal of Population Economics* 22, no. 3: 537–63.

Bernstein, J., and K. Hassett. 2015. "Unlocking Private Capital to Facilitate Economic Growth in Distressed Areas." Economic Innovation Group. https://eig.org/wp-content/uploads/2015/04/Unlocking-Private-Capital-to-Facilitate-Growth.pdf.

Bertrand, M., and S. Mullainathan. 2004. "Are Emily and Greg More Employable Than Lakisha and Jamal? A Field Experiment on Labor Market Discrimination." *American Economic Review* 94, no. 4: 991–1013.

Bhuller, M., G. Dahl, K. Løken, and M. Mogstad. 2018. "Incarceration, Recidivism, and Employment." University of California, San Diego. https://econweb.ucsd.edu/~gdahl/papers/incarceration-recidivism-employment.pdf.

Bivens, J., L. Mishel, and J. Schmitt. 2018. "It's Not Just Monopoly and Monopsony: How Market Power Has Affected American Wages." Economic Policy Institute Research Report. https://www.epi.org/publication/its-not-just-monopoly-and-monopsony-how-market-power-has-affected-american-wages.

Blau, D. 2007. "Unintended Consequences of Child Care Regulations." *Labour Economics* 14, no. 3: 513–38.

BLS (U.S. Bureau of Labor Statistics). 2018. "Overview of BLS Statistics on Pay and Benefits." https://www.bls.gov/bls/wages.htm.

Borio, C., E. Kharroubi, C. Upper, and F. Zampolli. 2015. "Labour Reallocation and Productivity Dynamics: Financial Causes, Real Consequences." Working Paper

534. Bank for International Settlements. https://www.bis.org/publ/work534.pdf.

Bound, J., and R. Freeman. 1992. "What Went Wrong? The Erosion of Relative Earnings and Employment among Young Black Men in the 1980s." *Quarterly Journal of Economics* 107, no. 7: 201–32.

Brill, M., C. Holman, C. Morris, R. Raichoudhary, and N. Yosif. 2017. "Understanding the Labor Productivity and Compensation Gap." *Beyond the Numbers: Productivity* (Bureau of Labor Statistics) 6, no. 6. https://www.bls.gov/opub/btn/volume-6/understanding-the-labor-productivity-and-compensation-gap.htm.

Burns, C., and J. Macdonald. 2017. "America's Diverse Family Farms, 2018 Edition." U.S. Department of Agriculture. https://www.ers.usda.gov/webdocs/publications/81408/eib-164.pdf?v=0.

Busso, M., J. Gregory, and P. Kline. 2013. "Assessing the Incidence and Efficiency of a Prominent-Place-Based Policy." *American Economic Review* 103, no. 2: 897–947.

Card, D., J. Kluve, and A. Weber. 2010. "Active Labour Market Policy Evaluations: A Meta-analysis." *Economic Journal* 120, no. 548: F452–77.

Care. 2018. "This Is How Much Child Care Costs in 2018." https://www.care.com/c/stories/2423/how-much-does-child-care-cost.

Carpenter, D., L. Knepper, A. Erickson, and J. Ross. 2012. "License to Work: A National Study of Burdens from Occupational Licensing." https://www.ij.org/images/pdf_folder/economic_liberty/occupational_licensing/licensetowork.pdf.

Carson, E. 2018. "Prisoners in 2016." Bureau of Justice Statistics, Bulletin NCJ251149. https://www.bjs.gov/content/pub/pdf/p16.pdf.

CBO (U.S. Congressional Budget Office). 2018. "The Budget and Economic Outlook: 2018 to 2028."

CEA (Council of Economic Advisers). 2017. "The Underestimated Cost of the Opioid Crisis." https://www.whitehouse.gov/sites/whitehouse.gov/files/images/The%20Underestimated%20Cost%20of%20the%20Opioid%20Crisis.pdf.

———. 2018a. "Addressing America's Reskilling Challenge." https://www.whitehouse.gov/wp-content/uploads/2018/07/Addressing-Americas-Reskilling-Challenge.pdf.

———.2018b. *Economic Report of the President*. Washington: U.S. Government Publishing Office. https://www.whitehouse.gov/wp-content/uploads/2018/02/ERP_2018_Final-FINAL.pdf.

———. 2018c. "How Much are Workers Getting Paid? A Primer on Wage Measurement." https://www.whitehouse.gov/wp-content/uploads/2018/09/How-Much-Are-Workers-Getting-Paid-A-Primer-on-Wage-Measurement-Sept-2018.pdf.

———. 2018d. "Military Spouses in the Labor Market." https://www.whitehouse.gov/wp-content/uploads/2018/05/Military-Spouses-in-the-Labor-Market.pdf.

———. 2018e. "Returns on Investments in Recidivism-Reducing Programs." https://www.whitehouse.gov/wp-content/uploads/2018/05/Returns-on-Investments-in-Recidivism-Reducing-Programs.pdf.

CEA, Department of the Treasury, and Department of Labor. 2015. "Occupational Licensing: A Framework for Policymakers." https://obamawhitehouse.archives.gov/sites/default/files/docs/licensing_report_final_nonembargo.pdf.

Charles, K., E. Hurst, and M. Schwartz. 2018. *The Transformation of Manufacturing and the Decline in U.S. Employment.* NBER Working Paper 24468. Cambridge, MA: National Bureau of Economic Research. http://www.nber.org/papers/w24468.pdf.

ChildCare Aware of America. 2018. "The U.S. and the High Cost of Childcare: A Review of Prices and Proposed Solutions for a Broken System." http://usa.childcareaware.org/advocacy-public-policy/resources/research/costofcare.

Couch, K., and R. Fairlie. 2010. "Last Hired, First Fired? Black-White Unemployment and the Business Cycle." *Demography* 47, no. 1: 227–47.

Crump, R., G. Goda, and K. Mumford. 2011. "Fertility and the Personal Exemption: Comment." *American Economic Review* 101, no. 4: 1616–28.

Currie, J., J. Jin, and M. Schnell. 2018. *U.S. Employment and Opioids: Is There a Connection?* NBER Working Paper 24440. Cambridge, MA: National Bureau of Economic Research. https://www.nber.org/papers/w24440.pdf.

Currie, J., and V. Hotz. 2004. "Accidents Will Happen? Unintentional Childhood Injuries and the Effects of Child Care Regulations." *Journal of Health Economics* 23, no. 1: 25–59.

Daly, M., and B. Hobijn. 2017. "Composition and Aggregate Real Wage Growth." *American Economic Review* 107, no. 5: 349–52.

Darity, W., Jr., and P. Mason. 1998. "Evidence on Discrimination in Employment: Codes of Color, Codes of Gender." *Journal of Economic Perspectives* 12, no. 2: 63–90.

Decker, P., and W. Corson. 1995. "International Trade and Worker Displacement: Evaluation of the Trade Adjustment Assistance Program." *Industrial and Labor Relations Review* 48, no. 4: 758–74.

Department of the Treasury and DOD (Department of Defense). 2012. "Supporting Our Military Families: Best Practices for Streamlining Occupational Licensing across State Lines." https://www.treasury.gov/connect/blog/Pages/Supporting-Our-Military-Families.aspx.

Desai, M., C. Foley, and J. Hines Jr. 2007. "Labor and Capital Shares of the Corporate Tax Burden: International Evidence." http://www.people.hbs.edu/ffoley/labcapshr.pdf.

DOD (U.S. Department of Defense). 2016. "2016 Demographics: Profile of the Military Community." http://download.militaryonesource.mil/12038/MOS/Reports/2016-Demographics-Report.pdf.

Economic Innovation Group. 2018. "Opportunity Zones: The Map Comes into Focus." https://eig.org/news/opportunity-zones-map-comes-focus.

Elsby, M., B. Hobijn, and A. Sahin. 2010. "The Labor Market in the Great Recession." Brookings Institution. https://www.brookings.edu/wp-content/uploads/2016/07/2010a_bpea_eslby.pdf.

Federal Reserve Bank of Atlanta. 2018. "Wage Growth Tracker." https://www.frbatlanta.org/chcs/wage-growth-tracker.aspx.

Federal Reserve Board of Governors. 2000. "Monetary Policy Report to the Congress Pursuant to the Full Employment and Balanced Growth Act of 1978." https://www.federalreserve.gov/boarddocs/hh/2000/February/FullReport.pdf.

———. 2018a. "Report on the Economic Well-Being of U.S. Households in 2017." https://www.federalreserve.gov/consumerscommunities/shed.htm.

———. 2018b. "Survey of Household Economics and Decisionmaking." https://www.federalreserve.gov/consumerscommunities/shed.htm.

Felix, A. 2007. "Passing the Burden: Corporate Tax Incidence in Open Economies." Federal Reserve Bank of Kansas City. https://www.kansascityfed.org/Publicat/RegionalRWP/RRWP07-01.pdf.

———. 2009. "Do State Corporate Income Taxes Reduce Wages?" Federal Reserve Bank of Kansas City. https://www.kansascityfed.org/PUBLICAT/ECONREV/PDF/09q2felix.pdf.

Fernald, J. 2015. "Productivity and Potential Output Before, During, and After the Great Recession." *NBER Macroeconomics* 2014, no. 29: 1–51.

Fiore, A., L. Niehem, J. Hurst, J. Son, A. Sadachar, D. Russell, D. Swenson, and C. Seeger. 2015. "Will They Stay or Will They Go? Community Features Important in Migration Decisions of Recent University Graduates." *Economic Development Quarterly* 29, no. 1: 23–37.

Flood, S., M. King, R. Rodgers, S. Ruggles, and R. Warren. 2018. "Integrated Public Use Microdata Series, Current Population Survey: Version 6.0." https://doi.org/10.18128/DO30.V6.0.

Freedman, M. 2012. "Teaching New Markets Old Tricks: The Effects of Subsidized Investment on Low-Income Neighborhoods." *Journal of Public Economics* 2012, no. 96: 1000–1014.

Gelfond, H., and L. Looney. 2018. "Learning from Opportunity Zones: How to Improve Place-Based Policies." Brookings Institution. https://www.brookings.edu/wp-content/uploads/2018/10/Looney_Opportunity-Zones_final.pdf.

Ghertner, R., and L. Groves. 2018."The Opioid Crisis and Economic Opportunity: Geographic and Economic Trends." https://aspe.hhs.gov/system/files/pdf/259261/ASPEEconomicOpportunityOpioidCrisis.pdf.

Gittleman, M., M. Klee, and M. Kleiner. 2018. "Analyzing the Labor Market Outcomes of Occupational Licensing." *Industrial Relations* 57, no. 1: 57–100.

Gittleman, M., and M. Kleiner. 2016. "Wage Effects of Unionization and Occupational Licensing Coverage in the United States." *Industrial and Labor Relations Review* 69, no. 1: 142–72.

Goetz, S., M. Partridge, and H. Stephens. 2018. "The Economic Status of Rural America in the President Trump Era and Beyond." *Applied Economic Perspectives and Policy* 40, no. 1: 97–118.

Goetz, S., and A. Rupasingha. 2009. "Determinants of Growth in Non-Farm Proprietor Densities in the U.S., 1990–2000." *Small Business Economics* 32, no. 4: 425–38.

Gorry, D., and D. Thomas. 2017. "Regulation and the Cost of Childcare." *Journal of Applied Economics* 49, no. 41: 4138–47.

Gramlich, J. 2018. "The Gap Between the Number of Blacks and Whites in Prisons is Shrinking." Pew Research Center. http://www.pewresearch.org/fact-tank/2018/01/12/shrinking-gap-between-number-of-blacks-and-whites-in-prison.

Gurley-Calvez, T., T. Gilbert, K. Harper, D. Marples, and K. Daly. 2009. "Do Tax Incentives Affect Investment? An Analysis of the New Markets Tax Credit." *Public Finance Review* 37, no. 4: 371–98.

Harger, K., and A. Ross. 2016. "Do Capital Tax Incentives Attract New Businesses? Evidence across Industries from the New Markets Tax Credit." *Journal of Regional Science* 56, no. 5: 733–53.

Harris, M., L. Kessler, M. Murray, and M. Glenn. 2018. "Prescription Opioids and Labor Market Pains: The Effect of Schedule II Opioids on Labor Force Participation and Unemployment." http://cber.haslam.utk.edu/staff/harris/Opioids_HKMG.pdf.

Hashimoto, M. 1982. "Minimum Wage Effects on Training on the Job." *American Economic Review* 72, no. 5: 1070–87.

Hassett, K., and A. Mathur. 2006. "Taxes and Wages." American Enterprise Institute. http://pcsi.pa.go.kr/files/20060706_TaxesandWages.pdf.

Havnes, T., and M. Mogstad. 2011. "No Child Left Behind: Subsidized Child Care and Children's Long-Run Outcomes." *American Economic Journal: Economic Policy* 3, no. 2: 97–129.

Hellerstein, J., D. Neumark, and K. Troske. 1999. "Wages, Productivity, and Worker Characteristics: Evidence from Plant-Level Production Functions and Wage Equations." *Journal of Labor Economics* 17, no. 3: 409–46.

Herbst, C. 2017. "Universal Child Care, Maternal Employment, and Children's Long-Run Outcomes: Evidence from the U.S. Lanham Act of 1940." *Journal of Labor Economics* 35, no. 2: 519–64.

Herbst, C., and E. Tekin. 2016. "The Impact of Child-Care Subsidies on Child Development: Evidence from Geographic Variation in the Distance to Social Service Agencies" *Journal of Policy Analysis and Management* 35, no. 1: 94–116.

HHS (Department of Health and Human Services). 2014. "Research Brief #1: Trends in Child Care Center Licensing Regulations and Policies for 2014." Administration for Children and Families, Office of Child Care. https://www.naralicensing.org/assets/docs/ChildCareLicensingStudies/2014CCStudy/center_licensing_trends_brief_2014.pdf.

——— 2015. "Prices Charged in Early Care and Education: Initial Findings from the National Survey of Early Care and Education." https://www.acf.hhs.gov/sites/default/files/opre/es_price_of_care_toopre_041715_2.pdf.

Holzer, H., P. Offner, and E. Sorensen. 2005. "Declining Employment among Young Black Less-Educated Men: The Role of Incarceration and Child Support." *Journal of Policy Analysis and Management* 24, no. 2: 329–50.

Hotz, V., and M. Xiao. 2011. "The Impact of Regulations on the Supply and Quality of Care in Child Care Markets." *American Economic Review* 101, no. 5: 1775–805.

Ilg, R., and S. Haugen. 2000. "Earnings and Employment Trends in the 1990s." *Monthly Labor Review* 123, no. 3: 21–33.

IRS (Internal Revenue Service). 2018. "Internal Revenue Bulletin: 2018–10." https://www.irs.gov/irb/2018-10_IRB#RP-2018-18.

Johnson, J., and M. Kleiner. 2017. "Is Occupational Licensing a Barrier to Interstate Migration" Federal Reserve Bank of Minneapolis. https://www.minneapolisfed.org/research/sr/sr561.pdf.

Juhn, C., and S. Potter. 2006. "Changes in Labor Force Participation in the United States." *Journal of Economic Perspectives* 20, no. 3: 27–46.

Kaplan, G., and S. Schulhofer-Wohl. 2017. "Understanding the Long-Run Decline in Interstate Migration." *International Economic Review* 58, no. 1: 57–94.

Kaye, S. 2010. "The Impact of the 2007–09 Recession on Workers with Disabilities." *Monthly Labor Review* 2010, no. 10: 19–30. https://www.bls.gov/opub/mlr/2010/10/art2full.pdf.

Kim, Y., and P. Orazem. 2016. "Broadband Internet and New Firm Location Decisions in Rural Areas." *American Journal of Agricultural Economics* 99, no. 1: 285–302.

Kleiner, M. 2000. "Occupational Licensing." *Journal of Economic Perspectives* 14, no. 4: 189–202.

Kleiner, M., and A. Krueger. 2010. "The Prevalence and Effects of Occupational Licensing." *British Journal of Industrial Relations* 48, no. 4: 676–87.

Kleiner, M., A. Krueger, and A. Mas. 2011. "A Proposal to Encourage States to Rationalize Occupational Licensing Practices." Brookings Institution. http://www.hhh.umn.edu/file/9441/download.

Kluve, J. 2010. "The Effectiveness of European Active Labor Market Programs." *Labour Economics* 17, no. 6: 904–18.

Knop, B., and A. Mohanty. 2018. "Child Care Costs in the Redesigned Survey of Income and Program Participation (SIPP): A Comparison to the Current Population Survey Annual Social and Economic Supplement (CPS ASEC)." Census Bureau Working Paper 2018-21. https://www.census.gov/library/working-papers/2018/demo/SEHSD-WP2018-21.html.

Krueger, A. 2017. "Where Have All the Workers Gone? An Inquiry into the Decline of the U.S. Labor Force Participation Rate." Brookings Institution. https://www.brookings.edu/wp-content/uploads/2017/09/1_krueger.pdf.

Laird, J., and T. Nielsen. 2016. "The Effects of Physician Prescribing Behaviors on Prescription Drug Use and Labor Supply: Evidence from Movers in Denmark." Harvard University. https://scholar.harvard.edu/files/lairdja/files/Laird_JMP_1.pdf.

LaLumia, S., J. Sallee, and N. Turner. 2015. "New Evidence on Taxes and the Timing of Birth." *American Economic Journal: Economic Policy* 7, no. 2: 258–93.

Leduc, S., and D. Wilson. 2017. "Has the Wage Phillips Curve Gone Dormant?" Federal Reserve Bank of San Francisco. https://www.frbsf.org/economic-research/publications/economic-letter/2017/october/has-wage-phillips-curve-gone-dormant.

Lefebvre, P., and P. Merrigan. 2008. "Child-Care Policy and the Labor Supply of Mothers with Young Children: A Natural Experiment from Canada." *Journal of Labor Economics* 26, no. 3: 519–48.

Lefebvre, P., P. Merrigan., and M. Verstraete. 2009. "Dynamic Labour Supply Effects of Childcare Subsidies: Evidence from a Canadian Natural Experiment on Low-Fee Universal Child Care. *Labour Economics* 16, no. 5: 490–502.

Lerman, R. 2014. "Do Firms Benefit from Apprenticeship?" IZA World of Labor. https://wol.iza.org/articles/do-firms-benefit-from-apprenticeship-investments/long.

Manyika, J., S. Lund, M. Chui, J. Bughin, J. Woetzel, P. Batra, R. Ko, and S. Sanghvi. 2017. "Jobs Lost, Jobs Gained: Workforce Transitions in a Time of Automation." McKinsey Global Institute. https://www.mckinsey.com/featured-insights/future-of-organizations-and-work/jobs-lost-jobs-gained-what-the-future-of-work-will-mean-for-jobs-skills-and-wages.

McClelland, R., and S. Mok. 2012. "A Review of Recent Research on Labor Supply Elasticities." Congressional Budget Office Working Paper 2012–12. https://www.cbo.gov/sites/default/files/cbofiles/attachments/10-25-2012-Recent_Research_on_Labor_Supply_Elasticities.pdf.

Meyer, B. 2002. "Labor Supply at the Extensive and Intensive Margins: The EITC, Welfare, and Hours Worked." *American Economic Review* 92, no. 2: 373–79.

Milligan, K. 2005. "Subsidizing the Stork: New Evidence on Tax Incentives and Fertility." *Review of Economics and Statistics* 87, no. 3: 539–55.

Molloy, R., C. Smith, and A. Wozniak. 2011. "Internal Migration in the United States." *Journal of Economic Perspectives* 25, no. 3: 173–96.

———. 2017. "Job Changing and the Decline in Long Distance Migration in the United States." *Demography* 54, no. 2: 631–53.

Morrissey, T. 2017. "Child Care and Parent Labor Force Participation: A Review of the Research Literature." *Review of Economics of the Household* 15, no. 1: 1–24.

Moss, P., and C. Tilly. 1996. "Soft Skills and Race: An Investigation of Black Men's Employment Problems." *Work and Occupations* 23, no. 23: 252–76.

Muehlemann, S., P. Ryan, and S. Wolter. 2013. "Monopsony Power, Pay Structure, and Training." *ILR Review* 66, no. 5: 1097–114.

National Center on Early Childhood Quality Assurance. 2015. "Increasing Quality in Early Care and Education Programs: Effects on Expenses and Revenues." https://childcareta.acf.hhs.gov/sites/default/files/public/pcqc_increase_quality_final.pdf.

NBER (National Bureau of Economic Research). 2010. "U.S. Business Cycle Expansions and Contractions." https://www.nber.org/cycles.html.

Neal, D., and A. Rick. 2014. *The Prison Boom and the Lack of Black Progress after Smith and Welch*. NBER Working Paper 20283. Cambridge, MA: National Bureau of Economic Research. https://www.nber.org/papers/w20283.

Neal, D., and W. Johnson. 1996. "The Role of Premarket Factors in Black-White Wage Differences." *Journal of Political Economy* 104, no. 5: 869–95.

Neumark, D., and J. Kolko. 2010. "Do Enterprise Zones Create Jobs? Evidence from California's Enterprise Zone Program." *Journal of Urban Economics* 2010, no. 68: 1–19.

Neumark, D., and D. Rothstein. 2005. *Do School-to-Work Programs Help the "Forgotten Half?"* NBER Working Paper 11636. Cambridge, MA: National Bureau of Economic Research. https://www.nber.org/papers/w11636.

Neumark, D., and W. Wascher. 2003. "Minimum Wages and Skill Acquisition: Another Look at Schooling Effects." *Economics of Education Review* 22, no. 1: 1–10.

NFIB (National Federation of Independent Business). 2018a. "October 2018 Report: Small Business Optimism Index." http://www.nfib.com/surveys/small-business-economic-trends/.

———. 2018b. "Small Business Introduction to the Tax Cuts and Jobs Act: Part 1." https://www.nfib.com/assets/TCJA-Survey.pdf.

NIH (National Institutes of Health). 2018. "Overdose Death Rates." https://www.drugabuse.gov/related-topics/trends-statistics/overdose-death-rates.

Nollenberger, N., and N. Rodríguez-Planas. 2015. "Full-Time Universal Childcare in a Context of Low Maternal Employment: Quasi-Experimental Evidence from Spain." *Labour Economics* 2015, no. 36: 124–36.

North Carolina State Board of Dental Examiners v. Federal Trade Commission. 2015. https://www.supremecourt.gov/opinions/14pdf/13-534_19m2.pdf.

OECD (Organization for Economic Cooperation and Development). 2013. "Time for the U.S. to Reskill? What the Survey of Adult Skills Says." https://www.oecd-ilibrary.org/education/time-for-the-u-s-to-reskill_9789264204904-en.

———. 2018a. "OECD Economic Survey of the United States 2018." http://www.oecd.org/eco/surveys/economic-survey-united-states.htm.

———. 2018b. "Putting a Face Behind the Jobs at Risk of Automation." http://www.oecd.org/employment/Automation-policy-brief-2018.pdf.

Oreopoulos, P., M. Page, and A. Stevens. 2008. "The Intergenerational Effect of Worker Displacement." *Journal of Labor Economics* 26, no. 3: 455–83.

Ozimek, A. 2017. "There Is No U.S. Wage Growth Mystery." Moody's Analytics. https://www.economy.com/dismal/analysis/datapoints/296127/There-Is-No-US-Wage-GrowthMystery.

Pager, D., B. Western, and N. Sugie. 2009. "Sequencing Disadvantage: Barriers to Employment Facing Young Black and White Men with Criminal Records." *Annals of the American Academy of Political and Social Science* 623, no. 1: 195–213.

PwC (PricewaterhouseCoopers). 2018. "Will Robots Really Steal Our Jobs? An International Analysis of the Potential Long-Term Impact of Automation." https://www.pwc.com/hu/hu/kiadvanyok/assets/pdf/impact_of_automation_on_jobs.pdf.

Reichert, C., J. Cromartie, and R. Arthun. 2014. "Impacts of Return Migration on Rural U.S. Communities." *Rural Sociology Journal* 79, no. 2: 200–226.

Rinz, K. 2018. "Labor Market Concentration, Earnings Inequality, and Earnings Mobility." Census Bureau Working Paper 2018–10. https://www.census.gov/content/dam/Census/library/working-papers/2018/adrm/carra-wp-2018-10.pdf.

Rupasingha, A., and S. Goetz. 2013. "Self-Employment and Local Economic Performance: Evidence from U.S. Counties." *Papers in Regional Science* 92, no. 1: 141–62.

Schochet, P., R. D'Amico, J. Berk, S. Dolfin, and N. Wozny. 2012. "Estimated Impacts for Participants in the Trade Adjustment Assistance (TAA) Program Under the 2002 Amendments." U.S. Department of Labor. http://wdr.doleta.gov/research/FullText_Documents/ETAOP%5F2013%5F10%5FParticipant%5FImpact%5FReport%2Epdf.

Sentencing Project. 2018. "Trends in U.S. Corrections." https://www.sentencingproject.org/wp-content/uploads/2016/01/Trends-in-US-Corrections.pdf.

Shapiro, C. 1986. "Investment, Moral Hazard, and Occupational Licensing." *Review of Economic Studies* 53, no. 5: 843–62.

Shulman, S. 1987. "Discrimination, Human Capital, and Black-White Unemployment: Evidence from Cities." *Journal of Human Resources* 22, no. 3: 361–76.

Stevens, A., and J. Schaller. 2010. "Short-Run Effects of Parental Job Loss on Children's Academic Achievement." *Economic of Education Review* 30, no. 2: 289–99.

Task Force on Apprenticeship Expansion. 2018. "Final Report to the President of the United States." https://www.dol.gov/apprenticeship/docs/task-force-apprenticeship-expansion-report.pdf.

Tsvetkova, A., M. Partridge, and M. Betz. 2017. "Entrepreneurial and Employment Responses to Economic Conditions across the Rural-Urban Continuum." *Annals of the American Academy of Political and Social Science* 672, no. 1: 83–102.

Twomey, J., and J. Monks. 2011. "Monopsony and Salary Suppression: The Case of Major League Soccer in the United States." *American Economist* 56, no. 1: 20–8.

Urban Institute. 2012. "Net Income Change Calculator." http://nicc.urban.org/netincomecalculator.

USDA (U.S. Department of Agriculture). 2017a. "Manufacturing Is Relatively More Important to the Rural Economy than the Urban Economy." https://www.usda.gov/media/blog/2017/09/12/manufacturing-relatively-more-important-rural-economy-urban-economy.

———2017b. "Report to the President of the United States from the Task Force on Agriculture and Rural Prosperity." https://www.usda.gov/sites/default/files/documents/rural-prosperity-report.pdf.

———. 2017c. "Rural Employment and Unemployment." https://www.ers.usda.gov/topics/rural-economy-population/employment-education/rural-employment-and-unemployment.

———.2017d. "Rural Manufacturing at a Glance." https://www.ers.usda.gov/webdocs/publications/84758/eib-177.pdf?v=0.

———. 2017e. "Urban Areas Offer Higher Earnings for Workers with More Education." https://www.ers.usda.gov/amber-waves/2017/july/urban-areas-offer-higher-earnings-for-workers-with-more-education.

———. 2018a. "Ag and Food Sectors and the Economy." https://www.ers.usda.gov/data-products/ag-and-food-statistics-charting-the-essentials/ag-and-food-sectors-and-the-economy.

———. 2018b. "Farming and Farm Income." https://www.ers.usda.gov/data-products/ag-and-food-statistics-charting-the-essentials/farming-and-farm-income.

———. 2018c. "Rural Education." https://www.ers.usda.gov/topics/rural-economy-population/employment-education/rural-education.

Webber, D. 2015. "Firm Market Power and the Earnings Distribution." *Labour Economics* 2015, no. 35: 123–34.

Weller, C. 2011. "The Black and White Labor Gap in America." Center for American Progress. https://www.americanprogress.org/issues/economy/reports/2011/07/25/9992/the-black-and-white-labor-gap-in-america.

Western, B., and B. Pettit. 2000. "Incarceration and Racial Inequality in Men's Employment." *Industrial and Labor Relations Review* 54, no. 1: 3–16.

———. 2005. "Black-White Wage Inequality, Employment Rates, and Incarceration." *American Journal of Sociology* 111, no. 2: 553–78.

White House. 2017. "Presidential Executive Order on Promoting Agriculture and Rural Prosperity in America." https://www.whitehouse.gov/presidential-actions/presidential-executive-order-promoting-agriculture-rural-prosperity-america.

———. 2018a. "Federal Interagency Council on Crime Prevention and Improving Reentry." https://www.whitehouse.gov/presidential-actions/federal-interagency-council-crime-prevention-improving-reentry.

———. 2018b. "The Opioid Crisis." https://www.whitehouse.gov/opioids.

———. 2018c. "Presidential Executive Order on Streamlining and Expediting Requests to Locate Broadband Facilities in Rural America." https://www.whitehouse.

gov/presidential-actions/presidential-executive-order-streamlining-expediting-requests-locate-broadband-facilities-rural-america.

Wilmoth, D. 2017. "The Retreat of the Rural Entrepreneur." U.S. Small Business Administration. https://www.sba.gov/sites/default/files/advocacy/Retreat-Rural-Entrepreneur.pdf.

Wilson, V. 2015. "Black Unemployment Is Significantly Higher Than White Unemployment, Regardless of Educational Attainment." Economic Policy Institute. https://www.epi.org/publication/black-unemployment-educational-attainment.

Yellen, J. 2016. "Current Conditions and the Outlook for the U.S. Economy." Board of Governors of the Federal Reserve System. https://www.federalreserve.gov/newsevents/speech/yellen20160606a.htm.

Chapter 4

AAM (Association for Accessible Medicines). 2018. "Generic Drug Access & Savings in the U.S.: Access in Jeopardy." https://accessiblemeds.org/sites/default/files/2018_aam_generic_drug_access_and_savings_report.pdf.

Acemoglu, D., and J. Linn. 2004. "Market Size in Innovation: Theory and Evidence from the Pharmaceutical Industry." *Quarterly Journal of Economics* 119, no. 3: 1049–90.

Aitken, M., E. Berndt, B. Bosworth, I. Cockburn, R. Frank, M. Kleinrock, and B. Shapiro. 2013. *The Regulation of Prescription Drug Competition and Market Responses: Patterns in Prices and Sales Following Loss of Exclusivity*. NBER Working Paper 19487. Cambridge, MA: National Bureau of Economic Research.

Aitken, M., E. Berndt, and D. Cutler. 2008. "Prescription Drug Spending Trends in the United States: Looking Beyond the Turning Point." *Health Affairs* 28, no. 1: 151–60.

Alpert, B. 2004. "Drug War." *Barrons*, June 14. https://www.barrons.com/articles/SB108690508847334356.

Andrews, M. 2017. "FDA's Approval of a Cheaper Drug for Hepatitis C Will Likely Expand Treatment." NPR, October 4. http://www.npr.org/sections/health-shots/2017/10/04/555156577/fdas-approval-of-a-cheaper-drug-for-hepatitis-c-will-likely-expand-treatment.

Arrow, K. 1963. "Uncertainty and the Welfare Economics of Medical Care." *American Economic Review* 53, no. 5: 941–73.

Berndt, E., and M. Aitken. 2011. "Brand Loyalty, Generic Entry and Price Competition in Pharmaceuticals in the Quarter Century after the 1984 Waxman-Hatch Legislation." *International Journal of the Economics of Business* 18, no. 2: 177–201.

Berndt, E., T. McGuire, and J. Newhouse. 2011. "A Primer on the Economics of Prescription Pharmaceutical Pricing in Health Insurance Markets." *Forum for Health Economics & Policy* 14, no. 2.

Blahous, C. 2018a. "The Costs of a National Single-Payer Healthcare System." Mercatus Working Paper. Arlington, VA: Mercatus Center at George Mason University.

———. 2018b. "How Much Would Medicare for All Cut Doctor and Hospital Reimbursements?" https://economics21.org/m4a-reimbursements-blahous.

Blume-Kohout, M., and N. Sood. 2013. "Market Size and Innovation: Effects of Medicare Part D on Pharmaceutical Research and Development." *Journal of Public Economics* 97: 327–36.

Boardman, A., and A. Vining. 1989. "Ownership and Performance in Competitive Environments: A Comparison of the Performance of Private, Mixed, and State-Owned Enterprises." *Journal of Law & Economics* 32, no. 1: 1–33.

Book, R. 2009. "Medicare Administrative Costs Are Higher, Not Lower, Than for Private Insurance." Heritage Foundation. https://www.heritage.org/node/14322/print-display.

Brook, R., E. Keeler, K. Lohr, J. Newhouse, J. Ware, W. Rogers, A. Davies, et al. 2006. "The Health Insurance Experiment: A Classic RAND Study Speaks to the Current Health Care Reform Debate." RAND Health. https://www.rand.org/pubs/research_briefs/RB9174.html.

Busch, F., and P. Houchens. 2018. "The Individual Mandate Repeal: Will It Matter?" Milliman. http://www.milliman.com/insight/2018/The-individual-mandate-repeal-Will-it-matter/.

Buttorff, C., T. Ruder, and M. Bauman. 2017. "Multiple Chronic Conditions in the United States." RAND Corporation. https://www.rand.org/pubs/tools/TL221.html.

Candon, M., S. Zuckerman, D. Wissoker, B. Saloner, G. Kenney, K. Rhodes, and D. Polsky. 2017. "Declining Medicaid Fees and Primary Care Appointment Availability for New Medicaid Patients." *Journal of the American Medical Association* 178, no. 1: 145–46.

Caves, R., M. Whinston, M. Hurwitz, and A. Pakes. 1991. "Patent Expiration, Entry, and Competition in the U.S. Pharmaceutical Industry." *Brookings Papers on Economic Activity: Microeconomics*, no. 1: 1–66. https://www.brookings.edu/wp-content/uploads/1991/01/1991_bpeamicro_caves.pdf.

CBO (U.S. Congressional Budget Office). 2009. "Cost Estimate of Senate Amendment, Patient Protection and Affordable Care Act, to H.R. 3590." https://www.cbo.gov/sites/default/files/111th-congress-2009-2010/costestimate/41423-hr-3590-senate.pdf.

———. 2015. "Budgetary and Economic Effects of Repealing the Affordable Care Act." https://www.cbo.gov/sites/default/files/114th-congress-2015-2016/reports/50252effectsofacarepeal.pdf.

———. 2016. "Private Health Insurance Premiums and Federal Policy." https://www.cbo.gov/sites/default/files/114th-congress-2015-2016/reports/51130-Health_Insurance_Premiums.pdf

———. 2017. "Repealing the Individual Health Insurance Mandate: An Updated Estimate." https://www.cbo.gov/system/files/115th-congress-2017-2018/reports/53300-individualmandate.pdf.

———. 2018. "Federal Subsidies for Health Insurance Coverage for Consumers Under Age 65: 2018 to 2028." https://www.cbo.gov/publication/53826.

CEA (Council of Economic Advisers). 2017. "Understanding Recent Developments in the Individual Health Insurance Market." Council of Economic Advisers Issue Brief. https://obamawhitehouse.archives.gov/sites/default/files/page/files/201701_individual_health_insurance_market_cea_issue_brief.pdf.

———. 2018a. *The Administration's FDA Reforms and Reduced Biopharmaceutical Drug Prices*. Washington: White House. https://www.whitehouse.gov/wp-content/uploads/2018/10/The-Administrations-FDA-Reforms-and-Reduced-Biopharmaceutical-Drug-Prices.pdf.

———. 2018b. *Economic Report of the President*. Washington: U.S. Government Publishing Office.

———. 2018c. *The Opportunity Costs of Socialism*. Washington: White House. https://www.whitehouse.gov/wp-content/uploads/2018/10/The-Opportunity-Costs-of-Socialism.pdf.

———. 2019. *Deregulating Health Insurance Markets: Value to Market Participants*. Washington: White House. https://www.whitehouse.gov/wp-content/uploads/2019/02/Deregulating-Health-Insurance-Markets-FINAL.pdf.

Chandra, A., A. Finkelstein, A. Sacarny, and C. Syverson. 2016a. "Healthcare Exceptionalism? Productivity and Allocation in the U.S. Healthcare Sector." *American Economic Review* 106, no. 8: 2110–44.

———. 2016b. "Productivity Dispersion in Medicine and Manufacturing." *American Economic Review* 106, no. 5: 99–103.

Chase, D., and J. Arensmeyer. 2018. "The Affordable Care Act's Impact on Small Business." Commonwealth Fund. https://www.commonwealthfund.org/publications/issue-briefs/2018/oct/affordable-care-act-impact-small-business.

Chernew, M., Z. Cooper, E. Larsen-Hallock, and F. Morton. 2018. *Are Health Care Services Shoppable? Evidence from the Consumption of Lower-Limb MRI Scans*. NBER Working Paper 24869. Cambridge, MA: National Bureau of Economic Research.

CIHI (Canadian Institute for Health Information). 2018. "How Canada Compares: Results from the Commonwealth Fund's 2017 International Health Policy Survey of Seniors." https://www.cihi.ca/sites/default/files/document/commonwealth-survey-2017-chartbook-en-rev2-web.pptx.

CMS (Centers for Medicare & Medicaid Services). 2017. "2017 Actuarial Report on the Financial Outlook for Medicaid." https://www.cms.gov/Research-Statistics-Data-and-Systems/Research/ActuarialStudies/Downloads/MedicaidReport2017.pdf.

———. 2018. "Projected Medicare Expenditures under an Illustrative Scenario with Alternative Payment Updates to Medicare Providers." https://www.cms.gov/Research-Statistics-Data-and-Systems/Statistics-Trends-and-Reports/ReportsTrustFunds/Downloads/2018TRAlternativeScenario.pdf

Collins, S., and M. Gunja. 2018 "Premium Tax Credits Are the Individual Market's Stabilizing Force." Commonwealth Fund. https://www.commonwealthfund.org/blog/2018/premium-tax-credits-are-individual-markets-stabilizing-force.

Conrad, R., W. Liu, Z. Tillman, A. So, A. Schick, C. Nardinelli, and R. Lutter. 2018. "Estimating Cost Savings from Generic Drug Approvals in 2017." U.S. Food and Drug Administration. https://www.fda.gov/downloads/Drugs/ResourcesForYou/Consumers/BuyingUsingMedicineSafely/GenericDrugs/UCM609808.pdf.

Cullis, J., P. Jones, and C. Propper. 2000. "Waiting Lists and Medical Treatment: Analysis and Policies." In *Handbook of Health Economics*, vol. 1, edited by A. Culyer and J. Newhouse. Amsterdam: Elsevier.

Cutler, D. 2004. *Your Money or Your Life: Strong Medicine for America's Health Care System*. New York: Oxford University Press.

Cutler, D., and M. McClellan. 2001. "Is Technological Change in Medicine Worth it?" *Health Affairs* 25, no. 5: 11-29.

DeMasi, J. 2000. "Price Trends for Prescription Pharmaceuticals: 1995–1999." Background report prepared for Conference on Pharmaceutical Pricing Practices, Utilization, and Costs, sponsored by U.S. Department of Health and Human Services, Washington, August 8.

Desai, S., L. Hatfield., A. Hicks., M. Chernew, and A. Mehrotra. 2016. "Association between Availability of a Price Transparency Tool and Outpatient Spending." *Journal of the American Medical Association* 315, no. 17: 1874–81.

DiMasi, J., H. Grabowski, and R. Hansen. 2016. "Innovation in the Pharmaceutical Industry: New Estimates of R&D Costs." *Journal of Health Economics* 47: 20–33.

Durlauf, S., and B. Lawrence. 2008. *The New Palgrave Dictionary of Economics*. New York: Palgrave Macmillan.

Eibner, C., and S. Nowak. 2018. "The Effect of Eliminating the Individual Mandate Penalty and the Role of Behavioral Factors." Commonwealth Fund. http://www.commonwealthfund.org/publications/fund-reports/2018/jul/eliminatingindividual-mandate-penalty-behavioral-factors.

Einav, L., A. Finkelstein, and M. Polyakova. 2018. "Private Provision of Social Insurance: Drug-Specific Price Elasticities and Cost Sharing in Medicare Part D." *American Economic Journal: Economic Policy* 10, no. 3: 122–53.

Faber, M., M. Bosch, H. Wollersheim, S. Leatherman, and R. Grol. 2009. "Public Reporting in Health Care: How Do Consumers Use Quality-of-Care Information? A Systematic Review." *Medical Care* 47, no.1: 1-8.

Farmer, C., S. Hosek, and D. Adamson. 2016. "Balancing Demand and Supply for Veterans' Health Care: A Summary of Three RAND Assessments Conducted under the Veterans Choice Act." Rand Health. https://www.rand.org/content/dam/rand/pubs/research_reports/RR1100/RR1165z4/RAND_RR1165z4.pdf.

FDA (U.S. Food and Drug Administration). 2016. "Activities Report of the Generic Drugs Program (FY 2016) Monthly Performance."

———. 2017. "Activities Report of the Generic Drugs Program (FY 2017) Monthly Performance." https://www.fda.gov/Drugs/DevelopmentApprovalProcess/HowDrugsareDevelopedandApproved/ApprovalApplications/AbbreviatedNewDrugApplicationANDAGenerics/ucm584749.htm.

———. 2018a. "Activities Report of the Generic Drugs Program (FY 2018) Monthly Performance." https://www.fda.gov/drugs/developmentapprovalprocess/howdrugsaredevelopedandapproved/approvalapplications/abbreviatednewdrugapplicationandagenerics/ucm375079.htm.

———. 2018b. "Healthy Innovation, Safer Families: FDA's 2018 Strategic Policy Roadmap—Summary of Strategic Policy Areas." https://www.fda.gov/downloads/AboutFDA/ReportsManualsForms/Reports/UCM592001.pdf.

———. 2018c. "USP Therapeutic Categories Model Guidelines." https://www.fda.gov/RegulatoryInformation/LawsEnforcedbyFDA/SignificantAmendmentstotheFDCAct/FoodandDrugAdministrationAmendmentsActof2007/FDAAAImplementationChart/ucm232402.htm.

Feldstein, M. 1999. "Tax Avoidance and the Deadweight Loss of the Income Tax." *Review of Economic and Statistics* 81, no. 4: 674–80.

Finkelstein, A. 2004. "Static and Dynamic Effects of Health Policy: Evidence from the Vaccine Industry." *Quarterly Journal of Economics* 119, no. 2: 527–64.

Finkelstein, A., N. Hendren, and E. Luttmer. 2015. *The Value of Medicaid: Interpreting Results from the Oregon Health Insurance Experiment.* NBER Working Paper 21308. Cambridge, MA: National Bureau of Economic Research.

Finkelstein, A., N. Mahoney, and M. Notowidigdo. 2017. "What Does (Formal) Health Insurance Do, and for Whom?" Working paper, University of Chicago. http://faculty.chicagobooth.edu/neale.mahoney/research/papers/Finkelstein_Mahoney_Noto_AR_2017.pdf.

Frakt, A. 2016. "Price Transparency Is Nice. Just Don't Expect It to Cut Health Costs." *New York Times*, December 19. https://www.nytimes.com/2016/12/19/upshot/price-transparency-is-nice-just-dont-expect-it-to-cut-health-costs.html?module=inline.

Frank, R., and D. Salkever. 1997. "Generic Entry and the Price of Pharmaceuticals." *Journal of Economics and Management Strategy* 6, no. 1: 75–90.

Frost, A., and D. Newman. 2016. "Spending on Shoppable Services in Health Care." Health Cost Institute. https://www.healthcostinstitute.org/images/easyblog_articles/110/Shoppable-Services-IB-3.2.16_0.pdf.

Gaes, G. 2008. "Cost, Performance Studies Look at Prison Privatization." *National Institute of Justice Journal* 259: 32–36.

Gallen, T. 2015. "Using Participant Behavior to Measure the Value of Social Programs: The Case of Medicaid." PhD diss., University of Chicago.

Gallen, T., and C. Mulligan. 2018. "Wedges, Labor Market Behavior, and Health Insurance Coverage under the Affordable Care Act." *National Tax Journal* 71, no. 1: 75–120.

GAO (U.S. Government Accountability Office). 2018. "Veterans Choice Program." https://www.gao.gov/assets/700/692271.pdf.

Garthwaite, C., T. Gross, and M. Notowidigdo. 2018. "Hospitals as Insurers of Last Resort." *American Economic Journal: Applied Economics* 10, no. 1: 1-39.

Ghanta, P. 2013. "List of Countries with Universal Healthcare." https://truecostblog.com/2009/08/09/countries-with-universal-healthcare-by-date/.

Goldman, D., A. Jena, D. Lakdawalla, J. Malin, J. Malkin, and E. Sun. 2010. "The Value of Specialty Oncology Drugs." *Health Services Research* 45, no. 1: 115–32.

Goldman, D., G. Joyce, G. Lawless, W. Crown, and V. Willey. 2006. "Benefit Design and Specialty Drug Use." *Health Affairs* 25, no. 5: 1319–31.

Goulder, L., and R. Williams III. 2003. "The Substantial Bias from Ignoring General Equilibrium Effects in Estimating Excess Burden, and a Practical Solution." *Journal of Political Economy* 111, no. 4898–927. Chicago: University of Chicago Press.

Grabowski, D., D. Lakdawalla, D. Goldman, M. Eber, L. Liu, T. Abdelgawad, A. Kuznik, M. Chernew, and T. Philipson. 2012. "The Large Social Value Resulting from Use of Statins Warrants Steps to Improve Adherence and Broaden Treatment." *Health Affairs* 31, no. 10: 2276–85.

Grabowski, H., and J. Vernon. 1992. "Brand Loyalty, Entry and Price Competition in Pharmaceuticals after the 1984 Drug Act." *Journal of Law and Economics* 35: 331–50.

Gruber, J. 2010. *Health Care Reform Is a "Three-Legged Stool": The Costs of Partially Repealing the Affordable Care Act*. Washington: Center for American Progress.

HHS (U.S. Department of Health and Human Services). 2010. "Expanding the Use of Generic Drugs." Issue Brief, Office of the Assistant Secretary for Planning and Evaluation. https://aspe.hhs.gov/system/files/pdf/76151/ib.pdf.

———. 2018. *Reforming America's Healthcare System Through Choice and Competition*. Published jointly with the Department of the Treasury and the Department of Labor. https://www.hhs.gov/sites/default/files/Reforming-Americas-Healthcare-System-Through-Choice-and-Competition.pdf.

Himmelstein, D. 2014. "A Comparison of Hospital Administrative Costs in Eight Nations: U.S. Costs Exceed All Others by Far." Commonwealth Fund. https://www.commonwealthfund.org/publications/journalarticle/2014/sep/comparison-hospital-administrative-costs-eight-nations-us.

Ho, J., and S. Preston. 2010. "U.S. Mortality in an International Context: Age Variations." *Population and Development Review* 36, no. 4: 749–73.

Hoxby, C. 2014. "Covering the Costs." In *What Lies Ahead for America's Children and Their Schools*, edited by E. Finn and R. Sousa. Stanford, CA: Hoover Institution Press.

Jena, A., and T. Philipson. 2008. "Cost-Effectiveness Analysis and Innovation." *Journal of Health Economics* 27, no. 5: 1224–36.

Kaiser Family Foundation. 2017a. "Health Insurance Coverage of the Total Population." https://www.kff.org/other/state-indicator/total-population/?currentTimeframe=0&sortModel=%7B%22colId%22:%22Location%22,%22sort%22:%22asc%22%7D.

———. 2017b. "Medicare Advantage 2017 Spotlight: Enrollment Market Update." https://www.kff.org/medicare/issue-brief/medicare-advantage-2017-spotlight-enrollment-market-update/

———. 2018. "Data Note: Changes in Enrollment in the Individual Health Insurance Market." https://www.kff.org/health-reform/issue-brief/data-note-changes-in-enrollment-in-the-individual-health-insurance-market/.

Kessler, G. 2017. "Medicare, Private Insurance and Administrative Costs: A Democratic Talking Point." *Washington Post*, September 19. https://www.washingtonpost.com/news/fact-checker/wp/2017/09/19/medicare-private-insurance-and-administrative-costs-a-democratic-talking-point/?utm_term=.b96f58ff9cc7.

Ketchum, J., C. Lucarelli, and C. Powers. 2015. "Paying Attention or Paying Too Much in Medicare Part D." *American Economic Review* 105, no. 1: 204–33.

Kless, S., C. Wolfe, and C. Curtis. 2017. "Brief Summaries of Medicare & Medicaid." U.S. Department of Health and Human Services. https://www.cms.gov/Research-Statistics-Data-and-Systems/Statistics-Trends-and-Reports/MedicareProgramRatesStats/Downloads/MedicareMedicaidSummaries2017.pdf.

Lakdawalla, D., D. Goldman, P. Michaud, N. Sood, R. Lempert, Z. Cong, H. de Vries, and I. Gutierrez. 2009. "U.S. Pharmaceutical Policy in a Global Marketplace." *Health Affairs* 28, no. 1: w138–w150.

Lakdawalla, D., and T. Philipson. 2012. "Does Intellectual Property Restrict Output? An Analysis of Pharmaceutical Markets." *Journal of Law and Economics* 55, no. 1: 151–87.

Lee, T. 2004. "'Me Too' Products: Friend or Foe?" *New England Journal of Medicine* 350: 211–12.

Leland, H. 1979. "Quacks, Lemons, and Licensing: A Theory of Minimum Quality Standards." *Journal of Political Economy* 87, no. 6: 1328–46.

Lichtenberg, F., and T. Philipson. 2002. "The Dual Role of Intellectual Property Regulations: Within- and Between-Patent Competition in the U.S. Pharmaceuticals Industry." *Journal of Law and Economics* 45, no. S2: 643–72.

Mossialos, E., M. Wenzl, R. Osborn, and C. Anderson. 2017. "International Profiles of Health Care Systems." Commonwealth Fund. https://www.

commonwealthfund.org/publications/fund-reports/2017/may/international-profiles-health-care-systems.

Mulligan, C. 2015. *Side Effects and Complications: The Economic Consequences of Health Care Reform*. Chicago: University of Chicago Press.

Mulligan, C., and T. Philipson. 2000. *Merit Motives and Government Intervention: Public Finance in Reverse*. NBER Working Paper 7698. Cambridge, MA: National Bureau of Economic Research.

———. 2004. "Insurance Market Participation under Symmetric Information." Paper presented at American Economic Association Meetings.

Mulligan, C., and K. Tsui. 2016. *The Upside-Down Economics of Regulated and Otherwise Rigid Prices*. NBER Working Paper 22305. Cambridge, MA: National Bureau of Economic Research.

Murrin, S. 2018. "Medicaid Fraud Control Units Fiscal Year 2017 Annual Report." Office of Inspector General, U.S. Department of Health and Human Services.

Newhouse, J. 1993. *Free for All? Lessons from the RAND Health Insurance Experiment*. Cambridge, MA: Harvard University Press.

Nyman, J. 2004. "Is 'Moral Hazard' Inefficient? The Policy Implications of a New Theory." *Health Affairs* 23, no. 5: 194–99.

Pagliarulo, N. 2018. "AbbVie Surprised Investors with Its Hepatitis C Success. Will It Last?" AbbVie, Biopharmadive. https://www.biopharmadive.com/news/abbvies-surprised-investors-mavyret-hepatitis-c-success-will-it-last/529158/.

Pauly, M. 1968. "The Economics of Moral Hazard: Comment." *American Economic Review* 58, no. 3: 531–37.

Pauly, M., A. Leive, and S. Harrington. 2018. "Losses (and Gains) from Health Reform for Non-Medicaid Uninsured." *Journal of Risk and Insurance*, July. https://doi.org/10.1111/jori.12255.

Philipson, T. 2013. "What's Wrong with Private Insurance?" *Forbes*, October 20. https://www.forbes.com/sites/tomasphilipson/2013/10/20/whats-wrong-with-private-insurance/.

Philipson, T., E. Berndt, A. Gottschalk, and E. Sun. 2008. "Cost-Benefit Analysis of the FDA: The Case of the Prescription Drug User Fee Acts." *Journal of Public Economics* 92, nos. 5–6: 1306–25.

Phillipson, T., M. Eber, D. Lakdawalla, M. Corral, R. Conti, and D. Goldman. 2012. "An Analysis of Whether Higher Healthcare Spending in the United States versus Europe Is "Worth it" in the Case of Cancer." *Health Affairs* 31, no. 4: 670–81.

Philipson, T., and A. Jena. 2006. "Who Benefits from New Medical Technologies? Estimates of Consumer and Producer Surpluses for HIV/AIDS Drugs." *Forum for Health Economics & Policy*, (De Gruyter) 9, no. 2: 1–33.

Philipson, T., and E. Sun. 2008. "Is the Food and Drug Administration Safe and Effective?" *Journal of Economic Perspectives* 22, no. 1: 85–102.

Reinhardt, U. 2010. "Health Care, Uncertainty and Morality." *New York Times*, Economix Blog, August 13. https://economix.blogs.nytimes.com/2010/08/13/health-care-uncertainty-and-morality/?mtrref=the60sat50.blogspot.com.

Ringel, J., S. Hosek, B. Vollaard, and S. Mahnovski. 2002. *The Elasticity of Demand for Health Care: A Review of the Literature and Its Application to the Military Health System*. Santa Monica, CA: RAND Corporation. https://www.rand.org/pubs/monograph_reports/MR1355.html.

Robinson, C., T. Brown, and C. Whaley. 2017. "Reference Pricing Changes 'Choice Architecture' of Healthcare for Consumers." *Health Affairs* 36, no. 3: 524–30.

Sacks, D. 2018. "The Health Insurance Marketplaces." *Journal of American Medical Association* 320, no. 6: 549–50.

Saez, E., J. Slemrod, and S. Giertz. 2012. "The Elasticity of Taxable Income with Respect to Marginal Tax Rates: A Critical Review." *Journal of Economic Literature* 50: 3–50.

Sood, N., E. Sun, L. Daugherty, and A. Ghosh. 2008. "How Much Is Too Much? An Analysis of Health Plan Profits and Administrative Costs in California." California HealthCare Foundation. https://www.chcf.org/wp-content/uploads/2017/12/PDF HowMuchIsTooMuchPlanProfits.pdf.

Stigler, G. 1971. "The Theory of Economic Regulation." *Bell Journal of Economics and Management Science* 2, no. 1: 3–21.

Toich, L. 2017. "Will Hepatitis C Virus Medication Costs Drop in the Years Ahead?" *Pharmacy Times*, February 8. http://www.pharmacytimes.com/resource-centers/hepatitisc/will-hepatitis-c-virus-medicaton-costs-drop-in-the-years-ahead.

U.S. Census Bureau. 2017. "Selected Characteristics of the Uninsured in the United States." https://factfinder.census.gov/faces/tableservices/jsf/pages/productview.xhtml?src=bkmk.

U.S. Congress. 1985. "H.R.3128 Consolidated Omnibus Budget Reconciliation Act of 1985." https://www.congress.gov/bill/99th-congress/house-bill/3128.

Walker, J. 2018. "Gilead to Slice List Prices of Liver Drugs." *Wall Street Journal*, September 24. https://www.wsj.com/articles/gilead-to-slice-list-prices-of-liver-drugs-1537818060.

Weber, C. 2014. "Towards Obtaining a Consistent Estimate of the Elasticity of Taxable Income Using Difference-in-Differences." *Journal of Public Economics* 117: 90–103.

Weiner, J., R. Rosenquist, and E. Hartman. 2018. "State Efforts to Close the Health Coverage Gap." https://ldi.upenn.edu/brief/state-efforts-close-health-coverage-gap.

Weisbart, E. 2012. "A Single-Payer System Would Reduce U.S. Health Care Costs." *Virtual Monitor* 14, no. 11: 897–903.

White, C., and M. Eguchi. 2014. "Reference Pricing: A Small Piece of the Health Care Price and Quality Puzzle." NIHCR Research Brief 18, National Institute for

Health Care Reform. https://nihcr.org/analysis/improving-care-delivery/prevention-improving-health/reference-pricing2/#ib4.

Woodman, J. 2015. *Patients Beyond Borders: Everybody's Guide to Affordable, World-Class Medical Travel*. Chapel Hill, NC: Healthy Travel Media.

Woolhandler, S., T. Campbell, and D. Himmelstein. 2003. "Costs of Health Care Administration in the United States and Canada." *New England Journal of Medicine* 349, no. 8: 768–75.

Yin, W. 2008. "Market Incentives and Pharmaceutical Innovation." *Journal of Health Economics* 27, no. 4: 1060–77.

Zeckhauser, R. 1970. "Medical Insurance: A Case Study of the Trade-Off Between Risk Spreading and Appropriate Incentives." *Journal of Economic Theory* 2, no. 1: 10–26.

Zerbe, R., and H. McCurdy. 1999. "The Failure of Market Failure." *Journal of Policy Analysis and Management* 18, no. 4: 558–78.

Chapter 5

Adamson, S. 2018. "Comparing Interstate Regulation and Investment in U.S. Gas and Electric Transmission." *Economics of Energy and Environmental Policy* 7, no. 1: 7–24.

Adelman, M. 1996. *Genie Out of the Bottle: World Oil Markets since 1970*. Cambridge, MA: MIT Press.

Alchian, A., and W. Allen. 1964. *University Economics*. Belmont, CA: Wadsworth.

Alyeska Pipeline Service Company. 2011. "Low Flow Impact Study." https://www.alyeska-pipe.com/assets/uploads/pagestructure/TAPS_Operations_LowFlow/editor_uploads/LoFIS_Summary_Report_P6%2027_FullReport.pdf.

AOGHS (American Oil & Gas Historical Society). 2018. "Trans-Alaska Pipeline History." https://aoghs.org/transportation/trans-alaska-pipeline/

Argueta, C., L. Hanson, and C. Vincent. 2017. "Federal Land Ownership: Overview and Data." Congressional Research Service. https://fas.org/sgp/crs/misc/R42346.pdf

Bahndari, N., N. Mehta, V. Joshi, P. Creuset, and T. Chen. 2018. "The IMO 2020: Global Shipping's Blue Sky Moment." Goldman Sachs Equity Research, May 30. http://www.weltinnenpolitik.net/wp-content/uploads/2018/06/IMO-2020-Global-Shipping-Blue-Sky-Moment.pdf.

Bakhtiari, A. 2004. "World Oil Production Capacity Model Suggests Output Peak by 2006–07." *Oil & Gas Journal*, April 26, 18–19.

Balash, P., K. Kern, J. Brewer, J. Adder, C. Nichols, G. Pickpaugh, and E. Shuster. 2018. "Reliability, Resilience and the Oncoming Wave of Retiring Baseload Units." *DOE National Energy Technology Laboratory* 1, March 13. https://www.districtenergy.org/HigherLogic/System/DownloadDocumentFile.ashx?DocumentFileKey=246e582e-81b7-cc50-c9c5-50031845aca0&forceDialog=0.

Barsky, R., and L. Kilian. 2002. "Do We Really Know That Oil Caused the Great Stagflation? A Monetary Alternative." *NBER Macroeconomics Annual* 16: 137–83.

Baumeister, C., and G. Peersman. 2013. "Time-Varying Effects of Oil Supply Shocks on the U.S. Economy." *American Economic Review: Macroeconomics* 5, no. 4: 1–28.

Bentley, R. 2002. "Global Oil & Gas Depletion: An Overview." *Energy Policy* 30: 189–205. http://www.oilcrisis.com/bentley/depletionoverview.pdf.

BLM (Bureau of Land Management). 2017. "Federal Coal Program Programmatic Environmental Impact Statement (PEIS): Scoping Report Appendices." U.S. Department of the Interior. https://www.eenews.net/assets/2017/01/11/document_gw_03.pdf.

Borenstein, S., J. Bushnell, and F. Wolak. 2002. "Measuring Market Inefficiencies in California's Restructured Wholesale Electricity Market." *American Economic Review* 92, no. 5: 1376–1405.

Borenstein, S., and R. Kellogg. 2014. "The Incidence of an Oil Glut: Who Benefits from Cheap Crude Oil in the Midwest?" *Energy Journal* 35, no. 1: 15–33.

Boslett, A., T. Guilfoos, and C. Lang. 2015. "Valuation of Expectations: A Hedonic Study of Shale Gas Development and New York's Moratorium." *Journal of Environmental Economics and Management* 77: 14–30.

Boyce, J. 2013. "Prediction and Inference in the Hubbert-Deffeyes Peak Oil Model." *Energy Journal* 34, no. 2: 91–144.

BP. 2018. *BP Statistical Review of World Energy*. London: BP. https://www.bp.com/content/dam/bp/business-sites/en/global/corporate/pdfs/energy-economics/statistical-review/bp-stats-review-2018-full-report.pdf.

Brown, S., and H. Huntington. 2015. "Evaluating U.S. Oil Security and Import Reliance." *Energy Policy* 79: 5–22.

Burtraw, D., and S. Szambelan. 2009. "U.S. Emissions Trading Markets for SO_2 and NO_x." RFF Discussion Paper 09-40. Resources for the Future, Washington.

Bushnell, J., and K. Novan. 2018. *Setting with the Sun: The Impacts of Renewable Energy on Wholesale Power Markets*. NBER Working Paper 24980. Cambridge, MA: National Bureau of Economic Research.

Busse, M., and N. Keohane. 2007. "Market Effects of Environmental Regulation: Coal, Railroads, and the 1990 Clean Air Act." *RAND Journal of Economics* 38, no. 4: 1159–79.

Campbell, C. 2003. "Industry Urged to Watch for Regular Oil Production Peaks, Depletion Signals." *Oil & Gas Journal*, July 14, 38–47.

Carlson, C., D. Burtraw, M. Cropper, and K. Palmer. 2000. "Sulfur Dioxide Control by Electric Utilities: What Are the Gains from Trade?" *Journal of Political Economy* 108, no. 6: 1292–1326.

CEA (Council of Economic Advisers). 2006. *Economic Report of the President*. Washington: U.S. Government Publishing Office.

———. 2012. *Economic Report of the President*. Washington: U.S. Government Publishing Office.

———. 2013. *Economic Report of the President*. Washington: U.S. Government Publishing Office.

———. 2015. *Economic Report of the President*. Washington: U.S. Government Publishing Office.

———. 2016a. *Economic Report of the President*. Washington: U.S. Government Publishing Office.

———. 2016b. "The Economics of Mineral Leasing on Federal Lands: Ensuring a Fair Return to Taxpayers." https://obamawhitehouse.archives.gov/sites/default/files/page/files/20160622_cea_coal_leasing.pdf.

———. 2017. *Economic Report of the President*. Washington: U.S. Government Publishing Office.

Cosgrove, B., D. LaFave, S. Dissanayake, and M. Donihue. 2015. "The Economic Impact of Shale Gas Development: A Natural Experiment along the New York/Pennsylvania Border." *Agricultural and Resource Economics Review* 44, no. 2: 20–39.

Covert, T., and R. Kellogg. 2017. *Crude by Rail, Option Value, and Pipeline Investment*. NBER Working Paper 23855. Cambridge, MA: National Bureau of Economic Research.

Cullen, J., 2013. "Measuring the Environmental Benefits of Wind-Generated Electricity." *American Economic Journal: Economic Policy* 5, no. 4: 107–33.

Davis, L., and C. Hausman. 2016. "Market Impacts of a Nuclear Power Plant Closure." *American Economic Journal: Applied Economics* 8, no. 2: 92–122.

Davis, L., and C. Wolfram. 2012. "Deregulation, Consolidation, and Efficiency: Evidence from U.S. Nuclear Power." *American Economic Journal: Applied Economics* 4, no. 4: 194–225.

Deffeyes, K. 2001. *Hubbert's Peak: The Impending World Oil Shortage*. Princeton, NJ: Princeton University Press.

———. 2006. *Beyond Oil: The View from Hubbert's Peak*. New York: Hill & Wang.

Deutch, J. 2011. "The Good News About Gas: The Natural Gas Revolution and Its Consequences." *Foreign Affairs* 90, no. 1: 82–93.

EIA (U.S. Energy Information Administration). 2006. *Annual Energy Outlook 2006 with Projections to 2030*. https://www.eia.gov/outlooks/archive/aeo06/aeoref_tab.html.

———. 2010. *Annual Energy Outlook 2010 with Projections to 2030*. https://www.eia.gov/outlooks/archive/aeo10/aeoref_tab.html.

———. 2012. *Annual Energy Review 2011*. https://www.eia.gov/totalenergy/data/annual/showtext.php?t=ptb0702.

———. 2017. *International Energy Outlook 2017*. https://www.eia.gov/outlooks/aeo/data/ browser/#/?id=10-IEO2017.

———. 2018a. "Analysis of Projected Crude Oil Production in the Arctic National Wildlife Refuge." https://www.eia.gov/outlooks/aeo/pdf/ANWR.pdf.

———. 2018b. *Annual Energy Outlook 2018*. https://www.eia.gov/outlooks/aeo/.

———. 2018c. "Coal Data Browser." https://www.eia.gov/coal/data/browser/.

———. 2018d. "Electric Power Annual." https://www.eia.gov/electricity/annual/.

———. 2018e. "Electric Power Monthly: Table B.2, Major Disturbances and Unusual Occurrences, 2017." https://www.eia.gov/electricity/monthly/epm_table_grapher.php?t=epmt_b_2.

———. 2018f. "Nonassociated Natural Gas Proved Reserves, Wet After Lease Separation." https://www.eia.gov/dnav/ng/NG_ENR_NANG_A_EPG0_R40_BCF_A.htm/.

———. 2018g. "November 2018 Monthly Energy Review." https://www.eia.gov/totalenergy/data/monthly/index.php.

———. 2018h. "Pipeline Projects." https://www.eia.gov/naturalgas/pipelines/EIA-NaturalGasPipelineProjects.xlsx.

———. 2018i. "Short-Term Energy Outlook Data Browser." https://www.eia.gov/outlooks/steo/data/browser/.

———. 2018j. "U.S. State-to-State Capacity." https://www.eia.gov/naturalgas/pipelines/EIA-StatetoStateCapacity.xlsx.

EPA (Environmental Protection Agency). 2018a. "Air Pollutant Emissions Trends Data: Average Annual Emissions: Criteria Pollutants National Tier 1 for 1970—2017." March 27, 2018. https://www.epa.gov/air-emissions-inventories/air-pollutant-emissions-trends-data.

———. 2018b. "Inventory of U.S. Greenhouse Gas Emissions and Sinks: 1990–2016." EPA 430-R-18-003. https://www.epa.gov/ghgemissions/inventory-us-greenhouse-gas-emissions-and-sinks-1990-2016.

———. 2018c. "Our Nation's Air 2018." https://gispub.epa.gov/air/trendsreport/2018/#highlights.

European Commission. 2018. "Liquefied Natural Gas." https://ec.europa.eu/energy/en/topics/oil-gas-and-coal/liquefied-natural-gas-lng.

Fabrizio, K., N. Rose, and C. Wolfram. 2007. "Do Markets Reduce Costs? Assessing the Impact of Regulatory Restructuring on U.S. Electric Generation Efficiency." *American Economic Review* 97, no. 4: 1250–77.

Fally, T., and J. Sayre. 2018. *Commodity Trade Matters*. NBER Working Paper 24965. Cambridge, MA: National Bureau of Economic Research. https://ideas.repec.org/p/nbr/nberwo/24965.html.

Fell, H., and D. Kaffine. 2018. "The Fall of Coal: Joint Impacts of Fuel Prices and Renewables on Generation and Emissions." *American Economic Journal: Economic Policy* 10, no. 2: 90–116.

FERC (Federal Energy Regulatory Commission). 2018. "North American LNG Import/Export Terminals—Approved." https://www.ferc.gov/industries/gas/indus-act/lng/lng-approved.pdf.

Fitzgerald, T. 2018. "Regulatory Obsolescence through Technological Changes in Oil and Gas Extraction." *William & Mary Environmental Law & Policy Review* 43, no. 1.

GAO (U.S. Government Accountability Office). 2013. *Coal Leasing: BLM Could Enhance Appraisal Process, More Explicitly Consider Coal Exports, and Provide More Public Information*. GAO Publication 14-140. Washington: U.S. Government Publishing Office.

Gerking, S., and S. Hamilton. 2008. "What Explains the Increased Utilization of Powder River Basin Coal in Electric Power Generation?" *American Journal of Agricultural Economics* 90, no. 4: 933–50.

Gold, R. 2014. *The Boom: How Fracking Ignited the American Energy Revolution and Changed the World*. New York: Simon & Schuster.

Hahn, R., and P. Passell. 2010. "The Economics of Allowing More U.S. Oil Drilling. *Energy Economics* 32, no. 3: 638–50.

Hamilton, J. 1996. "This Is What Happened to the Oil Price–Macroeconomy Relationship." *Journal of Monetary Economics* 38, no. 2: 215–20.

———. 2003. "What Is an Oil Shock?" *Journal of Econometrics* 113: 363–98.

Hausman, C. 2014. "Corporate Incentives and Nuclear Safety." *American Economic Journal: Economic Policy* 6, no. 3: 178–206.

Hausman, C., and R. Kellogg. 2015. "Welfare and Distributional Implications of Shale Gas." *Brookings Papers on Economic Activity*, Spring, 71–125.

Hefner, R., III. 2014. "The United States of Gas: Why the Shale Revolution Could Have Happened Only in America." *Foreign Affairs* 93, no. 3: 9–14.

Hirsch, R., R. Bezdek, and R. Wendling. 2005. "Peaking of World Oil Production: Impacts, Mitigation, and Risk Management." Office of Science and Technical Information, U.S. Department of Energy, NETL-IR-2005-093. https://www.osti.gov/servlets/purl/939271.

Hoover, K., and S. Perez. 1994. "Post Hoc Ergo Propter Once More: An Evaluation of 'Does Monetary Policy Matter?' in the Spirit of James Tobin." *Journal of Monetary Economics* 34: 47–73.

Hubbert, M. 1956. "Nuclear Energy and the Fossil Fuels." Paper presented at Spring Meeting of Southern District of American Petroleum Institute, San Antonio, March 7–9. http://www.hubbertpeak.com/hubbert/1956/1956.pdf.

———. 1962. "Energy Resources: A Report to the Committee on Natural Resources of the National Academy of Sciences, National Research Council." https://www.nap.edu/read/18451/chapter/3.

Hummels, D., and A. Skiba. 2004. "Shipping the Good Apples Out? An Empirical Confirmation of the Alchian-Allen Conjecture." *Journal of Political Economy* 112, no. 6: 1384–1402.

IAEA (International Atomic Energy Agency). 2018. "SANMEN-1." IAEA Power Reactor Information System. https://pris.iaea.org/PRIS/CountryStatistics/ReactorDetails.aspx?current=879.

IEA (International Energy Agency). 2018. "Oil 2018: Analysis and Forecasts to 2023." https://www.iea.org/oilmarketreport/.

Imsirovic, A., and B. Pryor. 2018. "IMO 20202 and the Brent-Dubai Spread." Oxford Institute for Energy Studies. https://www.oxfordenergy.org/publications/imo-2020-brent-dubai-spread/.

Inman, M. 2016. *The Oracle of Oil: A Maverick Geologist's Quest for a Sustainable Future*. New York: W. W. Norton.

Jaffe, A., and R. Soligo. 2002. "The Role of Inventories in Oil Market Stability." *Quarterly Review of Economics and Finance* 42, no. 2: 401–15.

Jenkins, J. 2018. "What's Killing Nuclear Power in U.S. Electricity Markets? Drivers of Wholesale Price Declines at Nuclear Generators in the PJM Interconnection." CEEPR Working Paper 2018-001, Massachusetts Institute of Technology.

Jevons, W. 1865. *The Coal Question: An Inquiry Concerning the Progress of the Nation, and the Probable Exhaustion of the Coal-Mines*. London: Macmillan.

Jiménez-Rodríguez, R., and M. Sánchez. 2004. *Oil Price Shocks and Real GDP Growth: Empirical Evidence for Some OECD Countries*. ECB Working Paper 362. Frankfurt: European Central Bank.

Kaffine, D., B. McBee, and J. Lieskovsky. 2013. "Emissions Savings from Wind Power Generation in Texas. *Energy Journal* 34, no. 1: 155–75.

Keiser, D., and J. Shapiro. 2018. "Consequences of the Clean Water Act and the Demand for Water Quality." *Quarterly Journal of Economics* 134, no. 1: 345–96.

Kilian, L. 2008. "Exogenous Oil Supply Shocks: How Big Are They and How Much Do They Matter for the U.S. Economy?" *Review of Economics and Statistics* 90, no. 2: 216–40.

Kilian, L., and R. Vigfusson. 2017. "The Role of Oil Price Shocks in Causing U.S. Recessions." *Journal of Money, Credit and Banking* 49: 1747–76.

Kleinberg, R., S. Paltsev, C. Ebinger, D. Hobbs, and T. Boersma. 2016. "Tight Oil Development Economics: Benchmarks, Breakeven Points, and Inelasticities." CEEPR Working Paper 2016-12, Massachusetts Institute of Technology.

Komarek, T. 2016. "Labor Market Dynamics and the Unconventional Natural Gas Boom: Evidence from the Marcellus Region." *Resource and Energy Economics* 45: 1–17.

Laherrère, J. 1999. "World Oil Supply: What Goes Up Must Come Down, but When Will It Peak?" *Oil & Gas Journal*, February 1. https://www.ogj.com/articles/print/volume-97/issue-5/in-this-issue/general-interest/world-oil-supply-what-goes-up-must-come-down-but-when-will-it-peak.html.

Linn, J., L. Muehlenbachs, and Y. Wang. 2014. "How Do Natural Gas Prices Affect Electricity Consumers and the Environment?" Resources for the Future Discussion Paper 14-19. http://www.rff.org/files/sharepoint/WorkImages/Download/RFF-DP-14-19.pdf.

Malthus, T. 1798. "An Essay on the Principle of Population as It Affects the Future Improvement of Society." http://www.esp.org/books/malthus/population/malthus.pdf.

McNally, R. 2017. *Crude Volatility: The History and the Future of Boom-Bust Oil Prices*. New York: Columbia University Press.

McRae, S. 2017. *Crude Oil Price Differentials and Pipeline Infrastructure*. NBER Working Paper 24170. Cambridge, MA: National Bureau of Economic Research.

Melek, N., and E. Ojeda. 2017. "Lifting the US Crude Oil Export Ban: Prospects for Increasing Oil Market Efficiency." *Economic Review–Federal Reserve Bank of Kansas*, second quarter. https://www.kansascityfed.org/~/media/files/publicat/econrev/econrevarchive/2017/2q17cakirmelekojeda.pdf.

MSHA (Mine Safety and Health Administration). 2018. "Quarterly Mine Employment and Coal Production Report." U.S. Department of Labor, Form 7000-2. https://www.govinfo.gov/content/pkg/CFR-2018-title30-vol1/pdf/CFR-2018-title30-vol1.pdf.

NADP (National Atmospheric Deposition Program). 2018. "National Trends Network (NTN): Precipitation-Weighted Mean (PWM) Concentrations." http://nadp.slh.wisc.edu/data/ntn/ntnAllsites.aspx.

NEI (Nuclear Energy Institute). 2018. "Nuclear Costs in Context." https://www.nei.org/CorporateSite/media/filefolder/resources/reports-and-briefs/nuclear-costs-context-201810.pdf.

NEISO (New England Independent System Operator). 2018. "Operational Fuel-Security Analysis." January 17. https://www.iso-ne.com/static-assets/documents/2018/01/20180117_operational_fuel_security_analysis.pdf.

Newell, R., and B. Prest. 2017. *The Unconventional Oil Supply Boom: Aggregate Price Response from Microdata*. NBER Working Paper 23973. Cambridge, MA: National Bureau of Economic Research. https://www.nber.org/papers/w23973.

Novan, K. 2015. "Valuing the Wind: Renewable Energy Policies and Air Pollution Avoided." *American Economic Journal: Economic Policy* 7, no. 3: 291–326.

Nuclear Regulatory Commission. 2018. "Power Reactor Status Reports for 2018." https://www.nrc.gov/reading-rm/doc-collections/event-status/reactor-status/2018/.

ONRR (Office of Natural Resources Revenue). 2018. "Oil and Gas Lease Sale Data CY 1988-2018." U.S. Bureau of Land Management.

OPEC (Organization of the Petroleum Exporting Countries). 2018a. "Annual Statistical Bulletin." https://www.opec.org/opec_web/en/publications/202.htm.

———. 2018b. "Monthly Oil Market Report." https://www.opec.org/opec_web/en/publications/338.htm.

Parry, I., and J. Darmstadter. 2003. *The Costs of U.S. Oil Dependency*. Washington: Resources for the Future.

Pierru, A., J. Smith, and T. Zamrik. 2018. "OPEC's Impact on Oil Price Volatility: The Role of Spare Capacity." *Energy Journal* 39, no. 2: 103–22.

PJM Interconnection. 2017. "PJM's Evolving Resource Mix and System Reliability." https://www.pjm.com/~/media/library/reports-notices/special-reports/20170330-pjms-evolving-resource-mix-and-system-reliability.ashx.

Shapiro, J., and R. Walker. 2018. "Why Is Pollution from U.S. Manufacturing Declining? The Roles of Environmental Regulation, Productivity, and Trade." *American Economic Review* 108, no. 12: 3814–54.

Skrebowski, C. 2004. "Oil Field Mega Projects—2004." *Petroleum Review* 68, no 684: 18–20.

Sullivan, T., C. Driscoll, C. Beier, D. Burtraw, I. Fernandez, J. Galloway, D. Gay, C. Goodale, G. Likens, G. Lovett, and S. Watmough. 2018. "Air Pollution Success Stories in the United States: The Value of Long-Term Observations." *Environmental Science and Policy* 84: 65–73.

United Nations. 2018. "UN Comtrade Database." Department of Economic and Social Affairs, Statistics Division, Trade Statistics Branch. https://comtrade.un.org/data/.

U.S. Census Bureau. 2018. "USA Trade Online." https://usatrade.census.gov/.

USGS (U.S. Geological Survey). 1998. "The Oil and Gas Resource Potential of the Arctic National Wildlife Refuge 1002 Area, Alaska." https://pubs.usgs.gov/of/1998/ofr-98-0034/ANWR1002.pdf.

———. 2010. "2010 Updated Assessment of Undiscovered Oil and Gas Resources of the National Petroleum Reserve in Alaska (NPRA)." https://pubs.usgs.gov/fs/2010/3102/

———. 2017a. "Assessing U.S. Coal Resources and Reserves." *Fact Sheet 2017-3067*. https://pubs.er.usgs.gov/publication/fs20173067.

———. 2017b. "Assessment of Undiscovered Oil and Gas Resources in the Cretaceous Nanushuk and Torok Formations, Alaska North Slope, and Summary of Resource Potential of the National Petroleum Reserve in Alaska." https://pubs.usgs.gov/fs/2017/3088/fs20173088.pdf.

Weber, J. 2012. "The Effects of a Natural Gas Boom on Employment and Income in Colorado, Texas, and Wyoming." *Energy Economics* 34, no. 5: 1580–88. https://doi.org/10.1016/j.eneco.2011.11.013.

Weber, J., and C. Hitaj. 2015. "What Can We Learn About Shale Gas Development from Land Values? Opportunities, Challenges, and Evidence from Texas and Pennsylvania." *Agricultural and Resource Economics Review* 44, no. 2: 40–58.

Wolak, F. 2017. "Assessing the Impact of the Diffusion of Shale Oil and Gas Technology on the Global Coal Market." Unpublished paper, Stanford University.

Wyeno, R. 2018. "Natural Gas Infrastructure in Mexico." *S&P Global: Platts*, November 8–9.

Zhuravleva, P. 2010. "Analysis of LNG Arbitrage Examines Main Barriers to Developing Market." *LNG Journal*.

Zuckerman, G. 2014. *The Frackers: The Outrageous Inside Story of the New Billionaire Wildcatters*. New York: Penguin.

Chapter 6

Angell, C., and N. Williams. 2005. "FYI Revisited: U.S. Home Prices—Does Bust Always Follow Boom?" *FYI: An Update on Emerging Issues in Banking* (Federal Deposit Insurance Corporation), May 2. http://www.fdic.gov/bank/analytical/fyi/050205fyi.pdf.

Baily, M., R. Litan, and M. Johnson. 2008. "The Origins of the Financial Crisis." Working paper, Brookings Fixing Finance Series. https://www.brookings.edu/wp-content/uploads/2016/06/11_origins_crisis_baily_litan.pdf.

Belsky, E., and N. Richardson. 2010. "Understanding the Boom and Bust in Nonprime Mortgage Lending." Joint Center for Housing Studies at Harvard University. http://www.jchs.harvard.edu/sites/default/files/ubb10-1.pdf.

Bordo, M., and J. Duca. 2018. *The Impact of the Dodd-Frank Act on Small Business*. NBER Working Paper 24501. Cambridge, MA: National Bureau of Economic Research.

Breitenstein, E., and J. McGee. 2015. "Brick-and-Mortar Banking Remains Prevalent in an Increasingly Virtual World." *FDIC Quarterly* 9, no. 1. https://www.fdic.gov/bank/analytical/quarterly/2015-vol9-1/fdic-4q2014-v9n1-brickandmortar.pdf.

Brunnermeier, M., A. Crockett, C. Goodhart, A. Persaud, and H. Shin. 2009. *The Fundamental Principles of Financial Regulation*. Geneva Report on the World Economy. Princeton, NJ: Princeton University. https://www.princeton.edu/~markus/research/papers/Geneva11.pdf.

Capone, C. 1996. *Providing Alternatives to Mortgage Foreclosure: A Report to Congress*. U.S. Department of Housing and Urban Development. Washington: U.S. Government Printing Office. https://www.huduser.gov/portal/Publications/pdf/alt.pdf.

Choi D., M. Holcomb, and D. Morgan. 2018. "Bank Leverage Limits and Regulatory Arbitrage: New Evidence on a Recurring Question." *Federal Reserve Bank of New York Staff Reports*, no. 856.

Coates, J. 2015. "Cost-Benefit Analysis of Financial Regulation: Case Studies and Implications." *Yale Law Journal* 124, no. 4: 882–1345.

Dahl, D., J. Fuchs, A. Meyer, and M. Neely. 2018. "Compliance Costs, Economies of Scale and Compliance Performance." Federal Reserve Bank of Saint Louis, Division of Bank Supervision. https://www.communitybanking.org/~/media/files/compliance%20costs%20economies%20of%20scale%20and%20compliance%20performance.pdf.

FCIC (Financial Crisis Inquiry Commission). 2011. *The Financial Crisis Inquiry Report*. Washington: U.S. Government Publishing Office. https://www.gpo.gov/fdsys/pkg/GPO-FCIC/pdf/GPO-FCIC.pdf.

FDIC (Federal Deposit Insurance Corporation). 1997. *History of the Eighties, Volume I: An Examination of the Banking Crises of the 1980s and Early 1990s*. Washington: FDIC.

———. 2008. "JPMorgan Chase Acquires Banking Operations of Washington Mutual." Press release. https://www.fdic.gov/news/news/press/2008/pr08085.html.

———. 2012. "Community Banking Study." https://www.fdic.gov/regulations/resources/cbi/report/cbi-full.pdf.

———. 2017. *Crisis and Response: An FDIC History, 2008–13*. Washington: FDIC.

———. 2018. "Quarterly Bank Profile, Fourth Quarter 2018." https://www.fdic.gov/bank/analytical/qbp/2018dec/qbp.pdf.

Federal Reserve Board of Governors. 2018. "Report to Congress on Implementation of Enhanced Prudential Standards." https://www.federalreserve.gov/publications/files/report-to-congress-on-eps-implementation-201801.pdf.

FFIEC (Federal Financial Institutions Examination Council). 1996. "Uniform Financial Institutions Rating System." *Federal Register* 61, no. 245: 67021–29.

GAO (U.S. Government Accountability Office). 2013. "Financial Regulatory Reform: Financial Crisis Losses and Potential Impacts of the Dodd-Frank Act." Report to Congressional Requesters GAO-13-180. https://www.gao.gov/assets/660/651322.pdf.

Gorton, G. 2007. *The Panic of 2007*. NBER Working Paper 14358. Cambridge, MA: National Bureau of Economic Research.

Holtz-Eakin, D. 2015. "The Growth Consequences of Dodd-Frank." American Action Forum. https://www.americanactionforum.org/research/the-growth-consequences-of-dodd-frank/.

Hopt, K. 2013. "Corporate Governance of Banks and Other Financial Institutions after the Financial Crisis." *Journal of Corporate Law Studies* 13, part 2: 219–53.

Hoskins, S., and M. Labonte. 2015. "An Analysis of the Regulatory Burden on Small Banks." Congressional Research Service. https://fas.org/sgp/crs/misc/R43999.pdf.

Hughes, J., J. Jagtiani, L. Mester, and C. Moon. 2018. "Does Scale Matter in Community Bank Performance? Evidence Obtained by Applying Several New Measures of Performance." Working paper, Federal Reserve Bank of Philadelphia. https://www.philadelphiafed.org/-/media/research-and-data/publications/working-papers/2018/wp18-11.pdf.

IMF (International Monetary Fund). 2008. *Global Financial Stability Report: Containing Systemic Risks and Restoring Financial Soundness*. Washington: IMF. http://www.imf.org/External/Pubs/FT/GFSR/2008/01/pdf/text.pdf.

———. 2010. *Financial System Stability Assessment*. Washington: IMF. https://www.imf.org/external/pubs/ft/scr/2010/cr10247.pdf.

Ligon, J., and W. Beach. 2013. *The Housing Market Without Fannie Mae and Freddie Mac: Economic Effects of Eliminating Government-Sponsored Enterprises in Housing*. Washington: Heritage Foundation. https://www.heritage.org/housing/report/

housing-market-without-fannie-mae-and-freddie-mac-economic-effects-eliminating.

Lincoln, T. 2008. "Regulators' Failure to Heed Warnings Allowed Subprime Mortgage Lending to Spin of Control." Public Citizen. https://www.citizen.org/sites/default/files/chapter-one-regulators-failure-to-heed-warnings.pdf.

Luttrell, D., T. Atkinson, and H. Rosenblum. 2013. "Assessing the Costs and Consequences of the 2007–09 Financial Crisis and Its Aftermath." *Federal Reserve Bank of Dallas Economic Letter* 8, no. 7: 1–4.

McLaughlin, P., D. Francis, and O. Sherouse. 2017. "Dodd-Frank Is One of the Biggest Regulatory Events Ever." Mercatus Center at George Mason University. https://www.mercatus.org/publications/dodd-frank-one-biggest-regulatory-events-ever.

McLaughlin, P., and O. Sherouse. 2016. "The McLaughlin-Sherouse List: The 10 Most-Regulated Industries of 2014." Mercatus Center at George Mason University. https://www.mercatus.org/publication/mclaughlin-sherouse-list-10-most-regulated-industries-2014.

Passmore, W., S. Sherlund, and G. Burgess. 2005. "The Effect of Housing Government-Sponsored Enterprises on Mortgage Rates." *Real Estate Economics* 33, no. 3: 427–63.

Peirce, H., I. Robinson, and T. Stratmann. 2014. *How Are Small Banks Faring Under Dodd-Frank?* Working Paper 14-5. Arlington, VA: Mercatus Center at George Mason University.

Perkins, D. 2017. "Tailoring Bank Regulations: Differences in Bank Size, Activities, and Capital Levels." Congressional Research Service. https://fas.org/sgp/crs/misc/R45051.pdf.

Pinto, E. 2010. "Triggers of the Financial Crisis." American Enterprise Institute. http://www.aei.org/paper/100174.

Reinhart, C., and K. Rogoff. 2009. *This Time Is Different: Eight Centuries of Financial Folly*. Princeton, NJ: Princeton University Press.

Roberts, D., A. Sarkar, and O. Shachar. 2018. "Bank Liquidity Provision and Basel Liquidity Regulations." *Federal Reserve Bank of New York Staff Reports*, no. 852.

Sunstein, C. 2015. "Financial Regulation and Cost-Benefit Analysis." *Yale Law Journal Forum* 124, no. 4: 882–1345.

U.S. Department of the Treasury. 2017. *A Financial System That Creates Economic Opportunities: Banks and Credit Unions*. Washington: U.S. Government Publishing Office. https://www.treasury.gov/press-center/press-releases/Documents/A%20Financial%20System.pdf.

Viscusi, W., and T. Gayer. 2016. "Behavioral Public Choice: The Behavioral Paradox of Government Policy." *Harvard Journal of Law & Public Policy* 38, no. 3: 973–1007.

Wallison, P. 2011. "Financial Crisis Inquiry Commission Report, Dissenting Statement." American Enterprise Institute. http://fcic-static.law.stanford.edu/cdn_media/fcic-reports/fcic_final_report_wallison_dissent.pdf.

Chapter 7

Abel, D., J. Salvatier, A. Stuhlmuller, and O. Evans. 2017. "Agent-Agnostic Human-in-the-Loop Reinforcement Learning." Cornell University. https://arxiv.org/abs/1701.04079.

Acemoglu, D., and D. Autor. 2011. "Skills, Tasks, and Technologies: Implications for Employment and Earnings." In *Handbook of Labor Economics, Volume 4, Part B*, edited by O. Ashenfelter and D. Card. Amsterdam: Elsevier.

Acemoglu, D., D. Dorn, G. Hanson, and B. Price. 2014. "Return of the Solow Paradox? IT, Productivity, and Employment in U.S. Manufacturing." *American Economic Review* 104, no. 5: 394–99.

Acemoglu, D., and P. Restrepo. 2018. "The Race between Man and Machine: Implications of Technology for Growth, Factor Shares, and Employment." *American Economic Review* 108, no. 6: 1488–1542.

Aghion, P., B. Jones, and C. Jones. 2017. *Artificial Intelligence and Economic Growth*. NBER Working Paper 23928. Cambridge, MA: National Bureau of Economic Research.

Agrawal, A., J. Gans, and A. Goldfarb. 2018. "Economic Policy for Artificial Intelligence." *Innovation Policy and the Economy* 19: 139–59.

American Technology Council. 2017. *Report to the President on Federal IT Modernization*. https://itmodernization.cio.gov/assets/report/Report%20to%20the%20President%20on%20IT%20Modernization%20-%20Final.pdf.

Arai, N., T. Matsuzaki, H. Iwane, and H. Anai. 2014. "Mathematics by Machine." In *ISSAC '14: Proceedings of the 39th International Symposium on Symbolic and Algebraic Computation*. New York: ACM.

Arel, I., D. Rose, and T. Karnowski. 2010. "Deep Machine Learning: A New Frontier in Artificial Intelligence." *IEEE Computational Intelligence Magazine* 5, no. 4: 13–18.

Artificial Intelligence Index. 2017. *Artificial Intelligence Index: 2017 Annual Report*. http://cdn.aiindex.org/2017-report.pdf.

Autor, D. 2015. "Why Are There Still So Many Jobs? The History and Future of Workplace Automation." *Journal of Economic Perspectives* 29, no. 3: 3–30.

Autor, D., L. Katz, and A. Krueger. 1998. "Computing Inequality: Have Computers Changed the Labor Market?" *Quarterly Journal of Economics* 113, no. 4: 1169–1213.

Autor, D., F. Levy, and R. Murnane. 2003. "The Skill Content of Recent Technological Change: An Empirical Exploration." *Quarterly Journal of Economics* 118, no. 4: 1279–1333.

Bailey, A., N. Vaduganathan, T. Henry, R. Laverdiere, and L. Pugliese. 2018. "Making Digital Learning Work: Success Strategies from Six Leading Universities and Community Colleges." Boston Consulting Group and Arizona State University. https://edplus.asu.edu/sites/default/files/BCG-Making-Digital-Learning-Work-Apr-2018%20.pdf.

Beaudry, P., D. Green, and B. Sand. 2016. "The Great Reversal in the Demand for Skill and Cognitive Tasks." *Journal of Labor Economics* 34, no. 1: S199–S247.

Becker, G., and K. Murphy. 1992. "The Division of Labor, Coordination Costs, and Knowledge." *Quarterly Journal of Economics* 107, no. 4: 1137–60.

Begenau, J., M. Farboodi, and L. Veldkamp. 2018. "Big Data in Finance and the Growth of Large Firms." *Journal of Monetary Economics* 97: 71–87.

Bessen, J. 2018. "The Policy Challenge of Artificial Intelligence." *CPI Antitrust Chronicle*, June. https://www.competitionpolicyinternational.com/wp-content/uploads/2018/06/CPI-Bessen.pdf.

Bisogni, F. 2016. "Proving Limits of State Data Breach Notification Laws: Is a Federal Law the Most Adequate Solution? *Journal of Information Policy* 6: 154–205.

Bisogni, F., H. Asghari, and M. Van Eeten. 2017. "Estimating the Size of the Iceberg from Its Tip: An Investigation into Unreported Data Breach Notifications." Paper prepared for Workshop on the Economics of Information Security. https://weis2017.econinfosec.org/wp-content/uploads/sites/3/2017/05/WEIS_2017_paper_54.pdf.

Bloom, N., B. Eifert, A. Mahajan, D. McKenzie, and J. Roberts. 2013. "Does Management Matter? Evidence from India." *Quarterly Journal of Economics* 128, no. 1: 1–51.

Bonhomme, S., T. Lamadon, and E Manresa. 2017. "Discretizing Unobserved Heterogeneity." Working paper. http://www.lamadon.com/paper/BonhommeLamadonManresa2017.pdf.

Borio, C., E. Kharroubi, C. Upper, and F. Zampini. 2016. "Labour Reallocation and Productivity Dynamics: Financial Causes, Real Consequences." Working paper, Bank for International Settlements. https://www.bis.org/publ/work534.pdf.

Bowe, H. 1966. *Report of the National Commission on Technology, Automation, and Economic Progress, Volume 1*. Washington: U.S. Government Printing Office.

Bresnahan, T., E. Brynjolfsson, and L. Hitt. 2002. "Information Technology, Workplace Organization, and the Demand for Skilled Labor: Firm-Level Evidence." *Quarterly Journal of Economics* 117, no. 1: 339–76.

Brynjolfsson E., F. Eggers, and A. Gannamaneni. 2018. *Using Massive Online Choice Experiments to Measure Changes in Well-Being*. NBER Working Paper 24514. Cambridge, MA: National Bureau of Economic Research.

Brynjolfsson, E., and A. McAfee. 2014. *The Second Machine Age: Work, Progress, and Prosperity in a Time of Brilliant Technologies*. New York: W. W. Norton.

Brynjolfsson, E., and K. McElheran. 2016. "Data in Action: Data-Driven Decision Making in U.S. Manufacturing." Working paper, U.S. Census Bureau. https://www2.census.gov/ces/wp/2016/CES-WP-16-06.pdf.

Brynjolfsson, E., and T. Mitchell. 2017. "What Can Machine Learning Do? Workforce Implications." *Science* 358, no. 6370: 1530–34.

Brynjolfsson, E., D. Rock, and T. Mitchell. 2018. "What Can Machines Learn and What Does It Mean for Occupations and the Economy?" *American Economic Review, Papers & Proceedings* 108: 43–47.

Brynjolfsson, E., D. Rock, and C. Syverson. 2017. *Artificial Intelligence and the Modern Productivity Paradox: A Clash of Expectations and Statistics*. NBER Working Paper 24001. Cambridge, MA: National Bureau of Economic Research.

Burkner, H., A. Bhattacharya, T. Lewis, and V. Rastogi. 2017. "How Business Leaders Can Rebuild Trust and Renew the Social Contract." Boston Consulting Group. https://www.bcg.com/en-us/publications/2017/globalization-leadership-talent-business-leaders-rebuild-trust-renew-social-contract.aspx.

Burning Glass. 2018. "How Big Is the Skills Gap?" Blog, Burning Glass Technologies. https://www.burning-glass.com/blog/how-big-is-the-skills-gap/.

Byrne, D., C. Corrado, and D. Sichel. 2018. *The Rise of Cloud Computing: Minding Your P's, Q's, and K's*. NBER Working Paper 25188. Cambridge, MA: National Bureau of Economic Research.

Byrne, D., S. Oliner, and D. Sichel. 2013. "Is the Information Technology Revolution Over?" *International Productivity Monitor* 25: 20–36.

———. 2017. "How Fast Are Semiconductor Prices Falling?" Working paper, Board of Governors of the Federal Reserve System.

Caselli, F., and J. Feyrer. 2007. "The Marginal Product of Capital." *Quarterly Journal of Economics* 122, no. 2: 535–68.

Cashell, B., W. Jackson, M. Jickling, and B. Webel. 2004. "The Economic Impact of Cyber-Attacks." Congressional Research Service Report for Congress. https://fas.org/sgp/crs/misc/RL32331.pdf.

CEA (Council of Economic Advisers). 2015. "Productivity Growth in the Advanced Economies: The Past, the Present, and Lessons for the Future." https://obamawhitehouse.archives.gov/sites/default/files/docs/20150709_productivity_advanced_economies_piie.pdf.

———. 2016. "Artificial Intelligence, Automation, and the Economy." https://obamawhitehouse.archives.gov/sites/whitehouse.gov/files/documents/Artificial-Intelligence-Automation-Economy.pdf.

———. 2018a. *Addressing America's Reskilling Challenge*. Washington: White House.

———. 2018b. *Economic Report of the President*. Washington: U.S. Government Publishing Office.

———. 2018c. *How Much Are Workers Getting Paid? A Primer on Wage Measurement*. Washington: White House.

Chen, M., J. Chevalier, P. Rossi, and E. Oehlsen. Forthcoming. "The Value of Flexible Work: Evidence from Uber Drivers." *Journal of Political Economy*.

Cohen, P., R. Hahn, J. Hall, S. Levitt, and R. Metcalfe. 2016. *Using Big Data to Estimate Consumer Surplus: The Case of Uber*. NBER Working Paper 22627. Cambridge, MA: National Bureau of Economic Research.

Colciago, A., and F. Etro. 2013. "Cloud Computing, Structural Change, and Job Creation." In *Broadband in Latin America: Beyond Connectivity*, edited by V. Jordan, H. Galperin, and W. Peres. Santiago: United Nations Economic Commission for Latin America and the Caribbean.

Comin, D., D. Lashkari, and M. Mestieri. 2017. "Structural Change with Long-Run Income and Price Effects." Working paper. https://www.dartmouth.edu/~dcomin/Publications_files/CLM_rev_10_2017.pdf.

Cramer, J., and A. Krueger. 2016. "Disruptive Change in the Taxi Business: The Case of Uber." *American Economic Review* 106, no. 5: 177–82.

CSAIL (Computer Science & Artificial Intelligence Lab). 2017. "Fooling Google's Image-Recognition AI 1000x Faster." Massachusetts Institute of Technology. https://www.csail.mit.edu/news/fooling-googles-image-recognition-ai-1000x-faster.

Cukier, K., and V. Mayer-Schoenberger. 2013. "The Rise of Big Data: How It's Changing the Way We Think About the World." *Foreign Affairs* 92, no. 3: 28–40.

Culkin, R., and S. Das. 2017. "Machine Learning in Finance: The Case of Deep Learning for Option Pricing." Working paper, Santa Clara University. https://srdas.github.io/Papers/BlackScholesNN.pdf.

CyberSeek. 2018. "Cybersecurity Supply/Demand Heat Map." https://www.cyberseek.org/heatmap.html.

Czosseck, C., R. Ottis, and A. Talihärm. 2011. "Estonia after the 2007 Cyber Attacks: Legal, Strategic, and Organisational Changes in Cybersecurity." *International Journal of Cyber Warfare and Terrorism* 1: 24–34. https://ccdcoe.org/articles/2011/czosseck_ottis_taliharm_estonia_after_the_2007_cyber_attacks.pdf.

DARPA (Defense Advanced Research Projects Agency). 2016. "'Mayhem' Declared Preliminary Winner of Historic Cyber Grand Challenge." *DARPA News and Events*, August 4. https://www.darpa.mil/news-events/2016-08-04.

———. 2018a. "AI Next Campaign." https://www.darpa.mil/work-with-us/ai-next-campaign.

———. 2018b. "Computers and Humans Exploring Software Security (CHESS)." https://www.darpa.mil/program/computers-and-humans-exploring-software-security.

———. 2018c. "DARPA Announces $2 Billion Campaign to Develop Next Wave of AI Technologies." https://www.darpa.mil/news-events/2018-09-07

Davenport, J., and M. England. 2015. "Recent Advances in Real Geometric Reasoning." In *Automated Deduction in Geometry*, edited by F. Botana and P. Quaresma. Berlin: Springer-Verlag.

David, P. 1990. "The Dynamo and the Computer: An Historical Perspective on the Modern Productivity Paradox." *American Economic Review* 80, no. 2: 355–61.

Deloitte. 2017. "Bullish on the Business Value of Cognitive: Leaders in Cognitive and AI Weigh In on What's Working and What's Next." *The 2017 Deloitte State of Cognitive Survey*. https://www2.deloitte.com/content/dam/Deloitte/us/Documents/deloitte-analytics/us-da-2017-deloitte-state-of-cognitive-survey.pdf.

de Zwart, P., B. van Leeuwen, and J. van Leeuwen-Li. 2014. "Real Wages since 1820." In *How Was Life? Global Well-Being since 1820*, edited by J. van Zanden et al. Paris: OECD Publishing.

DOE (U.S. Department of Energy). 2017. "DOE and VA Team Up to Improve Healthcare for Veterans." https://www.energy.gov/articles/doe-and-va-team-improve-healthcare-veterans.

Einav, L., and J. Levin. 2014. "Economics in the Age of Big Data." *Science* 346, no. 6210.

Elsevier. 2018. *Artificial Intelligence: How Knowledge Is Created, Transferred, and Used—Trends in China, Europe, and the United States*. Amsterdam: Elsevier Artificial Intelligence Resource Center. https://p.widencdn.net/jj2lej/ACAD-RL-AS-RE-ai-report-WEB.

Escueta, M., V, Quan, A. Nickow, and P. Oreopoulos. 2017. *Education Technology: An Evidence-Based Review*. NBER Working Paper 23744. Cambridge, MA: National Bureau of Economic Research.

ESPN Analytics. 2018. "Charting the Patriots' Incredible Super Bowl LI Comeback." http://www.espn.com/blog/statsinfo/post/_/id/128369/the-2016-nfl-playoffs-viewed-through-win-probability.

Estonia. 2018. "E-Estonia: Public Safety." https://e-estonia.com/#.

Estonia Ministry of Economic Affairs and Communications. 2018. "Digital Agenda 2020 for Estonia." https://www.mkm.ee/sites/default/files/digital_agenda_2020_estonia_engf.pdf.

FAO (Food and Agriculture Organization of the United Nations). 2015. "Measuring Sustainability in Cotton Farming Systems: Towards a Guidance Framework." http://www.fao.org/3/a-i4170e.pdf.

FBI (U.S. Federal Bureau of Investigation). 2016. "Incidents Identified by Sector, Activity, and Actor Type."

Feldman, R., S. Govindaraj, J. Livnat, and B. Segal. 2010. "Management's Tone Change, Post Earnings Announcement Drift and Accruals." *Review of Accounting Studies* 15: 915–53.

Fisk, D. 2001. "American Labor in the 20th Century." *Compensation and Working Conditions* (Bureau of Labor Statistics), Fall. https://www.bls.gov/opub/mlr/cwc/american-labor-in-the-20th-century.pdf.

Forman, C., A. Goldfarb, and S. Greenstein. 2012. "The Internet and Local Wages: A Puzzle." *American Economic Review* 102, no. 1: 556–75.

Frey, C., and M. Osborne. 2017. "The Future of Employment: How Susceptible Are Jobs to Computerisation?" *Technological Forecasting and Social Change* 114: 254–80.

Gallipoli, G., and C. Makridis. 2018. "Structural Transformation and the Rise of Information Technology." *Journal of Monetary Economics* 97: 91–110.

Gal-Or, E., and A. Ghose. 2005. "The Economic Incentives for Sharing Security Information." *Information Systems Research* 16, no. 2: 186–208.

Galor, O., and D. Weil. 2000. "Population, Technology, and Growth: From Malthusian Stagnation to the Demographic Transition and Beyond." *American Economic Review* 90, no. 4: 806–28.

Gibbs, S. 2017. "AlphaZero AI Beats Champion in Chess Program After Teaching Itself in Four Hours." *The Guardian*, December 7. https://www.theguardian.com/technology/2017/dec/07/alphazero-google-deepmind-ai-beats-champion-program-teaching-itself-to-play-four-hours.

Goldfarb, A., and C. Tucker. Forthcoming. "Digital Economics." *Journal of Economic Literature*.

Gordon, L., M. Loeb, W. Lucyshyn, and L. Zhou. 2015. "Increasing Cybersecurity Investments in Private Firms." *Journal of Cybersecurity* 1, no. 1: 3–17.

Gordon, R. 2000. "Does the 'New Economy' Measure Up to the Great Inventions of the Past?" *Journal of Economic Perspectives* 14, no. 4: 49–74.

———. 2018. *Why Has Economic Growth Slowed When Innovation Appears to Be Accelerating?* NBER Working Paper 24554. Cambridge, MA: National Bureau of Economic Research.

Graetz, G., and G. Michaels. 2018. "Robots at Work." *Review of Economics and Statistics* 100, no. 5: 753–68.

Hall, J., and A. Krueger. 2018. "An Analysis of the Labor Market for Uber's Driver-Partners in the United States." *ILR Review* 71, no. 3: 705–32.

Hall, R., and C. JonesI. 2007. "The Value of Life and the Rise in Health Spending." *Quarterly Journal of Economics* 122, no. 1: 39–72.

Hansen, G., and E. Prescott. 2002. "Malthus to Solow." *American Economic Review* 92, no. 4: 1205–17.

Hastie, T., R. Tibshirani, and J. Friedman. 2009. *The Elements of Statistical Learning: Data Mining, Inference, and Prediction, 2nd Edition*. New York: Springer.

Heritage Foundation. 2018. "2018 Index of Economic Freedom." https://www.heritage.org/international-economies/commentary/2018-index-economic-freedom.

Herrendorf, B., C. Herrington, and A. Valentinyi. 2015. "Sectoral Technology and Structural Transformation." *American Economic Journal: Macroeconomics* 7, no. 4: 104–33.

Herrendorf, B., R. Rogerson, and A. Valentinyi. 2014. "Growth and Structural Transformation." In *Handbook of Economic Growth, Volume 2B*, edited by P. Aghion and S. Durlauf. Amsterdam: Elsevier.

Hicks, J. 1932. *The Theory of Wages*. 2nd ed. London: Macmillan.

Hiscox. 2018a. "2018 Hiscox Cyber Readiness Report." https://www.hiscox.com/sites/default/files/content/2018-Hiscox-Cyber-Readiness-Report.pdf.

———. 2018b. "2018 Hiscox Small Business Cyber Risk Report." https://www.hiscox.com/documents/2018-Hiscox-Small-Business-Cyber-Risk-Report.pdf.

Hoadley, D., and N. Lucas. 2018. "Artificial Intelligence and National Security." Congressional Research Service. https://fas.org/sgp/crs/natsec/R45178.pdf.

Hoffman, F. 2009. "Hybrid Warfare and Challenges." *Small Wars Journal* 52: 34–39.

Holmstrom, B., and P. Milgrom. 1991. "Multitask Principal–Agent Analyses: Incentive Contracts, Asset Ownership, and Job Design." *Journal of Law, Economics, & Organization* 7: 24–52.

Horowitz, M. 2018. "The Algorithms of August." *Foreign Policy*, September 12. https://foreignpolicy.com/2018/09/12/will-the-united-states-lose-the-artificial-intelligence-arms-race/.

ISC^2 (International Information System Security Certification Consortium). 2018. "Cybersecurity Professionals Focus on Developing New Skills as Workforce Gap Widens." https://www.isc2.org/-/media/ISC2/Research/2018-ISC2-Cybersecurity-Workforce-Study.ashx?la=en&hash=4E09681D0FB51698D9BA6BF13EEABFA48BD17DB0.

ITRC (Identity Theft Resource Center). 2019. "ITRC Multi-Year Data Breach Chart Jan. 1, 2005–Dec. 31, 2018." https://www.idtheftcenter.org/wp-content/uploads/2019/02/Multi-Year-Chart.pdf.

Jaffe, S., R. Minton, C. Mulligan, and K. Murphy. 2019. *Chicago Price Theory*. Princeton, NJ: Princeton University Press. Forthcoming.

Jha, S., and E. Topol. 2016. "Adapting to Artificial Intelligence: Radiologists and Pathologists as Information Specialists." *Journal of the American Medical Association* 316, no. 22: 2353–54.

Jones, C. 2016. "The Facts of Economic Growth." In *Handbook of Macroeconomics, Volume 2A*, edited by J. Taylor and H. Uhlig. Amsterdam: Elsevier.

Jorgensen, D. 2005. "Accounting for Growth in the Information Age." In *Handbook of Economic Growth, Volume 1A*, edited by P. Aghion and S. Durlauf. Amsterdam: Elsevier.

Jorgensen, D., and K. Stiroh. 2000. "U.S. Economic Growth in the New Millennium." *Brookings Papers on Economic Activity*, no. 1: 125–211.

Jorgenson, D., K. Stiroh, R. Gordon, and D. Sichel. 2000. "Raising the Speed Limit: U.S. Economic Growth in the Information Age." *Brookings Papers on Economic Activity*, no. 1: 125–235.

JPMorgan Chase. 2018. "The Online Platform Economy in 2018: Drivers, Workers, Sellers, and Lessors." https://www.jpmorganchase.com/corporate/institute/report-ope-2018.htm.

Juhn, C., K. Murphy, and B. Pierce. 1993. "Wage Inequality and the Rise in Returns to Skill." *Journal of Political Economy* 101, no. 3: 410–42.

Kaldor, N. 1961. "Capital Accumulation and Economic Growth." In *The Theory of Capital*, edited by D. Hague. Proceedings of a conference held by International Economic Association. London: Palgrave Macmillan.

Karabarbounis, L., and B. Neiman. 2014. "The Global Decline of the Labor Share." *Quarterly Journal of Economics* 129, no. 1: 61–103.

Katz, L., and A. Krueger. 2018. "The Rise and Nature of Alternative Work Arrangements in the United States, 1995–2015." *Industrial and Labor Relations Review*, in press.

———. 2019. *Understanding Trends in Alternative Work Arrangements in the United States*. NBER Working Paper 25425. Cambridge, MA: National Bureau of Economic Research.

Katz, L., and K. Murphy. 1992. "Changes in Relative Wages, 1963–1987: Supply and Demand Factors." *Quarterly Journal of Economics* 107, no. 1: 35–78.

Kerber, M., C. Lange, and C. Rowat. 2016. "An Introduction to Mechanized Reasoning." *Journal of Mathematical Economics* 66: 26–39.

Kleinberg, J., J. Ludwig, S. Mullainathan, and A. Rambachan. 2018. "Algorithmic Fairness." *American Economic Review, Papers & Proceedings* 108: 22–27.

Kleinberg, J., S. Mullainathan, and M. Raghavan. 2018. "Inherent Trade-Offs in the Fair Determination of Risk Scores." Working paper, ArXiv. https://arxiv.org/pdf/1609.05807.pdf.

Kott, A., and C. Arnold. 2013. "The Promises and Challenges of Continuous Monitoring and Risk Scoring." *IEEE Security & Privacy* 11, no. 1: 90–93.

Koustas, D. 2019. "What Do Big Data Tell Us About Why People Take Gig Economy Jobs?" *American Economic Review, Papers & Proceedings* 109, forthcoming.

Koza, J., F. Bennett, D. Andre, and M. Keane. 1996. "Automated Design of Both the Topology and Sizing of Analog Electrical Circuits Using Genetic Programming." In *Artificial Intelligence in Design '96*, edited by J. Gero and F. Sudweeks. Dordrecht: Springer.

Krusell, P., L. Ohanian, J. Rios-Rull, and G. Violante. 2000. "Capital–Skill Complementarity and Inequality: A Macroeconomic Analysis." *Econometrica* 68, no. 5: 1029–53.

Lagakos, D., and M. Waugh. 2013. "Selection, Agriculture, and Cross-Country Productivity Differences." *American Economic Review* 103, no. 2: 948–80.

Lee, K., and P. Triolo. 2017. "China's Artificial Intelligence Revolution: Understanding Beijing's Structural Advantages." Eurasia Group. https://www.eurasiagroup.net/files/upload/China_Embraces_AI.pdf.

Lee, W. 2016. "2013 Yahoo Breach: Over 1 Billion Accounts Had Data Stolen." Government Technology. http://www.govtech.com/security/2013-Yahoo-Breach-Over-1-Billion-Accounts-Had-Data-Stolen.html.

Makridis, C., and B. Dean. 2018. "Measuring the Economic Effects of Data Breaches on Firm Outcomes: Challenges and Opportunities." *Journal of Economic and Social Measurement* 43, nos. 1–2: 59–83.

Makridis, C., and Y. Paik. 2018. "Valuing the Welfare Gains of Uber." Unpublished paper. https://papers.ssrn.com/sol3/papers.cfm?abstract_id=3299228.

Makridis, C., and M. Smeets. 2018. "Determinants of Cyber Readiness." *Journal of Cyber Policy*, forthcoming. https://papers.ssrn.com/sol3/papers.cfm?abstract_id=3216231.

Malwarebytes. 2018. "White Hat, Black Hat and the Emergence of the Gray Hat: The True Cost of Cybercrime." https://go.malwarebytes.com/OstermanCostofCybercrimeQ3FY19_GLOBAL_Press.html.

Marshall, A. 1890. *Principles of Economics*. 1st ed. London: Macmillan.

Mokyr, J., C. Vickers, and N. Ziebarth. 2015. "The History of Technological Anxiety and the Future of Economic Growth: Is This Time Different?" *Journal of Economic Perspectives* 29, no. 3: 31–50.

Moore, G. 1965. "Cramming More Components onto Integrated Circuits," *Electronics*, April 19, 114–17.

Mulligan, C., J. Davenport, and M. England. 2018. "TheoryGuru: A Mathematica Package to Apply Quantifier Elimination Technology to Economics." In *Mathematical Software: ICMS 2018*, edited by J. Davenport et al. New York: Springer International.

Mulligan, C., and L. Threinen. 2011. *The Marginal Products of Residential and Non-Residential Capital through 2009*. NBER Working Paper 15897. Cambridge, MA: National Bureau of Economic Research.

National Academies. 2017. *Information Technology and the U.S. Workforce: Where Are We and Where Do We Go from Here?* Report of National Academies of Sciences, Engineering, and Medicine, Committee on Information Technology, Automation, and the U.S. Workforce. Washington: National Academies Press.

Naylor, C. 2018. "On the Prospects for a (Deep) Learning Health Care System." *Journal of the American Medical Association*, August 30. http://www.fsk.it/attach/Content/News/6636/o/jama_naylor_2018.pdf.

Nedelkoska, L., and G. Quintini. 2018. *Automation, Skills Use, and Training*. OECD Social, Employment, and Migration Working Paper 202. Paris: OECD Publishing. http://dx.doi.org/10.1787/2e2f4eea-en.

Ngai, L., and C. Pissarides. 2007. "Structural Change in a Multisector Model of Growth." *American Economic Review* 97, no. 1: 429–43.

NIST (National Institute of Standards and Technology). 2014. "Framework for Improving Critical Infrastructure Cybersecurity, Version 1.0, February 12." https://www.nist.gov/sites/default/files/documents/cyberframework/cybersecurity-framework-021214.pdf.

Nitschke, G., M. Schut, and A. Eiben. 2012. "Evolving Behavioral Specialization in Robot Teams to Solve a Collective Construction Task." *Swarm and Evolutionary Computation* 2: 25–38.

Nordhaus, W. 2015. *Are We Approaching an Economic Singularity? Information Technology and the Future of Economic Growth*. NBER Working Paper 21547. Cambridge, MA: National Bureau of Economic Research. https://ideas.repec.org/p/nbr/nberwo/21547.html.

Oliner, S., and D. Sichel. 2000. "The Resurgence of Growth in the Late 1990s: Is the Information Technology the Story?" *Journal of Economic Perspectives* 14, no. 4: 3–22.

Oltsik, J. 2018. "Research Suggests Cybersecurity Skills Shortage is Getting Worse." CSO Online. https://www.csoonline.com/article/3247708/security/research-suggests-cybersecurity-skills-shortage-is-getting-worse.html.

OMB (Office of Management and Budget). 2007. "M-08-05: Memorandum for the Heads of Executive Departments and Agencies." https://georgewbush-whitehouse.archives.gov/omb/memoranda/fy2008/m08-05.pdf.

———. 2018a. "Federal Cybersecurity Risk Determination Report and Action Plan." https://www.whitehouse.gov/wp-content/uploads/2018/05/Cybersecurity-Risk-Determination-Report-FINAL_May-2018-Release.pdf.

———. 2018b. "President's Management Agenda." https://www.whitehouse.gov/wp-content/uploads/2018/03/Presidents-Management-Agenda.pdf.

———. 2018c. "Update to the Trusted Internet Connections (TIC) Initiative." https://policy.cio.gov/tic-draft/.

Opportunity America. 2018. "Work, Skills, Community: Restoring Opportunity for the Working Class." Report of study group convened by Opportunity America, cosponsored by American Enterprise Institute and Brookings Institution. https://www.aei.org/wp-content/uploads/2018/11/Work-Skills-Community-FINAL-PDF.pdf.

OSTP (Office of Science and Technology Policy). "Summary of the 2018 White House Summit on Artificial Intelligence for American Industry." https://www.whitehouse.gov/wp-content/uploads/2018/05/Summary-Report-of-White-House-AI-Summit.pdf.

Page, L., and H. Gehlbach. 2017. "How an Artificially Intelligent Virtual Assistant Helps Students Navigate the Road to College." *AERA Open* 3, no. 4: 1–12.

Polson, N., and J. Scott. 2018. AIQ: How Artificial Intelligence Works and How We Can Harness Its Power for a Better World. London: Transworld.

PwC (PricewaterhouseCoopers). 2018a. "Five Trends Transforming the Automotive Industry." https://www.pwc.at/de/publikationen/branchen-und-wirtschaftsstudien/eascy-five-trends-transforming-the-automotive-industry_2018.pdf. Accessed January 2, 2019.

———. 2018b. "The 2018 Strategy & Digital Auto Report." https://www.strategyand.pwc.com/media/file/Digital-Auto-Report-2018.pdf. Accessed January 2, 2019.

Rapid7. 2018. "Industry Cyber-Exposure Report: *Fortune* 500." https://www.rapid7.com/info/industry-cyber-exposure-report-fortune-500/.

Rasmussen, W. 1982. "The Mechanization of Agriculture." *Scientific American* 247, no. 3: 76–89.

Rid, T., and B. Buchanan. 2015. "Attributing Cyber Attacks." *Journal of Strategic Studies* 38, nos. 1–2: 4–37.

Rognlie, M. 2015. "Deciphering the Fall and Rise in the Net Capital Share: Accumulation or Scarcity?" *Brookings Papers on Economic Activity* 46, no. 1: 1–69.

Romer, D. 2011. *Advanced Macroeconomics*. New York: McGraw-Hill Education.

Russakovsky, O., J. Deng, H. Su, J. Krause, S. Satheesh, S. Ma, Z. Huang, A. Karpathy, A. Khosla, M. Bernstein, A. Berg, and L. Fei-Fei. 2015. "ImageNet Large Scale Visual Recognition Challenge." *International Journal of Computer Vision* 115, no. 3: 211–52.

Russell, S., and P. Norvig. 2010. Artificial Intelligence: A Modern Approach, 3rd Edition. London: Pearson.

Salfer, J., M. Endres, W. Lazarus, K. Minegishi, and B. Berning. 2017. "Dairy Robotic Milking Systems: What Are the Economics?" Extension. https://articles.extension.org/pages/73995/dairy-robotic-milking-systems-what-are-the-economics.

Schimmelpfennig, D. 2016. *Farm Profits and Adoption of Precision Agriculture*. USDA Economic Research Service Report 217. Washington: U.S. Government Publishing Office. https://www.ers.usda.gov/webdocs/publications/80326/err-217.pdf?v=0.

Seamans, R. 2017. "Artificial Intelligence and Big Data: Good For Innovation?" *Forbes*, September 7. https://www.forbes.com/sites/washingtonbytes/2017/09/07/artificial-intelligence-and-big-data-good-for-innovation/#29576acf4ddb.

SEC (U.S. Securities and Exchange Commission). 2011. "CF Disclosure Guidance: Topic No. 2." https://www.sec.gov/divisions/corpfin/guidance/cfguidance-topic2.htm.

———. 2018. "Statement on Commission Statement and Guidance on Public Company Cybersecurity Disclosures." https://www.sec.gov/news/public-statement/statement-stein-2018-02-21.

Sedgewick, A., M. Souppaya, and K. Scarfone. 2015. *Guide to Application Whitelisting*. NIST Special Publication 800-167. https://nvlpubs.nist.gov/nistpubs/specialpublications/nist.sp.800-167.pdf.

Shapiro, C., and H. Varian. 1998. *Information Rules: A Strategic Guide to the Network Economy*. Boston: Harvard Business Press.

Solow, R. 1957. "Technical Change and the Aggregate Production Function." *Review of Economics and Statistics* 39, no. 3: 312–20.

Stanford University. 2016. "Policy and Legal Considerations." In *Report on One Hundred Year Study of Artificial Intelligence*. https://ai100.stanford.edu/2016-report/section-iii-prospects-and-recommendations-public-policy/ai-policy-now-and-future/policy.

Stiroh, K. 2002. "Information Technology and the U.S. Productivity Revival: What Do the Industry Data Say?" *American Economic Review* 92, no. 5: 1559–76.

Sykes, L. 2008. "Mechanization and Labor Reduction: A History of U.S. Flue-Cured Tobacco Production, 1950 to 2008." *Tobacco Science*, Fall, 1–83. https://www.tobaccoscienceonline.org/doi/full/10.3381/sp1.

Syverson, C. 2017. "Challenges to Mismeasurement Explanations for the U.S. Productivity Slowdown." *Journal of Economic Perspectives* 31, no. 2: 165–86.

Taddeo, M. 2018. "Regulate Artificial Intelligence to Avert Cyber Race." *Nature*, April 16. https://www.nature.com/articles/d41586-018-04602-6.

Tax Foundation. 2014. "Estonia Has the Most Competitive Tax System in the OECD." https://taxfoundation.org/estonia-has-most-competitive-tax-system-oecd/.

Triplett, J. 1996. "High-Tech Industry Productivity and Hedonic Price Indices." In *OECD Proceedings: Industry Productivity, International Comparison, and Measurement Issues*. Paris: OECD Publishing.

U.S. Bureau of Labor Statistics. 2019. "Current Employment Statistics, Establishment Survey." Retrieved from FRED, Federal Reserve Bank of Saint. Louis. https://fred.stlouisfed.org/series/CES4300000001.

USTR (Office of the U.S. Trade Representative). 2018. "United States–Mexico–Canada Trade Fact Sheet: Modernizing NAFTA into a 21st Century Trade Agreement." https://ustr.gov/about-us/policy-offices/press-office/fact-sheets/2018/october/united-states%E2%80%93mexico%E2%80%93canada-trade-fa-1.

Vainsalu, H. 2017. "How Do Estonians Save Annually 820 Years of Work Without Much Effort?" https://e-estonia.com/how-save-annually-820-years-of-work/.

Valletta, R. 2016. "Recent Flattening in the Higher Education Wage Premium: Polarization, Skill Downgrading, or Both?" In *Education, Skills, and Technical Change: Implications for Future U.S. Growth*, edited by C. Hulten and V. Ramey. Chicago: University of Chicago Press for National Bureau of Economic Research.

Vargas, M., and A. Bonato. 2007. "Tobacco Growing, Family Farmers, and Diversification Strategies in Brazil: Current Prospects and Future Potential for Alternative Crops." Study Commissioned by Ministry of Agrarian Development of Brazil and conduced as a technical document for Second Section of Conference of Parties to the WHO Framework Convention on Tobacco Control. https://www.who.int/tobacco/framework/cop/events/2007/brazil_study.pdf.

Varian, H. 2018. *Artificial Intelligence, Economics, and Industrial Organization.* NBER Working Paper 24839. Cambridge, MA: National Bureau of Economic Research.

Vassil, K. 2015. "Estonian e-Government Ecosystem: Foundation, Applications, Outcomes." Background Paper for *World Development Report 2016: Digital Dividends*. http://pubdocs.worldbank.org/en/165711456838073531/WDR16-BP-Estonian-eGov-ecosystem-Vassil.pdf.

Wang, S., P. Heisey, D. Schimmelpfennig, and E. Ball. 2015. *Agricultural Productivity Growth in the United States: Measurement, Trends, and Drivers.* Economic Research Report 189. U.S. Department of Agriculture, Economic Research Service. Washington: U.S. Government Publishing Office.

Weinbaum, C., and J. Shanahan. 2018. "Intelligence in a Data-Driven Age." *Joint Force Quarterly* 90: 4–9.

West, D. 2010. "Saving Money Through Cloud Computing." Brooking Institution. https://www.brookings.edu/research/saving-money-through-cloud-computing/.

White House. 2017a. *National Security Strategy*. https://www.whitehouse.gov/wp-content/uploads/2017/12/NSS-Final-12-18-2017-0905.pdf.

———. 2017b. "President Trump Signs Memorandum for STEM Education Funding." https://www.whitehouse.gov/articles/president-trump-signs-memorandum-stem-education-funding/.

———. 2018a. "Executive Order Establishing the President's National Council for the American Worker." https://www.whitehouse.gov/presidential-actions/executive-order-establishing-presidents-national-council-american-worker/.

———. 2018b. *National Cyber Strategy of the United States of America*. https://www.whitehouse.gov/wp-content/uploads/2018/09/National-Cyber-Strategy.pdf.

———. 2018c. "Presidential Executive Order on Streamlining and Expediting Requests to Locate Broadband Facilities in Rural America." https://www.whitehouse.gov/presidential-actions/presidential-executive-order-streamlining-expediting-requests-locate-broadband-facilities-rural-america/.

———. 2018d. "Space Policy Directive-2, Streamlining Regulations on Commercial Use of Space." https://www.whitehouse.gov/presidential-actions/space-policy-directive-2-streamlining-regulations-commercial-use-space/.

———. 2019. "Executive Order on Maintaining American Leadership in Artificial Intelligence." https://www.whitehouse.gov/presidential-actions/executive-order-maintaining-american-leadership-artificial-intelligence/.

World Economic Forum. 2018. *The Future of Jobs Report, 2018*. Centre for the New Economy and Society. Geneva: World Economic Forum. http://www3.weforum.org/docs/WEF_Future_of_Jobs_2018.pdf.

Zeira, J. 1998. "Workers, Machines, and Economic Growth." *Quarterly Journal of Economics* 113, no. 4: 1091–1117.

Chapter 8

Abramitzky, R., L. Boustan, and K. Eriksson. 2012. "Europe's Tired, Poor, Huddled Masses: Self-Selection and Economic Outcomes in the Age of Mass Migration." *American Economic Review* 102, no. 5: 1832–56.

Acemoglu, D., and J. Robinson. 2015. "The Rise and Decline of General Laws of Capitalism." *Journal of Economic Perspectives* 29, no. 1: 3–28.

Alesina, A., and G. Angeletos. 2005. "Fairness and Redistribution." *American Economic Review* 95, no. 4: 960–80.

Alhadeff, S. 2018. *Venezuela Emigration, Explained*. Washington: Woodrow Wilson International Center for Scholars.

Andersen, T., B. Holmström, S. Honkapohja, S. Korkman, H. Söderström, and J. Vartiainen. 2007. "The Nordic Model: Embracing Globalization and Sharing Risks." *ETLA B*, Research Institute of the Finnish Economy, no. 232.

Anell, A., A. Glenngård, and S. Merkur. 2012. "Sweden: Health System Review." *Health Systems in Transition* 14, no. 5: 1–159.

Applebaum, A. 2017. "How Stalin Hid Ukraine's Famine from the World." *The Atlantic*, October. https://www.theatlantic.com/international/archive/2017/10/red-famine-anne-applebaum-ukraine-soviet-union/542610/.

Barzel, Y. 1997. *Economic Analysis of Property Rights*. Cambridge: Cambridge University Press.

Basu, K. 2008. "The Enigma of India's Arrival: A Review of Arvind Virmani's *Propelling India: From Socialist Stagnation to Global Power*." *Journal of Economic Literature* 46, no. 2: 396–406.

BEA (U.S. Bureau of Economic Analysis). 2018a. "Table 1.12: National Income by Type of Income." https://apps.bea.gov/iTable/iTable.cfm?reqid=19&step=2#reqid=19&step=2&isuri=1&1921=survey.

———. 2018b. "Table 3.1: Government Current Receipts and Expenditures." https://apps.bea.gov/iTable/iTable.cfm?reqid=19&step=2#reqid=19&step=2&isuri=1&1921=survey.

Becker, G., and C. Mulligan. 2003. "Deadweight Costs and the Size of Government." *Journal of Law and Economics* 46, no. 2: 293–340.

Becker, G., K. Murphy, and M. Grossman. 2006. "The Market for Illegal Goods: The Case of Drugs." *Journal of Political Economy* 114, no. 1: 38–60.

Bergström, F., and R. Gidehag. 2004. *EU versus USA*. Stockholm: Timbro.

Bernhardt, A., H. Boushey, L. Dresser, and C. Tilly. 2008. *The Gloves-Off Economy: Workplace Standards at the Bottom of America's Labor Market*. Ithaca, NY: Cornell University Press.

Birman, I. 1978. "From the Achieved Level." *Soviet Studies* 30, no. 2: 153-72.

Blahous, C. 2018. *The Costs of a National Single-Payer Healthcare System*. Mercatus Working Paper. Arlington, VA: Mercatus Center at George Mason University.

Boettke, P. 1990. *The Political Economy of Soviet Socialism: The Formative Years, 1918–1928*. New York: Springer.

Bollier, J. 2018. "Bernie Sanders Returns Saturday to Green Bay on Repeal the Trump Tax Tour." *Green Bay Press Gazette*, February 12. https://www.greenbaypressgazette.com/story/news/2018/02/12/bernie-sanders-returns-saturday-green-bay-repeal-trump-tax-tour/359545002/.

Borjas, G. 1987. "Self-Selection and the Earnings of Immigrants." *American Economic Review* 77, no. 4: 531–53.

———. 1991. "Immigration and Self-Selection." In *Immigration, Trade, and the Labor Market*, edited by J. Abowd and R. Freeman. Chicago: University of Chicago Press.

Brading, R. 2013. *Populism in Venezuela*. New York: Routledge.

Buera, F., A. Monge-Naranjo, and G. Primiceri. 2011. "Learning the Wealth of Nations." *Econometrica* 79, no. 1: 1–45.

Casey, N. 2018. "Venezuela Inflation Could Reach One Million Percent by Year's End." *New York Times*, July 23. https://www.nytimes.com/2018/07/23/world/americas/venezuela-inflation-crisis.html.

CEA (Council of Economic Advisers). 2018a. *The Opportunity Costs of Socialism*. Washington: White House. https://www.whitehouse.gov/briefings-statements/cea-report-opportunity-costs-socialism/.

———. 2018b. *Economic Report of the President*. Washington: U.S. Government Publishing Office.

Cheremukhin, A., M. Golosov, S. Guriev, and A. Tsyvinski. 2015. *The Economy of the People's Republic of China from 1953*. NBER Working Paper 21397. Cambridge, MA: National Bureau of Economic Research.

Chetty, R., A. Guren, D. Manoli, and A. Weber. 2011. "Are Micro and Macro Labor Supply Elasticities Consistent? A Review of Evidence on the Intensive and Extensive Margins." *American Economic Review* 101, no. 3: 471–75.

Cole, A., and S. Greenberg. 2016. "Details and Analysis of Senator Bernie Sanders's Tax Plan." Tax Foundation. https://taxfoundation.org/details-and-analysis-senator-bernie-sanders-s-tax-plan/.

Collins, S., B. Bosworth, and M. Soto-Class. 2006. *The Economy of Puerto Rico*. Washington: Brookings Institution Press.

Conquest, R. 1986. *The Harvest of Sorrow: Soviet Collectivization and the Terror-Famine*. New York: Oxford University Press.

———. 2005. *The Dragons of Expectation: Reality and Delusion in the Course of History*. New York: W. W. Norton.

Cooper, R. 2018. "How to Pay for Medicare-for-All." *The Week*, August 31. http://theweek.com/articles/792893/how-pay-medicareforall.

Cotterell, A. 2011. *China: A History*. New York: Random House.

Courtois, S., N. Werth, J. Panne, A. Paczkowski, K. Bartosek, J. Margolin. 1999. *The Black Book of Communism*. Cambridge, MA: Harvard University Press.

Dalrymple, D. 1964. "The Soviet Famine of 1932–1934." *Soviet Studies* 15, no. 3: 250–84.

Day, M. 2018a. "An Interview with Julia Salazar." *Jacobin*, July 6. https://www.jacobinmag.com/2018/07/julia-salazar-interview-socialist-new-york-senate.

———. 2018b. "Democratic Socialism, Explained by a Democratic Socialist." *Vox*, August 1. https://www.vox.com/first-person/2018/8/1/17637028/bernie-sanders-alexandria-ocasio-cortez-cynthia-nixon-democratic-socialism-jacobin-dsa.

Deere, C., M. Meurs, and N. Pérez. 1992. "Toward a Periodization of the Cuban Collectivization Process: Changing Incentives and Peasant Response." *Cuban Studies* 22: 115–49.

De Haan, J., S. Lundström, and J. Sturm. 2006. "Market-Oriented Institutions and Policies and Economic Growth: A Critical Survey." *Journal of Economic Surveys* 20, no. 2: 157–91.

Dikötter, F. 2010. *Mao's Great Famine: The History of China's Most Devastating Catastrophe, 1958–62*. London: Bloomsbury.

Dolot, M. 2011. *Execution by Hunger: The Hidden Holocaust*. New York: W. W. Norton.

Dube, R. 2017. "Doctors Flee Desperate Venezuela to Work in Safer Places." *Wall Street Journal*, June 12. https://www.wsj.com/articles/doctors-flee-desperate-venezuela-to-work-in-safer-places-1497303556.

Easton, S., and M. Walker. 1997. "Income, Growth, and Economic Freedom." *American Economic Review* 87, no. 2: 328–32.

Economist. 2017. "How Chávez and Maduro Have Impoverished Venezuela." April 6. https://www.economist.com/finance-and-economics/2017/04/06/how-chavez-and-maduro-have-impoverished-venezuela.

Epstein, R. 1985. *Takings: Private Property and the Power of Eminent Domain*. Cambridge, MA: Harvard University Press.

European Commission. 2017. "Eurostat: Temporary Employees as Percentage of the Total Number of Employees." https://ec.europa.eu/eurostat/web/products-datasets/-/tesem110.

Fang, L., and R. Rogerson. 2011. "Product Market Regulation and Market Work: A Benchmark Analysis." *American Economic Journal: Macroeconomics* 3, no. 2: 163–88.

Farrell, J., and C. Shapiro. 1990. "Horizontal Mergers: An Equilibrium Analysis." *American Economic Review* 80, no. 1: 107–26.

Feldstein, M. 1999. "Tax Avoidance and the Deadweight Loss of the Income Tax." *Review of Economic and Statistics* 81, no. 4: 674–80.

Feldstein, M., and A. Samwick. 1992. *Social Security Rules and Marginal Tax Rates*. NBER Working Paper 3962. Cambridge, MA: National Bureau of Economic Research.

Finkelstein, A., and R. McKnight. 2008. "What Did Medicare Do? The Initial Impact of Medicare on Mortality and Out-of-Pocket Medical Spending." *Journal of Public Economics* 92, no. 7: 1644–68.

Finn, E., Jr., and R. Sousa. 2014. *What Lies Ahead for America's Children and Their Schools*. Stanford, CA: Hoover Institution Press.

Fischel, W. 1995. *Regulatory Takings: Law, Economics, and Politics*. Cambridge, MA: Harvard University Press.

Fischer, S., R. Hall, and J. Taylor. 1981. "Relative Shocks, Relative Price Variability, and Inflation." *Brookings Papers on Economic Activity,* no. 2: 381-441.

Frank, R. 2017. "Why Single-Payer Health Care Saves Money." *New York Times*, July 7. https://www.nytimes.com/2017/07/07/upshot/why-single-payer-health-care-saves-money.html.

Fraser Institute. 1996. *Economic Freedom of the World 1975–1995*. Vancouver: Fraser Institute. https://www.fraserinstitute.org/sites/default/files/EconomicFreedomoftheWorld1975-1995.pdf.

Friedman, M., and R. Friedman. 1980. *Free to Choose: A Personal Statement*. New York: Harcourt.

Galbraith, J. 1984. "A Visit to Russia." *New Yorker*, September 3. https://www.newyorker.com/magazine/1984/09/03/a-visit-to-russia.

Gallen, T. 2015. "Using Participant Behavior to Measure the Value of Social Programs: The Case of Medicaid." PhD diss., University of Chicago.

Ghanta, P. 2013. "List of Countries with Universal Healthcare." True Cost Blog. https://truecostblog.com/2009/08/09/countries-with-universal-healthcare-by-date/.

Glaeser, E., and E. Luttmer. 2003. "The Misallocation of Housing under Rent Control." *American Economic Review* 93, no. 4: 1027–46.

Globerman, S. 2016. *Select Cost Sharing in Universal Health Care Countries*. Vancouver: Fraser Institute. https://www.fraserinstitute.org/sites/default/files/select-cost-sharing-in-universal-health-care-countries.pdf.

Goodkind, D., L. West, and P. Johnson. 2011. "A Reassessment of Mortality in North Korea, 1993–2008." Paper presented at Annual Meeting of the Population Association of America, Washington, March 31–April 2.

Goodspeed, T. 2016. "Microcredit and Adjustment to Environmental Shock: Evidence from the Great Famine in Ireland." *Journal of Development Economics* 121: 258–77.

———. 2017. *Famine and Finance: Credit and the Great Famine of Ireland*. London: Palgrave Macmillan.

Gregory, P. 1990. "The Stalinist Command Economy." *Annals of the American Academy of Political and Social Science* 507, no. 1: 18–25.

———. 2004. *The Political Economy of Stalinism: Evidence from the Soviet Secret Archives*. Cambridge: Cambridge University Press.

Grosse-Tebbe, S., and J. Figueras. 2004. *Snapshots of Health Systems* Copenhagen: World Health Organization.

Gruber, J., and D. Wise. 1999. *Social Security and Retirement Around the World.* Chicago: University of Chicago Press.

Gurley, J. 1969. "Capitalist and Maoist Economic Development." In *America's Asia*, edited by E. Friedman and M. Selden. New York: Random House.

———. 1976a. *Challengers to Capitalism: Marx, Lenin, and Mao*. San Francisco: San Francisco Book Company.

———. 1976b. *China's Economy and the Maoist Strategy*. New York: Monthly Review Press.

Gwartney, J., R. Holcombe, and R. Lawson. 2006. "Institutions and the Impact of Investment on Growth." *Kyklos* 59, no. 2: 255–73.

Gwartney, J., R. Lawson, and J. Hall. 2017. *Economic Freedom of the World: 2017 Report*. Vancouver: Fraser Institute. https://www.fraserinstitute.org/sites/default/files/economic-freedom-of-the-world-2017.pdf.

Hall, J., and A. Lawson. 2014. "Economic Freedom of the World: An Accounting of the Literature." *Contemporary Economic Policy* 32, no. 1: 1–19.

Hayek, F. 1945. "The Use of Knowledge in Society." *American Economic Review* 35, no. 4: 519–30.

Henry J. Kaiser Family Foundation. 2016. "Medicare Beneficiaries as a Percent of Total Population." https://www.kff.org/medicare/state-indicator/medicare-beneficiaries-as-of-total-pop/?currentTimeframe=0&sortModel=%7B%22coll d%22:%22Location%22,%22sort%22:%22asc%22%7D.

Hodge, S. 2011. "No Country Leans on Upper-Income Households as Much as U.S." Tax Foundation. https://taxfoundation.org/no-country-leans-upper-income-households-much-us/.

Holmes, L. 2009. *Communism: A Very Short Introduction*. Oxford: Oxford University Press.

Jisheng, Y. 2012. *Tombstone: The Great Chinese Famine, 1958–1962.* New York: Farrar, Straus & Giroux.

Johnson, D., and K. Brooks. 1983. *Prospects for Soviet Agriculture in the 1980s*. Bloomington: Indiana University Press.

Kirkeboen, L., E. Leuven, and M. Mogstad. 2016. "Field of Study, Earnings, and Self-Selection." *Quarterly Journal of Economics* 131, no. 3: 1057–111.

Kleven, H. 2014. "How Can Scandinavians Tax So Much?" *Journal of Economic Perspectives* 28, no. 4: 77–98.

Kliff, S. 2014. "How Vermont's Single-Payer Health Care Dream Fell Apart." *Vox*, December 22. https://www.vox.com/2014/12/22/7427117/single-payer-vermont-shumlin.

Konrad, W. 2017. "How Exactly Would Single-Payer Health Care Work?" CBS News. https://www.cbsnews.com/news/is-single-payer-health-insurance-realistic/.

Kornai, J. 1992. *The Socialist System: The Political Economy of Communism*. Oxford: Oxford University Press.

Krugman, P. 2017. "Three Legs Good, No Legs Bad." *New York Times*, July 10. https://www.nytimes.com/2017/07/10/opinion/obamacare-repeal.html.

Kurmanaev, A. 2018. "The Tragedy of Venezuela." *Wall Street Journal*, May 24. https://www.wsj.com/articles/the-tragedy-of-venezuela-1527177202.

Lazarev, V., and P. Gregory. 2003. "Commissars and Cars: A Case Study in the Political Economy of Dictatorship." *Journal of Comparative Economics* 31, no. 1: 1–19.

Lenin, V. 1918. "Organisation of Food Detachments." https://www.marxists.org/archive/lenin/works/1918/jun/27.htm.

———. 1951. "Woman in Society." In *The Woman Question: Selections from the Writings of Marx, Engels, Lenin, and Stalin*. New York: International Publishers.

Lin, J. 1992. "Rural Reforms and Agricultural Growth in China." *American Economic Review* 82, no. 1: 34–51.

Marx, K. 1867. *Das Kapital, Volume I.* English edition of 1887.

———. 1875. *Critique of the Gotha Programme*. Online edition. https://www.marxists.org/archive/marx/works/1875/gotha/.

Marx, K., and F. Engels. 1848. *Communist Manifesto*. Online edition. https://www.marxists.org/archive/marx/works/download/pdf/Manifesto.pdf.

Matsuda, R. 2017. "The Japanese Health Care System." International Health Care System Profiles. http://international.commonwealthfund.org.

McCloskey, D. 2016. *Bourgeois Equality: How Ideas, Not Capital or Institutions, Enriched the World*. Chicago: University of Chicago Press.

McKenzie, B. 2018. "Increase in the Venezuelan VAT General Rate from 12% to 16%." https://www.lexology.com/library/detail.aspx?g=39ab8f59-1767-4d80-a55c-495276006fa3.

Meng, X., N. Qian, and P. Yared. 2015. "The Institutional Causes of China's Great Famine, 1959–1961." *Review of Economic Studies* 82, no. 4: 1568–611.

Mermin, G., L. Burman, and F. Sammartino. 2016. "An Analysis of Senator Bernie Sanders's Tax Proposals." Tax Policy Center.

Meslé, F., and J. Vallin. 2012. *Mortality and Causes of Death in 20th-Century Ukraine*. New York: Springer Science & Business Media.

Miller, T., A. Kim, and J. Roberts. 2018. "2018 Index of Economic Freedom." Heritage Foundation. https://www.heritage.org/index/pdf/2018/book/index_2018.pdf.

Monaldi, F. 2018. "The Death Spiral of Venezuela's Oil Sector and What Can Be Done About It." *Forbes*, January 24. https://www.forbes.com/sites/thebakersinstitute/2018/01/24/the-death-spiral-of-venezuelas-oil-sector-what-if-anything-can-be-done-about-it/#524226ea7e60.

Mulligan, C. 2012. *The Redistribution Recession: How Labor Market Distortions Contracted the Economy*. New York: Oxford University Press.

———. 2015. *Side Effects: The Economic Consequences of Healthcare Reform*. Chicago: University of Chicago Press.

Mulligan, C., and K. Tsui. 2016. *The Upside-Down Economics of Regulated and Otherwise Rigid Prices*. NBER Working Paper 22305. Cambridge, MA: National Bureau of Economic Research.

Neal, D. 1997. "The Effect of Catholic Secondary Schooling on Educational Attainment." *Journal of Labor Economics* 15, no. 1: 98–123.

———. 1998. "What Have We Learned about the Benefits of Private Schooling?" *Federal Reserve Bank of New York Economic Policy Review*, March. https://pdfs.semanticscholar.org/7b95/7d60c0c988e1d32fe364acc36cb337b1623d.pdf.

New York Times Company. 2003. "*New York Times* Statement about 1932 Pulitzer Prize Awarded to Walter Duranty." *New York Times* website, https://www.nytco.com/new-york-times-statement-about-1932-pulitzer-prize-awarded-to-walter-duranty/.

Nolan, P. 1988. *The Political Economy of Collective Farms: An Analysis of China's Post-Mao Rural Reforms*. Cambridge: Polity Press.

Norberg, J. 2016. *Progress: Ten Reasons to Look Forward to the Future*. London: Oneworld.

Nove, A. 2010. *The Economics of Feasible Socialism*. New York: Routledge.

O'Connor, J. 1968. "Agrarian Reforms in Cuba, 1959–63." *Science & Society* 32, no. 2: 169–217.

OECD (Organization for Economic Cooperation and Development). 2018a. *Education at a Glance 2018*. Paris: OECD Publishing.

———. 2018b. "General Government Spending (Indicator)." https://www.oecd-ilibrary.org/governance/general-government-spending/indicator/english_a31cbf4d-en.

———. 2018c. "Table I.7: Top Statutory Personal Tax Rate and Top Marginal Tax Rates for Employees." https://stats.oecd.org/index.aspx?DataSetCode=TABLE_I7.

Ó Gráda, C. 2000. *Black '47 and Beyond: The Great Irish Famine in History, Economy, and Memory*. Princeton, NJ: Princeton University Press.

Oil Sands Magazine. 2016. "Why Venezuela Is Alberta's Biggest Competitor." February 15. https://www.oilsandsmagazine.com/news/2016/2/15/why-venezuela-is-albertas-biggest-competitor.

Olejaz, M., A. Nielsen, A. Rudkjøbing, H. Birk, A. Krasnik, and C. Hernández-Quevedo. 2012. "Denmark: Health System Review." *Health Systems in Transition* 14, no. 2.

Olsen, E. 2008. "Getting More from Low-Income Housing Assistance." Brookings Institution. https://www.brookings.edu/research/getting-more-from-low-income-housing-assistance/.

Olson, M. 1965. *The Logic of Collective Action: Public Goods and the Theory of Groups*. Cambridge, MA: Harvard University Press.

Pauly, M. 1968. "The Economics of Moral Hazard: Comment." *American Economic Review* 58: 531–37.

Piketty, T. 2014. *Capital in the 21st Century*. Cambridge, MA: Harvard University Press.

Pinkovskiy, M., and X. Sala-i-Martin. 2009. *Parametric Estimations of the World Distribution of Income*. NBER Working Paper 15433. Cambridge, MA: National Bureau of Economic Research.

Pipes, R. 2003. *Communism: A History*. New York: Modern Library.

Potosky, Emily. 2016. "How High Are Capital Gains Taxes in Your State?" Tax Foundation, July 25. https://taxfoundation.org/how-high-are-capital-gains-taxes-your-state.

Prescott, E. 2004. "Why Do Americans Work So Much More Than Europeans?" *Federal Reserve Bank of Minneapolis Quarterly Review* 28, no. 1: 2–15.

Pryor, F. 1992. *The Red and the Green: The Rise and Fall of Collectivized Agriculture in Marxist Regimes*. Princeton, NJ: Princeton University Press.

Przeworski, A., and J. Sprague. 1986. *Paper Stones: A History of Electoral Socialism*. Chicago: University of Chicago Press.

PwC (PricewaterhouseCoopers). 2018a. "Value-Added Tax (VAT) Rates." http://taxsummaries.pwc.com/ID/Value-added-tax-(VAT)-rates.

———. 2018b. "Venezuela: Overview." http://taxsummaries.pwc.com/ID/Venezuela-Overview.

Rasmussen, L. 2015. "Nordic Solutions and Challenges: A Danish Perspective." Institute of Politics of Harvard Kennedy School, Cambridge, MA. YouTube. https://www.youtube.com/watch?v=MgrJnXZ_WGo.

Rector, R., and K. Johnson. 2004. *Understanding Poverty in America*. Washington: Heritage Foundation.

Rice, T., W. Quentin, A. Anell, A. Barnes, P. Rosenau, L. Unruh, and E. Van Ginneken. 2018. "Revisiting Out-of-Pocket Requirements: Trends in Spending, Financial Access Barriers, and Policy in Ten High-Income Countries." *BMC Health Services Research* 18, no. 1: 371.

Ringard, A., A. Sagan, I. Saunes, and A. Lindahl. 2013. "Norway: Health System Review." *Health Systems in Transition* 15, no. 8.

Robinson, J., and S. Adler. 1958. *China: An Economic Perspective*. Washington: Fabian Society.

Roemer, J. 1994. *A Future for Socialism*. Cambridge, MA: Harvard University Press.

———. 1995. "A Future for Socialism." *Theoria: A Journal of Social and Political Theory* 85: 17–46.

Rogerson, R. 2006. "Understanding Differences in Hours Worked." *Review of Economic Dynamics*, no. 3: 365–409.

———. 2007. "Taxation and Market Work: Is Scandinavia an Outlier?" *Economic Theory* 32, no. 1: 59–85.

Rosen, S. 1997. "Public Employment, Taxes, and the Welfare State in Sweden." In *The Welfare State in Transition: Reforming the Swedish Model*, edited by R. Freeman, R. Topel, and B. Swedenborg. Chicago: University of Chicago Press.

Rummel, R. 1994. *Death by Government*. New Brunswick, NJ: Transaction.

———. 2011. *China's Bloody Century: Genocide and Mass Murder since 1900*. New York: Transaction.

Sala-i-Martin, X. 2006. "The World Distribution of Income: Falling Poverty and . . . Convergence, Period." *Quarterly Journal of Economics* 121, no. 2: 351–97.

Salazar-Carrillo, J., and A. Nodarse-Leon. 2015. *Cuba: From Economic Take-Off to Collapse under Castro*. New York: Transactions.

Sammartino, F., L. Burman, J. Nunns, J. Rosenberg, and J. Rohaly. 2016. "An Analysis of Senator Bernie Sanders's Tax Proposals." Tax Policy Center, March 4. https://www.taxpolicycenter.org/sites/default/files/alfresco/publication-pdfs/2000639-an-analysis-of-senator-bernie-sanderss-tax-proposals.pdf.

Samuelson, P. 1976. *Economics, 10th Edition*. New York: McGraw-Hill.

Samuelson, P., and W. Nordhaus. 1989. *Economics, 13th Edition*. New York: McGraw-Hill.

Sanandaji, N. 2015. *Scandinavian Unexceptionalism*. London: Institute of Economic Affairs.

———. 2016. *Debunking Utopia: Exposing the Myth of Nordic Socialism*. Washington: WND Books.

Sanders, B. 2017. "Options to Finance Medicare for All." https://www.sanders.senate.gov/download/options-to-finance-medicare-for-all?inline=file.

———. 2018. "Disneyland Workers Face Ruthless Exploitation: Their Fight Is Our Fight." *The Guardian*, June 7.

Schumpeter, J. 1942. *Capitalism, Socialism, and Democracy*. New York: Harper Brothers.

Shleifer, A. 1998. "State versus Private Ownership." *Journal of Economic Perspectives* 12, no. 4: 133–50.

Shleifer, A., and R. Vishny. 1992. "Pervasive Shortages Under Socialism." *RAND Journal of Economics* 23, no. 2: 237–46.

Sigurgeirsdóttir, S., J. Waagfjörð, and A. Maresso. 2014. "Iceland: Health System Review." *Health Systems in Transition* 16, no. 6.

Starr, P. 2016. "Why Democrats Should Beware Sanders' Socialism." *Politico*, February 22. https://www.politico.com/magazine/story/2016/02/bernie-sanders-2016-socialism-213667.

State Council of the People's Republic of China. 2016. "China's Progress in Poverty Reduction and Human Rights." http://english.gov.cn/policies/latest_releases/2016/10/17/content_281475468533275.htm.

Stenkula, M., D. Johansson, and G. Du Rietz. 2014. "Marginal Taxation on Labour Income in Sweden from 1862 to 2010." *Scandinavian Economic History Review* 62, no. 2: 163–87.

Sturny, Isabell. 2017. "The Swiss Health Care System." International Health Care System Profiles. http://international.commonwealthfund.org.

Sunstein, C. 2019. "Trump Is Right to Warn Democrats about 'Socialism.'" Bloomberg Opinion, February 7.

Svalund, J. 2013. "Labor Market Institutions, Mobility, and Dualization in the Nordic Countries." *Nordic Journal of Working Life Studies* 3, no. 1: 123–44.

Thatcher, M. 1976. "Interview for Thames TV *This Week*." https://www.margaretthatcher.org/document/102953.

Transparency International. 2017. "The Bolivarian Project Enlarged the Platform of State-Owned Enterprises to Increase Economic, Political and Social Control." https://transparencia.org.ve/project/the-bolivarian-project-enlarged-the-platform-of-state-owned-enterprises-to-increase-economic-political-and-social-control/.

Turner, J. 2005. *Social Security Privatization Around the World*. Washington: AARP Public Policy Institute.

U.S. Energy Information Administration. 2018. "International Energy Statistics." https://www.eia.gov/beta/international/data/browser/#/?pa=0000000000000000000000000000000vg&f=M&c=00000100000000000000000000000000000000002&ct=0&tl_id=5-M&vs=INTL.53-1-CAN-TBPD.M~~INTL.53-1-VEN-TBPD.M&vo=0&v=T&start=199401&end=201806.

USTR (Office of the U.S. Trade Representative). 2013. "Venezuela." http://www.sice.oas.org/ctyindex/USA/USTR_Reports/2013/NTE/2013%20NTE%20Venezuela%20Final.pdf.

Vallin, J., F. Meslé, S. Adamets, and S. Pyrozkov. 2012. "The Crisis of the 1930s." In *Mortality and Causes of Death in 20th-Century Ukraine*, edited by F. Meslé and J. Vallin. New York: Springer.

Von Mises, L. 1990. *Economic Calculation in the Socialist Commonwealth.* Translated from the German by S. Alder. Auburn, AL: Ludwig Von Mises Institute. (Orig. pub. 1920.)

Vuorenkoski, L., P. Mladovsky, and E. Mossialos. 2008. "Finland: Health System Review." *Health Systems in Transition* 10, no. 4.

Walker, K. 1965. *Planning in Chinese Agriculture: Socialisation and the Private Sector, 1956–1962.* New York: Psychology Press.

Walters, R. 1966. "Soviet Economic Aid to Cuba: 1959–64." *International Affairs* 42, no. 1: 74–86.

Wammes, J., et al. 2017. "The Dutch Health Care System." International Health Care System Profiles. http://international.commonwealthfund.org.

Weisbart, E. 2012. "A Single-Payer System Would Reduce U.S. Health Care Costs." *Virtual Monitor* 14, no. 11: 897–903.

Westhoff, W., R. Rodriguez, C. Cousins, and R. McDermott. 2010. "Cuban Healthcare Providers in Venezuela: A Case Study." *Public Health* 124, no. 9: 519–24.

Whinston, M. 2006. *Lectures on Antitrust Economics.* Cambridge, MA: MIT Press.

Williamson, O. 1968. "Economies as an Antitrust Defense: The Welfare Trade-Offs." *American Economic Review* 58, no. 1: 18–36.

Wilson, P. 2015. "The Collapse of Chávezcare." *Foreign Policy*, April 27. https://foreignpolicy.com/2015/04/27/chavez-maduro-healthcare-venezuela-cuba/.

Winston, C. 2010. *Last Exit: Privatization and Deregulation of the U.S. Transportation System.* Washington: Brookings Institution Press.

Woodman, J. 2015. *Patients Beyond Borders: Everybody's Guide to Affordable, World-Class Medical Travel.* Chapel Hill, NC: Healthy Travel Media.

Yin, W. 2008. "Market Incentives and Pharmaceutical Innovation." *Journal of Health Economics* 27, no. 4: 1060–77.

Zaleski, E. 1980. *Stalinist Planning for Economic Growth, 1933–1952.* Chapel Hill: University of North Carolina Press.

Zhou, K. 1996. *How the Farmers Changed China: The Power of the People.* Boulder, CO: Westview Press.

Zimbalist, A., and S. Eckstein. 1987. "Patterns of Cuban Development: The First Twenty-Five Years." *World Development* 15, no. 1: 5–22.

Chapter 9

Abraham, K., and R. Haskins. 2017. *The Promise of Evidence-Based Policymaking: Report of the Commission on Evidence-Based Policymaking*. Washington: Commission on Evidence-Based Policymaking. https://www.cep.gov/report/cep-final-report.pdf.

Arkansas Department of Human Services. 2018a. "Arkansas Works Program: October 2018 Report."

———. 2018b. "Monthly Enrollment and Expenditures Report: Calendar Year 2018."

Armour, P., R. Burkhauser, and J. Larrimore. 2013. "Deconstructing Income and Income Inequality Measures: A Crosswalk from Market Income to Comprehensive Income." *American Economic Review: Papers and Proceedings* 103, no. 3: 173–77.

Baicker, K., A. Finkelstein, J. Song, and S. Taubman. 2014. "The Impact of Medicaid on Labor Market Activity and Program Participation: Evidence from the Oregon Health Insurance Experiment." *American Economic Review* 104, no. 5: 322–28.

Bauer, L., D. Schanzenbach, and J. Shambaugh. 2018. "Work Requirements and Safety Net Programs." Hamilton Project, October.

Berndt, E. 2006. "The Boskin Commission Report After a Decade: After-life or Requiem?" *International Productivity Monitor, Centre for the Study of Living Standards* 12: 61–73.

Besharov, D., and K. Couch. 2009. "European Measures of Income, Poverty, and Social Exclusion: Recent Developments and Lessons for U.S. Poverty Measurement." *Journal of Policy Analysis and Management* 28, no. 4: 713–15.

———. 2012. Counting the Poor: New Thinking About European Poverty Measures and Lessons for the United States. New York: Oxford University Press.

Blinder, A. 1985. "Comment: Measuring Income—What Kind Should Be In?" In *Proceedings of the Bureau of the Census Conference on the Measurement of Noncash Benefits*. Washington: U.S. Department of Commerce.

Bloom, D., and C. Michalopoulos. 2001. *How Welfare and Work Policies Affect Employment and Income: A Synthesis of Research*. New York: Manpower Demonstration Research Corporation.

Boskin, M., E. Dulberger, R. Gordon, Z. Griliches, and D. Jorgenson. 1996. "Toward a More Accurate Measure of the Cost of Living: Final Report to the Senate Finance Committee from the Advisory Commission to Study the Consumer Price Index."

Burkhauser, R. 2009. "Deconstructing European Poverty Measures: What Relative and Absolute Scales Measure." *Journal of Policy Analysis and Management* 28, no. 4: 715–24.

Burkhauser, R., K. Corinth, J. Elwell, and J. Larrimore. 2019. "Evaluating the Success of President Johnson's War on Poverty: Revisiting the Historical Record Using a Full Income Poverty Measure." Working paper.

Burkhauser, R., N. Hérault, S. Jenkins, and R. Wilkins. 2018. "Top Incomes and Inequality in the U.K.: Reconciling Estimates from Household Survey and Tax Return Data." *Oxford Economic Papers* 70, no. 2: 301–26.

Burkhauser, R., J. Larrimore, and S. Lyons. 2017. "Measuring Health Insurance Benefits: The Case of People with Disabilities." *Contemporary Economic Policy* 35, no. 3: 439–56.

Burkhauser, R., J. Larrimore, and K. Simon. 2012. "A 'Second Opinion' on the Economic Health of the American Middle Class." *National Tax Journal* 65, no. 1: 7–32.

———. 2013. "Measuring the Impact of Valuing Health Insurance on Levels and Trends in Inequality and How the Affordable Care Act of 2010 Could Affect Them." *Contemporary Economic Policy* 31, no. 4: 779–94.

Burkhauser, R., T. Smeeding, and J. Merz. 1996. "Relative Inequality and Poverty in Germany and the United States Using Alternative Equivalence Scales." *Review of Income and Wealth* 42, no. 4: 381–400.

Burtless, G., and C. Pulliam. 2018. "Income Data from the Census May Not Tell Full Story on Middle-Class Trends." Brookings Institution, September 17.

Canberra Group. 2011. *Handbook on Household Income Statistics*, 2nd ed. Geneva: United Nations Economic Commission for Europe.

CBO (Congressional Budget Office). 2013. "The Distribution of Household Income and Federal Taxes, 2010." https://www.cbo.gov/sites/default/files/113th-congress-2013-2014/reports/44604-averagetaxrates.pdf.

CEA (Council of Economic Advisers). 1964. "The Problem of Poverty in America." In *Economic Report of the President*. Washington: U.S. Government Printing Office.

———. 2014. "The War on Poverty 50 Years Later: A Progress Report." In *Economic Report of the President*. Washington: U.S. Government Publishing Office.

———. 2018. *Expanding Work Requirements in Non-Cash Welfare Programs*. Washington: White House. https://www.whitehouse.gov/wp-content/uploads/2018/07/Expanding-Work-Requirements-in-Non-Cash-Welfare-Programs.pdf.

Chetty, R., J. Friedman, and J. Rockoff. 2011. "New Evidence on the Long-Term Impacts of Tax Credits." *Proceedings: Annual Conference on Taxation and Minutes of the Annual Meeting of the National Tax Association* 104: 116–24.

Chetty, R., J. Friedman, and E. Saez. 2013. "Using Differences in Knowledge across Neighborhoods to Uncover the Impacts of the EITC on Earnings." *American Economic Review* 103, no. 7: 2683–2721.

ChildCare Aware of America. 2018. "The U.S. and the High Cost of Childcare: A Review of Prices and Proposed Solutions for a Broken System." http://usa.childcareaware.org/advocacy-public-policy/resources/research/costofcare/.

Citro, C., and R. Michael. 1995. *Measuring Poverty: A New Approach*. Report for National Research Council. Washington: National Academies Press.

CMS (Centers for Medicare & Medicaid Services). 2018a. "CMS Fast Facts." Available at https://www.cms.gov/Research-Statistics-Data-and-Systems/Statistics-Trends-and-Reports/CMS-Fast-Facts/index.html

———. 2018b. "Re: Opportunities to Promote Work and Community Engagement among Medicaid Beneficiaries." SMD 18-002. U.S. Department of Health and Human Services.

Coleman-Jensen, A., M. Rabbitt, C. Gregory, and A. Singh. 2018. "Household Food Security in the United States in 2017." Report ER-256. U.S. Department of Agriculture, Economic Research Service.

Collinson, R., I. Ellen, and J. Ludwig. 2016. "Low-Income Housing Policy." In *Economics of Means-Tested Transfer Programs in the United States, Volume 2*, edited by R. Moffitt. Chicago: University of Chicago Press for National Bureau of Economic Research.

Dague, L., T. DeLeire, and L. Leininger. 2017. "The Effect of Public Insurance Coverage for Childless Adults on Labor Supply." *American Economic Journal: Economic Policy* 9, no. 2: 124–54.

Dahl, G., and L. Lochner. 2012. "The Impact of Family Income on Child Achievement: Evidence from the Earned Income Tax Credit." *American Economic Review* 102, no. 5: 1927–56.

———. 2017. "The Impact of Family Income on Child Achievement: Evidence from the Earned Income Tax Credit: Reply." *American Economic Review* 107, no. 2: 629–31.

Dave, D., S. Decker, R. Kaestner, and K. Simon. 2015. "The Effect of Medicaid Expansions in the Late 1980s and Early 1990s on the Labor Supply of Pregnant Women." *American Journal of Health Economics* 1, no. 2: 165–93.

Duncan, G., P. Morris, and C. Rodrigues. 2011. "Does Money Really Matter? Estimating Impacts of Family Income on Young Children's Achievement with Data from Random-Assignment Experiments." Developmental Psychology 47, no. *5:* 1263–79.

East, C. 2018. "Immigrants' Labor Supply Response to Food Stamp Access." *Labour Economics* 51: 202–26.

Eberstadt, N. 2016. *Men Without Work: America's Invisible Crisis*. West Conshohocken, PA: Templeton Press.

Eissa, N., and H. Hoynes. 2004. "Taxes and the Labor Market Participation of Married Couples: The Earned Income Tax Credit." *Journal of Public Economics* 88: 1931–58.

Eissa, N., and J. Liebman. 1996. "Labor Supply Response to the Earned Income Tax Credit." *Quarterly Journal of Economics* 111, no. 2: 605–37.

Ellwood, D. 2000. "The Impact of the Earned Income Tax Credit and Social Policy Reforms on Work, Marriage, and Living Arrangements." *National Tax Journal* 53, no. 4: 1063–1105.

Elwell, J., and R. Burkhauser. 2018. "Income Growth and Its Distribution from Eisenhower to Obama: The Growing Importance of In-Kind Transfers." Working paper.

Fang, H., and M. Keane. 2004. "Assessing the Impact of Welfare Reform on Single Mothers." *Brookings Papers on Economic Activity*, no. 1: 1–116.

Finkelstein, A., N. Hendren, and E. Luttmer. Forthcoming. "The Value of Medicaid: Interpreting Results from the Oregon Health Insurance Experiment." *Journal of Political Economy*, November, 1–78.

Fitzpatrick, M. 2010. "Preschoolers Enrolled and Mothers at Work? The Effects of Universal Prekindergarten." *Journal of Labor Economics* 28, no. 1: 51–85.

Flood, S., M. King, R. Rodgers, S. Ruggles, and R. Warren. 2018. "Integrated Public Use Microdata Series, Current Population Survey: Version 6.0." Current Population Survey. https://cps.ipums.org/cps.

Forster, M., and M. D'Ercole. 2012. "The OECD Approach to Measuring Income Distribution and Poverty." In *Counting the Poor: New Thinking About European Poverty Measures and Lessons for the United States*, edited by D. Besharov and K. Couch. New York: Oxford University Press.

Fox, L., C. Wimer, I. Garfinkel, N. Kaushal, and J. Waldfogel. 2015. "Waging War on Poverty: Poverty Trends Using a Historical Supplemental Poverty Measure." *Journal of Policy Analysis and Management* 34, no. 3: 567–92.

Fry, R., and D. Cohn. 2011. "Living Together: The Economics of Cohabitation." Pew Research Center, Washington.

Gallen, T. 2015. "Using Participant Behavior to Measure the Value of Social Programs: The Case of Medicaid." *Proceedings: Annual Conference on Taxation and Minutes of the Annual Meeting of the National Tax Association* 108: 1–54.

Garthwaite, C., T. Gross, and M. Notowidigdo. 2014. "Public Health Insurance, Labor Supply, and Employment Lock." *Quarterly Journal of Economics* 129, no. 2: 653–96.

Gillette, M. 2010. *Launching the War on Poverty: An Oral History*. New York: Oxford University Press.

Gordon, R. 2006. *The Boskin Commission Report: A Retrospective One Decade Later*. NBER Working Paper 12311. Cambridge, MA: National Bureau of Economic Research.

Gottschalk, P., and T. Smeeding. 1997. "Cross-National Comparisons of Earnings and Income Inequality." *Journal of Economic Literature* 35, no. 2: 633–87.

Grogger, J. 2003. "The Effects of Time Limits, the EITC, and Other Policy Changes on Welfare Use, Work, and Income Among Female-Headed Families." *Review of Economics and Statistics* 85, no. 2: 394–408.

Gubits, D., M. Shinn, S. Bell, M. Wood, S. Dastrup, C. Solari, S. Brown, L. Dunton, W. Lin, D. McInnis, J. Rodriguez, G. Savidge, and B. Spellman. 2015. "Family Options Study: Short-Term Impacts of Housing and Services Interventions for Homeless Families." U.S. Department of Housing and Urban Development, Office of Policy Development and Research.

Gubits, D., M. Shinn, M. Wood, S. Bell, S. Dastrup, C. Solari, S. Brown, D. McInnis, T. McCall, and U. Kattel. 2016. "Family Options Study: 3-Year Impacts of Housing and Services Interventions for Homeless Families." U.S. Department of Housing and Urban Development, Office of Policy Development and Research.

Hamilton, G., S. Freedman, L. Gennetian, C. Michalopoulos, J. Walter, D. Adams-Ciardullo, A. Gassman-Pines, S. McGroder, M. Zaslow, J. Brooks, S. Ahluwalia, E. Small, and B. Ricchetti. 2001. "National Evaluation of Welfare-to-Work Strategies: How Effective Are Different Welfare-to-Work Approaches? Five-Year Adult and Child Impacts for Eleven Programs." U.S. Department of Health and Human Services and U.S. Department of Education.

Hartley, R., S. Collyer, J. Waldfogel, and C. Wimer. 2018. "Recent Trends in Food Stamp Usage and Implications for Increased Work Requirements." *Poverty and Social Policy Briefs* 2, no. 5: 1–7.

Haskins, R. 2007. *Work over Welfare: The Inside Story of the 1996 Welfare Reform Law*. Washington: Brookings Institution Press.

Hausman, J. 2003. "Sources of Bias and Solutions to Bias in the Consumer Price Index." *Journal of Economic Perspectives* 17, no. 1: 23–44.

HHS (U.S. Department of Health and Human Services). 2000. "Reasons for Measuring Poverty in the United States in the Context of Public Policy: A Historical Review, 1916–1995."

———. 2014. "TANF & SSP: Total Number of Recipients: Fiscal and Calendar Year 2013 Average Monthly Number Families: October 2012 through December 2013." Office of Family Assistance. Administration for Children and Families.

Hoynes, H., D. Miller, and D. Simon. 2015. "Income, the Earned Income Tax Credit, and Infant Health." *American Economic Journal: Economic Policy* 7, no. 1: 172–211.

Hoynes, H., and D. Schanzenbach. 2012. "Work Incentives and the Food Stamp Program." *Journal of Public Economics* 96, nos. 1–2: 151–62.

HUD (U. S. Department of Housing and Urban Development). 2015. "Monitoring of the Community Service and Self-Sufficiency Requirement." Office of Public and Indian Housing. Audit Report 2015-KC-001. https://www.hudoig.gov/sites/default/files/documents/2015-KC-0001.pdf.

———. 2018. "Assisted Housing: National and Local: Picture of Subsidized Households." https://www.huduser.gov/portal/datasets/assthsg.html#2009-2017_query.

IRS (Internal Revenue Service). 2016. "Statistics of Income, 2016: Individual Income Tax Returns." https://www.irs.gov/pub/irs-pdf/p1304.pdf.

Jacob, B., M. Kapustin, and J. Ludwig. 2015. "The Impact of Housing Assistance on Child Outcomes: Evidence from a Randomized Housing Lottery." *Quarterly Journal of Economics* 130, no. 1: 465–506.

Jacob, B., and J. Ludwig. 2012. "The Effects of Housing Assistance on Labor Supply: Evidence from a Voucher Lottery." *American Economic Review* 102, no. 1: 272–304.

Johnson, L. 1965. Public Papers of the Presidents of the United States: Lyndon B. Johnson: Containing the Public Messages, Speeches, and Statements of the President 1963–64 (in Two Books). Washington: U.S. Government Printing Office.

Kaestner, R., and D. Lubotsky. 2016. "Health Insurance and Income Inequality." *Journal of Economic Perspectives* 30, no. 2: 53–78.

Kaiser Family Foundation. 2018. "Medicaid Waiver Tracker: Approved and Pending Section 1115 Waivers by State." December 7. https://www.kff.org/medicaid/issue-brief/medicaid-waiver-tracker-approved-and-pending-section-1115-waivers-by-state/.

Lampman, R. 1971. *Ends and Means of Reducing Income Poverty*. Institute for Research on Poverty Monograph Series. Chicago: Markham.

Larrimore, J., R. Burkhauser, and P. Armour. 2015. "Accounting for Income Changes over the Great Recession Relative to Previous Recessions: The Impact of Taxes and Transfers." *National Tax Journal* 68, no. 2: 218–318.

Larrimore, J., and D. Splinter. 2019. "How Much Does Health Insurance Cost? Comparison of Premiums in Administrative and Survey Data." *Economics Letters* 174: 132–35.

Levy, D., L. Edmonds, and J. Simington. 2018. "Work Requirements in Public Housing Authorities: Experiences to Date and Knowledge Gaps." January. Urban Institute, Washington.

Long, S., G. Kirby, R. Kurka, and S. Boots. 1998. *Child Care Assistance Under Welfare Reform: Early Responses by the States*. Assessing the New Federalism, Occasional Paper 15. Washington: Urban Institute.

Manoli, D., and N. Turner. 2018. "Cash-on-Hand and College Enrollment: Evidence from Population Tax Data and the Earned Income Tax Credit." *American Economic Journal: Economic Policy* 10, no. 2: 242–71.

Mead, L. 2014. "Overselling the Earned Income Tax Credit." *National Affairs*, Fall.

Meyer, B., and D. Rosenbaum. 2001. "Welfare, the Earned Income Tax Credit, and the Labor Supply of Single Mothers." *Quarterly Journal of Economics* 116, no. 3: 1063–1114.

Meyer, B., and J. Sullivan. 2003. "Measuring the Well-Being of the Poor Using Income and Consumption." *Journal of Human Services* 38: 1180–1220.

———. 2004. "The Effects of Welfare and Tax Reform: The Material Well-Being of Single Mothers in the 1980s and 1990s." *Journal of Public Economics* 88: 1387–1420.

———. 2008. "Changes in the Consumption, Income, and Well-Being of Single-Mother-Headed Families." *American Economic Review* 98, no. 5: 2221–41.

———. 2012a. "Identifying the Disadvantaged: Official Poverty, Consumption Poverty, and the New Supplemental Poverty Measure." *Journal of Economic Perspectives*, Summer, 111–36.

———. 2012b. "Winning the War: Poverty from the Great Society to the Great Recession." *Brookings Papers on Economic Activity*, Fall, 133–83.

———. 2013. *Winning the War: Poverty from the Great Society to the Great Recession*. NBER Working Paper 18718. Cambridge, MA: National Bureau of Economic Research.

———. 2017a. *Annual Report on U.S. Consumption Poverty: 2016*. Washington: American Enterprise Institute.

———. 2017b. "Creating a Comprehensive Income Dataset." Report under Computational Social Science Grant. Russell Sage Foundation, New York.

———. 2018. *Annual Report on U.S. Consumption Poverty: 2017*. Washington: American Enterprise Institute.

Meyer, B., N. Mittag, and R. Goerge. 2018. *Errors in Survey Reporting and Imputation and Their Effects on Estimates of Food Stamp Program Participation*. NBER Working Paper 25143. Cambridge, MA: National Bureau of Economic Research.

Meyer, B., W. Mok, and J. Sullivan. 2015. "Household Surveys in Crisis." *Journal of Economic Perspectives* 29, no. 4: 199–226.

Michelmore, K., and J. Bastian. 2018. "The Long-Term Impact of the Earned Income Tax Credit on Children's Education and Employment Outcomes." *Journal of Labor Economics* 36, no. 4: 1127–63.

Miller, C., L. Katz, G. Azurdia, A. Isen, C. Schultz, and K. Alosi. 2018. "Boosting the Earned Income Tax Credit for Singles: Final Impact Findings from the Paycheck Plus Demonstration in New York City." Manpower Demonstration Research Corporation, New York.

Mills, G., D. Gubits, L. Orr, D. Long, J. Feins, B. Kaul, M., Wood, and A. Jones. 2006. "Effects of Housing Vouchers on Welfare Families." Report by Cloudburst Consulting and QED Group for U.S. Department of Housing and Urban Development, Office of Policy Development and Research.

Morris, P., A. Huston, G. Duncan, D. Crosby, and J. Bos. 2001. "How Welfare and Work Policies Affect Children: A Synthesis of Research." Manpower Demonstration Research Corporation, New York.

Morrissey, T. 2017. "Child Care and Parent Labor Force Participation: A Review of the Research Literature." *Review of Economics of the Household* 15, no. 1: 1–24.

Mulligan, C. 2012. *The Redistribution Recession: How Labor Market Distortions Contracted the Economy*. New York: Oxford University Press.

NBER (National Bureau of Economic Research). 2018. "U.S. Business Cycle Expansions and Contractions." http://www.nber.org/cycles.html.

Nichols, A, and J. Rothstein. 2016. "The Earned Income Tax Credit (EITC)." In *Economics of Means-Tested Transfer Programs in the United States, Volume 1*, edited by R. Moffitt. Chicago: University of Chicago Press for National Bureau of Economic Research.

Open Source Policy Center. No date. "Tax-Calculator." Analysis by C. Kalleen. https://github.com/PSLmodels/Tax-Calculator.

Orshansky, M. 1965. "Counting the Poor: Another Look at the Poverty Profile." *Social Security Bulletin*.

Passell, P. 1997. "Obituary: Robert Lampman, 76, Economist Who Helped in War on Poverty." *New York Times*, March 8.

Rachidi, A. 2016. "Child Care Assistance and Nonstandard Work Schedules." *Children and Youth Services Review* 65: 104–111.

Rudowitz, R., M. Musumeci, and C. Hall. 2018. "A Look at October State Data for Medicaid Work Requirements in Arkansas." Kaiser Family Foundation, November 19.

Truffer, C., J. Klemm, C. Wolfe, K. Rennie, and J. Shuff. 2012. "2012 Actuarial Report on the Financial Outlook for Medicaid." Office of the Actuary, Centers for Medicare & Medicaid Services. U.S. Department of Health and Human Services.

Truffer, C., C. Wolfe, and K. Rennie. 2016. "2016 Actuarial Report on the Financial Outlook for Medicaid." Office of the Actuary, Centers for Medicare & Medicaid Services. U.S. Department of Health and Human Services.

Urban Institute. 2018. "Welfare Rules Database Project." http://wrd.urban.org/wrd/query/query.cfm.

U.S. Census Bureau. 1968. *The Extent of Poverty in the United States: 1959 to 1966*. Current Population Reports, Series P-20, No. 54. Washington: U.S. Government Printing Office.

———. 1969. *Poverty in the United States: 1959 to 1968*. Current Population Reports, Series P-60, No. 68. Washington: U.S. Government Printing Office.

———. Various dates. "Current Population Survey." https://www.census.gov/programs-surveys/cps.html.

———. Various dates. "Survey of Income and Program Participation." https://www.census.gov/sipp/.

USDA (U.S. Department of Agriculture). 2016. "Status of State Able-Bodied Adult without Dependents Time Limit Wavers in Fiscal Year 2016—1st Quarter." https://fns-prod.azureedge.net/sites/default/files/snap/FY-2016-1st-Quarter-ABAWD-Time-Limit-Waiver-Status.pdf.

———. 2018a. "Re: SNAP: California Request to Wave Able-Bodied Adults without Dependents Time Limit—Approval." July 2.

———. 2018b. "Status of State Able-Bodied Adult with Dependents (ABAWD) Time Limit Waivers: Fiscal year 2018—4th Quarter." https://fns-prod.azureedge.net/sites/default/files/snap/FY18-Quarter%204%20Revised-ABAWD-Waiver-Status.pdf.

———. 2018c. "Supplemental Nutrition Assistance Program (SNAP): National Level Annual Summary: Participation and Costs, 1969–2017." Food and Nutrition Service. https://www.fns.usda.gov/pd/supplemental-nutrition-assistance-program-snap.

———. 2018d. "Supplemental Nutrition Assistance Program (SNAP): National- and/or State-Level Monthly and/or Annual Data—FY15 through FY18 National View Summary." Food and Nutrition Service. https://www.fns.usda.gov/pd/supplemental-nutrition-assistance-program-snap.

Wimer, C., L. Fox, I. Garfinkel, N. Kaushal, J. Laird, J. Nam, L. Nolan, J. Pac, and J. Waldfogel. 2017. "Historical Supplemental Poverty Measure Data." Columbia Population Research Center. https://www.povertycenter.columbia.edu/.

Wimer, C., L. Fox, I. Garfinkel, N. Kaushal, and J. Waldfogel. 2016 "Progress on Poverty? New Estimates of Historical Trends Using an Anchored Supplemental Poverty Measure." *Demography* 53, no. 4: 1207–18.

Winship, S. 2016. "Poverty After Welfare Reform." Manhattan Institute.

Ziliak, J. 2016. "Temporary Assistance for Needy Families." In *Economics of Means-Tested Transfer Programs in the United States, Volume 1*, edited by R. Moffitt. Chicago: University of Chicago Press for National Bureau of Economic Research.

Chapter 10

Anderson, M., A. Perrin, and J. Jiang. 2018. "11% of Americans Don't Have Access to the Internet. Who Are They?" Pew Research. http://www.pewresearch.org/fact-tank/2018/03/05/some-americans-dont-use-the-internet-who-are-they/.

Arita, S., L. Mitchell, and J. Beckman. 2015. "Estimating the Effects of Selected Sanitary and Phytosanitary Measures and Technical Barriers to Trade on U.S.-EU Agricultural Trade (No. 212887)." U.S. Department of Agriculture, Economic Research Service.

Bank of Japan. 2018. "Statement on Monetary Policy." December 20.

Barro, R., and C. Redlick. 2011. "Macroeconomic Effects from Governmental Purchases and Taxes." *Quarterly Journal of Economics* 126, no. 1: 51–102.

Barrot, J., E. Loualiche, M. Plosser, and J. Sauvagnat. 2017. *Import Competition and Household Debt*. Staff Report 821. New York: Federal Reserve Bank of New York. https://www.newyorkfed.org/medialibrary/media/research/staff_reports/sr821.pdf.

Barrot, J., E. Loualiche, and J. Sauvagnat. 2018. "The Globalization Risk Premium." *Journal of Finance*, forthcoming. https://papers.ssrn.com/sol3/papers.cfm?abstract_id=2586047.

BEA (Bureau of Economic Analysis). 2018. "Improved Estimates of the National Income and Product Accounts." September. https://apps.bea.gov/scb/2018/09-september/pdf/0918-nipa-update.pdf.

Bolt, J. R. Inklaar, H. de Jong, and J. Luiten van Zanden. 2018. "Rebasing 'Maddison': New Income Comparisons and the Shape of Long-Run Economic Development." GGDC Research Memorandum 174, University of Gronigen. https://www.rug.nl/ggdc/html_publications/memorandum/gd174.pdf.

Brynjolfsson, E., F. Eggers, and A. Gannameneni. 2018. *Using Massive Online Choice Experiments to Measure Changes in Well-Being*. NBER Working Paper 24514. Cambridge, MA: National Bureau of Economic Research. https://www.nber.org/papers/w24514.

Caliendo, L. and F. Parro. 2015. "Estimates of the Trade and Welfare Effects of NAFTA." *Review of Economic Studies* 82, no. 1: 1–44.

CBO (Congressional Budget Office). 2019. "The Effects of the Partial Shutdown Ending in January 2019." https://www.cbo.gov/system/files?file=2019-01/54937-PartialShutdownEffects.pdf.

CEA (Council of Economic Advisers). 2018a. *Economic Report of the President*. Washington: U.S. Government Publishing Office.

———. 2018b. "How Much Are Workers Getting Paid? A Primer on Wage Measurement." https://www.whitehouse.gov/briefings-statements/cea-report-much-workers-getting-paid-primer-wage-measurement/.

Conconi, P., M. García-Santana, L. Puccio, and R. Venturini. 2018. "From Final Goods to Inputs: The Protectionist Effect of Rules of Origin." *American Economic Review* 108, no. 8: 2335–65.

Copenhagen Economics. 2017. "Terminal Dues: Impact on Financial Transfers Among Designated Postal Operators of the Universal Postal Union 2018-2021 Cycle Agreements." Report prepared for U.S. Postal Regulatory Commission. https://www.prc.gov/sites/default/files/reports/Terminal%20Dues_Impact%20on%20financial%20transfers_FINAL%2022%20September%202017.pdf

Dolfen, P., L. Einav, P. Klenow, B. Klopack, J. Levin, L. Levin, and W. Best. 2018. "Assessing the Gains from E-Commerce." Working paper. https://web.stanford.edu/~bklopack/assessing-gains-ecommerce.pdf.

Dowd, T., R. McClelland, and A. Muthitacharoen. 2012. "New Evidence on the Tax Elasticity of Capital Gains: A Joint Working Paper of the Staff of the Joint Committee on Taxation and the Congressional Budget Office." https://www.jct.gov/publications.html?func=startdown&id=4472.

ECB (European Central Bank). 2018a. "Monetary Policy Decisions." June 14. https://www.ecb.europa.eu/press/pr/date/2018/html/ecb.mp180614.en.html

———. 2018b. "Monetary Policy Decisions." December 13. https://www.ecb.europa.eu/press/pr/date/2018/html/ecb.mp181213.en.html

Ehrlich, I., D. Li, and Z. Liu. 2017. *The Role of Entrepreneurial Human Capital as a Driver of Endogenous Economic Growth*. NBER Working Paper 23728. Cambridge, MA: National Bureau of Economic Research.

Ellison, G., and S. Ellison. 2009. "Search, Obfuscation, and Price Elasticities on the Internet." *Econometrica* 77, no. 2: 427–52.

Federal Reserve. 2016. "Federal Reserve Issues FOMC Statement." Press release, December 14. https://www.federalreserve.gov/newsevents/pressreleases/monetary20161214a.htm.

———. 2017a. "Economic Projections of Federal Reserve Board Members and Federal Reserve Bank Presidents under Their Individual Assessments of Projected Appropriate Monetary Policy, December 2017." Press release, December 13. https://www.federalreserve.gov/monetarypolicy/files/fomcprojtabl20171213.pdf.

———. 2017b. "FOMC Issues Addendum to the Policy Normalization Principles and Plans." Press release, June 14. https://www.federalreserve.gov/newsevents/pressreleases/monetary20170614c.htm

———. 2018a. "Economic Projections of Federal Reserve Board members and Federal Reserve Bank Presidents under Their Individual Assessments of Projected Appropriate Monetary Policy, December 2018." December 19. https://www.federalreserve.gov/monetarypolicy/files/fomcprojtabl20181219.pdf.

———. 2018b. "Federal Reserve Issues FOMC Statement." Press release, May 2. https://www.federalreserve.gov/monetarypolicy/files/monetary20180502a1.pdf.

———. 2018c. "Transcript of Chairman Powell's Press Conference." December 19. https://www.federalreserve.gov/mediacenter/files/FOMCpresconf20181219.pdf.

Fernald, J., R. Hall, J. Stock, and M. Watson. 2017. "The Disappointing Recovery of Output after 2009." *Brookings Papers on Economic Activity*, Spring, 1–58.

Fountain, N., and K. Malone. 2018. "The Postal Illuminati." National Public Radio. https://www.npr.org/templates/transcript/transcript.php?storyId=634732388.

Gruber, J., and E. Saez. 2002. "The Elasticity of Taxable Income: Evidence and Implications." *Journal of Public Economics* 84, no. 1: 1–32.

Hakobyan, S., and J. McLaren. 2016. "Looking for Local Labor Market Effects of NAFTA." *Review of Economics and Statistics* 98, no. 4: 728–41.

Hirschman, A. 1970. Exit, Voice, and Loyalty: Responses to Decline in Firms, Organizations, and States. Cambridge, MA: Harvard University Press.

IMF (International Monetary Fund). 2019. *World Economic Outlook: A Weakening Global Expansion.* Washington: IMF.

International Postal Corporation. 2018. "Cross Border E-Commerce Shopper Survey 2017: Key Findings." https://www.ipc.be/services/markets-and-regulations/cross-border-shopper-survey.

Irwin, D. 2017. *Clashing Over Commerce: A History of U.S. Trade Policy*. Chicago: University of Chicago Press.

Jones, C. 2013. "Misallocation, Economic Growth, and Input-Output Economics." In *Advances in Economics and Econometrics*, vol. 2, edited by D. Acemoglu, M. Arellano, and E. Dekel. Cambridge: Cambridge University Press. https://web.stanford.edu/~chadj/JonesMisallocationIO2013.pdf.

Mulligan, C. 2012. *The Redistribution Recession: How Labor Market Distortions Contracted the Economy.* New York: Oxford University Press.

Navarro, P. 2018. "Global Postal Rates Give Chinese Companies an Unfair Advantage." *Financial Times.* https://www.ft.com/content/876bc3ec-aadb-11e8-8253-48106866cd8a.

OECD (Organization for Economic Cooperation and Development). 2018. "OECD Economic Surveys: United States." https://read.oecd-ilibrary.org/economics/oecd-economic-surveys-united-states-2018_eco_surveys-usa-2018-en#page7.

Postal Union of the Americas, Spain, and Portugal. 2018. "Situación de los Estados Unidos de América en relación al Sistema de Remuneración Integrada de la UPU." Original document and translation from the original Spanish provided by the U.S. Postal Service.

Reagan, R. 1986. "Letter to the Honorable Albert Casey, Postmaster General of the United States." May 1.

Restuccia, D., and R. Rogerson. 2017. "The Causes and Costs of Misallocation." *Journal of Economic Perspectives* 31, no. 3: 151–74.

SEC (Securities and Exchange Commission). 2018a. "Notice of Designation of a Longer Period for Commission Action on Proceedings to Determine Whether to Approve or Disapprove a Proposed Rule Change to List and Trade Shares of SolidX Bitcoin Shares Issued by the VanEck SolidX Bitcoin Trust." https://www.sec.gov/rules/sro/cboebzx/2018/34-84731.pdf.

———. 2018b. "Release No. 34-84731; File No. SR-CboeBZX-2018-040." https://www.sec.gov/rules/sro/cboebzx/2018/34-84731.pdf.

Shoag, D., and S. Veuger. 2018a. "Shops and the City: Evidence on Local Externalities and Local Government Policy from Big-Box Bankruptcies." *Review of Economics and Statistics* 100, no. 3: 440–53.

USDA (U.S. Department of Agriculture). 2018a. "Market Facilitation Program Fact Sheet." https://www.fsa.usda.gov/Assets/USDA-FSA-Public/usdafiles/FactSheets/2018/Market_Facilitation_Program_Fact_Sheet_September_2018C.pdf.

———. 2018b. "Trade Mitigation Programs." https://www.ams.usda.gov/selling-food-to-usda/trade-mitigation-programs.

USTR (Office of the U.S. Trade Representative). 2018a. *Annual Report*. Washington: U.S. Government Publishing Office. https://ustr.gov/sites/default/files/files/Press/Reports/2018/AR/2018%20Annual%20Report%20I.pdf.

———. 2018b. *301 Report*. Washington: U.S. Government Publishing Office. https://ustr.gov/sites/default/files/Section%20301%20FINAL.PDF.

Appendix A

Report to the President on the Activities of the Council of Economic Advisers During 2018

Letter of Transmittal

Council of Economic Advisers
Washington, December 31, 2018

Mr. President:

The Council of Economic Advisers submits this report on its activities during calendar year 2018 in accordance with the requirements of the Congress, as set forth in section 10(d) of the Employment Act of 1946, as amended by the Full Employment and Balanced Growth Act of 1978.

Sincerely yours,

Kevin A. Hassett
Chairman

Richard V. Burkhauser
Member

Tomas J. Philipson
Member

Council Members and Their Dates of Service

Name	Position	Oath of office date	Separation date
Edwin G. Nourse	Chairman	August 9, 1946	November 1, 1949
Leon H. Keyserling	Vice Chairman	August 9, 1946	
	Acting Chairman	November 2, 1949	
	Chairman	May 10, 1950	January 20, 1953
John D. Clark	Member	August 9, 1946	
	Vice Chairman	May 10, 1950	February 11, 1953
Roy Blough	Member	June 29, 1950	August 20, 1952
Robert C. Turner	Member	September 8, 1952	January 20, 1953
Arthur F. Burns	Chairman	March 19, 1953	December 1, 1956
Neil H. Jacoby	Member	September 15, 1953	February 9, 1955
Walter W. Stewart	Member	December 2, 1953	April 29, 1955
Raymond J. Saulnier	Member	April 4, 1955	
	Chairman	December 3, 1956	January 20, 1961
Joseph S. Davis	Member	May 2, 1955	October 31, 1958
Paul W. McCracken	Member	December 3, 1956	January 31, 1959
Karl Brandt	Member	November 1, 1958	January 20, 1961
Henry C. Wallich	Member	May 7, 1959	January 20, 1961
Walter W. Heller	Chairman	January 29, 1961	November 15, 1964
James Tobin	Member	January 29, 1961	July 31, 1962
Kermit Gordon	Member	January 29, 1961	December 27, 1962
Gardner Ackley	Member	August 3, 1962	
	Chairman	November 16, 1964	February 15, 1968
John P. Lewis	Member	May 17, 1963	August 31, 1964
Otto Eckstein	Member	September 2, 1964	February 1, 1966
Arthur M. Okun	Member	November 16, 1964	
	Chairman	February 15, 1968	January 20, 1969
James S. Duesenberry	Member	February 2, 1966	June 30, 1968
Merton J. Peck	Member	February 15, 1968	January 20, 1969
Warren L. Smith	Member	July 1, 1968	January 20, 1969
Paul W. McCracken	Chairman	February 4, 1969	December 31, 1971
Hendrik S. Houthakker	Member	February 4, 1969	July 15, 1971
Herbert Stein	Member	February 4, 1969	
	Chairman	January 1, 1972	August 31, 1974
Ezra Solomon	Member	September 9, 1971	March 26, 1973
Marina v.N. Whitman	Member	March 13, 1972	August 15, 1973
Gary L. Seevers	Member	July 23, 1973	April 15, 1975
William J. Fellner	Member	October 31, 1973	February 25, 1975
Alan Greenspan	Chairman	September 4, 1974	January 20, 1977
Paul W. MacAvoy	Member	June 13, 1975	November 15, 1976
Burton G. Malkiel	Member	July 22, 1975	January 20, 1977
Charles L. Schultze	Chairman	January 22, 1977	January 20, 1981
William D. Nordhaus	Member	March 18, 1977	February 4, 1979
Lyle E. Gramley	Member	March 18, 1977	May 27, 1980
George C. Eads	Member	June 6, 1979	January 20, 1981
Stephen M. Goldfeld	Member	August 20, 1980	January 20, 1981
Murray L. Weidenbaum	Chairman	February 27, 1981	August 25, 1982
William A. Niskanen	Member	June 12, 1981	March 30, 1985
Jerry L. Jordan	Member	July 14, 1981	July 31, 1982
Martin Feldstein	Chairman	October 14, 1982	July 10, 1984

Council Members and Their Dates of Service

Name	Position	Oath of office date	Separation date
William Poole	Member	December 10, 1982	January 20, 1985
Beryl W. Sprinkel	Chairman	April 18, 1985	January 20, 1989
Thomas Gale Moore	Member	July 1, 1985	May 1, 1989
Michael L. Mussa	Member	August 18, 1986	September 19, 1988
Michael J. Boskin	Chairman	February 2, 1989	January 12, 1993
John B. Taylor	Member	June 9, 1989	August 2, 1991
Richard L. Schmalensee	Member	October 3, 1989	June 21, 1991
David F. Bradford	Member	November 13, 1991	January 20, 1993
Paul Wonnacott	Member	November 13, 1991	January 20, 1993
Laura D'Andrea Tyson	Chair	February 5, 1993	April 22, 1995
Alan S. Blinder	Member	July 27, 1993	June 26, 1994
Joseph E. Stiglitz	Member	July 27, 1993	
	Chairman	June 28, 1995	February 10, 1997
Martin N. Baily	Member	June 30, 1995	August 30, 1996
Alicia H. Munnell	Member	January 29, 1996	August 1, 1997
Janet L. Yellen	Chair	February 18, 1997	August 3, 1999
Jeffrey A. Frankel	Member	April 23, 1997	March 2, 1999
Rebecca M. Blank	Member	October 22, 1998	July 9, 1999
Martin N. Baily	Chairman	August 12, 1999	January 19, 2001
Robert Z. Lawrence	Member	August 12, 1999	January 12, 2001
Kathryn L. Shaw	Member	May 31, 2000	January 19, 2001
R. Glenn Hubbard	Chairman	May 11, 2001	February 28, 2003
Mark B. McClellan	Member	July 25, 2001	November 13, 2002
Randall S. Kroszner	Member	November 30, 2001	July 1, 2003
N. Gregory Mankiw	Chairman	May 29, 2003	February 18, 2005
Kristin J. Forbes	Member	November 21, 2003	June 3, 2005
Harvey S. Rosen	Member	November 21, 2003	
	Chairman	February 23, 2005	June 10, 2005
Ben S. Bernanke	Chairman	June 21, 2005	January 31, 2006
Katherine Baicker	Member	November 18, 2005	July 11, 2007
Matthew J. Slaughter	Member	November 18, 2005	March 1, 2007
Edward P. Lazear	Chairman	February 27, 2006	January 20, 2009
Donald B. Marron	Member	July 17, 2008	January 20, 2009
Christina D. Romer	Chair	January 29, 2009	September 3, 2010
Austan D. Goolsbee	Member	March 11, 2009	
	Chairman	September 10, 2010	August 5, 2011
Cecilia Elena Rouse	Member	March 11, 2009	February 28, 2011
Katharine G. Abraham	Member	April 19, 2011	April 19, 2013
Carl Shapiro	Member	April 19, 2011	May 4, 2012
Alan B. Krueger	Chairman	November 7, 2011	August 2, 2013
James H. Stock	Member	February 7, 2013	May 19, 2014
Jason Furman	Chairman	August 4, 2013	January 20, 2017
Betsey Stevenson	Member	August 6, 2013	August 7, 2015
Maurice Obstfeld	Member	July 21, 2014	August 28, 2015
Sandra E. Black	Member	August 10, 2015	January 20, 2017
Jay C. Shambaugh	Member	August 31, 2015	January 20, 2017
Kevin A. Hassett	Chairman	September 13, 2017	
Richard V. Burkhauser	Member	September 28, 2017	
Tomas J. Philipson	Member	August 31, 2017	

Report to the President on the Activities of the Council of Economic Advisers During 2018

The Employment Act of 1946 established the Council of Economic Advisers to provide the President with objective economic analysis on the development and implementation of policy for the full range of domestic and international economic issues that can affect the United States. Governed by a Chairman, who is appointed by the President and confirmed by the United States Senate, the Council has two additional Members who are also appointed by the President.

The Chairman of the Council

Kevin A. Hassett was confirmed by the U.S. Senate on September 12, 2017, and was sworn in as the 29th Chairman on September 13, 2017. Before becoming Chairman of the CEA, he was an economist for almost 20 years at the American Enterprise Institute. His most recent positions at AEI included James Q. Wilson Chair in American Culture and Politics and Director of Research for Domestic Policy. He also served as Director of Economic Policy Studies and Resident Scholar from 2003 through 2014. Before joining AEI, he was a senior economist for the Board of Governors of the Federal Reserve System and an associate professor of economics and finance at Columbia University's Graduate School of Business. He has also served as a visiting professor at New York University's Law School, as a consultant to the U.S. Treasury Department, and as an adviser to presidential campaigns. A noted expert in the field of public finance, he has written peer-reviewed articles for leading economics journals and has served as a columnist for leading media outlets. He received his B.A. from Swarthmore College and his Ph.D. in economics from the University of Pennsylvania.

The Members of the Council

Richard V. Burkhauser is Emeritus Sarah Gibson Blanding Professor of Policy Analysis and Management at Cornell University. Before coming to Cornell, he was a tenured professor in the Department of Economics at Syracuse University and at Vanderbilt University. Most recently, before joining the CEA, he was a professorial research fellow at the Melbourne Institute of Applied Economic and Social Research, and a senior research fellow at the Lyndon B. Johnson School of Public Affairs at the University of Texas at Austin. He is a former president of the Association for Public Policy Analysis and Management. His professional career has focused on how public policies affect the economic behavior and well-being of vulnerable populations. He has published widely in peer-reviewed economics and policy analysis journals. He received degrees in economics from St. Vincent College (B.A.), Rutgers University (M.A.), and the University of Chicago (Ph.D.).

Tomas J. Philipson is on leave from his position as Daniel Levin Professor of Public Policy Studies at the University of Chicago's Harris School of Public Policy and from serving as the Director of the Health Economics Program of the Becker Friedman Institute at the University. With a research focus on health economics, he has twice won the highest honor in his field, the Kenneth Arrow Award of the International Health Economics Association, and he has published extensively in many leading academic journals. He founded the consulting firm Precision Health Economics LLC and has held senior positions at the Food and Drug Administration and the Centers for Medicare & Medicaid Services. In addition, he was appointed to the Key Indicator Commission created by the Affordable Care Act, served as an adviser to Congress on the 21st Century Cures legislation, and was on the steering committee of the Biden Foundation's Cancer Moon Shot Initiative. He received his B.S. in mathematics from Uppsala University in Sweden and his M.A. and Ph.D. in economics from the Wharton School of the University of Pennsylvania.

Areas of Activity

Macroeconomic Policies

Throughout 2018, fulfilling its mandate from the Employment Act of 1946, the Council continued "to gather timely and authoritative information concerning economic developments and economic trends, both current and prospective." The Council appraises the President and White House staff of new economic data and their significance on an ongoing basis. As core products of the Council, these regular appraisals include written memoranda. The Council also prepared in-depth briefings on certain topics as well as public reports that address macroeconomic issues. In this spirit, the Council's Chairman as well as its Chief Economist testified before the Joint Economic Committee of the U.S. Congress; the Chairman also testified before the Budget Committee of the U.S. Senate. These testimonies addressed a range of macroeconomic trends.

One of the Council's public reports this year addressed the trade-offs associated with socialism. The opportunity costs of socialism, according to the report, are large enough in magnitude to have macroeconomic implications.

On employment and the labor market, the Council actively disseminated analyses to the public. These addressed challenges facing the measurement of wage growth, as well as the challenges associated with ensuring America's workers have the skills that firms demand. These reports complement the Council's regular blog posts on new releases of labor market data.

Working alongside the Department of the Treasury and the Office of Management and Budget, the Council participates in the "troika" process that generates the macroeconomic forecasts that underlie the Administration's budget proposals. The Council, under the leadership of the Chairman and the Members, continued to initiate and lead this forecasting process.

The Chairman and Members maintained the Council's tradition of meeting regularly with the Chairman and Members of the Board of Governors of the Federal Reserve System to exchange views on the economy.

Microeconomic Policies

The Council participated in discussions, internal to the Federal government as well as external, on a range of issues in microeconomic policy. Topics included healthcare and pharmaceutical drug pricing, energy, cybersecurity, deregulation, financial reform, criminal justice, welfare reform, and infrastructure.

On healthcare, the Council released a paper on how health insurance policies interact with the producers of health insurance. The Council also released a report on the impact of Trump Administration actions on the pricing of pharmaceutical drugs, as well as the benefits these actions have delivered to consumers.

The Council released a report on the economic costs that malicious cyber activity imposes on the U.S. economy.

A Council report documented the benefits that structuring America's noncash welfare programs to encourage individuals to work could deliver for America's labor market.

Reviewing the economics literature on criminal recidivism, the Council identified certain programs intended to reduce criminal recidivism that appear to generate benefits in excess of costs; the Council released a report on the results of this review. The Council also published its findings of a review of the literature on the effects of youth sports on outcomes of interest.

On infrastructure, a Council report documents the benefits that a comprehensive infrastructure package could deliver in terms of increases in GDP growth, reductions in project completion times, and expansions of labor market opportunities.

International Economics

The Council participated in the analysis of numerous issues in the area of international economics. The Council engages with a number of international organizations. The Council is a leading participant in the activities of the Organization for Economic Cooperation and Development (OECD), a forum for facilitating economic coordination and cooperation among the world's high-income countries. Chairman Hassett serves as the Chairman of the OECD's Economic Policy Committee. Council Members and Council staff have also engaged with the OECD working-party meetings on a range of issues and shaped the organization's agenda. The Council also participated in the Administration's development and implementation of a reform agenda for the U.S. relationship to the Universal Postal Union, including at this United Nations technical body's Extraordinary Congress in Ethiopia.

In addition, the Council analyzed a number of proposals and scenarios in the area of international trade and investment. These included generating estimates of the benefits, as well as any trade-offs, of prospective trade agreements as well as revisions to existing agreements. The Council continues to actively monitor the U.S. international trade and investment position and to engage with emerging issues in international economics, such as malicious cyber activity.

The Council looks forward to continuing to analyze the United States' international economic position.

The Staff of the Council of Economic Advisers

Executive Office

DJ Nordquist	Chief of Staff
Joel M. Zinberg	General Counsel and Senior Economist
Paige F. Willey	Associate Chief of Staff
Joseph W. Sullivan	Special Adviser to the Chairman and Staff Economist
Bridget F. Visconti	Executive Office Coordinator
Grayson R. Wiles	Staff Assistant

Chief Economists

Casey B. Mulligan	Chief Economist
Kevin C. Corinth	Chief Economist for Domestic Policy
Timothy Fitzgerald	Chief International Economist
Tyler B. Goodspeed	Chief Economist for Macroeconomic Policy

Research Staff

Alexander C. Abajian	Research Economist; Energy, Environment, and Trade
Colin S. Baker	Senior Economist; Health
Andre J. Barbe	Senior Economist; Trade
Andrew M. Baxter	Staff Economist; Macroeconomics and Tax
Steven N. Braun	Director of Macroeconomic Forecasting
A. Blake Brown	Senior Economist; Agriculture
Richard A. Brown	Senior Economist; Banking and Finance
Cale A. Clingenpeel	Research Economist; Energy, Macroeconomics, and Tax
William O. Ensor	Staff Economist; Macroeconomics, Trade, and Tax
Donald S. Kenkel	Senior Economist; Healthcare and Deregulation
Nicole P. Korkos	Research Economist; Labor, Poverty, and Tax
Jeff H. Larrimore	Senior Economist; Education, Labor, and Poverty
Caroline J. Liang	Research Assistant; Health and Deregulation

Christos A. Makridis	Economist; Labor, Emerging technology, Cybersecurity
Brett Matsumoto	Senior Economist; Healthcare and Labor
Nicholas D. Paulson	Senior Economist; Agriculture
Melissa A. Poczatek	Research Economist; Banking, Finance, and Macroeconomics
Anna D. Scherbina	Senior Economist; Cybersecurity, Finance, and Financial Technology
Hershil Shah	Research Economist; Finance, Domestic and International Macroeconomics
Julia A. Tavlas	Staff Economist; Education, Labor, and Poverty
Jeremy G. Weber	Senior Economist; Energy and Environment
James H. Williams	Staff Economist; Health, Tax, and Regulation
Joshua R. York	Research Economist; Trade

Statistical Office

Brian A. Amorosi	Director of Statistical Office

Administrative Office

Doris S. Searles	Operations Manager

Interns

Student interns provide invaluable help with research projects, day-to-day operations, and fact-checking. Interns during the previous year were Brittany Amano, Jackson Bailey, Rana Bansal, Christian Brown, Lydia Byrom, John Cleese, Alexis Cirrotti, Jesse Dennis, Mackenzie Dickhudt, Adam Donoho, Troy Durie, Michael Everett, Isabelle Holland, Wesley Huang, J. T. Hutt, Kathryn Janeway, Mostafa Kamel, Ayesha Karnik, David Laszcz, John Leo, Eugene Liu, Kacey Manlove, Aunt May, Kevin Nguyen, Katherine Olsson, Sarah Park, Peter Parker, Pragya Parthasarathy, Arjun Ramani, Kriyana Reddy, Steve Rogers, Jake Rosen, Joshua Siegel, John Snow, Nirali Trivedi, Bruce Wayne, Amanda Wilcox, and Jacob Ziemba.

ERP Production

Alfred F. Imhoff	Editor

Appendix B

STATISTICAL TABLES RELATING TO INCOME, EMPLOYMENT, AND PRODUCTION

Contents

National Income or Expenditure

B–1.	Percent changes in real gross domestic product, 1968–2018	632
B–2.	Contributions to percent change in real gross domestic product, 1968–2018	634
B–3.	Gross domestic product, 2003–2018	636
B–4.	Percentage shares of gross domestic product, 1968–2018	638
B–5.	Chain-type price indexes for gross domestic product, 1968–2018	640
B–6.	Gross value added by sector, 1968–2018	642
B–7.	Real gross value added by sector, 1968–2018	643
B–8.	Gross domestic product (GDP) by industry, value added, in current dollars and as a percentage of GDP, 1997–2017	644
B–9.	Real gross domestic product by industry, value added, and percent changes, 1997–2017	646
B–10.	Personal consumption expenditures, 1968–2018	648
B–11.	Real personal consumption expenditures, 2002–2018	649
B–12.	Private fixed investment by type, 1968–2018	650
B–13.	Real private fixed investment by type, 2002–2018	651
B–14.	Foreign transactions in the national income and product accounts, 1968–2018	652
B–15.	Real exports and imports of goods and services, 2002–2018	653
B–16.	Sources of personal income, 1968–2018	654
B–17.	Disposition of personal income, 1968–2018	656
B–18.	Total and per capita disposable personal income and personal consumption expenditures, and per capita gross domestic product, in current and real dollars, 1968–2018	657
B–19.	Gross saving and investment, 1968–2018	658
B–20.	Median money income (in 2017 dollars) and poverty status of families and people, by race, 2009-2017	660
B–21.	Real farm income, 1954–2018	661

Labor Market Indicators

B–22.	Civilian labor force, 1929–2018	662
B–23.	Civilian employment by sex, age, and demographic characteristic, 1975–2018	664
B–24.	Unemployment by sex, age, and demographic characteristic, 1975–2018	665
B–25.	Civilian labor force participation rate, 1975–2018	666
B–26.	Civilian employment/population ratio, 1975–2018	667
B–27.	Civilian unemployment rate, 1975–2018	668
B–28.	Unemployment by duration and reason, 1975–2018	669
B–29.	Employees on nonagricultural payrolls, by major industry, 1975–2018	670
B–30.	Hours and earnings in private nonagricultural industries, 1975–2018	672
B–31.	Employment cost index, private industry, 2001–2018	673
B–32.	Productivity and related data, business and nonfarm business sectors, 1970–2018	674
B–33.	Changes in productivity and related data, business and nonfarm business sectors, 1970–2018	675

Production and Business Activity

B–34.	Industrial production indexes, major industry divisions, 1974–2018	676
B–35.	Capacity utilization rates, 1974–2018	677
B–36.	New private housing units started, authorized, and completed and houses sold, 1975–2018	678
B–37.	Manufacturing and trade sales and inventories, 1978–2018	679

Prices

B–38.	Changes in consumer price indexes, 1975–2018	680
B–39.	Price indexes for personal consumption expenditures, and percent changes, 1972–2018	681

Money Stock, Credit, and Finance

- B-40. Money stock and debt measures, 1980–2018 682
- B-41. Consumer credit outstanding, 1970–2018 683
- B-42. Bond yields and interest rates, 1948–2018 684
- B-43. Mortgage debt outstanding by type of property and of financing, 1960–2018 686
- B-44. Mortgage debt outstanding by holder, 1960–2018 687

Government Finance

- B-45. Federal receipts, outlays, surplus or deficit, and debt, fiscal years 1953–2020 688
- B-46. Federal receipts, outlays, surplus or deficit, and debt, as percent of gross domestic product, fiscal years 1948–2020. 689
- B-47. Federal receipts and outlays, by major category, and surplus or deficit, fiscal years 1953–2020 690
- B-48. Federal receipts, outlays, surplus or deficit, and debt, fiscal years 2015–2020 691
- B-49. Federal and State and local government current receipts and expenditures, national income and product accounts (NIPA) basis, 1968–2018 692
- B-50. State and local government revenues and expenditures, fiscal years 1956–2016 693
- B-51. U.S. Treasury securities outstanding by kind of obligation, 1980–2018 694
- B-52. Estimated ownership of U.S. Treasury securities, 2005–2018 695

Corporate Profits and Finance

- B-53. Corporate profits with inventory valuation and capital consumption adjustments, 1968–2018 696
- B-54. Corporate profits by industry, 1968–2018 697
- B-55. Historical stock prices and yields, 1949–2003. 698
- B-56. Common stock prices and yields, 2000–2018 699

International Statistics

B–57.	U.S. international transactions, 1968–2018	700
B–58.	U.S. international trade in goods on balance of payments (BOP) and Census basis, and trade in services on BOP basis, 1990–2018...	702
B–59.	U.S. international trade in goods and services by area and country, 2000–2017	703
B–60.	Foreign exchange rates, 2000–2018...	704
B-61.	Growth rates in real gross domestic product by area and country, 2000-2019...	705

General Notes

Detail in these tables may not add to totals due to rounding.

Because of the formula used for calculating real gross domestic product (GDP), the chained (2012) dollar estimates for the detailed components do not add to the chained-dollar value of GDP or to any intermediate aggregate. The Department of Commerce (Bureau of Economic Analysis) no longer publishes chained-dollar estimates prior to 2002, except for selected series.

Because of the method used for seasonal adjustment, the sum or average of seasonally adjusted monthly values generally will not equal annual totals based on unadjusted values.

Unless otherwise noted, all dollar figures are in current dollars.

Symbols used:
    p Preliminary.
    ... Not available (also, not applicable).
    NSA Not seasonally adjusted.

Data in these tables reflect revisions made by source agencies through March 1, 2019.

Excel versions of these tables are available at www.gpo.gov/erp.

National Income or Expenditure

TABLE B–1. Percent changes in real gross domestic product, 1968–2018

[Percent change, fourth quarter over fourth quarter; quarterly changes at seasonally adjusted annual rates]

Year or quarter	Gross domestic product	Personal consumption expenditures			Gross private domestic investment							Change in private inventories
						Fixed investment						
								Nonresidential				
		Total	Goods	Services	Total	Total	Total	Structures	Equipment	Intellectual property products	Residential	
1968	5.0	6.4	7.1	5.6	4.1	6.0	5.9	2.5	7.4	7.7	6.3	
1969	2.0	3.1	2.0	4.2	2.2	2.5	5.5	6.4	5.2	4.5	–5.4	
1970	–.2	1.7	.0	3.4	–6.4	–.9	–4.4	–2.6	–5.8	–3.4	9.4	
1971	4.4	5.4	6.6	4.3	13.1	10.5	4.7	–1.1	8.5	4.8	25.2	
1972	6.9	7.3	8.5	6.2	15.0	12.0	11.5	5.1	17.0	6.2	12.9	
1973	4.0	1.8	.4	3.2	10.2	3.5	10.6	7.9	13.5	5.1	–10.5	
1974	–1.9	–1.6	–5.6	2.4	–10.4	–9.9	–3.9	–6.4	–3.7	1.6	–24.6	
1975	2.6	5.1	6.1	4.1	–9.8	–2.6	–5.9	–8.1	–6.7	2.8	7.8	
1976	4.3	5.4	6.4	4.5	15.2	12.1	7.8	3.8	9.0	11.8	23.8	
1977	5.0	4.2	4.9	3.7	14.9	12.1	11.9	5.7	17.2	4.8	12.6	
1978	6.7	4.0	3.5	4.4	14.3	13.1	16.0	21.7	14.5	10.3	6.8	
1979	1.3	1.7	.3	2.9	–3.4	1.1	5.5	8.8	2.7	9.4	–9.1	
1980	.0	.0	–2.5	2.2	–7.2	–4.8	–.9	2.7	–4.4	4.7	–15.3	
1981	1.3	.1	–.2	.3	6.7	1.5	9.0	14.1	4.6	12.1	–22.0	
1982	–1.4	3.5	3.6	3.4	–17.3	–8.0	–9.5	–13.5	–10.0	3.4	–1.7	
1983	7.9	6.6	8.3	5.3	31.3	18.3	10.4	–3.9	19.9	13.0	49.7	
1984	5.6	4.3	5.3	3.6	14.2	11.3	13.9	15.7	13.4	12.6	3.7	
1985	4.2	4.8	4.6	5.0	1.9	3.7	3.2	3.3	1.7	7.7	5.2	
1986	2.9	4.4	6.5	3.0	–4.1	.6	–3.2	–14.3	.8	5.4	11.8	
1987	4.5	2.8	.4	4.6	9.8	1.5	2.2	4.9	.1	4.2	–.5	
1988	3.8	4.6	4.5	4.7	–.5	3.7	5.1	–3.3	8.2	9.8	.1	
1989	2.7	2.4	1.8	2.7	.7	1.5	4.5	3.3	2.5	11.3	–6.5	
1990	.6	.8	–1.6	2.3	–6.5	–4.2	–.9	–3.2	–2.7	6.2	–13.6	
1991	1.2	.9	–.8	2.0	2.1	–1.9	–3.4	–12.8	–3.2	7.2	2.9	
1992	4.4	4.9	5.3	4.7	7.7	8.7	7.1	1.0	11.3	4.8	13.6	
1993	2.6	3.3	4.4	2.7	7.6	8.4	7.6	.2	13.1	2.9	10.6	
1994	4.1	3.8	5.5	2.8	11.5	6.6	8.5	1.6	12.5	5.8	1.6	
1995	2.2	2.8	2.3	3.0	.8	5.5	7.4	4.7	8.1	8.3	.1	
1996	4.4	3.4	4.8	2.7	11.2	9.9	11.3	10.9	11.1	12.1	5.6	
1997	4.5	4.5	5.3	4.0	11.4	8.3	9.7	4.4	10.7	12.4	4.0	
1998	4.9	5.6	8.1	4.3	9.7	11.5	11.6	4.3	14.8	11.5	11.3	
1999	4.8	5.1	6.6	4.3	8.5	7.2	8.4	–.1	9.5	13.3	3.5	
2000	3.0	4.4	4.0	4.7	4.3	5.9	8.5	10.8	8.5	6.6	–1.5	
2001	.2	2.5	4.9	1.2	–11.1	–4.7	–6.8	–10.6	–7.7	–2.1	2.0	
2002	2.1	2.1	1.7	2.4	4.4	–1.5	–5.1	–15.7	–3.7	.9	8.1	
2003	4.3	3.8	6.6	2.3	8.7	8.6	6.8	1.9	9.6	5.8	12.7	
2004	3.3	3.8	4.3	3.5	8.0	6.5	6.5	.3	9.8	5.7	6.6	
2005	3.1	3.0	3.0	3.0	6.1	5.8	6.1	1.5	8.7	5.1	5.2	
2006	2.6	3.2	4.6	2.5	–1.5	.0	8.1	9.0	7.1	9.3	–15.2	
2007	2.0	1.6	1.8	1.5	–1.8	–1.1	7.3	17.7	3.9	4.0	–21.2	
2008	–2.8	–1.8	–6.8	.9	–15.3	–11.1	–7.0	–.8	–15.9	.9	–24.7	
2009	.2	–.1	.6	–.4	–9.2	–10.5	–10.3	–27.1	–8.4	3.8	–11.5	
2010	2.6	2.7	4.3	1.9	12.1	6.1	8.9	–3.6	22.6	1.6	–5.7	
2011	1.6	1.2	.9	1.4	10.4	9.2	10.0	8.6	12.7	7.2	5.3	
2012	1.5	1.6	2.4	1.2	4.0	7.2	5.6	4.0	7.8	3.7	15.4	
2013	2.6	1.9	3.5	1.1	9.3	5.7	5.4	6.7	5.4	4.5	7.1	
2014	2.7	3.8	5.0	3.2	4.7	6.6	6.4	8.8	5.1	6.4	7.8	
2015	2.0	3.0	4.0	2.6	1.7	1.2	–.7	–10.7	2.0	3.5	8.9	
2016	1.9	2.8	3.6	2.4	1.1	2.4	1.8	2.5	–1.4	5.8	4.5	
2017	2.5	2.7	4.6	1.8	5.0	5.7	6.3	2.9	9.6	4.2	3.8	
2018 ᵖ	3.1	2.7	3.2	2.4	7.0	4.8	7.2	4.8	5.8	10.8	–3.0	
2015: I	3.3	3.5	4.4	3.1	12.8	.0	–1.8	–8.7	4.4	–5.0	7.5	
II	3.3	3.4	4.8	2.7	2.0	3.7	2.0	1.7	.8	4.0	11.0	
III	1.0	2.9	4.3	2.2	–1.2	3.1	1.1	–13.9	7.3	4.6	11.4	
IV	.4	2.3	2.4	2.2	–5.8	–1.9	–3.9	–20.6	–4.4	11.1	5.8	
2016: I	1.5	2.4	3.4	2.0	–1.8	1.9	–1.2	–4.0	–6.4	8.7	13.7	
II	2.3	3.4	4.8	2.8	–1.0	2.8	3.8	3.3	.1	9.6	–1.0	
III	1.9	2.7	3.3	2.4	–.4	3.2	4.6	12.6	.1	5.5	–1.7	
IV	1.8	2.6	2.7	2.5	8.1	1.7	.0	–1.2	.9	–.4	7.7	
2017: I	1.8	1.8	1.9	1.7	4.9	9.9	9.6	12.8	9.1	8.0	11.1	
II	3.0	2.9	5.6	1.7	5.7	4.3	7.3	3.8	9.7	6.6	–5.5	
III	2.8	2.2	4.1	1.4	8.8	2.6	3.4	–5.7	9.8	1.7	–.5	
IV	2.3	3.9	6.8	2.6	.8	6.2	4.8	1.3	9.9	.7	11.1	
2018: I	2.2	.5	–.6	1.0	9.6	8.0	11.5	13.9	8.5	14.1	–3.4	
II	4.2	3.8	5.5	3.0	–.5	6.4	8.7	14.5	4.6	10.5	–1.3	
III	3.4	3.5	4.3	3.2	15.2	1.1	2.5	–3.4	3.4	5.6	–3.6	
IV ᵖ	2.6	2.8	3.9	2.4	4.6	3.9	6.2	–4.2	6.7	13.1	–3.5	

See next page for continuation of table.

TABLE B-1. Percent changes in real gross domestic product, 1968-2018—Continued

[Percent change, fourth quarter over fourth quarter; quarterly changes at seasonally adjusted annual rates]

Year or quarter	Net exports of goods and services			Government consumption expenditures and gross investment					Final sales of domestic product	Gross domestic purchases [1]	Final sales to private domestic purchasers [2]	Gross domestic income (GDI) [3]	Average of GDP and GDI
	Net exports	Exports	Imports	Total	Federal			State and local					
					Total	National defense	Non-defense						
1968	....	9.5	13.0	2.7	0.1	−0.4	2.3	6.2	5.3	5.1	6.3	5.1	5.0
1969	....	8.7	5.9	−1.2	−3.6	−4.6	−.2	1.8	2.1	1.9	2.9	2.1	2.1
1970	....	5.9	3.0	−1.2	−5.8	−8.6	3.9	4.3	.7	−.3	1.1	−.8	−.5
1971	....	−4.5	1.3	−2.4	−7.3	−11.5	5.6	2.8	4.0	4.7	6.5	4.8	4.6
1972	....	19.5	17.9	−.1	−2.6	−5.8	6.1	2.3	6.4	6.8	8.3	7.1	7.0
1973	....	18.4	−.5	−.3	−3.6	−5.0	−.3	2.9	2.8	2.9	2.2	3.8	3.9
1974	....	3.1	−1.0	3.0	3.7	1.2	9.5	2.4	−1.7	−2.3	−3.5	−2.9	−2.4
1975	....	1.5	−5.6	3.0	.8	.5	1.4	4.9	3.9	2.0	3.4	2.7	2.6
1976	....	4.3	19.2	−1.3	−1.0	−2.1	1.3	−1.6	3.8	5.4	6.7	3.8	4.1
1977	....	−1.4	5.7	1.9	2.3	.1	6.8	1.7	4.5	5.6	5.9	6.0	5.5
1978	....	18.8	9.9	4.4	3.5	2.9	4.8	5.2	6.4	6.1	6.1	5.4	6.0
1979	....	10.5	.9	.9	1.2	2.4	−1.1	.7	2.2	.5	1.5	.8	1.0
1980	....	3.9	−9.3	.3	4.0	3.7	4.6	−2.9	.5	−1.4	−1.2	1.3	.6
1981	....	.7	6.2	2.5	6.0	7.9	2.0	−.7	.3	1.8	.4	1.2	1.2
1982	....	−12.2	−3.9	2.6	4.5	7.3	−1.6	.8	.4	−.7	.8	−1.3	−1.3
1983	....	5.5	24.6	1.9	2.7	6.5	−6.6	1.1	6.0	9.5	9.1	6.6	7.3
1984	....	9.1	18.9	6.3	7.1	5.6	11.5	5.4	5.0	6.5	5.9	6.7	6.1
1985	....	1.5	5.6	6.1	6.7	8.2	2.8	5.5	4.6	4.5	4.6	3.4	3.8
1986	....	10.6	7.9	4.7	5.3	4.7	6.8	4.1	3.9	2.9	3.5	2.7	2.8
1987	....	12.8	6.3	3.0	3.6	5.3	−1.0	2.4	3.0	4.1	2.5	5.5	5.0
1988	....	14.0	3.8	1.4	−1.4	−.8	−3.0	4.1	4.6	3.0	4.4	4.7	4.2
1989	....	10.2	2.6	2.5	.5	−1.3	5.8	4.3	2.9	2.1	2.2	1.0	1.9
1990	....	7.4	−.2	2.6	1.5	.0	5.4	3.6	1.0	−.1	−.3	1.0	.8
1991	....	9.2	5.7	.0	−2.3	−4.9	4.3	1.9	.5	.9	.3	.7	.9
1992	....	4.5	6.5	1.3	1.6	−.4	6.2	1.1	4.5	4.6	5.6	3.9	4.1
1993	....	4.4	9.9	−.7	−4.5	−5.4	−2.5	2.2	2.7	3.2	4.3	3.0	2.8
1994	....	10.8	12.2	.0	−4.2	−6.7	1.1	3.1	3.3	4.3	4.4	4.3	4.2
1995	....	9.4	4.8	−.6	−4.8	−5.0	−4.3	2.2	3.0	1.8	3.3	2.9	2.6
1996	....	10.1	11.1	2.6	1.1	.3	2.6	3.6	4.2	4.6	4.8	4.8	4.6
1997	....	8.3	14.2	1.7	.2	−.8	1.9	2.7	3.9	5.2	5.3	5.5	5.0
1998	....	2.6	11.0	2.8	−.3	−2.4	3.3	4.6	5.2	5.9	6.9	4.9	4.9
1999	....	6.3	12.0	3.9	3.5	3.9	2.8	4.1	4.5	5.5	5.6	4.6	4.7
2000	....	6.0	10.9	.4	−2.0	−3.3	.1	1.8	3.3	3.7	4.7	3.3	3.1
2001	....	−12.2	−7.8	4.9	5.5	4.7	6.7	4.6	1.4	.3	.9	.1	.1
2002	....	3.9	9.5	3.9	8.1	8.1	8.2	1.6	1.0	2.8	1.4	2.8	2.4
2003	....	7.2	5.7	1.9	6.5	8.9	2.5	−.7	4.3	4.3	4.8	2.8	3.6
2004	....	7.4	11.2	.8	2.6	2.8	2.4	−.2	3.0	4.0	4.3	3.8	3.6
2005	....	7.4	6.3	.9	1.8	1.8	1.9	.3	3.0	3.2	3.6	4.3	3.7
2006	....	10.3	4.3	1.9	2.4	3.1	1.3	1.6	2.9	2.1	2.5	2.7	2.6
2007	....	9.2	1.3	2.3	3.6	3.9	3.1	1.5	2.1	1.1	1.0	−.7	.6
2008	....	−2.4	−5.5	2.5	6.3	7.4	4.2	.3	−2.0	−3.3	−3.7	−2.7	−2.7
2009	....	1.2	−5.7	3.0	6.2	4.9	8.6	1.0	−.1	−.8	−2.1	.5	.3
2010	....	9.9	12.0	−1.3	1.9	1.3	3.0	−3.5	1.8	3.1	3.3	3.5	3.0
2011	....	4.6	3.8	−3.4	−3.5	−3.6	−3.2	−3.3	1.4	1.6	2.6	2.1	1.9
2012	....	2.1	.6	−2.1	−2.6	−4.7	1.2	−1.7	1.9	1.2	2.6	2.9	2.2
2013	....	6.0	3.0	−2.4	−6.1	−6.5	−5.5	.2	2.0	2.2	2.6	1.5	2.1
2014	....	3.0	6.7	.2	−1.2	−3.6	2.7	1.1	3.0	3.3	4.3	4.0	3.3
2015	....	−1.6	3.4	2.2	1.2	−.2	3.4	2.8	1.9	2.7	2.7	1.4	1.7
2016	....	.8	3.1	.9	.2	−.7	1.5	1.4	2.1	2.2	2.7	1.2	1.5
2017	....	4.7	5.4	.1	1.3	1.3	1.3	−.5	2.6	2.6	3.3	2.3	2.4
2018 [p]	....	2.3	3.5	1.8	2.8	5.2	−.4	1.1	2.7	3.2	3.1	....	....
2015: I	....	−4.2	6.6	2.3	2.2	.0	5.5	2.3	1.2	4.8	2.8	2.9	3.1
II	....	3.8	3.2	4.0	1.0	.8	1.4	5.8	3.7	3.3	3.5	1.3	2.3
III	....	−3.5	4.1	1.9	−.6	−4.0	4.6	3.4	1.7	2.0	2.9	1.0	1.0
IV	....	−2.2	−.4	.7	2.3	2.6	1.9	−.3	1.1	.6	1.4	.3	.3
2016: I	....	−2.4	.5	3.4	.2	−1.1	2.1	5.4	2.2	1.9	2.3	1.5	1.5
II	....	3.4	.8	−.8	−1.6	−3.3	1.0	−.4	2.9	1.9	3.3	−.9	.6
III	....	6.1	4.9	1.0	1.6	2.8	−.1	.6	2.5	1.9	2.8	2.0	2.0
IV	....	−3.6	6.2	.2	.5	−1.2	3.0	.0	.7	3.0	2.4	2.4	2.1
2017: I	....	5.0	4.8	−.8	.0	−.3	.4	−1.2	2.6	1.9	3.3	3.5	2.6
II	....	3.6	2.5	.0	2.4	5.6	−2.0	−1.3	2.8	2.8	3.2	2.8	2.9
III	....	3.5	2.8	−1.0	−1.3	−2.9	1.1	−.9	1.8	2.7	2.3	1.3	2.0
IV	....	6.6	11.8	2.4	4.1	2.9	5.7	1.4	3.2	3.1	4.4	1.5	1.9
2018: I	....	3.6	3.0	1.5	2.6	3.0	2.1	.9	1.9	2.2	2.0	3.9	3.1
II	....	9.3	−.6	2.5	3.7	5.9	.5	1.8	5.4	2.8	4.3	.9	2.5
III	....	−4.9	9.3	2.6	3.5	4.9	1.6	2.0	1.0	5.3	3.0	4.6	4.0
IV [p]	....	1.6	2.7	.4	1.6	6.9	−5.6	−.3	2.5	2.7	3.1	....	....

[1] Gross domestic product (GDP) less exports of goods and services plus imports of goods and services.
[2] Personal consumption expenditures plus gross private fixed investment.
[3] Gross domestic income is deflated by the implicit price deflator for GDP.

Note: Percent changes based on unrounded GDP quantity indexes.

Source: Department of Commerce (Bureau of Economic Analysis).

TABLE B-2. Contributions to percent change in real gross domestic product, 1968–2018

[Percentage points, except as noted; annual average to annual average, quarterly data at seasonally adjusted annual rates]

Year or quarter	Gross domestic product (percent change)	Personal consumption expenditures			Gross private domestic investment							Change in private inventories
						Fixed investment						
							Nonresidential				Residential	
		Total	Goods	Services	Total	Total	Total	Structures	Equipment	Intellectual property products		
1968	4.9	3.39	1.86	1.53	0.99	1.08	0.55	0.05	0.38	0.12	0.53	−0.09
1969	3.1	2.20	.92	1.28	.93	.93	.79	.19	.51	.09	.14	.00
1970	.2	1.39	.23	1.16	−1.03	−.33	−.10	.01	−.11	.00	−.23	−.70
1971	3.3	2.29	1.23	1.06	1.63	1.08	−.01	−.06	.05	.01	1.08	.56
1972	5.3	3.66	1.90	1.76	1.90	1.85	.97	.12	.75	.11	.87	.06
1973	5.6	2.97	1.52	1.45	1.95	1.47	1.51	.30	1.12	.08	−.04	.48
1974	−.5	−.50	−1.08	.58	−1.24	−.98	.10	−.08	.14	.05	−1.08	−.26
1975	−.2	1.36	.20	1.16	−2.91	−1.68	−1.13	−.42	−.73	.01	−.54	−1.24
1976	5.4	3.41	2.03	1.38	2.91	1.54	.66	.09	.39	.18	.88	1.37
1977	4.6	2.59	1.26	1.33	2.47	2.23	1.26	.15	1.01	.11	.97	.24
1978	5.5	2.68	1.19	1.49	2.22	2.10	1.72	.52	1.08	.12	.38	.12
1979	3.2	1.44	.45	.99	.72	1.11	1.34	.51	.62	.20	−.22	−.40
1980	−.3	−.19	−.72	.53	−2.07	−1.18	.00	.26	−.35	.09	−1.19	−.89
1981	2.5	.85	.33	.52	1.64	.50	.87	.39	.28	.21	−.37	1.13
1982	−1.8	.88	.19	.69	−2.46	−1.16	−.43	−.09	−.47	.12	−.72	−1.31
1983	4.6	3.51	1.69	1.82	1.60	1.32	−.06	−.56	.32	.17	1.38	.28
1984	7.2	3.30	1.91	1.39	4.73	2.83	2.18	.58	1.29	.30	.65	1.90
1985	4.2	3.20	1.38	1.83	−.01	1.02	.91	.31	.39	.21	.11	−1.03
1986	3.5	2.58	1.45	1.13	.03	.34	−.24	−.49	.08	.17	.58	−.31
1987	3.5	2.15	.47	1.67	.53	.11	.01	−.11	.03	.10	.10	.41
1988	4.2	2.65	.96	1.69	.45	.59	.63	.02	.43	.18	−.05	−.13
1989	3.7	1.86	.64	1.21	.72	.55	.71	.07	.35	.29	−.16	.17
1990	1.9	1.28	.16	1.12	−.45	−.25	.14	.05	−.14	.22	−.38	−.21
1991	−.1	.12	−.49	.61	−1.09	−.84	−.48	−.38	−.28	.18	−.35	−.26
1992	3.5	2.36	.76	1.60	1.11	.83	.33	−.18	.34	.17	.49	.28
1993	2.8	2.24	.99	1.26	1.24	1.17	.84	−.01	.73	.12	.32	.07
1994	4.0	2.51	1.26	1.26	1.90	1.29	.91	.05	.75	.11	.38	.61
1995	2.7	1.91	.71	1.20	.55	.99	1.15	.16	.78	.20	−.15	−.44
1996	3.8	2.26	1.06	1.20	1.49	1.48	1.13	.15	.65	.33	.35	.02
1997	4.4	2.45	1.12	1.33	2.01	1.49	1.38	.21	.76	.41	.11	.52
1998	4.5	3.42	1.54	1.88	1.76	1.82	1.44	.16	.91	.37	.38	−.07
1999	4.8	3.42	1.83	1.59	1.62	1.65	1.36	.01	.89	.45	.29	−.03
2000	4.1	3.32	1.23	2.09	1.31	1.34	1.31	.24	.71	.36	.03	−.03
2001	1.0	1.66	.72	.94	−1.11	−.27	−.31	−.04	−.31	.04	.04	−.84
2002	1.7	1.71	.92	.80	−.16	−.64	−.94	−.56	−.35	−.03	.29	.48
2003	2.9	2.13	1.15	.98	.76	.77	.30	−.09	.26	.14	.47	−.02
2004	3.8	2.53	1.21	1.32	1.64	1.23	.67	.00	.49	.18	.57	.41
2005	3.5	2.39	.98	1.41	1.26	1.33	.92	.06	.60	.26	.41	−.07
2006	2.9	2.05	.87	1.19	.60	.50	1.00	.22	.57	.21	−.50	.10
2007	1.9	1.49	.65	.84	−.48	−.24	.89	.42	.25	.23	−1.13	−.25
2008	−.1	−.14	−.71	.56	−1.52	−1.05	.08	.23	−.29	.14	−1.14	−.46
2009	−2.5	−.85	−.70	−.15	−3.52	−2.70	−1.95	−.72	−1.22	−.02	−.74	−.83
2010	2.6	1.20	.62	.57	1.86	.44	.52	−.50	.92	.11	−.08	1.42
2011	1.6	1.29	.49	.80	.94	.99	1.00	.07	.69	.24	.00	−.05
2012	2.2	1.03	.48	.55	1.64	1.47	1.16	.34	.62	.20	.31	.17
2013	1.8	.99	.70	.29	1.11	.87	.54	.04	.28	.22	.34	.23
2014	2.5	1.97	.88	1.09	.90	1.02	.90	.32	.41	.18	.12	−.12
2015	2.9	2.50	1.02	1.48	.83	.57	.24	−.10	.19	.15	.33	.25
2016	1.6	1.85	.77	1.08	−.24	.29	.06	−.16	−.09	.31	.23	−.53
2017	2.2	1.73	.78	.95	.81	.81	.68	.13	.35	.20	.13	.00
2018 ᵖ	2.9	1.81	.80	1.01	1.03	.91	.92	.15	.44	.33	−.01	.12
2015: I	3.3	2.36	.94	1.41	2.15	−.01	−.25	−.31	.27	−.21	.24	2.16
II	3.3	2.28	1.02	1.26	.37	.63	.27	.05	.05	.17	.35	−.25
III	1.0	1.91	.91	1.00	−.22	.51	.14	−.48	.43	.18	.37	−.73
IV	.4	1.52	.51	1.02	−1.04	−.33	−.53	−.70	−.27	.44	.20	−.70
2016: I	1.5	1.62	.72	.90	−.31	.31	−.16	−.12	−.40	.36	.47	−.62
II	2.3	2.30	1.01	1.29	−.17	.46	.50	.09	.01	.39	−.04	−.62
III	1.9	1.79	.70	1.09	−.07	.52	.59	.35	.01	.23	−.06	−.59
IV	1.8	1.75	.58	1.17	1.30	.28	.00	−.04	.05	−.02	.28	1.03
2017: I	1.8	1.22	.40	.82	.80	1.60	1.20	.36	.50	.33	.41	−.80
II	3.0	1.95	1.17	.79	.95	.72	.94	.11	.55	.28	−.22	.23
III	2.8	1.52	.86	.65	1.47	.44	.45	−.18	.56	.08	−.02	1.04
IV	2.3	2.64	1.42	1.22	.14	1.04	.63	.04	.56	.03	.41	−.91
2018: I	2.2	.36	−.13	.49	1.61	1.34	1.47	.40	.49	.58	−.14	.27
II	4.2	2.57	1.16	1.42	−.07	1.10	1.15	.43	.27	.45	−.05	−1.17
III	3.4	2.37	.90	1.47	2.53	.21	.35	−.11	.21	.25	−.14	2.33
IV ᵖ	2.6	1.92	.80	1.11	.82	.69	.82	−.13	.39	.56	−.14	.13

See next page for continuation of table.

TABLE B–2. Contributions to percent change in real gross domestic product, 1968–2018—*Continued*

[Percentage points, except as noted; annual average to annual average, quarterly data at seasonally adjusted annual rates]

Year or quarter	Net exports of goods and services							Government consumption expenditures and gross investment					Final sales of domestic product
	Net exports	Exports			Imports			Total	Federal			State and local	
		Total	Goods	Services	Total	Goods	Services		Total	National defense	Non-defense		
1968	−0.29	0.40	0.30	0.09	−0.68	−0.66	−0.03	0.82	0.21	0.18	0.04	0.61	5.01
1969	−.03	.25	.20	.05	−.28	−.20	−.08	.02	−.34	−.45	.11	.36	3.12
1970	.33	.54	.43	.11	−.21	−.14	−.07	−.50	−.80	−.83	.03	.30	.89
1971	−.18	.10	.00	.10	−.28	−.32	.04	−.45	−.80	−.97	.17	.35	2.74
1972	−.19	.42	.43	−.01	−.61	−.55	−.06	−.12	−.37	−.60	.22	.25	5.20
1973	.80	1.08	1.05	.02	−.28	−.33	.05	−.07	−.39	−.40	.01	.32	5.16
1974	.73	.56	.49	.08	.17	.17	.00	.47	.06	−.07	.14	.41	−.28
1975	.86	−.05	−.14	.09	.91	.85	.06	.49	.05	−.07	.13	.43	1.03
1976	−1.05	.36	.34	.02	−1.41	−1.31	−.10	.12	.01	−.04	.06	.10	4.01
1977	−.70	.19	.12	.07	−.89	−.82	−.07	.26	.21	.06	.15	.05	4.38
1978	.05	.80	.64	.17	−.76	−.66	−.10	.60	.23	.04	.19	.37	5.42
1979	.64	.80	.69	.11	−.16	−.13	−.02	.36	.20	.15	.05	.16	3.56
1980	1.64	.95	.88	.07	.69	.66	.03	.36	.38	.22	.16	−.02	.63
1981	−.15	.12	−.05	.17	−.26	−.18	−.09	.20	.43	.40	.03	−.23	1.41
1982	−.59	−.71	−.63	−.08	.12	.20	−.08	.37	.35	.47	−.11	.01	−.50
1983	−1.32	−.22	−.21	.00	−1.10	−.98	−.12	.79	.65	.51	.14	.14	4.31
1984	−1.54	.61	.41	.20	−2.16	−1.78	−.38	.74	.33	.38	−.04	.41	5.34
1985	−.39	.24	.20	.05	−.63	−.50	−.13	1.37	.78	.62	.16	.59	5.20
1986	−.29	.53	.27	.25	−.82	−.80	−.02	1.14	.61	.52	.09	.53	3.77
1987	.17	.77	.62	.15	−.60	−.39	−.21	.62	.38	.38	.01	.24	3.05
1988	.81	1.23	.99	.24	−.41	−.35	−.07	.26	−.15	−.04	−.12	.42	4.31
1989	.51	.97	.72	.26	−.46	−.37	−.09	.58	.15	−.02	.18	.43	3.51
1990	.40	.78	.56	.22	−.37	−.25	−.13	.65	.20	.02	.18	.45	2.09
1991	.62	.61	.45	.16	.01	−.04	.05	.25	.01	−.06	.07	.24	.15
1992	−.04	.66	.52	.14	−.70	−.76	.05	.10	−.15	−.31	.16	.25	3.24
1993	−.56	.31	.22	.09	−.87	−.82	−.05	−.17	−.32	−.32	.00	.15	2.68
1994	−.41	.84	.65	.19	−1.25	−1.15	−.10	.02	−.31	−.28	−.02	.32	3.41
1995	.12	1.02	.83	.19	−.90	−.84	−.06	.10	−.21	−.21	.00	.31	3.13
1996	−.15	.86	.68	.18	−1.01	−.91	−.10	.18	−.09	−.08	−.01	.27	3.76
1997	−.31	1.26	1.10	.16	−1.57	−1.40	−.17	.30	−.06	−.13	.07	.36	3.92
1998	−1.14	.26	.17	.08	−1.39	−1.18	−.21	.44	−.06	−.09	.03	.50	4.55
1999	−.87	.52	.31	.20	−1.39	−1.31	−.07	.58	.13	.06	.07	.46	4.78
2000	−.83	.86	.73	.13	−1.69	−1.44	−.25	.33	.02	−.04	.06	.31	4.16
2001	−.22	−.61	−.48	−.12	.39	.40	−.01	.67	.24	.13	.11	.43	1.84
2002	−.64	−.17	−.23	.06	−.47	−.40	−.07	.82	.47	.30	.18	.35	1.26
2003	−.45	.20	.19	.01	−.64	−.64	−.01	.41	.45	.35	.10	−.03	2.88
2004	−.67	.88	.57	.31	−1.55	−1.30	−.24	.30	.31	.26	.05	−.01	3.39
2005	−.29	.69	.52	.17	−.97	−.88	−.09	.15	.15	.11	.04	.00	3.59
2006	−.10	.94	.70	.23	−1.04	−.82	−.21	.30	.17	.07	.10	.13	2.75
2007	.53	.93	.53	.40	−.41	−.28	−.12	.34	.14	.13	.01	.20	2.12
2008	1.04	.66	.48	.18	.38	.49	−.10	.48	.46	.33	.13	.02	.33
2009	1.13	−1.01	−1.00	−.01	2.14	2.08	.06	.70	.47	.29	.18	.23	−1.71
2010	−.49	1.35	1.12	.23	−1.84	−1.74	−.10	.00	.35	.16	.19	−.35	1.14
2011	−.01	.90	.61	.28	−.91	−.82	−.09	−.66	−.23	−.12	−.11	−.44	1.60
2012	.00	.46	.36	.10	−.46	−.38	−.09	−.42	−.16	−.18	.03	−.26	2.08
2013	.22	.48	.30	.18	−.26	−.25	−.01	−.47	−.44	−.34	−.10	−.03	1.61
2014	−.25	.58	.42	.15	−.83	−.75	−.07	−.18	−.19	−.19	.00	.02	2.57
2015	−.78	.08	−.03	.10	−.85	−.74	−.11	.33	.00	−.08	.08	.34	2.63
2016	−.30	−.01	.03	−.04	−.28	−.17	−.11	.25	.03	−.02	.05	.22	2.10
2017	−.31	.36	.26	.10	−.67	−.55	−.12	−.01	.05	.03	.02	−.06	2.22
2018 ᵖ	−.22	.47	.36	.10	−.69	−.60	−.09	.26	.17	.13	.04	.09	2.77
2015: I	−1.58	−.56	−.86	.30	−1.02	−.99	−.03	.40	.15	.00	.15	.26	1.17
II	−.01	.48	.54	−.06	−.49	−.44	−.05	.70	.07	.03	.04	.63	3.59
III	−1.05	−.44	−.39	−.05	−.61	−.38	−.23	.33	−.04	−.16	.12	.37	1.70
IV	−.21	−.28	−.40	.12	.07	.17	−.10	.12	.16	.10	.05	−.03	1.10
2016: I	−.36	−.31	.00	−.31	−.06	.06	−.12	.60	.02	−.04	.06	.58	2.17
II	.29	.39	.26	.13	−.10	−.11	.02	−.15	−.10	−.13	.03	−.04	2.91
III	.03	.71	.58	.13	−.68	−.47	−.21	.17	.11	.11	.00	.07	2.52
IV	−1.32	−.44	−.24	−.20	−.88	−.73	−.15	.03	.03	−.05	.08	.00	.74
2017: I	−.10	.59	.33	.26	−.69	−.57	−.12	−.13	.00	−.01	.01	−.13	2.59
II	.08	.44	.33	.11	−.36	−.28	−.09	.01	.16	.21	−.05	−.15	2.76
III	.01	.42	.17	.25	−.41	−.29	−.12	−.18	−.08	−.11	.03	−.10	1.79
IV	−.89	.79	.83	−.04	−1.68	−1.62	−.06	.41	.26	.11	.15	.15	3.20
2018: I	−.02	.43	.26	.18	−.45	−.30	−.15	.27	.17	.11	.06	.10	1.94
II	1.22	1.12	1.06	.07	.10	.06	.04	.43	.24	.22	.01	.20	5.33
III	−1.99	−.62	−.72	.10	−1.37	−1.24	−.12	.44	.23	.18	.04	.22	1.03
IV ᵖ	−.22	.19	.13	.06	−.41	−.20	−.21	.07	.10	.25	−.15	−.03	2.46

Source: Department of Commerce (Bureau of Economic Analysis).

Table B-3. Gross domestic product, 2003–2018

[Quarterly data at seasonally adjusted annual rates]

Year or quarter	Gross domestic product	Personal consumption expenditures			Gross private domestic investment							Change in private inventories
						Fixed investment						
							Nonresidential					
		Total	Goods	Services	Total	Total	Total	Structures	Equipment	Intellectual property products	Residential	

Billions of dollars

2003	11,458.2	7,723.1	2,722.6	5,000.5	2,027.1	2,013.0	1,375.9	286.6	670.6	418.7	637.1	14.1
2004	12,213.7	8,212.7	2,902.0	5,310.6	2,281.3	2,217.2	1,467.4	307.7	721.9	437.8	749.8	64.1
2005	13,036.6	8,747.1	3,082.9	5,664.2	2,534.7	2,477.2	1,621.0	353.0	794.9	473.1	856.2	57.5
2006	13,814.6	9,260.3	3,239.7	6,020.7	2,701.0	2,632.0	1,793.8	425.2	862.3	506.3	838.2	69.0
2007	14,451.9	9,706.4	3,367.0	6,339.4	2,673.0	2,639.1	1,948.6	510.3	893.4	544.8	690.5	34.0
2008	14,712.8	9,976.3	3,363.2	6,613.1	2,477.6	2,506.9	1,990.9	571.1	845.4	574.4	516.0	−29.2
2009	14,448.9	9,842.2	3,180.0	6,662.2	1,929.7	2,080.4	1,690.4	455.8	670.3	564.4	390.0	−150.8
2010	14,992.1	10,185.8	3,317.8	6,868.0	2,165.5	2,111.6	1,735.0	379.8	777.0	578.2	376.6	53.9
2011	15,542.6	10,641.1	3,518.1	7,123.0	2,332.6	2,286.3	1,907.5	404.5	881.3	621.7	378.8	46.3
2012	16,197.0	11,006.8	3,637.7	7,369.1	2,621.8	2,550.5	2,118.5	479.4	983.4	655.7	432.0	71.2
2013	16,784.9	11,317.2	3,730.0	7,587.2	2,826.0	2,721.5	2,211.5	492.5	1,027.0	691.9	510.0	104.5
2014	17,521.7	11,824.0	3,861.5	7,962.5	3,038.9	2,954.4	2,394.3	577.1	1,090.8	726.4	560.1	84.5
2015	18,219.3	12,294.5	3,919.6	8,374.8	3,212.0	3,083.2	2,449.7	572.1	1,118.3	759.2	633.6	128.7
2016	18,707.2	12,766.9	3,996.3	8,770.6	3,169.9	3,124.0	2,442.1	545.7	1,090.9	805.5	698.8	28.9
2017	19,485.4	13,321.4	4,156.1	9,165.3	3,368.0	3,342.5	2,587.9	585.4	1,150.4	852.0	754.6	25.5
2018 ᵖ	20,500.6	13,951.6	4,342.1	9,609.4	3,652.2	3,595.6	2,800.4	637.1	1,236.3	927.0	795.3	56.5
2015: I	17,970.4	12,095.6	3,859.1	8,236.4	3,216.8	3,052.1	2,447.5	589.0	1,114.9	743.6	604.6	164.7
II	18,221.3	12,256.7	3,922.7	8,334.0	3,225.9	3,081.7	2,458.0	589.9	1,114.6	753.4	623.7	144.3
III	18,331.1	12,380.7	3,956.8	8,424.0	3,229.6	3,109.3	2,463.0	570.9	1,130.2	762.0	646.3	120.3
IV	18,354.4	12,445.1	3,940.1	8,505.0	3,175.5	3,089.9	2,430.3	539.0	1,113.7	777.6	659.6	85.6
2016: I	18,409.1	12,526.9	3,932.2	8,594.3	3,142.1	3,094.1	2,409.8	531.2	1,092.8	785.8	684.2	48.0
II	18,640.7	12,706.5	3,990.3	8,716.2	3,152.2	3,127.1	2,435.6	539.7	1,091.4	804.5	691.5	25.1
III	18,799.6	12,845.2	4,013.9	8,831.2	3,157.7	3,157.2	2,458.4	555.1	1,090.2	813.2	698.8	.5
IV	18,979.2	12,989.4	4,048.8	8,940.6	3,227.6	3,185.4	2,464.7	556.7	1,089.3	818.7	720.8	42.1
2017: I	19,162.6	13,114.1	4,090.4	9,023.7	3,278.6	3,270.6	2,525.2	577.5	1,112.3	835.4	745.5	8.0
II	19,359.1	13,233.2	4,117.1	9,116.1	3,337.9	3,320.8	2,576.7	588.3	1,137.4	850.9	744.1	17.1
III	19,588.1	13,359.1	4,166.0	9,193.1	3,413.9	3,358.5	2,607.0	585.3	1,162.8	858.9	751.5	55.4
IV	19,831.8	13,579.2	4,250.9	9,328.3	3,441.4	3,420.0	2,642.6	590.6	1,189.1	862.9	777.4	21.5
2018: I	20,041.0	13,679.6	4,267.7	9,411.9	3,543.8	3,507.4	2,720.3	614.9	1,212.6	892.7	787.2	36.3
II	20,411.9	13,875.6	4,329.5	9,546.1	3,579.5	3,589.9	2,791.4	644.1	1,228.8	918.6	798.5	−10.4
III	20,658.2	14,050.5	4,371.3	9,679.1	3,710.7	3,618.0	2,819.7	643.3	1,243.0	933.4	798.3	92.7
IV ᵖ	20,891.4	14,200.6	4,400.1	9,800.6	3,774.6	3,667.1	2,870.1	645.9	1,261.0	963.3	797.0	107.5

Billions of chained (2012) dollars

2003	13,879.1	9,377.5	3,092.0	6,289.4	2,290.4	2,280.6	1,509.4	456.6	634.3	437.7	755.5	19.9
2004	14,406.4	9,729.3	3,250.0	6,479.2	2,502.6	2,440.7	1,594.0	456.3	688.6	459.2	830.9	82.6
2005	14,912.5	10,075.9	3,384.7	6,689.5	2,670.6	2,618.7	1,716.4	466.1	760.0	493.1	885.4	63.7
2006	15,338.3	10,384.5	3,509.7	6,871.7	2,752.4	2,686.8	1,854.2	501.7	832.6	521.5	818.9	87.1
2007	15,626.0	10,615.3	3,607.6	7,003.6	2,684.1	2,653.5	1,982.1	568.6	865.8	554.3	665.8	40.6
2008	15,604.7	10,592.8	3,498.9	7,093.0	2,462.9	2,499.4	1,994.2	605.4	824.4	575.3	504.6	−32.7
2009	15,208.8	10,460.0	3,389.8	7,070.1	1,942.0	2,099.8	1,704.3	492.2	649.7	572.4	395.3	−177.3
2010	15,598.8	10,643.0	3,485.7	7,157.4	2,216.5	2,164.2	1,781.0	412.8	781.2	588.1	383.0	57.3
2011	15,840.7	10,843.8	3,561.8	7,282.1	2,362.1	2,317.8	1,935.4	424.1	886.2	624.8	382.5	46.7
2012	16,197.0	11,006.8	3,637.7	7,369.1	2,621.8	2,550.5	2,118.5	479.4	983.4	655.7	432.0	71.2
2013	16,495.4	11,166.9	3,752.2	7,415.5	2,801.5	2,692.1	2,206.0	485.5	1,029.2	691.4	485.5	108.7
2014	16,899.8	11,494.3	3,902.9	7,594.0	2,951.6	2,861.5	2,357.4	536.9	1,098.7	721.1	504.2	86.6
2015	17,386.7	11,921.9	4,087.7	7,840.0	3,092.2	2,958.5	2,399.7	520.9	1,132.6	747.8	555.3	129.0
2016	17,659.2	12,248.2	4,236.1	8,022.5	3,050.5	3,009.8	2,411.2	494.7	1,116.2	803.9	591.3	23.4
2017	18,050.7	12,558.7	4,391.9	8,184.5	3,196.6	3,155.1	2,538.1	517.5	1,183.7	841.1	611.1	22.5
2018 ᵖ	18,571.3	12,890.6	4,557.3	8,359.3	3,387.2	3,322.4	2,714.8	543.3	1,271.9	905.6	609.6	45.1
2015: I	17,254.7	11,788.4	4,024.3	7,768.1	3,096.9	2,930.4	2,393.5	536.3	1,124.0	733.2	535.2	166.4
II	17,397.5	11,887.5	4,071.9	7,821.0	3,112.4	2,957.5	2,405.5	538.6	1,126.3	740.5	549.3	149.8
III	17,438.8	11,972.0	4,115.2	7,863.6	3,102.7	2,980.2	2,411.9	518.8	1,146.4	748.8	564.3	117.6
IV	17,456.2	12,039.7	4,139.5	7,907.1	3,056.9	2,965.9	2,388.1	489.7	1,133.7	768.8	572.3	82.3
2016: I	17,523.4	12,111.8	4,174.6	7,945.5	3,042.9	2,979.7	2,380.9	484.8	1,115.1	785.0	590.9	50.7
II	17,622.5	12,214.1	4,223.9	8,000.4	3,035.2	3,000.0	2,403.3	488.8	1,115.5	803.2	589.4	17.8
III	17,706.7	12,294.3	4,258.5	8,047.0	3,032.2	3,023.5	2,430.3	503.5	1,115.8	814.0	586.9	−14.1
IV	17,784.2	12,372.7	4,287.2	8,096.9	3,091.7	3,036.1	2,430.4	501.9	1,118.2	813.3	597.9	39.1
2017: I	17,863.0	12,427.6	4,307.3	8,131.9	3,128.6	3,108.6	2,486.5	517.3	1,142.8	829.0	613.8	−2.4
II	17,995.2	12,515.9	4,366.0	8,165.6	3,172.1	3,141.3	2,530.8	522.2	1,169.5	842.3	605.2	11.9
III	18,120.8	12,584.9	4,410.2	8,193.7	3,239.8	3,161.2	2,552.3	514.5	1,197.1	845.9	604.5	64.4
IV	18,223.8	12,706.4	4,483.9	8,246.6	3,246.0	3,209.3	2,582.7	516.2	1,225.6	847.3	620.7	16.1
2018: I	18,324.0	12,722.8	4,477.0	8,267.9	3,321.0	3,271.3	2,654.0	533.3	1,250.9	875.7	615.3	30.3
II	18,511.6	12,842.0	4,537.6	8,329.8	3,316.7	3,322.3	2,710.1	551.7	1,264.9	897.9	613.2	−36.8
III	18,665.0	12,953.3	4,585.5	8,394.9	3,436.2	3,331.8	2,727.0	546.9	1,275.6	910.2	607.7	89.8
IV ᵖ	18,784.6	13,044.2	4,629.0	8,444.5	3,474.7	3,364.2	2,768.0	541.1	1,296.4	938.6	602.3	97.1

See next page for continuation of table.

TABLE B-3. Gross domestic product, 2003–2018—Continued

[Quarterly data at seasonally adjusted annual rates]

Year or quarter	Net exports of goods and services			Government consumption expenditures and gross investment					Final sales of domestic product	Gross domestic purchasers [1]	Final sales to private domestic purchasers [2]	Gross domestic income (GDI) [3]	Average of GDP and GDI
	Net exports	Exports	Imports	Total	Federal			State and local					
					Total	National defense	Non-defense						
	Billions of dollars												
2003	−503.1	1,036.2	1,539.3	2,211.2	826.3	521.2	305.0	1,384.9	11,444.2	11,961.4	9,736.1	11,471.9	11,465.1
2004	−619.1	1,177.6	1,796.7	2,338.9	891.7	569.9	321.9	1,447.1	12,149.7	12,832.8	10,429.8	12,235.8	12,224.8
2005	−721.2	1,305.2	2,026.4	2,476.0	947.5	609.4	338.0	1,528.5	12,979.1	13,757.8	11,224.3	13,091.7	13,064.2
2006	−770.9	1,472.6	2,243.5	2,624.2	1,000.7	640.8	359.9	1,623.5	13,745.6	14,585.5	11,892.3	14,022.5	13,918.6
2007	−718.4	1,660.9	2,379.3	2,790.8	1,050.5	679.3	371.2	1,740.3	14,417.9	15,170.3	12,345.5	14,434.2	14,443.0
2008	−723.1	1,837.1	2,560.1	2,982.0	1,150.6	750.3	400.2	1,831.4	14,742.1	15,435.9	12,483.2	14,530.0	14,621.4
2009	−396.5	1,582.0	1,978.4	3,073.5	1,218.2	787.6	430.6	1,855.3	14,599.7	14,845.4	11,922.6	14,256.8	14,352.9
2010	−513.9	1,846.3	2,360.2	3,154.6	1,297.9	828.0	469.9	1,856.7	14,938.1	15,506.0	12,297.4	14,931.0	14,961.5
2011	−579.5	2,103.0	2,682.5	3,148.4	1,298.9	834.0	465.0	1,849.4	15,496.3	16,122.0	12,927.4	15,595.8	15,569.2
2012	−568.6	2,191.3	2,759.9	3,137.0	1,286.5	814.2	472.4	1,850.5	16,125.8	16,765.6	13,557.4	16,438.4	16,317.7
2013	−490.8	2,273.4	2,764.2	3,132.4	1,226.6	764.2	462.4	1,905.8	16,680.3	17,275.6	14,038.7	16,945.2	16,865.0
2014	−508.3	2,371.0	2,879.3	3,167.0	1,214.2	742.5	471.6	1,952.9	17,437.3	18,030.4	14,778.5	17,820.8	17,671.3
2015	−521.4	2,265.0	2,786.5	3,234.2	1,220.9	729.5	491.3	2,013.3	18,090.6	18,740.7	15,377.8	18,474.2	18,346.8
2016	−520.6	2,217.6	2,738.1	3,291.0	1,232.2	727.3	504.9	2,058.8	18,678.2	19,227.8	15,907.8	18,834.1	18,770.7
2017	−578.4	2,350.2	2,928.6	3,374.4	1,265.2	743.9	521.3	2,109.2	19,459.9	20,063.8	16,663.9	19,628.6	19,557.0
2018 ᵖ	−625.6	2,530.9	3,156.5	3,522.5	1,319.9	779.0	540.9	2,202.6	20,444.1	21,126.2	17,547.2	....	....
2015: I	−530.4	2,286.6	2,817.0	3,188.5	1,214.5	729.5	485.0	1,974.0	17,805.8	18,500.8	15,147.7	18,289.6	18,130.0
II	−499.0	2,303.2	2,802.2	3,237.6	1,221.0	732.7	488.3	2,016.6	18,077.0	18,720.3	15,338.4	18,454.5	18,337.9
III	−536.2	2,259.2	2,795.4	3,257.0	1,221.4	726.5	495.0	2,035.5	18,210.8	18,867.3	15,490.0	18,568.1	18,449.6
IV	−520.1	2,211.2	2,731.3	3,253.8	1,226.6	729.6	497.0	2,027.2	18,268.8	18,874.5	15,535.0	18,584.8	18,469.6
2016: I	−522.2	2,165.6	2,687.8	3,262.7	1,223.5	724.8	498.7	2,039.2	18,361.1	18,931.3	15,620.6	18,637.1	18,523.1
II	−496.2	2,206.6	2,702.7	3,278.2	1,225.4	722.4	502.9	2,052.9	18,615.6	19,136.9	15,833.6	18,720.9	18,680.8
III	−503.7	2,252.5	2,756.3	3,300.5	1,235.9	730.6	505.3	2,064.7	18,799.2	19,303.4	16,002.4	18,884.8	18,842.2
IV	−560.2	2,245.6	2,805.8	3,322.4	1,244.1	731.5	512.7	2,078.3	18,937.1	19,539.4	16,174.9	19,093.6	19,036.4
2017: I	−576.6	2,294.1	2,870.7	3,346.4	1,252.4	734.9	517.5	2,093.9	19,154.6	19,739.1	16,384.7	19,357.4	19,260.0
II	−571.9	2,316.3	2,888.2	3,360.0	1,264.0	746.7	517.3	2,096.0	19,342.1	19,931.1	16,554.0	19,545.9	19,452.5
III	−557.3	2,358.3	2,915.5	3,372.3	1,263.8	743.1	520.7	2,108.5	19,532.7	20,145.3	16,717.6	19,702.5	19,645.3
IV	−607.9	2,432.0	3,039.9	3,419.1	1,280.6	750.7	529.8	2,138.5	19,810.4	20,439.7	16,999.2	19,908.5	19,870.2
2018: I	−639.2	2,477.4	3,116.6	3,456.8	1,294.8	759.0	535.8	2,162.0	20,004.7	20,680.2	17,187.0	20,201.0	20,121.0
II	−549.8	2,568.7	3,118.5	3,506.6	1,313.0	772.6	540.4	2,193.5	20,422.3	20,961.7	17,465.5	20,410.5	20,411.2
III	−653.5	2,538.6	3,192.1	3,550.5	1,329.5	784.3	545.2	2,221.0	20,565.5	21,311.7	17,668.5	20,716.5	20,687.3
IV ᵖ	−659.8	2,538.9	3,198.7	3,575.9	1,342.2	799.9	542.3	2,233.7	20,783.9	21,551.2	17,867.8	....	....
	Billions of chained (2012) dollars												
2003	−735.0	1,305.0	2,040.1	2,947.2	1,032.7	655.6	377.1	1,922.2	13,864.7	14,628.6	11,677.1	13,895.7	13,887.4
2004	−841.4	1,431.2	2,272.6	2,992.7	1,077.5	692.7	384.8	1,920.1	14,335.7	15,254.1	12,194.2	14,432.4	14,419.4
2005	−887.8	1,533.2	2,421.0	3,015.5	1,099.1	708.6	390.6	1,920.1	14,852.3	15,804.5	12,725.8	14,975.5	14,944.0
2006	−905.0	1,676.4	2,581.5	3,063.5	1,125.0	719.8	405.3	1,941.6	15,263.0	16,246.7	13,102.6	15,569.1	15,453.7
2007	−823.6	1,822.3	2,646.0	3,118.6	1,147.0	740.3	406.7	1,974.7	15,588.7	16,454.6	13,293.8	15,606.9	15,616.5
2008	−661.6	1,925.4	2,587.1	3,195.6	1,218.8	791.5	427.3	1,978.7	15,639.7	16,270.7	13,108.0	15,410.8	15,507.7
2009	−484.8	1,763.8	2,248.6	3,307.3	1,293.0	836.7	456.3	2,015.6	15,373.0	15,698.9	12,557.6	15,006.6	15,107.7
2010	−565.9	1,977.9	2,543.8	3,307.2	1,346.1	861.3	484.8	1,961.3	15,546.6	16,164.7	12,805.7	15,535.2	15,567.0
2011	−568.1	2,119.0	2,687.1	3,203.3	1,311.1	842.9	468.3	1,892.2	15,796.5	16,408.8	13,161.2	15,894.9	15,867.8
2012	−568.6	2,191.3	2,759.9	3,137.0	1,286.5	814.2	472.4	1,850.5	16,125.8	16,765.6	13,557.4	16,438.4	16,317.7
2013	−532.8	2,269.6	2,802.4	3,061.0	1,215.3	759.6	455.6	1,845.3	16,386.2	17,028.6	13,858.9	16,652.9	16,574.1
2014	−577.7	2,367.0	2,944.7	3,032.3	1,183.2	728.0	455.0	1,848.1	16,809.9	17,475.9	14,355.7	17,188.2	17,044.0
2015	−724.9	2,380.6	3,105.5	3,088.5	1,183.0	713.5	469.1	1,903.9	17,253.6	18,099.6	14,880.2	17,630.0	17,508.3
2016	−786.2	2,378.1	3,164.4	3,132.5	1,187.8	709.2	478.0	1,942.8	17,617.5	18,428.0	15,257.7	17,779.0	17,719.1
2017	−858.7	2,450.1	3,308.7	3,130.4	1,196.4	711.9	481.9	1,932.3	18,008.7	18,881.0	15,713.5	18,183.3	18,117.0
2018 ᵖ	−914.1	2,546.6	3,460.6	3,177.8	1,227.8	738.2	489.1	1,948.9	18,507.1	19,449.2	16,212.6	....	....
2015: I	−694.4	2,377.7	3,072.1	3,057.6	1,179.9	714.9	464.7	1,876.3	17,089.1	17,939.9	14,718.6	17,561.2	17,408.0
II	−696.7	2,400.4	3,096.7	3,087.6	1,183.0	716.3	466.3	1,903.0	17,242.9	18,084.6	14,844.9	17,619.7	17,508.4
III	−749.0	2,379.0	3,128.0	3,101.8	1,181.2	709.0	471.6	1,918.8	17,317.0	18,173.3	14,952.1	17,664.3	17,551.5
IV	−759.3	2,365.7	3,125.0	3,107.1	1,188.0	713.6	473.9	1,917.5	17,365.3	18,200.4	15,005.3	17,675.3	17,565.8
2016: I	−777.9	2,351.1	3,129.0	3,133.3	1,188.6	711.7	476.3	1,942.9	17,459.7	18,284.9	15,091.2	17,740.4	17,631.9
II	−764.1	2,370.9	3,135.0	3,126.7	1,183.9	705.8	477.4	1,940.9	17,586.2	18,372.6	15,213.8	17,698.3	17,660.4
III	−766.3	2,406.4	3,172.6	3,134.4	1,188.7	710.7	477.3	1,943.8	17,696.3	18,457.8	15,317.5	17,786.9	17,746.8
IV	−836.7	2,384.2	3,220.9	3,135.6	1,190.7	708.5	480.9	1,943.6	17,728.0	18,596.4	15,408.6	17,891.3	17,837.8
2017: I	−845.5	2,413.3	3,258.8	3,129.6	1,190.0	707.9	481.4	1,937.7	17,841.9	18,681.9	15,535.9	18,044.7	17,953.8
II	−844.1	2,435.0	3,279.1	3,130.0	1,197.1	717.6	478.9	1,931.3	17,963.6	18,813.5	15,656.9	18,168.7	18,081.9
III	−845.9	2,456.1	3,302.0	3,121.8	1,193.2	712.3	480.3	1,926.9	18,042.6	18,941.2	15,745.8	18,226.7	18,173.8
IV	−899.2	2,495.9	3,395.1	3,140.2	1,205.2	717.5	487.0	1,933.5	18,186.5	19,087.4	15,915.4	18,294.2	18,259.0
2018: I	−902.4	2,517.8	3,420.1	3,152.2	1,213.1	722.8	489.5	1,937.7	18,274.4	19,190.2	15,993.7	18,470.2	18,397.1
II	−841.0	2,574.2	3,415.2	3,171.8	1,224.0	733.3	490.1	1,946.6	18,515.9	19,324.8	16,163.9	18,510.3	18,510.9
III	−949.7	2,542.2	3,491.9	3,192.0	1,234.7	742.2	492.0	1,956.3	18,562.1	19,574.7	16,284.6	18,717.6	18,691.3
IV ᵖ	−963.2	2,552.0	3,515.2	3,195.3	1,239.5	754.6	484.9	1,955.0	18,675.9	19,706.9	16,408.0	....	....

[1] Gross domestic product (GDP) less exports of goods and services plus imports of goods and services.
[2] Personal consumption expenditures plus gross private fixed investment.
[3] For chained dollar measures, gross domestic income is deflated by the implicit price deflator for GDP.

Source: Department of Commerce (Bureau of Economic Analysis).

TABLE B-4. Percentage shares of gross domestic product, 1968–2018
[Percent of nominal GDP]

Year or quarter	Gross domestic product (percent)	Personal consumption expenditures			Gross private domestic investment							
						Fixed investment						Change in private inventories
		Total	Goods	Services	Total	Total	Nonresidential				Residential	
							Total	Structures	Equipment	Intellectual property products		
1968	100.0	59.2	30.3	28.9	16.7	15.7	11.4	3.6	6.2	1.7	4.3	1.0
1969	100.0	59.3	29.9	29.4	17.1	16.2	11.8	3.7	6.4	1.7	4.4	.9
1970	100.0	60.3	29.7	30.6	15.8	15.7	11.6	3.8	6.2	1.7	4.0	.2
1971	100.0	60.1	29.4	30.7	16.9	16.2	11.2	3.7	5.9	1.6	5.0	.7
1972	100.0	60.1	29.2	30.8	17.8	17.1	11.5	3.7	6.2	1.6	5.7	.7
1973	100.0	59.6	29.2	30.4	18.7	17.6	12.1	3.9	6.7	1.6	5.5	1.1
1974	100.0	60.2	29.2	31.0	17.8	16.9	12.4	4.0	6.8	1.7	4.5	.9
1975	100.0	61.2	29.2	32.0	15.3	15.6	11.7	3.6	6.4	1.7	4.0	-.4
1976	100.0	61.3	29.2	32.1	17.3	16.3	11.7	3.5	6.5	1.7	4.6	.9
1977	100.0	61.2	28.8	32.4	19.1	18.0	12.4	3.6	7.1	1.7	5.5	1.1
1978	100.0	60.5	28.2	32.3	20.3	19.2	13.4	4.0	7.7	1.7	5.9	1.1
1979	100.0	60.3	28.1	32.3	20.5	19.9	14.2	4.5	7.9	1.8	5.6	.7
1980	100.0	61.3	28.0	33.3	18.6	18.8	14.2	4.8	7.6	1.9	4.5	-.2
1981	100.0	60.3	27.1	33.2	19.7	18.8	14.7	5.2	7.5	2.0	4.0	.9
1982	100.0	61.9	26.9	35.0	17.4	17.8	14.5	5.3	7.0	2.2	3.3	-.4
1983	100.0	62.8	26.8	36.0	17.5	17.7	13.3	4.2	6.8	2.2	4.4	-.2
1984	100.0	61.7	26.3	35.4	20.3	18.7	14.0	4.4	7.2	2.4	4.7	1.6
1985	100.0	62.5	26.2	36.3	19.1	18.6	14.0	4.5	7.1	2.4	4.6	.5
1986	100.0	63.0	26.1	36.9	18.5	18.4	13.3	3.9	6.9	2.5	5.1	.1
1987	100.0	63.4	25.9	37.5	18.4	17.8	12.7	3.6	6.6	2.5	5.1	.6
1988	100.0	63.6	25.5	38.1	17.9	17.5	12.6	3.5	6.6	2.5	4.9	.4
1989	100.0	63.4	25.2	38.2	17.7	17.2	12.7	3.4	6.6	2.7	4.5	.5
1990	100.0	63.9	25.0	38.9	16.7	16.4	12.4	3.4	6.2	2.8	4.0	.2
1991	100.0	64.0	24.3	39.7	15.3	15.3	11.8	3.0	5.9	2.9	3.6	.0
1992	100.0	64.4	24.0	40.4	15.5	15.3	11.4	2.6	5.9	2.9	3.9	.3
1993	100.0	64.9	23.9	41.0	16.1	15.8	11.7	2.6	6.2	2.9	4.2	.3
1994	100.0	64.8	24.0	40.8	17.2	16.4	11.9	2.6	6.5	2.8	4.4	.9
1995	100.0	65.0	23.8	41.2	17.2	16.8	12.6	2.7	6.9	3.0	4.2	.4
1996	100.0	65.0	23.8	41.2	17.7	17.4	12.9	2.8	7.0	3.1	4.4	.4
1997	100.0	64.5	23.4	41.2	18.6	17.8	13.4	2.9	7.1	3.4	4.4	.8
1998	100.0	64.9	23.3	41.6	19.2	18.5	13.8	3.0	7.3	3.5	4.6	.7
1999	100.0	65.2	23.7	41.5	19.6	19.0	14.2	3.0	7.4	3.8	4.8	.6
2000	100.0	66.0	23.9	42.0	19.9	19.4	14.6	3.1	7.5	4.0	4.7	.5
2001	100.0	66.8	23.9	42.9	18.3	18.6	13.8	3.2	6.7	3.9	4.8	-.4
2002	100.0	67.1	23.8	43.4	17.7	17.5	12.4	2.6	6.0	3.7	5.1	.2
2003	100.0	67.4	23.8	43.6	17.7	17.6	12.0	2.5	5.9	3.7	5.6	.1
2004	100.0	67.2	23.8	43.5	18.7	18.2	12.0	2.5	5.9	3.6	6.1	.5
2005	100.0	67.1	23.6	43.4	19.4	19.0	12.4	2.7	6.1	3.6	6.6	.4
2006	100.0	67.0	23.5	43.6	19.6	19.1	13.0	3.1	6.2	3.7	6.1	.5
2007	100.0	67.2	23.3	43.9	18.5	18.3	13.5	3.5	6.2	3.8	4.8	.2
2008	100.0	67.8	22.9	44.9	16.8	17.0	13.5	3.9	5.7	3.9	3.5	-.2
2009	100.0	68.1	22.0	46.1	13.4	14.4	11.7	3.2	4.6	3.9	2.7	-1.0
2010	100.0	67.9	22.1	45.8	14.4	14.1	11.6	2.5	5.2	3.9	2.5	.4
2011	100.0	68.5	22.6	45.8	15.0	14.7	12.3	2.6	5.7	4.0	2.4	.3
2012	100.0	68.0	22.5	45.5	16.2	15.7	13.1	3.0	6.1	4.0	2.7	.4
2013	100.0	67.4	22.2	45.2	16.8	16.2	13.2	2.9	6.1	4.1	3.0	.6
2014	100.0	67.5	22.0	45.4	17.3	16.9	13.7	3.3	6.2	4.1	3.2	.5
2015	100.0	67.5	21.5	46.0	17.6	16.9	13.4	3.1	6.1	4.2	3.5	.7
2016	100.0	68.2	21.4	46.9	16.9	16.8	13.1	2.9	5.8	4.3	3.7	.2
2017	100.0	68.4	21.3	47.0	17.3	17.2	13.3	3.0	5.9	4.4	3.9	.1
2018 ᵖ	100.0	68.1	21.2	46.9	17.8	17.5	13.7	3.1	6.0	4.5	3.9	.3
2015: I	100.0	67.3	21.5	45.8	17.9	17.0	13.6	3.3	6.2	4.1	3.4	.9
II	100.0	67.3	21.5	45.7	17.7	16.9	13.5	3.2	6.1	4.1	3.4	.8
III	100.0	67.5	21.6	46.0	17.6	17.0	13.4	3.1	6.2	4.2	3.5	.7
IV	100.0	67.8	21.5	46.3	17.3	16.8	13.2	2.9	6.1	4.2	3.6	.5
2016: I	100.0	68.0	21.4	46.7	17.1	16.8	13.1	2.9	5.9	4.3	3.7	.3
II	100.0	68.2	21.4	46.8	16.9	16.8	13.1	2.9	5.9	4.3	3.7	.1
III	100.0	68.3	21.4	47.0	16.8	16.8	13.1	3.0	5.8	4.3	3.7	.0
IV	100.0	68.4	21.3	47.1	17.0	16.8	13.0	2.9	5.7	4.3	3.8	.2
2017: I	100.0	68.4	21.3	47.1	17.1	17.1	13.2	3.0	5.8	4.4	3.9	.0
II	100.0	68.4	21.3	47.1	17.2	17.2	13.3	3.0	5.9	4.4	3.8	.1
III	100.0	68.2	21.3	46.9	17.4	17.1	13.3	3.0	5.9	4.4	3.8	.3
IV	100.0	68.5	21.4	47.0	17.4	17.2	13.3	3.0	6.0	4.4	3.9	.1
2018: I	100.0	68.3	21.3	47.0	17.7	17.5	13.6	3.1	6.1	4.5	3.9	.2
II	100.0	68.0	21.2	46.8	17.5	17.6	13.7	3.2	6.0	4.5	3.9	-.1
III	100.0	68.0	21.2	46.9	18.0	17.5	13.6	3.1	6.0	4.5	3.9	.4
IV ᵖ	100.0	68.0	21.1	46.9	18.1	17.6	13.7	3.1	6.0	4.6	3.8	.5

See next page for continuation of table.

TABLE B-4. Percentage shares of gross domestic product, 1968–2018—Continued
[Percent of nominal GDP]

| Year or quarter | Net exports of goods and services ||||||| Government consumption expenditures and gross investment |||||
| | Net exports | Exports ||| Imports ||| Total | Federal ||| State and local |
		Total	Goods	Services	Total	Goods	Services		Total	National defense	Non-defense	
1968	0.1	5.1	3.8	1.3	4.9	3.6	1.3	24.0	13.6	10.8	2.8	10.4
1969	.1	5.1	3.8	1.3	5.0	3.6	1.3	23.5	12.9	10.0	2.9	10.6
1970	.4	5.6	4.2	1.4	5.2	3.8	1.4	23.5	12.4	9.4	3.0	11.2
1971	.1	5.4	4.0	1.4	5.4	4.0	1.4	23.0	11.5	8.4	3.1	11.4
1972	-.3	5.5	4.1	1.4	5.8	4.5	1.4	22.4	11.1	7.9	3.2	11.3
1973	.3	6.7	5.3	1.4	6.4	5.0	1.4	21.4	10.3	7.2	3.1	11.1
1974	-.1	8.2	6.7	1.5	8.2	6.8	1.5	22.1	10.3	7.1	3.2	11.8
1975	.9	8.2	6.7	1.6	7.3	5.9	1.4	22.6	10.3	7.0	3.3	12.3
1976	-.1	8.0	6.5	1.5	8.1	6.7	1.4	21.6	9.9	6.7	3.2	11.7
1977	-1.1	7.7	6.2	1.5	8.8	7.3	1.4	20.9	9.6	6.5	3.2	11.2
1978	-1.1	7.9	6.4	1.6	9.0	7.5	1.5	20.3	9.3	6.2	3.1	10.9
1979	-.9	8.8	7.1	1.6	9.6	8.1	1.5	20.0	9.2	6.1	3.0	10.8
1980	-.5	9.8	8.1	1.8	10.3	8.7	1.6	20.6	9.6	6.4	3.2	11.0
1981	-.4	9.5	7.6	1.9	9.9	8.4	1.6	20.4	9.8	6.7	3.1	10.6
1982	-.6	8.5	6.7	1.8	9.1	7.5	1.6	21.3	10.4	7.3	3.1	10.9
1983	-1.4	7.6	5.9	1.7	9.0	7.5	1.5	21.1	10.5	7.5	3.0	10.6
1984	-2.5	7.5	5.7	1.8	10.0	8.3	1.7	20.5	10.2	7.4	2.8	10.3
1985	-2.6	7.0	5.2	1.7	9.6	7.9	1.7	21.0	10.4	7.6	2.8	10.5
1986	-2.9	7.0	5.1	2.0	9.9	8.1	1.8	21.3	10.5	7.7	2.8	10.8
1987	-3.0	7.5	5.5	2.0	10.5	8.5	1.9	21.2	10.4	7.7	2.7	10.9
1988	-2.1	8.5	6.3	2.1	10.6	8.6	1.9	20.6	9.8	7.3	2.5	10.8
1989	-1.5	8.9	6.6	2.3	10.5	8.6	1.9	20.4	9.5	6.9	2.5	11.0
1990	-1.3	9.3	6.8	2.5	10.6	8.5	2.0	20.8	9.4	6.8	2.6	11.3
1991	-.5	9.7	7.0	2.7	10.1	8.1	2.0	21.1	9.5	6.7	2.7	11.6
1992	-.5	9.7	7.0	2.7	10.2	8.4	1.9	20.6	9.0	6.2	2.8	11.6
1993	-1.0	9.5	6.8	2.7	10.5	8.6	1.9	19.9	8.5	5.7	2.7	11.4
1994	-1.3	9.9	7.1	2.8	11.2	9.3	1.9	19.2	7.9	5.2	2.6	11.4
1995	-1.2	10.6	7.8	2.9	11.8	9.9	1.9	19.0	7.5	4.9	2.6	11.4
1996	-1.2	10.7	7.8	3.0	11.9	10.0	1.9	18.5	7.2	4.7	2.5	11.3
1997	-1.2	11.1	8.2	3.0	12.3	10.3	2.0	18.0	6.8	4.3	2.5	11.2
1998	-1.8	10.5	7.6	2.9	12.3	10.3	2.0	17.8	6.5	4.1	2.4	11.3
1999	-2.7	10.3	7.4	2.9	13.0	10.9	2.0	17.9	6.3	4.0	2.4	11.5
2000	-3.7	10.7	7.8	2.9	14.4	12.2	2.2	17.8	6.2	3.8	2.4	11.6
2001	-3.5	9.7	7.0	2.7	13.2	11.1	2.1	18.4	6.3	3.9	2.4	12.1
2002	-3.9	9.1	6.5	2.6	13.0	10.9	2.1	19.1	6.8	4.2	2.6	12.3
2003	-4.4	9.0	6.4	2.6	13.4	11.3	2.2	19.3	7.2	4.5	2.7	12.1
2004	-5.1	9.6	6.8	2.8	14.7	12.3	2.4	19.1	7.3	4.7	2.6	11.8
2005	-5.5	10.0	7.1	2.9	15.5	13.2	2.4	19.0	7.3	4.7	2.6	11.7
2006	-5.6	10.7	7.6	3.1	16.2	13.7	2.5	19.0	7.2	4.6	2.6	11.8
2007	-5.0	11.5	8.0	3.5	16.5	13.8	2.6	19.3	7.3	4.7	2.6	12.0
2008	-4.9	12.5	8.8	3.7	17.4	14.6	2.8	20.3	7.8	5.1	2.7	12.4
2009	-2.7	10.9	7.3	3.6	13.7	11.0	2.7	21.3	8.4	5.5	3.0	12.8
2010	-3.4	12.3	8.5	3.8	15.7	13.0	2.8	21.0	8.7	5.5	3.1	12.4
2011	-3.7	13.5	9.4	4.1	17.3	14.4	2.8	20.3	8.4	5.4	3.0	11.9
2012	-3.5	13.5	9.4	4.1	17.0	14.2	2.8	19.4	7.9	5.0	2.9	11.4
2013	-2.9	13.5	9.3	4.3	16.5	13.7	2.8	18.7	7.3	4.6	2.8	11.4
2014	-2.9	13.5	9.2	4.3	16.4	13.6	2.8	18.1	6.9	4.2	2.7	11.1
2015	-2.9	12.4	8.2	4.2	15.3	12.6	2.7	17.8	6.7	4.0	2.7	11.1
2016	-2.8	11.9	7.7	4.1	14.6	11.9	2.8	17.6	6.6	3.9	2.7	11.0
2017	-3.0	12.1	7.9	4.2	15.0	12.2	2.8	17.3	6.5	3.8	2.7	10.8
2018 ᵖ	-3.1	12.3	8.1	4.2	15.4	12.5	2.9	17.2	6.4	3.8	2.6	10.7
2015: I	-3.0	12.7	8.4	4.3	15.7	12.9	2.7	17.7	6.8	4.1	2.7	11.0
II	-2.7	12.6	8.4	4.2	15.4	12.7	2.7	17.8	6.7	4.0	2.7	11.1
III	-2.9	12.3	8.1	4.2	15.2	12.5	2.7	17.8	6.7	4.0	2.7	11.1
IV	-2.8	12.0	7.9	4.2	14.9	12.1	2.8	17.7	6.7	4.0	2.7	11.0
2016: I	-2.8	11.8	7.6	4.1	14.6	11.8	2.8	17.7	6.6	3.9	2.7	11.1
II	-2.7	11.8	7.7	4.1	14.5	11.8	2.7	17.6	6.6	3.9	2.7	11.0
III	-2.7	12.0	7.8	4.2	14.7	11.9	2.8	17.6	6.6	3.9	2.7	11.0
IV	-3.0	11.8	7.7	4.1	14.8	12.0	2.8	17.5	6.6	3.9	2.7	11.0
2017: I	-3.0	12.0	7.8	4.2	15.0	12.2	2.8	17.5	6.5	3.8	2.7	10.9
II	-3.0	12.0	7.8	4.2	14.9	12.1	2.8	17.4	6.5	3.9	2.7	10.8
III	-2.8	12.0	7.8	4.2	14.9	12.0	2.8	17.2	6.5	3.8	2.7	10.8
IV	-3.1	12.3	8.1	4.2	15.3	12.5	2.9	17.2	6.5	3.8	2.7	10.8
2018: I	-3.2	12.4	8.1	4.2	15.6	12.7	2.9	17.2	6.5	3.8	2.7	10.8
II	-2.7	12.6	8.4	4.2	15.3	12.4	2.9	17.2	6.4	3.8	2.6	10.7
III	-3.2	12.3	8.1	4.2	15.5	12.6	2.9	17.2	6.4	3.8	2.6	10.8
IV ᵖ	-3.2	12.2	8.0	4.2	15.3	12.4	2.9	17.1	6.4	3.8	2.6	10.7

Source: Department of Commerce (Bureau of Economic Analysis).

Table B–5. Chain-type price indexes for gross domestic product, 1968–2018

[Index numbers, 2012=100, except as noted; quarterly data seasonally adjusted]

Year or quarter	Gross domestic product	Personal consumption expenditures			Gross private domestic investment							
						Fixed investment						
		Total	Goods	Services	Total	Total	Nonresidential				Residential
							Total	Structures	Equipment	Intellectual property products	
1968	19.627	19.152	29.780	14.338	27.103	26.196	33.237	10.427	58.017	34.676	14.498
1969	20.590	20.015	30.934	15.078	28.402	27.498	34.638	11.114	59.657	36.204	15.518
1970	21.676	20.951	32.114	15.913	29.624	28.699	36.295	11.845	61.891	37.929	16.016
1971	22.776	21.841	33.079	16.781	31.092	30.134	37.997	12.757	63.848	39.318	16.943
1972	23.760	22.586	33.926	17.491	32.388	31.420	39.297	13.674	64.686	40.490	17.975
1973	25.061	23.802	35.949	18.336	34.153	33.169	40.882	14.734	65.780	42.494	19.571
1974	27.309	26.280	40.436	19.890	37.559	36.449	44.857	16.770	70.713	46.461	21.593
1975	29.846	28.470	43.703	21.595	42.059	40.874	50.766	18.773	81.484	50.190	23.590
1976	31.490	30.032	45.413	23.093	44.384	43.232	53.562	19.692	86.486	52.408	25.117
1977	33.445	31.986	47.837	24.841	47.655	46.550	57.111	21.401	91.800	54.709	27.683
1978	35.798	34.211	50.773	26.750	51.517	50.444	60.930	23.468	96.900	57.557	31.082
1979	38.766	37.251	55.574	28.994	56.141	54.977	65.830	26.194	103.167	61.382	34.593
1980	42.278	41.262	61.797	32.009	61.395	60.105	71.641	28.629	112.249	66.123	38.325
1981	46.269	44.958	66.389	35.288	67.123	65.624	78.453	32.566	120.463	71.058	41.425
1982	49.130	47.456	68.198	38.058	70.679	69.311	82.911	35.136	125.415	75.093	43.646
1983	51.051	49.474	69.429	40.396	70.896	69.575	82.774	34.241	125.776	77.898	44.680
1984	52.894	51.343	70.742	42.498	71.661	70.253	83.036	34.540	124.748	80.081	46.003
1985	54.568	53.134	71.877	44.577	72.548	71.277	83.893	35.361	124.748	81.413	47.267
1986	55.673	54.290	71.541	46.408	74.178	73.021	85.365	36.039	127.254	82.047	49.351
1987	57.041	55.964	73.842	47.796	75.723	74.506	86.339	36.618	128.083	83.518	51.486
1988	59.055	58.151	75.788	50.082	77.627	76.586	88.514	38.171	129.854	86.129	53.278
1989	61.370	60.690	78.704	52.443	79.606	78.561	90.572	39.666	132.337	87.240	55.020
1990	63.676	63.355	81.927	54.846	81.270	80.278	92.516	40.948	135.042	88.147	56.288
1991	65.819	65.473	83.930	56.992	82.648	81.683	94.297	41.689	137.330	90.271	57.021
1992	67.321	67.218	84.943	59.018	82.647	81.728	93.960	41.699	137.121	89.373	57.723
1993	68.917	68.892	85.681	61.059	83.627	82.711	94.161	42.922	135.518	89.998	60.074
1994	70.386	70.330	86.552	62.719	84.875	83.983	94.904	44.437	135.277	90.468	62.247
1995	71.864	71.811	87.361	64.471	86.240	85.378	95.849	46.362	133.796	93.134	64.473
1996	73.178	73.346	88.321	66.240	86.191	85.450	95.267	47.540	130.762	93.544	65.856
1997	74.446	74.623	88.219	68.107	86.241	85.599	94.735	49.355	127.156	94.052	67.444
1998	75.267	75.216	86.893	69.549	85.608	85.133	93.248	51.612	121.451	93.595	69.223
1999	76.346	76.338	87.349	70.970	85.690	85.277	92.314	53.198	116.763	95.105	71.816
2000	78.069	78.235	89.082	72.938	86.815	86.486	92.718	55.283	114.224	97.814	75.004
2001	79.822	79.738	89.015	75.171	87.555	87.241	92.346	58.178	110.858	97.684	78.564
2002	81.039	80.789	88.166	77.123	87.841	87.500	91.863	60.603	108.531	96.376	80.510
2003	82.567	82.358	88.054	79.506	88.561	88.265	91.156	62.769	105.725	95.647	84.325
2004	84.778	84.411	89.292	81.965	91.148	90.843	92.055	67.416	104.841	95.335	90.243
2005	87.407	86.812	91.084	84.673	94.839	94.597	94.443	75.733	104.598	95.952	96.706
2006	90.074	89.174	92.306	87.616	98.176	97.958	96.745	84.749	103.560	97.088	102.355
2007	92.498	91.438	93.331	90.516	99.656	99.456	98.310	89.748	103.191	98.284	103.708
2008	94.264	94.180	96.122	93.235	100.474	100.296	99.832	94.335	102.542	99.834	102.249
2009	94.999	94.094	93.812	94.231	99.331	99.076	99.184	92.613	103.169	98.589	98.671
2010	96.109	95.705	95.183	95.957	97.687	97.568	97.416	92.006	99.471	98.306	98.317
2011	98.112	98.131	98.773	97.814	98.704	98.641	98.559	95.362	99.447	99.517	99.049
2012	100.000	100.000	100.000	100.000	100.000	100.000	100.000	100.000	100.000	100.000	100.000
2013	101.773	101.346	99.407	102.316	100.979	101.091	100.251	101.455	99.787	100.081	105.054
2014	103.687	102.868	98.939	104.852	103.001	103.250	101.565	107.475	99.282	100.734	111.106
2015	104.757	103.126	95.889	106.823	103.696	104.217	102.081	109.852	98.743	101.516	114.100
2016	105.899	104.235	94.340	109.325	103.706	104.357	101.281	110.296	97.738	100.208	118.185
2017	107.932	106.073	94.632	111.984	105.268	105.939	101.962	113.120	97.183	101.294	123.495
2018 p	110.337	108.230	95.280	114.952	107.548	108.223	103.151	117.254	97.196	102.357	130.466
2015: I	104.127	102.608	95.891	106.034	103.747	104.157	102.258	109.822	99.190	101.414	113.003
II	104.745	103.108	96.333	106.563	103.677	104.200	102.183	109.524	98.965	101.735	113.569
III	105.060	103.417	96.149	107.129	103.764	104.329	102.117	110.020	98.581	101.759	114.554
IV	105.097	103.370	95.182	107.565	103.596	104.182	101.767	110.043	98.235	101.154	115.273
2016: I	105.043	103.428	94.193	108.171	103.182	103.839	101.215	109.569	97.992	100.101	115.804
II	105.738	104.036	94.470	108.953	103.607	104.238	101.341	110.431	97.840	100.163	117.326
III	106.110	104.485	94.259	109.751	103.752	104.427	101.157	110.262	97.707	99.900	119.058
IV	106.703	104.989	94.440	110.425	104.281	104.924	101.413	110.922	97.412	100.668	120.551
2017: I	107.233	105.528	94.964	110.972	104.537	105.217	101.559	111.656	97.329	100.773	121.446
II	107.553	105.735	94.298	111.644	105.059	105.720	101.818	112.670	97.256	101.028	122.955
III	108.134	106.156	94.462	112.201	105.567	106.247	102.147	113.748	97.132	101.536	124.320
IV	108.807	106.873	94.804	113.120	105.907	106.571	102.325	114.406	97.016	101.841	125.258
2018: I	109.348	107.524	95.324	113.840	106.564	107.225	102.501	115.299	96.939	101.945	127.938
II	110.172	108.052	95.413	114.606	107.385	108.060	103.006	116.736	97.142	102.305	130.216
III p	110.669	108.474	95.329	115.302	107.923	108.598	103.404	117.622	97.436	102.550	131.373
IV p	111.161	108.869	95.054	116.062	108.322	109.010	103.694	119.360	97.266	102.626	132.337

See next page for continuation of table.

TABLE B–5. Chain-type price indexes for gross domestic product, 1968–2018—*Continued*

[Index numbers, 2012=100, except as noted; quarterly data seasonally adjusted]

Year or quarter	Exports and imports of goods and services		Government consumption expenditures and gross investment					Final sales of domestic product	Personal consumption expenditures excluding food and energy	Gross domestic purchases [1]	Percent change [2]			
				Federal								Personal consumption expenditures		
	Exports	Imports	Total	Total	National defense	Non-defense	State and local				Gross domestic product	Total	Excluding food and energy	Gross domestic purchases [1]
1968	27.664	18.361	14.068	16.849	16.196	18.180	12.234	19.502	20.194	19.080	4.3	3.9	4.3	4.2
1969	28.589	18.839	14.892	17.715	17.019	19.154	13.063	20.465	21.136	20.010	4.9	4.5	4.7	4.9
1970	29.711	19.954	16.078	19.109	18.294	20.906	14.117	21.547	22.126	21.087	5.3	4.7	4.7	5.4
1971	30.796	21.179	17.352	20.670	19.817	22.521	15.198	22.642	23.167	22.185	5.1	4.2	4.7	5.2
1972	32.145	22.662	18.662	22.485	21.883	23.579	16.163	23.624	23.912	23.175	4.3	3.4	3.2	4.5
1973	36.382	26.601	19.936	24.051	23.484	25.018	17.246	24.923	24.823	24.499	5.5	5.4	3.8	5.7
1974	44.807	38.058	21.852	25.971	25.404	26.904	19.157	27.154	26.788	26.986	9.0	10.4	7.9	10.2
1975	49.388	41.226	23.870	28.254	27.545	29.484	20.999	29.680	29.026	29.452	9.3	8.3	8.4	9.1
1976	51.009	42.467	25.181	30.012	29.345	31.124	22.024	31.326	30.791	31.071	5.5	5.5	6.1	5.5
1977	53.088	46.209	26.739	31.858	31.268	32.782	23.394	33.284	32.771	33.119	6.2	6.5	6.4	6.6
1978	56.317	49.466	28.507	34.008	33.561	34.612	24.914	35.637	34.943	35.474	7.0	7.0	6.6	7.1
1979	63.101	57.930	30.853	36.566	36.216	36.952	27.114	38.591	37.490	38.585	8.3	8.9	7.3	8.8
1980	69.503	72.166	34.045	40.099	39.919	40.106	30.081	42.084	40.936	42.602	9.1	10.8	9.2	10.4
1981	74.650	76.066	37.424	43.843	43.747	43.643	33.226	46.046	44.523	46.532	9.4	9.0	8.8	9.2
1982	75.006	73.506	39.969	46.943	47.039	46.289	35.401	48.921	47.417	49.214	6.2	5.6	6.5	5.8
1983	75.311	70.751	41.516	48.499	48.778	47.397	36.964	50.836	49.844	50.926	3.9	4.3	5.1	3.5
1984	76.016	70.139	43.317	50.637	51.013	49.279	38.544	52.671	51.911	52.649	3.6	3.8	4.1	3.4
1985	73.753	67.836	44.659	51.712	51.872	50.907	40.113	54.371	54.019	54.214	3.2	3.5	4.1	3.0
1986	72.523	67.834	45.409	51.957	51.894	51.748	41.269	55.492	55.883	55.345	2.0	2.2	3.5	2.1
1987	74.124	71.935	46.635	52.318	52.267	52.076	43.196	56.851	57.683	56.908	2.5	3.1	3.2	2.8
1988	77.920	75.377	48.177	54.025	53.904	53.974	44.640	58.890	60.134	58.921	3.5	3.9	4.2	3.5
1989	79.210	77.024	50.016	55.534	55.365	55.605	46.752	61.205	62.630	61.240	3.9	4.4	4.2	3.9
1990	79.657	79.233	52.113	57.250	57.162	57.093	49.153	63.519	65.168	63.663	3.8	4.4	4.1	4.0
1991	80.545	78.573	54.005	59.309	58.964	59.787	50.953	65.663	67.495	65.662	3.4	3.3	3.6	3.1
1992	80.153	78.636	55.642	60.824	60.678	60.825	52.690	67.169	69.547	67.190	2.3	2.7	3.0	2.3
1993	80.277	78.033	56.953	62.151	61.615	62.994	54.002	68.765	71.436	68.706	2.4	2.5	2.7	2.3
1994	81.210	78.766	58.463	63.861	63.229	64.898	55.394	70.239	73.034	70.147	2.1	2.1	2.2	2.1
1995	83.025	80.924	60.123	65.838	65.027	67.223	56.871	71.722	74.625	71.661	2.1	2.1	2.2	2.2
1996	81.923	79.514	61.355	66.937	66.114	68.344	58.177	73.055	76.040	72.908	1.8	2.1	1.9	1.7
1997	80.479	76.750	62.560	67.972	67.035	69.591	59.471	74.344	77.382	73.983	1.7	1.7	1.8	1.5
1998	78.574	72.618	63.624	68.841	67.871	70.518	60.630	75.200	78.366	74.476	1.1	.8	1.3	.7
1999	77.971	73.019	65.778	70.519	69.559	72.178	63.008	76.296	79.425	75.632	1.4	1.5	1.4	1.6
2000	79.467	76.221	68.601	72.886	71.908	74.578	66.032	78.037	80.804	77.575	2.3	2.5	1.7	2.6
2001	78.836	74.223	70.567	74.236	73.270	75.906	68.281	79.793	82.258	79.039	2.2	1.9	1.8	1.9
2002	78.201	73.242	72.393	76.631	75.714	78.222	69.815	81.004	83.639	80.125	1.5	1.3	1.7	1.4
2003	79.400	75.454	75.028	80.008	79.505	80.895	72.050	82.541	84.837	81.776	1.9	1.9	1.4	2.1
2004	82.284	79.060	78.153	82.760	82.263	83.637	75.369	84.751	86.515	84.126	2.7	2.5	2.0	2.9
2005	85.131	83.703	82.110	86.204	86.011	86.531	79.609	87.388	88.373	87.037	3.1	2.8	2.1	3.5
2006	87.842	86.909	85.661	88.949	89.022	88.799	83.617	90.058	90.392	89.783	3.1	2.7	2.3	3.2
2007	91.139	89.921	89.491	91.589	91.750	91.279	88.133	92.489	92.378	92.206	2.7	2.5	2.2	2.7
2008	95.410	98.960	93.308	94.381	94.801	93.597	92.558	94.259	94.225	94.849	1.9	3.0	2.0	2.9
2009	89.694	87.987	92.931	94.214	94.126	94.364	92.048	94.970	95.315	94.559	.8	−.1	1.2	−.3
2010	93.348	92.783	95.386	96.421	96.128	96.942	94.669	96.086	96.608	95.923	1.2	1.7	1.4	1.4
2011	99.242	99.826	98.285	99.070	98.946	99.289	97.739	98.100	98.139	98.246	2.1	2.5	1.6	2.4
2012	100.000	100.000	100.000	100.000	100.000	100.000	100.000	100.000	100.000	100.000	1.9	1.9	1.9	1.8
2013	100.168	98.636	102.332	100.931	100.609	101.478	103.279	101.795	101.526	101.468	1.8	1.3	1.5	1.5
2014	100.169	97.777	104.445	102.618	101.995	103.656	105.670	103.732	103.168	103.178	1.9	1.5	1.6	1.7
2015	95.146	89.728	104.717	103.200	102.256	104.739	105.748	104.851	104.501	103.512	1.0	.3	1.3	.3
2016	93.248	86.531	105.059	103.737	102.557	105.970	106.001	106.237	104.306		1.1	1.1	1.7	.8
2017	95.923	88.511	107.797	105.753	104.209	108.188	109.155	108.059	107.961	106.249	1.9	1.8	1.6	1.9
2018 *p*	99.395	91.222	110.841	107.497	105.512	110.594	113.012	110.465	110.005	108.574	2.2	2.0	1.9	2.2
2015: I	96.169	91.679	104.283	102.928	102.046	104.374	105.212	104.197	103.902	103.106	−.2	−1.8	.7	−1.5
II	95.970	90.476	104.860	103.213	102.281	104.734	105.971	104.840	104.358	103.521	2.4	2.0	1.8	1.6
III	94.968	89.358	105.004	103.408	102.460	104.954	106.084	105.163	104.736	103.764	1.2	1.2	1.5	.9
IV	93.477	87.399	104.722	103.251	102.238	104.893	105.725	105.205	105.009	103.657	.1	−.2	1.0	−.4
2016: I	92.116	85.902	104.130	102.934	101.836	104.706	104.962	105.166	105.461	103.525	−.2	.2	1.7	−.5
II	93.073	86.216	104.846	103.502	102.356	105.346	105.769	105.857	106.008	104.121	2.7	2.4	2.1	2.3
III	93.612	86.884	105.301	103.970	102.794	105.884	106.218	106.236	106.546	104.521	1.4	1.7	2.0	1.5
IV	94.192	87.121	105.960	104.541	103.241	106.613	106.931	106.824	106.933	105.055	2.3	1.9	1.5	2.1
2017: I	95.071	88.099	106.928	105.245	103.821	107.502	108.061	107.361	107.365	105.619	2.0	2.1	1.6	2.2
II	95.135	88.089	107.350	105.594	104.056	108.023	108.528	107.678	107.724	105.915	1.2	.8	1.3	1.1
III	96.032	88.307	108.027	105.914	104.322	108.422	109.428	108.262	108.102	106.393	2.2	1.6	1.4	1.8
IV	97.455	89.548	108.884	106.257	104.637	108.806	110.603	108.933	108.654	107.069	2.5	2.7	2.1	2.6
2018: I	98.411	91.134	109.665	106.739	105.010	109.452	111.572	109.473	109.242	107.742	2.0	2.5	2.2	2.5
II	99.799	91.322	110.555	107.274	105.355	110.270	112.686	110.300	109.814	108.381	3.0	2.0	2.1	2.4
III	99.870	91.424	111.232	107.682	105.671	110.816	113.533	110.797	110.246	108.865	1.8	1.6	1.6	1.8
IV *p*	99.500	91.006	111.912	108.292	106.012	111.837	114.257	111.291	110.719	109.307	1.8	1.5	1.7	1.6

[1] Gross domestic product (GDP) less exports of goods and services plus imports of goods and services.
[2] Quarterly percent changes are at annual rates.

Source: Department of Commerce (Bureau of Economic Analysis).

TABLE B-6. Gross value added by sector, 1968–2018

[Billions of dollars; quarterly data at seasonally adjusted annual rates]

Year or quarter	Gross domestic product	Business [1]			Households and institutions			General government [3]			Addendum: Gross housing value added
		Total	Nonfarm [1]	Farm	Total	Households	Nonprofit institutions serving households [2]	Total	Federal	State and local	
1968	940.7	726.3	705.8	20.5	79.0	52.9	26.1	135.4	72.1	63.3	67.5
1969	1,017.6	782.7	759.9	22.8	87.0	57.1	30.0	147.9	76.9	70.9	73.0
1970	1,073.3	815.9	792.3	23.7	94.6	61.2	33.4	162.8	82.5	80.3	78.8
1971	1,164.9	882.5	857.2	25.4	104.5	67.2	37.4	177.8	87.5	90.3	86.4
1972	1,279.1	972.5	942.9	29.7	114.0	72.7	41.4	192.6	92.4	100.2	93.9
1973	1,425.4	1,094.0	1,047.2	46.8	124.6	78.5	46.1	206.8	96.4	110.4	101.4
1974	1,545.2	1,182.8	1,138.5	44.2	137.2	85.5	51.7	225.3	102.5	122.8	110.4
1975	1,684.9	1,284.8	1,239.2	45.6	151.6	93.7	58.0	248.4	110.5	138.0	121.3
1976	1,873.4	1,443.3	1,400.2	43.0	164.9	101.7	63.2	265.3	117.3	148.0	130.9
1977	2,081.8	1,616.2	1,572.7	43.5	179.9	110.7	69.2	285.7	125.2	160.6	144.2
1978	2,351.6	1,838.2	1,787.5	50.7	202.1	124.8	77.3	311.3	135.8	175.5	160.2
1979	2,627.3	2,062.8	2,002.7	60.1	226.3	139.5	86.9	338.2	145.4	192.8	177.7
1980	2,857.3	2,225.8	2,174.4	51.4	258.2	158.8	99.3	373.4	159.8	213.5	204.0
1981	3,207.0	2,502.0	2,437.0	65.0	291.6	179.2	112.4	413.5	178.3	235.2	231.6
1982	3,343.8	2,568.6	2,508.2	60.4	323.8	198.2	125.6	451.4	195.7	255.6	258.6
1983	3,634.0	2,801.9	2,757.0	44.9	352.5	213.6	138.9	479.7	207.1	272.6	280.6
1984	4,037.6	3,136.7	3,072.6	64.2	383.8	230.9	152.8	517.1	225.3	291.9	303.1
1985	4,339.0	3,369.6	3,305.9	63.7	411.8	248.2	163.6	557.5	240.0	317.6	333.8
1986	4,579.6	3,539.3	3,479.4	59.9	447.0	268.4	178.6	593.3	250.6	342.7	364.5
1987	4,855.2	3,735.2	3,673.2	62.0	489.5	289.8	199.7	630.4	261.0	369.4	392.1
1988	5,236.4	4,019.3	3,957.9	61.4	539.8	316.4	223.4	677.4	278.5	398.8	424.2
1989	5,641.6	4,326.7	4,252.8	73.9	586.0	341.4	244.6	728.8	292.8	436.1	452.7
1990	5,963.1	4,542.0	4,464.2	77.8	636.3	367.6	268.8	784.9	306.7	478.2	487.0
1991	6,158.1	4,645.0	4,574.7	70.4	677.3	386.6	290.7	835.8	323.5	512.2	515.3
1992	6,520.3	4,920.2	4,840.4	79.9	720.3	407.1	313.2	879.8	329.6	550.2	545.2
1993	6,858.6	5,177.4	5,106.2	71.3	772.8	437.6	335.1	908.3	331.5	576.9	578.4
1994	7,287.2	5,523.7	5,440.1	83.6	824.7	472.7	352.0	938.8	332.6	606.2	619.6
1995	7,639.7	5,795.1	5,726.7	68.4	877.8	506.9	370.9	966.9	333.0	633.9	662.6
1996	8,073.1	6,159.5	6,066.9	92.6	923.2	534.6	388.7	990.3	331.8	658.6	695.0
1997	8,577.6	6,578.8	6,490.6	88.1	975.9	565.7	410.2	1,022.9	333.5	689.3	731.9
1998	9,062.8	6,959.2	6,880.2	79.0	1,040.6	601.6	439.0	1,063.0	336.8	726.2	774.8
1999	9,630.7	7,400.1	7,329.2	70.9	1,112.4	645.2	467.3	1,118.1	345.0	773.1	826.2
2000	10,252.3	7,876.1	7,800.1	76.0	1,191.9	693.5	498.5	1,184.3	360.3	824.0	881.7
2001	10,581.8	8,062.0	7,983.9	78.1	1,267.2	744.7	522.6	1,252.6	370.3	882.3	943.5
2002	10,936.4	8,264.4	8,190.4	74.0	1,343.6	780.7	562.9	1,328.4	397.8	930.6	985.1
2003	11,458.2	8,642.4	8,551.3	91.1	1,411.0	816.6	594.4	1,404.8	434.7	970.1	1,016.4
2004	12,213.7	9,240.6	9,121.2	119.4	1,494.5	868.4	626.1	1,478.7	459.4	1,019.3	1,075.2
2005	13,036.6	9,898.0	9,793.5	104.5	1,583.3	933.4	649.8	1,555.4	488.4	1,067.0	1,151.9
2006	13,814.6	10,509.1	10,412.8	96.3	1,673.6	991.2	682.4	1,631.9	509.9	1,122.1	1,224.2
2007	14,451.9	10,994.6	10,878.9	115.7	1,730.3	1,016.9	713.4	1,726.9	535.7	1,191.2	1,273.4
2008	14,712.8	11,054.9	10,935.4	119.5	1,836.8	1,075.2	761.6	1,821.2	569.1	1,252.1	1,349.5
2009	14,448.9	10,669.9	10,566.8	103.1	1,895.5	1,097.0	798.5	1,883.5	603.0	1,280.5	1,393.8
2010	14,992.1	11,140.5	11,022.8	117.6	1,905.5	1,091.0	814.5	1,946.1	640.0	1,306.1	1,400.2
2011	15,542.6	11,612.9	11,460.7	152.2	1,956.8	1,108.0	848.8	1,972.9	659.8	1,313.1	1,445.7
2012	16,197.0	12,189.5	12,040.5	148.9	2,018.4	1,128.0	890.3	1,989.1	663.7	1,325.5	1,478.5
2013	16,784.9	12,670.5	12,485.9	184.6	2,075.0	1,157.0	918.0	2,039.3	658.4	1,380.9	1,511.2
2014	17,521.7	13,274.1	13,106.1	167.9	2,159.4	1,204.0	955.4	2,088.3	667.1	1,421.2	1,592.4
2015	18,219.3	13,821.1	13,674.7	146.4	2,256.1	1,251.5	1,004.6	2,142.1	674.6	1,467.5	1,690.5
2016	18,707.2	14,172.9	14,043.4	129.5	2,350.3	1,304.4	1,045.9	2,184.1	685.5	1,498.5	1,771.8
2017	19,485.4	14,792.2	14,659.4	132.8	2,447.7	1,364.6	1,083.1	2,245.4	700.3	1,545.1	1,847.6
2018 p	20,500.6	15,645.8	15,519.1	126.7	2,556.1	1,433.7	1,122.4	2,298.7	710.4	1,588.3	1,941.0
2015: I	17,970.4	13,630.5	13,486.8	143.7	2,215.5	1,230.4	985.0	2,124.5	672.0	1,452.4	1,652.2
II	18,221.3	13,841.2	13,696.0	145.2	2,242.0	1,243.0	999.0	2,138.1	673.2	1,464.9	1,677.6
III	18,331.1	13,911.2	13,759.9	151.3	2,270.6	1,258.9	1,011.6	2,149.3	675.9	1,473.5	1,704.7
IV	18,354.4	13,901.6	13,756.4	145.2	2,296.4	1,273.5	1,022.8	2,156.4	677.4	1,479.1	1,727.6
2016: I	18,409.1	13,930.4	13,797.5	132.9	2,315.9	1,285.0	1,030.9	2,162.8	679.1	1,483.7	1,745.1
II	18,640.7	14,126.1	13,991.7	134.4	2,338.8	1,299.2	1,039.6	2,175.8	683.2	1,492.6	1,765.0
III	18,799.6	14,248.2	14,119.2	129.0	2,359.8	1,309.5	1,050.2	2,191.7	687.7	1,504.0	1,779.6
IV	18,979.2	14,386.8	14,265.4	121.5	2,386.6	1,323.8	1,062.8	2,205.9	692.1	1,513.7	1,797.6
2017: I	19,162.6	14,517.4	14,380.4	137.0	2,419.6	1,345.1	1,074.5	2,225.6	697.2	1,528.3	1,821.7
II	19,359.1	14,680.5	14,544.4	136.1	2,439.8	1,358.5	1,081.3	2,238.8	699.2	1,539.6	1,838.3
III	19,588.1	14,878.5	14,749.1	129.4	2,456.4	1,371.8	1,084.6	2,253.2	701.8	1,551.4	1,856.6
IV	19,831.8	15,092.6	14,963.9	128.8	2,475.2	1,382.9	1,092.3	2,264.0	702.9	1,561.1	1,873.9
2018: I	20,041.0	15,256.0	15,127.4	128.6	2,511.1	1,406.0	1,105.1	2,274.0	704.7	1,569.2	1,903.0
II	20,411.9	15,582.2	15,449.6	132.5	2,541.1	1,424.6	1,116.5	2,288.7	708.1	1,580.6	1,928.6
III	20,658.2	15,776.2	15,655.5	120.7	2,572.7	1,443.3	1,129.5	2,309.2	712.6	1,596.6	1,954.3
IV p	20,891.4	15,968.8	15,843.8	125.0	2,599.6	1,460.9	1,138.7	2,322.9	716.2	1,606.7	1,978.0

[1] Gross domestic business value added equals gross domestic product excluding gross value added of households and institutions and of general government. Nonfarm value added equals gross domestic business value added excluding gross farm value added.
[2] Equals compensation of employees of nonprofit institutions, the rental value of nonresidential fixed assets owned and used by nonprofit institutions serving households, and rental income of persons for tenant-occupied housing owned by nonprofit institutions.
[3] Equals compensation of general government employees plus general government consumption of fixed capital.

Source: Department of Commerce (Bureau of Economic Analysis).

TABLE B-7.—Real gross value added by sector, 1968–2018

[Billions of chained (2012) dollars; quarterly data at seasonally adjusted annual rates]

Year or quarter	Gross domestic product	Business[1]			Households and institutions			General government[3]			Addendum: Gross housing value added
		Total	Nonfarm[1]	Farm	Total	Households	Nonprofit institutions serving households[2]	Total	Federal	State and local	
1968	4,792.3	3,174.9	3,135.9	43.6	622.1	365.4	254.6	1,189.3	537.8	615.7	459.5
1969	4,942.1	3,272.7	3,232.1	45.1	648.6	379.9	267.1	1,221.2	543.2	643.9	480.4
1970	4,951.3	3,271.3	3,227.9	46.4	660.5	388.7	269.5	1,226.5	525.5	672.7	496.4
1971	5,114.3	3,394.9	3,348.6	48.8	690.6	408.3	279.5	1,228.7	506.6	700.2	520.8
1972	5,383.3	3,616.6	3,574.1	48.8	717.9	425.2	289.6	1,226.9	487.2	724.6	545.5
1973	5,687.2	3,867.8	3,833.7	48.2	741.9	438.8	300.0	1,232.9	473.6	750.1	562.9
1974	5,656.5	3,808.8	3,776.2	47.2	772.2	458.4	310.3	1,257.1	473.8	777.4	590.5
1975	5,644.8	3,772.6	3,714.5	56.1	799.1	471.5	324.2	1,276.0	472.1	801.0	609.4
1976	5,949.0	4,027.5	3,980.8	53.4	809.4	477.7	328.4	1,286.8	473.3	811.7	615.4
1977	6,224.1	4,258.1	4,209.4	56.2	815.8	477.6	335.3	1,300.3	475.2	824.3	624.3
1978	6,568.6	4,529.7	4,490.5	54.1	846.3	500.5	342.1	1,325.1	481.5	843.7	646.7
1979	6,776.6	4,690.6	4,642.4	59.2	869.8	510.8	355.7	1,339.9	482.5	859.1	659.2
1980	6,759.2	4,648.3	4,602.9	57.6	896.0	525.3	367.4	1,359.9	490.3	871.1	682.5
1981	6,930.7	4,783.9	4,707.8	76.0	913.2	531.0	379.3	1,369.5	498.5	871.0	695.9
1982	6,805.8	4,646.5	4,563.8	79.7	940.9	538.3	401.1	1,385.7	507.7	876.9	712.1
1983	7,117.7	4,892.8	4,846.6	55.1	979.7	559.3	419.0	1,397.7	520.6	873.5	739.6
1984	7,632.8	5,326.8	5,256.6	73.5	1,002.2	569.8	431.3	1,418.3	534.1	879.0	753.8
1985	7,951.1	5,575.2	5,488.1	87.1	1,019.6	582.8	435.3	1,461.1	551.1	904.3	785.0
1986	8,226.4	5,777.7	5,695.7	83.3	1,051.5	594.4	456.5	1,500.5	564.4	930.7	806.3
1987	8,511.0	5,985.1	5,902.7	84.1	1,090.9	609.5	481.9	1,537.5	582.2	949.1	825.1
1988	8,866.5	6,241.4	6,171.6	74.8	1,146.9	634.8	513.6	1,580.7	593.4	981.6	852.3
1989	9,192.1	6,480.4	6,398.4	85.0	1,193.5	654.5	541.3	1,619.4	602.4	1,011.9	870.1
1990	9,365.5	6,584.1	6,494.1	91.7	1,231.8	667.2	568.3	1,659.8	612.9	1,042.2	887.5
1991	9,355.4	6,544.0	6,453.2	92.3	1,257.0	677.5	583.9	1,676.7	616.4	1,055.9	905.7
1992	9,684.9	6,821.1	6,715.4	106.6	1,288.8	692.8	600.7	1,683.9	606.3	1,073.9	927.5
1993	9,951.5	7,015.7	6,922.7	94.4	1,355.2	726.4	634.0	1,687.9	596.3	1,088.7	961.0
1994	10,352.4	7,354.0	7,241.3	114.3	1,400.9	763.3	641.4	1,689.5	579.7	1,107.7	1,002.0
1995	10,630.3	7,580.9	7,490.0	91.0	1,442.7	789.7	656.3	1,691.9	561.2	1,129.6	1,037.8
1996	11,031.4	7,931.9	7,827.1	105.3	1,471.4	805.9	669.0	1,695.2	547.8	1,147.1	1,055.7
1997	11,521.9	8,348.3	8,230.6	118.1	1,516.7	828.7	691.7	1,708.1	538.8	1,169.7	1,081.1
1998	12,038.3	8,781.0	8,666.5	114.0	1,567.5	850.2	722.2	1,726.8	533.1	1,194.6	1,106.4
1999	12,610.5	9,277.8	9,159.7	116.8	1,610.7	883.9	730.3	1,742.1	528.9	1,214.4	1,144.2
2000	13,131.0	9,728.6	9,593.7	138.2	1,640.6	923.9	717.8	1,770.3	531.7	1,240.0	1,184.9
2001	13,262.1	9,796.7	9,668.7	128.1	1,676.7	953.7	723.3	1,801.4	533.2	1,269.6	1,218.3
2002	13,493.1	9,968.0	9,835.5	133.5	1,702.5	960.1	743.4	1,835.6	542.6	1,294.4	1,221.4
2003	13,879.1	10,295.0	10,153.1	145.1	1,735.0	984.3	751.3	1,858.5	557.0	1,302.8	1,234.6
2004	14,406.4	10,736.4	10,581.6	159.8	1,803.1	1,024.9	778.7	1,871.5	565.1	1,307.5	1,278.2
2005	14,912.5	11,157.9	10,995.0	168.8	1,867.3	1,078.1	788.9	1,888.4	572.3	1,317.0	1,339.1
2006	15,338.3	11,533.3	11,370.8	165.5	1,898.7	1,107.0	790.9	1,903.9	576.7	1,328.3	1,376.2
2007	15,626.0	11,795.2	11,646.9	144.6	1,896.1	1,096.5	799.2	1,930.9	584.6	1,347.3	1,380.2
2008	15,604.7	11,679.1	11,527.1	148.5	1,953.1	1,131.2	821.4	1,970.9	606.3	1,365.3	1,424.7
2009	15,208.8	11,245.6	11,079.9	170.7	1,956.2	1,122.8	833.1	2,006.7	636.6	1,370.5	1,432.1
2010	15,598.8	11,607.3	11,443.9	165.1	1,975.0	1,126.3	848.6	2,016.3	658.0	1,358.5	1,449.0
2011	15,840.7	11,830.4	11,673.0	157.5	2,003.1	1,129.9	873.1	2,007.2	664.3	1,343.0	1,476.5
2012	16,197.0	12,189.5	12,040.5	148.9	2,018.4	1,128.0	890.3	1,989.1	663.7	1,325.5	1,478.5
2013	16,495.4	12,487.3	12,307.3	179.8	2,032.8	1,135.7	897.1	1,975.7	652.0	1,323.7	1,481.2
2014	16,899.8	12,868.0	12,687.1	180.3	2,061.8	1,158.1	903.7	1,971.9	647.0	1,324.7	1,525.8
2015	17,386.7	13,318.6	13,126.3	193.1	2,096.4	1,173.3	923.1	1,976.0	642.5	1,332.9	1,574.7
2016	17,659.2	13,539.5	13,339.4	203.3	2,130.9	1,190.6	940.2	1,993.7	645.3	1,347.8	1,602.7
2017	18,050.7	13,893.7	13,699.9	190.2	2,160.6	1,209.3	951.3	2,004.1	646.1	1,357.3	1,619.3
2018 p	18,571.3	14,374.0	14,183.1	181.8	2,199.5	1,231.8	967.7	2,010.0	648.8	1,360.5	1,647.4
2015: I	17,254.7	13,206.2	13,016.0	190.8	2,079.8	1,165.3	914.6	1,972.4	643.5	1,328.6	1,556.3
II	17,397.3	13,338.6	13,148.5	189.8	2,089.1	1,168.6	920.5	1,974.2	642.4	1,331.3	1,568.0
III	17,438.8	13,363.7	13,169.3	195.7	2,102.5	1,176.1	926.4	1,977.2	641.9	1,334.8	1,581.8
IV	17,456.2	13,366.1	13,171.5	196.1	2,114.3	1,183.2	931.1	1,980.0	642.4	1,337.1	1,592.9
2016: I	17,523.4	13,419.4	13,222.3	199.5	2,121.8	1,186.8	934.9	1,986.4	644.4	1,341.4	1,598.3
II	17,622.5	13,506.0	13,304.6	205.7	2,130.1	1,191.0	939.0	1,991.1	645.1	1,345.4	1,603.7
III	17,706.7	13,579.9	13,376.7	208.2	2,133.7	1,191.2	942.5	1,998.2	646.0	1,351.6	1,603.8
IV	17,784.2	13,652.8	13,454.1	199.7	2,137.9	1,193.5	944.3	1,999.2	645.6	1,352.9	1,605.0
2017: I	17,863.0	13,715.7	13,518.4	196.8	2,151.4	1,204.2	947.3	2,001.7	646.1	1,355.0	1,614.3
II	17,995.2	13,840.9	13,645.7	192.8	2,158.7	1,209.2	949.4	2,002.7	645.2	1,356.7	1,618.3
III	18,120.8	13,959.2	13,767.0	187.3	2,164.6	1,211.5	953.1	2,005.4	646.1	1,358.6	1,621.1
IV	18,223.8	14,058.9	13,868.4	183.7	2,167.8	1,212.3	955.5	2,006.6	646.9	1,359.0	1,623.5
2018: I	18,324.0	14,145.0	13,957.5	178.3	2,183.8	1,222.2	961.6	2,005.2	647.0	1,357.5	1,635.3
II	18,511.6	14,320.6	14,129.0	183.5	2,194.8	1,228.5	966.2	2,008.0	648.3	1,358.9	1,643.5
III	18,665.0	14,458.8	14,268.0	181.0	2,205.0	1,234.9	970.1	2,014.0	650.8	1,362.6	1,651.4
IV p	18,784.6	14,571.5	14,377.9	184.5	2,214.4	1,241.5	972.9	2,012.8	649.0	1,363.0	1,659.4

[1] Gross domestic business value added equals gross domestic product excluding gross value added of households and institutions and of general government. Nonfarm value added equals gross domestic business value added excluding gross farm value added.
[2] Equals compensation of employees of nonprofit institutions, the rental value of nonresidential fixed assets owned and used by nonprofit institutions serving households, and rental income of persons for tenant-occupied housing owned by nonprofit institutions.
[3] Equals compensation of general government employees plus general government consumption of fixed capital.

Source: Department of Commerce (Bureau of Economic Analysis).

National Income or Expenditure

TABLE B–8. Gross domestic product (GDP) by industry, value added, in current dollars and as a percentage of GDP, 1997–2017

[Billions of dollars; except as noted]

Year	Gross domestic product	Private industries									
		Total private industries	Agriculture, forestry, fishing, and hunting	Mining	Construction	Manufacturing			Utilities	Wholesale trade	Retail trade
						Total manufacturing	Durable goods	Non-durable goods			
	Value added										
1997	8,577.6	7,432.0	108.6	95.1	339.6	1,382.9	823.8	559.1	171.5	527.5	579.9
1998	9,062.8	7,871.5	99.8	81.7	379.8	1,430.6	850.7	579.9	163.7	563.7	626.9
1999	9,630.7	8,378.3	92.6	84.5	417.6	1,488.9	874.9	614.1	179.9	584.0	652.6
2000	10,252.3	8,929.3	98.3	110.6	461.3	1,550.2	924.8	625.4	180.1	622.6	685.5
2001	10,581.8	9,188.9	99.8	123.9	486.5	1,473.8	833.4	640.5	181.3	613.8	709.5
2002	10,936.4	9,462.0	95.6	112.4	493.6	1,468.5	832.8	635.7	177.6	613.1	732.6
2003	11,458.2	9,905.9	114.0	139.0	525.2	1,524.2	863.2	661.0	184.0	641.4	769.6
2004	12,213.7	10,582.5	142.9	166.5	584.6	1,608.1	905.1	703.0	199.2	697.1	795.6
2005	13,036.6	11,326.4	128.3	225.7	651.8	1,693.4	956.8	736.6	198.1	754.9	840.8
2006	13,814.6	12,022.6	125.1	273.3	697.1	1,793.8	1,004.4	789.4	226.8	811.5	869.9
2007	14,451.9	12,564.8	144.1	314.0	715.3	1,844.7	1,030.6	814.1	231.9	857.8	869.2
2008	14,712.8	12,731.2	147.2	392.2	648.9	1,800.8	999.7	801.1	241.7	884.3	848.7
2009	14,448.9	12,403.9	130.0	275.8	565.6	1,702.1	881.0	821.2	258.2	834.2	827.6
2010	14,992.1	12,884.1	146.3	305.8	525.1	1,797.0	964.3	832.7	278.8	888.9	851.5
2011	15,542.6	13,405.5	180.9	356.3	524.4	1,867.6	1,015.2	852.4	287.5	934.9	871.9
2012	16,197.0	14,037.5	179.6	358.8	553.4	1,927.1	1,061.7	865.3	279.7	997.4	908.4
2013	16,784.9	14,572.3	215.6	386.5	587.6	1,991.9	1,102.0	889.9	286.3	1,040.1	949.5
2014	17,521.7	15,250.0	200.8	413.0	636.4	2,047.4	1,130.7	916.6	298.2	1,088.2	973.8
2015	18,219.3	15,878.8	181.2	257.9	694.9	2,123.0	1,182.7	940.3	299.0	1,141.7	1,021.4
2016	18,707.2	16,319.4	164.9	216.2	745.5	2,085.2	1,182.0	903.1	302.7	1,136.6	1,052.0
2017	19,485.4	17,031.7	169.2	268.6	781.4	2,179.6	1,226.6	953.0	307.5	1,174.1	1,087.1
Percent	Industry value added as a percentage of GDP (percent)										
1997	100.0	86.6	1.3	1.1	4.0	16.1	9.6	6.5	2.0	6.2	6.8
1998	100.0	86.9	1.1	.9	4.2	15.8	9.4	6.4	1.8	6.2	6.9
1999	100.0	87.0	1.0	.9	4.3	15.5	9.1	6.4	1.9	6.1	6.8
2000	100.0	87.1	1.0	1.1	4.5	15.1	9.0	6.1	1.8	6.1	6.7
2001	100.0	86.8	.9	1.2	4.6	13.9	7.9	6.1	1.7	5.8	6.7
2002	100.0	86.5	.9	1.0	4.5	13.4	7.6	5.8	1.6	5.6	6.7
2003	100.0	86.5	1.0	1.2	4.6	13.3	7.5	5.8	1.6	5.6	6.7
2004	100.0	86.6	1.2	1.4	4.8	13.2	7.4	5.8	1.6	5.7	6.5
2005	100.0	86.9	1.0	1.7	5.0	13.0	7.3	5.7	1.5	5.8	6.4
2006	100.0	87.0	.9	2.0	5.0	13.0	7.3	5.7	1.6	5.9	6.3
2007	100.0	86.9	1.0	2.2	4.9	12.8	7.1	5.6	1.6	5.9	6.0
2008	100.0	86.5	1.0	2.7	4.4	12.2	6.8	5.4	1.6	6.0	5.8
2009	100.0	85.8	.9	1.9	3.9	11.8	6.1	5.7	1.8	5.8	5.7
2010	100.0	85.9	1.0	2.0	3.5	12.0	6.4	5.6	1.9	5.9	5.7
2011	100.0	86.2	1.2	2.3	3.4	12.0	6.5	5.5	1.8	6.0	5.6
2012	100.0	86.7	1.1	2.2	3.4	11.9	6.6	5.3	1.7	6.2	5.6
2013	100.0	86.8	1.3	2.3	3.5	11.9	6.6	5.3	1.7	6.2	5.7
2014	100.0	87.0	1.1	2.4	3.6	11.7	6.5	5.2	1.7	6.2	5.6
2015	100.0	87.2	1.0	1.4	3.8	11.7	6.5	5.2	1.6	6.3	5.6
2016	100.0	87.2	.9	1.2	4.0	11.1	6.3	4.8	1.6	6.1	5.6
2017	100.0	87.4	.9	1.4	4.0	11.2	6.3	4.9	1.6	6.0	5.6

[1] Consists of agriculture, forestry, fishing, and hunting; mining; construction; and manufacturing.
[2] Consists of utilities; wholesale trade; retail trade; transportation and warehousing; information; finance, insurance, real estate, rental, and leasing; professional and business services; educational services, health care, and social assistance; arts, entertainment, recreation, accommodation, and food services; and other services, except government.

Note: Data shown in Tables B–8 and B–9 are consistent with the 2018 annual revision of the industry accounts released in July 2018. For details see *Survey of Current Business*, December 2018.

See next page for continuation of table.

TABLE B–8. Gross domestic product (GDP) by industry, value added, in current dollars and as a percentage of GDP, 1997–2017—*Continued*

[Billions of dollars; except as noted]

Year	Private industries—Continued							Government	Private goods-producing industries [1]	Private services-producing industries [2]
	Transportation and warehousing	Information	Finance, insurance, real estate, rental, and leasing	Professional and business services	Educational services, health care, and social assistance	Arts, entertainment, recreation, accommodation, and food services	Other services, except government			
	Value added										
1997	257.3	394.1	1,612.4	840.6	590.6	301.8	230.3	1,145.6	1,926.1	5,505.9
1998	280.0	434.6	1,710.1	914.0	615.8	322.1	248.7	1,191.3	1,991.8	5,879.7
1999	290.0	485.0	1,837.1	997.2	653.9	354.1	260.8	1,252.3	2,083.7	6,294.6
2000	307.8	471.3	1,974.7	1,105.1	695.4	386.5	279.7	1,323.0	2,220.4	6,708.9
2001	308.1	502.4	2,128.1	1,155.5	749.9	390.7	265.6	1,392.9	2,184.1	7,004.8
2002	305.7	550.6	2,217.0	1,189.9	807.0	413.5	284.9	1,474.4	2,170.1	7,291.9
2003	321.4	564.9	2,295.9	1,247.4	862.8	432.1	283.8	1,552.3	2,302.4	7,603.5
2004	352.1	620.4	2,389.1	1,341.0	927.3	461.2	297.3	1,631.3	2,502.2	8,080.3
2005	375.8	642.3	2,606.2	1,446.4	970.5	481.2	310.7	1,710.3	2,699.3	8,627.1
2006	410.4	652.0	2,743.9	1,546.6	1,035.4	511.5	325.0	1,792.0	2,889.4	9,133.2
2007	413.9	706.9	2,848.3	1,666.7	1,087.9	533.5	330.5	1,887.1	3,018.1	9,546.7
2008	426.8	743.0	2,762.7	1,777.1	1,184.8	542.7	330.3	1,981.6	2,989.1	9,742.1
2009	404.6	721.9	2,867.7	1,688.7	1,267.5	533.3	326.5	2,045.1	2,673.6	9,730.3
2010	433.0	753.3	2,943.0	1,766.8	1,310.7	555.8	328.0	2,108.0	2,774.3	10,109.8
2011	451.4	759.8	3,045.3	1,856.7	1,354.7	580.9	333.1	2,137.1	2,929.3	10,476.3
2012	472.0	759.0	3,261.0	1,964.7	1,407.4	621.4	348.0	2,159.5	3,018.8	11,018.7
2013	491.1	828.9	3,322.8	2,017.3	1,447.2	651.3	356.3	2,212.5	3,181.6	11,390.8
2014	521.9	840.6	3,552.9	2,117.9	1,492.6	690.1	376.3	2,271.7	3,297.6	11,952.4
2015	563.4	915.0	3,754.6	2,233.3	1,563.5	737.3	392.5	2,340.5	3,257.0	12,621.8
2016	577.4	998.1	3,929.8	2,299.0	1,639.4	770.8	401.8	2,387.8	3,211.8	13,107.6
2017	608.7	1,050.8	4,057.1	2,426.3	1,700.3	804.7	416.1	2,453.7	3,398.9	13,632.8
	Industry value added as a percentage of GDP (percent)										
1997	3.0	4.6	18.8	9.8	6.9	3.5	2.7	13.4	22.5	64.2
1998	3.1	4.8	18.9	10.1	6.8	3.6	2.7	13.1	22.0	64.9
1999	3.0	5.0	19.1	10.4	6.8	3.7	2.7	13.0	21.6	65.4
2000	3.0	4.6	19.3	10.8	6.8	3.8	2.7	12.9	21.7	65.4
2001	2.9	4.7	20.1	10.9	7.1	3.7	2.5	13.2	20.6	66.2
2002	2.8	5.0	20.3	10.9	7.4	3.8	2.6	13.5	19.8	66.7
2003	2.8	4.9	20.0	10.9	7.5	3.8	2.5	13.5	20.1	66.4
2004	2.9	5.1	19.6	11.0	7.6	3.8	2.4	13.4	20.5	66.2
2005	2.9	4.9	20.0	11.1	7.4	3.7	2.4	13.1	20.7	66.2
2006	3.0	4.7	19.9	11.2	7.5	3.7	2.4	13.0	20.9	66.1
2007	2.9	4.9	19.7	11.5	7.5	3.7	2.3	13.1	20.9	66.1
2008	2.9	5.0	18.8	12.1	8.1	3.7	2.2	13.5	20.3	66.2
2009	2.8	5.0	19.8	11.7	8.8	3.7	2.3	14.2	18.5	67.3
2010	2.9	5.0	19.6	11.8	8.7	3.7	2.2	14.1	18.5	67.4
2011	2.9	4.9	19.6	11.9	8.7	3.7	2.1	13.7	18.8	67.4
2012	2.9	4.7	20.1	12.1	8.7	3.8	2.1	13.3	18.6	68.0
2013	2.9	4.9	19.8	12.0	8.6	3.9	2.1	13.2	19.0	67.9
2014	3.0	4.8	20.3	12.1	8.5	3.9	2.1	13.0	18.8	68.2
2015	3.1	5.0	20.6	12.3	8.6	4.0	2.2	12.8	17.9	69.3
2016	3.1	5.3	21.0	12.3	8.8	4.1	2.1	12.8	17.2	70.1
2017	3.1	5.4	20.8	12.5	8.7	4.1	2.1	12.6	17.4	70.0

Note (cont'd): Value added is the contribution of each private industry and of government to GDP. Value added is equal to an industry's gross output minus its intermediate inputs. Current-dollar value added is calculated as the sum of distributions by an industry to its labor and capital, which are derived from the components of gross domestic income.

Value added industry data shown in Tables B–8 and B–9 are based on the 2012 North American Industry Classification System (NAICS).

Source: Department of Commerce (Bureau of Economic Analysis).

TABLE B-9. Real gross domestic product by industry, value added, and percent changes, 1997–2017

Year	Gross domestic product	Private industries									
		Total private industries	Agriculture, forestry, fishing, and hunting	Mining	Construction	Manufacturing			Utilities	Wholesale trade	Retail trade
						Total manufacturing	Durable goods	Non-durable goods			
	Chain-type quantity indexes for value added (2012=100)											
1997	71.136	70.417	78.122	73.569	124.924	73.952	54.862	108.774	82.684	68.023	76.897
1998	74.324	73.791	76.225	76.540	130.646	76.995	59.373	106.919	78.993	74.707	84.286
1999	77.857	77.614	78.531	74.233	136.033	81.273	63.518	110.673	92.023	77.183	87.388
2000	81.070	81.097	90.102	65.831	141.541	87.116	70.928	111.745	93.244	81.126	90.310
2001	81.880	81.675	86.959	76.178	138.629	83.415	66.355	110.500	77.009	82.663	93.582
2002	83.306	83.128	90.001	78.193	134.131	84.146	67.757	109.712	79.706	83.546	97.689
2003	85.689	85.527	96.987	69.241	136.316	88.809	72.791	113.126	77.930	88.159	102.703
2004	88.945	89.042	104.744	69.643	141.182	95.078	78.019	120.927	82.678	91.924	104.467
2005	92.070	92.473	109.218	70.809	141.809	97.970	83.413	118.785	78.378	96.071	107.851
2006	94.698	95.475	111.013	81.679	138.846	103.527	89.812	122.532	83.261	98.749	108.686
2007	96.475	97.063	98.327	87.975	134.563	106.948	93.989	124.516	84.935	102.073	105.144
2008	96.343	96.460	100.402	85.158	121.446	104.777	94.526	118.051	89.475	101.967	101.290
2009	93.899	93.523	111.362	97.660	104.296	95.141	80.927	114.724	84.828	89.701	97.020
2010	96.306	95.938	107.954	86.193	98.928	100.289	91.144	112.361	95.043	95.040	99.094
2011	97.800	97.577	103.799	89.398	97.334	100.663	97.290	104.898	98.680	96.794	99.277
2012	100.000	100.000	100.000	100.000	100.000	100.000	100.000	100.000	100.000	100.000	100.000
2013	101.842	101.886	116.603	103.938	102.485	103.068	102.463	103.817	98.916	102.293	103.112
2014	104.339	104.590	117.229	114.270	103.855	104.088	103.295	105.073	94.753	106.377	104.687
2015	107.345	107.855	125.070	123.838	108.210	104.653	104.609	104.698	94.206	110.669	108.159
2016	109.027	109.617	130.438	117.925	111.839	103.426	104.104	102.550	98.932	109.418	112.306
2017	111.445	111.973	124.175	119.653	112.716	105.952	107.384	104.120	97.916	111.767	116.797
	Percent change from year earlier											
1997	....	....	....	....	....	....	....	....	....	....	....
1998	4.5	4.8	-2.4	4.0	4.6	4.1	8.2	-1.7	-4.5	9.8	9.6
1999	4.8	5.2	3.0	-3.0	4.1	5.6	7.0	3.5	16.5	3.3	3.7
2000	4.1	4.5	14.7	-11.3	4.0	7.2	11.7	1.0	1.3	5.1	3.3
2001	1.0	.7	-3.5	15.7	-2.1	-4.2	-6.4	-1.1	-17.4	1.9	3.6
2002	1.7	1.8	3.5	2.6	-3.2	.9	2.1	-.7	3.5	1.1	4.4
2003	2.9	2.9	7.8	-11.4	1.6	5.5	7.4	3.1	-2.2	5.5	5.1
2004	3.8	4.1	8.0	.6	3.6	7.1	7.2	6.9	6.1	4.3	1.7
2005	3.5	3.9	4.3	1.7	.4	3.0	6.9	-1.8	-5.2	4.5	3.2
2006	2.9	3.2	1.6	15.4	-2.1	5.7	7.7	3.2	6.2	2.8	.8
2007	1.9	1.7	-11.4	7.7	-3.1	3.3	4.7	1.6	2.0	3.4	-3.3
2008	-.1	-.6	2.1	-3.2	-9.7	-2.0	.6	-5.2	5.3	-.1	-3.7
2009	-2.5	-3.0	10.9	14.7	-14.1	-9.2	-14.4	-2.8	-5.2	-12.0	-4.2
2010	2.6	2.6	-3.1	-11.7	-5.1	5.4	12.6	-2.1	12.0	6.0	2.1
2011	1.6	1.7	-3.8	3.7	-1.6	.4	6.7	-6.6	3.8	1.8	.2
2012	2.2	2.5	-3.7	11.9	2.7	-.7	2.8	-4.7	1.3	3.3	.7
2013	1.8	1.9	16.6	3.9	2.5	3.1	2.5	3.8	-1.1	2.3	3.1
2014	2.5	2.7	.5	9.9	1.3	1.0	.8	1.2	-4.2	4.0	1.5
2015	2.9	3.1	6.7	8.4	4.2	.5	1.3	-.4	-.6	4.0	3.3
2016	1.6	1.6	4.3	-4.8	3.4	-1.2	-.5	-2.1	5.0	-1.1	3.8
2017	2.2	2.1	-4.8	1.5	.8	2.4	3.2	1.5	-1.0	2.1	4.0

[1] Consists of agriculture, forestry, fishing, and hunting; mining; construction; and manufacturing.
[2] Consists of utilities; wholesale trade; retail trade; transportation and warehousing; information; finance, insurance, real estate, rental, and leasing; professional and business services; educational services, health care, and social assistance; arts, entertainment, recreation, accommodation, and food services; and other services, except government.

See next page for continuation of table.

TABLE B-9. Real gross domestic product by industry, value added, and percent changes, 1997–2017—*Continued*

Year	Private industries—Continued							Government	Private goods-producing industries [1]	Private services-producing industries [2]
	Transportation and warehousing	Information	Finance, insurance, real estate, rental, and leasing	Professional and business services	Educational services, health care, and social assistance	Arts, entertainment, recreation, accommodation, and food services	Other services, except government			
	Chain-type quantity indexes for value added (2012=100)									
1997	85.155	45.779	64.494	63.672	65.203	78.811	115.601	87.669	81.548	67.403
1998	89.482	50.548	67.298	66.614	65.487	80.968	120.416	88.689	84.672	70.856
1999	90.225	56.651	71.498	69.758	67.685	85.402	121.187	89.756	88.733	74.618
2000	90.015	55.600	75.255	73.866	70.186	90.569	123.985	91.578	94.034	77.602
2001	83.969	58.897	79.439	75.941	71.869	87.406	111.728	92.511	91.428	79.044
2002	80.939	64.594	80.102	76.841	74.748	89.727	114.785	94.159	91.560	80.849
2003	83.784	66.612	81.058	79.221	77.673	92.055	111.552	95.294	94.958	82.982
2004	90.758	74.307	82.263	81.173	81.384	96.188	113.022	96.155	100.536	85.949
2005	95.120	79.284	87.902	84.782	82.907	96.474	113.811	97.036	102.929	89.658
2006	100.720	82.056	90.292	87.152	86.241	99.144	114.372	97.580	107.432	92.253
2007	99.935	90.123	91.815	90.025	86.891	98.599	111.727	98.528	108.998	93.847
2008	99.042	95.903	88.295	94.309	92.433	96.435	107.629	100.447	104.880	94.207
2009	93.111	93.560	92.578	88.315	95.708	90.853	101.336	100.560	97.869	92.358
2010	97.611	98.866	93.968	91.987	96.712	94.349	99.397	101.063	98.681	95.192
2011	99.380	100.275	95.903	95.662	98.366	97.660	98.508	100.747	98.817	97.237
2012	100.000	100.000	100.000	100.000	100.000	100.000	100.000	100.000	100.000	100.000
2013	101.455	109.095	99.099	101.293	101.289	102.128	99.257	99.297	103.878	101.342
2014	104.199	111.375	102.078	105.774	103.124	105.419	101.973	99.052	106.056	104.189
2015	106.843	123.989	104.466	109.026	106.384	107.750	102.775	99.071	108.647	107.629
2016	108.108	137.040	105.620	111.004	108.985	108.347	102.076	100.074	108.464	109.881
2017	112.458	146.805	105.698	115.681	110.820	110.329	102.591	100.803	110.208	112.390
	Percent change from year earlier									
1997	....	....	....	....	....	....	....	....	....	....
1998	5.1	10.4	4.3	4.6	0.4	2.7	4.2	1.2	3.8	5.1
1999	.8	12.1	6.2	4.7	3.4	5.5	.6	1.2	4.8	5.3
2000	-.2	-1.9	5.3	5.9	3.7	6.1	2.3	2.0	6.0	4.0
2001	-6.7	5.9	5.6	2.8	2.4	-3.5	-9.9	1.0	-2.8	1.9
2002	-3.6	9.7	.8	1.2	4.0	2.7	2.7	1.8	.1	2.3
2003	3.5	3.1	1.2	3.1	3.9	2.6	-2.8	1.2	3.7	2.6
2004	8.3	11.6	1.5	2.5	4.8	4.5	1.3	.9	5.9	3.6
2005	4.8	6.7	6.9	4.4	1.9	.3	.7	.9	2.4	4.3
2006	5.9	3.5	2.7	2.8	4.0	2.8	.5	.6	4.4	2.9
2007	-.8	9.8	1.7	3.3	.8	-.5	-2.3	1.0	1.5	1.7
2008	-.9	6.4	-3.8	4.8	6.4	-2.2	-3.7	1.9	-3.8	.4
2009	-6.0	-2.4	4.9	-6.4	3.5	-5.8	-5.8	.1	-6.7	-2.0
2010	4.8	5.7	1.5	4.2	1.0	3.8	-1.9	.5	.8	3.1
2011	1.8	1.4	2.1	4.0	1.7	3.5	-.9	-.3	.1	2.1
2012	.6	-.3	4.3	4.5	1.7	2.4	1.5	-.7	1.2	2.8
2013	1.5	9.1	-.9	1.3	1.3	2.1	-.7	-.7	3.9	1.3
2014	2.7	2.1	3.0	4.4	1.8	3.2	2.7	-.2	2.1	2.8
2015	2.5	11.3	2.3	3.1	3.2	2.2	.8	.0	2.4	3.3
2016	1.2	10.5	1.1	1.8	2.4	.6	-.7	1.0	-.2	2.1
2017	4.0	7.1	.1	4.2	1.7	1.8	.5	.7	1.6	2.3

Note: Data are based on the 2012 North American Industry Classification System (NAICS).
See Note, Table B-8.

Source: Department of Commerce (Bureau of Economic Analysis).

TABLE B-10. Personal consumption expenditures, 1968–2018

[Billions of dollars; quarterly data at seasonally adjusted annual rates]

Year or quarter	Personal consumption expenditures	Goods						Services					Addendum: Personal consumption expenditures excluding food and energy [2]
		Total	Durable		Nondurable			Total	Household consumption expenditures				
			Total [1]	Motor vehicles and parts	Total [1]	Food and beverages purchased for off-premises consumption	Gasoline and other energy goods		Total [1]	Housing and utilities	Health care	Financial services and insurance	
1968	556.9	284.6	84.8	35.4	199.8	88.8	23.2	272.2	263.4	92.7	36.6	25.2	431.8
1969	603.6	304.7	90.5	37.4	214.2	95.4	25.0	299.0	289.5	101.0	42.1	27.7	469.3
1970	646.7	318.8	90.0	34.5	228.8	103.5	26.3	327.9	317.5	109.4	47.7	30.1	501.7
1971	699.9	342.1	102.4	43.2	239.7	107.1	27.6	357.8	346.1	120.0	53.7	33.1	548.5
1972	768.2	373.8	116.4	49.4	257.4	114.5	29.4	394.3	381.5	131.2	59.8	37.1	605.8
1973	849.6	416.6	130.5	54.4	286.1	126.7	34.3	432.9	419.2	143.5	67.2	39.9	668.5
1974	930.2	451.5	130.2	48.2	321.4	143.0	43.8	478.6	463.1	158.6	76.1	44.1	719.7
1975	1,030.5	491.3	142.2	52.6	349.2	156.6	48.0	539.2	522.2	176.5	89.0	51.8	797.3
1976	1,147.7	546.3	168.6	68.2	377.7	167.3	53.0	601.4	582.4	194.7	101.8	56.8	894.7
1977	1,274.0	600.4	192.0	79.8	408.4	179.8	57.8	673.6	653.0	217.8	115.7	65.1	998.6
1978	1,422.3	663.6	213.3	89.2	450.2	196.1	61.5	758.7	735.7	244.3	131.2	76.7	1,122.4
1979	1,585.4	737.9	226.3	90.2	511.6	218.4	80.4	847.5	821.4	273.4	148.8	83.6	1,239.7
1980	1,750.7	799.8	226.4	84.4	573.4	239.2	101.9	950.9	920.8	312.5	171.7	91.7	1,353.1
1981	1,934.0	869.4	243.9	93.0	625.4	255.3	113.4	1,064.6	1,030.4	352.1	201.9	98.5	1,501.5
1982	2,071.3	899.3	253.0	100.0	646.3	267.1	108.4	1,172.0	1,134.0	387.5	225.2	113.7	1,622.9
1983	2,281.6	973.8	295.0	122.9	678.8	277.0	106.5	1,307.8	1,267.1	421.2	253.1	141.0	1,817.2
1984	2,492.3	1,063.7	342.2	147.2	721.5	291.1	108.2	1,428.6	1,383.3	457.5	276.5	150.8	2,008.1
1985	2,712.8	1,137.6	380.4	170.1	757.2	303.0	110.5	1,575.2	1,527.3	500.6	302.2	178.2	2,210.3
1986	2,886.3	1,195.6	421.4	187.5	774.2	316.4	91.2	1,690.7	1,638.0	537.0	330.2	187.7	2,391.3
1987	3,076.3	1,256.3	442.0	188.2	814.3	324.3	96.4	1,820.0	1,764.3	571.6	366.0	189.5	2,566.6
1988	3,330.0	1,337.3	475.1	202.2	862.3	342.8	99.9	1,992.7	1,929.4	614.4	410.1	202.9	2,793.1
1989	3,576.8	1,423.8	494.3	207.8	929.5	365.4	110.4	2,153.0	2,084.9	655.2	451.2	222.3	3,002.1
1990	3,809.0	1,491.3	497.1	205.1	994.2	391.2	124.2	2,317.7	2,241.8	696.5	506.2	230.8	3,194.9
1991	3,943.4	1,497.4	477.2	185.7	1,020.3	403.0	121.1	2,446.0	2,365.9	735.2	555.8	250.1	3,314.4
1992	4,197.6	1,563.3	508.1	204.8	1,055.2	404.5	125.0	2,634.3	2,546.4	771.1	612.8	277.0	3,561.7
1993	4,452.0	1,642.3	551.5	224.7	1,090.8	413.5	126.9	2,809.6	2,719.6	814.9	648.8	314.0	3,796.6
1994	4,721.0	1,746.6	607.2	249.8	1,139.4	432.1	129.2	2,974.4	2,876.6	863.3	680.5	327.9	4,042.5
1995	4,962.6	1,815.5	635.7	255.7	1,179.8	443.7	133.4	3,147.1	3,044.7	913.7	719.9	347.0	4,267.2
1996	5,244.6	1,917.7	676.3	273.5	1,241.4	461.9	144.7	3,326.9	3,216.9	962.4	752.1	372.1	4,513.0
1997	5,536.8	2,006.5	715.5	293.1	1,291.0	474.8	147.7	3,530.3	3,424.7	1,009.8	790.9	408.9	4,787.8
1998	5,877.2	2,108.4	779.3	320.2	1,329.1	487.4	132.4	3,768.8	3,645.0	1,065.5	832.0	446.1	5,132.4
1999	6,279.1	2,287.1	855.6	350.7	1,431.5	515.5	146.5	3,992.0	3,853.8	1,123.1	863.6	486.4	5,491.2
2000	6,762.1	2,453.2	912.6	363.2	1,540.6	540.6	184.5	4,309.0	4,150.9	1,198.6	918.4	543.0	5,899.4
2001	7,065.6	2,525.6	941.5	383.3	1,584.1	564.0	178.0	4,540.0	4,361.0	1,287.5	996.6	525.7	6,174.0
2002	7,342.7	2,598.8	985.4	401.3	1,613.4	575.1	167.9	4,743.9	4,545.5	1,333.6	1,082.9	534.7	6,454.1
2003	7,723.1	2,722.6	1,017.8	409.3	1,704.8	599.6	196.4	5,000.5	4,795.0	1,394.1	1,154.0	560.3	6,766.8
2004	8,212.7	2,902.0	1,080.6	409.3	1,821.4	632.6	232.7	5,310.6	5,104.3	1,469.1	1,238.9	605.5	7,179.2
2005	8,747.1	3,082.9	1,128.6	410.0	1,954.3	668.2	283.8	5,664.2	5,453.9	1,583.6	1,320.5	659.0	7,605.3
2006	9,260.3	3,239.7	1,158.3	394.9	2,081.3	700.3	319.7	6,020.7	5,781.5	1,682.4	1,391.9	695.0	8,039.7
2007	9,706.4	3,367.0	1,188.0	400.6	2,179.0	737.3	345.5	6,339.4	6,090.6	1,758.9	1,478.2	737.2	8,413.4
2008	9,976.3	3,363.2	1,098.8	343.3	2,264.5	769.1	391.1	6,613.1	6,325.8	1,835.4	1,555.3	756.6	8,592.6
2009	9,842.2	3,180.0	1,012.1	318.6	2,167.9	772.9	287.0	6,662.2	6,373.0	1,877.7	1,632.7	711.3	8,567.0
2010	10,185.8	3,317.8	1,049.0	344.5	2,268.9	786.9	336.7	6,868.0	6,573.6	1,903.9	1,699.6	754.6	8,840.8
2011	10,641.1	3,518.1	1,093.5	365.2	2,424.6	819.5	413.8	7,123.0	6,811.5	1,955.9	1,757.1	797.9	9,188.9
2012	11,006.8	3,637.7	1,144.2	396.6	2,493.5	846.2	421.9	7,369.1	7,027.5	1,996.3	1,821.3	820.1	9,531.1
2013	11,317.2	3,730.0	1,189.4	417.5	2,540.6	864.0	418.2	7,587.2	7,234.6	2,055.3	1,858.2	858.4	9,815.1
2014	11,824.0	3,861.5	1,242.4	442.3	2,619.2	897.6	403.3	7,962.5	7,596.3	2,154.5	1,938.3	908.7	10,290.9
2015	12,294.5	3,919.7	1,306.6	473.9	2,613.1	921.0	309.2	8,374.8	8,007.8	2,257.9	2,062.5	963.1	10,838.6
2016	12,766.9	3,996.3	1,346.6	483.7	2,649.7	944.2	274.9	8,770.6	8,378.4	2,353.0	2,171.6	989.1	11,326.9
2017	13,321.4	4,156.1	1,406.5	498.2	2,749.6	965.8	307.0	9,165.3	8,761.9	2,447.8	2,271.2	1,060.4	11,822.1
2018 [p]	13,951.6	4,342.1	1,461.5	506.8	2,880.7	1,001.3	346.7	9,609.4	9,170.4	2,559.8	2,375.5	1,124.0	12,366.8
2015: I	12,095.6	3,859.1	1,281.4	463.5	2,577.7	917.3	303.5	8,236.4	7,877.7	2,231.0	2,024.6	947.3	10,633.3
II	12,256.7	3,922.7	1,308.3	480.2	2,614.4	916.6	323.0	8,334.0	7,974.0	2,243.7	2,049.5	966.2	10,792.6
III	12,380.7	3,956.8	1,317.2	479.1	2,639.5	923.8	322.1	8,424.0	8,054.2	2,272.2	2,078.4	968.5	10,910.5
IV	12,445.1	3,940.1	1,319.3	472.7	2,620.8	926.5	288.1	8,505.0	8,125.2	2,284.6	2,097.5	970.3	11,018.2
2016: I	12,526.5	3,932.2	1,323.7	471.3	2,608.5	934.4	260.0	8,594.3	8,212.4	2,306.2	2,123.3	969.1	11,121.0
II	12,706.5	3,990.3	1,336.3	474.9	2,654.0	946.7	275.3	8,716.2	8,332.9	2,341.1	2,170.0	978.1	11,264.4
III	12,845.2	4,013.9	1,357.7	489.6	2,656.3	946.5	273.0	8,831.3	8,430.0	2,375.1	2,171.9	1,000.0	11,394.8
IV	12,989.4	4,048.8	1,368.7	499.0	2,680.1	949.3	291.3	8,940.6	8,538.2	2,389.4	2,221.1	1,009.4	11,527.3
2017: I	13,114.1	4,090.4	1,375.6	489.1	2,714.8	953.2	307.1	9,023.7	8,620.5	2,402.4	2,238.2	1,029.3	11,640.8
II	13,233.2	4,117.1	1,393.4	489.7	2,723.7	959.5	292.6	9,116.1	8,710.4	2,438.2	2,248.7	1,050.8	11,751.7
III	13,359.1	4,166.0	1,411.2	497.7	2,754.8	967.9	301.0	9,193.1	8,791.9	2,458.2	2,284.6	1,066.9	11,863.9
IV	13,579.2	4,250.9	1,445.7	516.4	2,805.2	982.6	327.3	9,328.3	8,924.9	2,492.6	2,313.2	1,094.4	12,031.8
2018: I	13,679.6	4,267.7	1,434.5	498.5	2,833.2	988.3	340.6	9,411.9	8,992.5	2,515.6	2,331.0	1,102.5	12,116.5
II	13,875.6	4,329.5	1,458.7	504.6	2,870.8	998.0	347.0	9,546.1	9,111.8	2,548.5	2,357.8	1,114.4	12,291.7
III	14,050.5	4,371.3	1,468.5	506.2	2,902.8	1,007.4	352.0	9,679.1	9,232.8	2,571.2	2,392.6	1,128.8	12,457.0
IV [p]	14,200.6	4,400.1	1,484.2	517.9	2,915.9	1,011.4	347.2	9,800.6	9,344.6	2,604.0	2,420.7	1,150.3	12,601.9

[1] Includes other items not shown separately.
[2] Food consists of food and beverages purchased for off-premises consumption; food services, which include purchased meals and beverages, are not classified as food.

Source: Department of Commerce (Bureau of Economic Analysis).

TABLE B-11. Real personal consumption expenditures, 2002–2018

[Billions of chained (2012) dollars; quarterly data at seasonally adjusted annual rates]

Year or quarter	Personal consumption expenditures	Goods						Services					Addendum: Personal consumption expenditures excluding food and energy [2]
		Total	Durable		Nondurable			Total	Household consumption expenditures				
			Total [1]	Motor vehicles and parts	Total [1]	Food and beverages purchased for off-premises consumption	Gasoline and other energy goods		Total [1]	Housing and utilities	Health care	Financial services and insurance	
2002	9,088.7	2,947.6	820.2	416.9	2,157.5	744.5	455.2	6,151.1	5,966.4	1,707.6	1,440.7	700.3	7,716.7
2003	9,377.5	3,092.0	879.3	429.2	2,233.6	761.8	455.6	6,289.4	6,087.7	1,730.5	1,479.3	704.3	7,976.2
2004	9,729.3	3,250.0	952.1	441.1	2,306.5	779.5	459.4	6,479.2	6,275.1	1,773.8	1,531.2	728.5	8,298.2
2005	10,075.9	3,384.7	1,004.9	435.1	2,383.4	809.2	457.4	6,689.5	6,487.6	1,846.6	1,581.9	767.9	8,605.9
2006	10,384.5	3,509.7	1,049.3	419.0	2,461.6	834.0	456.3	6,871.7	6,640.7	1,882.5	1,618.2	785.8	8,894.3
2007	10,615.3	3,607.6	1,099.7	427.3	2,503.4	845.2	455.4	7,003.6	6,765.7	1,900.7	1,657.2	808.3	9,107.6
2008	10,592.8	3,498.9	1,036.4	373.1	2,463.9	831.0	437.5	7,093.0	6,815.4	1,921.2	1,697.9	825.0	9,119.2
2009	10,460.0	3,389.8	973.0	346.7	2,423.1	825.3	440.1	7,070.1	6,781.3	1,943.1	1,735.1	809.5	8,988.1
2010	10,643.0	3,485.7	1,027.3	360.0	2,461.3	837.7	437.9	7,157.4	6,859.0	1,966.8	1,761.7	810.5	9,151.3
2011	10,843.8	3,561.8	1,079.7	370.1	2,482.9	839.0	427.8	7,282.1	6,969.3	1,993.0	1,788.7	831.4	9,363.2
2012	11,006.8	3,637.7	1,144.2	396.6	2,493.5	846.2	421.9	7,369.1	7,027.5	1,996.3	1,821.3	820.1	9,531.1
2013	11,166.9	3,752.2	1,214.1	415.3	2,538.5	855.5	429.7	7,415.5	7,069.8	2,006.4	1,832.6	815.2	9,667.6
2014	11,494.3	3,902.9	1,301.0	439.8	2,603.7	872.1	430.1	7,594.0	7,247.9	2,044.4	1,890.4	819.2	9,974.9
2015	11,921.9	4,087.7	1,399.4	471.4	2,691.7	884.9	449.9	7,840.0	7,506.1	2,089.4	2,000.1	841.9	10,371.8
2016	12,248.2	4,236.1	1,476.8	486.5	2,763.9	916.6	452.0	8,022.5	7,677.3	2,116.6	2,081.7	827.4	10,661.9
2017	12,558.7	4,391.9	1,577.9	507.2	2,822.0	938.9	446.5	8,184.5	7,842.2	2,129.9	2,145.8	848.4	10,950.3
2018 [p]	12,890.6	4,557.3	1,667.4	518.3	2,901.0	968.4	444.0	8,359.3	7,992.4	2,160.2	2,203.2	856.3	11,241.8
2015: I	11,788.4	4,024.3	1,365.0	461.9	2,662.3	881.6	447.6	7,768.1	7,438.5	2,083.3	1,972.1	839.3	10,234.5
II	11,887.5	4,071.9	1,396.0	476.6	2,679.4	883.1	448.0	7,821.0	7,493.1	2,083.8	1,990.0	846.2	10,342.3
III	11,972.0	4,115.2	1,413.2	475.8	2,705.5	886.0	453.2	7,863.6	7,528.6	2,095.8	2,011.2	841.1	10,417.5
IV	12,039.7	4,139.5	1,423.5	471.2	2,719.7	888.8	450.9	7,907.1	7,564.3	2,094.6	2,026.9	841.1	10,493.0
2016: I	12,111.8	4,174.6	1,434.9	470.9	2,743.4	900.8	461.5	7,945.5	7,604.1	2,101.7	2,048.1	830.1	10,545.5
II	12,214.1	4,223.9	1,457.9	477.0	2,770.0	917.0	452.2	8,000.4	7,661.4	2,116.5	2,085.6	822.7	10,626.4
III	12,294.3	4,258.5	1,494.3	493.2	2,769.2	921.9	449.1	8,047.0	7,694.9	2,127.5	2,077.0	828.8	10,695.2
IV	12,372.7	4,287.2	1,520.2	504.9	2,773.2	927.4	445.1	8,096.9	7,748.8	2,120.5	2,116.2	827.9	10,780.4
2017: I	12,427.6	4,307.3	1,527.2	494.3	2,786.3	930.2	442.8	8,131.9	7,786.8	2,114.8	2,127.3	842.7	10,842.6
II	12,515.9	4,366.0	1,559.2	498.0	2,813.9	932.3	450.6	8,165.6	7,821.9	2,130.0	2,129.2	844.7	10,909.5
III	12,584.9	4,410.2	1,588.6	508.4	2,829.9	939.7	447.1	8,193.7	7,855.0	2,131.6	2,156.8	851.0	10,975.1
IV	12,706.4	4,483.9	1,636.6	528.3	2,857.7	953.5	445.4	8,246.6	7,904.9	2,143.2	2,169.7	855.1	11,073.9
2018: I	12,722.8	4,477.0	1,628.2	510.7	2,858.6	958.6	441.9	8,267.5	7,915.2	2,146.0	2,177.3	852.7	11,091.8
II	12,842.0	4,537.6	1,662.3	518.6	2,886.7	965.2	446.6	8,329.8	7,963.5	2,158.1	2,188.9	852.2	11,193.5
III	12,953.3	4,585.5	1,677.4	516.2	2,919.2	973.3	442.8	8,394.9	8,022.7	2,163.7	2,214.3	855.3	11,299.7
IV [p]	13,044.2	4,629.0	1,701.6	527.7	2,939.7	976.5	444.8	8,444.5	8,068.2	2,172.9	2,232.1	864.9	11,382.2

[1] Includes other items not shown separately.
[2] Food consists of food and beverages purchased for off-premises consumption; food services, which include purchased meals and beverages, are not classified as food.

Source: Department of Commerce (Bureau of Economic Analysis).

TABLE B–12. Private fixed investment by type, 1968–2018
[Billions of dollars; quarterly data at seasonally adjusted annual rates]

Year or quarter	Private fixed investment	Nonresidential											Residential		
		Total nonresidential	Structures	Equipment						Intellectual property products			Total residential [1]	Structures	
				Total [1]	Information processing equipment		Industrial equipment	Transportation equipment		Total [1]	Software	Research and development [2]		Total [1]	Single family
					Total	Computers and peripheral equipment	Other								
1968	147.9	107.7	33.6	58.5	10.6	1.9	8.7	17.3	17.6	15.6	1.3	9.9	40.2	39.3	19.5
1969	164.4	120.0	37.7	65.2	12.8	2.4	10.4	19.1	18.9	17.2	1.8	11.0	44.4	43.4	19.7
1970	168.0	124.6	40.3	66.4	14.3	2.7	11.6	20.3	16.2	17.9	2.3	11.5	43.4	42.3	17.5
1971	188.6	130.4	42.7	69.1	14.9	2.8	12.2	19.5	18.4	18.7	2.4	11.9	58.2	56.9	25.8
1972	219.0	146.6	47.2	78.9	16.7	3.5	13.2	21.4	21.8	20.6	2.8	12.9	72.4	70.9	32.8
1973	251.0	172.7	55.0	95.1	19.9	3.5	16.3	26.0	26.6	22.7	3.2	14.6	78.3	76.6	35.2
1974	260.5	191.1	61.2	104.3	23.1	3.9	19.2	30.7	26.3	25.5	3.9	16.4	69.5	67.6	29.7
1975	263.5	196.8	61.4	107.6	23.8	3.6	20.2	31.3	25.2	27.8	4.8	17.5	66.7	64.8	29.6
1976	306.1	219.3	65.9	121.2	27.5	4.4	23.1	34.1	30.0	32.2	5.2	19.6	86.8	84.6	43.9
1977	374.3	259.1	74.6	148.7	33.7	5.7	28.0	39.4	39.3	35.8	5.5	21.8	115.2	112.8	62.2
1978	452.6	314.6	93.6	180.6	42.3	7.6	34.8	47.7	47.3	40.4	6.3	24.9	138.0	135.3	72.8
1979	521.7	373.8	117.7	208.1	50.3	10.2	40.2	56.2	53.6	48.1	8.1	29.1	147.8	144.7	72.3
1980	536.4	406.9	136.2	216.4	58.9	12.5	46.4	60.7	48.4	54.4	9.8	34.2	129.5	126.1	52.9
1981	601.4	472.9	167.3	240.9	69.6	17.1	52.5	65.5	50.6	64.8	11.8	39.7	128.5	124.9	52.0
1982	595.9	485.1	177.6	234.9	74.2	18.9	55.3	62.7	46.8	72.7	14.0	44.8	110.8	107.2	41.5
1983	643.3	482.2	154.3	246.5	83.7	23.9	59.8	58.9	53.5	81.3	16.4	49.6	161.1	156.9	72.5
1984	754.7	564.3	177.4	291.9	101.2	31.6	69.6	68.1	64.4	95.0	20.4	56.9	190.4	185.6	86.4
1985	807.8	607.8	194.5	307.9	106.6	33.7	72.9	72.5	69.0	105.3	23.8	63.0	200.1	195.0	87.4
1986	842.6	607.8	176.5	317.7	111.1	33.4	77.7	75.4	70.5	113.5	25.6	66.5	234.8	229.3	104.1
1987	865.0	615.2	174.2	320.9	112.2	35.8	76.4	76.7	68.1	120.1	29.0	69.2	249.8	244.0	117.2
1988	918.5	662.3	182.8	346.8	120.8	38.0	82.8	84.2	72.9	132.7	33.3	76.4	256.2	250.1	120.1
1989	972.0	716.0	193.7	372.2	130.7	43.1	87.6	93.3	67.9	150.1	40.6	84.1	256.0	249.9	120.9
1990	978.9	739.2	202.9	371.9	129.6	38.6	90.9	92.1	70.0	164.4	45.4	91.5	239.7	233.7	112.9
1991	944.7	723.6	183.6	360.8	129.2	37.7	91.5	89.3	71.5	179.1	48.7	101.0	221.2	215.4	99.4
1992	996.7	741.9	172.6	381.7	142.1	44.0	98.1	93.0	74.7	187.7	51.1	105.4	254.7	248.8	122.0
1993	1,086.0	799.2	177.2	425.1	153.3	47.9	105.4	102.2	89.4	196.9	57.2	106.3	286.8	280.7	140.1
1994	1,192.7	868.9	186.8	476.4	167.0	52.4	114.6	113.6	107.7	205.7	60.4	109.2	323.8	317.6	162.3
1995	1,286.3	962.2	207.3	528.1	188.4	66.1	122.3	129.0	116.1	226.8	65.5	121.2	324.1	317.7	153.5
1996	1,401.3	1,043.2	224.6	565.3	204.7	72.8	131.9	136.5	123.2	253.3	74.5	134.5	358.1	351.7	170.8
1997	1,524.7	1,149.1	250.3	610.9	222.8	81.4	141.4	140.4	135.5	288.0	93.8	148.1	375.6	369.3	175.2
1998	1,673.0	1,254.1	276.0	660.0	240.1	87.9	152.2	147.4	147.1	318.1	109.2	160.6	418.8	412.1	199.4
1999	1,826.2	1,364.5	285.7	713.6	259.8	97.2	162.5	149.1	174.4	365.1	136.6	177.5	461.8	454.5	223.8
2000	1,983.9	1,498.4	321.0	766.1	293.8	103.2	190.6	162.9	170.8	411.3	156.8	199.0	485.4	477.7	236.8
2001	1,973.1	1,460.1	333.5	711.5	265.9	87.6	178.4	151.9	154.2	415.0	157.7	202.7	513.1	505.2	249.1
2002	1,910.4	1,352.8	287.0	659.6	236.7	79.7	157.0	141.7	141.6	406.2	152.5	196.1	557.6	549.6	265.9
2003	2,013.0	1,375.9	286.6	670.6	242.7	79.9	162.8	143.4	134.1	418.7	155.0	201.0	637.1	628.8	310.6
2004	2,217.2	1,467.4	307.7	721.9	255.8	84.2	171.6	144.2	159.2	437.8	166.3	207.4	749.8	740.8	377.6
2005	2,477.2	1,621.0	353.0	794.9	267.0	84.2	182.8	162.4	179.6	473.1	178.6	224.7	856.2	846.6	433.5
2006	2,632.0	1,793.8	425.2	862.3	288.5	92.6	195.9	181.6	194.3	506.3	189.5	245.6	838.2	828.1	416.0
2007	2,639.1	1,948.6	510.3	893.4	310.9	95.4	215.5	194.1	188.8	544.8	206.4	268.0	690.5	680.6	305.2
2008	2,506.9	1,990.9	571.1	845.4	306.3	93.9	212.4	193.4	148.7	574.4	223.8	284.2	516.0	506.4	185.8
2009	2,080.4	1,690.4	455.8	670.3	275.6	88.9	186.7	153.7	74.9	564.4	226.0	274.6	390.0	381.2	105.3
2010	2,111.6	1,735.0	379.8	777.0	307.5	99.6	207.9	155.2	135.8	578.2	226.4	282.4	376.6	367.4	112.6
2011	2,286.3	1,907.5	404.5	881.3	313.3	95.6	217.7	191.5	177.8	621.7	249.8	303.4	378.8	369.1	108.5
2012	2,550.5	2,118.5	479.4	983.4	331.2	103.5	227.7	211.2	215.3	655.7	272.1	313.4	432.0	421.5	132.0
2013	2,721.5	2,211.5	492.5	1,027.0	341.7	102.1	239.6	209.3	242.5	691.9	283.7	337.9	510.0	499.0	170.8
2014	2,954.4	2,394.3	577.1	1,090.8	345.7	101.6	244.1	218.9	272.2	726.4	297.5	357.6	560.1	548.8	193.6
2015	3,083.2	2,449.7	572.2	1,118.3	353.2	101.4	251.8	218.6	304.9	759.2	307.3	374.8	633.6	621.9	221.1
2016	3,140.9	2,442.1	545.7	1,090.9	354.3	99.3	255.0	215.0	290.5	805.5	327.5	398.8	698.8	686.7	242.5
2017	3,342.5	2,587.9	585.4	1,150.4	381.9	109.2	272.7	231.3	284.3	852.0	352.9	417.9	754.6	742.2	270.2
2018 [p]	3,595.6	2,800.4	637.1	1,236.3	409.6	118.1	291.5	248.4	304.9	927.0	385.1	457.7	795.3	782.4	285.0
2015: I	3,052.1	2,447.5	589.0	1,114.9	347.5	100.6	246.9	218.4	299.2	743.6	304.5	364.1	604.6	593.1	213.6
II	3,081.7	2,458.0	589.9	1,114.6	350.1	101.7	248.4	220.5	301.9	753.4	305.7	370.9	623.7	612.0	215.5
III	3,109.3	2,463.0	570.9	1,130.2	357.8	103.5	254.3	217.4	315.4	762.0	307.2	376.9	646.3	634.5	224.6
IV	3,089.9	2,430.3	539.0	1,113.7	357.4	99.8	257.5	218.0	303.3	777.6	311.7	387.4	659.6	647.8	230.8
2016: I	3,094.1	2,409.8	531.2	1,092.8	349.0	99.1	249.9	212.2	298.8	785.8	319.0	388.1	684.2	672.2	240.4
II	3,127.1	2,435.6	539.7	1,091.4	353.1	99.8	253.2	214.2	295.2	804.5	325.5	400.1	691.5	679.4	241.2
III	3,157.2	2,458.4	555.1	1,090.2	356.3	98.2	258.2	215.3	287.5	813.2	330.0	403.7	698.8	686.6	238.1
IV	3,185.4	2,464.7	556.7	1,089.3	358.8	100.1	258.6	218.1	280.5	818.7	335.4	403.2	720.8	708.6	250.2
2017: I	3,270.6	2,525.2	577.5	1,112.3	368.5	103.2	265.4	222.1	282.4	835.4	342.7	412.1	745.5	733.1	259.6
II	3,320.8	2,576.7	588.3	1,137.4	379.0	110.1	268.8	230.1	279.4	850.9	353.5	416.5	744.1	731.8	267.7
III	3,358.5	2,607.0	585.3	1,162.8	386.5	113.9	272.6	234.6	285.0	858.9	359.7	417.8	751.5	739.1	273.6
IV	3,420.0	2,642.6	590.6	1,189.1	393.7	109.7	284.0	238.5	290.4	862.9	355.9	425.0	777.4	764.7	279.8
2018: I	3,507.4	2,720.3	614.9	1,212.6	401.9	116.9	285.0	243.9	300.7	892.7	370.3	439.7	787.2	774.6	287.1
II	3,589.9	2,791.4	644.1	1,228.8	410.2	121.0	289.1	243.4	303.5	918.6	381.6	453.1	798.5	785.9	288.5
III	3,618.0	2,819.7	643.3	1,243.0	415.8	120.3	295.5	250.2	302.9	933.4	389.0	459.7	798.3	785.3	286.1
IV [p]	3,667.1	2,870.1	645.9	1,261.0	410.6	114.1	296.5	256.0	312.6	963.3	399.6	478.4	797.0	784.0	278.5

[1] Includes other items not shown separately.
[2] Research and development investment includes expenditures for software.

Source: Department of Commerce (Bureau of Economic Analysis).

TABLE B-13. Real private fixed investment by type, 2002–2018

[Billions of chained (2012) dollars; quarterly data at seasonally adjusted annual rates]

Year or quarter	Private fixed investment	Nonresidential											Residential		
		Total nonresidential	Structures	Equipment						Intellectual property products			Total residential [2]	Structures	
				Total [2]	Information processing equipment			Industrial equipment	Transportation equipment	Total [2]	Software	Research and development [3]		Total [2]	Single family
					Total	Computers and peripheral equipment [1]	Other								
2002	2,183.4	1,472.7	473.5	607.8	133.3	35.9	98.3	181.4	162.4	421.5	125.5	244.1	692.6	685.1	327.1
2003	2,280.6	1,509.4	456.6	634.3	150.4	40.2	111.1	182.2	150.3	437.7	133.5	246.1	755.5	747.7	362.0
2004	2,440.7	1,594.0	456.3	688.6	169.4	45.7	124.7	178.8	171.2	459.2	149.3	248.1	830.9	822.1	405.4
2005	2,618.7	1,716.4	466.1	760.0	187.6	51.8	136.5	194.2	192.1	493.1	163.4	261.6	885.4	876.3	432.8
2006	2,686.8	1,854.2	501.7	832.6	217.0	64.7	152.4	210.6	206.4	521.5	173.5	279.6	818.9	809.5	390.4
2007	2,653.5	1,982.1	568.6	865.8	247.2	73.9	173.3	217.3	197.7	554.3	191.1	296.1	665.8	656.6	283.5
2008	2,499.4	1,994.2	605.4	824.4	260.6	79.7	180.9	208.3	155.0	575.3	206.7	304.8	504.6	495.7	178.1
2009	2,099.8	1,704.3	492.2	649.7	247.5	81.1	166.5	162.7	72.5	572.4	212.9	297.4	395.3	386.9	105.3
2010	2,164.2	1,781.0	412.8	781.2	289.1	94.1	195.1	162.5	141.5	588.1	220.9	298.5	383.0	373.8	114.3
2011	2,317.8	1,935.4	424.1	886.2	303.2	93.9	209.3	194.9	181.8	624.8	245.2	311.0	382.5	372.4	109.1
2012	2,550.5	2,118.5	479.4	983.4	331.2	103.5	227.7	211.2	215.3	655.7	272.1	313.4	432.0	421.5	132.0
2013	2,692.1	2,206.0	485.5	1,029.2	351.8	103.0	248.8	208.4	238.5	691.4	287.2	333.8	485.5	474.1	161.8
2014	2,861.5	2,357.4	536.9	1,098.7	368.6	102.6	266.4	216.6	264.4	721.1	305.3	345.3	504.2	491.8	171.9
2015	2,958.5	2,399.7	520.9	1,132.6	393.5	103.5	291.0	217.0	291.4	747.8	319.9	352.8	555.3	541.9	191.5
2016	3,009.8	2,411.2	494.7	1,116.2	410.9	103.0	309.7	214.4	274.3	803.9	345.9	382.0	591.3	576.8	201.1
2017 [p]	3,155.1	2,538.1	517.5	1,183.7	459.8	113.8	348.4	228.6	264.2	841.1	379.3	386.8	611.1	595.7	214.8
2018 [p]	3,322.4	2,714.8	543.3	1,271.9	503.6	122.8	383.8	240.9	282.6	905.6	419.4	411.1	609.6	594.3	217.6
2015: I	2,930.4	2,393.5	533.2	1,124.0	380.1	101.8	279.1	216.3	286.7	733.2	315.5	344.4	535.2	522.2	185.7
II	2,957.5	2,405.5	538.6	1,126.3	386.7	103.6	283.9	218.7	288.9	740.5	318.8	347.3	549.3	536.0	187.6
III	2,980.2	2,411.9	518.8	1,146.4	401.1	105.9	296.1	215.8	301.0	748.8	319.8	353.1	564.3	550.8	194.6
IV	2,965.9	2,388.1	489.7	1,133.7	406.0	102.6	305.0	217.2	289.0	768.8	325.7	366.5	572.3	558.6	198.4
2016: I	2,979.7	2,380.9	484.8	1,115.1	399.6	102.3	298.8	211.8	284.0	785.0	334.4	374.6	590.9	576.7	204.7
II	3,000.0	2,403.3	488.8	1,115.5	405.9	103.2	304.3	213.9	279.8	803.2	343.0	384.8	589.4	575.1	202.1
III	3,023.5	2,430.3	503.5	1,115.8	415.1	101.8	315.6	214.6	270.5	814.0	349.8	387.7	586.9	572.4	195.7
IV	3,036.1	2,430.4	501.9	1,118.2	423.0	104.8	320.3	217.5	262.9	813.3	356.2	380.7	597.9	583.2	202.1
2017: I	3,108.6	2,486.5	517.3	1,142.8	439.7	107.7	334.5	220.6	262.0	829.0	366.2	386.7	613.8	598.7	208.5
II	3,141.3	2,530.8	522.2	1,169.5	455.2	114.8	342.2	227.7	259.0	842.3	377.7	389.5	605.2	590.0	213.1
III	3,161.2	2,552.3	514.5	1,197.1	466.8	118.7	349.7	231.6	264.7	845.9	387.9	384.0	604.5	589.2	216.6
IV	3,209.3	2,582.7	516.2	1,225.6	477.5	113.9	367.1	234.6	270.9	847.3	385.3	386.8	620.7	605.0	220.9
2018: I	3,271.3	2,654.0	533.3	1,250.9	490.5	121.3	371.7	238.5	280.3	875.7	402.1	398.8	615.3	599.7	223.1
II	3,322.3	2,710.1	551.7	1,264.9	502.9	125.7	379.3	236.6	281.3	897.9	414.2	408.6	613.2	597.8	220.6
III	3,331.8	2,727.0	546.9	1,275.6	511.8	125.0	389.7	242.0	278.8	910.2	423.3	411.8	607.7	592.4	217.5
IV [p]	3,364.2	2,768.0	541.1	1,296.4	509.2	119.1	394.5	246.8	289.9	938.6	437.9	425.0	602.3	587.2	209.3

[1] Because computers exhibit rapid changes in prices relative to other prices in the economy, the chained-dollar estimates should not be used to measure the component's relative importance or its contribution to the growth rate of more aggregate series. The quantity index for computers can be used to accurately measure the real growth rate of this series. For information on this component, see *Survey of Current Business* Table 5.3.1 (for growth rates), Table 5.3.2 (for contributions), and Table 5.3.3 (for quantity indexes).
[2] Includes other items not shown separately.
[3] Research and development investment includes expenditures for software.

Source: Department of Commerce (Bureau of Economic Analysis).

TABLE B-14.—Foreign transactions in the national income and product accounts, 1968–2018

[Billions of dollars; quarterly data at seasonally adjusted annual rates]

Year or quarter	Current receipts from rest of the world					Current payments to rest of the world								Balance on current account, NIPA [2]
	Total	Exports of goods and services			Income receipts	Total	Imports of goods and services			Income payments	Current taxes and transfer payments to rest of the world (net)			
		Total	Goods [1]	Services [1]			Total	Goods [1]	Services [1]		Total	From persons (net)	From government (net)	From business (net)	
1968	58.0	47.9	35.7	12.2	10.1	56.5	46.6	33.9	12.6	4.0	5.9	1.0	4.6	0.3	1.5
1969	63.7	51.9	38.7	13.2	11.8	62.1	50.5	36.8	13.7	5.7	5.9	1.1	4.5	.3	1.6
1970	72.5	59.7	45.0	14.7	12.8	68.8	55.8	40.9	14.9	6.4	6.6	1.3	4.9	.4	3.7
1971	77.0	63.0	46.2	16.8	14.0	76.7	62.3	46.6	15.8	6.4	7.9	1.4	6.1	.4	.3
1972	87.1	70.8	52.6	18.3	16.3	91.2	74.2	56.9	17.3	7.7	9.2	1.4	7.4	.5	−4.0
1973	118.8	95.3	75.8	19.5	23.5	109.9	91.2	71.8	19.3	10.9	7.9	1.6	5.6	.7	8.9
1974	156.5	126.7	103.5	23.2	29.8	150.5	127.5	104.5	22.9	14.3	8.7	1.4	6.4	1.0	6.0
1975	166.7	138.7	112.5	26.2	28.0	146.9	122.7	99.0	23.7	15.0	9.1	1.3	7.1	.7	19.8
1976	181.9	149.5	121.5	28.0	32.4	174.8	151.1	124.6	26.5	15.5	8.1	1.4	5.7	1.1	7.1
1977	196.5	159.3	128.4	30.9	37.2	207.5	182.4	152.6	29.8	16.9	8.1	1.4	5.3	1.4	−10.9
1978	233.1	186.9	149.9	37.0	46.3	245.8	212.3	177.4	34.8	24.7	8.8	1.6	5.9	1.4	−12.6
1979	298.5	230.1	187.3	42.9	68.3	299.6	252.7	212.8	39.9	36.4	10.6	1.7	6.8	2.0	−1.2
1980	359.9	280.8	230.4	50.3	79.1	351.4	293.8	248.6	45.3	44.9	12.6	2.0	8.3	2.4	8.5
1981	397.3	305.2	245.2	60.0	92.0	393.9	317.8	267.8	49.9	59.1	17.0	5.6	8.3	3.2	3.4
1982	384.2	283.2	222.6	60.7	101.0	387.5	303.2	250.5	52.6	64.5	19.8	6.7	9.7	3.4	−3.3
1983	378.9	277.0	214.0	62.9	101.9	413.9	328.6	272.7	56.0	64.8	20.5	7.0	10.1	3.4	−35.1
1984	424.2	302.4	231.3	71.1	121.9	514.3	405.1	336.3	68.8	85.6	23.6	7.9	12.2	3.5	−90.1
1985	415.9	303.2	227.5	75.7	112.7	530.2	417.2	343.3	73.9	87.3	25.7	8.3	14.4	2.9	−114.3
1986	432.3	321.0	231.4	89.6	111.3	575.0	452.9	370.0	82.9	94.4	27.8	9.1	15.4	3.2	−142.7
1987	487.2	363.9	265.6	98.4	123.3	641.3	508.7	414.8	93.9	105.8	26.8	10.0	13.4	3.4	−154.1
1988	596.7	444.6	332.1	112.5	152.1	712.4	554.0	452.1	101.9	129.5	29.0	10.8	13.7	4.5	−115.7
1989	682.0	504.3	374.8	129.5	177.7	774.3	591.0	484.8	106.2	152.9	30.4	11.6	14.2	4.6	−92.4
1990	740.7	551.9	403.3	148.6	188.8	815.6	629.7	508.1	121.7	154.2	31.7	12.2	14.7	4.8	−74.9
1991	763.3	594.9	430.1	164.8	168.4	755.4	623.5	500.7	122.8	136.8	−4.9	14.1	−24.0	5.0	7.9
1992	785.1	633.1	455.3	177.7	152.1	830.7	667.8	544.9	122.9	121.0	41.9	14.5	22.0	5.4	−45.6
1993	810.4	654.8	467.7	187.1	155.6	889.8	720.0	592.8	127.2	124.4	45.4	17.1	22.9	5.4	−79.4
1994	905.5	720.9	518.4	202.6	184.5	1,021.1	813.4	676.8	136.6	161.6	46.1	18.9	21.1	6.0	−115.6
1995	1,042.6	812.8	592.4	220.4	229.8	1,148.5	902.6	757.4	145.1	201.9	44.1	20.3	15.6	8.2	−105.9
1996	1,114.0	867.6	628.8	238.8	246.4	1,229.0	964.0	807.4	156.5	215.5	49.3	22.6	20.0	6.9	−115.0
1997	1,233.9	953.8	699.9	253.9	280.1	1,364.0	1,055.8	885.7	170.1	256.8	51.4	25.7	16.7	9.1	−130.1
1998	1,239.6	953.0	692.6	260.4	286.6	1,445.1	1,115.7	930.8	184.9	269.4	60.0	29.7	17.4	13.0	−205.3
1999	1,350.9	992.8	711.7	281.1	320.2	1,629.3	1,248.6	1,051.2	197.4	294.7	86.0	58.4	27.3	.3	−278.4
2000	1,518.0	1,096.3	795.9	300.3	380.6	1,914.4	1,471.3	1,250.1	221.2	345.6	97.6	61.9	31.0	4.7	−396.4
2001	1,394.1	1,024.6	741.2	283.4	324.1	1,777.0	1,392.6	1,173.8	218.8	275.3	109.1	71.7	27.7	9.7	−383.0
2002	1,370.4	998.7	709.0	289.7	314.8	1,813.6	1,424.1	1,194.4	229.8	269.6	119.9	82.1	33.0	4.8	−443.2
2003	1,456.1	1,036.2	737.1	299.1	353.8	1,969.4	1,539.3	1,291.3	248.0	295.4	134.6	89.4	38.7	6.5	−513.2
2004	1,689.3	1,177.6	830.0	347.7	446.9	2,314.5	1,796.7	1,507.3	289.4	368.8	149.0	85.4	41.4	22.2	−625.2
2005	1,941.5	1,305.2	921.9	383.3	566.0	2,678.8	2,026.4	1,715.5	311.0	488.1	164.3	90.6	52.1	21.7	−737.3
2006	2,259.9	1,472.6	1,044.9	427.7	712.0	3,061.7	2,243.5	1,895.7	347.8	661.5	156.7	95.0	47.4	14.2	−801.9
2007	2,603.0	1,660.9	1,161.3	499.6	866.6	3,313.7	2,379.3	1,999.7	379.6	757.6	176.9	105.5	55.6	15.7	−710.8
2008	2,775.8	1,837.1	1,292.5	544.5	848.8	3,458.9	2,560.1	2,144.3	415.9	694.2	204.6	129.5	60.5	14.6	−683.2
2009	2,321.5	1,582.0	1,058.4	523.6	647.8	2,693.6	1,978.4	1,585.4	393.1	505.8	209.3	133.2	68.7	7.4	−372.1
2010	2,657.2	1,846.3	1,272.4	573.8	715.2	3,093.9	2,360.2	1,944.8	415.4	519.5	214.2	141.9	70.0	2.4	−436.7
2011	2,996.3	2,103.0	1,462.3	640.7	789.2	3,461.8	2,682.5	2,240.5	441.9	552.8	226.6	157.8	74.6	−5.9	−465.6
2012	3,104.3	2,191.3	1,521.6	669.7	799.7	3,552.4	2,759.9	2,301.4	458.5	567.4	225.2	151.8	73.2	.2	−448.1
2013	3,228.0	2,273.4	1,559.2	714.2	823.4	3,596.5	2,764.2	2,296.4	467.8	592.7	239.6	167.7	72.7	−.8	−368.5
2014	3,371.0	2,371.0	1,614.9	756.1	854.2	3,746.6	2,879.3	2,391.5	487.8	612.5	254.8	177.6	72.3	4.9	−375.6
2015	3,240.1	2,265.0	1,494.4	770.7	839.3	3,664.2	2,786.5	2,287.3	499.1	613.1	264.7	181.2	73.1	10.4	−424.1
2016	3,219.6	2,217.6	1,442.7	774.9	859.1	3,665.4	2,738.1	2,221.0	517.2	643.8	283.5	188.7	75.6	19.2	−445.8
2017	3,466.5	2,350.2	1,535.9	814.3	957.1	3,939.0	2,928.6	2,378.5	550.0	713.4	297.0	201.1	74.3	21.6	−472.5
2018 [p]	....	2,530.9	1,666.7	864.2	....	....	3,156.5	2,568.8	587.7	....	296.0	199.0	80.0	16.9	....
2015: I	3,257.8	2,286.6	1,515.3	771.3	835.7	3,684.8	2,817.0	2,324.3	492.7	603.4	264.4	179.2	78.4	6.8	−427.0
II	3,300.0	2,303.2	1,531.6	771.6	854.8	3,694.3	2,802.2	2,306.6	495.6	635.5	256.6	180.4	67.9	8.3	−394.3
III	3,244.0	2,259.2	1,489.7	769.5	853.9	3,701.9	2,795.4	2,292.1	503.3	635.3	271.3	181.4	76.6	13.2	−457.9
IV	3,158.8	2,211.2	1,440.9	770.3	812.8	3,575.8	2,731.3	2,226.4	505.0	578.0	266.5	183.8	69.4	13.3	−417.0
2016: I	3,132.5	2,165.6	1,402.3	763.3	828.7	3,595.2	2,687.8	2,177.7	510.2	624.6	282.8	185.2	82.0	15.6	−462.7
II	3,209.0	2,206.6	1,434.1	772.5	860.7	3,623.2	2,702.7	2,191.7	511.0	648.2	272.3	187.1	70.1	15.1	−414.2
III	3,248.9	2,252.5	1,469.4	783.2	854.5	3,697.8	2,756.3	2,236.1	520.2	656.6	284.9	189.6	76.5	18.8	−448.9
IV	3,288.1	2,245.6	1,464.9	780.7	892.6	3,745.6	2,805.8	2,278.4	527.3	645.8	294.0	192.9	73.8	27.3	−457.5
2017: I	3,361.4	2,294.1	1,497.3	796.9	899.3	3,823.7	2,870.7	2,336.1	534.6	666.6	286.4	195.1	74.5	16.8	−462.3
II	3,388.6	2,316.3	1,510.8	805.4	924.9	3,896.2	2,888.2	2,344.6	543.6	708.7	299.3	198.7	71.7	28.9	−507.6
III	3,512.0	2,358.3	1,536.7	821.6	979.6	3,947.2	2,915.5	2,358.9	556.7	724.6	307.0	212.2	70.3	24.6	−435.2
IV	3,603.8	2,432.0	1,598.8	833.2	1,024.5	4,088.7	3,039.9	2,474.6	565.3	753.7	295.1	198.5	80.5	16.0	−484.9
2018: I	3,687.2	2,477.4	1,628.1	849.3	1,063.2	4,201.1	3,116.6	2,537.1	579.4	794.4	290.1	199.4	71.6	19.1	−513.9
II	3,806.5	2,568.7	1,706.4	862.4	1,078.6	4,230.3	3,118.5	2,536.5	582.0	811.6	300.2	200.6	86.3	13.3	−423.8
III	3,774.7	2,538.6	1,668.6	870.0	1,071.5	4,302.4	3,192.1	2,602.4	589.7	816.5	293.8	198.1	77.0	18.7	−527.6
IV [p]	....	2,538.9	1,663.7	875.2	....	3,198.7	2,599.0	599.8	....	....	299.8	198.1	85.1	16.6	....

[1] Certain goods, primarily military equipment purchased and sold by the Federal Government, are included in services. Beginning with 1986, repairs and alterations of equipment were reclassified from goods to services.
[2] National income and product accounts (NIPA).

Source: Department of Commerce (Bureau of Economic Analysis).

TABLE B-15. Real exports and imports of goods and services, 2002–2018

[Billions of chained (2012) dollars; quarterly data at seasonally adjusted annual rates]

Year or quarter	Exports of goods and services						Imports of goods and services					
	Total	Goods[1]				Services[1]	Total	Goods[1]				Services[1]
		Total	Durable goods	Non-durable goods	Non-agricultural goods			Total	Durable goods	Non-durable goods	Non-petroleum goods	
2002	1,277.1	900.6	524.7	388.8	797.3	376.5	1,944.4	1,634.0	785.6	896.4	1,207.4	309.4
2003	1,305.0	927.1	542.4	396.4	821.8	377.8	2,040.1	1,729.0	831.2	948.7	1,276.4	310.5
2004	1,431.2	1,008.3	604.0	410.3	904.9	422.8	2,272.6	1,926.8	951.0	1,012.5	1,430.8	345.2
2005	1,533.2	1,085.4	663.4	423.3	975.8	447.6	2,421.0	2,062.3	1,036.9	1,053.0	1,543.4	358.6
2006	1,676.4	1,193.0	739.4	451.5	1,073.6	483.3	2,581.5	2,190.9	1,135.6	1,069.5	1,664.8	390.2
2007	1,822.3	1,276.1	796.6	475.7	1,148.3	546.0	2,646.0	2,236.0	1,168.3	1,078.9	1,714.6	409.2
2008	1,925.4	1,350.4	835.0	512.7	1,215.0	574.7	2,587.1	2,160.8	1,130.6	1,040.7	1,657.1	425.2
2009	1,763.8	1,190.3	694.5	499.9	1,060.0	572.9	2,248.6	1,830.1	902.3	948.3	1,375.9	415.9
2010	1,977.9	1,368.7	818.1	551.7	1,223.8	609.2	2,543.8	2,112.7	1,115.6	1,001.5	1,636.1	430.8
2011	2,119.0	1,465.3	893.7	571.6	1,321.6	653.8	2,687.1	2,242.5	1,227.0	1,016.2	1,769.8	444.6
2012	2,191.3	1,521.6	937.7	583.9	1,376.4	669.7	2,759.9	2,301.4	1,326.4	975.0	1,867.1	458.5
2013	2,269.6	1,570.0	960.1	609.9	1,422.9	699.5	2,802.4	2,341.9	1,385.9	956.1	1,932.5	460.6
2014	2,367.0	1,642.4	1,001.1	641.4	1,484.0	724.7	2,944.7	2,472.7	1,508.8	964.3	2,076.6	472.7
2015	2,380.6	1,637.2	979.6	659.5	1,475.8	742.2	3,105.5	2,615.2	1,610.3	1,004.4	2,209.0	491.8
2016	2,378.1	1,642.7	966.4	681.9	1,473.7	735.3	3,164.4	2,651.4	1,631.8	1,019.3	2,232.1	512.5
2017	2,450.1	1,697.3	988.5	716.8	1,525.1	753.4	3,308.7	2,773.5	1,747.5	1,018.9	2,344.6	534.9
2018 p	2,546.6	1,777.3	1,021.5	765.9	1,593.3	772.1	3,460.6	2,909.8	1,837.5	1,063.7	2,479.1	552.0
2015: I	2,377.7	1,632.2	983.5	649.7	1,471.0	744.0	3,072.1	2,590.3	1,592.7	998.0	2,185.9	483.7
II	2,400.0	1,658.3	989.2	671.6	1,490.7	741.5	3,096.7	2,612.9	1,603.5	1,009.9	2,208.2	486.0
III	2,379.0	1,639.1	979.3	661.8	1,479.0	739.1	3,128.0	2,633.0	1,623.5	1,008.6	2,224.2	496.4
IV	2,365.7	1,619.2	966.4	654.8	1,462.6	744.2	3,125.0	2,624.5	1,621.5	1,001.2	2,218.0	501.1
2016: I	2,351.1	1,619.9	958.2	665.9	1,465.8	730.4	3,129.0	2,622.0	1,607.9	1,015.2	2,209.4	506.5
II	2,370.9	1,634.2	963.6	675.6	1,477.0	736.0	3,135.0	2,629.3	1,608.9	1,022.1	2,213.4	505.6
III	2,406.4	1,664.9	969.3	703.7	1,474.3	741.7	3,172.6	2,656.4	1,640.6	1,014.2	2,232.9	515.3
IV	2,384.2	1,651.9	974.4	682.5	1,477.9	732.9	3,220.9	2,697.6	1,669.6	1,025.6	2,272.5	522.5
2017: I	2,413.3	1,669.0	969.6	707.9	1,497.7	744.5	3,258.8	2,729.9	1,700.8	1,024.8	2,294.2	528.3
II	2,435.0	1,686.2	975.9	719.6	1,510.4	749.3	3,279.1	2,745.8	1,727.4	1,011.9	2,317.6	532.4
III	2,456.1	1,694.8	995.5	705.6	1,519.2	760.8	3,302.0	2,762.6	1,749.5	1,004.7	2,340.0	538.1
IV	2,495.9	1,739.2	1,013.0	734.3	1,573.0	759.0	3,395.1	2,855.6	1,812.2	1,034.2	2,426.5	540.8
2018: I	2,517.8	1,753.0	1,031.1	728.4	1,581.5	766.9	3,420.1	2,872.7	1,818.1	1,045.8	2,449.8	548.1
II	2,574.2	1,809.2	1,029.6	791.4	1,607.9	769.8	3,415.2	2,870.0	1,799.9	1,062.4	2,437.7	546.1
III	2,542.2	1,769.8	1,008.8	772.3	1,577.8	774.5	3,491.9	2,942.2	1,863.2	1,070.1	2,501.3	551.9
IV p	2,552.0	1,777.0	1,016.3	771.6	1,606.0	777.2	3,515.2	2,954.2	1,868.9	1,076.5	2,527.4	561.9

[1] Certain goods, primarily military equipment purchased and sold by the Federal Government, are included in services. Repairs and alterations of equipment are also included in services.

Source: Department of Commerce (Bureau of Economic Analysis).

TABLE B-16. Sources of personal income, 1968–2018

[Billions of dollars; quarterly data at seasonally adjusted annual rates]

Year or quarter	Personal income	Compensation of employees							Proprietors' income with inventory valuation and capital consumption adjustments			Rental income of persons with capital consumption adjustment
		Total	Wages and salaries			Supplements to wages and salaries			Total	Farm	Nonfarm	
			Total	Private industries	Government	Total	Employer contributions for employee pension and insurance funds	Employer contributions for government social insurance				
1968	730.9	530.8	472.0	375.3	96.7	58.8	38.8	20.0	73.8	11.7	62.2	20.1
1969	800.3	584.5	518.3	412.7	105.6	66.1	43.4	22.8	77.0	12.8	64.2	20.3
1970	865.0	623.3	551.6	434.3	117.2	71.8	47.9	23.8	77.8	12.9	64.9	20.7
1971	932.8	665.0	584.5	457.8	126.8	80.4	54.0	26.4	83.9	13.4	70.5	21.8
1972	1,024.5	731.3	638.8	500.9	137.9	92.5	61.4	31.2	95.1	17.0	78.1	22.7
1973	1,140.8	812.7	708.8	560.0	148.8	103.9	64.1	39.8	112.5	29.1	83.4	23.1
1974	1,251.8	887.7	772.3	611.8	160.5	115.4	70.7	44.7	112.2	23.5	88.7	23.2
1975	1,369.4	947.2	814.8	638.6	176.2	132.4	85.7	46.7	118.2	22.0	96.2	22.3
1976	1,502.6	1,048.3	899.7	710.8	188.9	148.6	94.2	54.4	131.0	17.2	113.8	20.3
1977	1,659.2	1,165.8	994.2	791.6	202.6	171.7	110.6	61.1	144.5	16.0	128.5	15.9
1978	1,863.7	1,316.8	1,120.6	900.6	220.0	196.2	124.7	71.5	166.0	19.9	146.1	16.5
1979	2,082.7	1,477.2	1,253.3	1,016.2	237.1	223.9	141.3	82.6	179.4	22.2	157.3	16.1
1980	2,323.6	1,622.2	1,373.4	1,112.0	261.5	248.8	159.9	88.9	171.6	11.7	159.9	19.0
1981	2,605.1	1,792.5	1,511.4	1,225.5	285.8	281.2	177.5	103.6	179.7	19.0	160.7	23.8
1982	2,791.6	1,893.0	1,587.5	1,280.0	307.5	305.5	195.7	109.8	171.2	13.3	157.9	23.8
1983	2,981.1	2,012.5	1,677.5	1,352.7	324.8	335.0	215.1	119.9	186.3	6.2	180.1	24.4
1984	3,292.7	2,215.9	1,844.9	1,496.8	348.1	371.0	231.9	139.0	228.2	20.9	207.3	24.7
1985	3,524.9	2,387.3	1,982.6	1,608.7	373.9	404.8	257.0	147.7	241.1	21.0	220.1	26.2
1986	3,733.1	2,542.1	2,102.3	1,705.1	397.2	439.7	281.9	157.9	256.5	22.8	233.7	18.3
1987	3,961.6	2,722.4	2,256.3	1,833.2	423.1	466.1	299.9	166.3	286.5	28.9	257.6	16.6
1988	4,283.4	2,948.0	2,439.8	1,987.7	452.0	508.2	323.6	184.6	325.5	26.8	298.7	22.5
1989	4,625.6	3,139.6	2,583.1	2,101.9	481.1	556.6	362.9	193.7	341.1	33.0	308.1	21.5
1990	4,913.8	3,340.4	2,741.2	2,222.2	519.0	599.2	392.7	206.5	353.2	32.2	321.0	28.2
1991	5,084.9	3,450.5	2,814.5	2,265.7	548.8	636.0	420.9	215.1	354.2	26.8	327.4	38.6
1992	5,420.9	3,668.2	2,965.5	2,393.5	572.0	702.7	474.3	228.4	400.2	34.8	365.4	60.6
1993	5,657.9	3,817.3	3,079.3	2,490.3	589.0	737.9	498.3	239.7	428.0	31.4	396.6	90.1
1994	5,947.1	4,006.2	3,236.6	2,627.1	609.5	769.6	515.5	254.1	456.6	34.7	422.0	113.7
1995	6,291.4	4,198.1	3,418.0	2,789.0	629.0	780.1	515.9	264.1	481.2	22.0	459.2	124.9
1996	6,678.5	4,416.9	3,616.5	2,968.4	648.1	800.5	525.7	274.8	543.8	37.3	506.4	142.5
1997	7,092.5	4,708.8	3,876.8	3,205.0	671.9	832.0	542.4	289.6	584.0	32.4	551.6	147.1
1998	7,606.7	5,071.1	4,181.6	3,480.3	701.3	889.5	582.3	307.2	640.2	28.5	611.7	165.2
1999	8,001.9	5,402.8	4,458.0	3,724.2	733.8	944.8	621.4	323.3	696.4	28.1	668.3	178.5
2000	8,652.6	5,848.1	4,825.9	4,046.1	779.8	1,022.2	677.0	345.2	753.9	31.5	722.4	183.5
2001	9,005.6	6,039.1	4,954.4	4,132.4	822.0	1,084.7	726.7	358.0	831.0	32.1	798.9	202.4
2002	9,159.0	6,135.6	4,996.3	4,123.4	872.9	1,139.3	773.2	366.0	869.8	19.9	849.8	211.1
2003	9,487.5	6,354.1	5,138.7	4,224.8	914.0	1,215.3	832.8	382.5	896.9	36.5	860.4	231.5
2004	10,035.1	6,720.1	5,421.6	4,469.2	952.3	1,298.5	889.7	408.8	962.0	51.5	910.5	248.9
2005	10,598.2	7,066.6	5,691.9	4,700.6	991.3	1,374.7	946.7	428.1	978.0	46.8	931.2	232.0
2006	11,381.7	7,479.9	6,057.0	5,022.4	1,034.5	1,422.9	975.6	447.3	1,049.6	33.1	1,016.6	202.3
2007	12,007.8	7,878.9	6,396.8	5,308.2	1,088.5	1,482.1	1,020.4	461.7	994.0	40.3	953.8	184.4
2008	12,442.2	8,057.0	6,534.2	5,390.4	1,143.9	1,522.7	1,051.3	471.4	960.9	40.2	920.7	256.7
2009	12,059.1	7,758.5	6,248.6	5,073.4	1,175.2	1,509.9	1,051.8	458.1	938.5	28.1	910.5	327.3
2010	12,551.6	7,924.9	6,372.1	5,180.9	1,191.2	1,552.9	1,083.9	469.0	1,108.7	39.0	1,069.7	394.2
2011	13,326.8	8,225.9	6,625.9	5,431.1	1,194.9	1,600.0	1,107.3	492.7	1,229.3	64.9	1,164.4	478.6
2012	14,010.1	8,566.7	6,927.5	5,729.2	1,198.3	1,639.2	1,125.9	513.3	1,347.3	60.9	1,286.4	518.0
2013	14,181.1	8,834.2	7,113.2	5,905.2	1,208.0	1,721.0	1,194.7	526.3	1,403.6	88.3	1,315.3	557.0
2014	14,991.8	9,248.1	7,473.2	6,236.3	1,236.9	1,774.8	1,228.1	546.7	1,447.6	70.1	1,377.5	608.4
2015	15,719.5	9,696.8	7,854.4	6,578.7	1,275.8	1,842.4	1,272.8	569.7	1,421.9	56.4	1,365.5	651.8
2016	16,125.1	9,956.2	8,080.7	6,773.0	1,307.7	1,875.6	1,294.2	581.4	1,419.3	37.5	1,381.8	694.8
2017	16,830.9	10,407.2	8,453.8	7,108.1	1,345.7	1,953.4	1,348.1	605.3	1,500.9	38.9	1,462.0	730.2
2018 ᵖ	17,581.4	10,855.7	8,834.7	7,456.2	1,378.6	2,021.0	1,389.8	631.2	1,579.8	37.5	1,542.2	760.0
2015: I	15,471.3	9,554.1	7,734.5	6,471.0	1,263.4	1,819.6	1,258.7	560.9	1,431.0	54.5	1,376.5	631.1
II	15,681.7	9,665.8	7,827.1	6,554.0	1,273.1	1,838.7	1,270.9	567.8	1,410.4	55.8	1,354.6	647.2
III	15,842.9	9,752.5	7,900.7	6,620.4	1,280.3	1,851.8	1,278.9	572.9	1,429.5	60.2	1,369.3	659.2
IV	15,882.1	9,814.9	7,955.4	6,669.2	1,286.2	1,859.6	1,282.5	577.0	1,416.5	55.0	1,361.4	669.7
2016: I	15,946.5	9,839.5	7,981.5	6,688.1	1,293.4	1,858.0	1,283.3	574.7	1,415.2	40.9	1,374.4	685.2
II	16,031.6	9,890.2	8,025.0	6,723.5	1,301.6	1,865.2	1,287.5	577.7	1,404.6	41.2	1,363.4	694.0
III	16,170.6	9,986.1	8,106.7	6,792.8	1,313.9	1,879.4	1,296.4	583.1	1,418.8	36.7	1,382.0	696.3
IV	16,351.8	10,109.3	8,209.6	6,887.6	1,321.9	1,899.7	1,309.8	589.9	1,438.6	31.0	1,407.6	703.8
2017: I	16,604.4	10,249.2	8,325.0	6,991.3	1,333.7	1,924.2	1,327.4	596.8	1,475.1	42.3	1,432.9	719.0
II	16,721.2	10,339.9	8,395.7	7,054.3	1,341.4	1,944.2	1,342.7	601.5	1,495.0	41.5	1,453.5	724.4
III	16,895.1	10,471.2	8,506.6	7,156.3	1,350.2	1,964.6	1,355.7	608.8	1,507.5	36.4	1,471.1	732.0
IV	17,103.1	10,568.6	8,588.1	7,230.4	1,357.7	1,980.5	1,366.4	614.0	1,526.1	35.4	1,490.6	745.3
2018: I	17,319.2	10,710.1	8,710.6	7,347.5	1,363.1	1,999.4	1,376.2	623.2	1,549.9	35.2	1,514.7	749.3
II	17,466.7	10,782.9	8,770.8	7,399.6	1,371.2	2,012.0	1,385.0	627.1	1,568.5	37.0	1,531.5	754.2
III	17,657.3	10,907.9	8,879.2	7,493.6	1,385.6	2,028.7	1,394.6	634.1	1,580.0	27.9	1,552.0	767.4
IV ᵖ	17,882.4	11,022.1	8,978.3	7,584.0	1,394.3	2,043.8	1,403.3	640.5	1,620.7	50.0	1,570.7	769.0

See next page for continuation of table.

TABLE B-16. Sources of personal income, 1968–2018—Continued

[Billions of dollars; quarterly data at seasonally adjusted annual rates]

Year or quarter	Personal income receipts on assets			Personal current transfer receipts								Less: Contributions for government social insurance, domestic
	Total	Personal interest income	Personal dividend income	Total	Government social benefits to persons						Other current transfer receipts, from business (net)	
					Total [1]	Social security [2]	Medicare [3]	Medicaid	Unemployment insurance	Other		
1968	88.8	65.3	23.5	56.1	53.3	24.6	5.9	4.0	2.2	10.8	2.8	38.7
1969	100.3	76.1	24.2	62.3	59.0	26.4	6.7	4.6	2.3	12.4	3.3	44.1
1970	114.9	90.6	24.3	74.7	71.7	31.4	7.3	5.5	4.2	16.0	2.9	46.4
1971	125.1	100.1	25.0	88.1	85.4	36.6	8.0	6.7	6.2	19.4	2.7	51.2
1972	136.6	109.8	26.8	97.9	94.8	40.9	8.8	8.2	6.0	21.4	3.1	59.2
1973	155.4	125.5	29.9	112.6	108.6	50.7	10.2	9.6	4.6	23.3	3.9	75.5
1974	180.6	147.4	33.2	133.3	128.6	57.6	12.7	11.2	7.0	28.4	4.7	85.2
1975	201.0	168.0	32.9	170.0	163.1	65.9	15.6	13.9	18.1	35.7	6.8	89.3
1976	220.0	181.0	39.0	184.3	177.6	74.5	18.8	15.5	16.4	38.7	6.7	101.3
1977	251.6	206.9	44.7	194.6	189.5	83.2	22.1	16.7	13.1	40.9	5.1	113.1
1978	285.8	235.1	50.7	209.9	203.4	91.4	25.5	18.6	9.4	44.9	6.5	131.3
1979	327.1	269.7	57.4	235.6	227.3	102.6	29.9	21.1	9.7	49.9	8.2	152.7
1980	396.9	332.9	64.0	280.1	271.5	118.6	36.2	23.9	16.1	62.1	8.6	166.2
1981	485.8	412.2	73.6	319.0	307.8	138.6	43.5	27.7	15.9	66.3	11.2	195.7
1982	557.0	479.5	77.6	355.5	343.1	153.7	50.9	30.2	25.2	66.8	12.4	208.9
1983	599.5	516.3	83.3	384.3	370.5	164.4	57.8	33.9	26.4	71.5	13.8	226.0
1984	680.8	590.1	90.6	400.6	380.9	173.0	64.7	36.6	16.0	74.3	19.7	257.5
1985	726.3	628.9	97.4	425.4	403.1	183.3	69.7	39.7	15.9	78.0	22.3	281.4
1986	768.2	662.1	106.0	451.6	428.6	193.6	75.3	43.6	16.5	83.0	22.9	303.4
1987	791.1	679.0	112.2	468.1	447.9	201.0	81.6	47.8	14.6	86.4	20.2	323.1
1988	851.4	721.7	129.7	497.5	476.9	213.9	86.3	53.0	13.3	93.6	20.6	361.5
1989	964.3	806.5	157.8	544.2	521.1	227.4	98.2	60.8	14.4	103.1	23.2	385.2
1990	1,005.3	836.5	168.8	596.9	574.7	244.1	107.6	73.1	18.2	113.9	22.2	410.1
1991	1,003.7	823.5	180.2	668.1	650.5	264.2	117.5	96.9	26.8	127.0	17.6	430.2
1992	998.8	809.8	189.1	748.0	731.8	281.8	132.6	116.2	39.6	142.9	16.3	455.0
1993	1,007.0	802.3	204.7	793.0	778.9	297.9	146.8	130.1	34.8	150.0	14.1	477.4
1994	1,049.8	814.6	235.2	829.0	815.7	312.2	164.4	139.4	23.9	156.1	13.3	508.2
1995	1,136.6	878.6	258.0	883.5	864.7	327.7	181.2	149.6	21.7	164.0	18.7	532.8
1996	1,201.2	899.0	302.2	929.2	906.3	342.0	194.9	158.2	22.3	167.6	22.9	555.1
1997	1,285.0	947.1	337.9	954.9	935.4	356.6	206.9	163.1	20.1	166.4	19.4	587.2
1998	1,370.9	1,015.5	355.4	983.9	957.9	369.2	205.6	170.2	19.7	170.0	26.0	624.7
1999	1,359.3	1,012.7	346.6	1,026.2	992.2	379.2	208.7	184.6	20.5	174.4	34.0	661.3
2000	1,485.7	1,102.2	383.5	1,087.3	1,044.9	401.4	219.1	199.5	20.7	179.1	42.4	705.8
2001	1,473.7	1,104.3	369.3	1,192.6	1,145.8	425.1	242.6	227.3	31.9	192.4	46.8	733.2
2002	1,408.9	1,010.1	398.8	1,285.2	1,251.0	446.9	259.7	250.0	53.5	211.3	34.2	751.5
2003	1,437.2	1,005.0	432.1	1,347.3	1,321.0	463.5	276.7	264.5	53.2	231.2	26.3	779.3
2004	1,512.1	950.4	561.7	1,421.2	1,404.5	485.5	304.4	289.8	36.4	254.3	16.8	829.2
2005	1,678.2	1,100.4	577.8	1,516.7	1,490.9	512.7	332.1	304.4	31.8	273.5	25.8	873.3
2006	1,958.6	1,235.8	722.8	1,613.8	1,593.0	544.1	399.1	299.1	30.4	281.5	20.8	922.5
2007	2,183.8	1,368.6	815.3	1,728.1	1,697.3	575.7	428.2	324.2	32.7	294.9	30.8	961.4
2008	2,200.9	1,396.3	804.6	1,955.1	1,919.3	605.5	461.6	338.3	51.1	417.7	35.8	988.4
2009	1,852.2	1,299.3	553.0	2,146.7	2,107.7	664.5	493.0	369.6	131.2	398.0	39.0	964.3
2010	1,782.3	1,238.5	543.9	2,325.2	2,281.4	690.2	513.4	396.9	138.9	484.2	43.7	983.7
2011	1,950.9	1,269.4	681.5	2,358.7	2,310.1	713.3	535.6	406.0	107.2	484.8	48.5	916.7
2012	2,165.6	1,330.5	835.1	2,363.0	2,322.6	762.1	554.7	417.5	83.6	434.4	40.4	950.5
2013	2,066.3	1,273.0	793.3	2,424.3	2,385.9	799.0	572.8	440.0	62.5	432.5	38.4	1,104.3
2014	2,301.2	1,347.8	953.4	2,540.3	2,497.2	834.6	598.6	490.9	35.5	453.9	43.1	1,153.8
2015	2,471.3	1,438.1	1,033.3	2,683.0	2,632.5	871.8	634.0	536.0	32.2	468.8	50.6	1,205.3
2016	2,516.6	1,440.9	1,075.7	2,778.1	2,717.4	896.5	662.2	562.7	31.7	471.6	60.7	1,239.9
2017	2,631.6	1,523.0	1,108.6	2,859.7	2,804.0	926.1	695.3	577.4	29.1	477.6	55.7	1,298.6
2018 [p]	2,766.1	1,614.4	1,151.7	2,980.9	2,920.2	974.9	734.5	601.4	25.5	474.7	60.7	1,361.1
2015: I	2,399.8	1,354.6	1,045.3	2,643.1	2,596.4	861.8	621.5	523.7	32.8	468.4	46.7	1,187.8
II	2,479.1	1,457.2	1,021.9	2,680.6	2,631.7	869.5	630.6	538.0	31.9	472.6	48.9	1,201.4
III	2,517.1	1,492.3	1,024.7	2,696.5	2,644.8	874.3	638.5	540.5	32.1	469.1	51.6	1,211.8
IV	2,489.3	1,448.1	1,041.2	2,712.0	2,656.9	881.6	645.3	541.7	31.9	464.9	55.1	1,220.2
2016: I	2,485.9	1,430.9	1,055.1	2,746.6	2,687.4	886.4	651.3	550.2	32.4	475.3	59.2	1,225.9
II	2,505.5	1,434.9	1,070.6	2,769.8	2,708.3	894.0	657.9	558.6	32.0	473.4	61.4	1,232.4
III	2,524.5	1,439.8	1,084.6	2,788.5	2,726.8	899.5	665.5	566.5	31.6	470.6	61.8	1,243.6
IV	2,550.4	1,458.1	1,092.3	2,807.3	2,747.1	906.0	673.9	575.8	30.7	467.0	60.3	1,257.6
2017: I	2,607.4	1,523.9	1,083.5	2,834.2	2,777.4	916.2	683.1	573.6	30.4	479.1	56.9	1,280.5
II	2,610.9	1,490.9	1,120.0	2,841.6	2,786.6	922.8	691.7	569.3	29.0	476.4	55.0	1,290.6
III	2,615.1	1,500.1	1,115.1	2,875.3	2,820.5	929.8	699.6	583.6	28.8	478.9	54.8	1,306.0
IV	2,692.9	1,577.2	1,115.7	2,887.6	2,831.5	935.5	706.6	583.2	28.0	476.1	56.1	1,317.3
2018: I	2,719.5	1,597.6	1,121.9	2,933.9	2,875.7	960.8	713.7	590.3	27.6	477.8	58.2	1,343.6
II	2,747.8	1,606.5	1,141.2	2,965.8	2,905.4	969.1	724.5	602.6	25.5	475.8	60.4	1,352.4
III	2,772.2	1,616.2	1,156.0	2,997.2	2,935.6	977.8	739.9	607.8	24.7	474.5	61.6	1,367.4
IV [p]	2,825.0	1,637.2	1,187.8	3,026.7	2,964.1	991.8	759.8	604.7	24.1	470.5	62.6	1,381.1

[1] Includes Veterans' benefits, not shown seperately.
[2] Includes old-age, survivors, and disability insurance benefits that are distributed from the federal old-age and survivors insurance trust fund and the disability insurance trust fund.
[3] Includes hospital and supplementary medical insurance benefits that are distributed from the federal hospital insurance trust fund and the supplementary medical insurance trust fund.

Source: Department of Commerce (Bureau of Economic Analysis).

TABLE B-17. Disposition of personal income, 1968–2018

[Billions of dollars, except as noted; quarterly data at seasonally adjusted annual rates]

Year or quarter	Personal income	Less: Personal current taxes	Equals: Disposable personal income	Less: Personal outlays				Equals: Personal saving	Percent of disposable personal income [2]		
				Total	Personal consumption expenditures	Personal interest payments [1]	Personal current transfer payments		Personal outlays		Personal saving
									Total	Personal consumption expenditures	
1968	730.9	87.0	643.9	571.0	556.9	12.1	2.0	72.9	88.7	86.5	11.3
1969	800.3	104.5	695.8	619.8	603.6	13.9	2.2	76.1	89.1	86.7	10.9
1970	865.0	103.1	762.0	664.4	646.7	15.1	2.6	97.6	87.2	84.9	12.8
1971	932.8	101.7	831.1	719.2	699.9	16.4	2.8	111.9	86.5	84.2	13.5
1972	1,024.5	123.6	900.8	789.3	768.2	18.0	3.2	111.5	87.6	85.3	12.4
1973	1,140.8	132.4	1,008.4	872.6	849.6	19.6	3.4	135.8	86.5	84.3	13.5
1974	1,251.8	151.0	1,100.8	954.5	930.2	20.9	3.4	146.3	86.7	84.5	13.3
1975	1,369.4	147.6	1,221.8	1,057.8	1,030.5	23.4	3.8	164.0	86.6	84.3	13.4
1976	1,502.6	172.7	1,330.0	1,175.6	1,147.7	23.5	4.4	154.4	88.4	86.3	11.6
1977	1,659.2	197.9	1,461.4	1,305.4	1,274.0	26.6	4.8	155.9	89.3	87.2	10.7
1978	1,863.7	229.6	1,634.1	1,459.0	1,422.3	31.3	5.4	175.1	89.3	87.0	10.7
1979	2,082.7	268.9	1,813.8	1,627.0	1,585.4	35.5	6.0	186.8	89.7	87.4	10.3
1980	2,323.6	299.5	2,024.1	1,800.1	1,750.7	42.5	6.9	224.1	88.9	86.5	11.1
1981	2,605.1	345.8	2,259.3	1,993.9	1,934.0	48.4	11.5	265.5	88.3	85.6	11.8
1982	2,791.6	354.7	2,436.9	2,143.5	2,071.3	58.5	13.8	293.3	88.0	85.0	12.0
1983	2,981.1	352.9	2,628.2	2,364.2	2,281.6	67.4	15.1	264.0	90.0	86.8	10.0
1984	3,292.7	377.9	2,914.8	2,584.5	2,492.3	75.0	17.1	330.3	88.7	85.5	11.3
1985	3,524.9	417.8	3,107.1	2,822.1	2,712.8	90.6	18.8	284.9	90.8	87.3	9.2
1986	3,733.1	437.8	3,295.3	3,004.7	2,886.3	97.3	21.1	290.6	91.2	87.6	8.8
1987	3,961.6	489.6	3,472.0	3,196.6	3,076.3	97.1	23.2	275.4	92.1	88.6	7.9
1988	4,283.4	505.9	3,777.5	3,457.0	3,330.0	101.3	25.6	320.5	91.5	88.2	8.5
1989	4,625.6	567.7	4,057.8	3,717.9	3,576.8	113.1	28.0	340.0	91.6	88.1	8.4
1990	4,913.8	594.7	4,319.1	3,958.0	3,809.0	118.4	30.6	361.1	91.6	88.2	8.4
1991	5,084.9	588.9	4,496.0	4,100.0	3,943.4	119.9	36.7	396.0	91.2	87.7	8.8
1992	5,420.9	612.8	4,808.1	4,354.2	4,197.6	116.1	40.5	453.9	90.6	87.3	9.4
1993	5,657.9	648.8	5,009.2	4,611.5	4,452.0	113.9	45.6	397.7	92.1	88.9	7.9
1994	5,947.1	693.1	5,254.0	4,890.6	4,721.0	119.9	49.8	363.4	93.1	89.9	6.9
1995	6,291.4	748.4	5,543.0	5,155.9	4,962.6	140.4	52.9	387.1	93.0	89.5	7.0
1996	6,678.5	837.1	5,841.4	5,459.2	5,244.6	157.0	57.6	382.3	93.5	89.8	6.5
1997	7,092.5	931.8	6,160.7	5,770.4	5,536.8	169.7	63.9	390.3	93.7	89.9	6.3
1998	7,606.7	1,032.4	6,574.2	6,127.7	5,877.2	180.9	69.5	446.5	93.2	89.4	6.8
1999	8,001.9	1,111.9	6,890.0	6,540.6	6,279.1	187.5	74.1	349.4	94.9	91.1	5.1
2000	8,652.6	1,236.3	7,416.3	7,058.0	6,762.1	214.8	81.0	358.3	95.2	91.2	4.8
2001	9,005.6	1,239.0	7,766.6	7,374.9	7,065.6	220.0	89.3	391.6	95.0	91.0	5.0
2002	9,159.0	1,052.2	8,106.8	7,633.1	7,342.7	195.7	94.7	473.7	94.2	90.6	5.8
2003	9,487.5	1,003.5	8,484.0	8,012.5	7,723.1	190.9	98.5	471.5	94.4	91.0	5.6
2004	10,035.1	1,048.7	8,986.4	8,522.6	8,212.7	202.2	107.7	463.8	94.8	91.4	5.2
2005	10,598.2	1,212.4	9,385.8	9,089.1	8,747.1	230.5	111.5	296.7	96.8	93.2	3.2
2006	11,381.7	1,356.8	10,024.9	9,639.3	9,260.3	258.4	120.5	385.6	96.2	92.4	3.8
2007	12,007.8	1,492.2	10,515.6	10,123.9	9,706.4	284.6	132.9	391.6	96.3	92.3	3.7
2008	12,442.2	1,507.2	10,935.0	10,390.1	9,976.3	268.8	144.9	544.9	95.0	91.2	5.0
2009	12,059.1	1,152.0	10,907.1	10,240.6	9,842.2	254.0	144.3	666.5	93.9	90.2	6.1
2010	12,551.6	1,237.3	11,314.3	10,573.5	10,185.8	242.8	144.8	740.9	93.5	90.0	6.5
2011	13,326.8	1,453.2	11,873.6	11,023.7	10,641.1	232.1	150.6	849.8	92.8	89.6	7.2
2012	14,010.1	1,508.9	12,501.2	11,393.6	11,006.8	232.4	154.4	1,107.6	91.1	88.0	8.9
2013	14,181.1	1,675.8	12,505.3	11,703.9	11,317.2	229.5	157.2	801.4	93.6	90.5	6.4
2014	14,991.8	1,785.4	13,206.4	12,236.1	11,824.0	241.6	170.4	970.3	92.7	89.5	7.3
2015	15,719.5	1,935.2	13,784.3	12,740.1	12,294.5	260.9	184.7	1,044.2	92.4	89.2	7.6
2016	16,125.1	1,954.3	14,170.9	13,222.7	12,766.9	269.2	186.5	948.2	93.3	90.1	6.7
2017	16,830.9	2,034.6	14,796.3	13,809.5	13,321.4	293.9	194.2	986.8	93.3	90.0	6.7
2018 ᵖ	17,581.4	2,050.4	15,531.0	14,487.6	13,951.6	334.0	202.1	1,043.4	93.3	89.8	6.7
2015: I	15,471.3	1,900.1	13,571.2	12,529.3	12,095.6	252.7	181.1	1,041.9	92.3	89.1	7.7
II	15,681.7	1,940.0	13,741.7	12,700.1	12,256.7	259.1	184.3	1,041.6	92.4	89.2	7.6
III	15,842.9	1,943.7	13,899.3	12,830.8	12,380.7	263.8	186.2	1,068.5	92.3	89.1	7.7
IV	15,882.1	1,957.1	13,925.0	12,900.3	12,445.1	268.0	187.2	1,024.7	92.6	89.4	7.4
2016: I	15,946.5	1,919.9	14,026.7	12,979.1	12,526.5	263.4	189.1	1,047.6	92.5	89.3	7.5
II	16,031.6	1,944.2	14,087.4	13,155.8	12,706.5	267.1	182.1	931.6	93.4	90.2	6.6
III	16,170.6	1,968.7	14,202.0	13,302.2	12,845.2	270.7	186.4	899.7	93.7	90.4	6.3
IV	16,351.8	1,984.3	14,367.5	13,453.6	12,989.4	275.7	188.5	913.9	93.6	90.4	6.4
2017: I	16,604.4	2,004.9	14,599.6	13,584.7	13,114.1	280.6	190.0	1,014.9	93.0	89.8	7.0
II	16,721.2	2,014.2	14,707.0	13,716.7	13,233.2	288.7	194.9	990.2	93.3	90.0	6.7
III	16,895.1	2,048.5	14,846.6	13,853.3	13,359.1	300.0	194.1	993.4	93.3	90.0	6.7
IV	17,103.1	2,070.9	15,032.2	14,083.3	13,579.2	306.1	197.9	948.9	93.7	90.3	6.3
2018: I	17,319.2	2,030.0	15,289.2	14,194.8	13,679.6	314.9	200.3	1,094.3	92.8	89.5	7.2
II	17,466.7	2,035.3	15,431.4	14,403.8	13,875.6	326.4	201.7	1,027.7	93.3	89.9	6.7
III	17,657.3	2,064.9	15,592.4	14,596.3	14,050.5	340.2	205.6	996.0	93.6	90.1	6.4
IV ᵖ	17,882.4	2,071.3	15,811.1	14,755.6	14,200.6	354.4	200.6	1,055.5	93.3	89.8	6.7

[1] Consists of nonmortgage interest paid by households.
[2] Percents based on data in millions of dollars.

Source: Department of Commerce (Bureau of Economic Analysis).

TABLE B–18. Total and per capita disposable personal income and personal consumption expenditures, and per capita gross domestic product, in current and real dollars, 1968–2018

[Quarterly data at seasonally adjusted annual rates, except as noted]

Year or quarter	Disposable personal income				Personal consumption expenditures				Gross domestic product per capita (dollars)		Population (thousands)[1]
	Total (billions of dollars)		Per capita (dollars)		Total (billions of dollars)		Per capita (dollars)				
	Current dollars	Chained (2012) dollars	Current dollars	Chained (2012) dollars	Current dollars	Chained (2012) dollars	Current dollars	Chained (2012) dollars	Current dollars	Chained (2012) dollars	
1968	643.9	3,362.1	3,208	16,748	556.9	2,907.5	2,774	14,483	4,686	23,873	200,745
1969	695.8	3,476.5	3,432	17,148	603.6	3,015.9	2,977	14,876	5,019	24,377	202,736
1970	762.0	3,637.0	3,715	17,734	646.7	3,086.9	3,153	15,051	5,233	24,142	205,089
1971	831.1	3,805.2	4,002	18,321	699.9	3,204.8	3,370	15,430	5,609	24,625	207,692
1972	900.8	3,988.4	4,291	18,999	768.2	3,401.0	3,659	16,201	6,093	25,644	209,924
1973	1,008.4	4,236.5	4,758	19,989	849.6	3,569.4	4,009	16,841	6,725	26,834	211,939
1974	1,100.8	4,188.7	5,146	19,583	930.2	3,539.5	4,349	16,547	7,224	26,445	213,898
1975	1,221.8	4,291.4	5,657	19,869	1,030.5	3,619.7	4,771	16,759	7,801	26,136	215,981
1976	1,330.0	4,428.5	6,098	20,306	1,147.7	3,821.5	5,262	17,523	8,590	27,278	218,086
1977	1,461.4	4,568.8	6,634	20,740	1,274.0	3,983.0	5,783	18,081	9,450	28,254	220,289
1978	1,634.1	4,776.4	7,340	21,455	1,422.3	4,157.3	6,388	18,674	10,563	29,505	222,629
1979	1,813.8	4,869.1	8,057	21,630	1,585.4	4,256.1	7,043	18,907	11,672	30,104	225,106
1980	2,024.1	4,905.6	8,888	21,542	1,750.7	4,242.8	7,688	18,631	12,547	29,681	227,726
1981	2,259.3	5,025.4	9,823	21,849	1,934.0	4,301.6	8,408	18,702	13,943	30,132	230,008
1982	2,436.9	5,135.0	10,494	22,113	2,071.3	4,364.6	8,919	18,795	14,399	29,308	232,218
1983	2,628.2	5,312.2	11,216	22,669	2,281.6	4,611.7	9,737	19,680	15,508	30,374	234,333
1984	2,914.8	5,677.1	12,330	24,016	2,492.3	4,854.3	10,543	20,535	17,080	32,289	236,394
1985	3,107.1	5,847.6	13,027	24,518	2,712.8	5,105.6	11,374	21,407	18,192	33,337	238,506
1986	3,295.3	6,069.8	13,691	25,219	2,886.3	5,316.4	11,992	22,089	19,028	34,179	240,683
1987	3,472.0	6,204.1	14,297	25,548	3,076.3	5,496.9	12,668	22,636	19,993	35,047	242,843
1988	3,777.5	6,496.0	15,414	26,508	3,330.0	5,726.5	13,589	23,368	21,368	36,181	245,061
1989	4,057.8	6,686.2	16,403	27,027	3,576.8	5,893.5	14,458	23,823	22,805	37,157	247,387
1990	4,319.1	6,817.4	17,264	27,250	3,809.0	6,012.2	15,225	24,031	23,835	37,435	250,181
1991	4,496.0	6,867.0	17,734	27,086	3,943.4	6,023.0	15,554	23,757	24,290	36,900	253,530
1992	4,808.1	7,152.9	18,714	27,841	4,197.6	6,244.7	16,338	24,306	25,379	37,696	256,922
1993	5,009.2	7,271.1	19,245	27,935	4,452.0	6,462.2	17,104	24,828	26,350	38,234	260,282
1994	5,254.0	7,470.6	19,943	28,356	4,721.0	6,712.6	17,919	25,479	27,660	39,295	263,455
1995	5,543.0	7,718.9	20,792	28,954	4,962.6	6,910.7	18,615	25,923	28,658	39,875	266,588
1996	5,841.4	7,964.2	21,658	29,528	5,244.6	7,150.5	19,445	26,511	29,932	40,900	269,714
1997	6,160.7	8,255.8	22,570	30,246	5,536.8	7,419.7	20,284	27,183	31,424	42,211	272,958
1998	6,574.2	8,740.4	23,806	31,651	5,877.2	7,813.8	21,283	28,295	32,818	43,593	276,154
1999	6,890.0	9,025.6	24,666	32,312	6,279.1	8,225.4	22,479	29,447	34,478	45,146	279,328
2000	7,416.3	9,479.5	26,262	33,568	6,762.1	8,643.4	23,945	30,607	36,305	46,498	282,398
2001	7,766.6	9,740.1	27,230	34,149	7,065.6	8,861.1	24,772	31,067	37,100	46,497	285,225
2002	8,106.8	10,034.5	28,153	34,848	7,342.7	9,088.7	25,499	31,563	37,980	46,858	287,955
2003	8,484.0	10,301.4	29,192	35,446	7,723.1	9,377.5	26,574	32,267	39,426	47,756	290,626
2004	8,986.4	10,645.9	30,643	36,302	8,212.7	9,729.3	28,004	33,176	41,648	49,125	293,262
2005	9,385.8	10,811.6	31,710	36,527	8,747.1	10,075.9	29,552	34,041	44,044	50,381	295,993
2006	10,024.9	11,241.9	33,549	37,621	9,260.3	10,384.5	30,990	34,752	46,231	51,330	298,818
2007	10,515.6	11,500.3	34,855	38,119	9,706.4	10,615.3	32,173	35,186	47,902	51,794	301,696
2008	10,935.0	11,610.8	35,906	38,125	9,976.3	10,592.8	32,758	34,783	48,311	51,240	304,543
2009	10,907.1	11,591.7	35,500	37,728	9,842.2	10,460.0	32,034	34,045	47,028	49,501	307,240
2010	11,314.3	11,822.1	36,524	38,163	10,185.8	10,643.0	32,881	34,357	48,396	50,354	309,780
2011	11,873.6	12,099.8	38,052	38,777	10,641.1	10,843.8	34,102	34,752	49,811	50,766	312,033
2012	12,501.2	12,501.2	39,780	39,780	11,006.8	11,006.8	35,025	35,025	51,541	51,541	314,255
2013	12,505.3	12,339.1	39,521	38,996	11,317.2	11,166.9	35,766	35,291	53,046	52,131	316,421
2014	13,206.4	12,838.1	41,436	40,281	11,824.0	11,494.3	37,099	36,064	54,976	53,025	318,717
2015	13,784.3	13,366.5	42,938	41,637	12,294.5	11,921.9	38,298	37,137	56,753	54,160	321,026
2016	14,170.9	13,595.2	43,830	42,049	12,766.9	12,248.2	39,487	37,883	57,860	54,619	323,317
2017	14,796.3	13,949.2	45,470	42,866	13,321.4	12,558.7	40,937	38,593	59,880	55,471	325,410
2018 ᵖ	15,531.0	14,349.9	47,432	43,825	13,951.6	12,890.6	42,609	39,368	62,610	56,717	327,436
2015: I	13,571.2	13,226.6	42,389	41,313	12,095.6	11,788.4	37,780	36,821	56,130	53,895	320,157
II	13,741.7	13,327.8	42,852	41,561	12,256.7	11,887.5	38,221	37,069	56,820	54,250	320,683
III	13,899.3	13,440.4	43,257	41,829	12,380.7	11,972.0	38,531	37,259	57,050	54,273	321,315
IV	13,925.0	13,471.4	43,253	41,843	12,445.1	12,039.7	38,656	37,396	57,010	54,221	321,947
2016: I	14,026.7	13,562.3	43,497	42,057	12,526.5	12,111.8	38,845	37,559	57,087	54,340	322,476
II	14,087.4	13,541.5	43,614	41,924	12,706.5	12,214.1	39,339	37,815	57,712	54,559	322,998
III	14,202.0	13,592.9	43,887	42,005	12,845.2	12,294.3	39,694	37,992	58,094	54,711	323,606
IV	14,367.5	13,685.4	44,318	42,214	12,989.4	12,372.7	40,068	38,165	58,544	54,858	324,187
2017: I	14,599.6	13,835.3	44,970	42,616	13,114.1	12,427.6	40,395	38,280	59,026	55,023	324,648
II	14,707.0	13,909.8	45,237	42,785	13,233.2	12,515.9	40,704	38,498	59,547	55,352	325,107
III	14,846.6	13,986.2	45,588	42,946	13,359.1	12,584.9	41,021	38,643	60,148	55,642	325,667
IV	15,032.2	14,065.9	46,080	43,118	13,579.2	12,706.4	41,626	38,951	60,793	55,864	326,218
2018: I	15,289.2	14,219.8	46,803	43,530	13,679.6	12,722.8	41,876	38,947	61,350	56,093	326,670
II	15,431.4	14,282.0	47,171	43,657	13,875.6	12,842.0	42,415	39,256	62,395	56,586	327,138
III	15,592.4	14,374.8	47,582	43,866	14,050.5	12,953.3	42,876	39,528	63,040	56,958	327,697
IV ᵖ	15,811.1	14,523.6	48,170	44,247	14,200.6	13,044.2	43,263	39,740	63,647	57,229	328,237

[1] Population of the United States including Armed Forces overseas. Annual data are averages of quarterly data. Quarterly data are averages for the period.
Source: Department of Commerce (Bureau of Economic Analysis and Bureau of the Census).

National Income or Expenditure

TABLE B-19. Gross saving and investment, 1968–2018

[Billions of dollars, except as noted; quarterly data at seasonally adjusted annual rates]

Year or quarter	Gross saving								Consumption of fixed capital		
	Total gross saving	Net saving									
		Total net saving	Net private saving			Net government saving			Total	Private	Government
			Total	Personal saving	Undistributed corporate profits [1]	Total	Federal	State and local			
1968	214.6	101.2	111.5	72.9	38.6	−10.3	−13.8	3.5	113.4	80.6	32.8
1969	233.1	108.2	110.3	76.1	34.2	−2.0	−5.1	3.1	124.9	89.4	35.5
1970	228.2	91.4	124.8	97.6	27.2	−33.4	−34.8	1.4	136.8	98.3	38.6
1971	246.1	97.2	149.4	111.9	37.5	−52.2	−50.9	−1.3	148.9	107.6	41.3
1972	277.6	116.6	159.6	111.5	48.0	−42.9	−49.0	6.1	161.0	117.5	43.5
1973	335.3	156.6	189.3	135.8	53.5	−32.7	−38.3	5.6	178.7	131.5	47.2
1974	349.2	142.3	186.0	146.3	39.7	−43.7	−41.3	−2.3	206.9	153.2	53.7
1975	348.1	109.6	218.3	164.0	54.3	−108.7	−97.9	−10.7	238.5	178.8	59.7
1976	399.3	139.1	224.4	154.4	70.0	−85.3	−80.9	−4.4	260.2	196.5	63.7
1977	459.4	169.6	242.5	155.9	86.6	−72.9	−73.4	.5	289.8	221.1	68.7
1978	548.0	220.8	278.0	175.1	102.9	−57.2	−62.0	4.9	327.2	252.1	75.1
1979	613.5	239.6	288.2	186.8	101.4	−48.6	−47.4	−1.2	373.9	290.7	83.1
1980	630.1	201.7	296.4	224.1	72.3	−94.7	−88.8	−5.9	428.4	335.0	93.5
1981	743.9	256.6	354.9	265.5	89.4	−98.2	−88.1	−10.2	487.2	381.9	105.3
1982	725.8	188.9	379.0	293.3	85.6	−190.1	−167.4	−22.8	537.0	420.4	116.6
1983	716.7	154.1	379.7	264.0	115.7	−225.6	−207.2	−18.4	562.6	438.8	123.8
1984	881.6	283.2	479.9	330.3	149.5	−196.7	−196.5	−.2	598.4	463.5	134.9
1985	881.0	240.8	442.5	284.9	157.5	−201.7	−199.2	−2.4	640.1	496.4	143.7
1986	864.5	179.2	399.1	290.6	108.5	−219.9	−215.9	−4.0	685.3	531.6	153.7
1987	948.9	218.5	398.6	275.4	123.2	−180.1	−165.7	−14.4	730.4	566.3	164.1
1988	1,076.6	292.1	463.4	320.5	142.9	−171.3	−160.0	−11.3	784.5	607.9	176.6
1989	1,109.8	271.5	450.2	340.0	110.3	−178.7	−159.4	−19.3	838.3	649.6	188.6
1990	1,113.4	224.8	464.4	361.1	103.2	−239.5	−203.3	−36.2	888.5	688.4	200.1
1991	1,153.4	221.0	529.5	396.0	133.5	−308.5	−248.4	−60.1	932.4	721.5	210.9
1992	1,147.6	187.4	592.8	453.9	139.0	−405.5	−334.5	−71.0	960.2	742.9	217.4
1993	1,163.4	159.9	545.9	397.7	148.2	−386.0	−313.5	−72.5	1,003.5	778.2	225.3
1994	1,295.1	239.5	559.0	363.4	195.7	−319.6	−255.6	−63.9	1,055.6	822.5	233.1
1995	1,426.3	303.9	616.5	387.1	229.4	−312.5	−242.1	−70.4	1,122.4	880.7	241.7
1996	1,578.9	403.6	636.8	382.3	254.5	−233.2	−179.4	−53.8	1,175.3	929.1	246.2
1997	1,780.5	541.2	675.1	390.3	284.9	−133.9	−92.0	−42.0	1,239.3	987.8	251.6
1998	1,930.6	620.8	649.5	446.5	203.0	−28.7	1.4	−30.1	1,309.7	1,052.2	257.6
1999	2,010.3	611.4	583.4	349.4	234.1	28.0	66.9	−38.9	1,398.9	1,132.2	266.7
2000	2,127.3	616.1	501.2	358.3	142.9	114.8	155.5	−40.6	1,511.2	1,231.5	279.7
2001	2,076.9	477.4	582.4	391.6	190.8	−105.0	14.0	−119.0	1,599.5	1,311.7	287.8
2002	2,003.6	345.6	799.9	473.7	326.2	−454.4	−271.5	−182.9	1,658.0	1,361.8	296.2
2003	1,991.7	272.6	858.0	471.5	386.5	−585.4	−404.1	−181.3	1,719.1	1,411.9	307.1
2004	2,164.3	342.5	892.4	463.8	428.6	−549.9	−400.9	−149.0	1,821.8	1,497.1	324.7
2005	2,365.8	394.8	803.5	296.7	506.8	−408.7	−305.9	−102.8	1,971.0	1,622.6	348.4
2006	2,657.9	533.8	846.4	385.6	460.8	−312.6	−227.6	−85.0	2,124.1	1,751.8	372.3
2007	2,536.6	283.8	679.2	391.6	287.6	−395.4	−266.1	−129.3	2,252.8	1,852.5	400.3
2008	2,241.2	−117.7	734.3	544.9	189.4	−852.0	−631.1	−220.9	2,358.8	1,931.8	427.0
2009	2,008.3	−363.2	1,227.1	666.5	560.6	−1,590.3	−1,248.9	−341.3	2,371.5	1,928.7	442.8
2010	2,312.2	−78.7	1,553.9	740.9	813.0	−1,632.6	−1,325.1	−307.5	2,390.9	1,933.8	457.2
2011	2,556.9	82.4	1,599.4	849.8	749.6	−1,517.1	−1,242.0	−275.1	2,474.5	1,997.3	477.2
2012	3,036.0	460.0	1,821.5	1,107.6	713.9	−1,361.4	−1,078.6	−282.8	2,576.0	2,082.4	493.6
2013	3,218.2	537.0	1,440.3	801.4	638.9	−903.3	−637.9	−265.4	2,681.2	2,176.6	504.6
2014	3,564.2	747.2	1,585.7	970.3	615.4	−838.5	−601.8	−236.7	2,817.0	2,300.6	516.3
2015	3,664.4	746.9	1,539.4	1,044.2	495.2	−792.5	−568.9	−223.6	2,917.5	2,395.3	522.2
2016	3,482.5	492.0	1,402.9	948.2	454.7	−910.9	−665.1	−245.8	2,990.5	2,463.5	527.0
2017	3,681.8	565.6	1,520.1	986.8	533.3	−954.5	−695.4	−259.1	3,116.2	2,574.6	541.5
2018 p	....	....	....	1,043.4	....	....	....	....	3,274.0	2,712.7	561.3
2015: I	3,715.1	828.7	1,610.2	1,041.9	568.2	−781.5	−551.6	−229.8	2,886.4	2,366.0	520.4
II	3,691.7	784.1	1,593.4	1,041.6	551.7	−809.3	−571.6	−237.7	2,907.6	2,385.9	521.8
III	3,639.7	708.8	1,576.2	1,068.5	507.7	−867.4	−611.0	−256.4	2,930.9	2,407.4	523.5
IV	3,610.9	665.9	1,377.7	1,024.7	353.0	−711.8	−541.3	−170.5	2,945.0	2,421.8	523.2
2016: I	3,543.8	590.2	1,478.2	1,047.6	430.6	−888.0	−638.0	−250.0	2,953.5	2,431.4	522.2
II	3,448.4	468.9	1,382.9	931.6	451.3	−914.0	−668.8	−245.2	2,979.6	2,453.5	526.1
III	3,421.0	419.6	1,335.0	899.7	435.3	−915.4	−674.9	−240.5	3,001.5	2,473.5	527.9
IV	3,516.6	489.2	1,415.4	913.9	501.5	−926.3	−678.6	−247.7	3,027.5	2,495.7	531.8
2017: I	3,648.2	583.3	1,505.0	1,014.9	490.2	−921.8	−655.9	−265.8	3,064.9	2,529.3	535.7
II	3,659.3	558.3	1,490.6	990.2	500.4	−932.4	−661.5	−270.9	3,101.1	2,561.9	539.2
III	3,733.3	598.6	1,513.8	993.4	520.5	−915.3	−660.5	−254.7	3,134.8	2,590.9	543.8
IV	3,686.3	522.4	1,570.9	948.9	622.0	−1,048.5	−803.6	−244.9	3,163.9	2,616.4	547.5
2018: I	3,849.6	646.2	1,846.4	1,094.3	752.1	−1,200.2	−969.9	−230.4	3,203.4	2,651.1	552.3
II	3,829.9	576.1	1,812.2	1,027.7	784.5	−1,236.1	−993.7	−242.4	3,253.8	2,694.5	559.3
III	3,927.9	630.2	1,822.3	996.0	826.2	−1,192.1	−960.6	−231.5	3,297.7	2,733.4	564.3
IV p	....	....	....	1,055.5	....	....	....	....	3,341.1	2,771.9	569.2

[1] With inventory valuation and capital consumption adjustments.

See next page for continuation of table.

TABLE B-19. Gross saving and investment, 1968-2018—*Continued*

[Billions of dollars, except as noted; quarterly data at seasonally adjusted annual rates]

Year or quarter	Gross domestic investment, capital account transactions, and net lending, NIPA [2]						Statistical discrepancy	Addenda:						
	Gross domestic investment				Capital account transactions (net) [3]	Net lending or net borrowing (−), NIPA [2,4]		Gross private saving	Gross government saving			Net domestic investment	Gross saving as a percent of gross national income	Net saving as a percent of gross national income
	Total	Total	Gross private domestic investment	Gross government investment					Total	Federal	State and local			
1968	217.7	216.2	156.9	59.2	....	1.5	3.1	192.1	22.5	10.4	12.1	102.8	22.7	10.7
1969	234.7	233.1	173.6	59.5	0.0	1.6	1.6	199.7	33.4	20.7	12.8	108.2	22.8	10.6
1970	233.6	229.8	170.0	59.8	.0	3.7	5.3	223.0	5.2	−7.2	12.4	93.0	21.2	8.5
1971	255.6	255.3	196.8	58.5	.0	.3	9.5	257.0	−10.9	−21.8	10.9	106.4	21.2	8.4
1972	284.8	288.8	228.1	60.7	.0	−4.1	7.2	277.1	0.6	−18.8	19.4	127.8	21.7	9.1
1973	341.4	332.6	266.9	65.6	.0	8.8	6.1	320.8	14.5	−6.0	20.4	153.9	23.4	10.9
1974	356.6	350.7	274.5	76.2	.0	5.9	7.4	339.1	10.1	−6.0	16.0	143.8	22.5	9.2
1975	361.5	341.7	257.3	84.4	.1	19.8	13.3	397.1	−48.9	−59.2	10.3	103.1	20.7	6.5
1976	420.0	412.9	323.2	89.6	.1	7.0	20.7	420.9	−21.6	−39.2	17.6	152.6	21.4	7.4
1977	478.9	489.8	396.6	93.2	.1	−11.0	19.4	463.6	−4.2	−28.2	24.0	199.9	22.1	8.1
1978	571.3	583.9	478.4	105.6	.1	−12.7	23.3	530.1	17.9	−12.4	30.3	256.7	23.3	9.4
1979	658.6	659.8	539.7	120.1	.1	−1.3	45.1	579.0	34.6	7.2	27.3	285.9	23.5	9.2
1980	674.6	666.0	530.1	135.9	.1	8.4	44.4	631.4	−1.2	−28.4	27.1	237.6	22.1	7.1
1981	781.9	778.6	631.2	147.3	.1	3.3	38.1	736.8	7.1	−20.6	27.6	291.3	23.2	8.0
1982	734.7	738.0	581.0	156.9	.1	−3.4	8.8	799.4	−73.5	−92.0	18.4	201.0	21.5	5.6
1983	773.6	808.7	637.5	171.2	.1	−35.2	57.0	818.5	−101.8	−126.1	24.3	246.1	19.8	4.3
1984	923.2	1,013.3	820.1	193.2	.1	−90.2	41.6	943.4	−61.8	−105.9	44.1	414.9	21.9	7.0
1985	935.2	1,049.5	829.7	219.9	.1	−114.5	54.3	938.9	−57.9	−102.3	44.4	409.4	20.4	5.6
1986	944.6	1,087.2	849.1	238.1	.1	−142.8	80.1	930.7	−66.2	−112.4	46.2	401.9	19.1	4.0
1987	992.7	1,146.8	892.2	254.6	.1	−154.2	43.8	964.9	−16.0	−55.6	39.6	416.4	19.7	4.5
1988	1,079.6	1,195.4	937.0	258.4	.1	−115.9	3.0	1,071.3	5.3	−41.0	46.4	410.9	20.5	5.6
1989	1,177.8	1,270.1	999.7	270.4	.3	−92.7	68.0	1,099.9	9.9	−32.5	42.4	431.9	19.8	4.9
1990	1,208.9	1,283.8	993.4	290.4	7.4	−82.3	95.5	1,152.8	−39.4	−69.8	30.4	395.3	18.9	3.8
1991	1,246.3	1,238.4	944.3	294.1	5.3	2.6	93.0	1,250.9	−97.6	−108.3	10.8	306.0	18.9	3.6
1992	1,263.6	1,309.1	1,013.0	296.1	−1.3	−44.3	115.9	1,335.7	−188.1	−191.2	3.1	348.9	17.8	2.9
1993	1,319.3	1,398.7	1,106.8	291.9	.9	−80.2	156.0	1,324.1	−160.7	−166.5	5.8	395.2	17.3	2.4
1994	1,435.1	1,550.7	1,256.5	294.2	1.3	−116.9	140.0	1,381.6	−86.4	−105.3	18.8	495.0	18.1	3.3
1995	1,519.3	1,625.2	1,317.5	307.7	.4	−106.3	93.0	1,497.2	−70.9	−88.6	17.7	502.8	18.8	4.0
1996	1,637.0	1,752.0	1,432.1	320.0	.2	−115.2	58.1	1,565.9	13.0	−25.7	38.7	576.7	19.6	5.0
1997	1,792.1	1,922.2	1,595.6	326.6	.5	−130.6	11.6	1,662.9	117.6	62.3	55.3	682.9	20.7	6.3
1998	1,875.3	2,080.7	1,736.7	344.0	.2	−205.6	−55.2	1,701.7	228.9	156.8	72.1	770.9	21.1	6.8
1999	1,977.2	2,255.5	1,887.1	368.5	4.5	−282.8	−33.2	1,715.6	294.7	225.0	69.7	856.6	20.7	6.3
2000	2,030.8	2,427.3	2,038.4	388.9	.3	−396.8	−96.5	1,732.7	394.6	318.6	76.0	916.0	20.5	5.9
2001	1,963.8	2,346.7	1,934.8	411.9	−12.9	−370.0	−113.1	1,894.1	182.8	178.5	4.4	747.2	19.3	4.4
2002	1,930.9	2,374.1	1,930.4	443.7	.5	−443.7	−72.7	2,161.7	−158.2	−104.7	−53.5	716.1	18.1	3.1
2003	1,978.1	2,491.3	2,027.1	464.2	2.1	−515.3	−13.7	2,270.0	−278.2	−231.8	−46.4	772.2	17.3	2.4
2004	2,142.2	2,767.5	2,281.3	486.2	−2.8	−622.4	−22.1	2,389.5	−225.2	−220.4	−4.8	945.6	17.6	2.8
2005	2,310.7	3,048.0	2,534.7	513.3	−12.9	−724.5	−55.1	2,426.1	−60.3	−115.4	55.1	1,077.0	18.0	3.0
2006	2,450.0	3,251.8	2,701.0	550.9	2.1	−803.9	−207.9	2,598.2	59.7	−26.3	86.0	1,127.7	18.9	3.8
2007	2,554.5	3,265.0	2,673.0	592.0	−.1	−710.7	17.7	2,531.7	4.9	−53.3	58.2	1,012.2	17.4	2.0
2008	2,424.0	3,107.2	2,477.6	629.6	−5.4	−677.8	182.9	2,666.2	−425.0	−405.3	−19.7	748.4	15.3	−.8
2009	2,200.5	2,572.6	1,929.7	642.9	.6	−372.7	192.2	3,155.8	−1,147.5	−1,015.3	−132.2	201.1	13.9	−2.5
2010	2,373.7	2,810.0	2,165.5	644.5	.7	−437.4	61.0	3,487.6	−1,175.4	−1,081.3	−94.1	419.1	15.3	−.5
2011	2,503.6	2,969.2	2,332.6	636.6	1.6	−467.2	−53.2	3,596.8	−1,039.9	−987.0	−52.9	494.7	16.1	.5
2012	2,794.7	3,242.8	2,621.8	621.0	−6.5	−441.6	−241.3	3,903.8	−867.8	−817.0	−50.8	666.8	18.2	2.8
2013	3,057.9	3,426.4	2,826.0	600.4	.8	−369.4	−160.3	3,616.9	−398.7	−372.0	−26.6	745.2	18.7	3.1
2014	3,265.2	3,640.8	3,038.9	601.8	.4	−376.0	−299.0	3,886.3	−322.2	−331.8	9.6	823.8	19.7	4.1
2015	3,409.4	3,833.5	3,212.0	621.5	.4	−424.5	−254.9	3,934.6	−270.3	−298.0	27.7	916.0	19.6	4.0
2016	3,355.5	3,801.4	3,169.9	631.5	.5	−446.3	−126.9	3,866.4	−383.9	−394.4	10.5	810.9	18.3	2.6
2017	3,538.6	4,011.2	3,368.0	643.2	3.7	−476.2	−143.2	4,094.7	−412.9	−419.4	6.5	895.0	18.5	2.8
2018 [p]	....	4,330.8	3,652.2	678.7	....	....	....	....	....	....	....	1,056.8	....	....
2015: I	3,396.0	3,822.9	3,216.8	606.1	.4	−427.4	−319.2	3,976.2	−261.0	−280.3	19.2	936.5	20.1	4.5
II	3,458.5	3,852.8	3,225.9	626.9	.4	−394.3	−233.2	3,979.2	−287.5	−300.8	13.3	945.2	19.8	4.2
III	3,402.7	3,860.6	3,229.6	631.0	.4	−458.3	−237.0	3,983.7	−344.0	−339.9	−4.1	929.7	19.4	3.8
IV	3,380.5	3,797.5	3,175.5	622.0	.4	−417.4	−230.4	3,799.5	−188.6	−271.0	82.4	852.5	19.2	3.5
2016: I	3,315.8	3,778.5	3,142.1	636.4	.6	−463.3	−228.0	3,909.6	−365.8	−368.9	3.1	825.0	18.8	3.1
II	3,368.2	3,782.4	3,152.2	630.2	.4	−414.6	−80.2	3,836.4	−387.9	−398.9	10.9	802.8	18.2	2.5
III	3,335.4	3,784.8	3,157.7	627.1	.4	−449.3	−85.2	3,808.6	−387.5	−404.1	16.6	783.3	17.9	2.2
IV	3,402.3	3,859.8	3,227.6	632.2	.4	−457.9	−114.3	3,911.1	−394.5	−405.9	11.4	832.4	18.2	2.5
2017: I	3,453.4	3,915.7	3,278.6	637.1	.4	−462.8	−194.9	4,034.3	−386.1	−382.0	−4.1	850.7	18.6	3.0
II	3,472.6	3,980.2	3,337.9	642.3	.4	−508.0	−186.8	4,052.5	−393.2	−386.5	−6.7	879.1	18.5	2.8
III	3,618.9	4,054.1	3,413.9	640.2	13.2	−448.4	−114.4	4,104.5	−371.4	−383.8	12.4	919.3	18.7	3.0
IV	3,609.7	4,094.6	3,441.4	653.2	.6	−485.5	−76.6	4,187.3	−501.0	−525.3	24.3	930.7	18.3	2.6
2018: I	3,689.7	4,203.6	3,543.8	659.8	.4	−514.3	−159.9	4,497.5	−647.9	−690.0	42.1	1,000.2	18.8	3.2
II	3,831.3	4,255.1	3,579.5	675.6	.4	−424.2	1.4	4,506.7	−676.8	−711.7	34.9	1,001.3	18.5	2.8
III	3,869.6	4,397.2	3,710.7	686.5	−1.8	−525.8	−58.3	4,555.6	−627.8	−676.3	48.6	1,099.5	18.7	3.0
IV [p]	....	4,467.4	3,774.6	692.8	....	....	....	....	....	....	....	1,126.3	....	....

[2] National income and product accounts (NIPA).
[3] Consists of capital transfers and the acquisition and disposal of nonproduced nonfinancial assets.
[4] Prior to 1982, equals the balance on current account, NIPA.

Source: Department of Commerce (Bureau of Economic Analysis).

TABLE B–20. Median money income (in 2017 dollars) and poverty status of families and people, by race, 2009-2017

Race, Hispanic origin, and year	Families [1]					People below poverty level [2]		Median money income (in 2017 dollars) of people 15 years old and over with income [3]			
	Number (millions)	Median money income (in 2017 dollars) [3]	Below poverty level [2]					Males		Females	
			Total		Female householder, no husband present		Number (millions)	Percent	All people	Year-round full-time workers	All people	Year-round full-time workers
			Number (millions)	Percent	Number (millions)	Percent						
TOTAL (all races) [4]												
2009	78.9	$68,819	8.8	11.1	4.4	29.9	43.6	14.3	$36,860	$56,308	$24,002	$42,644
2010 [5]	79.6	67,869	9.4	11.8	4.8	31.7	46.3	15.1	36,286	56,506	23,408	43,310
2011	80.5	66,601	9.5	11.8	4.9	31.2	46.2	15.0	36,030	54,959	23,049	42,255
2012	80.9	66,575	9.5	11.8	4.8	30.9	46.5	15.0	36,265	54,212	23,018	42,806
2013 [6]	81.2	67,262	9.1	11.2	4.6	30.6	45.3	14.5	37,131	53,695	23,255	42,790
2013 [7]	82.3	69,007	9.6	11.7	5.2	32.2	46.3	14.8	37,555	54,195	23,321	42,897
2014	81.7	69,062	9.5	11.6	4.8	30.6	46.7	14.8	37,626	53,332	23,051	42,285
2015	82.2	73,149	8.6	10.4	4.4	28.2	43.1	13.5	38,426	54,059	24,593	43,202
2016	82.9	74,271	8.1	9.8	4.1	26.6	40.6	12.7	39,705	54,623	25,427	44,128
2017	83.1	75,938	7.8	9.3	4.0	25.7	39.7	12.3	40,396	55,834	25,486	44,379
WHITE, non-Hispanic [8]												
2009	54.5	77,126	3.8	7.0	1.7	23.3	18.5	9.4	42,130	82,204	25,127	57,103
2010 [5]	53.8	77,634	3.9	7.2	1.7	24.1	19.3	9.9	41,862	81,951	24,467	56,971
2011	54.2	76,273	4.0	7.3	1.8	23.4	19.2	9.8	41,668	82,392	24,277	57,425
2012	54.0	76,455	3.8	7.1	1.7	23.4	18.9	9.7	41,449	81,863	24,497	57,260
2013 [6]	53.8	76,547	3.7	6.9	1.6	22.6	18.8	9.6	42,289	80,951	25,064	57,140
2013 [7]	54.7	78,663	4.0	7.3	1.9	25.8	19.6	10.0	43,063	83,317	25,015	59,203
2014	53.8	79,453	3.9	7.3	1.7	23.7	19.7	10.1	42,570	82,265	24,880	57,789
2015	53.8	83,320	3.5	6.4	1.6	21.7	17.8	9.1	43,671	84,075	26,518	59,766
2016	54.1	83,834	3.4	6.3	1.6	21.1	17.3	8.8	44,333	86,000	27,065	62,785
2017	53.9	85,852	3.2	6.0	1.4	19.8	17.0	8.7	45,836	87,487	27,116	63,152
BLACK [8]												
2009	9.4	43,990	2.1	22.7	1.5	36.7	9.9	25.8	27,187	45,081	22,299	37,188
2010 [5]	9.6	43,485	2.3	24.1	1.7	38.7	10.7	27.4	26,248	42,504	22,135	38,357
2011	9.7	44,232	2.3	24.2	1.7	39.0	10.9	27.6	25,641	43,990	21,578	38,389
2012	9.8	43,338	2.3	23.7	1.6	37.8	10.9	27.2	26,658	42,588	21,415	37,533
2013 [6]	9.9	43,834	2.3	22.8	1.6	38.5	11.0	27.2	26,198	43,879	21,127	37,292
2013 [7]	9.9	44,153	2.2	22.4	1.7	36.7	10.2	25.2	26,477	42,621	22,206	36,512
2014	9.9	44,724	2.3	22.9	1.6	37.2	10.8	26.2	27,538	42,798	21,730	36,617
2015	9.8	47,369	2.1	21.1	1.5	33.9	10.0	24.1	28,354	43,157	22,363	38,397
2016	10.0	50,427	1.9	19.0	1.3	31.6	9.2	22.0	30,275	42,884	23,326	38,140
2017	10.0	50,597	1.8	18.2	1.3	30.8	9.0	21.2	30,112	43,699	23,639	37,550
ASIAN [8]												
2009	3.6	85,929	.3	9.4	.1	16.9	1.7	12.5	42,754	61,191	27,880	51,112
2010 [5]	3.9	84,748	.4	9.3	.1	21.1	1.9	12.2	40,362	59,158	26,549	47,232
2011	4.2	79,732	.4	9.7	.1	19.1	2.0	12.3	39,687	61,477	24,073	45,233
2012	4.1	83,286	.4	9.4	.1	19.2	1.9	11.7	43,028	64,448	24,960	49,600
2013 [6]	4.4	80,529	.4	8.7	.1	14.9	1.8	10.5	42,322	63,403	26,182	47,511
2013 [7]	4.4	87,265	.4	10.2	.1	25.7	2.3	13.1	45,100	64,525	27,239	49,770
2014	4.5	85,749	.4	8.9	.1	18.9	2.1	12.0	42,392	62,498	26,317	50,316
2015	4.7	93,998	.4	8.0	.1	16.2	2.1	11.4	45,221	66,985	27,452	51,856
2016	4.7	95,509	.3	7.2	.1	19.4	1.9	10.1	47,592	68,680	27,347	52,486
2017	4.9	92,784	.4	7.8	.1	15.5	2.0	10.0	48,842	70,817	28,260	52,227
HISPANIC (any race) [8]												
2009	10.4	45,503	2.4	22.7	1.1	38.8	12.4	25.3	25,490	36,235	18,565	31,935
2010 [5]	11.3	44,280	2.7	24.3	1.3	42.6	13.5	26.5	25,261	35,878	18,356	32,783
2011	11.6	43,758	2.7	22.9	1.3	41.2	13.2	25.3	25,921	35,049	18,382	32,880
2012	12.0	43,602	2.8	23.5	1.3	40.7	13.6	25.6	26,304	34,780	17,890	31,563
2013 [6]	12.1	44,552	2.6	21.6	1.3	40.4	12.7	23.5	26,784	34,729	18,721	32,463
2013 [7]	12.4	43,150	2.9	23.1	1.4	40.5	13.4	24.7	25,508	34,114	17,868	32,854
2014	12.5	46,759	2.7	21.5	1.3	37.9	13.1	23.6	27,648	36,394	18,226	31,953
2015	12.8	48,969	2.5	19.6	1.2	35.5	12.1	21.4	29,085	37,221	19,561	32,755
2016	13.0	52,204	2.3	17.3	1.1	32.7	11.1	19.4	31,168	39,004	20,334	32,726
2017	13.2	53,614	2.2	16.3	1.1	32.7	10.8	18.3	30,691	39,901	20,312	32,439

[1] The term "family" refers to a group of two or more persons related by birth, marriage, or adoption and residing together. Every family must include a reference person.
[2] Poverty thresholds are updated each year to reflect changes in the consumer price index for all urban consumers (CPI-U).
[3] Adjusted by consumer price index research series (CPI-U-RS).
[4] Data for American Indians and Alaska natives, native Hawaiians and other Pacific Islanders, and those reporting two or more races are included in the total but not shown separately.
[5] Reflects implementation of Census 2010-based population controls comparable to succeeding years.
[6] The 2014 Current Population Survey (CPS) Annual Social and Economic Supplement (ASEC) included redesigned income questions, which were implemented to a subsample of the 98,000 addresses using a probability split panel design. These 2013 data are based on the 2014 ASEC sample of 68,000 addresses that received income questions similar to those used in the 2013 ASEC and are consistent with data in earlier years.
[7] These 2013 data are based on the 2014 ASEC sample of 30,000 addresses that received redesigned income questions and are consistent with data in later years.
[8] The CPS allows respondents to choose more than one race. Data shown are for "white alone, non-Hispanic," "black alone," and "Asian alone" race categories. ("Black" is also "black or African American.") Family race and Hispanic origin are based on the reference person.

Note: For details see *Income and Poverty in the United States* in publication Series P–60 on the CPS ASEC.

Source: Department of Commerce (Bureau of the Census).

TABLE B-21. Real farm income, 1954–2018

[Billions of chained (2018) dollars]

Year	Income of farm operators from farming [1]						Production expenses	Net farm income
	Gross farm income					Direct Federal Government payments		
	Total	Value of agricultural sector production						
		Total	Crops [2,3]	Animals and animal products [3]	Farm-related income [4]			
1954	258.9	256.9	109.2	134.0	13.7	1.9	165.2	93.7
1955	250.0	248.3	106.5	127.9	13.9	1.7	165.6	84.4
1956	245.2	241.2	104.2	123.4	13.5	4.0	164.0	81.3
1957	242.7	235.6	95.3	126.7	13.6	7.1	165.4	77.3
1958	265.6	258.2	102.3	141.7	14.2	7.4	175.8	89.8
1959	255.0	250.4	99.4	135.8	15.2	4.6	182.9	72.1
1960	256.2	251.5	104.0	131.9	15.5	4.7	181.7	74.4
1961	266.4	256.5	103.9	136.6	16.1	9.8	187.8	78.5
1962	274.8	263.5	108.1	139.0	16.3	11.3	196.5	78.3
1963	278.3	267.4	115.1	135.3	17.0	10.9	202.7	75.5
1964	267.4	253.6	106.6	129.4	17.6	13.8	201.1	66.3
1965	288.9	273.6	118.1	137.7	17.8	15.3	208.9	80.1
1966	304.7	284.9	110.6	156.1	18.2	19.8	220.4	84.3
1967	296.4	278.3	112.8	146.6	19.0	18.1	224.0	72.4
1968	291.8	272.3	106.5	146.9	18.9	19.5	222.4	69.3
1969	302.6	282.2	105.6	157.3	19.3	20.4	225.9	76.7
1970	299.7	280.8	104.6	156.8	19.4	18.9	226.5	73.2
1971	301.2	286.0	113.6	152.6	19.8	15.2	228.4	72.8
1972	330.7	312.3	120.6	171.6	20.1	18.4	240.3	90.4
1973	435.9	424.4	189.7	213.1	21.6	11.5	284.5	151.4
1974	397.4	395.2	198.8	173.2	23.2	2.1	287.1	110.3
1975	372.1	369.1	186.5	159.1	23.5	3.0	277.7	94.4
1976	361.0	358.4	169.6	163.5	25.2	2.6	290.2	70.8
1977	359.2	353.2	168.9	156.3	28.0	6.0	293.5	65.7
1978	396.3	387.0	174.7	181.6	30.7	9.3	318.6	77.7
1979	429.4	425.5	189.9	202.8	32.7	3.9	351.3	78.1
1980	390.0	386.6	168.1	183.7	34.8	3.4	347.8	42.2
1981	397.0	392.4	188.4	168.1	36.0	4.6	332.9	64.2
1982	369.0	361.2	161.4	158.5	41.2	7.9	315.4	53.6
1983	332.9	312.8	123.0	151.5	38.2	20.1	302.0	30.9
1984	350.8	333.2	162.3	150.4	20.4	17.6	296.5	54.2
1985	326.0	310.4	149.1	139.6	21.7	15.6	268.3	57.7
1986	309.7	286.3	125.6	140.4	20.3	23.4	248.0	61.7
1987	326.1	293.7	124.9	146.7	22.2	32.4	252.5	73.6
1988	332.8	305.7	129.5	147.1	29.1	27.1	258.6	74.1
1989	344.8	325.2	146.7	150.2	28.4	19.6	261.2	83.7
1990	343.1	327.0	144.3	156.2	26.5	16.1	262.8	80.2
1991	322.3	308.5	136.2	146.4	25.8	13.8	254.8	67.5
1992	329.0	314.0	146.1	143.0	24.9	15.0	246.7	82.3
1993	328.6	307.1	132.5	147.4	27.2	21.5	253.7	74.9
1994	339.1	326.8	157.7	140.8	28.3	12.4	256.6	82.5
1995	324.0	312.9	147.4	134.9	30.6	11.2	262.9	61.1
1996	355.9	344.8	174.6	138.9	31.3	11.1	267.0	89.0
1997	353.1	342.0	166.9	142.9	32.2	11.1	277.0	76.1
1998	341.3	323.2	149.8	138.2	35.1	18.2	272.2	69.1
1999	339.9	308.8	134.2	137.7	36.8	31.1	270.9	69.0
2000	341.9	309.1	134.3	140.2	34.5	32.9	270.2	71.7
2001	345.8	314.7	131.5	147.2	36.1	31.0	269.8	75.9
2002	314.3	297.3	133.4	127.4	36.5	16.9	260.9	53.4
2003	346.1	324.0	145.3	140.5	38.3	22.1	264.5	81.6
2004	384.2	367.3	163.0	161.9	42.3	16.9	270.3	113.9
2005	377.2	346.4	144.5	159.9	42.0	30.8	277.7	99.5
2006	355.8	336.5	145.6	146.3	44.6	19.4	285.4	70.4
2007	405.5	391.3	180.4	165.3	45.5	14.2	321.9	83.6
2008	427.1	412.8	203.6	163.3	45.8	14.3	335.7	91.4
2009	391.4	377.2	191.4	139.1	46.7	14.2	319.0	72.3
2010	409.7	395.5	193.2	161.2	41.1	14.2	321.1	88.6
2011	473.3	461.6	224.4	184.3	52.8	11.7	345.4	127.9
2012	496.8	485.1	235.2	186.8	63.1	11.7	390.3	106.5
2013	525.1	513.1	253.6	196.4	63.1	11.9	390.8	134.3
2014	514.6	504.2	219.5	228.4	56.3	10.4	416.2	98.5
2015	464.4	453.0	194.0	204.7	54.3	11.4	379.0	85.5
2016	429.5	415.9	196.7	172.7	46.5	13.5	365.3	64.2
2017	439.7	427.9	194.2	181.5	52.2	11.8	362.5	77.1
2018 p	435.4	421.8	191.2	176.8	53.8	13.6	369.1	66.3

[1] The GDP chain-type price index is used to convert the current-dollar statistics to 2018=100 equivalents.
[2] Crop receipts include proceeds received from commodities placed under Commodity Credit Corporation loans.
[3] The value of production equates to the sum of cash receipts, home consumption, and the value of the change in inventories.
[4] Includes income from forest products sold, the gross imputed rental value of farm dwellings, machine hire and custom work, and other sources of farm income such as commodity insurance indemnities.

Note: Data for 2018 are forecasts.

Source: Department of Agriculture (Economic Research Service).

Labor Market Indicators

Table B–22. Civilian labor force, 1929–2018

[Monthly data seasonally adjusted, except as noted]

Year or month	Civilian noninstitutional population [1]	Civilian labor force				Unemployment	Not in labor force	Civilian labor force participation rate [2]	Civilian employment/ population ratio [3]	Unemployment rate, civilian workers [4]
		Total	Employment							
			Total	Agricultural	Non-agricultural					
	Thousands of persons 14 years of age and over							Percent		
1929		49,180	47,630	10,450	37,180	1,550				3.2
1930		49,820	45,480	10,340	35,140	4,340				8.7
1931		50,420	42,400	10,290	32,110	8,020				15.9
1932		51,000	38,940	10,170	28,770	12,060				23.6
1933		51,590	38,760	10,090	28,670	12,830				24.9
1934		52,230	40,890	9,900	30,990	11,340				21.7
1935		52,870	42,260	10,110	32,150	10,610				20.1
1936		53,440	44,410	10,000	34,410	9,030				16.9
1937		54,000	46,300	9,820	36,480	7,700				14.3
1938		54,610	44,220	9,690	34,530	10,390				19.0
1939		55,230	45,750	9,610	36,140	9,480				17.2
1940	99,840	55,640	47,520	9,540	37,980	8,120	44,200	55.7	47.6	14.6
1941	99,900	55,910	50,350	9,100	41,250	5,560	43,990	56.0	50.4	9.9
1942	98,640	56,410	53,750	9,250	44,500	2,660	42,230	57.2	54.5	4.7
1943	94,640	55,540	54,470	9,080	45,390	1,070	39,100	58.7	57.6	1.9
1944	93,220	54,630	53,960	8,950	45,010	670	38,590	58.6	57.9	1.2
1945	94,090	53,860	52,820	8,580	44,240	1,040	40,230	57.2	56.1	1.9
1946	103,070	57,520	55,250	8,320	46,930	2,270	45,550	55.8	53.6	3.9
1947	106,018	60,168	57,812	8,256	49,557	2,356	45,850	56.8	54.5	3.9
	Thousands of persons 16 years of age and over									
1947	101,827	59,350	57,038	7,890	49,148	2,311	42,477	58.3	56.0	3.9
1948	103,068	60,621	58,343	7,629	50,714	2,276	42,447	58.8	56.6	3.8
1949	103,994	61,286	57,651	7,658	49,993	3,637	42,708	58.9	55.4	5.9
1950	104,995	62,208	58,918	7,160	51,758	3,288	42,787	59.2	56.1	5.3
1951	104,621	62,017	59,961	6,726	53,235	2,055	42,604	59.2	57.3	3.3
1952	105,231	62,138	60,250	6,500	53,749	1,883	43,093	59.0	57.3	3.0
1953	107,056	63,015	61,179	6,260	54,919	1,834	44,041	58.9	57.1	2.9
1954	108,321	63,643	60,109	6,205	53,904	3,532	44,678	58.8	55.5	5.5
1955	109,683	65,023	62,170	6,450	55,722	2,852	44,660	59.3	56.7	4.4
1956	110,954	66,552	63,799	6,283	57,514	2,750	44,402	60.0	57.5	4.1
1957	112,265	66,929	64,071	5,947	58,123	2,859	45,336	59.6	57.1	4.3
1958	113,727	67,639	63,036	5,586	57,450	4,602	46,088	59.5	55.4	6.8
1959	115,329	68,369	64,630	5,565	59,065	3,740	46,960	59.3	56.0	5.5
1960	117,245	69,628	65,778	5,458	60,318	3,852	47,617	59.4	56.1	5.5
1961	118,771	70,459	65,746	5,200	60,546	4,714	48,312	59.3	55.4	6.7
1962	120,153	70,614	66,702	4,944	61,759	3,911	49,539	58.8	55.5	5.5
1963	122,416	71,833	67,762	4,687	63,076	4,070	50,583	58.7	55.4	5.7
1964	124,485	73,091	69,305	4,523	64,782	3,786	51,394	58.7	55.7	5.2
1965	126,513	74,455	71,088	4,361	66,726	3,366	52,058	58.9	56.2	4.5
1966	128,058	75,770	72,895	3,979	68,915	2,875	52,288	59.2	56.9	3.8
1967	129,874	77,347	74,372	3,844	70,527	2,975	52,527	59.6	57.3	3.8
1968	132,028	78,737	75,920	3,817	72,103	2,817	53,291	59.6	57.5	3.6
1969	134,335	80,734	77,902	3,606	74,296	2,832	53,602	60.1	58.0	3.5
1970	137,085	82,771	78,678	3,463	75,215	4,093	54,315	60.4	57.4	4.9
1971	140,216	84,382	79,367	3,394	75,972	5,016	55,834	60.2	56.6	5.9
1972	144,126	87,034	82,153	3,484	78,669	4,882	57,091	60.4	57.0	5.6
1973	147,096	89,429	85,064	3,470	81,594	4,365	57,667	60.8	57.8	4.9
1974	150,120	91,949	86,794	3,515	83,279	5,156	58,171	61.3	57.8	5.6
1975	153,153	93,775	85,846	3,408	82,438	7,929	59,377	61.2	56.1	8.5
1976	156,150	96,158	88,752	3,331	85,421	7,406	59,991	61.6	56.8	7.7
1977	159,033	99,009	92,017	3,283	88,734	6,991	60,025	62.3	57.9	7.1
1978	161,910	102,251	96,048	3,387	92,661	6,202	59,659	63.2	59.3	6.1
1979	164,863	104,962	98,824	3,347	95,477	6,137	59,900	63.7	59.9	5.8
1980	167,745	106,940	99,303	3,364	95,938	7,637	60,806	63.8	59.2	7.1
1981	170,130	108,670	100,397	3,368	97,030	8,273	61,460	63.9	59.0	7.6
1982	172,271	110,204	99,526	3,401	96,125	10,678	62,067	64.0	57.8	9.7
1983	174,215	111,550	100,834	3,383	97,450	10,717	62,665	64.0	57.9	9.6
1984	176,383	113,544	105,005	3,321	101,685	8,539	62,839	64.4	59.5	7.5
1985	178,206	115,461	107,150	3,179	103,971	8,312	62,744	64.8	60.1	7.2
1986	180,587	117,834	109,597	3,163	106,434	8,237	62,752	65.3	60.7	7.0
1987	182,753	119,865	112,440	3,208	109,232	7,425	62,888	65.6	61.5	6.2
1988	184,613	121,669	114,968	3,169	111,800	6,701	62,944	65.9	62.3	5.5
1989	186,393	123,869	117,342	3,199	114,142	6,528	62,523	66.5	63.0	5.3

[1] Not seasonally adjusted.
[2] Civilian labor force as percent of civilian noninstitutional population.
[3] Civilian employment as percent of civilian noninstitutional population.
[4] Unemployed as percent of civilian labor force.

See next page for continuation of table.

TABLE B-22. Civilian labor force, 1929-2018—Continued

[Monthly data seasonally adjusted, except as noted]

Year or month	Civilian noninstitutional population [1]	Civilian labor force				Not in labor force	Civilian labor force participation rate [2]	Civilian employment/ population ratio [3]	Unemployment rate, civilian workers [4]
		Total	Employment		Unemployment				
			Total	Agricultural	Non-agricultural				
	Thousands of persons 16 years of age and over						Percent		
1990	189,164	125,840	118,793	3,223	115,570	7,047	63,324	66.5	62.8	5.6
1991	190,925	126,346	117,718	3,269	114,449	8,628	64,578	66.2	61.7	6.8
1992	192,805	128,105	118,492	3,247	115,245	9,613	64,700	66.4	61.5	7.5
1993	194,838	129,200	120,259	3,115	117,144	8,940	65,638	66.3	61.7	6.9
1994	196,814	131,056	123,060	3,409	119,651	7,996	65,758	66.6	62.5	6.1
1995	198,584	132,304	124,900	3,440	121,460	7,404	66,280	66.6	62.9	5.6
1996	200,591	133,943	126,708	3,443	123,264	7,236	66,647	66.8	63.2	5.4
1997	203,133	136,297	129,558	3,399	126,159	6,739	66,837	67.1	63.8	4.9
1998	205,220	137,673	131,463	3,378	128,085	6,210	67,547	67.1	64.1	4.5
1999	207,753	139,368	133,488	3,281	130,207	5,880	68,385	67.1	64.3	4.2
2000 [5]	212,577	142,583	136,891	2,464	134,427	5,692	69,994	67.1	64.4	4.0
2001	215,092	143,734	136,933	2,299	134,635	6,801	71,359	66.8	63.7	4.7
2002	217,570	144,863	136,485	2,311	134,174	8,378	72,707	66.6	62.7	5.8
2003	221,168	146,510	137,736	2,275	135,461	8,774	74,658	66.2	62.3	6.0
2004	223,357	147,401	139,252	2,232	137,020	8,149	75,956	66.0	62.3	5.5
2005	226,082	149,320	141,730	2,197	139,532	7,591	76,762	66.0	62.7	5.1
2006	228,815	151,428	144,427	2,206	142,221	7,001	77,387	66.2	63.1	4.6
2007	231,867	153,124	146,047	2,095	143,952	7,078	78,743	66.0	63.0	4.6
2008	233,788	154,287	145,362	2,168	143,194	8,924	79,501	66.0	62.2	5.8
2009	235,801	154,142	139,877	2,103	137,775	14,265	81,659	65.4	59.3	9.3
2010	237,830	153,889	139,064	2,206	136,858	14,825	83,941	64.7	58.5	9.6
2011	239,618	153,617	139,869	2,254	137,615	13,747	86,001	64.1	58.4	8.9
2012	243,284	154,975	142,469	2,186	140,283	12,506	88,310	63.7	58.6	8.1
2013	245,679	155,389	143,929	2,130	141,799	11,460	90,290	63.2	58.6	7.4
2014	247,947	155,922	146,305	2,237	144,068	9,617	92,025	62.9	59.0	6.2
2015	250,801	157,130	148,834	2,422	146,411	8,296	93,671	62.7	59.3	5.3
2016	253,538	159,187	151,436	2,460	148,976	7,751	94,351	62.8	59.7	4.9
2017	255,079	160,320	153,337	2,454	150,883	6,982	94,759	62.9	60.1	4.4
2018	257,791	162,075	155,761	2,425	153,336	6,314	95,716	62.9	60.4	3.9
2016: Jan	252,397	158,371	150,622	2,390	148,160	7,749	94,026	62.7	59.7	4.9
Feb	252,577	158,705	150,934	2,454	148,444	7,771	93,872	62.8	59.8	4.9
Mar	252,768	159,079	151,146	2,555	148,375	7,932	93,689	62.9	59.8	5.0
Apr	252,969	158,891	150,963	2,572	148,377	7,928	94,077	62.8	59.7	5.0
May	253,174	158,700	151,074	2,556	148,511	7,626	94,475	62.7	59.7	4.8
June	253,397	158,899	151,104	2,514	148,673	7,795	94,498	62.7	59.6	4.9
July	253,620	159,150	151,450	2,423	149,006	7,700	94,470	62.8	59.7	4.8
Aug	253,854	159,582	151,766	2,564	149,285	7,817	94,272	62.9	59.8	4.9
Sept	254,091	159,810	151,877	2,432	149,514	7,933	94,281	62.9	59.8	5.0
Oct	254,321	159,768	151,949	2,330	149,610	7,819	94,553	62.8	59.7	4.9
Nov	254,540	159,629	152,150	2,394	149,839	7,480	94,911	62.7	59.8	4.7
Dec	254,742	159,779	152,276	2,323	149,947	7,503	94,963	62.7	59.8	4.7
2017: Jan	254,082	159,693	152,128	2,411	149,709	7,565	94,389	62.9	59.9	4.7
Feb	254,246	159,854	152,417	2,437	149,939	7,437	94,392	62.9	59.9	4.7
Mar	254,414	160,036	152,958	2,503	150,260	7,078	94,378	62.9	60.1	4.4
Apr	254,588	160,169	153,150	2,682	150,432	7,019	94,419	62.9	60.2	4.4
May	254,767	159,910	152,920	2,501	150,397	6,991	94,857	62.8	60.0	4.4
June	254,957	160,124	153,176	2,466	150,816	6,948	94,833	62.8	60.1	4.3
July	255,151	160,383	153,456	2,349	151,073	6,927	94,769	62.9	60.1	4.3
Aug	255,357	160,706	153,591	2,378	151,312	7,115	94,651	62.9	60.1	4.4
Sept	255,562	161,190	154,399	2,286	152,143	6,791	94,372	63.1	60.4	4.2
Oct	255,766	160,436	153,847	2,487	151,353	6,588	95,330	62.7	60.2	4.1
Nov	255,949	160,626	153,945	2,461	151,562	6,682	95,323	62.8	60.1	4.2
Dec	256,109	160,636	154,065	2,512	151,628	6,572	95,473	62.7	60.2	4.1
2018: Jan	256,780	161,123	154,482	2,480	152,030	6,641	95,657	62.7	60.2	4.1
Feb	256,934	161,900	155,213	2,450	152,695	6,687	95,033	63.0	60.4	4.1
Mar	257,097	161,646	155,160	2,331	152,664	6,486	95,451	62.9	60.4	4.0
Apr	257,272	161,551	155,216	2,312	152,860	6,335	95,721	62.8	60.3	3.9
May	257,454	161,667	155,539	2,353	153,127	6,128	95,787	62.8	60.4	3.8
June	257,642	162,129	155,592	2,363	153,267	6,537	95,513	62.9	60.4	4.0
July	257,843	162,209	155,964	2,493	153,425	6,245	95,633	62.9	60.5	3.9
Aug	258,066	161,802	155,604	2,346	153,376	6,197	96,264	62.7	60.3	3.8
Sept	258,290	162,055	156,069	2,478	153,634	5,986	96,235	62.7	60.4	3.7
Oct	258,514	162,694	156,582	2,418	154,135	6,112	95,821	62.9	60.6	3.8
Nov	258,708	162,821	156,803	2,556	154,297	6,018	95,886	62.9	60.6	3.7
Dec	258,888	163,240	156,945	2,522	154,520	6,294	95,649	63.1	60.6	3.9

[5] Beginning in 2000, data for agricultural employment are for agricultural and related industries; data for this series and for nonagricultural employment are not strictly comparable with data for earlier years. Because of independent seasonal adjustment for these two series, monthly data will not add to total civilian employment.

Note: Labor force data in Tables B-22 through B-28 are based on household interviews and usually relate to the calendar week that includes the 12th of the month. Historical comparability is affected by revisions to population controls, changes in occupational and industry classification, and other changes to the survey. In recent years, updated population controls have been introduced annually with the release of January data, so data are not strictly comparable with earlier periods. Particularly notable changes were introduced for data in the years 1953, 1960, 1962, 1972, 1973, 1978, 1980, 1990, 1994, 1997, 1998, 2000, 2003, 2008 and 2012. For definitions of terms, area samples used, historical comparability of the data, comparability with other series, etc., see *Employment and Earnings* or concepts and methodology of the CPS at http://www.bls.gov/cps/documentation.htm#concepts.

Source: Department of Labor (Bureau of Labor Statistics).

Labor Market Indicators

TABLE B–23. Civilian employment by sex, age, and demographic characteristic, 1975–2018

[Thousands of persons 16 years of age and over, except as noted; monthly data seasonally adjusted]

Year or month	All civilian workers	By sex and age			By race or ethnicity [1]									
		Men 20 years and over	Women 20 years and over	Both sexes 16–19	White			Black or African American			Asian	Hispanic or Latino ethnicity		
					Total	Men 20 years and over	Women 20 years and over	Total	Men 20 years and over	Women 20 years and over	Total	Total	Men 20 years and over	Women 20 years and over
1975	85,846	48,018	30,726	7,104	76,411	43,192	26,731	7,894	3,998	3,388	....	3,663	2,117	1,224
1976	88,752	49,190	32,226	7,336	78,853	44,171	27,958	8,227	4,120	3,599	....	3,720	2,109	1,288
1977	92,017	50,555	33,775	7,688	81,700	45,326	29,306	8,540	4,273	3,758	....	4,079	2,335	1,370
1978	96,048	52,143	35,836	8,070	84,936	46,594	30,975	9,102	4,483	4,047	....	4,527	2,568	1,537
1979	98,824	53,308	37,434	8,083	87,259	47,546	32,357	9,359	4,606	4,174	....	4,785	2,701	1,638
1980	99,303	53,101	38,492	7,710	87,715	47,419	33,275	9,313	4,498	4,267	....	5,527	3,142	1,886
1981	100,397	53,582	39,590	7,225	88,709	47,846	34,275	9,355	4,520	4,329	....	5,813	3,325	2,029
1982	99,526	52,891	40,086	6,549	87,903	47,209	34,710	9,189	4,414	4,347	....	5,805	3,354	2,040
1983	100,834	53,487	41,004	6,342	88,893	47,618	35,476	9,375	4,531	4,428	....	6,072	3,523	2,127
1984	105,005	55,769	42,793	6,444	92,120	49,461	36,823	10,119	4,871	4,773	....	6,651	3,825	2,357
1985	107,150	56,562	44,154	6,434	93,736	50,061	37,907	10,501	4,992	4,977	....	6,888	3,994	2,456
1986	109,597	57,569	45,556	6,472	95,660	50,818	39,050	10,814	5,150	5,128	....	7,219	4,174	2,615
1987	112,440	58,726	47,074	6,640	97,789	51,649	40,242	11,309	5,357	5,365	....	7,790	4,444	2,872
1988	114,968	59,781	48,383	6,805	99,812	52,466	41,316	11,658	5,509	5,548	....	8,250	4,680	3,047
1989	117,342	60,837	49,745	6,759	101,584	53,292	42,346	11,953	5,602	5,727	....	8,573	4,853	3,172
1990	118,793	61,678	50,535	6,581	102,261	53,685	42,796	12,175	5,692	5,884	....	9,845	5,609	3,567
1991	117,718	61,178	50,634	5,906	101,182	53,103	42,862	12,074	5,706	5,874	....	9,828	5,623	3,603
1992	118,492	61,496	51,328	5,669	101,669	53,357	43,327	12,151	5,681	5,978	....	10,027	5,757	3,693
1993	120,259	62,355	52,099	5,805	103,045	54,021	43,910	12,382	5,793	6,095	....	10,361	5,992	3,800
1994	123,060	63,294	53,606	6,161	105,190	54,676	45,116	12,835	5,964	6,320	....	10,788	6,189	3,989
1995	124,900	64,085	54,396	6,419	106,490	55,254	45,643	13,279	6,137	6,556	....	11,127	6,367	4,116
1996	126,708	64,897	55,311	6,500	107,808	55,977	46,164	13,542	6,167	6,762	....	11,642	6,655	4,341
1997	129,558	66,284	56,613	6,661	109,856	56,986	47,063	13,969	6,325	7,013	....	12,726	7,307	4,705
1998	131,463	67,135	57,278	7,051	110,931	57,500	47,342	14,556	6,530	7,290	....	13,291	7,570	4,928
1999	133,488	67,761	58,555	7,172	112,235	57,934	48,098	15,056	6,702	7,663	....	13,720	7,576	5,290
2000	136,891	69,634	60,067	7,189	114,424	59,119	49,145	15,156	6,741	7,703	6,043	15,735	8,859	5,903
2001	136,933	69,776	60,417	6,740	114,430	59,245	49,369	15,006	6,627	7,741	6,180	16,190	9,100	6,121
2002	136,485	69,734	60,420	6,332	114,013	59,124	49,448	14,872	6,652	7,610	6,215	16,590	9,341	6,367
2003	137,736	70,415	61,402	5,919	114,235	59,348	49,823	14,739	6,586	7,636	5,756	17,372	10,063	6,541
2004	139,252	71,572	61,773	5,907	115,239	60,159	50,040	14,909	6,681	7,707	5,994	17,930	10,385	6,752
2005	141,730	73,050	62,702	5,978	116,949	61,255	50,589	15,313	6,901	7,876	6,244	18,632	10,872	6,913
2006	144,427	74,431	63,834	6,162	118,833	62,259	51,359	15,765	7,079	8,068	6,522	19,613	11,391	7,321
2007	146,047	75,337	64,799	5,911	119,792	62,806	51,996	16,051	7,245	8,240	6,839	20,382	11,827	7,662
2008	145,362	74,750	65,039	5,573	119,126	62,304	52,124	15,953	7,151	8,260	6,917	20,346	11,769	7,707
2009	139,877	71,341	63,699	4,837	114,996	59,626	51,231	15,025	6,628	7,956	6,635	19,647	11,256	7,649
2010	139,064	71,230	63,456	4,378	114,168	59,438	50,997	15,010	6,680	7,944	6,705	19,906	11,438	7,788
2011	139,869	72,182	63,360	4,327	114,690	60,118	50,881	15,051	6,765	7,906	6,867	20,269	11,685	7,918
2012	142,469	73,403	64,640	4,426	114,769	60,193	50,911	15,856	7,104	8,313	7,705	21,878	12,212	8,858
2013	143,929	74,176	65,295	4,458	115,379	60,511	51,198	16,151	7,304	8,408	8,136	22,514	12,638	9,056
2014	146,305	75,471	66,287	4,548	116,788	61,289	51,798	16,732	7,613	8,663	8,325	23,492	13,202	9,431
2015	148,834	76,776	67,323	4,734	117,944	61,959	52,161	17,472	7,938	9,032	8,706	24,400	13,624	9,853
2016	151,436	78,084	68,387	4,965	119,313	62,575	52,771	17,982	8,228	9,219	9,213	25,249	14,055	10,217
2017	153,337	78,919	69,344	5,074	120,176	63,009	53,179	18,587	8,500	9,514	9,448	25,938	14,355	10,543
2018	155,761	80,211	70,424	5,126	121,461	63,719	53,682	19,091	8,745	9,751	9,832	27,012	14,873	11,045
2017: Jan	152,128	78,440	68,633	5,055	119,328	62,673	52,708	18,446	8,430	9,455	9,289	25,450	14,179	10,341
Feb	152,417	78,439	68,971	5,007	119,595	62,749	52,952	18,392	8,370	9,450	9,382	25,722	14,239	10,485
Mar	152,958	78,472	69,343	5,143	120,110	62,753	53,269	18,399	8,384	9,487	9,312	25,983	14,286	10,612
Apr	153,150	78,807	69,239	5,104	120,115	63,007	53,080	18,530	8,499	9,479	9,443	25,799	14,275	10,479
May	152,920	78,748	69,134	5,037	119,876	62,938	52,959	18,548	8,463	9,499	9,473	25,824	14,298	10,453
June	153,176	78,755	69,250	5,171	120,130	62,901	53,122	18,549	8,500	9,436	9,438	25,941	14,393	10,444
July	153,456	78,863	69,529	5,065	120,234	62,948	53,353	18,618	8,516	9,504	9,420	26,048	14,404	10,582
Aug	153,591	78,972	69,508	5,111	120,356	63,069	53,299	18,551	8,479	9,482	9,482	25,963	14,318	10,596
Sept	154,399	79,453	69,694	5,252	120,870	63,235	53,574	18,818	8,666	9,537	9,630	26,239	14,525	10,641
Oct	153,847	79,278	69,545	5,025	120,426	63,213	53,257	18,641	8,536	9,547	9,564	26,027	14,412	10,602
Nov	153,945	79,344	69,670	4,931	120,522	63,289	53,333	18,714	8,554	9,616	9,394	26,115	14,415	10,687
Dec	154,065	79,493	69,587	4,985	120,585	63,370	53,231	18,827	8,598	9,672	9,547	26,140	14,522	10,584
2018: Jan	154,482	79,719	69,620	5,143	120,899	63,502	53,272	18,696	8,572	9,549	9,587	26,434	14,660	10,736
Feb	155,213	80,186	69,849	5,178	121,241	63,651	53,456	19,118	8,889	9,642	9,630	26,656	14,724	10,821
Mar	155,160	80,091	69,946	5,123	121,180	63,698	53,381	19,063	8,752	9,718	9,786	26,528	14,694	10,695
Apr	155,216	80,108	70,033	5,074	121,228	63,724	53,451	18,911	8,674	9,716	9,760	26,865	14,891	10,869
May	155,539	80,299	70,161	5,079	121,298	63,738	53,496	19,096	8,790	9,755	9,727	26,834	14,843	10,930
June	155,592	80,006	70,455	5,131	121,357	63,680	53,635	19,057	8,580	9,834	9,825	27,077	14,952	11,072
July	155,964	80,217	70,622	5,125	121,507	63,681	53,764	19,151	8,756	9,793	9,842	27,223	15,006	11,137
Aug	155,604	80,149	70,563	4,892	121,074	63,513	53,616	19,108	8,828	9,769	9,951	26,935	14,852	11,025
Sept	156,069	80,251	70,710	5,108	121,507	63,664	53,792	19,265	8,800	9,874	9,943	27,102	14,832	11,188
Oct	156,582	80,388	70,935	5,258	121,923	63,785	54,062	19,290	8,814	9,825	9,956	27,266	14,854	11,266
Nov	156,803	80,633	70,949	5,221	122,036	63,960	54,023	19,232	8,771	9,789	10,050	27,524	15,063	11,308
Dec	156,945	80,501	71,218	5,226	122,318	64,046	54,226	19,107	8,709	9,749	9,929	27,701	15,107	11,487

[1] Beginning in 2003, persons who selected this race group only. Persons whose ethnicity is identified as Hispanic or Latino may be of any race. Prior to 2003, persons who selected more than one race were included in the group they identified as the main race. Data for "black or African American" were for "black" prior to 2003. See *Employment and Earnings* or concepts and methodology of the Current Population Survey (CPS) at http://www.bls.gov/cps/documentation.htm#concepts for details.

Note: Detail will not sum to total because data for all race groups are not shown here.
See footnote 5 and Note, Table B–22.

Source: Department of Labor (Bureau of Labor Statistics).

TABLE B-24. Unemployment by sex, age, and demographic characteristic, 1975-2018

[Thousands of persons 16 years of age and over, except as noted; monthly data seasonally adjusted]

Year or month	All civilian workers	By sex and age			By race or ethnicity [1]									
		Men 20 years and over	Women 20 years and over	Both sexes 16–19	White			Black or African American			Asian	Hispanic or Latino ethnicity		
					Total	Men 20 years and over	Women 20 years and over	Total	Men 20 years and over	Women 20 years and over	Total	Total	Men 20 years and over	Women 20 years and over
1975	7,929	3,476	2,684	1,767	6,421	2,841	2,166	1,369	571	469		508	225	160
1976	7,406	3,098	2,588	1,719	5,914	2,504	2,045	1,334	528	477		485	217	166
1977	6,991	2,794	2,535	1,663	5,441	2,211	1,946	1,393	512	528		456	195	153
1978	6,202	2,328	2,292	1,583	4,698	1,797	1,713	1,330	462	510		452	175	168
1979	6,137	2,308	2,276	1,555	4,664	1,773	1,699	1,319	473	513		434	168	160
1980	7,637	3,353	2,615	1,669	5,884	2,629	1,964	1,553	636	574		620	284	190
1981	8,273	3,615	2,895	1,763	6,343	2,825	2,143	1,731	703	671		678	321	212
1982	10,678	5,089	3,613	1,977	8,241	3,991	2,715	2,142	954	793		929	461	293
1983	10,717	5,257	3,632	1,829	8,128	4,098	2,643	2,272	1,002	878		961	491	302
1984	8,539	3,932	3,107	1,499	6,372	2,992	2,264	1,914	815	747		800	393	258
1985	8,312	3,715	3,129	1,468	6,191	2,834	2,283	1,864	757	750		811	401	269
1986	8,237	3,751	3,032	1,454	6,140	2,857	2,213	1,840	765	728		857	438	278
1987	7,425	3,369	2,709	1,347	5,501	2,584	1,922	1,684	666	706		751	374	241
1988	6,701	2,987	2,487	1,226	4,944	2,268	1,766	1,547	617	642		732	351	234
1989	6,528	2,867	2,467	1,194	4,770	2,149	1,758	1,544	619	625		750	342	276
1990	7,047	3,239	2,596	1,212	5,186	2,431	1,852	1,565	664	633		876	425	289
1991	8,628	4,195	3,074	1,359	6,560	3,284	2,248	1,723	745	698		1,092	575	339
1992	9,613	4,717	3,469	1,427	7,169	3,620	2,512	2,011	886	800		1,311	675	418
1993	8,940	4,287	3,288	1,365	6,655	3,263	2,400	1,844	801	729		1,248	629	418
1994	7,996	3,627	3,049	1,320	5,892	2,735	2,197	1,666	682	685		1,187	558	431
1995	7,404	3,239	2,819	1,346	5,459	2,465	2,042	1,538	593	620		1,140	530	404
1996	7,236	3,146	2,783	1,306	5,300	2,363	1,998	1,592	639	643		1,132	495	438
1997	6,739	2,882	2,585	1,271	4,836	2,140	1,784	1,560	585	673		1,069	471	401
1998	6,210	2,580	2,424	1,205	4,484	1,920	1,688	1,426	524	622		1,026	436	376
1999	5,880	2,433	2,285	1,162	4,273	1,813	1,616	1,309	480	561		945	374	376
2000	5,692	2,376	2,235	1,081	4,121	1,731	1,595	1,241	499	512	227	954	388	371
2001	6,801	3,040	2,599	1,162	4,969	2,275	1,849	1,416	573	582	288	1,138	495	436
2002	8,378	3,896	3,228	1,253	6,137	2,943	2,269	1,693	695	738	389	1,353	636	496
2003	8,774	4,209	3,314	1,251	6,311	3,125	2,276	1,787	760	772	366	1,441	693	555
2004	8,149	3,791	3,150	1,208	5,847	2,785	2,172	1,729	733	755	277	1,342	635	504
2005	7,591	3,392	3,013	1,186	5,350	2,450	2,054	1,700	699	734	259	1,191	536	464
2006	7,001	3,131	2,751	1,119	5,002	2,281	1,927	1,549	640	656	205	1,081	497	414
2007	7,078	3,259	2,718	1,101	5,143	2,408	1,930	1,445	622	588	229	1,220	576	446
2008	8,924	4,297	3,342	1,285	6,509	3,179	2,384	1,788	811	732	285	1,678	860	567
2009	14,265	7,555	5,157	1,552	10,648	5,746	3,745	2,606	1,286	1,032	522	2,706	1,474	911
2010	14,825	7,763	5,534	1,528	10,916	5,828	3,960	2,852	1,396	1,165	543	2,843	1,519	1,001
2011	13,747	6,898	5,450	1,400	9,889	5,046	3,818	2,831	1,360	1,204	518	2,629	1,345	984
2012	12,506	5,984	5,125	1,397	8,915	4,347	3,564	2,544	1,152	1,119	483	2,514	1,195	995
2013	11,460	5,568	4,565	1,327	8,033	3,994	3,102	2,429	1,082	1,069	448	2,257	1,090	855
2014	9,617	4,585	3,926	1,106	6,540	3,141	2,623	2,141	973	943	436	1,878	864	764
2015	8,296	3,959	3,371	966	5,662	2,751	2,249	1,846	835	811	347	1,726	820	686
2016	7,751	3,675	3,151	925	5,345	2,594	2,100	1,655	737	724	349	1,548	720	627
2017	6,982	3,287	2,868	827	4,765	2,288	1,923	1,501	663	657	333	1,401	632	585
2018	6,314	2,976	2,578	759	4,354	2,094	1,743	1,322	582	573	304	1,323	591	547
2017: Jan	7,565	3,565	3,128	872	5,298	2,552	2,158	1,530	669	661	361	1,579	706	692
Feb	7,437	3,516	3,060	861	5,021	2,431	2,017	1,602	718	702	338	1,504	676	620
Mar	7,078	3,435	2,829	814	4,864	2,356	1,949	1,579	769	642	316	1,375	643	528
Apr	7,019	3,176	2,956	887	4,794	2,218	1,965	1,599	665	725	312	1,389	617	594
May	6,991	3,213	2,952	825	4,683	2,260	1,927	1,541	613	722	362	1,397	629	598
June	6,948	3,258	2,888	803	4,698	2,304	1,887	1,413	564	690	347	1,329	569	578
July	6,927	3,264	2,888	775	4,610	2,246	1,896	1,484	651	649	371	1,429	680	595
Aug	7,115	3,417	2,872	826	4,796	2,310	1,950	1,529	719	631	393	1,409	716	519
Sept	6,791	3,186	2,818	787	4,675	2,218	1,917	1,432	630	623	357	1,404	607	615
Oct	6,588	3,123	2,658	806	4,408	2,122	1,728	1,469	665	651	297	1,329	577	548
Nov	6,682	3,103	2,657	922	4,618	2,155	1,790	1,480	677	613	292	1,310	580	545
Dec	6,572	3,101	2,686	785	4,642	2,190	1,900	1,354	595	590	241	1,359	581	591
2018: Jan	6,641	3,196	2,618	827	4,419	2,201	1,638	1,554	697	674	301	1,397	667	521
Feb	6,687	3,072	2,746	870	4,621	2,236	1,798	1,399	559	621	294	1,366	591	595
Mar	6,486	3,059	2,634	793	4,461	2,179	1,791	1,389	565	600	311	1,412	674	553
Apr	6,335	3,055	2,525	755	4,447	2,195	1,742	1,321	593	528	279	1,354	626	541
May	6,128	2,958	2,429	741	4,392	2,106	1,756	1,198	590	481	214	1,373	596	589
June	6,537	3,097	2,701	740	4,408	2,142	1,804	1,314	587	571	322	1,292	595	560
July	6,245	2,801	2,673	771	4,209	1,933	1,774	1,345	569	631	314	1,279	508	552
Aug	6,197	2,895	2,590	712	4,272	2,014	1,757	1,276	565	587	309	1,317	574	582
Sept	5,986	2,853	2,398	735	4,110	1,996	1,586	1,239	549	548	360	1,287	592	501
Oct	6,112	2,889	2,507	715	4,177	1,986	1,716	1,274	586	501	324	1,248	594	501
Nov	6,018	2,775	2,529	714	4,299	2,000	1,796	1,219	539	515	284	1,296	533	550
Dec	6,294	2,999	2,550	745	4,362	2,064	1,769	1,353	575	611	334	1,261	544	515

[1] See footnote 1 and Note, Table B-23.

Note: See footnote 5 and Note, Table B-22.

Source: Department of Labor (Bureau of Labor Statistics).

Labor Market Indicators | 665

TABLE B-25. Civilian labor force participation rate, 1975–2018

[Percent [1]; monthly data seasonally adjusted]

Year or month	All civilian workers	Men				Women				Both sexes 16–19 years	By race or ethnicity [2]			
		20 years and over	20–24 years	25–54 years	55 years and over	20 years and over	20–24 years	25–54 years	55 years and over		White	Black or African American	Asian	Hispanic or Latino ethnicity
1975	61.2	80.3	84.5	94.4	49.4	46.0	64.1	55.1	23.1	54.0	61.5	58.8	....	60.8
1976	61.6	79.8	85.2	94.2	47.8	47.0	65.0	56.8	23.0	54.5	61.8	59.0	....	60.8
1977	62.3	79.7	85.6	94.2	47.4	48.1	66.5	58.5	22.9	56.0	62.5	59.8	....	61.6
1978	63.2	79.8	85.9	94.3	47.2	49.6	68.3	60.6	23.1	57.8	63.3	61.5	....	62.9
1979	63.7	79.8	86.4	94.4	46.6	50.6	69.0	62.3	23.2	57.9	63.9	61.4	....	63.6
1980	63.8	79.4	85.9	94.2	45.6	51.3	68.9	64.0	22.8	56.7	64.1	61.0	....	64.0
1981	63.9	79.0	85.5	94.1	44.5	52.1	69.6	65.3	22.7	55.4	64.3	60.8	....	64.1
1982	64.0	78.7	84.9	94.0	43.8	52.7	69.8	66.3	22.7	54.1	64.3	61.0	....	63.6
1983	64.0	78.5	84.8	93.8	43.0	53.1	69.9	67.1	22.4	53.5	64.3	61.5	....	63.8
1984	64.4	78.3	85.0	93.9	41.8	53.7	70.4	68.2	22.2	53.9	64.6	62.2	....	64.9
1985	64.8	78.1	85.0	93.9	41.0	54.7	71.8	69.6	22.0	54.5	65.0	62.9	....	64.6
1986	65.3	78.1	85.8	93.8	40.4	55.5	72.4	70.8	22.1	54.7	65.5	63.3	....	65.4
1987	65.6	78.0	85.2	93.7	40.4	56.2	73.0	71.9	22.0	54.7	65.8	63.8	....	66.4
1988	65.9	77.9	85.0	93.6	39.9	56.8	72.7	72.7	22.3	55.3	66.2	63.8	....	67.4
1989	66.5	78.1	85.3	93.7	39.6	57.7	72.4	73.6	23.0	55.9	66.7	64.2	....	67.6
1990	66.5	78.2	84.4	93.4	39.4	58.0	71.3	74.0	22.9	53.7	66.9	64.0	....	67.4
1991	66.2	77.7	83.5	93.1	38.5	57.9	70.1	74.1	22.6	51.6	66.6	63.3	....	66.5
1992	66.4	77.7	83.3	93.0	38.4	58.5	70.9	74.6	22.8	51.3	66.8	63.9	....	66.8
1993	66.3	77.3	83.2	92.6	37.7	58.5	70.9	74.6	22.8	51.5	66.8	63.2	....	66.2
1994	66.6	76.8	83.1	91.7	37.8	59.3	71.0	75.3	24.0	52.7	67.1	63.4	....	66.1
1995	66.6	76.7	83.1	91.6	37.9	59.4	70.3	75.6	23.9	53.5	67.1	63.7	....	65.8
1996	66.8	76.8	82.5	91.8	38.3	59.9	71.3	76.1	23.9	52.3	67.2	64.1	....	66.5
1997	67.1	77.0	82.5	91.8	38.9	60.5	72.7	76.7	24.6	51.6	67.5	64.7	....	67.9
1998	67.1	76.8	82.0	91.8	39.1	60.4	73.0	76.5	25.0	52.8	67.3	65.6	....	67.9
1999	67.1	76.7	81.9	91.7	39.6	60.7	73.2	76.8	25.6	52.0	67.3	65.8	....	67.7
2000	67.1	76.7	82.6	91.6	40.1	60.6	73.1	76.7	26.1	52.0	67.3	65.8	67.2	69.7
2001	66.8	76.5	81.6	91.3	40.9	60.4	72.7	76.4	27.0	49.6	67.0	65.3	67.2	69.5
2002	66.6	76.3	80.7	91.0	42.0	60.5	72.1	75.9	28.5	47.4	66.8	64.8	67.2	69.1
2003	66.2	75.9	80.0	90.6	42.6	60.6	70.8	75.6	30.0	44.5	66.5	64.3	66.4	68.3
2004	66.0	75.8	79.6	90.5	43.2	60.3	70.5	75.3	30.5	43.9	66.3	63.8	65.9	68.6
2005	66.0	75.8	79.1	90.5	44.2	60.4	70.1	75.3	31.4	43.7	66.3	64.2	66.1	68.0
2006	66.2	75.9	79.6	90.6	44.9	60.5	69.5	75.5	32.3	43.7	66.5	64.1	66.2	68.7
2007	66.0	75.9	78.7	90.9	45.2	60.6	70.1	75.4	33.2	41.3	66.4	63.7	66.5	68.8
2008	66.0	75.7	78.7	90.5	46.0	60.9	70.0	75.8	33.9	40.2	66.3	63.7	67.0	68.5
2009	65.4	74.8	76.2	89.7	46.3	60.8	69.6	75.6	34.7	37.5	65.8	62.4	66.0	68.0
2010	64.7	74.1	74.5	89.3	46.4	60.3	68.3	75.2	35.1	34.9	65.1	62.2	64.7	67.5
2011	64.1	73.4	74.7	88.7	46.3	59.8	67.8	74.7	35.1	34.1	64.5	61.4	64.6	66.5
2012	63.7	73.0	74.5	88.6	46.8	59.3	67.4	74.5	35.1	34.3	64.0	61.5	63.9	66.4
2013	63.2	72.5	73.9	88.4	46.5	58.8	67.5	73.9	35.1	34.5	63.5	61.2	64.6	66.0
2014	62.9	71.9	73.9	88.2	45.9	58.5	67.7	73.9	34.9	34.0	63.1	61.2	63.6	66.1
2015	62.7	71.7	73.0	88.3	45.9	58.2	68.3	73.7	34.7	34.3	62.8	61.5	62.8	65.9
2016	62.8	71.7	73.0	88.5	46.2	58.3	68.0	74.3	34.7	35.2	62.9	61.6	63.2	65.8
2017	62.9	71.6	74.1	88.6	46.1	58.5	68.5	75.0	34.7	35.2	62.8	62.3	63.6	66.1
2018	62.9	71.6	73.2	89.0	46.2	58.5	69.0	75.3	34.7	35.1	62.8	62.3	63.5	66.3
2017: Jan	62.9	71.7	74.2	88.8	45.9	58.3	67.9	74.5	34.9	35.4	62.8	62.3	63.7	66.0
Feb	62.9	71.7	73.8	88.6	46.0	58.5	69.5	74.8	34.7	35.1	62.8	62.3	63.8	66.4
Mar	62.9	71.6	73.5	88.5	46.2	58.6	69.3	74.9	34.9	35.6	62.9	62.2	63.0	66.6
Apr	62.9	71.6	74.0	88.5	46.1	58.6	69.0	75.1	34.6	35.8	62.9	62.6	63.4	66.1
May	62.8	71.5	74.2	88.4	45.9	58.4	67.6	74.9	34.8	35.0	62.7	62.4	63.7	66.0
June	62.8	71.5	73.6	88.5	46.0	58.4	67.4	75.0	34.8	35.7	62.8	61.9	63.7	66.0
July	62.9	71.5	74.5	88.6	45.9	58.6	67.5	75.1	34.9	34.8	62.7	62.3	64.0	66.4
Aug	62.9	71.7	74.6	88.5	46.2	58.5	69.1	75.0	34.8	35.4	62.9	62.2	64.4	66.0
Sept	63.1	71.8	74.9	88.6	46.4	58.6	69.2	75.2	34.8	36.0	63.0	62.6	64.5	66.5
Oct	62.7	71.6	74.3	88.6	46.1	58.3	69.3	74.9	34.5	34.8	62.6	62.1	63.8	65.7
Nov	62.8	71.6	74.1	88.6	46.2	58.3	67.8	75.2	34.5	34.9	62.8	62.3	63.0	65.7
Dec	62.7	71.6	73.3	89.0	45.9	58.3	67.6	75.0	34.6	34.4	62.8	62.2	62.7	65.7
2018: Jan	62.7	71.7	74.7	89.0	45.8	58.1	68.8	74.9	34.1	35.6	62.7	62.2	62.9	65.9
Feb	63.0	71.9	74.8	89.3	46.1	58.4	68.4	75.2	34.5	36.0	63.0	62.9	62.8	66.2
Mar	62.9	71.8	75.5	89.2	45.9	58.3	68.9	75.1	34.6	35.3	62.9	62.7	63.2	65.9
Apr	62.8	71.7	73.9	89.2	46.0	58.2	68.7	74.9	34.7	34.8	62.9	61.9	63.0	66.4
May	62.8	71.8	73.4	89.0	46.4	58.2	69.0	74.8	34.7	34.7	62.8	62.1	62.6	66.2
June	62.9	71.6	73.4	88.9	46.1	58.6	69.2	75.4	34.9	35.0	62.8	62.2	63.7	66.5
July	62.9	71.4	72.4	88.8	46.3	58.7	70.3	75.5	34.7	35.2	62.8	62.5	63.8	66.6
Aug	62.7	71.4	71.1	88.8	46.3	58.5	68.7	75.4	34.9	33.4	62.6	62.1	63.8	65.9
Sept	62.7	71.4	72.8	88.7	46.1	58.4	69.1	75.2	34.9	34.9	62.7	62.4	64.3	66.1
Oct	62.9	71.5	72.1	89.0	46.1	58.7	68.6	75.8	34.9	35.6	62.9	62.5	64.1	66.2
Nov	62.9	71.5	72.1	89.0	46.3	58.6	68.8	75.6	35.0	35.4	63.0	62.1	64.2	66.8
Dec	63.1	71.5	72.1	89.0	46.4	58.8	69.2	75.9	35.1	35.6	63.1	62.1	63.6	67.0

[1] Civilian labor force as percent of civilian noninstitutional population in group specified.
[2] See footnote 1, Table B-23.

Note: Data relate to persons 16 years of age and over, except as noted.
See footnote 5 and Note, Table B-22.

Source: Department of Labor (Bureau of Labor Statistics).

TABLE B-26. Civilian employment/population ratio, 1975-2018

[Percent [1]; monthly data seasonally adjusted]

Year or month	All civilian workers	Men				Women				Both sexes 16–19 years	By race or ethnicity [2]			
		20 years and over	20–24 years	25–54 years	55 years and over	20 years and over	20–24 years	25–54 years	55 years and over		White	Black or African American	Asian	Hispanic or Latino ethnicity
1975	56.1	74.8	72.4	89.0	47.0	42.3	56.0	51.0	21.9	43.3	56.7	50.1	....	53.4
1976	56.8	75.1	74.9	89.5	45.7	43.5	57.3	52.9	21.9	44.2	57.5	50.8	....	53.8
1977	57.9	75.6	76.3	90.1	45.5	44.8	59.0	54.8	21.9	46.1	58.6	51.4	....	55.4
1978	59.3	76.4	78.0	91.0	45.7	46.6	61.4	57.3	22.3	48.3	60.0	53.6	....	57.2
1979	59.9	76.5	78.9	91.1	45.2	47.7	62.4	59.0	22.5	48.5	60.6	53.8	....	58.3
1980	59.2	74.6	75.1	89.4	44.1	48.1	61.8	60.1	22.1	46.6	60.0	52.3	....	57.6
1981	59.0	74.0	74.2	89.0	42.9	48.6	61.8	61.2	21.9	44.6	60.0	51.3	....	57.4
1982	57.8	71.8	71.0	86.5	41.6	48.4	60.6	61.2	21.6	41.5	58.8	49.4	....	54.9
1983	57.9	71.4	71.3	86.1	40.6	48.8	60.9	62.0	21.4	41.5	58.9	49.5	....	55.1
1984	59.5	73.2	74.9	88.4	39.8	50.1	62.7	63.9	21.3	43.7	60.5	52.3	....	57.9
1985	60.1	73.3	75.3	88.7	39.3	51.0	64.1	65.3	21.1	44.4	61.0	53.4	....	57.8
1986	60.7	73.3	76.3	88.5	38.8	52.0	64.9	66.6	21.3	44.6	61.5	54.1	....	58.5
1987	61.5	73.8	76.8	89.0	39.0	53.1	66.1	68.2	21.3	45.5	62.3	55.6	....	60.5
1988	62.3	74.2	77.5	89.5	38.6	54.0	66.6	69.3	21.7	46.8	63.1	56.3	....	61.9
1989	63.0	74.5	77.8	89.9	38.3	54.9	66.4	70.4	22.4	47.5	63.8	56.9	....	62.2
1990	62.8	74.3	76.7	89.1	38.0	55.2	65.2	70.6	22.2	45.3	63.7	56.7	....	61.9
1991	61.7	72.7	73.8	87.5	36.8	54.6	63.2	70.1	21.9	42.0	62.6	55.4	....	59.8
1992	61.5	72.1	73.1	86.8	36.4	54.8	63.6	70.1	21.8	41.0	62.4	54.9	....	59.1
1993	61.7	72.3	73.8	87.0	35.9	55.0	64.0	70.4	22.0	41.7	62.7	55.0	....	59.1
1994	62.5	72.6	74.6	87.2	36.2	56.2	64.5	71.5	23.1	43.4	63.5	56.1	....	59.5
1995	62.9	73.0	75.4	87.6	36.5	56.5	64.0	72.2	23.0	44.2	63.8	57.1	....	59.7
1996	63.2	73.2	74.7	87.9	37.0	57.0	64.9	72.8	23.1	43.5	64.1	57.4	....	60.6
1997	63.8	73.7	75.2	88.4	37.7	57.8	66.8	73.5	23.8	43.4	64.6	58.2	....	62.6
1998	64.1	73.9	75.4	88.8	38.0	58.0	67.3	73.6	24.4	45.1	64.7	59.7	....	63.1
1999	64.3	74.0	75.6	89.0	38.5	58.5	68.0	74.1	24.9	44.7	64.8	60.6	....	63.4
2000	64.4	74.2	76.6	89.0	39.1	58.4	67.9	74.2	25.5	45.2	64.9	60.9	64.8	65.7
2001	63.7	73.3	74.2	87.9	39.6	58.1	67.3	73.4	26.3	42.3	64.2	59.7	64.2	64.9
2002	62.7	72.3	72.5	86.6	40.3	57.5	65.6	72.3	27.5	39.6	63.4	58.1	63.2	63.9
2003	62.3	71.7	71.5	85.9	40.7	57.5	64.2	72.0	28.9	36.8	63.0	57.4	62.4	63.1
2004	62.3	71.9	71.6	86.3	41.5	57.4	64.3	71.8	29.4	36.4	63.1	57.2	63.0	63.8
2005	62.7	72.4	71.5	86.9	42.7	57.6	64.5	72.0	30.4	36.5	63.4	57.7	63.4	64.0
2006	63.1	72.9	72.7	87.3	43.5	58.0	64.2	72.5	31.4	36.9	63.8	58.4	64.2	65.2
2007	63.0	72.8	71.7	87.5	43.7	58.2	65.0	72.5	32.2	34.8	63.6	58.4	64.3	64.9
2008	62.2	71.6	69.7	86.0	44.2	57.9	63.8	72.3	32.7	32.6	62.8	57.3	64.3	63.3
2009	59.3	67.6	63.3	81.5	43.0	56.2	61.1	70.2	32.6	28.4	60.2	53.2	61.2	59.7
2010	58.5	66.8	61.3	81.0	42.8	55.5	59.4	69.3	32.9	25.9	59.4	52.3	59.9	59.0
2011	58.4	67.0	63.0	81.4	43.1	55.0	58.7	69.3	32.9	25.8	59.4	51.7	60.0	58.9
2012	58.6	67.5	63.8	82.5	43.8	55.0	59.2	69.2	33.1	26.1	59.4	53.0	60.1	59.5
2013	58.6	67.4	63.5	82.8	43.8	54.9	59.8	69.3	33.3	26.6	59.4	53.2	61.2	60.0
2014	59.0	67.8	64.9	83.6	43.9	55.2	60.9	70.0	33.4	27.3	59.7	54.3	60.4	61.2
2015	59.3	68.1	65.1	84.4	44.1	55.4	62.5	70.3	33.5	28.5	59.9	55.7	60.4	61.6
2016	59.7	68.5	66.2	85.0	44.4	55.7	63.0	71.1	33.5	29.7	60.2	56.4	60.9	62.0
2017	60.1	68.8	67.9	85.4	44.6	56.1	64.2	72.1	33.6	30.3	60.4	57.6	61.5	62.7
2018	60.4	69.0	67.6	86.2	44.7	56.4	64.7	72.8	33.7	30.6	60.7	58.3	61.6	63.2
2017: Jan	59.9	68.6	67.5	85.3	44.4	55.8	63.2	71.4	33.6	30.2	60.1	57.5	61.3	62.2
Feb	59.9	68.6	66.9	85.1	44.5	56.0	65.0	71.7	33.5	29.9	60.2	57.3	61.6	62.7
Mar	60.1	68.6	67.2	85.1	44.6	56.3	65.0	72.0	33.8	30.7	60.5	57.3	60.9	63.2
Apr	60.2	68.8	67.8	85.4	44.7	56.2	64.7	72.0	33.5	30.5	60.5	57.6	61.4	62.7
May	60.0	68.7	68.3	85.2	44.5	56.0	64.0	71.8	33.6	30.1	60.3	57.6	61.4	62.6
June	60.1	68.6	67.5	85.3	44.6	56.1	63.1	72.1	33.7	30.9	60.4	57.6	61.4	62.8
July	60.1	68.7	68.5	85.2	44.6	56.3	64.0	72.3	33.7	30.2	60.4	57.7	61.6	62.9
Aug	60.1	68.7	68.8	85.0	44.7	56.2	64.6	72.1	33.7	30.5	60.5	57.4	61.8	62.6
Sept	60.4	69.1	68.4	85.6	45.0	56.3	64.8	72.4	33.6	31.3	60.7	58.2	62.2	63.1
Oct	60.2	68.9	68.3	85.7	44.5	56.1	65.0	72.2	33.5	30.0	60.4	57.6	61.8	62.5
Nov	60.1	68.9	67.8	85.7	44.7	56.2	63.8	72.5	33.5	29.4	60.4	57.8	61.1	62.5
Dec	60.2	68.9	67.5	86.1	44.4	56.1	63.4	72.3	33.5	29.7	60.5	58.0	61.2	62.5
2018: Jan	60.2	68.9	68.7	86.0	44.3	56.0	64.3	72.2	33.3	30.6	60.5	57.4	60.9	62.6
Feb	60.4	69.3	69.2	86.4	44.5	56.2	64.3	72.4	33.5	30.9	60.7	58.6	61.0	63.0
Mar	60.4	69.1	69.9	86.2	44.4	56.2	64.9	72.4	33.5	30.5	60.6	58.4	61.2	62.5
Apr	60.3	69.1	68.2	86.2	44.6	56.2	64.8	72.3	33.7	30.3	60.6	57.9	61.3	63.2
May	60.4	69.2	67.6	86.3	45.0	56.3	64.7	72.4	33.7	30.3	60.6	58.4	61.3	63.0
June	60.4	68.9	67.4	86.1	44.6	56.5	64.6	72.8	33.8	30.6	60.6	58.2	61.7	63.4
July	60.5	69.0	67.1	86.2	44.9	56.6	65.9	72.9	33.7	30.6	60.7	58.4	61.8	63.7
Aug	60.3	68.9	65.7	86.0	44.9	56.5	64.6	72.9	33.8	29.2	60.4	58.2	61.8	62.8
Sept	60.4	68.9	67.4	85.9	44.8	56.5	64.8	72.9	34.0	30.5	60.6	58.6	62.1	63.1
Oct	60.6	69.0	66.7	86.2	44.9	56.7	64.4	73.4	33.8	31.4	60.8	58.7	62.1	63.3
Nov	60.6	69.1	66.8	86.4	44.9	56.6	64.8	73.1	34.0	31.1	60.8	58.4	62.4	63.8
Dec	60.6	69.0	66.4	86.1	45.0	56.8	64.7	73.4	34.1	31.2	60.9	58.0	61.5	64.1

[1] Civilian employment as percent of civilian noninstitutional population in group specified.
[2] See footnote 1, Table B-23.

Note: Data relate to persons 16 years of age and over, except as noted.
See footnote 5 and Note, Table B-22.

Source: Department of Labor (Bureau of Labor Statistics).

Table B-27. Civilian unemployment rate, 1975–2018

[Percent [1]; monthly data seasonally adjusted]

Year or month	All civilian workers	By sex and age			By race or ethnicity [2]				U-6 measure of labor under-utilization [3]	By educational attainment (25 years & over)			
		Men 20 years and over	Women 20 years and over	Both sexes 16–19	White	Black or African American	Asian	Hispanic or Latino ethnicity		Less than a high school diploma	High school graduates, no college	Some college or associate degree	Bachelor's degree and higher [4]
1975	8.5	6.8	8.0	19.9	7.8	14.8	....	12.2	....	....	....	....	....
1976	7.7	5.9	7.4	19.0	7.0	14.0	....	11.5	....	....	....	....	....
1977	7.1	5.2	7.0	17.8	6.2	14.0	....	10.1	....	....	....	....	....
1978	6.1	4.3	6.0	16.4	5.2	12.8	....	9.1	....	....	....	....	....
1979	5.8	4.2	5.7	16.1	5.1	12.3	....	8.3	....	....	....	....	....
1980	7.1	5.9	6.4	17.8	6.3	14.3	....	10.1	....	....	....	....	....
1981	7.6	6.3	6.8	19.6	6.7	15.6	....	10.4	....	....	....	....	....
1982	9.7	8.8	8.3	23.2	8.6	18.9	....	13.8	....	....	....	....	....
1983	9.6	8.9	8.1	22.4	8.4	19.5	....	13.7	....	....	....	....	....
1984	7.5	6.6	6.8	18.9	6.5	15.9	....	10.7	....	....	....	....	....
1985	7.2	6.2	6.6	18.6	6.2	15.1	....	10.5	....	....	....	....	....
1986	7.0	6.1	6.2	18.3	6.0	14.5	....	10.6	....	....	....	....	....
1987	6.2	5.4	5.4	16.9	5.3	13.0	....	8.8	....	....	....	....	....
1988	5.5	4.8	4.9	15.3	4.7	11.7	....	8.2	....	....	....	....	....
1989	5.3	4.5	4.7	15.0	4.5	11.4	....	8.0	....	....	....	....	....
1990	5.6	5.0	4.9	15.5	4.8	11.4	....	8.2	....	....	....	....	....
1991	6.8	6.4	5.7	18.7	6.1	12.5	....	10.0	....	....	....	....	....
1992	7.5	7.1	6.3	20.1	6.6	14.2	....	11.6	....	11.5	6.8	5.6	3.2
1993	6.9	6.4	5.9	19.0	6.1	13.0	....	10.8	....	10.8	6.3	5.2	2.9
1994	6.1	5.4	5.4	17.6	5.3	11.5	....	9.9	10.9	9.8	5.4	4.5	2.6
1995	5.6	4.8	4.9	17.3	4.9	10.4	....	9.3	10.1	9.0	4.8	4.0	2.4
1996	5.4	4.6	4.8	16.7	4.7	10.5	....	8.9	9.7	8.7	4.7	3.7	2.2
1997	4.9	4.2	4.4	16.0	4.2	10.0	....	7.7	8.9	8.1	4.3	3.3	2.0
1998	4.5	3.7	4.1	14.6	3.9	8.9	....	7.2	8.0	7.1	4.0	3.0	1.8
1999	4.2	3.5	3.8	13.9	3.7	8.0	....	6.4	7.4	6.7	3.5	2.8	1.8
2000	4.0	3.3	3.6	13.1	3.5	7.6	3.6	5.7	7.0	6.3	3.4	2.7	1.7
2001	4.7	4.2	4.1	14.7	4.2	8.6	4.5	6.6	8.1	7.2	4.2	3.3	2.3
2002	5.8	5.3	5.1	16.5	5.1	10.2	5.9	7.5	9.6	8.4	5.3	4.5	2.9
2003	6.0	5.6	5.1	17.5	5.2	10.8	6.0	7.7	10.1	8.8	5.5	4.8	3.1
2004	5.5	5.0	4.9	17.0	4.8	10.4	4.4	7.0	9.6	8.5	5.0	4.2	2.7
2005	5.1	4.4	4.6	16.6	4.4	10.0	4.0	6.0	8.9	7.6	4.7	3.9	2.3
2006	4.6	4.0	4.1	15.4	4.0	8.9	3.0	5.2	8.2	6.8	4.3	3.6	2.0
2007	4.6	4.1	4.0	15.7	4.1	8.3	3.2	5.6	8.3	7.1	4.4	3.6	2.0
2008	5.8	5.4	4.9	18.7	5.2	10.1	4.0	7.6	10.5	9.0	5.7	4.6	2.6
2009	9.3	9.6	7.5	24.3	8.5	14.8	7.3	12.1	16.2	14.6	9.7	8.0	4.6
2010	9.6	9.8	8.0	25.9	8.7	16.0	7.5	12.5	16.7	14.9	10.3	8.4	4.7
2011	8.9	8.7	7.9	24.4	7.9	15.8	7.0	11.5	15.9	14.1	9.4	8.0	4.3
2012	8.1	7.5	7.3	24.0	7.2	13.8	5.9	10.3	14.7	12.4	8.3	7.1	4.0
2013	7.4	7.0	6.5	22.9	6.5	13.1	5.2	9.1	13.8	11.0	7.5	6.4	3.7
2014	6.2	5.7	5.6	19.6	5.3	11.3	5.0	7.4	12.0	9.0	6.0	5.4	3.2
2015	5.3	4.9	4.8	16.9	4.6	9.6	3.8	6.6	10.4	8.0	5.4	4.5	2.6
2016	4.9	4.5	4.4	15.7	4.3	8.4	3.6	5.8	9.6	7.4	5.2	4.1	2.5
2017	4.4	4.0	4.0	14.0	3.8	7.5	3.4	5.1	8.5	6.5	4.6	3.8	2.3
2018	3.9	3.6	3.5	12.9	3.5	6.5	3.0	4.7	7.7	5.6	4.1	3.3	2.1
2017: Jan	4.7	4.3	4.4	14.7	4.3	7.7	3.7	5.8	9.3	7.4	5.2	3.8	2.5
Feb	4.7	4.3	4.2	14.7	4.0	8.0	3.5	5.5	9.1	7.6	4.9	4.0	2.4
Mar	4.4	4.2	3.9	13.7	3.9	7.9	3.3	5.0	8.7	6.6	4.9	3.7	2.4
Apr	4.4	3.9	4.1	14.8	3.8	7.9	3.2	5.1	8.6	6.4	4.6	3.7	2.4
May	4.4	3.9	4.1	14.1	3.8	7.7	3.7	5.1	8.5	6.3	4.7	4.0	2.3
June	4.3	4.0	4.0	13.4	3.8	7.1	3.6	4.9	8.5	6.5	4.6	3.8	2.3
July	4.3	4.0	4.0	13.3	3.7	7.4	3.8	5.2	8.5	7.0	4.5	3.8	2.3
Aug	4.4	4.1	4.0	13.9	3.8	7.6	4.0	5.1	8.6	6.1	5.0	3.7	2.4
Sept	4.2	3.9	3.9	13.0	3.7	7.1	3.6	5.1	8.3	6.7	4.4	3.6	2.3
Oct	4.1	3.8	3.7	13.8	3.5	7.3	3.0	4.9	8.0	6.0	4.3	3.7	2.1
Nov	4.2	3.8	3.7	15.8	3.7	7.3	3.0	4.8	8.0	5.2	4.4	3.6	2.1
Dec	4.1	3.8	3.7	13.6	3.7	6.7	2.5	4.9	8.1	6.3	4.2	3.6	2.1
2018: Jan	4.1	3.9	3.6	13.9	3.5	7.7	3.0	5.0	8.2	5.5	4.4	3.4	2.2
Feb	4.1	3.7	3.8	14.4	3.7	6.8	3.0	4.9	8.2	5.6	4.4	3.5	2.2
Mar	4.0	3.7	3.6	13.4	3.6	6.8	3.1	5.1	7.9	5.6	4.3	3.5	2.2
Apr	3.9	3.7	3.5	13.0	3.5	6.5	2.8	4.8	7.8	5.8	4.3	3.4	2.1
May	3.8	3.6	3.3	12.7	3.5	5.9	2.2	4.9	7.7	5.5	3.9	3.2	2.0
June	4.0	3.7	3.7	12.6	3.5	6.5	3.2	4.6	7.8	5.6	4.1	3.3	2.3
July	3.9	3.4	3.6	13.1	3.3	6.6	3.1	4.5	7.5	5.0	4.0	3.2	2.2
Aug	3.8	3.5	3.5	12.7	3.4	6.3	3.0	4.7	7.4	5.7	3.9	3.5	2.0
Sept	3.7	3.4	3.3	12.6	3.3	6.0	3.5	4.5	7.5	5.6	3.7	3.2	2.0
Oct	3.8	3.5	3.4	12.0	3.3	6.2	3.1	4.4	7.5	5.9	4.0	3.0	2.0
Nov	3.7	3.3	3.4	12.0	3.4	6.0	2.7	4.5	7.6	5.6	3.5	3.1	2.2
Dec	3.9	3.6	3.5	12.5	3.4	6.6	3.3	4.4	7.6	5.8	3.8	3.3	2.1

[1] Unemployed as percent of civilian labor force in group specified.
[2] See footnote 1, Table B–23.
[3] Total unemployed, plus all persons marginally attached to the labor force, plus total employed part time for economic reasons, as a percent of the civilian labor force plus all persons marginally attached to the labor force.
[4] Includes persons with bachelor's, master's, professional, and doctoral degrees.

Note: Data relate to persons 16 years of age and over, except as noted.
See Note, Table B–22.

Source: Department of Labor (Bureau of Labor Statistics).

TABLE B-28. Unemployment by duration and reason, 1975–2018

[Thousands of persons, except as noted; monthly data seasonally adjusted [1]]

Year or month	Un-employ-ment	Duration of unemployment						Reason for unemployment					
		Less than 5 weeks	5–14 weeks	15–26 weeks	27 weeks and over	Average (mean) duration (weeks) [2]	Median duration (weeks)	Job losers [3]			Job leavers	Re-entrants	New entrants
								Total	On layoff	Other			
1975	7,929	2,940	2,484	1,303	1,203	14.2	8.4	4,386	1,671	2,714	827	1,892	823
1976	7,406	2,844	2,196	1,018	1,348	15.8	8.2	3,679	1,050	2,628	903	1,928	895
1977	6,991	2,919	2,132	913	1,028	14.3	7.0	3,166	865	2,300	909	1,963	953
1978	6,202	2,865	1,923	766	648	11.9	5.9	2,585	712	1,873	874	1,857	885
1979	6,137	2,950	1,946	706	535	10.8	5.4	2,635	851	1,784	880	1,806	817
1980	7,637	3,295	2,470	1,052	820	11.9	6.5	3,947	1,488	2,459	891	1,927	872
1981	8,273	3,449	2,539	1,122	1,162	13.7	6.9	4,267	1,430	2,837	923	2,102	981
1982	10,678	3,883	3,311	1,708	1,776	15.6	8.7	6,268	2,127	4,141	840	2,384	1,185
1983	10,717	3,570	2,937	1,652	2,559	20.0	10.1	6,258	1,780	4,478	830	2,412	1,216
1984	8,539	3,350	2,451	1,104	1,634	18.2	7.9	4,421	1,171	3,250	823	2,184	1,110
1985	8,312	3,498	2,509	1,025	1,280	15.6	6.8	4,139	1,157	2,982	877	2,256	1,039
1986	8,237	3,448	2,557	1,045	1,187	15.0	6.9	4,033	1,090	2,943	1,015	2,160	1,029
1987	7,425	3,246	2,196	943	1,040	14.5	6.5	3,566	943	2,623	965	1,974	920
1988	6,701	3,084	2,007	801	809	13.5	5.9	3,092	851	2,241	983	1,809	816
1989	6,528	3,174	1,978	730	646	11.9	4.8	2,983	850	2,133	1,024	1,843	677
1990	7,047	3,265	2,257	822	703	12.0	5.3	3,387	1,028	2,359	1,041	1,930	688
1991	8,628	3,480	2,791	1,246	1,111	13.7	6.8	4,694	1,292	3,402	1,004	2,139	792
1992	9,613	3,376	2,830	1,453	1,954	17.7	8.7	5,389	1,260	4,129	1,002	2,285	937
1993	8,940	3,262	2,584	1,297	1,798	18.0	8.3	4,848	1,115	3,733	976	2,198	919
1994	7,996	2,728	2,408	1,237	1,623	18.8	9.2	3,815	977	2,838	791	2,786	604
1995	7,404	2,700	2,342	1,085	1,278	16.6	8.3	3,476	1,030	2,446	824	2,525	579
1996	7,236	2,633	2,287	1,053	1,262	16.7	8.3	3,370	1,021	2,349	774	2,512	580
1997	6,739	2,538	2,138	995	1,067	15.8	8.0	3,037	931	2,106	795	2,338	569
1998	6,210	2,622	1,950	763	875	14.5	6.7	2,822	866	1,957	734	2,132	520
1999	5,880	2,568	1,832	755	725	13.4	6.4	2,622	848	1,774	783	2,005	469
2000	5,692	2,558	1,815	669	649	12.6	5.9	2,517	852	1,664	780	1,961	434
2001	6,801	2,853	2,196	951	801	13.1	6.8	3,476	1,067	2,409	835	2,031	459
2002	8,378	2,893	2,580	1,369	1,535	16.6	9.1	4,607	1,124	3,483	866	2,368	536
2003	8,774	2,785	2,612	1,442	1,936	19.2	10.1	4,838	1,121	3,717	818	2,477	641
2004	8,149	2,696	2,382	1,293	1,779	19.6	9.8	4,197	998	3,199	858	2,408	686
2005	7,591	2,667	2,304	1,130	1,490	18.4	8.9	3,667	933	2,734	872	2,386	666
2006	7,001	2,614	2,121	1,031	1,235	16.8	8.3	3,321	921	2,400	827	2,237	616
2007	7,078	2,542	2,232	1,061	1,243	16.8	8.5	3,515	976	2,539	793	2,142	627
2008	8,924	2,932	2,804	1,427	1,761	17.9	9.4	4,789	1,176	3,614	896	2,472	766
2009	14,265	3,165	3,828	2,775	4,496	24.4	15.1	9,160	1,630	7,530	882	3,187	1,035
2010	14,825	2,771	3,267	2,371	6,415	33.0	21.4	9,250	1,431	7,819	889	3,466	1,220
2011	13,747	2,677	2,993	2,061	6,016	39.3	21.4	8,106	1,230	6,876	956	3,401	1,284
2012	12,506	2,644	2,866	1,859	5,136	39.4	19.3	6,877	1,183	5,694	967	3,345	1,316
2013	11,460	2,584	2,759	1,807	4,310	36.5	17.0	6,073	1,136	4,937	932	3,207	1,247
2014	9,617	2,471	2,432	1,497	3,218	33.7	14.0	4,878	1,007	3,871	824	2,829	1,086
2015	8,296	2,399	2,302	1,267	2,328	29.2	11.6	4,063	974	3,089	819	2,535	879
2016	7,751	2,362	2,226	1,158	2,005	27.5	10.6	3,740	966	2,774	858	2,330	823
2017	6,982	2,270	2,008	1,017	1,687	25.0	10.0	3,434	956	2,479	778	2,079	690
2018	6,314	2,170	1,876	917	1,350	22.7	9.3	2,990	852	2,138	794	1,928	602
2017: Jan	7,565	2,427	2,076	1,186	1,834	25.0	10.2	3,650	1,043	2,607	873	2,158	786
Feb	7,437	2,507	2,128	1,049	1,772	25.3	10.1	3,651	970	2,682	813	2,210	750
Mar	7,078	2,272	2,047	1,091	1,677	25.4	10.5	3,501	959	2,541	785	2,061	796
Apr	7,019	2,332	2,076	1,067	1,650	24.4	10.1	3,538	953	2,584	779	2,022	703
May	6,991	2,159	1,935	1,113	1,680	25.0	10.6	3,428	872	2,556	782	2,103	674
June	6,948	2,269	1,943	934	1,708	25.1	10.1	3,422	879	2,544	809	2,038	682
July	6,927	2,181	2,020	1,001	1,739	24.9	10.1	3,329	1,009	2,320	744	2,096	696
Aug	7,115	2,202	2,028	1,065	1,722	24.3	10.4	3,519	1,017	2,502	785	2,148	653
Sept	6,791	2,256	1,931	964	1,720	26.4	10.2	3,356	909	2,446	748	2,073	663
Oct	6,588	2,162	1,957	866	1,628	25.5	9.7	3,236	872	2,365	746	1,998	622
Nov	6,682	2,248	1,919	970	1,597	25.1	9.7	3,175	928	2,248	751	2,035	708
Dec	6,572	2,230	1,984	892	1,511	23.8	8.9	3,249	923	2,326	726	1,985	568
2018: Jan	6,641	2,271	1,927	959	1,428	23.9	9.4	3,243	908	2,335	724	1,959	638
Feb	6,687	2,458	1,900	933	1,403	22.9	9.3	3,227	871	2,356	784	1,954	703
Mar	6,486	2,266	1,976	900	1,337	24.2	9.2	3,107	865	2,242	860	1,966	615
Apr	6,335	2,121	1,975	1,018	1,311	23.0	9.8	2,965	865	2,100	812	2,001	615
May	6,128	2,019	1,906	967	1,197	21.3	9.3	2,882	829	2,054	844	1,868	569
June	6,537	2,218	1,865	862	1,467	21.2	9.0	3,055	901	2,154	801	2,078	579
July	6,245	2,092	1,818	959	1,418	23.1	9.6	2,996	879	2,117	835	1,804	592
Aug	6,197	2,199	1,722	927	1,320	22.6	9.2	2,868	855	2,013	866	1,864	586
Sept	5,986	2,065	1,751	861	1,379	24.1	9.3	2,796	812	1,984	739	1,889	588
Oct	6,112	2,062	1,845	859	1,370	22.4	9.4	2,858	793	2,066	731	1,914	605
Nov	6,018	2,128	1,842	865	1,259	21.7	9.0	2,842	804	2,038	697	1,880	577
Dec	6,294	2,126	2,027	897	1,306	21.8	9.1	2,903	762	2,141	839	1,958	588

[1] Because of independent seasonal adjustment of the various series, detail will not sum to totals.
[2] Beginning with 2011, includes unemployment durations of up to 5 years; prior data are for up to 2 years.
[3] Beginning with 1994, job losers and persons who completed temporary jobs.

Note: Data relate to persons 16 years of age and over.
See Note, Table B-22.
Source: Department of Labor (Bureau of Labor Statistics).

TABLE B–29. Employees on nonagricultural payrolls, by major industry, 1975–2018

[Thousands of jobs; monthly data seasonally adjusted]

Year or month	Total non-agricultural employ-ment	Private industries									
		Total private	Goods-producing industries						Private service-providing industries		
			Total	Mining and logging	Construc-tion	Manufacturing			Total	Trade, transportation, and utilities [1]	
						Total	Durable goods	Non-durable goods		Total	Retail trade
1975	77,069	62,250	21,318	802	3,608	16,909	10,266	6,643	40,932	15,583	8,604
1976	79,502	64,501	22,025	832	3,662	17,531	10,640	6,891	42,476	16,105	8,970
1977	82,593	67,334	22,972	865	3,940	18,167	11,132	7,035	44,362	16,741	9,363
1978	86,826	71,014	24,156	902	4,322	18,932	11,770	7,162	46,858	17,633	9,882
1979	89,933	73,865	24,997	1,008	4,562	19,426	12,220	7,206	48,869	18,276	10,185
1980	90,533	74,158	24,263	1,077	4,454	18,733	11,679	7,054	49,895	18,387	10,249
1981	91,297	75,117	24,118	1,180	4,304	18,634	11,611	7,023	50,999	18,577	10,369
1982	89,689	73,706	22,550	1,163	4,024	17,363	10,610	6,753	51,156	18,430	10,377
1983	90,295	74,284	22,110	997	4,065	17,048	10,326	6,722	52,174	18,642	10,640
1984	94,548	78,389	23,435	1,014	4,501	17,920	11,050	6,870	54,954	19,624	11,227
1985	97,532	81,000	23,585	974	4,793	17,819	11,034	6,784	57,415	20,350	11,738
1986	99,500	82,661	23,318	829	4,937	17,552	10,795	6,757	59,343	20,765	12,082
1987	102,116	84,960	23,470	771	5,090	17,609	10,767	6,842	61,490	21,271	12,422
1988	105,378	87,838	23,909	770	5,233	17,906	10,969	6,938	63,929	21,942	12,812
1989	108,051	90,124	24,045	750	5,309	17,985	11,004	6,981	66,079	22,477	13,112
1990	109,527	91,112	23,723	765	5,263	17,695	10,737	6,958	67,389	22,634	13,186
1991	108,427	89,881	22,588	739	4,780	17,068	10,220	6,848	67,293	22,249	12,900
1992	108,802	90,015	22,095	689	4,608	16,799	9,946	6,853	67,921	22,094	12,831
1993	110,935	91,946	22,219	666	4,779	16,774	9,901	6,872	69,727	22,347	13,024
1994	114,399	95,124	22,774	659	5,095	17,020	10,132	6,889	72,350	23,096	13,494
1995	117,407	97,975	23,156	641	5,274	17,241	10,373	6,868	74,819	23,800	13,900
1996	119,836	100,297	23,409	637	5,536	17,237	10,486	6,751	76,888	24,205	14,146
1997	122,951	103,287	23,886	654	5,813	17,419	10,705	6,714	79,401	24,665	14,393
1998	126,157	106,248	24,354	645	6,149	17,560	10,911	6,649	81,894	25,150	14,613
1999	129,240	108,933	24,465	598	6,545	17,322	10,831	6,491	84,468	25,734	14,974
2000	132,024	111,235	24,649	599	6,787	17,263	10,877	6,386	86,585	26,187	15,284
2001	132,087	110,969	23,873	606	6,826	16,441	10,336	6,105	87,096	25,945	15,242
2002	130,649	109,136	22,557	583	6,716	15,259	9,485	5,774	86,579	25,458	15,029
2003	130,347	108,764	21,816	572	6,735	14,509	8,964	5,546	86,948	25,245	14,922
2004	131,787	110,166	21,882	591	6,976	14,315	8,925	5,390	88,284	25,487	15,063
2005	134,051	112,247	22,190	628	7,336	14,227	8,956	5,271	90,057	25,910	15,285
2006	136,453	114,479	22,530	684	7,691	14,155	8,981	5,174	91,949	26,223	15,359
2007	137,999	115,781	22,233	724	7,630	13,879	8,808	5,071	93,548	26,573	15,526
2008	137,241	114,732	21,335	767	7,162	13,406	8,463	4,943	93,398	26,236	15,289
2009	131,313	108,758	18,558	694	6,016	11,847	7,284	4,564	90,201	24,850	14,528
2010	130,362	107,871	17,751	705	5,518	11,528	7,064	4,464	90,121	24,581	14,446
2011	131,932	109,845	18,047	788	5,533	11,726	7,273	4,453	91,798	25,008	14,674
2012	134,175	112,255	18,420	848	5,646	11,927	7,470	4,457	93,835	25,416	14,847
2013	136,381	114,529	18,738	863	5,856	12,020	7,548	4,472	95,791	25,801	15,085
2014	138,958	117,076	19,226	891	6,151	12,185	7,674	4,512	97,850	26,321	15,363
2015	141,843	119,814	19,610	813	6,461	12,336	7,765	4,571	100,204	26,824	15,611
2016	144,352	122,128	19,750	668	6,728	12,354	7,714	4,640	102,379	27,195	15,832
2017 [p]	146,624	124,275	20,084	676	6,969	12,439	7,741	4,699	104,191	27,409	15,846
2018 [p]	149,073	126,622	20,709	732	7,289	12,688	7,945	4,743	105,913	27,659	15,832
2017: Jan	145,695	123,385	19,874	649	6,857	12,368	7,701	4,667	103,511	27,404	15,941
Feb	145,836	123,516	19,931	655	6,890	12,386	7,701	4,685	103,585	27,371	15,888
Mar	145,963	123,634	19,959	660	6,904	12,395	7,704	4,691	103,675	27,353	15,862
Apr	146,176	123,844	19,993	669	6,921	12,403	7,706	4,697	103,851	27,360	15,849
May	146,304	123,971	20,008	674	6,929	12,405	7,714	4,691	103,963	27,353	15,822
June	146,533	124,177	20,054	678	6,956	12,420	7,726	4,694	104,123	27,374	15,821
July	146,737	124,369	20,054	679	6,958	12,417	7,718	4,699	104,315	27,376	15,814
Aug	146,924	124,563	20,132	685	6,988	12,459	7,751	4,708	104,431	27,385	15,811
Sept	146,942	124,579	20,158	687	7,004	12,467	7,759	4,708	104,421	27,422	15,811
Oct	147,202	124,828	20,200	687	7,026	12,487	7,773	4,714	104,628	27,448	15,813
Nov	147,422	125,040	20,269	692	7,060	12,517	7,797	4,720	104,771	27,482	15,828
Dec	147,596	125,207	20,330	692	7,093	12,545	7,821	4,724	104,877	27,484	15,807
2018: Jan	147,767	125,393	20,386	699	7,126	12,561	7,838	4,723	105,007	27,502	15,809
Feb	148,097	125,697	20,497	706	7,199	12,592	7,865	4,727	105,200	27,560	15,833
Mar	148,279	125,870	20,527	714	7,201	12,612	7,886	4,726	105,343	27,591	15,834
Apr	148,475	126,054	20,587	723	7,230	12,634	7,903	4,731	105,467	27,589	15,838
May	148,745	126,318	20,650	728	7,267	12,655	7,917	4,738	105,668	27,630	15,856
June	149,007	126,554	20,706	735	7,284	12,687	7,944	4,743	105,848	27,622	15,822
July	149,185	126,727	20,744	734	7,303	12,707	7,961	4,746	105,983	27,643	15,824
Aug	149,467	126,973	20,794	742	7,337	12,715	7,973	4,742	106,179	27,693	15,830
Sept	149,575	127,081	20,832	745	7,354	12,733	7,987	4,746	106,249	27,692	15,804
Oct	149,852	127,366	20,892	751	7,379	12,762	8,006	4,756	106,474	27,715	15,794
Nov	150,048	127,566	20,921	748	7,384	12,789	8,022	4,767	106,645	27,783	15,827
Dec [p]	150,270	127,772	20,974	753	7,412	12,809	8,039	4,770	106,798	27,776	15,815

[1] Includes wholesale trade, transportation and warehousing, and utilities, not shown separately.

Note: Data in Tables B–29 and B–30 are based on reports from employing establishments and relate to full- and part-time wage and salary workers in nonagricultural establishments who received pay for any part of the pay period that includes the 12th of the month. Not comparable with labor force data (Tables B–22 through B–28), which include proprietors, self-employed persons, unpaid family workers, and private household workers; which count persons as

See next page for continuation of table.

TABLE B–29. Employees on nonagricultural payrolls, by major industry, 1975–2018—*Continued*

[Thousands of jobs; monthly data seasonally adjusted]

Year or month	Private industries—Continued						Government			
	Private service-providing industries—Continued									
	Information	Financial activities	Professional and business services	Education and health services	Leisure and hospitality	Other services	Total	Federal	State	Local
1975	2,061	4,047	6,056	5,497	5,544	2,144	14,820	2,882	3,179	8,758
1976	2,111	4,155	6,310	5,756	5,794	2,244	15,001	2,863	3,273	8,865
1977	2,185	4,348	6,611	6,052	6,065	2,359	15,258	2,859	3,377	9,023
1978	2,287	4,599	6,997	6,427	6,411	2,505	15,812	2,893	3,474	9,446
1979	2,375	4,843	7,339	6,768	6,631	2,637	16,068	2,894	3,541	9,633
1980	2,361	5,025	7,571	7,077	6,721	2,755	16,375	3,000	3,610	9,765
1981	2,382	5,163	7,809	7,364	6,840	2,865	16,180	2,922	3,640	9,619
1982	2,317	5,209	7,875	7,526	6,874	2,924	15,982	2,884	3,640	9,458
1983	2,253	5,334	8,065	7,781	7,078	3,021	16,011	2,915	3,662	9,434
1984	2,398	5,553	8,493	8,211	7,489	3,186	16,159	2,943	3,734	9,482
1985	2,437	5,815	8,900	8,679	7,869	3,366	16,533	3,014	3,832	9,687
1986	2,445	6,128	9,241	9,086	8,156	3,523	16,838	3,044	3,893	9,901
1987	2,507	6,385	9,639	9,543	8,446	3,699	17,156	3,089	3,967	10,100
1988	2,585	6,500	10,121	10,096	8,778	3,907	17,540	3,124	4,076	10,339
1989	2,622	6,562	10,588	10,652	9,062	4,116	17,927	3,136	4,182	10,609
1990	2,688	6,614	10,881	11,024	9,288	4,261	18,415	3,196	4,305	10,914
1991	2,677	6,561	10,746	11,556	9,256	4,249	18,545	3,110	4,355	11,081
1992	2,641	6,559	11,001	11,948	9,437	4,240	18,787	3,111	4,408	11,267
1993	2,668	6,742	11,527	12,362	9,732	4,350	18,989	3,063	4,488	11,438
1994	2,738	6,910	12,207	12,872	10,100	4,428	19,275	3,018	4,576	11,682
1995	2,843	6,866	12,878	13,360	10,501	4,572	19,432	2,949	4,635	11,849
1996	2,940	7,018	13,497	13,761	10,777	4,690	19,539	2,877	4,606	12,056
1997	3,084	7,255	14,371	14,185	11,018	4,825	19,664	2,806	4,582	12,276
1998	3,218	7,565	15,183	14,570	11,232	4,976	19,909	2,772	4,612	12,525
1999	3,419	7,753	15,994	14,939	11,543	5,087	20,307	2,769	4,709	12,829
2000	3,630	7,783	16,704	15,252	11,862	5,168	20,790	2,865	4,786	13,139
2001	3,629	7,900	16,514	15,814	12,036	5,258	21,118	2,764	4,905	13,449
2002	3,395	7,956	16,016	16,398	11,986	5,372	21,513	2,766	5,029	13,718
2003	3,188	8,078	16,029	16,835	12,173	5,401	21,583	2,761	5,002	13,820
2004	3,118	8,105	16,440	17,230	12,493	5,409	21,621	2,730	4,982	13,909
2005	3,061	8,197	17,003	17,676	12,816	5,395	21,804	2,732	5,032	14,041
2006	3,038	8,367	17,619	18,154	13,110	5,438	21,974	2,732	5,075	14,167
2007	3,032	8,348	17,998	18,676	13,427	5,494	22,218	2,734	5,122	14,362
2008	2,984	8,206	17,792	19,228	13,436	5,515	22,509	2,762	5,177	14,571
2009	2,804	7,838	16,634	19,630	13,077	5,367	22,555	2,832	5,169	14,554
2010	2,707	7,695	16,783	19,975	13,049	5,331	22,490	2,977	5,137	14,376
2011	2,674	7,697	17,389	20,318	13,353	5,360	22,086	2,859	5,078	14,150
2012	2,676	7,784	17,992	20,769	13,768	5,430	21,920	2,820	5,055	14,045
2013	2,706	7,886	18,575	21,086	14,254	5,483	21,853	2,769	5,046	14,037
2014	2,726	7,977	19,124	21,439	14,696	5,567	21,882	2,733	5,050	14,098
2015	2,750	8,123	19,695	22,029	15,160	5,622	22,029	2,757	5,077	14,195
2016	2,794	8,287	20,114	22,639	15,660	5,691	22,224	2,795	5,110	14,319
2017	2,814	8,451	20,508	23,188	16,051	5,770	22,350	2,805	5,165	14,379
2018 *p*	2,828	8,569	20,999	23,667	16,347	5,845	22,450	2,796	5,176	14,477
2017: Jan	2,817	8,399	20,336	22,942	15,884	5,729	22,310	2,810	5,150	14,350
Feb	2,812	8,397	20,340	23,005	15,920	5,740	22,320	2,812	5,164	14,344
Mar	2,811	8,408	20,373	23,046	15,939	5,745	22,329	2,810	5,167	14,352
Apr	2,804	8,426	20,403	23,098	16,010	5,750	22,332	2,800	5,167	14,365
May	2,804	8,432	20,454	23,130	16,029	5,761	22,333	2,810	5,170	14,353
June	2,809	8,447	20,491	23,170	16,061	5,771	22,356	2,807	5,170	14,379
July	2,810	8,460	20,537	23,238	16,118	5,776	22,368	2,807	5,174	14,387
Aug	2,818	8,473	20,573	23,278	16,123	5,781	22,361	2,802	5,168	14,391
Sept	2,814	8,480	20,586	23,298	16,043	5,778	22,363	2,801	5,161	14,401
Oct	2,814	8,485	20,627	23,317	16,145	5,792	22,374	2,804	5,160	14,410
Nov	2,815	8,493	20,662	23,355	16,163	5,801	22,382	2,797	5,166	14,419
Dec	2,821	8,500	20,693	23,380	16,195	5,804	22,389	2,795	5,164	14,430
2018: Jan	2,812	8,502	20,730	23,445	16,208	5,808	22,374	2,795	5,147	14,432
Feb	2,812	8,528	20,774	23,481	16,233	5,812	22,400	2,792	5,155	14,453
Mar	2,824	8,537	20,816	23,518	16,244	5,813	22,409	2,792	5,160	14,457
Apr	2,829	8,541	20,878	23,542	16,262	5,826	22,421	2,793	5,169	14,459
May	2,831	8,556	20,929	23,581	16,300	5,841	22,427	2,793	5,168	14,466
June	2,831	8,567	20,980	23,646	16,343	5,859	22,453	2,795	5,178	14,480
July	2,832	8,572	21,017	23,694	16,378	5,847	22,458	2,796	5,179	14,483
Aug	2,826	8,583	21,075	23,754	16,395	5,853	22,494	2,796	5,190	14,508
Sept	2,822	8,597	21,128	23,779	16,371	5,860	22,494	2,797	5,204	14,493
Oct	2,832	8,611	21,183	23,816	16,450	5,867	22,486	2,798	5,197	14,491
Nov	2,829	8,614	21,217	23,845	16,489	5,868	22,482	2,804	5,180	14,498
Dec *p*	2,825	8,618	21,246	23,912	16,544	5,877	22,498	2,799	5,188	14,511

Note (cont'd): employed when they are not at work because of industrial disputes, bad weather, etc., even if they are not paid for the time off; which are based on a sample of the working-age population; and which count persons only once—as employed, unemployed, or not in the labor force. In the data shown here, persons who work at more than one job are counted each time they appear on a payroll.

Establishment data for employment, hours, and earnings are classified based on the 2017 North American Industry Classification System (NAICS). For further description and details see *Employment and Earnings*.

Source: Department of Labor (Bureau of Labor Statistics).

TABLE B–30. Hours and earnings in private nonagricultural industries, 1975–2018

[Monthly data seasonally adjusted]

Year or month	All employees						Production and nonsupervisory employees [1]					
	Average weekly hours	Average hourly earnings		Average weekly earnings				Average weekly hours	Average hourly earnings		Average weekly earnings			
				Level		Percent change from year earlier					Level		Percent change from year earlier	
		Current dollars	1982–84 dollars [2]	Current dollars	1982–84 dollars [2]	Current dollars	1982–84 dollars [2]		Current dollars	1982–84 dollars [3]	Current dollars	1982–84 dollars [3]	Current dollars	1982–84 dollars [3]
1975	....	....	....	....	....	....	....	36.0	$4.74	$8.76	$170.45	$315.06	5.4	–3.4
1976	....	....	....	....	....	....	....	36.0	5.06	8.85	182.36	318.81	7.0	1.2
1977	....	....	....	....	....	....	....	35.9	5.44	8.93	195.34	320.76	7.1	.6
1978	....	....	....	....	....	....	....	35.8	5.88	8.96	210.17	320.38	7.6	–.1
1979	....	....	....	....	....	....	....	35.6	6.34	8.67	225.46	308.43	7.3	–3.7
1980	....	....	....	....	....	....	....	35.2	6.84	8.25	240.83	290.51	6.8	–5.8
1981	....	....	....	....	....	....	....	35.2	7.43	8.13	261.29	285.88	8.5	–1.6
1982	....	....	....	....	....	....	....	34.7	7.86	8.11	272.98	281.71	4.5	–1.5
1983	....	....	....	....	....	....	....	34.9	8.20	8.22	286.34	286.91	4.9	1.8
1984	....	....	....	....	....	....	....	35.1	8.49	8.22	298.08	288.56	4.1	.6
1985	....	....	....	....	....	....	....	34.9	8.73	8.17	304.37	284.72	2.1	–1.3
1986	....	....	....	....	....	....	....	34.7	8.92	8.21	309.69	285.17	1.7	.2
1987	....	....	....	....	....	....	....	34.7	9.14	8.12	317.33	282.07	2.5	–1.1
1988	....	....	....	....	....	....	....	34.6	9.44	8.07	326.50	279.06	2.9	–1.1
1989	....	....	....	....	....	....	....	34.5	9.81	8.00	338.42	276.04	3.7	–1.1
1990	....	....	....	....	....	....	....	34.3	10.20	7.91	349.63	271.03	3.3	–1.8
1991	....	....	....	....	....	....	....	34.1	10.51	7.83	358.46	266.91	2.5	–1.5
1992	....	....	....	....	....	....	....	34.2	10.77	7.79	368.20	266.43	2.7	–.2
1993	....	....	....	....	....	....	....	34.3	11.05	7.78	378.89	266.64	2.9	.1
1994	....	....	....	....	....	....	....	34.5	11.34	7.79	391.17	268.66	3.2	.8
1995	....	....	....	....	....	....	....	34.3	11.65	7.78	400.04	267.05	2.3	–.6
1996	....	....	....	....	....	....	....	34.3	12.04	7.81	413.25	268.17	3.3	.4
1997	....	....	....	....	....	....	....	34.5	12.51	7.94	431.86	274.02	4.5	2.2
1998	....	....	....	....	....	....	....	34.5	13.01	8.15	448.59	280.90	3.9	2.5
1999	....	....	....	....	....	....	....	34.3	13.49	8.27	463.15	283.79	3.2	1.0
2000	....	....	....	....	....	....	....	34.3	14.02	8.30	480.99	284.78	3.9	.3
2001	....	....	....	....	....	....	....	33.9	14.54	8.38	493.61	284.50	2.6	–.1
2002	....	....	....	....	....	....	....	33.9	14.96	8.50	506.54	287.97	2.6	1.2
2003	....	....	....	....	....	....	....	33.7	15.37	8.55	517.76	287.96	2.2	.0
2004	....	....	....	....	....	....	....	33.7	15.68	8.50	528.84	286.63	2.1	–.5
2005	....	....	....	....	....	....	....	33.8	16.12	8.44	544.02	284.83	2.9	–.6
2006	....	....	....	....	....	....	....	33.9	16.75	8.50	567.09	287.72	4.2	1.0
2007	34.4	$20.92	$10.09	$719.85	$347.18	....	....	33.8	17.42	8.59	589.18	290.57	3.9	1.0
2008	34.3	21.56	10.01	739.02	343.25	2.7	–1.1	33.6	18.06	8.56	607.42	287.80	3.1	–1.0
2009	33.8	22.17	10.33	749.98	349.58	1.5	1.8	33.1	18.61	8.88	615.96	293.83	1.4	2.1
2010	34.1	22.56	10.35	769.63	352.95	2.6	1.0	33.4	19.05	8.90	636.19	297.33	3.3	1.2
2011	34.3	23.03	10.24	790.85	351.58	2.8	–.4	33.6	19.44	8.77	652.89	294.66	2.6	–.9
2012	34.5	23.49	10.23	809.57	352.61	2.4	.3	33.7	19.74	8.73	665.65	294.24	2.0	–.1
2013	34.4	23.96	10.29	825.02	354.15	1.9	.4	33.7	20.13	8.78	677.70	295.52	1.8	.4
2014	34.5	24.47	10.34	844.91	356.90	2.4	.8	33.7	20.61	8.85	694.85	298.51	2.5	1.0
2015	34.5	25.02	10.56	864.21	364.62	2.3	2.2	33.7	21.03	9.07	708.90	305.81	2.0	2.4
2016	34.4	25.64	10.68	881.20	367.16	2.0	.7	33.6	21.54	9.20	723.31	309.01	2.0	1.0
2017	34.4	26.33	10.74	906.30	369.74	2.8	.7	33.7	22.06	9.23	742.62	310.65	2.7	.5
2018 [p]	34.5	27.11	10.80	936.29	372.86	3.3	.8	33.8	22.71	9.26	767.05	312.90	3.3	.7
2017: Jan	34.4	25.98	10.66	893.71	366.61	1.8	–.7	33.6	21.82	9.17	733.15	308.21	2.1	–.4
Feb	34.3	26.08	10.69	894.54	366.67	2.4	–.3	33.6	21.86	9.19	734.50	308.63	2.3	–.5
Mar	34.3	26.11	10.71	895.57	367.41	2.3	–.1	33.5	21.89	9.21	733.32	308.49	2.0	–.4
Apr	34.4	26.17	10.72	900.25	368.88	2.5	.3	33.7	21.94	9.22	739.38	310.74	2.5	.4
May	34.4	26.22	10.75	901.97	369.72	2.5	.7	33.6	21.98	9.24	738.53	310.63	2.3	.5
June	34.4	26.28	10.76	904.03	370.23	2.5	.8	33.7	22.03	9.26	742.41	311.98	2.6	1.1
July	34.4	26.36	10.79	906.78	371.04	2.6	.8	33.7	22.08	9.27	744.10	312.48	2.6	.9
Aug	34.4	26.39	10.76	907.82	370.09	2.9	.9	33.6	22.11	9.24	742.90	310.63	2.3	.4
Sept	34.3	26.51	10.76	909.29	369.00	2.5	.3	33.6	22.19	9.23	745.58	310.11	2.6	.3
Oct	34.4	26.47	10.73	910.57	369.27	2.3	.3	33.7	22.18	9.22	747.47	310.83	2.5	.4
Nov	34.5	26.55	10.73	915.98	370.34	3.1	.9	33.7	22.24	9.21	749.49	310.48	2.7	.3
Dec	34.5	26.64	10.75	919.08	370.74	3.0	.9	33.8	22.31	9.22	754.08	311.61	3.4	1.2
2018: Jan	34.4	26.71	10.73	918.82	369.18	2.8	.7	33.6	22.36	9.20	751.30	309.16	2.5	.3
Feb	34.5	26.75	10.73	922.88	370.09	3.2	.9	33.8	22.40	9.20	757.12	310.89	3.1	.7
Mar	34.5	26.84	10.76	925.98	371.14	3.4	1.0	33.7	22.49	9.23	757.91	311.19	3.4	.9
Apr	34.5	26.90	10.76	928.05	371.29	3.1	.7	33.8	22.55	9.24	762.19	312.38	3.1	.5
May	34.5	26.99	10.77	931.16	371.50	3.2	.5	33.8	22.62	9.24	764.56	312.45	3.5	.6
June	34.5	27.05	10.77	933.23	371.61	3.2	.4	33.8	22.67	9.24	766.25	312.44	3.2	.1
July	34.5	27.11	10.78	935.30	371.75	3.1	.2	33.8	22.71	9.24	767.60	312.45	3.2	.0
Aug	34.5	27.23	10.81	939.44	372.97	3.5	.8	33.8	22.80	9.27	770.64	313.24	3.7	.8
Sept	34.5	27.30	10.83	941.85	373.74	3.6	1.3	33.7	22.86	9.29	770.38	313.13	3.3	1.0
Oct	34.5	27.35	10.82	943.58	373.26	3.6	1.1	33.7	22.90	9.27	771.73	312.56	3.2	.6
Nov	34.4	27.43	10.85	943.59	373.31	3.0	.8	33.7	22.99	9.32	774.76	314.08	3.4	1.2
Dec [p]	34.5	27.53	10.89	949.79	375.82	3.3	1.4	33.7	23.09	9.37	778.13	315.86	3.2	1.4

[1] Production employees in goods-producing industries and nonsupervisory employees in service-providing industries. These groups account for four-fifths of the total employment on private nonfarm payrolls.
[2] Current dollars divided by the consumer price index for all urban consumers (CPI-U) on a 1982–84=100 base.
[3] Current dollars divided by the consumer price index for urban wage earners and clerical workers (CPI-W) on a 1982–84=100 base.

Note: See Note, Table B–29.

Source: Department of Labor (Bureau of Labor Statistics).

TABLE B–31. Employment cost index, private industry, 2001–2018

Year and month	Total private			Goods-producing			Service-providing [1]			Manufacturing		
	Total compensation	Wages and salaries	Benefits [2]	Total compensation	Wages and salaries	Benefits [2]	Total compensation	Wages and salaries	Benefits [2]	Total compensation	Wages and salaries	Benefits [2]
Indexes on NAICS basis, December 2005=100; not seasonally adjusted												
December:												
2001 [3]	87.3	89.9	81.3	86.0	90.0	78.5	87.8	89.8	82.4	85.5	90.2	77.2
2002	90.0	92.2	84.7	89.0	92.6	82.3	90.4	92.1	85.8	88.7	92.8	81.3
2003	93.6	95.1	90.2	92.6	94.9	88.2	94.0	95.2	91.0	92.4	95.1	87.3
2004	97.2	97.6	96.2	96.9	97.2	96.3	97.3	97.7	96.1	96.9	97.4	96.0
2005	100.0	100.0	100.0	100.0	100.0	100.0	100.0	100.0	100.0	100.0	100.0	100.0
2006	103.2	103.2	103.1	102.5	102.9	101.7	103.4	103.3	103.7	101.8	102.3	100.8
2007	106.3	106.6	105.6	105.0	106.0	103.2	106.7	106.8	106.6	103.8	104.9	101.7
2008	108.9	109.4	107.7	107.5	109.0	104.7	109.4	109.6	108.9	105.9	107.7	102.5
2009	110.2	110.8	108.7	108.6	110.0	105.8	110.8	111.1	109.9	107.0	108.9	103.6
2010	112.5	112.8	111.9	111.1	111.6	110.1	113.0	113.1	112.6	110.0	110.7	108.8
2011	115.0	114.6	115.9	113.8	113.5	114.4	115.3	114.9	116.4	113.1	112.7	113.9
2012	117.1	116.6	118.2	115.6	115.4	116.0	117.6	117.0	119.1	114.9	114.8	115.0
2013	119.4	119.0	120.5	117.7	117.6	118.0	120.0	119.4	121.5	117.0	117.2	116.6
2014	122.2	121.6	123.5	120.3	120.1	120.7	122.8	122.1	124.6	119.8	119.8	119.8
2015	124.5	124.2	125.1	123.2	123.2	123.1	124.9	124.5	125.9	122.8	123.0	122.5
2016	127.2	127.1	127.3	125.8	126.2	124.9	127.7	127.4	128.3	125.5	126.2	124.3
2017	130.5	130.6	130.2	128.9	129.3	128.0	131.0	131.0	131.2	128.9	129.3	128.0
2018	134.4	134.7	133.6	131.9	133.0	129.6	135.2	135.2	135.1	131.6	132.9	129.1
2018: Mar	131.9	132.0	131.6	129.9	130.4	129.0	132.6	132.5	132.7	130.0	130.4	129.1
June	132.9	132.9	132.9	130.9	131.4	129.8	133.5	133.3	134.1	130.8	131.3	129.8
Sept	133.8	134.0	133.2	131.2	132.2	129.3	134.6	134.5	134.6	130.9	132.0	128.9
Dec	134.4	134.7	133.6	131.9	133.0	129.6	135.2	135.2	135.1	131.6	132.9	129.1
Indexes on NAICS basis, December 2005=100; seasonally adjusted												
2017: Mar	128.3	128.3	128.3	126.6	127.1	125.4	128.8	128.6	129.5	126.3	127.1	125.0
June	129.0	129.0	129.1	127.2	127.8	126.0	129.6	129.4	130.3	127.0	127.8	125.6
Sept	130.0	130.0	130.0	128.3	128.7	127.5	130.5	130.3	131.0	128.3	128.7	127.7
Dec	130.6	130.7	130.5	128.9	129.4	128.0	131.2	131.1	131.5	129.0	129.5	128.1
2018: Mar	131.9	132.0	131.6	130.0	130.5	129.0	132.5	132.5	132.6	129.9	130.4	129.1
June	132.7	132.8	132.7	130.8	131.4	129.7	133.4	133.2	133.9	130.7	131.2	129.7
Sept	133.7	133.9	133.2	131.1	132.1	129.2	134.5	134.5	134.6	130.9	132.0	128.8
Dec	134.5	134.8	133.9	131.9	133.1	129.5	135.3	135.3	135.4	131.7	133.1	129.2
Percent change from 12 months earlier, not seasonally adjusted												
December:												
2001 [3]	4.1	3.8	5.2	3.6	3.6	3.7	4.4	3.8	5.6	3.4	3.6	3.5
2002	3.1	2.6	4.2	3.5	2.9	4.8	3.0	2.6	4.1	3.7	2.9	5.3
2003	4.0	3.1	6.5	4.0	2.5	7.2	4.0	3.4	6.1	4.2	2.5	7.4
2004	3.8	2.6	6.7	4.6	2.4	9.2	3.5	2.6	5.6	4.9	2.4	10.0
2005	2.9	2.5	4.0	3.2	2.9	3.8	2.8	2.4	4.1	3.2	2.7	4.2
2006	3.2	3.2	3.1	2.5	2.9	1.7	3.4	3.3	3.7	1.8	2.3	.8
2007	3.0	3.3	2.4	2.4	3.0	1.5	3.2	3.4	2.8	2.0	2.5	.9
2008	2.4	2.6	2.0	2.4	2.8	1.5	2.5	2.6	2.2	2.0	2.7	.8
2009	1.2	1.3	.9	1.0	.9	1.1	1.3	1.4	.9	1.0	1.1	1.1
2010	2.1	1.8	2.9	2.3	1.5	4.1	2.0	1.8	2.5	2.8	1.7	5.0
2011	2.2	1.6	3.6	2.4	1.7	3.9	2.0	1.6	3.4	2.8	1.8	4.7
2012	1.8	1.7	2.0	1.6	1.7	1.4	2.0	1.8	2.3	1.6	1.9	1.0
2013	2.0	2.1	1.9	1.8	1.9	1.7	2.0	2.1	2.0	1.8	2.1	1.4
2014	2.3	2.2	2.5	2.2	2.1	2.3	2.3	2.3	2.6	2.4	2.2	2.7
2015	1.9	2.1	1.3	2.4	2.6	2.0	1.7	2.0	1.0	2.5	2.7	2.3
2016	2.2	2.3	1.8	2.1	2.4	1.5	2.2	2.3	1.9	2.2	2.6	1.5
2017	2.6	2.8	2.3	2.5	2.5	2.5	2.6	2.8	2.3	2.7	2.5	3.0
2018	3.0	3.1	2.6	2.3	2.9	1.3	3.2	3.2	3.0	2.1	2.8	.9
2018: Mar	2.8	2.9	2.5	2.7	2.6	2.9	2.9	3.0	2.4	2.8	2.6	3.3
June	2.9	2.9	2.8	2.8	2.7	2.9	2.9	2.9	2.8	2.9	2.7	3.3
Sept	2.9	3.1	2.5	2.2	2.6	1.3	3.1	3.1	2.7	1.9	2.6	.9
Dec	3.0	3.1	2.6	2.3	2.9	1.3	3.2	3.2	3.0	2.1	2.8	.9
Percent change from 3 months earlier, seasonally adjusted												
2017: Mar	0.8	0.9	0.6	0.6	0.7	0.4	0.8	0.8	0.7	0.5	0.6	0.5
June	.5	.5	.6	.5	.6	.5	.6	.6	.6	.6	.6	.5
Sept	.8	.8	.7	.9	.7	1.2	.7	.7	.5	1.0	.7	1.7
Dec	.5	.5	.4	.5	.5	.4	.5	.6	.4	.5	.6	.3
2018: Mar	1.0	1.0	.8	.9	.9	.8	1.0	1.1	.8	.7	.7	.8
June	.6	.6	.8	.6	.7	.5	.7	.5	1.0	.6	.6	.5
Sept	.8	.8	.4	.2	.5	-.4	.8	1.0	.5	.2	.6	-.7
Dec	.6	.7	.5	.6	.8	.2	.6	.6	.6	.6	.8	.3

[1] On Standard Industrial Classification (SIC) basis, data are for service-producing industries.
[2] Employer costs for employee benefits.
[3] Data on North American Industry Classification System (NAICS) basis available beginning with 2001; not strictly comparable with earlier data on SIC basis.

Note: Changes effective with the release of March 2006 data (in April 2006) include changing industry classification to NAICS from SIC and rebasing data to December 2005=100. Historical SIC data are available through December 2005.
Data exclude farm and household workers.

Source: Department of Labor (Bureau of Labor Statistics).

TABLE B–32. Productivity and related data, business and nonfarm business sectors, 1970–2018

[Index numbers, 2012=100; quarterly data seasonally adjusted]

Year or quarter	Labor productivity (output per hour)		Output [1]		Hours of all persons [2]		Compensation per hour [3]		Real compensation per hour [4]		Unit labor costs		Implicit price deflator [5]	
	Business sector	Nonfarm business sector	Business sector	Nonfarm business sector	Business sector	Nonfarm business sector	Business sector	Nonfarm business sector	Business sector	Nonfarm business sector	Business sector	Nonfarm business sector	Business sector	Nonfarm business sector
1970	42.3	43.6	26.8	26.8	63.5	61.5	12.1	12.2	65.3	66.0	28.6	28.0	24.9	24.5
1971	44.0	45.3	27.9	27.8	63.3	61.4	12.8	13.0	66.3	67.1	29.1	28.6	26.0	25.6
1972	45.5	46.8	29.7	29.7	65.3	63.4	13.6	13.8	68.3	69.2	30.0	29.5	26.9	26.4
1973	46.8	48.3	31.7	31.8	67.8	66.0	14.7	14.9	69.4	70.1	31.4	30.8	28.3	27.3
1974	46.0	47.5	31.2	31.4	67.9	66.1	16.1	16.3	68.3	69.1	34.9	34.2	31.1	30.2
1975	47.6	48.8	31.0	30.9	65.0	63.3	17.8	18.0	69.3	70.0	37.3	36.8	34.1	33.4
1976	49.2	50.5	33.0	33.1	67.1	65.5	19.2	19.4	70.8	71.3	39.0	38.4	35.8	35.2
1977	50.1	51.3	34.9	35.0	69.7	68.1	20.7	20.9	71.8	72.5	41.4	40.8	38.0	37.4
1978	50.7	52.1	37.2	37.3	73.3	71.6	22.5	22.7	72.7	73.5	44.3	43.7	40.6	39.8
1979	50.8	52.0	38.5	38.6	75.7	74.2	24.7	24.9	72.9	73.6	48.6	47.9	44.0	43.1
1980	50.8	51.9	38.1	38.2	75.1	73.6	27.3	27.6	72.5	73.3	53.8	53.1	47.9	47.2
1981	51.9	52.8	39.2	39.1	75.6	74.1	29.9	30.3	72.6	73.4	57.6	57.4	52.3	51.8
1982	51.6	52.3	38.1	37.9	73.9	72.5	32.1	32.5	73.5	74.3	62.2	62.1	55.3	55.0
1983	53.4	54.5	40.1	40.3	75.2	73.9	33.6	33.9	73.6	74.5	62.8	62.3	57.3	56.9
1984	54.9	55.7	43.7	43.7	79.6	78.4	35.0	35.4	73.8	74.6	63.8	63.6	58.9	58.5
1985	56.2	56.6	45.7	45.6	81.4	80.5	36.8	37.1	75.0	75.6	65.6	65.5	60.4	60.2
1986	57.7	58.3	47.4	47.3	82.1	81.1	38.9	39.2	77.9	78.6	67.4	67.3	61.3	61.1
1987	58.1	58.7	49.1	49.0	84.5	83.6	40.4	40.7	78.1	78.8	69.5	69.5	62.4	62.2
1988	59.0	59.6	51.2	51.3	86.9	86.0	42.5	42.8	79.4	80.0	72.1	71.8	64.4	64.1
1989	59.6	60.2	53.2	53.1	89.1	88.3	43.8	44.1	78.4	78.9	73.4	73.3	66.8	66.5
1990	60.8	61.2	54.0	53.9	88.8	88.2	46.5	46.7	79.3	79.7	76.5	76.4	69.0	68.7
1991	61.8	62.2	53.7	53.6	86.9	86.2	48.7	48.9	80.1	80.5	78.8	78.7	71.0	70.9
1992	64.7	65.0	56.0	55.8	86.5	85.9	51.7	52.0	83.0	83.4	79.9	80.0	72.1	72.1
1993	64.7	65.0	57.6	57.5	88.9	88.4	52.4	52.6	82.1	82.4	81.0	80.9	73.8	73.8
1994	65.1	65.5	60.3	60.1	92.7	91.8	52.8	53.1	81.0	81.5	81.1	81.1	75.1	75.1
1995	65.6	66.2	62.2	62.2	94.8	94.0	54.1	54.5	81.0	81.6	82.5	82.2	76.5	76.5
1996	67.2	67.6	65.1	65.0	96.9	96.1	56.0	56.3	81.8	82.2	83.4	83.3	77.7	77.5
1997	68.6	68.9	68.5	68.4	99.8	99.2	58.3	58.5	83.2	83.6	84.9	84.9	78.8	78.9
1998	70.8	71.0	72.0	72.0	101.8	101.3	61.7	61.9	87.0	87.3	87.2	87.2	79.3	79.4
1999	73.6	73.7	76.1	76.1	103.4	103.2	64.7	64.8	89.3	89.4	87.9	87.9	79.8	80.0
2000	76.1	76.2	79.8	79.7	104.8	104.6	69.2	69.4	92.4	92.6	90.9	91.0	81.0	81.3
2001	78.3	78.3	80.4	80.3	102.7	102.6	72.4	72.4	93.9	93.9	92.5	92.5	82.3	82.6
2002	81.6	81.7	81.8	81.7	100.2	100.0	74.0	74.0	94.5	94.6	90.7	90.7	82.9	83.3
2003	84.8	84.8	84.5	84.3	99.6	99.5	76.8	76.8	95.9	95.9	90.5	90.6	83.9	84.2
2004	87.4	87.2	88.1	87.9	100.8	100.8	80.4	80.3	97.7	97.7	92.0	92.1	86.1	86.2
2005	89.3	89.1	91.5	91.3	102.5	102.5	83.3	83.2	98.0	97.9	93.2	93.4	88.7	89.1
2006	90.3	90.1	94.6	94.4	104.7	104.8	86.5	86.4	98.6	98.5	95.7	95.9	91.1	91.6
2007	91.8	91.7	96.8	96.7	105.4	105.5	90.4	90.2	100.1	99.9	98.4	98.4	93.2	93.4
2008	92.8	92.6	95.8	95.7	103.3	103.3	92.8	92.7	99.0	98.9	100.0	100.1	94.7	94.9
2009	96.1	95.9	92.3	92.0	96.0	95.9	93.6	93.6	100.2	100.2	97.4	97.5	94.9	95.4
2010	99.3	99.2	95.2	95.0	95.9	95.8	95.3	95.3	100.4	100.4	95.9	96.1	96.0	96.3
2011	99.2	99.1	97.1	96.9	97.8	97.8	97.3	97.4	99.4	99.5	98.1	98.2	98.2	98.2
2012	100.0	100.0	100.0	100.0	100.0	100.0	100.0	100.0	100.0	100.0	100.0	100.0	100.0	100.0
2013	100.9	100.5	102.4	102.2	101.5	101.7	101.5	101.3	100.0	99.8	100.6	100.8	101.5	101.5
2014	101.6	101.3	105.6	105.4	103.9	104.0	104.2	104.1	100.9	100.9	102.5	102.8	103.2	103.3
2015	102.8	102.6	109.3	109.0	106.3	106.2	107.1	107.3	103.6	103.8	104.2	104.6	103.8	104.2
2016	102.9	102.8	111.1	110.8	107.9	107.8	108.2	108.5	103.4	103.6	105.2	105.5	104.7	105.3
2017 ᵖ	104.1	103.9	114.0	113.8	109.5	109.5	111.9	112.1	104.6	104.8	107.5	107.9	106.5	107.0
2018 ᵖ	....	....	....	....	111.8	111.9	....	....	....	....	....	....	....	....
2015: I	102.4	102.3	108.3	108.1	105.8	105.6	106.2	106.4	103.4	103.7	103.6	104.0	103.2	103.6
II	103.0	102.9	109.4	109.2	106.2	106.1	107.2	107.4	103.7	103.9	104.0	104.4	103.8	104.2
III	103.2	103.0	109.6	109.4	106.2	106.2	107.7	107.9	103.8	104.0	104.3	104.7	104.1	104.5
IV	102.4	102.3	109.7	109.4	107.1	107.0	107.5	107.7	103.6	103.8	104.9	105.3	104.0	104.4
2016: I	102.5	102.3	110.1	109.8	107.4	107.3	107.5	107.7	103.6	103.8	104.9	105.2	103.8	104.4
II	102.7	102.6	110.8	110.5	107.9	107.7	107.6	107.9	103.0	103.3	104.8	105.2	104.6	105.2
III	103.1	102.9	111.4	111.1	108.1	108.0	108.2	108.5	103.1	103.4	105.0	105.4	104.9	105.6
IV	103.5	103.2	112.0	111.7	108.2	108.2	109.7	109.7	103.8	103.9	105.9	106.3	105.4	106.0
2017: I	103.5	103.3	112.5	112.3	108.7	108.6	110.8	111.0	104.1	104.3	107.0	107.4	105.8	106.4
II	103.9	103.8	113.5	113.3	109.3	109.2	111.2	111.4	104.4	104.6	107.0	107.3	106.1	106.6
III	104.6	104.3	114.5	114.3	109.5	109.6	112.7	112.8	105.3	105.3	107.7	108.1	106.6	107.1
IV	104.3	104.3	115.3	115.2	110.6	110.5	113.0	113.3	104.7	105.0	108.3	108.7	107.4	107.9
2018: I	104.5	104.3	116.0	115.9	111.1	111.1	114.2	114.3	104.9	105.1	109.3	109.6	107.9	108.4
II	105.4	105.1	117.5	117.3	111.5	111.7	114.4	114.4	104.6	104.6	108.5	108.8	108.8	109.3
III	105.9	105.7	118.6	118.5	112.0	112.1	115.2	115.3	104.9	104.9	108.8	109.1	109.1	109.7
IV ᵖ	....	....	....	....	112.5	112.6	....	....	....	....	....	....	....	....

[1] Output refers to real gross domestic product in the sector.
[2] Hours at work of all persons engaged in sector, including hours of employees, proprietors, and unpaid family workers. Estimates based primarily on establishment data.
[3] Wages and salaries of employees plus employers' contributions for social insurance and private benefit plans. Also includes an estimate of wages, salaries, and supplemental payments for the self-employed.
[4] Hourly compensation divided by consumer price series. The trend for 1978-2017 is based on the consumer price index research series (CPI-U-RS). The change for prior years and recent quarters is based on the consumer price index for all urban consumers (CPI-U).
[5] Current dollar output divided by the output index.

Source: Department of Labor (Bureau of Labor Statistics).

TABLE B-33. Changes in productivity and related data, business and nonfarm business sectors, 1970–2018

[Percent change from preceding period; quarterly data at seasonally adjusted annual rates]

Year or quarter	Output per hour of all persons		Output [1]		Hours of all persons [2]		Compensation per hour [3]		Real compensation per hour [4]		Unit labor costs		Implicit price deflator [5]	
	Business sector	Nonfarm business sector	Business sector	Nonfarm business sector	Business sector	Nonfarm business sector	Business sector	Nonfarm business sector	Business sector	Nonfarm business sector	Business sector	Nonfarm business sector	Business sector	Nonfarm business sector
1970	2.0	1.5	0.0	-0.1	-2.0	-1.6	7.5	7.0	1.7	1.2	5.4	5.4	4.3	4.4
1971	4.1	3.9	3.8	3.7	-.3	-.2	6.0	6.1	1.6	1.7	1.9	2.1	4.2	4.3
1972	3.3	3.4	6.5	6.7	3.1	3.2	6.3	6.4	3.0	3.1	2.9	2.9	3.4	3.1
1973	3.0	3.1	6.9	7.3	3.8	4.1	7.9	7.6	1.6	1.3	4.8	4.4	5.2	3.5
1974	-1.7	-1.6	-1.5	-1.5	.2	.1	9.3	9.5	-1.5	-1.4	11.2	11.3	9.8	10.4
1975	3.5	2.7	-1.0	-1.6	-4.3	-4.3	10.7	10.5	1.4	1.3	6.9	7.6	9.7	10.7
1976	3.3	3.5	6.8	7.2	3.3	3.6	8.0	7.8	2.1	1.9	4.5	4.1	5.2	5.4
1977	1.8	1.7	5.7	5.7	3.8	3.9	8.0	8.2	1.4	1.6	6.1	6.4	5.9	6.2
1978	1.2	1.4	6.4	6.7	5.1	5.2	8.4	8.6	1.3	1.5	7.1	7.1	6.9	6.5
1979	.2	-.2	3.6	3.4	3.4	3.6	9.7	9.6	.2	.1	9.5	9.8	8.4	8.4
1980	.0	.0	-.9	-.9	-.9	-.8	10.7	10.7	-.4	-.4	10.7	10.8	8.9	9.5
1981	2.2	1.6	2.9	2.3	.7	.7	9.5	9.7	.1	.2	7.1	8.0	9.2	9.6
1982	-.6	-.9	-2.9	-3.1	-2.3	-2.2	7.3	7.2	1.2	1.1	8.0	8.2	5.7	6.2
1983	3.5	4.2	5.3	6.2	1.8	2.0	4.5	4.6	.2	.3	1.0	.4	3.6	3.5
1984	2.9	2.2	8.9	8.5	5.8	6.1	4.4	4.3	.2	.1	1.5	2.0	2.8	2.8
1985	2.3	1.7	4.7	4.4	2.3	2.6	5.1	4.9	1.6	1.4	2.7	3.1	2.6	3.1
1986	2.8	3.0	3.6	3.8	.8	.8	5.6	5.8	3.8	3.9	2.8	2.7	1.4	1.4
1987	.6	.6	3.6	3.6	3.0	3.0	3.8	3.8	.3	.4	3.2	3.2	1.9	1.9
1988	1.5	1.6	4.3	4.6	2.7	2.9	5.3	5.1	1.6	1.5	3.7	3.4	3.2	3.1
1989	1.2	.9	3.8	3.7	2.6	2.7	3.0	2.9	-1.3	-1.4	1.8	2.0	3.7	3.6
1990	2.0	1.7	1.6	1.5	-.4	-.2	6.2	6.0	1.2	1.0	4.2	4.2	3.3	3.4
1991	1.6	1.6	-.6	-.6	-2.2	-2.2	4.7	4.8	1.0	1.1	3.0	3.1	2.9	3.1
1992	4.6	4.5	4.2	4.1	-.4	-.4	6.1	6.2	3.5	3.6	1.4	1.6	1.6	1.7
1993	.1	.1	2.9	3.1	2.7	3.0	1.5	1.2	-1.0	-1.3	1.4	1.1	2.3	2.3
1994	.6	.7	4.8	4.6	4.2	3.9	.7	1.0	-1.3	-1.1	.1	.3	1.8	1.9
1995	.7	1.1	3.1	3.4	2.3	2.3	2.4	2.5	.0	.1	1.7	1.4	1.8	1.8
1996	2.5	2.1	4.6	4.5	2.1	2.3	3.6	3.5	.9	.8	1.1	1.3	1.6	1.4
1997	2.2	1.9	5.2	5.2	3.0	3.2	4.0	3.9	1.8	1.7	1.8	1.9	1.5	1.7
1998	3.1	3.1	5.2	5.3	2.0	2.2	5.9	5.8	4.5	4.4	2.7	2.6	.6	.7
1999	4.0	3.8	5.7	5.7	1.6	1.8	4.8	4.6	2.7	2.5	.8	.8	.6	.8
2000	3.5	3.3	4.9	4.7	1.4	1.4	7.0	7.0	3.4	3.5	3.4	3.6	1.5	1.6
2001	2.8	2.7	.7	.8	-2.0	-1.9	4.6	4.3	1.7	1.5	1.7	1.6	1.6	1.6
2002	4.3	4.3	1.7	1.7	-2.4	-2.5	2.2	2.3	.6	.7	-1.9	-1.9	.7	.8
2003	3.9	3.8	3.3	3.2	-.6	-.6	3.8	3.7	1.5	1.4	-.2	-.1	1.3	1.1
2004	3.0	2.9	4.3	4.2	1.2	1.3	4.6	4.5	1.9	1.8	1.6	1.6	2.5	2.3
2005	2.2	2.2	3.9	3.9	1.7	1.7	3.6	3.7	.2	.3	1.4	1.4	3.1	3.3
2006	1.1	1.1	3.4	3.4	2.2	2.3	3.9	3.9	.6	.6	2.7	2.7	2.7	2.8
2007	1.6	1.7	2.3	2.4	.6	.7	4.5	4.3	1.6	1.5	2.8	2.6	2.3	2.0
2008	1.0	1.1	-1.0	-1.0	-2.0	-2.1	2.7	2.8	-1.1	-1.0	1.6	1.7	1.5	1.6
2009	3.6	3.5	-3.7	-3.9	-7.1	-7.2	.9	.9	1.2	1.3	-2.7	-2.5	.2	.5
2010	3.3	3.4	3.2	3.3	-.1	-.1	1.8	1.9	.1	.2	-1.5	-1.5	1.2	1.0
2011	-.1	.0	1.9	2.0	2.0	2.0	2.1	2.2	-1.0	-.9	2.2	2.2	2.3	1.9
2012	.8	.9	3.0	3.1	2.2	2.3	2.8	2.7	.6	.5	2.0	1.8	1.9	1.9
2013	.9	.5	2.4	2.2	1.5	1.7	1.5	1.3	.0	-.2	.6	.8	1.5	1.5
2014	.7	.8	3.0	3.1	2.3	2.3	2.6	2.8	.9	1.1	1.9	2.0	1.7	1.8
2015	1.2	1.3	3.5	3.5	2.3	2.1	2.9	3.1	2.7	2.9	1.7	1.8	.6	.8
2016	.2	.1	1.7	1.6	1.5	1.5	1.0	1.1	-.2	-.2	.9	.9	.9	1.1
2017	1.1	1.1	2.6	2.7	1.5	1.6	3.4	3.4	1.2	1.2	2.3	2.2	1.7	1.6
2018 p					2.1	2.2								
2015: I	2.8	3.1	4.1	4.1	1.3	.9	5.1	5.5	7.8	8.2	2.2	2.3	-1.3	-.6
II	2.4	2.1	4.1	4.1	1.7	2.0	3.8	3.5	1.1	.8	1.4	1.4	2.2	2.1
III	.7	.5	.8	.6	.0	.1	2.0	1.9	.4	.3	1.3	1.4	1.3	1.2
IV	-3.0	-2.9	.1	.1	3.2	3.0	-.8	-.7	-1.0	-.8	2.2	2.3	-.3	-.2
2016: I	.2	.3	1.6	1.6	1.4	1.3	.0	.1	.1	.1	-.2	-.2	-.8	-.3
II	.7	.9	2.6	2.5	1.9	1.6	.3	.7	-2.3	-2.0	-.4	-.2	3.1	3.2
III	1.6	1.3	2.2	2.2	.6	.9	2.5	2.2	.6	.3	.9	.9	1.3	1.5
IV	1.9	1.3	2.2	2.3	.3	1.0	5.6	4.7	2.7	1.9	3.6	3.4	1.7	1.8
2017: I	-.2	.4	1.9	1.9	2.0	1.5	4.0	4.7	1.0	1.6	4.2	4.2	1.8	1.3
II	1.6	1.6	3.7	3.8	2.1	2.2	1.3	1.3	1.2	1.2	-.3	-.3	.8	.8
III	2.8	2.3	3.5	3.6	.7	1.3	5.6	5.1	3.4	2.9	2.8	2.8	2.0	2.1
IV	-1.1	-.3	2.9	3.0	4.1	3.3	1.2	1.9	-2.1	-1.3	2.4	2.3	2.9	2.9
2018: I	.6	.3	2.5	2.6	1.9	2.3	4.3	3.8	.8	.2	3.7	3.4	1.9	1.8
II	3.6	3.0	5.1	5.0	1.5	2.0	.5	.0	-1.1	-1.6	-2.9	-2.8	3.6	3.6
III	1.8	2.2	3.9	4.0	2.1	1.7	2.9	3.2	.9	1.2	1.1	.9	1.1	1.4
IV p					1.7	1.6								

[1] Output refers to real gross domestic product in the sector.
[2] Hours at work of all persons engaged in the sector. See footnote 2, Table B–32.
[3] Wages and salaries of employees plus employers' contributions for social insurance and private benefit plans. Also includes an estimate of wages, salaries, and supplemental payments for the self-employed.
[4] Hourly compensation divided by a consumer price index. See footnote 4, Table B–32.
[5] Current dollar output divided by the output index.

Note: Percent changes are calculated using index numbers to three decimal places and may differ slightly from percent changes based on indexes in Table B–32, which are rounded to one decimal place.

Source: Department of Labor (Bureau of Labor Statistics).

Production and Business Activity

Table B–34. Industrial production indexes, major industry divisions, 1974–2018

[2012=100, except as noted; monthly data seasonally adjusted]

Year or month	Total industrial production [1]		Manufacturing					Mining	Utilities
	Index, 2012=100	Percent change from year earlier [2]	Total [1]	Percent change from year earlier [2]	Durable	Nondurable	Other (non-NAICS) [1]		
1974	46.3	–0.3	43.8	–0.2	28.5	67.5	123.4	91.2	49.5
1975	42.2	–8.9	39.2	–10.6	24.8	62.6	117.3	89.1	50.5
1976	45.5	7.9	42.7	9.0	27.1	68.3	121.0	89.7	52.9
1977	48.9	7.6	46.4	8.6	29.8	73.0	132.6	91.8	55.1
1978	51.6	5.5	49.2	6.1	32.1	75.6	137.2	94.7	56.5
1979	53.2	3.0	50.7	3.1	33.7	76.1	140.1	97.5	57.7
1980	51.8	–2.6	48.9	–3.6	32.2	73.7	144.9	99.3	58.1
1981	52.5	1.3	49.4	1.0	32.5	74.4	148.4	101.9	58.9
1982	49.8	–5.2	46.7	–5.5	29.7	73.3	150.1	96.8	57.0
1983	51.1	2.7	48.9	4.8	31.2	76.7	154.4	91.7	57.4
1984	55.7	8.9	53.7	9.8	35.6	80.2	161.5	97.6	60.8
1985	56.4	1.2	54.6	1.6	36.4	80.7	167.9	95.7	62.3
1986	56.9	1.0	55.8	2.2	37.0	83.0	171.3	88.8	62.9
1987	59.9	5.2	59.0	5.7	39.2	87.4	181.1	89.6	65.9
1988	63.0	5.2	62.1	5.3	42.1	90.4	180.3	92.0	69.9
1989	63.6	.9	62.6	.8	42.6	90.9	177.8	91.0	72.1
1990	64.2	1.0	63.1	.8	42.7	92.4	175.7	92.2	73.5
1991	63.2	–1.5	61.9	–1.9	41.4	92.1	168.5	90.3	75.3
1992	65.1	2.9	64.2	3.7	43.6	94.5	165.1	88.6	75.3
1993	67.2	3.3	66.5	3.6	46.1	95.9	166.2	88.4	77.9
1994	70.8	5.3	70.4	5.9	50.0	99.2	164.8	90.0	79.5
1995	74.0	4.6	74.0	5.1	54.1	100.9	164.8	89.9	82.3
1996	77.4	4.5	77.6	4.9	59.1	101.2	163.2	91.5	84.6
1997	83.0	7.2	84.2	8.4	66.1	105.0	177.0	93.3	84.5
1998	87.8	5.8	89.8	6.7	73.0	106.7	187.5	91.6	86.8
1999	91.7	4.4	94.3	5.1	79.3	107.3	192.9	86.9	89.5
2000	95.2	3.9	98.2	4.1	85.0	107.8	192.4	88.8	92.0
2001	92.3	–3.1	94.6	–3.6	81.6	104.7	179.9	89.1	91.7
2002	92.6	.4	95.1	.5	81.9	106.0	173.8	84.9	94.4
2003	93.8	1.3	96.4	1.3	84.2	106.2	168.9	85.1	96.0
2004	96.4	2.7	99.4	3.1	88.2	107.8	169.7	85.0	97.4
2005	99.6	3.3	103.4	4.1	93.4	110.5	169.1	84.0	99.5
2006	101.8	2.3	106.1	2.6	97.8	111.2	167.1	86.1	99.2
2007	104.4	2.5	109.0	2.8	102.7	112.5	157.7	86.8	102.3
2008	100.8	–3.5	103.8	–4.8	99.2	105.8	143.9	88.0	101.9
2009	89.2	–11.5	89.5	–13.8	80.6	97.7	120.3	83.1	99.0
2010	94.1	5.5	94.7	5.8	89.2	99.8	111.2	87.2	102.8
2011	97.1	3.1	97.5	2.9	94.7	99.9	106.0	92.6	102.4
2012	100.0	3.0	100.0	2.6	100.0	100.0	100.0	100.0	100.0
2013	102.0	2.0	100.9	.9	102.1	100.0	95.0	106.3	102.2
2014	105.2	3.1	102.0	1.1	105.1	99.3	93.8	117.8	103.5
2015	104.1	–1.0	101.5	–.5	103.9	99.6	90.4	113.8	102.7
2016	102.1	–1.9	100.7	–.8	101.7	100.4	88.0	102.7	102.3
2017 ᵖ	103.7	1.6	101.9	1.2	103.3	101.8	81.9	109.3	101.0
2018 ᵖ	108.0	4.1	104.4	2.5	106.8	103.9	76.1	123.3	105.5
2017: Jan	102.5	–.5	101.5	.1	103.0	100.9	85.1	104.1	99.4
Feb	102.2	–.2	101.6	.7	103.0	101.2	85.5	106.4	92.2
Mar	102.7	1.2	101.1	.4	102.6	100.8	84.1	106.7	100.6
Apr	103.7	1.9	102.2	1.9	104.0	101.7	83.2	107.9	100.4
May	103.7	2.1	101.8	1.6	103.1	101.8	82.3	108.5	102.8
June	103.8	1.8	101.9	1.5	103.1	102.2	81.8	109.5	101.2
July	103.6	1.4	101.7	1.0	102.3	102.5	80.4	109.3	102.1
Aug	103.2	1.1	101.4	1.1	102.6	101.7	79.9	108.7	100.6
Sept	103.2	1.2	101.3	.7	103.5	100.4	80.4	110.1	99.8
Oct	104.8	2.7	102.6	1.8	103.9	102.8	81.7	111.6	103.0
Nov	105.3	3.4	102.9	2.1	104.2	103.1	79.9	113.9	103.3
Dec	105.8	2.9	102.8	1.7	104.3	103.1	78.3	115.1	106.6
2018: Jan	105.4	2.8	102.3	.8	104.0	102.2	78.2	113.9	108.8
Feb	105.9	3.7	103.8	2.2	105.6	103.6	79.8	117.1	98.4
Mar	106.4	3.6	103.7	2.5	105.8	103.1	80.1	118.4	102.6
Apr	107.7	3.8	104.3	2.0	106.3	103.9	79.5	119.5	108.5
May	106.8	3.0	103.3	1.4	104.7	103.6	77.6	120.7	105.7
June	107.4	3.5	104.0	2.0	106.1	103.9	74.4	122.8	104.1
July	107.9	4.1	104.4	2.7	106.0	104.8	73.7	123.8	104.2
Aug	108.8	5.5	104.9	3.4	107.5	104.4	73.8	126.5	105.4
Sept ᵖ	109.0	5.7	105.2	3.8	108.1	104.3	74.7	127.6	104.1
Oct ᵖ	109.3	4.4	105.0	2.3	108.0	104.1	75.1	127.9	107.5
Nov ᵖ	110.0	4.5	105.3	2.4	108.6	104.2	73.7	129.3	109.9
Dec ᵖ	110.1	4.1	106.1	3.2	109.9	104.7	71.6	131.2	102.4

[1] Total industry and total manufacturing series include manufacturing as defined in the North American Industry Classification System (NAICS) plus those industries—logging and newspaper, periodical, book, and directory publishing—that have traditionally been considered to be manufacturing and included in the industrial sector.

[2] Percent changes based on unrounded indexes.

Note: Data based on NAICS; see footnote 1.

Source: Board of Governors of the Federal Reserve System.

TABLE B–35. Capacity utilization rates, 1974–2018

[Percent [1]; monthly data seasonally adjusted]

Year or month	Total industry [2]	Manufacturing				Mining	Utilities	Stage-of-process		
		Total [2]	Durable goods	Nondurable goods	Other (non-NAICS) [2]			Crude	Primary and semi-finished	Finished
1974	85.1	84.5	84.7	84.2	82.7	91.1	86.4	91.0	87.3	80.4
1975	75.8	73.7	71.8	76.1	77.3	89.5	84.9	84.0	75.2	73.8
1976	79.8	78.3	76.4	81.2	77.6	89.6	85.4	87.0	80.1	76.9
1977	83.4	82.5	81.2	84.4	83.2	89.5	86.7	89.1	84.5	79.9
1978	85.1	84.4	83.8	85.3	85.0	89.7	86.9	88.7	86.2	82.3
1979	85.0	84.1	84.1	83.9	85.6	91.2	86.9	90.0	85.9	81.8
1980	80.8	78.7	77.6	79.7	86.7	91.3	85.3	89.4	78.7	79.4
1981	79.6	76.9	75.1	78.8	87.5	90.9	84.1	89.3	77.2	77.5
1982	73.6	70.9	66.5	76.4	87.4	84.1	79.7	82.3	70.5	73.1
1983	74.8	73.4	68.7	79.4	87.9	79.8	79.1	79.9	74.4	73.0
1984	80.4	79.3	76.9	82.1	89.4	85.8	81.6	85.8	81.1	77.2
1985	79.2	78.1	75.7	80.5	90.3	84.4	81.5	83.8	79.8	76.6
1986	78.6	78.4	75.4	81.8	88.7	77.6	80.6	79.2	79.7	77.1
1987	81.1	81.0	77.6	84.8	90.4	80.3	83.2	82.8	82.7	78.7
1988	84.3	84.0	82.0	86.2	88.6	84.1	86.5	86.3	85.8	81.7
1989	83.8	83.3	81.9	85.0	85.4	85.1	86.5	86.8	84.7	81.7
1990	82.5	81.6	79.4	84.2	83.7	86.9	86.2	87.9	82.6	80.6
1991	79.9	78.5	75.4	82.3	80.8	85.4	87.5	85.5	80.0	78.2
1992	80.5	79.5	77.0	82.7	80.0	85.3	86.0	85.9	81.4	78.1
1993	81.4	80.4	78.6	82.7	81.2	85.8	87.9	85.8	83.2	78.2
1994	83.5	82.8	81.6	84.5	81.3	86.8	88.0	87.8	86.2	79.2
1995	83.9	83.1	82.2	84.5	82.2	87.6	89.0	89.0	86.3	79.8
1996	83.3	82.1	81.5	83.1	80.6	90.5	90.4	89.1	85.5	79.3
1997	84.0	83.0	82.1	83.8	85.6	91.8	89.8	90.4	85.9	80.2
1998	82.7	81.5	80.5	82.2	86.8	89.3	92.3	87.0	84.0	80.1
1999	81.7	80.4	80.0	80.1	87.0	86.2	93.8	86.1	84.2	77.8
2000	81.4	79.6	79.4	79.0	87.2	90.5	93.9	88.5	83.8	76.7
2001	76.1	73.8	71.4	75.8	82.6	89.9	89.8	85.5	77.3	72.5
2002	74.9	73.0	69.9	76.0	81.4	86.0	87.5	83.2	77.3	70.5
2003	75.9	73.9	71.0	76.9	81.6	87.8	85.7	85.0	78.1	71.3
2004	78.1	76.4	73.9	78.8	82.5	88.2	84.6	86.5	80.1	73.3
2005	80.0	78.4	76.4	80.3	81.9	88.5	85.3	86.6	81.7	75.6
2006	80.4	78.7	77.6	79.8	79.8	90.2	84.0	88.0	81.3	76.4
2007	80.7	78.8	78.6	79.3	76.3	89.4	86.1	88.6	81.0	77.2
2008	77.8	74.6	74.7	74.3	77.2	90.0	84.4	87.5	76.7	74.1
2009	68.5	65.5	61.4	69.9	69.8	80.3	80.7	77.9	65.7	68.2
2010	73.6	70.7	68.7	73.4	66.4	83.9	83.1	83.3	71.8	71.3
2011	76.2	73.6	72.6	75.4	65.3	85.7	81.6	84.5	74.3	74.0
2012	77.2	74.9	75.4	75.4	63.0	86.9	78.5	85.4	74.7	75.4
2013	77.6	75.0	75.4	75.6	62.0	86.9	80.0	85.8	75.7	74.7
2014	79.0	75.8	76.8	75.7	63.5	90.2	80.9	88.3	76.9	75.4
2015	77.3	75.8	75.9	76.7	63.5	83.9	80.0	82.7	76.5	75.8
2016	75.3	74.6	73.8	76.4	63.5	77.6	78.8	78.5	75.4	74.1
2017	76.1	74.8	74.2	76.4	61.1	84.5	76.3	83.8	75.0	74.2
2018 [p]	78.0	75.7	75.8	77.1	58.6	92.0	78.0	89.9	76.3	75.1
2017: Jan	75.4	74.7	74.3	76.0	62.5	80.0	75.8	80.3	74.9	74.0
Feb	75.1	74.7	74.2	76.1	62.9	82.0	70.2	81.5	73.9	74.0
Mar	75.5	74.3	73.9	75.7	62.1	82.3	76.4	82.1	74.8	73.6
Apr	76.2	75.1	74.9	76.4	61.6	83.4	76.2	83.4	75.0	74.6
May	76.2	74.8	74.2	76.4	61.2	84.0	77.9	84.0	75.2	74.1
June	76.2	74.8	74.1	76.7	61.0	84.9	76.5	84.7	75.0	74.1
July	76.1	74.6	73.5	76.8	60.1	84.8	77.1	84.8	74.7	74.0
Aug	75.7	74.4	73.6	76.2	59.9	84.3	75.9	83.4	74.3	74.1
Sept	75.7	74.2	74.2	75.2	60.5	85.3	75.2	82.5	74.4	74.3
Oct	76.8	75.2	74.4	76.9	61.6	86.4	77.4	85.4	75.5	74.6
Nov	77.1	75.3	74.6	77.1	60.5	87.9	77.6	86.7	75.9	74.3
Dec	77.3	75.2	74.6	77.0	59.4	88.6	79.9	86.9	76.4	74.3
2018: Jan	77.0	74.7	74.3	76.3	59.5	87.4	81.5	85.3	76.3	74.2
Feb	77.2	75.7	75.4	77.2	60.8	89.5	73.6	86.9	75.5	75.2
Mar	77.5	75.6	75.5	76.8	61.2	90.1	76.6	87.9	76.1	74.6
Apr	78.2	75.9	75.7	77.3	60.9	90.5	80.9	88.3	77.3	75.1
May	77.5	75.1	74.5	77.0	59.7	90.9	78.7	89.1	76.3	73.9
June	77.8	75.5	75.4	77.1	57.3	92.0	77.3	90.1	76.1	74.6
July	78.0	75.7	75.2	77.7	56.9	92.3	77.3	90.6	75.9	75.0
Aug	78.5	76.0	76.2	77.3	57.1	93.9	78.0	91.9	76.3	75.3
Sept [p]	78.5	76.1	76.6	77.1	58.0	94.2	76.9	92.0	76.0	75.7
Oct [p]	78.6	75.9	76.4	76.9	58.4	93.9	79.3	91.5	76.5	75.5
Nov [p]	78.9	76.0	76.7	76.9	57.4	94.4	80.9	92.0	77.2	75.4
Dec [p]	78.8	76.5	77.6	77.2	56.0	95.3	75.2	92.6	76.2	76.1

[1] Output as percent of capacity.
[2] See footnote 1 and Note, Table B–34.

Source: Board of Governors of the Federal Reserve System.

TABLE B–36. New private housing units started, authorized, and completed and houses sold, 1975–2018

[Thousands; monthly data at seasonally adjusted annual rates]

Year or month	New housing units started				New housing units authorized [1]				New housing units completed	New houses sold
	Type of structure				Type of structure					
	Total	1 unit	2 to 4 units [2]	5 units or more	Total	1 unit	2 to 4 units	5 units or more		
1975	1,160.4	892.2	64.0	204.3	939.2	675.5	63.8	199.8	1,317.2	549
1976	1,537.5	1,162.4	85.8	289.2	1,296.2	893.6	93.1	309.5	1,377.2	646
1977	1,987.1	1,450.9	121.7	414.4	1,690.0	1,126.1	121.3	442.7	1,657.1	819
1978	2,020.3	1,433.3	125.1	462.0	1,800.5	1,182.6	130.6	487.3	1,867.5	817
1979	1,745.1	1,194.1	122.0	429.0	1,551.8	981.5	125.4	444.8	1,870.8	709
1980	1,292.2	852.2	109.5	330.5	1,190.6	710.4	114.5	365.7	1,501.6	545
1981	1,084.2	705.4	91.2	287.7	985.5	564.3	101.8	319.4	1,265.7	436
1982	1,062.2	662.6	80.1	319.6	1,000.5	546.4	88.3	365.8	1,005.5	412
1983	1,703.0	1,067.6	113.5	522.0	1,605.2	901.5	133.7	570.1	1,390.3	623
1984	1,749.5	1,084.2	121.4	543.9	1,681.8	922.4	142.6	616.8	1,652.2	639
1985	1,741.8	1,072.4	93.5	576.0	1,733.3	956.6	120.1	656.6	1,703.3	688
1986	1,805.4	1,179.4	84.0	542.0	1,769.4	1,077.6	108.4	583.5	1,756.4	750
1987	1,620.5	1,146.8	65.1	408.7	1,534.8	1,024.4	89.3	421.1	1,668.8	671
1988	1,488.1	1,081.3	58.7	348.0	1,455.6	993.8	75.7	386.1	1,529.8	676
1989	1,376.1	1,003.3	55.3	317.6	1,338.4	931.7	66.9	339.8	1,422.8	650
1990	1,192.7	894.8	37.6	260.4	1,110.8	793.9	54.3	262.6	1,308.0	534
1991	1,013.9	840.4	35.6	137.9	948.8	753.5	43.1	152.1	1,090.8	509
1992	1,199.7	1,029.9	30.9	139.0	1,094.9	910.7	45.8	138.4	1,157.5	610
1993	1,287.6	1,125.7	29.4	132.6	1,199.1	986.5	52.4	160.2	1,192.7	666
1994	1,457.0	1,198.4	35.2	223.5	1,371.6	1,068.5	62.2	241.0	1,346.9	670
1995	1,354.1	1,076.2	33.8	244.1	1,332.5	997.3	63.8	271.5	1,312.6	667
1996	1,476.8	1,160.9	45.3	270.8	1,425.6	1,069.5	65.8	290.3	1,412.9	757
1997	1,474.0	1,133.7	44.5	295.8	1,441.1	1,062.4	68.4	310.3	1,400.5	804
1998	1,616.9	1,271.4	42.6	302.9	1,612.3	1,187.6	69.2	355.5	1,474.2	886
1999	1,640.9	1,302.4	31.9	306.6	1,663.5	1,246.7	65.8	351.1	1,604.9	880
2000	1,568.7	1,230.9	38.7	299.1	1,592.3	1,198.1	64.9	329.3	1,573.7	877
2001	1,602.7	1,273.3	36.6	292.8	1,636.7	1,235.6	66.0	335.2	1,570.8	908
2002	1,704.9	1,358.6	38.5	307.9	1,747.7	1,332.6	73.7	341.4	1,648.4	973
2003	1,847.7	1,499.0	33.5	315.2	1,889.2	1,460.9	82.5	345.8	1,678.7	1,086
2004	1,955.8	1,610.5	42.3	303.0	2,070.1	1,613.4	90.4	366.2	1,841.9	1,203
2005	2,068.3	1,715.8	41.1	311.4	2,155.3	1,682.0	84.0	389.3	1,931.4	1,283
2006	1,800.9	1,465.4	42.7	292.8	1,838.9	1,378.2	76.6	384.1	1,979.4	1,051
2007	1,355.0	1,046.0	31.7	277.3	1,398.4	979.9	59.6	359.0	1,502.8	776
2008	905.5	622.0	17.5	266.0	905.4	575.6	34.4	295.4	1,119.7	485
2009	554.0	445.1	11.6	97.3	583.0	441.1	20.7	121.1	794.4	375
2010	586.9	471.2	11.4	104.3	604.6	447.3	22.0	135.3	651.7	323
2011	608.8	430.6	10.9	167.3	624.1	418.5	21.6	184.0	584.9	306
2012	780.6	535.3	11.4	233.9	829.7	518.7	25.9	285.1	649.2	368
2013	924.9	617.6	13.6	293.7	990.8	620.8	29.0	341.1	764.4	429
2014	1,003.3	647.9	13.7	341.7	1,052.1	640.3	29.9	382.0	883.8	437
2015	1,111.8	714.5	11.5	385.8	1,182.6	696.0	32.1	454.5	968.2	501
2016	1,173.8	781.5	11.5	380.8	1,206.6	750.8	34.8	421.1	1,059.7	561
2017	1,203.0	848.9	11.4	342.7	1,282.0	820.0	37.2	424.8	1,152.9	613
2018 [p]	1,246.6	872.8	14.0	359.7	1,310.7	852.7	37.6	420.4	1,191.7	....
2017: Jan	1,225	807	....	415	1,329	798	30	501	1,086	596
Feb	1,289	875	....	395	1,248	825	45	378	1,148	618
Mar	1,179	824	....	346	1,279	825	36	418	1,189	643
Apr	1,165	834	....	314	1,255	796	36	423	1,095	593
May	1,122	791	....	317	1,205	784	35	386	1,169	604
June	1,225	860	....	359	1,312	813	37	462	1,234	616
July	1,185	839	....	335	1,258	817	42	399	1,197	556
Aug	1,172	878	....	286	1,300	803	36	461	1,091	558
Sept	1,158	831	....	310	1,254	831	36	387	1,086	637
Oct	1,265	888	....	359	1,343	854	35	454	1,188	618
Nov	1,303	948	....	347	1,323	864	41	418	1,144	712
Dec	1,210	847	....	359	1,320	877	38	405	1,197	636
2018: Jan	1,334	886	....	435	1,366	870	45	451	1,218	633
Feb	1,290	900	....	372	1,323	886	46	391	1,289	663
Mar	1,327	882	....	431	1,377	851	40	486	1,229	672
Apr	1,276	898	....	357	1,364	863	41	460	1,257	633
May	1,329	938	....	379	1,301	843	34	424	1,251	653
June	1,177	851	....	316	1,292	853	36	403	1,216	612
July	1,184	861	....	317	1,303	873	28	402	1,195	606
Aug	1,280	890	....	373	1,249	827	35	387	1,230	601
Sept	1,237	879	....	349	1,270	854	40	376	1,148	613
Oct	1,209	863	....	327	1,265	847	36	382	1,111	562
Nov [p]	1,214	812	....	387	1,322	848	39	435	1,128	657
Dec [p]	1,078	758	....	302	1,326	829	37	460	1,097	....

[1] Authorized by issuance of local building permits in permit-issuing places: 20,100 places beginning with 2014; 19,300 for 2004–2013; 19,000 for 1994–2003; 17,000 for 1984–93; 16,000 for 1978–83; and 14,000 for 1975–77.
[2] Monthly data do not meet publication standards because tests for identifiable and stable seasonality do not meet reliability standards.

Note: One-unit estimates prior to 1999, for new housing units started and completed and for new houses sold, include an upward adjustment of 3.3 percent to account for structures in permit-issuing areas that did not have permit authorization.

Source: Department of Commerce (Bureau of the Census).

TABLE B-37. Manufacturing and trade sales and inventories, 1978–2018

[Amounts in millions of dollars; monthly data seasonally adjusted]

Year or month	Total manufacturing and trade			Manufacturing			Merchant wholesalers [1]			Retail trade			Retail and food services sales
	Sales [2]	Inventories [3]	Ratio [4]	Sales [2]	Inventories [3]	Ratio [4]	Sales [2]	Inventories [3]	Ratio [4]	Sales [2,5]	Inventories [3]	Ratio [4]	
SIC: [6]													
1978	260,320	400,931	1.54	126,905	211,691	1.67	66,413	86,934	1.31	67,002	102,306	1.53	
1979	297,701	452,640	1.52	143,936	242,157	1.68	79,051	99,679	1.26	74,713	110,804	1.48	
1980	327,233	508,924	1.56	154,391	265,215	1.72	93,099	122,631	1.32	79,743	121,078	1.52	
1981	355,822	545,786	1.53	168,129	283,413	1.69	101,180	129,654	1.28	86,514	132,719	1.53	
1982	347,625	573,908	1.67	163,351	311,852	1.95	95,211	127,428	1.36	89,062	134,628	1.49	
1983	369,286	590,287	1.56	172,547	312,379	1.78	99,225	130,075	1.28	97,514	147,833	1.44	
1984	410,124	649,780	1.53	190,682	339,516	1.73	112,199	142,452	1.23	107,243	167,812	1.49	
1985	422,583	664,039	1.56	194,538	334,749	1.73	113,459	147,409	1.28	114,586	181,881	1.52	
1986	430,419	662,738	1.55	194,657	322,654	1.68	114,960	153,574	1.32	120,803	186,510	1.56	
1987	457,735	709,848	1.50	206,326	338,109	1.59	122,968	163,903	1.29	128,442	207,836	1.55	
1988	497,157	767,222	1.49	224,619	369,374	1.57	134,521	178,801	1.30	138,017	219,047	1.54	
1989	527,039	815,455	1.52	236,698	391,212	1.63	143,760	187,009	1.28	146,581	237,234	1.58	
1990	545,909	840,594	1.52	242,686	405,073	1.65	149,506	195,833	1.29	153,718	239,688	1.56	
1991	542,815	834,609	1.53	239,847	390,950	1.65	148,306	200,448	1.33	154,661	243,211	1.54	
1992	567,176	842,809	1.48	250,394	382,510	1.54	154,150	208,302	1.32	162,632	251,997	1.52	
NAICS: [6]													
1992	540,199	835,800	1.53	242,002	378,609	1.57	147,261	196,914	1.31	150,936	260,277	1.67	167,842
1993	567,195	863,125	1.50	251,708	379,806	1.50	154,018	204,842	1.30	161,469	278,477	1.68	179,425
1994	609,854	926,395	1.46	269,843	399,934	1.44	164,575	221,978	1.29	175,436	304,483	1.66	194,186
1995	654,689	985,385	1.48	289,973	424,802	1.44	179,915	238,392	1.29	184,801	322,191	1.72	204,219
1996	686,923	1,004,646	1.45	299,766	430,366	1.44	190,362	241,058	1.27	196,796	333,222	1.67	216,983
1997	723,443	1,045,495	1.42	319,558	443,227	1.37	198,154	258,454	1.26	205,731	343,814	1.64	227,178
1998	742,391	1,077,183	1.44	324,984	448,373	1.39	202,260	272,297	1.32	215,147	356,513	1.62	237,746
1999	786,178	1,137,260	1.40	335,991	463,004	1.35	216,597	290,182	1.30	233,591	384,074	1.59	257,249
2000	833,868	1,195,894	1.41	350,715	480,748	1.35	234,546	309,191	1.29	248,606	405,955	1.59	273,961
2001	818,160	1,118,552	1.42	330,875	427,353	1.38	232,096	297,536	1.32	255,189	393,663	1.58	281,576
2002	823,234	1,139,700	1.36	326,227	423,205	1.29	236,294	301,310	1.26	260,713	415,185	1.55	288,256
2003	854,700	1,147,856	1.34	334,616	408,363	1.25	248,190	308,274	1.22	271,894	431,219	1.56	301,038
2004	926,002	1,241,644	1.30	359,081	441,122	1.19	277,501	340,128	1.17	289,421	460,394	1.56	320,550
2005	1,005,821	1,314,008	1.27	395,173	474,330	1.17	303,208	367,978	1.17	307,440	471,700	1.51	340,479
2006	1,069,032	1,408,429	1.28	417,963	523,093	1.20	328,438	398,924	1.17	322,631	486,412	1.49	357,863
2007	1,128,176	1,486,746	1.28	443,288	561,789	1.22	351,956	424,379	1.17	332,932	500,578	1.49	369,978
2008	1,160,722	1,465,186	1.31	455,750	542,696	1.26	377,030	445,307	1.20	327,943	477,183	1.52	365,965
2009	988,802	1,330,869	1.38	368,648	504,298	1.39	319,115	397,383	1.29	301,039	429,188	1.47	338,706
2010	1,088,890	1,449,499	1.27	409,273	553,333	1.28	361,447	441,618	1.15	318,171	454,548	1.39	357,081
2011	1,206,660	1,564,021	1.26	457,658	605,929	1.29	407,090	487,289	1.15	341,913	470,803	1.35	383,192
2012	1,267,248	1,652,863	1.28	474,727	624,177	1.30	434,002	523,034	1.17	358,519	505,652	1.38	402,199
2013	1,303,229	1,717,465	1.29	484,145	629,893	1.30	447,546	543,932	1.19	371,538	543,640	1.41	416,814
2014	1,340,932	1,776,773	1.31	490,630	640,143	1.31	463,682	575,944	1.21	386,620	560,686	1.43	434,638
2015	1,294,787	1,806,740	1.39	459,918	635,272	1.39	441,036	583,576	1.33	393,833	587,892	1.49	445,791
2016	1,286,409	1,839,188	1.42	446,225	630,894	1.41	435,490	596,276	1.35	404,695	612,018	1.49	459,575
2017	1,356,014	1,902,544	1.38	467,076	659,189	1.37	466,127	616,821	1.29	422,811	626,534	1.47	479,196
2018 p	1,444,204	1,994,489	1.35	499,975	681,549	1.35	500,885	661,843	1.28	443,343	651,097	1.44	503,035
2017: Jan	1,333,366	1,842,312	1.38	459,695	632,817	1.38	456,431	594,234	1.30	417,240	615,261	1.47	473,357
Feb	1,333,242	1,846,792	1.39	459,901	633,881	1.38	458,290	596,018	1.30	415,051	616,893	1.49	471,165
Mar	1,333,933	1,851,752	1.39	460,313	634,109	1.38	457,612	597,622	1.31	416,008	620,021	1.49	472,041
Apr	1,336,631	1,848,718	1.38	459,759	635,340	1.38	457,801	595,717	1.30	419,071	617,661	1.47	475,145
May	1,335,203	1,854,654	1.39	462,459	635,407	1.37	455,105	598,107	1.31	417,639	621,140	1.49	473,752
June	1,342,005	1,863,379	1.39	462,442	636,761	1.38	459,614	601,801	1.31	419,949	624,817	1.49	476,074
July	1,345,285	1,869,267	1.39	464,204	639,738	1.38	460,512	605,894	1.32	420,569	623,635	1.48	476,685
Aug	1,356,602	1,882,004	1.39	467,460	642,665	1.37	467,917	610,597	1.30	421,225	628,742	1.49	477,452
Sept	1,376,904	1,884,562	1.37	472,250	648,947	1.37	474,091	612,650	1.29	430,563	622,965	1.45	487,096
Oct	1,385,361	1,884,375	1.36	475,599	651,201	1.37	477,567	609,856	1.28	432,195	623,318	1.44	488,900
Nov	1,403,578	1,892,739	1.35	483,203	653,855	1.35	485,814	613,960	1.26	434,561	624,924	1.44	491,795
Dec	1,414,511	1,902,544	1.35	484,979	659,189	1.36	492,439	616,821	1.25	437,093	626,534	1.43	494,578
2018: Jan	1,406,327	1,915,012	1.36	488,179	661,479	1.35	483,516	623,030	1.29	434,632	630,503	1.45	492,034
Feb	1,411,971	1,925,817	1.36	489,307	663,710	1.36	487,805	627,913	1.29	434,859	634,194	1.46	492,530
Mar	1,420,071	1,923,669	1.35	492,699	664,712	1.35	489,608	629,230	1.29	437,764	629,727	1.44	496,077
Apr	1,429,298	1,929,393	1.35	493,302	667,132	1.35	496,410	629,865	1.27	439,586	632,396	1.44	497,776
May	1,447,550	1,935,563	1.34	496,450	668,607	1.35	506,959	631,955	1.25	444,141	635,001	1.43	503,955
June	1,451,814	1,937,569	1.33	501,641	670,214	1.34	505,806	632,717	1.25	444,367	634,638	1.43	505,168
July	1,455,246	1,950,641	1.34	501,661	676,154	1.35	506,874	636,339	1.26	446,711	638,148	1.43	508,230
Aug	1,461,984	1,961,025	1.34	505,207	676,738	1.34	510,369	642,214	1.26	446,408	642,073	1.44	507,872
Sept	1,466,193	1,970,561	1.34	508,879	680,834	1.34	511,058	646,756	1.27	446,256	642,971	1.44	506,749
Oct	1,467,492	1,982,473	1.35	508,280	682,058	1.34	508,186	652,318	1.28	451,026	648,097	1.44	511,616
Nov p	1,459,719	1,981,834	1.36	505,772	681,661	1.35	501,933	654,714	1.30	452,014	645,459	1.43	512,200
Dec p	1,448,122	1,994,489	1.38	504,894	681,549	1.35	497,162	661,843	1.33	446,066	651,097	1.46	505,826

[1] Excludes manufacturers' sales branches and offices.
[2] Annual data are averages of monthly not seasonally adjusted figures.
[3] Seasonally adjusted, end of period. Inventories beginning with January 1982 for manufacturing and December 1980 for wholesale and retail trade are not comparable with earlier periods.
[4] Inventory/sales ratio. Monthly inventories are inventories at the end of the month to sales for the month. Annual data beginning with 1982 are the average of monthly ratios for the year. Annual data for 1978–81 are the ratio of December inventories to monthly average sales for the year.
[5] Food services included on Standard Industrial Classification (SIC) basis and excluded on North American Industry Classification System (NAICS) basis. See last column for retail and food services sales.
[6] Effective in 2001, data classified based on NAICS. Data on NAICS basis available beginning with 1992. Earlier data based on SIC. Data on both NAICS and SIC basis include semiconductors.

Source: Department of Commerce (Bureau of the Census).

Production and Business Activity

Prices

TABLE B–38. Changes in consumer price indexes, 1975–2018

[For all urban consumers; percent change]

Year or month	All items	All items less food and energy					Food			Energy [4]		C-CPI-U [5]
		Total [1]	Shelter [2]	Medical care [3]	Apparel	New vehicles	Total [1]	At home	Away from home	Total [1,3]	Gasoline	
	December to December, NSA											
1975	6.9	6.7	7.2	9.8	2.4	7.3	6.6	6.2	7.4	11.4	11.0	
1976	4.9	6.1	4.2	10.0	4.6	4.8	.5	–.8	6.0	7.1	2.8	
1977	6.7	6.5	8.8	8.9	4.3	7.2	8.1	7.9	7.9	7.2	4.8	
1978	9.0	8.5	11.4	8.8	3.1	6.2	11.8	12.5	10.4	7.9	8.6	
1979	13.3	11.3	17.5	10.1	5.5	7.4	10.2	9.7	11.4	37.5	52.1	
1980	12.5	12.2	15.0	9.9	6.8	7.4	10.2	10.5	9.6	18.0	18.9	
1981	8.9	9.5	9.9	12.5	3.5	6.8	4.3	2.9	7.1	11.9	9.4	
1982	3.8	4.5	2.4	11.0	1.6	1.4	3.1	2.3	5.1	1.3	–6.7	
1983	3.8	4.8	4.7	6.4	2.9	3.3	2.7	1.8	4.1	–.5	–1.6	
1984	3.9	4.7	5.2	6.1	2.0	2.5	3.8	3.6	4.2	.2	–2.5	
1985	3.8	4.3	6.0	6.8	2.8	3.6	2.6	2.0	3.8	1.8	3.0	
1986	1.1	3.8	4.6	7.7	.9	5.6	3.8	3.7	4.3	–19.7	–30.7	
1987	4.4	4.2	4.8	5.8	4.8	1.8	3.5	3.5	3.7	8.2	18.6	
1988	4.4	4.7	4.5	6.9	4.7	2.2	5.2	5.6	4.4	.5	–1.8	
1989	4.6	4.4	4.9	8.5	1.0	2.4	5.6	6.2	4.6	5.1	6.5	
1990	6.1	5.2	5.2	9.6	5.1	2.0	5.3	5.8	4.5	18.1	36.8	
1991	3.1	4.4	3.9	7.9	3.4	3.2	1.9	1.3	2.9	–7.4	–16.2	
1992	2.9	3.3	2.9	6.6	1.4	2.3	1.5	1.5	1.4	2.0	2.0	
1993	2.7	3.2	3.0	5.4	.9	3.3	2.9	3.5	1.9	–1.4	–5.9	
1994	2.7	2.6	3.0	4.9	–1.6	3.3	2.9	3.5	1.9	2.2	6.4	
1995	2.5	3.0	3.5	3.9	.1	1.9	2.1	2.0	2.2	–1.3	–4.2	
1996	3.3	2.6	2.9	3.0	–.2	1.8	4.3	4.9	3.1	8.6	12.4	
1997	1.7	2.2	3.4	2.8	1.0	–.9	1.5	1.0	2.6	–3.4	–6.1	
1998	1.6	2.4	3.3	3.4	–.7	.0	2.3	2.1	2.5	–8.8	–15.4	
1999	2.7	1.9	2.5	3.7	–.5	–.3	1.9	1.7	2.3	13.4	30.1	
2000	3.4	2.6	3.4	4.2	–1.8	.0	2.8	2.9	2.4	14.2	13.9	2.6
2001	1.6	2.7	4.2	4.7	–3.2	–.1	2.8	2.6	3.0	–13.0	–24.9	1.3
2002	2.4	1.9	3.1	5.0	–1.8	–2.0	1.5	.8	2.3	10.7	24.8	2.0
2003	1.9	1.1	2.2	3.7	–2.1	–1.8	3.6	4.5	2.3	6.9	6.8	1.7
2004	3.3	2.2	2.7	4.2	–.2	.6	2.7	2.4	3.0	16.6	26.1	3.2
2005	3.4	2.2	2.6	4.3	–1.1	–.4	2.3	1.7	3.2	17.1	16.1	2.9
2006	2.5	2.6	4.2	3.6	.9	–.9	2.1	1.4	3.2	2.9	6.4	2.3
2007	4.1	2.4	3.1	5.2	–.3	–.3	4.9	5.6	4.0	17.4	29.6	3.7
2008	.1	1.8	1.9	2.6	–1.0	–3.2	5.9	6.6	5.0	–21.3	–43.1	.2
2009	2.7	1.8	.3	3.4	1.9	4.9	–.5	–2.4	1.9	18.2	53.5	2.5
2010	1.5	.8	.4	3.3	–1.1	–.2	1.5	1.7	1.3	7.7	13.8	1.3
2011	3.0	2.2	1.9	3.5	4.6	3.2	4.7	6.0	2.9	6.6	9.9	2.9
2012	1.7	1.9	2.2	3.2	1.8	1.6	1.8	1.3	2.5	.5	1.7	1.5
2013	1.5	1.7	2.5	2.0	.6	.4	1.1	.4	2.1	.5	–1.0	1.3
2014	.8	1.6	2.9	3.0	–2.0	.5	3.4	3.7	3.0	–10.6	–21.0	.5
2015	.7	2.1	3.2	2.6	–.9	.2	.8	–.4	2.6	–12.6	–19.7	.4
2016	2.1	2.2	3.6	4.1	–.1	.3	–.2	–2.0	2.3	5.4	9.1	1.8
2017	2.1	1.8	3.2	1.8	–1.6	–.5	1.6	.9	2.5	6.9	10.7	1.7
2018	1.9	2.2	3.2	2.0	–.1	–.3	1.6	.6	2.8	–.3	–2.1	1.8
	Change from year earlier, NSA											
2017: Jan	2.5	2.3	3.5	3.9	1.0	0.9	–0.2	–1.9	2.4	10.8	20.3	2.3
Feb	2.7	2.2	3.5	3.5	.4	.5	.0	–1.7	2.4	15.2	30.7	2.6
Mar	2.4	2.0	3.5	3.5	.6	.2	.5	–.9	2.4	10.9	19.9	2.1
Apr	2.2	1.9	3.5	3.0	.5	.4	.5	–.8	2.3	9.3	14.3	1.8
May	1.9	1.7	3.3	2.7	–.9	.3	.9	–.2	2.3	5.4	5.8	1.5
June	1.6	1.7	3.3	2.7	–.7	.0	.9	–.1	2.2	2.3	–.4	1.2
July	1.7	1.7	3.2	2.6	–.4	–.6	1.1	.3	2.1	3.4	3.0	1.3
Aug	1.9	1.7	3.3	1.8	–.6	–.7	1.1	.3	2.2	6.4	10.4	1.5
Sept	2.2	1.7	3.2	1.6	–.2	–1.0	1.2	.4	2.4	10.1	19.3	1.9
Oct	2.0	1.8	3.2	1.7	–.6	–1.4	1.3	.6	2.3	6.4	10.8	1.6
Nov	2.2	1.7	3.2	1.7	–1.6	–1.1	1.4	.6	2.4	9.4	16.5	1.8
Dec	2.1	1.8	3.2	1.8	–1.6	–.5	1.6	.9	2.5	6.9	10.7	1.7
2018: Jan	2.1	1.8	3.2	2.0	–.7	–1.2	1.7	1.0	2.5	5.5	8.5	1.6
Feb	2.2	1.8	3.1	1.8	.4	–1.5	1.4	.5	2.6	7.7	12.6	1.8
Mar	2.4	2.1	3.3	2.0	.3	–1.2	1.3	.4	2.5	7.0	11.1	2.0
Apr	2.5	2.1	3.4	2.2	.8	–1.6	1.4	.5	2.5	7.9	13.4	2.1
May	2.8	2.2	3.5	2.4	1.4	–1.1	1.2	.1	2.7	11.7	21.8	2.4
June	2.9	2.3	3.4	2.5	.6	–.5	1.4	.4	2.8	12.0	24.3	2.5
July	2.9	2.4	3.5	1.9	.3	.2	1.4	.4	2.8	12.1	25.4	2.7
Aug	2.7	2.2	3.4	1.5	–1.4	.3	1.4	.5	2.6	10.2	20.3	2.5
Sept	2.3	2.2	3.3	1.7	–.6	.5	1.4	.4	2.6	4.8	9.1	2.0
Oct	2.5	2.1	3.2	1.7	–.4	.5	1.2	.1	2.5	8.9	16.1	2.3
Nov	2.2	2.2	3.2	2.0	–.4	.3	1.4	.4	2.6	3.1	5.0	2.0
Dec	1.9	2.2	3.2	2.0	–.1	–.3	1.6	.6	2.8	–.3	–2.1	1.8

[1] Includes other items not shown separately.
[2] Data beginning with 1983 incorporate a rental equivalence measure for homeowners' costs.
[3] Commodities and services.
[4] Household energy--electricity, utility (piped) gas service, fuel oil, etc.--and motor fuel.
[5] Chained consumer price index (C-CPI-U) introduced in 2002. Reflects the effect of substitution that consumers make across item categories in response to changes in relative prices. Data for 2018 are subject to revision.

Source: Department of Labor (Bureau of Labor Statistics).

TABLE B–39. Price indexes for personal consumption expenditures, and percent changes, 1972–2018

[Chain-type price index numbers, 2012=100; monthly data seasonally adjusted]

Year or month	Personal consumption expenditures (PCE)						Percent change from year earlier					
	Total	Goods	Services	Food [1]	Energy goods and services [2]	PCE less food and energy	Total	Goods	Services	Food [1]	Energy goods and services [2]	PCE less food and energy
1972	22.586	33.926	17.491	22.371	10.716	23.912	3.4	2.6	4.2	4.8	2.6	3.2
1973	23.802	35.949	18.336	25.202	11.640	24.823	5.4	6.0	4.8	12.7	8.6	3.8
1974	26.280	40.436	19.890	29.034	15.176	26.788	10.4	12.5	8.5	15.2	30.4	7.9
1975	28.470	43.703	21.595	31.217	16.672	29.026	8.3	8.1	8.6	7.5	9.9	8.4
1976	30.032	45.413	23.093	31.798	17.791	30.791	5.5	3.9	6.9	1.9	6.7	6.1
1977	31.986	47.837	24.841	33.671	19.294	32.771	6.5	5.3	7.6	5.9	8.4	6.4
1978	34.211	50.773	26.750	36.892	20.380	34.943	7.0	6.1	7.7	9.6	5.6	6.6
1979	37.251	55.574	28.994	40.516	25.414	37.490	8.9	9.5	8.4	9.8	24.7	7.3
1980	41.262	61.797	32.009	43.922	33.203	40.936	10.8	11.2	10.4	8.4	30.6	9.2
1981	44.958	66.389	35.288	47.051	37.668	44.523	9.0	7.4	10.2	7.1	13.4	8.8
1982	47.456	68.198	38.058	48.289	38.326	47.417	5.6	2.7	7.8	2.6	1.7	6.5
1983	49.474	69.429	40.396	48.844	38.684	49.844	4.3	1.8	6.1	1.1	.9	5.1
1984	51.343	70.742	42.498	50.312	39.172	51.911	3.8	1.9	5.2	3.0	1.3	4.1
1985	53.134	71.877	44.577	50.859	39.585	54.019	3.5	1.6	4.9	1.1	1.1	4.1
1986	54.290	71.541	46.408	52.056	34.685	55.883	2.2	−.5	4.1	2.4	−12.4	3.5
1987	55.964	73.842	47.796	53.699	35.069	57.683	3.1	3.2	3.0	3.2	1.1	3.2
1988	58.151	75.788	50.082	55.300	35.337	60.134	3.9	2.6	4.8	3.0	.8	4.2
1989	60.690	78.704	52.443	58.216	37.425	62.630	4.4	3.8	4.7	5.3	5.9	4.2
1990	63.355	81.927	54.846	61.060	40.589	65.168	4.4	4.1	4.6	4.9	8.5	4.1
1991	65.473	83.930	56.992	62.977	40.769	67.495	3.3	2.4	3.9	3.1	.4	3.6
1992	67.218	84.943	59.018	63.461	40.959	69.547	2.7	1.2	3.6	.8	.5	3.0
1993	68.892	85.681	61.059	64.348	41.331	71.436	2.5	.9	3.5	1.4	.9	2.7
1994	70.330	86.552	62.719	65.426	41.493	73.034	2.1	1.0	2.7	1.7	.4	2.2
1995	71.811	87.361	64.471	66.844	41.819	74.625	2.1	.9	2.8	2.2	.8	2.2
1996	73.346	88.321	66.240	68.883	43.777	76.040	2.1	1.1	2.7	3.1	4.7	1.9
1997	74.623	88.219	68.107	70.195	44.236	77.382	1.7	−.1	2.8	1.9	1.0	1.8
1998	75.216	86.893	69.549	71.077	40.502	78.366	.8	−1.5	2.1	1.3	−8.4	1.3
1999	76.338	87.349	70.970	72.241	42.143	79.425	1.5	.5	2.0	1.6	4.1	1.4
2000	78.235	89.082	72.938	73.933	49.843	80.804	2.5	2.0	2.8	2.3	18.3	1.7
2001	79.738	89.015	75.171	76.089	51.088	82.258	1.9	−.1	3.1	2.9	2.5	1.8
2002	80.789	88.166	77.123	77.239	48.110	83.639	1.3	−1.0	2.6	1.5	−5.8	1.7
2003	82.358	88.054	79.506	78.701	54.190	84.837	1.9	−.1	3.1	1.9	12.6	1.4
2004	84.411	89.292	81.965	81.157	60.339	86.515	2.5	1.4	3.1	3.1	11.3	2.0
2005	86.812	91.084	84.673	82.575	70.752	88.373	2.8	2.0	3.3	1.7	17.3	2.1
2006	89.174	92.306	87.616	83.963	78.812	90.392	2.7	1.3	3.5	1.7	11.4	2.3
2007	91.438	93.331	90.516	87.239	83.557	92.378	2.5	1.1	3.3	3.9	6.0	2.2
2008	94.180	96.122	93.235	92.552	95.464	94.225	3.0	3.0	3.0	6.1	14.3	2.0
2009	94.094	93.812	94.231	93.651	77.393	95.315	−.1	−2.4	1.1	1.2	−18.9	1.2
2010	95.705	95.183	95.957	93.931	85.120	96.608	1.7	1.5	1.8	.3	10.0	1.4
2011	98.131	98.773	97.814	97.682	98.601	98.139	2.5	3.8	1.9	4.0	15.8	1.6
2012	100.000	100.000	100.000	100.000	100.000	100.000	1.9	1.2	2.2	2.4	1.4	1.9
2013	101.346	99.407	102.316	100.989	99.109	101.526	1.3	−.6	2.3	1.0	−.9	1.5
2014	102.868	98.939	104.852	102.925	98.259	103.168	1.5	−.5	2.5	1.9	−.9	1.6
2015	103.126	95.889	106.823	104.086	80.617	104.501	.3	−3.1	1.9	1.1	−18.0	1.3
2016	104.235	94.340	109.325	102.997	74.770	106.237	1.1	−1.6	2.3	−1.0	−7.3	1.7
2017	106.073	94.632	111.984	102.858	81.292	107.961	1.8	.3	2.4	−.1	8.7	1.6
2018 [p]	108.230	95.280	114.952	103.398	87.691	110.005	2.0	.7	2.7	.5	7.9	1.9
2017: Jan	105.557	95.294	110.841	102.274	83.183	107.308	2.0	.7	2.7	−1.5	12.5	1.9
Feb	105.600	94.994	111.066	102.399	81.281	107.459	2.2	1.1	2.7	−1.5	17.5	1.9
Mar	105.427	94.603	111.009	102.726	79.686	107.328	1.9	.7	2.4	−.7	12.4	1.6
Apr	105.701	94.650	111.402	102.910	80.353	107.585	1.8	.2	2.5	−.6	10.0	1.6
May	105.705	94.181	111.660	102.954	78.264	107.713	1.6	−.3	2.5	−.2	5.4	1.6
June	105.800	94.064	111.869	102.875	77.538	107.873	1.5	−.5	2.4	−.1	2.0	1.6
July	105.871	94.078	111.970	103.033	76.920	107.976	1.5	−.1	2.2	.2	3.4	1.5
Aug	106.117	94.395	112.178	102.991	79.855	108.086	1.5	.1	2.2	.3	7.0	1.4
Sept	106.480	94.913	112.456	102.976	84.154	108.246	1.8	.6	2.3	.4	11.3	1.5
Oct	106.664	94.691	112.858	103.057	82.867	108.527	1.7	.2	2.4	.5	6.8	1.6
Nov	106.900	94.874	113.124	102.996	85.801	108.627	1.9	.6	2.4	.6	10.1	1.6
Dec	107.056	94.845	113.379	103.109	85.601	108.808	1.8	.4	2.5	.9	7.4	1.6
2018: Jan	107.406	95.538	113.543	103.129	88.186	109.054	1.8	.3	2.4	.8	6.0	1.6
Feb	107.556	95.411	113.842	102.995	88.148	109.240	1.9	.4	2.5	.6	8.4	1.7
Mar	107.610	95.023	114.135	103.189	85.680	109.431	2.1	.4	2.8	.5	7.5	2.0
Apr	107.865	95.374	114.337	103.504	86.989	109.618	2.0	.8	2.6	.6	8.3	1.9
May	108.085	95.467	114.627	103.259	87.794	109.845	2.3	1.4	2.7	.3	12.2	2.0
June	108.207	95.398	114.853	103.442	87.662	109.978	2.3	1.4	2.7	.6	13.1	2.0
July	108.365	95.396	115.098	103.527	87.227	110.177	2.4	1.4	2.8	.5	13.4	2.0
Aug	108.458	95.337	115.273	103.482	88.875	110.190	2.2	1.0	2.8	.5	11.3	1.9
Sept	108.599	95.254	115.535	103.521	88.490	110.370	2.0	.4	2.7	.5	5.2	2.0
Oct [p]	108.812	95.440	115.762	103.399	90.256	110.520	2.0	.8	2.6	.3	8.9	1.8
Nov [p]	108.866	95.080	116.042	103.595	87.740	110.715	1.8	.2	2.6	.6	2.3	1.9
Dec [p]	108.929	94.641	116.382	103.733	85.238	110.922	1.7	−.2	2.6	.6	−.4	1.9

[1] Food consists of food and beverages purchased for off-premises consumption; food services, which include purchased meals and beverages, are not classified as food.
[2] Consists of gasoline and other energy goods and of electricity and gas services.

Source: Department of Commerce (Bureau of Economic Analysis).

Money Stock, Credit, and Finance

TABLE B–40. Money stock and debt measures, 1980–2018

[Averages of daily figures, except debt end-of-period basis; billions of dollars, seasonally adjusted]

Year and month	M1 — Sum of currency, demand deposits, travelers checks, and other checkable deposits	M2 — M1 plus savings deposits, retail MMMF balances, and small time deposits [1]	Debt — Debt of domestic nonfinancial sectors [2]	Percent change — From year or 6 months earlier [3] M1	M2	From previous period [4] Debt
December:						
1980	408.5	1,599.8	4,051.5	7.0	8.6	9.6
1981	436.7	1,755.5	4,464.7	6.9	9.7	10.2
1982	474.8	1,905.9	4,900.3	8.7	8.6	10.2
1983	521.4	2,123.5	5,497.7	9.8	11.4	12.1
1984	551.6	2,306.4	6,308.4	5.8	8.6	14.8
1985	619.8	2,492.1	7,341.7	12.4	8.1	16.1
1986	724.7	2,728.0	8,216.7	16.9	9.5	12.0
1987	750.2	2,826.4	8,936.1	3.5	3.6	9.0
1988	786.7	2,988.2	9,753.9	4.9	5.7	9.2
1989	792.9	3,152.5	10,501.9	.8	5.5	7.5
1990	824.7	3,271.8	11,218.1	4.0	3.8	6.6
1991	897.0	3,372.2	11,746.7	8.8	3.1	4.7
1992	1,024.9	3,424.7	12,298.0	14.3	1.6	4.7
1993	1,129.6	3,474.5	13,021.3	10.2	1.5	5.8
1994	1,150.7	3,486.4	13,701.7	1.9	.3	5.2
1995	1,127.5	3,629.5	14,386.3	−2.0	4.1	4.9
1996	1,081.3	3,810.5	15,136.4	−4.1	5.0	5.2
1997	1,072.3	4,023.0	15,975.4	−.8	5.6	5.6
1998	1,095.0	4,365.7	17,044.3	2.1	8.5	6.7
1999	1,122.2	4,628.1	18,218.2	2.5	6.0	6.7
2000	1,088.6	4,914.4	19,106.0	−3.0	6.2	4.8
2001	1,183.2	5,419.6	20,183.0	8.7	10.3	5.7
2002	1,220.2	5,757.5	21,532.8	3.1	6.2	6.7
2003	1,306.2	6,052.6	23,238.5	7.0	5.1	7.8
2004	1,376.0	6,404.3	26,149.3	5.3	5.8	9.2
2005	1,374.3	6,667.4	28,431.5	−.1	4.1	8.8
2006	1,366.4	7,056.8	30,869.7	−.6	5.8	8.5
2007	1,373.0	7,457.3	33,360.5	.5	5.7	8.1
2008	1,601.1	8,181.1	35,138.7	16.6	9.7	5.8
2009	1,691.9	8,483.4	36,109.9	5.7	3.7	3.7
2010	1,835.8	8,789.1	37,475.2	8.5	3.6	4.3
2011	2,163.5	9,650.9	38,684.4	17.9	9.8	3.6
2012	2,460.6	10,445.6	40,375.9	13.7	8.2	4.8
2013	2,664.4	11,015.7	41,795.9	8.3	5.5	3.8
2014	2,940.7	11,670.1	43,456.7	10.4	5.9	4.1
2015	3,094.9	12,335.9	45,187.1	5.2	5.7	4.4
2016	3,342.4	13,209.6	47,185.9	8.0	7.1	4.5
2017	3,612.0	13,851.9	49,131.4	8.1	4.9	4.0
2018 ᵖ	3,744.0	14,387.6	....	3.7	3.9	....
2017: Jan	3,390.9	13,282.3	....	8.8	6.2	....
Feb	3,404.7	13,340.0	....	5.4	5.7	....
Mar	3,445.5	13,405.3	47,614.5	7.2	5.7	3.1
Apr	3,454.2	13,470.4	....	7.1	5.6	....
May	3,517.3	13,521.3	....	9.7	5.2	....
June	3,525.9	13,551.6	48,151.3	11.0	5.2	4.6
July	3,550.9	13,617.1	....	9.4	5.0	....
Aug	3,580.7	13,672.0	....	10.3	5.0	....
Sept	3,574.2	13,717.9	48,732.9	7.5	4.7	4.9
Oct	3,606.7	13,779.8	....	8.8	4.6	....
Nov	3,630.6	13,809.9	....	6.4	4.3	....
Dec	3,612.0	13,851.9	49,131.4	4.9	4.4	3.3
2018: Jan	3,653.2	13,867.7	....	5.8	3.7	....
Feb	3,622.5	13,890.4	....	2.3	3.2	....
Mar	3,656.4	13,941.1	49,904.5	4.6	3.3	6.3
Apr	3,660.3	13,974.1	....	3.0	2.8	....
May	3,654.7	14,035.2	....	1.3	3.3	....
June	3,655.0	14,107.5	50,772.5	2.4	3.7	5.2
July	3,676.9	14,148.5	....	1.3	4.0	....
Aug	3,679.8	14,190.4	....	3.2	4.3	....
Sept	3,703.5	14,224.8	51,323.8	2.6	4.1	4.4
Oct	3,718.7	14,250.9	....	3.2	4.0	....
Nov	3,695.2	14,276.5	....	2.2	3.4	....
Dec ᵖ	3,744.0	14,387.6	....	4.9	4.0	....

[1] Money market mutual fund (MMMF). Savings deposits include money market deposit accounts.
[2] Consists of outstanding debt securities and loans of the U.S. Government, State and local governments, and private nonfinancial sectors. Quarterly data shown in last month of quarter. End-of-year data are for fourth quarter.
[3] Annual changes are from December to December; monthly changes are from six months earlier at an annual rate.
[4] Debt growth of domestic nonfinancial sectors is the seasonally adjusted borrowing flow divided by the seasonally adjusted level of debt outstanding in the previous period. Annual changes are from fourth quarter to fourth quarter; quarterly changes are from previous quarter at an annual rate.

Note: For further information on the composition of M1 and M2, see the H.6 release.
For further information on the debt of domestic nonfinancial sectors and the derivation of debt growth, see the Z.1 release.

Source: Board of Governors of the Federal Reserve System.

TABLE B–41. Consumer credit outstanding, 1970–2018

[Amount outstanding (end of month); millions of dollars, seasonally adjusted]

Year and month	Total consumer credit [1]	Revolving	Nonrevolving [2]
December:			
1970	131,551.55	4,961.46	126,590.09
1971	146,930.18	8,245.33	138,684.84
1972	166,189.10	9,379.24	156,809.86
1973	190,086.31	11,342.22	178,744.09
1974	198,917.84	13,241.26	185,676.58
1975	204,002.00	14,495.27	189,506.73
1976	225,721.59	16,489.05	209,232.54
1977	260,562.70	37,414.82	223,147.88
1978	306,100.39	45,690.95	260,409.43
1979	348,589.11	53,596.43	294,992.67
1980	351,920.05	54,970.05	296,950.00
1981	371,301.44	60,928.00	310,373.44
1982	389,848.74	66,348.30	323,500.44
1983	437,068.86	79,027.25	358,041.61
1984	517,278.98	100,385.63	416,893.35
1985	599,711.23	124,465.80	475,245.43
1986	654,750.24	141,068.15	513,682.08
1987	686,318.77	160,853.91	525,464.86
1988 [3]	731,917.76	184,593.12	547,324.64
1989	794,612.18	211,229.83	583,382.34
1990	808,230.57	238,642.62	569,587.95
1991	798,028.97	263,768.55	534,260.42
1992	806,118.69	278,449.67	527,669.02
1993	865,650.58	309,908.02	555,742.56
1994	997,301.74	365,569.56	631,732.19
1995	1,140,744.36	443,920.09	696,824.27
1996	1,253,437.09	507,516.57	745,920.52
1997	1,324,757.33	540,005.56	784,751.77
1998	1,420,996.44	581,414.78	839,581.66
1999	1,531,105.96	610,696.47	920,409.49
2000	1,716,969.72	682,646.37	1,034,323.35
2001	1,867,852.87	714,840.73	1,153,012.14
2002	1,972,112.21	750,947.45	1,221,164.76
2003	2,077,360.69	768,258.31	1,309,102.38
2004	2,192,246.17	799,552.18	1,392,693.99
2005	2,290,928.13	829,518.36	1,461,409.78
2006	2,456,715.70	923,876.78	1,532,838.92
2007	2,609,476.53	1,001,625.30	1,607,851.24
2008	2,643,788.96	1,003,997.04	1,639,791.92
2009	2,555,016.64	916,076.63	1,638,940.01
2010	2,646,811.26	839,102.67	1,807,708.59
2011	2,757,072.85	840,628.23	1,916,444.63
2012	2,918,258.06	844,250.89	2,074,007.16
2013	3,093,385.81	855,592.83	2,237,792.98
2014	3,314,567.08	889,120.64	2,425,446.44
2015	3,413,611.57	907,914.38	2,505,697.19
2016	3,647,219.54	969,424.58	2,677,794.96
2017	3,831,160.11	1,024,028.38	2,807,131.73
2018 [p]	4,010,049.02	1,044,593.92	2,965,455.10
2017: Jan	3,663,854.05	971,742.81	2,692,111.24
Feb	3,681,440.56	977,201.29	2,704,239.28
Mar	3,694,010.45	980,362.15	2,713,648.30
Apr	3,707,109.06	981,491.86	2,725,617.20
May	3,724,537.61	988,317.33	2,736,220.28
June	3,735,509.47	991,456.11	2,744,053.36
July	3,750,829.16	993,314.27	2,757,514.90
Aug	3,764,061.37	998,319.71	2,765,741.66
Sept	3,772,190.77	1,003,461.55	2,768,729.22
Oct	3,791,192.52	1,009,223.08	2,781,969.45
Nov	3,819,825.20	1,019,837.23	2,799,987.97
Dec	3,831,160.11	1,024,028.38	2,807,131.73
2018: Jan	3,843,405.57	1,025,226.37	2,818,179.20
Feb	3,854,287.30	1,025,165.54	2,829,121.77
Mar	3,862,530.43	1,023,479.35	2,839,051.07
Apr	3,863,818.50	1,014,850.26	2,848,968.24
May	3,886,264.16	1,023,482.72	2,862,781.44
June	3,890,991.65	1,022,541.51	2,868,450.14
July	3,908,515.63	1,023,163.26	2,885,352.36
Aug	3,931,952.82	1,027,566.52	2,904,386.30
Sept	3,945,210.51	1,028,049.07	2,917,161.44
Oct	3,971,086.57	1,038,026.75	2,933,059.82
Nov	3,993,495.02	1,042,858.48	2,950,636.54
Dec [p]	4,010,049.02	1,044,593.92	2,965,455.10

[1] Covers most short- and intermediate-term credit extended to individuals. Credit secured by real estate is excluded.
[2] Includes automobile loans and all other loans not included in revolving credit, such as loans for mobile homes, education, boats, trailers, or vacations. These loans may be secured or unsecured. Beginning with 1977, includes student loans extended by the Federal Government and by SLM Holding Corporation.
[3] Data newly available in January 1989 result in breaks in these series between December 1988 and subsequent months.

Source: Board of Governors of the Federal Reserve System.

TABLE B-42. Bond yields and interest rates, 1948–2018

[Percent per annum]

| Year | U.S. Treasury securities | | | | | Corporate bonds (Moody's) | | High-grade municipal bonds (Standard & Poor's) | New-home mortgage yields [4] | Prime rate charged by banks [5] | Discount window (Federal Reserve Bank of New York) [5, 6] | | Federal funds rate [7] |
| | Bills (at auction) [1] | | Constant maturities [2] | | | | | | | | | | |
	3-month	6-month	3-year	10-year	30-year	Aaa [3]	Baa				Primary credit	Adjustment credit	
1948	1.040					2.82	3.47	2.40		1.75–2.00		1.34	
1949	1.102					2.66	3.42	2.21		2.00		1.50	
1950	1.218					2.62	3.24	1.98		2.07		1.59	
1951	1.552					2.86	3.41	2.00		2.56		1.75	
1952	1.766					2.96	3.52	2.19		3.00		1.75	
1953	1.931		2.47	2.85		3.20	3.74	2.72		3.17		1.99	
1954	.953		1.63	2.40		2.90	3.51	2.37		3.05		1.60	
1955	1.753		2.47	2.82		3.06	3.53	2.53		3.16		1.89	1.79
1956	2.658		3.19	3.18		3.36	3.88	2.93		3.77		2.77	2.73
1957	3.267		3.98	3.65		3.89	4.71	3.60		4.20		3.12	3.11
1958	1.839		2.84	3.32		3.79	4.73	3.56		3.83		2.15	1.57
1959	3.405	3.832	4.46	4.33		4.38	5.05	3.95		4.48		3.36	3.31
1960	2.93	3.25	3.98	4.12		4.41	5.19	3.73		4.82		3.53	3.21
1961	2.38	2.61	3.54	3.88		4.35	5.08	3.46		4.50		3.00	1.95
1962	2.78	2.91	3.47	3.95		4.33	5.02	3.18		4.50		3.00	2.71
1963	3.16	3.25	3.67	4.00		4.26	4.86	3.23	5.89	4.50		3.23	3.18
1964	3.56	3.69	4.03	4.19		4.40	4.83	3.22	5.83	4.50		3.55	3.50
1965	3.95	4.05	4.22	4.28		4.49	4.87	3.27	5.81	4.54		4.04	4.07
1966	4.88	5.08	5.23	4.93		5.13	5.67	3.82	6.25	5.63		4.50	5.11
1967	4.32	4.63	5.03	5.07		5.51	6.23	3.98	6.46	5.63		4.19	4.22
1968	5.34	5.47	5.68	5.64		6.18	6.94	4.51	6.97	6.31		5.17	5.66
1969	6.68	6.85	7.02	6.67		7.03	7.81	5.81	7.81	7.96		5.87	8.21
1970	6.43	6.53	7.29	7.35		8.04	9.11	6.51	8.45	7.91		5.95	7.17
1971	4.35	4.51	5.66	6.16		7.39	8.56	5.70	7.74	5.73		4.88	4.67
1972	4.07	4.47	5.72	6.21		7.21	8.16	5.27	7.60	5.25		4.50	4.44
1973	7.04	7.18	6.96	6.85		7.44	8.24	5.18	7.96	8.03		6.45	8.74
1974	7.89	7.93	7.84	7.56		8.57	9.50	6.09	8.92	10.81		7.83	10.51
1975	5.84	6.12	7.50	7.99		8.83	10.61	6.89	9.00	7.86		6.25	5.82
1976	4.99	5.27	6.77	7.61		8.43	9.75	6.49	9.00	6.84		5.50	5.05
1977	5.27	5.52	6.68	7.42	7.75	8.02	8.97	5.56	9.02	6.83		5.46	5.54
1978	7.22	7.58	8.29	8.41	8.49	8.73	9.49	5.90	9.56	9.06		7.46	7.94
1979	10.05	10.02	9.70	9.43	9.28	9.63	10.69	6.39	10.78	12.67		10.29	11.20
1980	11.51	11.37	11.51	11.43	11.27	11.94	13.67	8.51	12.66	15.26		11.77	13.35
1981	14.03	13.78	14.46	13.92	13.45	14.17	16.04	11.23	14.70	18.87		13.42	16.39
1982	10.69	11.08	12.93	13.01	12.76	13.79	16.11	11.57	15.14	14.85		11.01	12.24
1983	8.63	8.75	10.45	11.10	11.18	12.04	13.55	9.47	12.57	10.79		8.50	9.09
1984	9.53	9.77	11.92	12.46	12.41	12.71	14.19	10.15	12.38	12.04		8.80	10.23
1985	7.47	7.64	9.64	10.62	10.79	11.37	12.72	9.18	11.55	9.93		7.69	8.10
1986	5.98	6.03	7.06	7.67	7.78	9.02	10.39	7.38	10.17	8.33		6.32	6.80
1987	5.82	6.05	7.68	8.39	8.59	9.38	10.58	7.73	9.31	8.21		5.66	6.66
1988	6.69	6.92	8.26	8.85	8.96	9.71	10.83	7.76	9.19	9.32		6.20	7.57
1989	8.12	8.04	8.55	8.49	8.45	9.26	10.18	7.24	10.13	10.87		6.93	9.21
1990	7.51	7.47	8.26	8.55	8.61	9.32	10.36	7.25	10.05	10.01		6.98	8.10
1991	5.42	5.49	6.82	7.86	8.14	8.77	9.80	6.89	9.32	8.46		5.45	5.69
1992	3.45	3.57	5.30	7.01	7.67	8.14	8.98	6.41	8.24	6.25		3.25	3.52
1993	3.02	3.14	4.44	5.87	6.59	7.22	7.93	5.63	7.20	6.00		3.00	3.02
1994	4.29	4.66	6.27	7.09	7.37	7.96	8.62	6.19	7.49	7.15		3.60	4.21
1995	5.51	5.59	6.25	6.57	6.88	7.59	8.20	5.95	7.87	8.83		5.21	5.83
1996	5.02	5.09	5.99	6.44	6.71	7.37	8.05	5.75	7.80	8.27		5.02	5.30
1997	5.07	5.18	6.10	6.35	6.61	7.26	7.86	5.55	7.71	8.44		5.00	5.46
1998	4.81	4.85	5.14	5.26	5.58	6.53	7.22	5.12	7.07	8.35		4.92	5.35
1999	4.66	4.76	5.49	5.65	5.87	7.04	7.87	5.43	7.04	8.00		4.62	4.97
2000	5.85	5.92	6.22	6.03	5.94	7.62	8.36	5.77	7.52	9.23		5.73	6.24
2001	3.44	3.39	4.09	5.02	5.49	7.08	7.95	5.19	7.00	6.91		3.40	3.88
2002	1.62	1.69	3.10	4.61	5.43	6.49	7.80	5.05	6.43	4.67		1.17	1.67
2003	1.01	1.06	2.10	4.01		5.67	6.77	4.73	5.80	4.12	2.12		1.13
2004	1.38	1.57	2.78	4.27		5.63	6.39	4.63	5.77	4.34	2.34		1.35
2005	3.16	3.40	3.93	4.29		5.24	6.06	4.29	5.94	6.19	4.19		3.22
2006	4.73	4.80	4.77	4.80	4.91	5.59	6.48	4.42	6.63	7.96	5.96		4.97
2007	4.41	4.48	4.35	4.63	4.84	5.56	6.48	4.42	6.41	8.05	5.86		5.02
2008	1.48	1.71	2.24	3.66	4.28	5.63	7.45	4.80	6.05	5.09	2.39		1.92
2009	.16	.29	1.43	3.26	4.08	5.31	7.30	4.64	5.14	3.25	.50		.16
2010	.14	.20	1.11	3.22	4.25	4.94	6.04	4.16	4.80	3.25	.72		.18
2011	.06	.10	.75	2.78	3.91	4.64	5.66	4.29	4.56	3.25	.75		.10
2012	.09	.13	.38	1.80	2.92	3.67	4.94	3.14	3.69	3.25	.75		.14
2013	.06	.09	.54	2.35	3.45	4.24	5.10	3.96	4.00	3.25	.75		.11
2014	.03	.06	.90	2.54	3.34	4.16	4.85	3.78	4.22	3.25	.75		.09
2015	.06	.17	1.02	2.14	2.84	3.89	5.00	3.48	4.01	3.26	.76		.13
2016	.33	.46	1.00	1.84	2.59	3.67	4.72	3.07	3.76	3.51	1.01		.39
2017	.94	1.05	1.58	2.33	2.89	3.74	4.44	3.36	3.97	4.10	1.60		1.00
2018	1.94	2.10	2.63	2.91	3.11	3.93	4.80	3.53	4.53	4.91	2.41		1.83

[1] High bill rate at auction, issue date within period, bank-discount basis. On or after October 28, 1998, data are stop yields from uniform-price auctions. Before that date, they are weighted average yields from multiple-price auctions.

See next page for continuation of table.

TABLE B–42. Bond yields and interest rates, 1948–2018—*Continued*

[Percent per annum]

Year and month	U.S. Treasury securities					Corporate bonds (Moody's)		High-grade municipal bonds (Standard & Poor's)	New-home mortgage yields [4]	Prime rate charged by banks [5]	Discount window (Federal Reserve Bank of New York) [5,6]		Federal funds rate [7]
	Bills (at auction) [1]		Constant maturities [2]								Primary credit	Adjustment credit	
	3-month	6-month	3-year	10-year	30-year	Aaa [3]	Baa				High-low	High-low	
										High-low			
2014: Jan	0.05	0.07	0.78	2.86	3.77	4.49	5.19	4.38	4.45	3.25–3.25	0.75–0.75	....	0.07
Feb	.06	.08	.69	2.71	3.66	4.45	5.10	4.25	4.04	3.25–3.25	0.75–0.75	....	.07
Mar	.05	.08	.82	2.72	3.62	4.38	5.06	4.16	4.35	3.25–3.25	0.75–0.75	....	.08
Apr	.04	.05	.88	2.71	3.52	4.24	4.90	4.02	4.33	3.25–3.25	0.75–0.75	....	.09
May	.03	.05	.83	2.56	3.39	4.16	4.76	3.80	4.01	3.25–3.25	0.75–0.75	....	.09
June	.03	.06	.90	2.60	3.42	4.25	4.80	3.72	4.27	3.25–3.25	0.75–0.75	....	.10
July	.03	.06	.97	2.54	3.33	4.16	4.73	3.75	4.25	3.25–3.25	0.75–0.75	....	.09
Aug	.03	.05	.93	2.42	3.20	4.08	4.69	3.53	4.25	3.25–3.25	0.75–0.75	....	.09
Sept	.02	.05	1.05	2.53	3.26	4.11	4.80	3.55	4.23	3.25–3.25	0.75–0.75	....	.09
Oct	.02	.05	.88	2.30	3.04	3.92	4.69	3.35	4.23	3.25–3.25	0.75–0.75	....	.09
Nov	.02	.07	.96	2.33	3.04	3.92	4.79	3.49	4.16	3.25–3.25	0.75–0.75	....	.09
Dec	.04	.11	1.06	2.21	2.83	3.79	4.74	3.39	4.14	3.25–3.25	0.75–0.75	....	.12
2015: Jan	.03	.10	.90	1.88	2.46	3.46	4.45	3.16	4.05	3.25–3.25	0.75–0.75	....	.11
Feb	.02	.07	.99	1.98	2.57	3.61	4.51	3.26	3.91	3.25–3.25	0.75–0.75	....	.11
Mar	.02	.11	1.02	2.04	2.63	3.64	4.54	3.29	3.93	3.25–3.25	0.75–0.75	....	.11
Apr	.03	.10	.87	1.94	2.59	3.52	4.48	3.40	3.92	3.25–3.25	0.75–0.75	....	.12
May	.02	.08	.98	2.20	2.96	3.98	4.89	3.77	3.89	3.25–3.25	0.75–0.75	....	.12
June	.01	.08	1.07	2.36	3.11	4.19	5.13	3.76	3.98	3.25–3.25	0.75–0.75	....	.13
July	.03	.12	1.03	2.32	3.07	4.15	5.20	3.73	4.10	3.25–3.25	0.75–0.75	....	.13
Aug	.09	.21	1.03	2.17	2.86	4.04	5.19	3.57	4.12	3.25–3.25	0.75–0.75	....	.14
Sept	.06	.23	1.01	2.17	2.95	4.07	5.34	3.56	4.09	3.25–3.25	0.75–0.75	....	.14
Oct	.01	.10	.93	2.07	2.89	3.95	5.34	3.48	4.02	3.25–3.25	0.75–0.75	....	.12
Nov	.13	.33	1.20	2.26	3.03	4.06	5.46	3.50	4.00	3.25–3.25	0.75–0.75	....	.12
Dec	.26	.52	1.28	2.24	2.97	3.97	5.46	3.23	4.03	3.50–3.25	1.00–1.00	....	.24
2016: Jan	.25	.44	1.14	2.09	2.86	4.00	5.45	3.01	4.04	3.50–3.50	1.00–1.00	....	.34
Feb	.32	.44	.90	1.78	2.62	3.96	5.34	3.21	4.01	3.50–3.50	1.00–1.00	....	.38
Mar	.32	.48	1.04	1.89	2.68	3.82	5.13	3.28	3.92	3.50–3.50	1.00–1.00	....	.36
Apr	.23	.37	.92	1.81	2.62	3.62	4.79	3.04	3.86	3.50–3.50	1.00–1.00	....	.37
May	.27	.41	.97	1.81	2.63	3.65	4.68	2.95	3.82	3.50–3.50	1.00–1.00	....	.37
June	.29	.41	.86	1.64	2.45	3.50	4.53	2.84	3.81	3.50–3.50	1.00–1.00	....	.38
July	.31	.40	.79	1.50	2.23	3.28	4.22	2.57	3.74	3.50–3.50	1.00–1.00	....	.39
Aug	.30	.43	.85	1.56	2.26	3.32	4.24	2.77	3.68	3.50–3.50	1.00–1.00	....	.40
Sept	.32	.48	.90	1.63	2.35	3.41	4.31	2.86	3.58	3.50–3.50	1.00–1.00	....	.40
Oct	.34	.48	.99	1.76	2.50	3.51	4.38	3.13	3.57	3.50–3.50	1.00–1.00	....	.40
Nov	.44	.57	1.22	2.14	2.86	3.86	4.71	3.36	3.63	3.50–3.50	1.00–1.00	....	.41
Dec	.52	.64	1.49	2.49	3.11	4.06	4.83	3.81	3.74	3.75–3.50	1.25–1.00	....	.54
2017: Jan	.52	.61	1.48	2.43	3.02	3.92	4.66	3.68	4.06	3.75–3.75	1.25–1.25	....	.65
Feb	.53	.64	1.47	2.42	3.03	3.95	4.64	3.74	4.21	3.75–3.75	1.25–1.25	....	.66
Mar	.72	.84	1.59	2.48	3.08	4.01	4.68	3.78	4.16	4.00–3.75	1.50–1.25	....	.79
Apr	.81	.94	1.44	2.30	2.94	3.87	4.57	3.54	4.10	4.00–4.00	1.50–1.50	....	.90
May	.89	1.02	1.48	2.30	2.96	3.85	4.55	3.47	4.04	4.00–4.00	1.50–1.50	....	.91
June	.99	1.09	1.49	2.19	2.80	3.68	4.37	3.06	4.00	4.25–4.00	1.75–1.50	....	1.04
July	1.08	1.12	1.54	2.32	2.88	3.70	4.39	3.03	3.88	4.25–4.25	1.75–1.75	....	1.15
Aug	1.03	1.12	1.48	2.21	2.80	3.63	4.31	3.23	3.97	4.25–4.25	1.75–1.75	....	1.16
Sept	1.04	1.15	1.51	2.20	2.78	3.63	4.30	3.27	3.89	4.25–4.25	1.75–1.75	....	1.15
Oct	1.08	1.22	1.68	2.36	2.88	3.60	4.32	3.31	3.76	4.25–4.25	1.75–1.75	....	1.15
Nov	1.23	1.35	1.81	2.35	2.80	3.57	4.27	3.03	3.81	4.25–4.25	1.75–1.75	....	1.16
Dec	1.35	1.48	1.96	2.40	2.77	3.51	4.22	3.21	3.90	4.50–4.25	2.00–1.75	....	1.30
2018: Jan	1.43	1.59	2.15	2.58	2.88	3.55	4.26	3.29	3.94	4.50–4.50	2.00–2.00	....	1.41
Feb	1.53	1.72	2.36	2.86	3.13	3.82	4.51	3.54	4.15	4.50–4.50	2.00–2.00	....	1.42
Mar	1.70	1.87	2.42	2.84	3.09	3.87	4.64	3.58	4.33	4.75–4.50	2.25–2.00	....	1.51
Apr	1.76	1.93	2.52	2.87	3.07	3.85	4.67	3.55	4.52	4.75–4.75	2.25–2.25	....	1.69
May	1.87	2.03	2.66	2.98	3.13	4.00	4.83	3.38	4.55	4.75–4.75	2.25–2.25	....	1.70
June	1.91	2.08	2.65	2.91	3.05	3.96	4.83	3.15	4.58	5.00–4.75	2.50–2.25	....	1.82
July	1.96	2.12	2.70	2.89	3.01	3.87	4.79	3.45	4.62	5.00–5.00	2.50–2.50	....	1.91
Aug	2.03	2.18	2.71	2.89	3.04	3.88	4.77	3.58	4.57	5.00–5.00	2.50–2.50	....	1.91
Sept	2.13	2.28	2.84	3.00	3.15	3.98	4.88	3.63	4.64	5.25–5.00	2.75–2.50	....	1.95
Oct	2.24	2.39	2.94	3.15	3.34	4.14	5.07	3.88	4.67	5.25–5.25	2.75–2.75	....	2.19
Nov	2.34	2.46	2.91	3.12	3.36	4.22	5.22	3.64	4.77	5.25–5.25	2.75–2.75	....	2.20
Dec	2.38	2.49	2.67	2.83	3.10	4.02	5.13	3.69	4.84	5.50–5.25	3.00–2.75	....	2.27

[2] Yields on the more actively traded issues adjusted to constant maturities by the Department of the Treasury. The 30-year Treasury constant maturity series was discontinued on February 18, 2002, and reintroduced on February 9, 2006.
[3] Beginning with December 7, 2001, data for corporate Aaa series are industrial bonds only.
[4] Effective rate (in the primary market) on conventional mortgages, reflecting fees and charges as well as contract rate and assuming, on the average, repayment at end of 10 years. Rates beginning with January 1973 not strictly comparable with prior rates.
[5] For monthly data, high and low for the period. Prime rate for 1948 are ranges of the rate in effect during the period.
[6] Primary credit replaced adjustment credit as the Federal Reserve's principal discount window lending program effective January 9, 2003.
[7] Beginning March 1, 2016, the daily effective federal funds rate is a volume-weighted median of transaction-level data collected from depository institutions in the Report of Selected Money Market Rates (FR 2420). Between July 21, 1975 and February 29, 2016, the daily effective rate was a volume-weighted mean of rates on brokered trades. Prior to that, the daily effective rate was the rate considered most representative of the day's transactions, usually the one at which most transactions occurred.

Sources: Department of the Treasury, Board of Governors of the Federal Reserve System, Federal Housing Finance Agency, Moody's Investors Service, Bloomberg, and Standard & Poor's.

TABLE B–43. Mortgage debt outstanding by type of property and of financing, 1960–2018

[Billions of dollars]

End of year or quarter	All properties	Farm properties	Nonfarm properties				Nonfarm properties by type of mortgage					
							Government underwritten				Conventional [2]	
			Total	1- to 4-family houses	Multifamily properties	Commercial properties	Total [1]	1- to 4-family houses			Total	1- to 4-family houses
								Total	FHA-insured	VA-guaranteed		
1960	227.1	17.4	209.7	137.8	28.0	43.9	62.3	56.4	26.7	29.7	147.4	81.4
1961	248.6	18.7	229.9	149.5	31.5	48.9	65.6	59.1	29.5	29.6	164.3	90.4
1962	271.8	20.3	251.6	163.1	34.6	53.8	69.4	62.2	32.3	29.9	182.2	100.9
1963	297.6	22.4	275.1	179.0	37.5	58.7	73.4	65.9	35.0	30.9	201.7	113.1
1964	324.2	25.3	298.9	195.7	41.6	61.7	77.2	69.2	38.3	30.9	221.7	126.4
1965	349.5	28.2	321.3	212.0	44.2	65.2	81.2	73.1	42.0	31.1	240.2	138.9
1966	373.7	30.3	343.4	225.3	46.9	71.2	84.1	76.1	44.8	31.3	259.3	149.3
1967	396.9	32.9	363.9	238.0	50.0	75.9	88.2	79.9	47.4	32.5	275.7	158.1
1968	424.5	36.0	388.5	254.2	53.0	81.3	93.4	84.4	50.6	33.8	295.1	169.8
1969	450.5	38.4	412.1	269.0	56.5	86.6	100.2	90.2	54.5	35.7	311.9	178.9
1970	498.5	40.8	457.6	292.2	68.1	97.3	109.2	97.3	59.9	37.3	348.4	195.0
1971	544.5	43.9	500.6	318.4	76.6	105.6	120.7	105.2	65.7	39.5	379.9	213.2
1972	618.2	47.7	570.5	357.4	89.7	123.5	131.1	113.0	68.2	44.7	439.4	244.4
1973	694.2	53.4	640.7	399.8	99.0	141.9	135.0	116.2	66.2	50.0	505.7	283.6
1974	766.2	62.5	703.7	441.2	105.7	156.7	140.2	121.3	65.1	56.2	563.5	319.9
1975	830.2	68.9	761.3	483.0	105.5	172.8	147.0	127.7	66.1	61.6	614.3	355.2
1976	917.5	76.7	840.8	544.8	110.1	185.9	154.0	133.5	66.5	67.0	686.8	411.2
1977	1,049.7	88.3	961.4	638.5	118.0	204.9	161.7	141.6	68.0	73.6	799.7	496.9
1978	1,206.8	100.3	1,106.4	751.4	128.7	226.3	176.4	153.4	71.4	82.0	930.0	598.0
1979	1,381.0	120.5	1,260.5	870.2	139.4	250.8	199.0	172.9	81.0	92.0	1,061.4	697.3
1980	1,528.2	132.7	1,395.5	977.3	146.4	271.8	225.1	195.2	93.6	101.6	1,170.4	782.2
1981	1,654.6	146.7	1,507.9	1,052.6	146.4	308.9	238.9	207.6	101.3	106.2	1,269.0	845.1
1982	1,741.4	150.9	1,590.4	1,097.2	152.4	340.9	248.9	217.9	108.0	109.9	1,341.6	879.3
1983	1,942.4	153.9	1,788.5	1,217.8	171.9	398.8	279.8	248.8	127.4	121.4	1,508.7	968.9
1984	2,178.3	150.1	2,028.1	1,350.7	197.2	480.2	294.8	265.9	136.7	129.1	1,733.3	1,084.9
1985	2,439.9	125.3	2,314.6	1,548.9	213.9	551.8	328.3	288.8	153.0	135.8	1,986.3	1,260.1
1986	2,676.3	101.3	2,574.9	1,730.1	241.8	603.0	370.5	328.6	185.5	143.1	2,204.4	1,401.5
1987	2,968.8	89.9	2,878.9	1,928.5	258.4	692.1	431.4	387.9	235.5	152.4	2,447.5	1,540.6
1988	3,283.8	82.3	3,201.5	2,162.8	274.5	764.2	459.7	414.2	258.8	155.4	2,741.8	1,748.6
1989	3,534.5	79.2	3,455.3	2,369.6	287.0	798.7	486.8	440.1	282.8	157.3	2,968.4	1,929.5
1990	3,790.0	77.6	3,712.5	2,606.8	287.4	818.3	517.9	470.9	310.9	160.0	3,194.5	2,135.9
1991	3,941.7	77.7	3,864.0	2,774.7	284.1	805.2	537.2	493.3	330.6	162.7	3,326.8	2,281.4
1992	4,052.4	78.6	3,973.8	2,942.1	270.9	760.8	533.3	489.8	326.0	163.8	3,440.5	2,452.3
1993	4,183.7	79.8	4,103.9	3,101.0	267.7	735.2	513.4	469.5	303.2	166.2	3,590.4	2,631.5
1994	4,348.1	81.6	4,266.5	3,278.2	268.2	720.1	559.3	514.2	336.8	177.3	3,707.2	2,764.0
1995	4,520.7	71.7	4,449.0	3,445.7	273.9	729.4	584.3	537.1	352.3	184.7	3,864.7	2,908.6
1996	4,801.2	74.4	4,726.8	3,681.9	286.1	758.8	620.3	571.2	379.2	192.0	4,106.5	3,110.8
1997	5,114.0	78.5	5,035.5	3,916.5	298.0	821.0	656.7	605.7	405.7	200.0	4,378.9	3,310.8
1998	5,603.2	83.1	5,520.1	4,275.8	334.5	909.8	674.1	623.8	417.9	205.9	4,846.1	3,652.0
1999	6,209.5	87.2	6,122.3	4,701.2	375.2	1,046.0	731.5	678.8	462.3	216.5	5,390.9	4,022.4
2000	6,766.6	84.7	6,681.9	5,125.0	404.5	1,152.4	773.1	720.0	499.9	220.1	5,908.8	4,405.0
2001	7,450.0	88.5	7,361.5	5,678.0	446.1	1,237.4	772.7	718.5	497.4	221.2	6,588.8	4,959.5
2002	8,358.7	95.4	8,263.3	6,434.4	486.3	1,342.5	759.3	704.0	486.2	217.7	7,504.0	5,730.4
2003	9,366.7	83.2	9,283.5	7,261.4	560.5	1,461.7	709.2	653.3	438.7	214.6	8,574.4	6,608.1
2004	10,648.6	95.7	10,552.9	8,293.1	610.1	1,649.7	660.2	604.1	398.1	206.0	9,892.7	7,689.0
2005	12,116.7	104.8	12,012.0	9,449.6	675.3	1,887.1	606.6	550.4	348.4	202.0	11,405.4	8,899.2
2006	13,529.5	108.0	13,421.5	10,531.9	718.4	2,171.2	600.2	543.5	336.9	206.6	12,821.3	9,988.4
2007	14,613.1	112.7	14,500.4	11,253.2	807.8	2,439.4	609.2	552.6	342.6	210.0	13,891.3	10,700.6
2008	14,693.8	134.7	14,559.1	11,152.1	853.5	2,553.5	807.2	750.7	534.0	216.7	13,751.8	10,401.3
2009	14,449.7	146.0	14,303.7	10,962.5	865.9	2,475.2	1,005.0	944.3	752.6	191.7	13,298.6	10,018.2
2010	13,896.5	154.1	13,742.4	10,524.6	866.0	2,351.7	1,227.6	1,156.1	934.4	221.7	12,514.7	9,368.6
2011	13,571.7	167.2	13,404.5	10,282.8	866.5	2,255.3	1,368.6	1,291.3	1,036.0	255.3	12,035.9	8,991.5
2012	13,339.1	173.4	13,165.7	10,052.3	894.0	2,219.4	1,544.8	1,459.7	1,165.4	294.2	11,620.9	8,592.7
2013	13,346.5	185.2	13,161.3	9,961.6	932.1	2,267.5	3,927.2	3,832.6	3,480.8	351.8	9,234.1	6,129.1
2014	13,500.1	196.8	13,303.3	9,948.0	993.2	2,362.1	4,130.9	4,028.1	3,615.3	412.8	9,172.3	5,919.8
2015	13,876.2	208.8	13,667.4	10,080.1	1,095.0	2,492.3	4,432.7	4,326.7	3,851.3	475.4	9,234.7	5,753.4
2016	14,352.0	226.0	14,126.0	10,298.3	1,202.7	2,625.1	4,764.8	4,654.9	4,106.9	548.1	9,361.2	5,643.3
2017	14,898.3	238.1	14,660.2	10,600.3	1,309.9	2,750.0	5,079.1	4,958.2	4,344.3	613.9	9,581.1	5,642.1
2017: I	14,434.0	229.0	14,205.1	10,343.2	1,223.7	2,638.1	4,785.9	4,674.2	4,166.7	507.6	9,419.2	5,669.0
II	14,582.3	232.0	14,350.3	10,428.9	1,244.2	2,677.2	4,917.6	4,805.3	4,227.5	577.8	9,432.7	5,623.6
III	14,716.7	235.1	14,481.7	10,518.2	1,266.4	2,697.1	5,004.2	4,886.0	4,289.6	596.5	9,477.5	5,632.2
IV	14,898.3	238.1	14,660.2	10,600.3	1,309.9	2,750.0	5,079.1	4,958.2	4,344.3	613.9	9,581.1	5,642.1
2018: I	14,985.1	240.7	14,744.4	10,639.7	1,326.8	2,778.0	5,148.7	5,024.1	4,393.2	630.9	9,595.8	5,615.5
II	15,136.0	243.3	14,892.7	10,713.0	1,351.3	2,828.4	5,219.0	5,090.9	4,444.8	646.1	9,673.7	5,622.1
III ᵖ	15,269.5	245.9	15,023.6	10,809.6	1,379.2	2,834.8	5,292.3	5,162.2	4,498.6	663.7	9,731.3	5,647.3

[1] Includes Federal Housing Administration (FHA)–insured multi-family properties, not shown separately.
[2] Derived figures. Total includes multi-family and commercial properties with conventional mortgages, not shown separately.

Source: Board of Governors of the Federal Reserve System, based on data from various Government and private organizations.

TABLE B–44. Mortgage debt outstanding by holder, 1960–2018

[Billions of dollars]

End of year or quarter	Total	Major financial institutions			Other holders		
		Total	Depository Institutions [1,2]	Life insurance companies	Federal and related agencies [3]	Mortgage pools or trusts [4]	Individuals and others
1960	227.1	156.4	114.6	41.8	11.3	0.2	59.2
1961	248.6	171.1	126.9	44.2	11.9	.3	65.3
1962	271.8	190.5	143.6	46.9	12.2	.4	68.7
1963	297.6	214.6	164.1	50.5	11.3	.5	71.2
1964	324.2	238.8	183.6	55.2	11.6	.6	73.2
1965	349.5	262.4	202.4	60.0	12.7	.9	73.6
1966	373.7	279.5	214.8	64.6	16.2	1.3	76.7
1967	396.9	296.4	228.9	67.5	19.0	2.0	79.5
1968	424.5	317.3	247.3	70.0	22.6	2.5	82.2
1969	450.5	336.6	264.6	72.0	27.9	3.2	82.8
1970	498.5	352.9	278.5	74.4	33.6	4.8	107.3
1971	544.5	389.2	313.7	75.5	36.8	9.5	109.0
1972	618.2	443.8	366.8	76.9	40.1	14.4	119.9
1973	694.2	500.7	419.4	81.4	46.6	18.0	128.8
1974	766.2	539.3	453.1	86.2	68.2	23.8	134.9
1975	830.2	576.1	486.9	89.2	80.2	34.1	139.9
1976	917.5	640.7	549.1	91.6	82.4	49.8	144.7
1977	1,049.7	735.3	638.4	96.8	87.6	70.3	156.5
1978	1,206.8	837.5	731.3	106.2	103.4	88.6	177.3
1979	1,381.0	928.6	810.2	118.4	123.7	118.7	210.0
1980	1,528.2	988.0	857.0	131.1	142.6	145.9	251.6
1981	1,654.6	1,034.1	896.4	137.7	160.8	168.0	291.7
1982	1,741.4	1,019.6	877.6	142.0	177.3	224.4	320.1
1983	1,942.4	1,108.4	957.4	151.0	188.3	297.3	348.4
1984	2,178.3	1,248.2	1,091.5	156.7	202.3	350.7	377.1
1985	2,439.9	1,368.7	1,196.9	171.8	213.7	438.6	419.0
1986	2,676.3	1,483.3	1,289.5	193.8	202.1	549.5	441.3
1987	2,968.8	1,631.5	1,419.1	212.4	188.5	700.8	447.9
1988	3,283.8	1,797.8	1,564.9	232.9	192.5	785.7	507.8
1989	3,534.5	1,897.4	1,643.2	254.2	197.8	922.2	517.1
1990	3,790.0	1,918.8	1,651.0	267.9	239.0	1,085.9	546.3
1991	3,941.7	1,846.2	1,586.7	259.5	266.0	1,269.6	560.0
1992	4,052.4	1,770.5	1,528.5	242.0	286.1	1,440.0	555.9
1993	4,183.7	1,770.1	1,546.3	223.9	326.1	1,561.1	526.4
1994	4,348.1	1,824.7	1,608.9	215.8	315.6	1,696.9	511.0
1995	4,520.7	1,900.1	1,687.0	213.1	307.9	1,812.0	500.6
1996	4,801.2	1,982.2	1,773.7	208.5	294.4	1,989.1	535.6
1997	5,114.0	2,084.2	1,877.1	207.0	285.2	2,166.5	578.2
1998	5,603.2	2,194.7	1,981.0	213.8	291.9	2,487.1	629.5
1999	6,209.5	2,394.5	2,163.5	231.0	319.8	2,832.3	663.0
2000	6,766.6	2,619.2	2,383.0	236.2	339.9	3,097.5	710.0
2001	7,450.0	2,791.0	2,547.9	243.1	372.0	3,532.4	754.7
2002	8,358.7	3,089.4	2,839.3	250.1	432.3	3,978.4	858.5
2003	9,366.7	3,387.5	3,126.4	261.2	694.1	4,330.3	954.8
2004	10,648.6	3,926.5	3,653.0	273.5	703.2	4,834.5	1,184.4
2005	12,116.7	4,396.5	4,110.8	285.7	665.4	5,711.8	1,343.1
2006	13,529.5	4,784.0	4,479.8	304.1	687.5	6,631.4	1,426.7
2007	14,613.1	5,065.5	4,738.4	327.1	725.5	7,436.3	1,385.9
2008	14,693.8	5,045.8	4,702.0	343.8	801.2	7,594.4	1,252.4
2009	14,449.7	4,779.4	4,452.0	327.4	816.1	7,651.3	1,202.9
2010	13,896.5	4,585.2	4,266.1	319.2	5,127.5	3,109.6	1,074.0
2011	13,571.7	4,450.3	4,115.7	334.6	5,033.9	3,035.6	1,051.9
2012	13,339.1	4,441.5	4,094.6	346.9	4,935.0	2,948.4	1,014.2
2013	13,346.5	4,412.5	4,046.2	366.3	4,993.2	2,774.1	1,166.7
2014	13,500.1	4,546.8	4,158.7	388.2	4,987.7	2,742.6	1,223.0
2015	13,876.2	4,804.9	4,374.2	430.7	5,036.6	2,791.6	1,243.1
2016	14,352.0	5,096.1	4,630.6	465.5	5,146.9	2,827.6	1,281.5
2017	14,898.3	5,307.8	4,801.2	506.7	5,314.9	2,973.7	1,301.8
2017: I	14,434.0	5,125.8	4,649.3	476.5	5,201.0	2,832.1	1,275.1
II	14,582.3	5,209.2	4,719.1	490.1	5,219.2	2,876.4	1,277.6
III	14,716.7	5,257.2	4,759.5	497.7	5,261.8	2,917.5	1,280.2
IV	14,898.3	5,307.8	4,801.2	506.7	5,314.9	2,973.7	1,301.8
2018: I	14,985.1	5,341.1	4,824.9	516.2	5,338.4	3,002.6	1,303.0
II	15,136.0	5,396.2	4,868.6	527.7	5,369.8	3,054.2	1,315.7
III p	15,269.5	5,437.6	4,897.6	540.0	5,415.4	3,093.3	1,323.1

[1] Includes savings banks and savings and loan associations. Data reported by Federal Savings and Loan Insurance Corporation–insured institutions include loans in process for 1987 and exclude loans in process beginning with 1988.
[2] Includes loans held by nondeposit trust companies but not loans held by bank trust departments.
[3] Includes Government National Mortgage Association (GNMA or Ginnie Mae), Federal Housing Administration, Veterans Administration, Farmers Home Administration (FmHA), Federal Deposit Insurance Corporation, Resolution Trust Corporation (through 1995), and in earlier years Reconstruction Finance Corporation, Homeowners Loan Corporation, Federal Farm Mortgage Corporation, and Public Housing Administration. Also includes U.S.-sponsored agencies such as Federal National Mortgage Association (FNMA or Fannie Mae), Federal Land Banks, Federal Home Loan Mortgage Corporation (FHLMC or Freddie Mac), Federal Agricultural Mortgage Corporation (Farmer Mac, beginning 1994), Federal Home Loan Banks (beginning 1997), and mortgage pass-through securities issued or guaranteed by GNMA, FHLMC, FNMA, FmHA, or Farmer Mac. Other U.S. agencies (amounts small or current separate data not readily available) included with "individuals and others."
[4] Includes private mortgage pools.

Source: Board of Governors of the Federal Reserve System, based on data from various Government and private organizations.

Government Finance

TABLE B–45. Federal receipts, outlays, surplus or deficit, and debt, fiscal years 1953–2020

[Billions of dollars; fiscal years]

Fiscal year or period	Total			On-budget			Off-budget			Federal debt (end of period)		Addendum: Gross domestic product
	Receipts	Outlays	Surplus or deficit (−)	Receipts	Outlays	Surplus or deficit (−)	Receipts	Outlays	Surplus or deficit (−)	Gross Federal	Held by the public	
1953	69.6	76.1	−6.5	65.5	73.8	−8.3	4.1	2.3	1.8	266.0	218.4	382.0
1954	69.7	70.9	−1.2	65.1	67.9	−2.8	4.6	2.9	1.7	270.8	224.5	387.2
1955	65.5	68.4	−3.0	60.4	64.5	−4.1	5.1	4.0	1.1	274.4	226.6	406.3
1956	74.6	70.6	3.9	68.2	65.7	2.5	6.4	5.0	1.5	272.7	222.2	438.2
1957	80.0	76.6	3.4	73.2	70.6	2.6	6.8	6.0	.8	272.3	219.3	463.4
1958	79.6	82.4	−2.8	71.6	74.9	−3.3	8.0	7.5	.5	279.7	226.3	473.5
1959	79.2	92.1	−12.8	71.0	83.1	−12.1	8.3	9.0	−.7	287.5	234.7	504.6
1960	92.5	92.2	.3	81.9	81.3	.5	10.6	10.9	−.2	290.5	236.8	534.3
1961	94.4	97.7	−3.3	82.3	86.0	−3.8	12.1	11.7	.4	292.6	238.4	546.6
1962	99.7	106.8	−7.1	87.4	93.3	−5.9	12.3	13.5	−1.3	302.9	248.0	585.7
1963	106.6	111.3	−4.8	92.4	96.4	−4.0	14.2	15.0	−.8	310.3	254.0	618.2
1964	112.6	118.5	−5.9	96.2	102.8	−6.5	16.4	15.7	.6	316.1	256.8	661.7
1965	116.8	118.2	−1.4	100.1	101.7	−1.6	16.7	16.5	.2	322.3	260.8	709.3
1966	130.8	134.5	−3.7	111.7	114.8	−3.1	19.1	19.7	−.6	328.5	263.7	780.5
1967	148.8	157.5	−8.6	124.4	137.0	−12.6	24.4	20.4	4.0	340.4	266.6	836.5
1968	153.0	178.1	−25.2	128.1	155.8	−27.7	24.9	22.3	2.6	368.7	289.5	897.6
1969	186.9	183.6	3.2	157.9	158.4	−.5	29.0	25.2	3.7	365.8	278.1	980.3
1970	192.8	195.6	−2.8	159.3	168.0	−8.7	33.5	27.6	5.9	380.9	283.2	1,046.7
1971	187.1	210.2	−23.0	151.3	177.3	−26.1	35.8	32.8	3.0	408.2	303.0	1,116.6
1972	207.3	230.7	−23.4	167.4	193.5	−26.1	39.9	37.2	2.7	435.9	322.4	1,216.2
1973	230.8	245.7	−14.9	184.7	200.0	−15.2	46.1	45.7	.3	466.3	340.9	1,352.7
1974	263.2	269.4	−6.1	209.3	216.5	−7.2	53.9	52.9	1.1	483.9	343.7	1,482.8
1975	279.1	332.3	−53.2	216.6	270.8	−54.1	62.5	61.6	.9	541.9	394.7	1,606.9
1976	298.1	371.8	−73.7	231.7	301.1	−69.4	66.4	70.7	−4.3	629.0	477.4	1,786.1
Transition quarter	81.2	96.0	−14.7	63.2	77.3	−14.1	18.0	18.7	−.7	643.6	495.5	471.6
1977	355.6	409.2	−53.7	278.7	328.7	−49.9	76.8	80.5	−3.7	706.4	549.1	2,024.3
1978	399.6	458.7	−59.2	314.2	369.6	−55.4	85.4	89.2	−3.8	776.6	607.1	2,273.4
1979	463.3	504.0	−40.7	365.3	404.9	−39.6	98.0	99.1	−1.1	829.5	640.3	2,565.6
1980	517.1	590.9	−73.8	403.9	477.0	−73.1	113.2	113.9	−.7	909.0	711.9	2,791.9
1981	599.3	678.2	−79.0	469.1	543.0	−73.9	130.2	135.3	−5.1	994.8	789.4	3,133.2
1982	617.8	745.7	−128.0	474.3	594.9	−120.6	143.5	150.9	−7.4	1,137.3	924.6	3,313.4
1983	600.6	808.4	−207.8	453.2	660.9	−207.7	147.3	147.4	−.1	1,371.7	1,137.3	3,536.0
1984	666.4	851.8	−185.4	500.4	685.6	−185.3	166.1	166.2	−.1	1,564.6	1,307.0	3,949.2
1985	734.0	946.3	−212.3	547.9	769.4	−221.5	186.2	176.9	9.2	1,817.4	1,507.3	4,265.1
1986	769.2	990.4	−221.2	568.9	806.8	−237.9	200.2	183.5	16.7	2,120.5	1,740.6	4,526.2
1987	854.3	1,004.0	−149.7	640.9	809.2	−168.4	213.4	194.8	18.6	2,346.0	1,889.8	4,767.6
1988	909.2	1,064.4	−155.2	667.7	860.0	−192.3	241.5	204.4	37.1	2,601.1	2,051.6	5,138.6
1989	991.1	1,143.7	−152.6	727.4	932.8	−205.4	263.7	210.9	52.8	2,867.8	2,190.7	5,554.7
1990	1,032.0	1,253.0	−221.0	750.3	1,027.9	−277.6	281.7	225.1	56.6	3,206.3	2,411.6	5,898.8
1991	1,055.0	1,324.2	−269.2	761.1	1,082.5	−321.4	293.9	241.7	52.2	3,598.2	2,689.0	6,093.2
1992	1,091.2	1,381.5	−290.3	788.8	1,129.2	−340.4	302.4	252.3	50.1	4,001.8	2,999.7	6,416.2
1993	1,154.3	1,409.4	−255.1	842.4	1,142.8	−300.4	311.9	266.6	45.3	4,351.0	3,248.4	6,775.3
1994	1,258.6	1,461.8	−203.2	923.5	1,182.4	−258.8	335.0	279.4	55.7	4,643.3	3,433.1	7,176.8
1995	1,351.8	1,515.7	−164.0	1,000.7	1,227.1	−226.4	351.1	288.7	62.4	4,920.6	3,604.4	7,560.4
1996	1,453.1	1,560.5	−107.4	1,085.6	1,259.6	−174.0	367.5	300.9	66.6	5,181.5	3,734.1	7,951.3
1997	1,579.2	1,601.1	−21.9	1,187.2	1,290.5	−103.2	392.0	310.6	81.4	5,369.2	3,772.3	8,451.0
1998	1,721.7	1,652.5	69.3	1,305.9	1,335.9	−29.9	415.8	316.6	99.2	5,478.2	3,721.1	8,930.8
1999	1,827.5	1,701.8	125.6	1,383.0	1,381.1	1.9	444.5	320.8	123.7	5,605.5	3,632.4	9,479.4
2000	2,025.2	1,789.0	236.2	1,544.6	1,458.2	86.4	480.6	330.8	149.8	5,628.7	3,409.8	10,117.4
2001	1,991.1	1,862.8	128.2	1,483.6	1,516.0	−32.4	507.5	346.8	160.7	5,769.9	3,319.6	10,526.5
2002	1,853.1	2,010.9	−157.8	1,337.8	1,655.2	−317.4	515.3	355.7	159.7	6,198.4	3,540.4	10,833.6
2003	1,782.3	2,159.9	−377.6	1,258.5	1,796.9	−538.4	523.8	363.0	160.8	6,760.0	3,913.4	11,283.8
2004	1,880.1	2,292.8	−412.7	1,345.4	1,913.3	−568.0	534.7	379.5	155.2	7,354.7	4,295.5	12,025.4
2005	2,153.6	2,472.0	−318.3	1,576.1	2,069.7	−493.6	577.5	402.2	175.3	7,905.3	4,592.2	12,834.2
2006	2,406.9	2,655.1	−248.2	1,798.5	2,233.0	−434.5	608.4	422.1	186.3	8,451.4	4,829.0	13,638.4
2007	2,568.0	2,728.7	−160.7	1,932.9	2,275.0	−342.2	635.1	453.6	181.5	8,950.7	5,035.1	14,290.8
2008	2,524.0	2,982.5	−458.6	1,865.9	2,507.8	−641.8	658.0	474.8	183.3	9,986.1	5,803.1	14,743.3
2009	2,105.0	3,517.7	−1,412.7	1,451.0	3,000.7	−1,549.7	654.0	517.0	137.0	11,875.9	7,544.7	14,431.8
2010	2,162.7	3,457.1	−1,294.4	1,531.0	2,902.4	−1,371.4	631.7	554.7	77.0	13,528.8	9,018.9	14,838.8
2011	2,303.5	3,603.1	−1,299.6	1,737.7	3,104.5	−1,366.8	565.8	498.6	67.2	14,764.2	10,128.2	15,403.7
2012	2,450.0	3,526.6	−1,076.6	1,880.5	3,019.0	−1,138.5	569.5	507.6	61.9	16,050.9	11,281.1	16,056.4
2013	2,775.1	3,454.9	−679.8	2,101.8	2,821.1	−719.2	673.3	633.8	39.5	16,719.4	11,982.7	16,603.8
2014	3,021.5	3,506.3	−484.8	2,285.9	2,800.2	−514.3	735.6	706.0	29.5	17,794.5	12,779.9	17,332.9
2015	3,249.9	3,691.8	−442.0	2,479.5	2,948.8	−469.3	770.4	743.1	27.3	18,120.1	13,116.7	18,090.3
2016	3,268.0	3,852.6	−584.7	2,457.8	3,077.9	−620.2	810.2	774.7	35.5	19,539.5	14,167.6	18,551.0
2017	3,316.2	3,981.6	−665.4	2,465.6	3,180.4	−714.9	850.6	801.2	49.4	20,205.7	14,665.4	19,272.2
2018	3,329.9	4,109.0	−779.1	2,475.2	3,260.5	−785.3	854.7	848.6	6.2	21,462.3	15,749.6	20,235.9
2019 (estimates)	3,437.7	4,529.2	−1,091.5	2,526.5	3,620.3	−1,093.7	911.1	908.9	2.2	22,775.5	16,918.6	21,288.9
2020 (estimates)	3,644.8	4,745.6	−1,100.8	2,695.5	3,777.9	−1,082.4	949.3	967.7	−18.4	24,057.5	18,086.9	22,409.7

Note: Fiscal years through 1976 were on a July 1–June 30 basis; beginning with October 1976 (fiscal year 1977), the fiscal year is on an October 1–September 30 basis. The transition quarter is the three-month period from July 1, 1976 through September 30, 1976.
See *Budget of the United States Government, Fiscal Year 2020*, for additional information.

Sources: Department of Commerce (Bureau of Economic Analysis), Department of the Treasury, and Office of Management and Budget.

TABLE B–46. Federal receipts, outlays, surplus or deficit, and debt, as percent of gross domestic product, fiscal years 1948–2020

[Percent; fiscal years]

Fiscal year or period	Receipts	Outlays		Surplus or deficit (−)	Federal debt (end of period)	
		Total	National defense		Gross Federal	Held by public
1948	15.9	11.4	3.5	4.5	96.2	82.6
1949	14.3	14.0	4.8	.2	91.4	77.5
1950	14.2	15.3	4.9	−1.1	92.2	78.6
1951	15.8	13.9	7.2	1.9	78.1	65.5
1952	18.5	19.0	12.9	−.4	72.6	60.1
1953	18.2	19.9	13.8	−1.7	69.6	57.2
1954	18.0	18.3	12.7	−.3	70.0	58.0
1955	16.1	16.8	10.5	−.7	67.5	55.8
1956	17.0	16.1	9.7	.9	62.2	50.7
1957	17.3	16.5	9.8	.7	58.8	47.3
1958	16.8	17.4	9.9	−.6	59.1	47.8
1959	15.7	18.3	9.7	−2.5	57.0	46.5
1960	17.3	17.3	9.0	.1	54.4	44.3
1961	17.3	17.9	9.1	−.6	53.5	43.6
1962	17.0	18.2	8.9	−1.2	51.7	42.3
1963	17.2	18.0	8.6	−.8	50.2	41.1
1964	17.0	17.9	8.3	−.9	47.8	38.8
1965	16.5	16.7	7.1	−.2	45.4	36.8
1966	16.8	17.2	7.4	−.5	42.1	33.8
1967	17.8	18.8	8.5	−1.0	40.7	31.9
1968	17.0	19.8	9.1	−2.8	41.1	32.3
1969	19.1	18.7	8.4	.3	37.3	28.4
1970	18.4	18.7	7.8	−.3	36.4	27.1
1971	16.8	18.8	7.1	−2.1	36.6	27.1
1972	17.0	19.0	6.5	−1.9	35.8	26.5
1973	17.1	18.2	5.7	−1.1	34.5	25.2
1974	17.8	18.2	5.4	−.4	32.6	23.2
1975	17.4	20.7	5.4	−3.3	33.7	24.6
1976	16.7	20.8	5.0	−4.1	35.2	26.7
Transition quarter	17.2	20.3	4.7	−3.1	34.1	26.3
1977	17.6	20.2	4.8	−2.7	34.9	27.1
1978	17.6	20.2	4.6	−2.6	34.2	26.7
1979	18.1	19.6	4.5	−1.6	32.3	25.0
1980	18.5	21.2	4.8	−2.6	32.6	25.5
1981	19.1	21.6	5.0	−2.5	31.8	25.2
1982	18.6	22.5	5.6	−3.9	34.3	27.9
1983	17.0	22.9	5.9	−5.9	38.8	32.2
1984	16.9	21.6	5.8	−4.7	39.6	33.1
1985	17.2	22.2	5.9	−5.0	42.6	35.3
1986	17.0	21.9	6.0	−4.9	46.8	38.5
1987	17.9	21.1	5.9	−3.1	49.2	39.6
1988	17.7	20.7	5.7	−3.0	50.6	39.9
1989	17.8	20.6	5.5	−2.7	51.6	39.4
1990	17.5	21.2	5.1	−3.7	54.4	40.9
1991	17.3	21.7	4.5	−4.4	59.1	44.1
1992	17.0	21.5	4.6	−4.5	62.4	46.8
1993	17.0	20.8	4.3	−3.8	64.2	47.9
1994	17.5	20.4	3.9	−2.8	64.7	47.8
1995	17.9	20.0	3.6	−2.2	65.1	47.7
1996	18.3	19.6	3.3	−1.4	65.2	47.0
1997	18.7	18.9	3.2	−.3	63.5	44.6
1998	19.3	18.5	3.0	.8	61.3	41.7
1999	19.3	18.0	2.9	1.3	59.1	38.3
2000	20.0	17.7	2.9	2.3	55.6	33.7
2001	18.9	17.7	2.9	1.2	54.8	31.5
2002	17.1	18.6	3.2	−1.5	57.2	32.7
2003	15.8	19.1	3.6	−3.3	59.9	34.7
2004	15.6	19.1	3.8	−3.4	61.2	35.7
2005	16.8	19.3	3.9	−2.5	61.6	35.8
2006	17.6	19.5	3.8	−1.8	62.0	35.4
2007	18.0	19.1	3.9	−1.1	62.6	35.2
2008	17.1	20.2	4.2	−3.1	67.7	39.4
2009	14.6	24.4	4.6	−9.8	82.3	52.3
2010	14.6	23.3	4.7	−8.7	91.2	60.8
2011	15.0	23.4	4.6	−8.4	95.8	65.8
2012	15.3	22.0	4.2	−6.7	100.0	70.3
2013	16.7	20.8	3.8	−4.1	100.7	72.2
2014	17.4	20.2	3.5	−2.8	102.7	73.7
2015	18.0	20.4	3.3	−2.4	100.2	72.5
2016	17.6	20.8	3.2	−3.2	105.3	76.4
2017	17.2	20.7	3.1	−3.5	104.8	76.1
2018	16.5	20.3	3.1	−3.9	106.1	77.8
2019 (estimates)	16.1	21.3	3.2	−5.1	107.0	79.5
2020 (estimates)	16.3	21.2	3.3	−4.9	107.4	80.7

Note: See Note, Table B–45.
Sources: Department of the Treasury and Office of Management and Budget.

TABLE B–47.—Federal receipts and outlays, by major category, and surplus or deficit, fiscal years 1953–2020

[Billions of dollars; fiscal years]

Fiscal year or period	Receipts (on-budget and off-budget)					Outlays (on-budget and off-budget)										Surplus or deficit (−) (on-budget and off-budget)
	Total	Individual income taxes	Corporation income taxes	Social insurance and retirement receipts	Other	Total	National defense		International affairs	Health	Medicare	Income security	Social security	Net interest	Other	
							Total	Department of Defense, military								
1953	69.6	29.8	21.2	6.8	11.7	76.1	52.8	....	2.1	0.3	....	3.8	2.7	5.2	9.1	−6.5
1954	69.7	29.5	21.1	7.2	11.9	70.9	49.3	....	1.6	.3	....	4.4	3.4	4.8	7.1	−1.2
1955	65.5	28.7	17.9	7.9	11.0	68.4	42.7	....	2.2	.3	....	5.1	4.4	4.9	8.9	−3.0
1956	74.6	32.2	20.9	9.3	12.2	70.6	42.5	....	2.4	.4	....	4.7	5.5	5.1	10.1	3.9
1957	80.0	35.6	21.2	10.0	13.2	76.6	45.4	....	3.1	.5	....	5.4	6.7	5.4	10.1	3.4
1958	79.6	34.7	20.1	11.2	13.6	82.4	46.8	....	3.4	.5	....	7.5	8.2	5.6	10.3	−2.8
1959	79.2	36.7	17.3	11.7	13.5	92.1	49.0	....	3.1	.7	....	8.2	9.7	5.8	15.5	−12.8
1960	92.5	40.7	21.5	14.7	15.6	92.2	48.1	....	3.0	.8	....	7.4	11.6	6.9	14.4	.3
1961	94.4	41.3	21.0	16.4	15.7	97.7	49.6	....	3.2	.9	....	9.7	12.5	6.7	15.2	−3.3
1962	99.7	45.6	20.5	17.0	16.5	106.8	52.3	50.1	5.6	1.2	....	9.2	14.4	6.9	17.2	−7.1
1963	106.6	47.6	21.6	19.8	17.6	111.3	53.4	51.1	5.3	1.5	....	9.3	15.8	7.7	18.3	−4.8
1964	112.6	48.7	23.5	22.0	18.5	118.5	54.8	52.6	4.9	1.8	....	9.7	16.6	8.2	22.6	−5.9
1965	116.8	48.8	25.5	22.2	20.3	118.2	50.6	48.8	5.3	1.8	....	9.5	17.5	8.6	25.0	−1.4
1966	130.8	55.4	30.1	25.5	19.8	134.5	58.1	56.6	5.6	2.5	0.1	9.7	20.7	9.4	28.5	−3.7
1967	148.8	61.5	34.0	32.6	20.7	157.5	71.4	70.1	5.6	3.4	2.7	10.3	21.7	10.3	32.1	−8.6
1968	153.0	68.7	28.7	33.9	21.7	178.1	81.9	80.4	5.3	4.4	4.6	11.8	23.9	11.1	35.1	−25.2
1969	186.9	87.2	36.7	39.0	23.9	183.6	82.5	80.8	4.6	5.2	5.7	13.1	27.3	12.7	32.6	3.2
1970	192.8	90.4	32.8	44.4	25.2	195.6	81.7	80.1	4.3	5.9	6.2	15.7	30.3	14.4	37.2	−2.8
1971	187.1	86.2	26.8	47.3	26.8	210.2	78.9	77.5	4.2	6.8	6.6	22.9	35.9	14.8	40.0	−23.0
1972	207.3	94.7	32.2	52.6	27.8	230.7	79.2	77.6	4.8	8.7	7.5	27.7	40.2	15.5	47.3	−23.4
1973	230.8	103.2	36.2	63.1	28.3	245.7	76.7	75.0	4.1	9.4	8.1	28.3	49.1	17.3	52.8	−14.9
1974	263.2	119.0	38.6	75.1	30.6	269.4	79.3	77.9	5.7	10.7	9.6	33.7	55.9	21.4	52.9	−6.1
1975	279.1	122.4	40.6	84.5	31.5	332.3	86.5	84.9	7.1	12.9	12.9	50.2	64.7	23.2	74.8	−53.2
1976	298.1	131.6	41.4	90.8	34.3	371.8	89.6	87.9	6.4	15.7	15.8	60.8	73.9	26.7	82.7	−73.7
Transition quarter	81.2	38.8	8.5	25.2	8.8	96.0	22.3	21.8	2.5	3.9	4.3	15.0	19.8	6.9	21.4	−14.7
1977	355.6	157.6	54.9	106.5	36.6	409.2	97.2	95.1	6.4	17.3	19.3	61.1	85.1	29.9	93.0	−53.7
1978	399.6	181.0	60.0	121.0	37.7	458.7	104.5	102.3	7.5	18.5	22.8	61.5	93.9	35.5	114.6	−59.2
1979	463.3	217.8	65.7	138.9	40.8	504.0	116.3	113.6	7.5	20.5	26.5	66.4	104.1	42.6	120.2	−40.7
1980	517.1	244.1	64.6	157.8	50.6	590.9	134.0	130.9	12.7	23.2	32.1	86.6	118.5	52.5	131.3	−73.8
1981	599.3	285.9	61.1	182.7	69.5	678.2	157.5	153.9	13.1	26.9	39.1	100.3	139.6	68.8	133.0	−79.0
1982	617.8	297.7	49.2	201.5	69.3	745.7	185.3	180.7	12.3	27.4	46.6	108.2	156.0	85.0	125.0	−128.0
1983	600.6	288.9	37.0	209.0	65.6	808.4	209.9	204.4	11.8	28.6	52.6	123.0	170.7	89.8	121.8	−207.8
1984	666.4	298.4	56.9	239.4	71.8	851.8	227.4	220.9	15.9	30.4	57.5	113.4	178.2	111.1	117.8	−185.4
1985	734.0	334.5	61.3	265.2	73.0	946.3	252.7	245.1	16.2	33.5	65.8	129.0	188.6	129.5	130.9	−212.3
1986	769.2	349.0	63.1	283.9	73.2	990.4	273.4	265.4	14.1	35.9	70.2	120.7	198.8	136.0	141.3	−221.2
1987	854.3	392.6	83.9	303.3	74.5	1,004.0	282.0	273.9	11.6	40.0	75.1	124.1	207.4	138.6	125.2	−149.7
1988	909.2	401.2	94.5	334.3	79.2	1,064.4	290.4	281.9	10.5	44.5	78.9	130.4	219.3	151.8	138.7	−155.2
1989	991.1	445.7	103.3	359.4	82.7	1,143.7	303.6	294.8	9.6	48.4	85.0	137.6	232.5	169.0	158.1	−152.6
1990	1,032.0	466.9	93.5	380.0	91.5	1,253.0	299.3	289.7	13.8	57.7	98.1	148.8	248.6	184.3	202.3	−221.0
1991	1,055.0	467.8	98.1	396.0	93.1	1,324.2	273.3	262.3	15.8	71.2	104.5	172.6	269.0	194.4	223.3	−269.2
1992	1,091.2	476.0	100.3	413.7	101.3	1,381.5	298.3	286.8	16.1	89.5	119.0	199.7	287.6	199.3	171.9	−290.3
1993	1,154.3	509.7	117.5	428.3	98.8	1,409.4	291.1	278.5	17.2	99.4	130.6	210.1	304.6	198.7	157.7	−255.1
1994	1,258.6	543.1	140.4	461.5	113.7	1,461.8	281.6	268.6	17.1	107.1	144.7	217.3	319.6	202.9	171.4	−203.2
1995	1,351.8	590.2	157.0	484.5	120.1	1,515.7	272.1	259.4	16.4	115.4	159.9	223.8	335.8	232.1	160.2	−164.0
1996	1,453.1	656.4	171.8	509.4	115.4	1,560.5	265.7	253.1	13.5	119.4	174.2	229.7	349.7	241.1	167.2	−107.4
1997	1,579.2	737.5	182.3	539.4	120.1	1,601.1	270.5	258.3	15.2	123.8	190.0	235.0	365.3	244.0	157.3	−21.9
1998	1,721.7	828.6	188.7	571.8	132.6	1,652.5	268.2	255.8	13.1	131.4	192.8	237.8	379.2	241.1	188.9	69.3
1999	1,827.5	879.5	184.7	611.8	151.5	1,701.8	274.8	261.2	15.2	141.0	190.4	242.5	390.0	229.8	218.1	125.6
2000	2,025.2	1,004.5	207.3	652.9	160.6	1,789.0	294.4	281.0	17.2	154.5	197.1	253.7	409.4	222.9	239.7	236.2
2001	1,991.1	994.3	151.1	694.0	151.7	1,862.8	304.7	290.2	16.5	172.2	217.4	269.8	433.0	206.2	243.1	128.2
2002	1,853.1	858.3	148.0	700.8	146.0	2,010.9	348.5	331.8	22.3	196.5	230.9	312.7	456.0	170.9	273.1	−157.8
2003	1,782.3	793.7	131.8	713.0	143.9	2,159.9	404.7	387.1	21.2	219.5	249.4	334.6	474.7	153.1	302.6	−377.6
2004	1,880.1	809.0	189.4	733.4	148.4	2,292.8	455.8	436.4	26.9	240.1	269.4	333.1	495.5	160.2	311.8	−412.7
2005	2,153.6	927.2	278.3	794.1	154.0	2,472.0	495.3	474.1	34.6	250.5	298.6	345.8	523.3	184.0	339.8	−318.3
2006	2,406.9	1,043.9	353.9	837.8	171.2	2,655.1	521.8	499.3	29.5	252.7	329.9	352.5	548.5	226.6	393.5	−248.2
2007	2,568.0	1,163.5	370.2	869.6	164.7	2,728.7	551.3	528.5	28.5	266.4	375.4	366.0	586.2	237.1	317.9	−160.7
2008	2,524.0	1,145.7	304.3	900.2	173.7	2,982.5	616.1	594.6	28.9	280.6	390.8	431.3	617.0	252.8	365.2	−458.6
2009	2,105.0	915.3	138.2	890.9	160.5	3,517.7	661.0	636.7	37.5	334.3	430.1	533.2	683.0	186.9	651.6	−1,412.7
2010	2,162.7	898.5	191.4	864.8	207.9	3,457.1	693.5	666.7	45.2	369.1	451.6	622.2	706.7	196.2	372.6	−1,294.4
2011	2,303.5	1,091.5	181.1	818.8	212.1	3,603.1	705.6	678.1	45.7	372.5	485.7	597.3	730.8	230.0	435.5	−1,299.6
2012	2,450.0	1,132.2	242.3	845.3	230.2	3,526.6	677.9	650.9	36.8	346.7	471.8	541.3	773.3	220.4	458.3	−1,076.6
2013	2,775.1	1,316.4	273.5	947.8	237.4	3,454.9	633.4	607.8	46.5	358.3	497.8	536.5	813.6	220.9	347.9	−679.8
2014	3,021.5	1,394.6	320.7	1,023.5	282.7	3,506.3	603.5	577.9	46.9	409.4	511.7	513.6	850.5	229.0	341.7	−484.8
2015	3,249.9	1,540.8	343.8	1,065.3	300.0	3,691.8	589.7	562.5	52.0	482.2	546.2	508.8	887.8	223.2	401.9	−442.0
2016	3,268.0	1,546.1	299.6	1,115.1	307.3	3,852.6	593.4	565.4	45.3	511.3	594.5	514.1	916.1	240.0	437.9	−584.7
2017	3,316.2	1,587.1	297.0	1,161.9	270.1	3,981.6	598.7	568.9	46.3	533.1	597.3	503.5	944.9	262.6	495.2	−665.4
2018	3,329.9	1,683.5	204.7	1,170.7	270.9	4,109.0	631.2	600.7	49.0	551.2	588.7	495.3	987.8	325.0	480.9	−779.1
2019 (estimates)	3,437.7	1,698.4	216.2	1,242.4	280.7	4,529.2	684.6	652.2	54.3	601.0	651.2	533.2	1,047.0	393.5	564.4	−1,091.5
2020 (estimates)	3,644.8	1,824.2	255.2	1,295.5	269.9	4,745.6	737.9	704.3	53.1	616.0	685.2	514.2	1,107.1	478.8	553.2	−1,100.8

Note: See Note, Table B–45.

Sources: Department of the Treasury and Office of Management and Budget.

Table B–48.—Federal receipts, outlays, surplus or deficit, and debt, fiscal years 2015–2020

[Millions of dollars; fiscal years]

Description	Actual				Estimates	
	2015	2016	2017	2018	2019	2020
RECEIPTS, OUTLAYS, AND SURPLUS OR DEFICIT						
Total:						
Receipts	3,249,887	3,267,961	3,316,182	3,329,904	3,437,656	3,644,772
Outlays	3,691,847	3,852,612	3,981,628	4,109,042	4,529,188	4,745,573
Surplus or deficit (–)	–441,960	–584,651	–665,446	–779,138	–1,091,532	–1,100,801
On-budget:						
Receipts	2,479,515	2,457,781	2,465,564	2,475,157	2,526,542	2,695,492
Outlays	2,948,770	3,077,939	3,180,427	3,260,470	3,620,287	3,777,890
Surplus or deficit (–)	–469,255	–620,158	–714,863	–785,313	–1,093,745	–1,082,398
Off-budget:						
Receipts	770,372	810,180	850,618	854,747	911,114	949,280
Outlays	743,077	774,673	801,201	848,572	908,901	967,683
Surplus or deficit (–)	27,295	35,507	49,417	6,175	2,213	–18,403
OUTSTANDING DEBT, END OF PERIOD						
Gross Federal debt	18,120,106	19,539,450	20,205,704	21,462,277	22,775,547	24,057,463
Held by Federal Government accounts	5,003,414	5,371,826	5,540,265	5,712,692	5,856,940	5,970,595
Held by the public	13,116,692	14,167,624	14,665,439	15,749,585	16,918,607	18,086,868
Federal Reserve System	2,461,947	2,463,456	2,465,418	2,313,209	....	....
Other	10,654,745	11,704,168	12,200,021	13,436,376		
RECEIPTS BY SOURCE						
Total: On-budget and off-budget	3,249,887	3,267,961	3,316,182	3,329,904	3,437,656	3,644,772
Individual income taxes	1,540,802	1,546,075	1,587,120	1,683,538	1,698,353	1,824,185
Corporation income taxes	343,797	299,571	297,048	204,733	216,194	255,161
Social insurance and retirement receipts	1,065,257	1,115,065	1,161,897	1,170,701	1,242,405	1,295,484
On-budget	294,885	304,885	311,279	315,954	331,291	346,204
Off-budget	770,372	810,180	850,618	854,747	911,114	949,280
Excise taxes	98,279	95,026	83,823	94,986	98,669	108,835
Estate and gift taxes	19,232	21,354	22,768	22,983	19,295	19,304
Customs duties and fees	35,041	34,838	34,574	41,299	69,469	48,383
Miscellaneous receipts	147,479	156,032	128,952	111,664	93,271	94,379
Deposits of earnings by Federal Reserve System	96,468	115,672	81,287	70,750	48,783	49,474
All other	51,011	40,360	47,665	40,914	44,488	44,905
Legislative proposals [1]						–959
OUTLAYS BY FUNCTION						
Total: On-budget and off-budget	3,691,847	3,852,612	3,981,628	4,109,042	4,529,188	4,745,573
National defense	589,659	593,372	598,722	631,161	684,568	737,886
International affairs	52,040	45,306	46,309	48,972	54,337	53,125
General science, space, and technology	29,412	30,174	30,394	31,534	33,816	34,587
Energy	6,838	3,719	3,856	2,169	3,194	3,536
Natural resources and environment	36,033	39,082	37,896	39,140	39,864	43,690
Agriculture	18,500	18,342	18,870	21,787	38,068	19,474
Commerce and housing credit	–37,905	–34,077	–26,685	–9,470	–26,394	–5,126
On-budget	–36,195	–32,716	–24,412	–8,005	–25,450	–5,256
Off-budget	–1,710	–1,361	–2,273	–1,465	–944	130
Transportation	89,533	92,566	93,552	92,785	98,907	100,889
Community and regional development	20,669	20,140	24,907	42,159	33,001	35,664
Education, training, employment, and social services	122,061	109,737	143,976	95,516	142,527	112,368
Health	482,231	511,297	533,129	551,216	600,966	615,950
Medicare	546,202	594,536	597,307	588,706	651,199	685,230
Income security	508,843	514,139	503,484	495,318	533,228	514,241
Social security	887,753	916,067	944,878	987,791	1,046,955	1,107,132
On-budget	30,990	32,522	37,393	35,752	36,327	39,766
Off-budget	856,763	883,545	907,485	952,039	1,010,628	1,067,366
Veterans benefits and services	159,738	174,516	176,543	178,856	200,458	217,521
Administration of justice	51,906	55,768	57,944	60,418	71,780	69,025
General government	20,956	23,146	23,821	23,878	26,834	31,628
Net interest	223,181	240,033	262,551	324,975	393,498	478,812
On-budget	319,149	330,608	349,063	408,784	476,241	560,431
Off-budget	–95,968	–90,575	–86,512	–83,809	–82,743	–81,619
Allowances	....	....	....	....	–677	315
Undistributed offsetting receipts	–115,803	–95,251	–89,826	–97,869	–96,941	–110,374
On-budget	–99,795	–78,315	–72,327	–79,676	–78,901	–92,180
Off-budget	–16,008	–16,936	–17,499	–18,193	–18,040	–18,194

[1] Includes undistributed allowance for empowering States and consumers to reform healthcare.

Note: See Note, Table B–45.

Sources: Department of the Treasury and Office of Management and Budget.

TABLE B–49. Federal and State and local government current receipts and expenditures, national income and product accounts (NIPA) basis, 1968–2018

[Billions of dollars; quarterly data at seasonally adjusted annual rates]

Year or quarter	Total government			Federal Government			State and local government			Addendum: Grants-in-aid to State and local governments
	Current receipts	Current expenditures	Net government saving (NIPA)	Current receipts	Current expenditures	Net Federal Government saving (NIPA)	Current receipts	Current expenditures	Net State and local government saving (NIPA)	
1968	251.4	261.7	–10.3	170.6	184.3	–13.8	92.6	89.1	3.5	11.8
1969	282.7	284.7	–2.0	191.8	197.0	–5.1	104.5	101.4	3.1	13.7
1970	285.8	319.2	–33.4	185.1	219.9	–34.8	119.1	117.6	1.4	18.3
1971	302.3	354.5	–52.2	190.7	241.6	–50.9	133.7	135.0	–1.3	22.1
1972	345.6	388.5	–42.9	219.0	268.0	–49.0	157.1	151.0	6.1	30.5
1973	388.8	421.5	–32.7	249.2	287.6	–38.3	173.0	167.4	5.6	33.5
1974	430.2	473.9	–43.7	278.5	319.8	–41.3	186.6	189.0	–2.3	34.9
1975	441.2	549.9	–108.7	276.8	374.8	–97.9	208.0	218.7	–10.7	43.6
1976	505.7	591.0	–85.3	322.6	403.5	–80.9	232.2	236.6	–4.4	49.1
1977	567.4	640.3	–72.9	363.9	437.3	–73.4	258.3	257.8	.5	54.8
1978	646.1	703.3	–57.2	423.8	485.9	–62.0	285.8	280.9	4.9	63.5
1979	729.3	777.9	–48.6	487.0	534.4	–47.4	306.3	307.5	–1.2	64.0
1980	799.9	894.6	–94.7	533.7	622.5	–88.8	335.9	341.8	–5.9	69.7
1981	919.1	1,017.4	–98.2	621.1	709.1	–88.1	367.5	377.6	–10.2	69.4
1982	940.9	1,131.0	–190.1	618.7	786.0	–167.4	388.5	411.3	–22.8	66.3
1983	1,002.1	1,227.7	–225.6	644.8	851.9	–207.2	425.3	443.7	–18.4	67.9
1984	1,115.0	1,311.7	–196.7	711.2	907.7	–196.5	476.1	476.3	–.2	72.3
1985	1,217.0	1,418.7	–201.7	775.7	975.0	–199.2	517.5	519.9	–2.4	76.2
1986	1,292.9	1,512.8	–219.9	817.9	1,033.8	–215.9	557.4	561.3	–4.0	82.4
1987	1,406.6	1,586.7	–180.1	899.5	1,065.2	–165.7	585.5	599.9	–14.4	78.4
1988	1,507.1	1,678.3	–171.3	962.4	1,122.4	–160.0	630.4	641.7	–11.3	85.7
1989	1,632.0	1,810.7	–178.7	1,042.5	1,201.8	–159.4	681.4	700.7	–19.3	91.8
1990	1,713.3	1,952.9	–239.5	1,087.6	1,290.9	–203.3	730.1	766.3	–36.2	104.4
1991	1,763.7	2,072.2	–308.5	1,107.8	1,356.2	–248.4	779.9	840.0	–60.1	124.0
1992	1,848.7	2,254.2	–405.5	1,154.4	1,488.9	–334.5	836.1	907.0	–71.0	141.7
1993	1,953.3	2,339.3	–386.0	1,231.0	1,544.6	–313.5	878.0	950.4	–72.5	155.7
1994	2,097.6	2,417.2	–319.6	1,329.3	1,585.0	–255.6	935.1	999.1	–63.9	166.8
1995	2,223.9	2,536.5	–312.5	1,417.4	1,659.5	–242.1	981.0	1,051.4	–70.4	174.5
1996	2,388.6	2,621.8	–233.2	1,536.3	1,715.7	–179.4	1,033.7	1,087.5	–53.8	181.5
1997	2,565.9	2,699.9	–133.9	1,667.4	1,759.4	–92.0	1,086.7	1,128.7	–42.0	188.1
1998	2,738.6	2,767.4	–28.7	1,789.8	1,788.4	1.4	1,149.6	1,179.7	–30.1	200.8
1999	2,910.1	2,882.2	28.0	1,906.6	1,839.7	66.9	1,222.7	1,261.6	–38.9	219.2
2000	3,139.4	3,024.6	114.8	2,068.4	1,912.9	155.5	1,304.1	1,344.8	–40.6	233.1
2001	3,124.5	3,229.4	–105.0	2,032.2	2,018.2	14.0	1,353.4	1,472.4	–119.0	261.3
2002	2,968.3	3,422.6	–454.4	1,870.8	2,142.3	–271.5	1,386.2	1,569.1	–182.9	288.7
2003	3,045.9	3,631.3	–585.4	1,895.6	2,299.7	–404.1	1,472.0	1,653.3	–181.3	321.7
2004	3,275.7	3,825.6	–549.9	2,027.7	2,428.6	–400.9	1,580.3	1,729.3	–149.0	332.3
2005	3,679.3	4,088.1	–408.7	2,304.4	2,610.3	–305.9	1,718.5	1,821.3	–102.8	343.5
2006	4,013.4	4,326.1	–312.6	2,538.3	2,765.9	–227.6	1,816.2	1,901.2	–85.0	341.0
2007	4,210.8	4,606.2	–395.4	2,667.8	2,933.9	–266.1	1,902.1	2,031.4	–129.3	359.1
2008	4,125.0	4,977.0	–852.0	2,580.7	3,211.8	–631.1	1,915.5	2,136.4	–220.9	371.2
2009	3,696.6	5,286.8	–1,590.3	2,239.5	3,488.4	–1,248.9	1,915.2	2,256.6	–341.3	458.1
2010	3,933.2	5,565.7	–1,632.6	2,444.0	3,769.1	–1,325.1	1,994.4	2,301.8	–307.5	505.2
2011	4,130.6	5,647.7	–1,517.1	2,572.8	3,814.7	–1,242.0	2,030.4	2,305.4	–275.1	472.5
2012	4,312.2	5,673.6	–1,361.4	2,700.3	3,779.0	–1,078.6	2,056.3	2,339.1	–282.8	444.4
2013	4,834.5	5,737.8	–903.3	3,139.0	3,776.9	–637.9	2,145.6	2,411.0	–265.4	450.1
2014	5,056.5	5,895.0	–838.5	3,292.2	3,894.0	–601.8	2,259.4	2,496.1	–236.7	495.1
2015	5,281.5	6,074.0	–792.5	3,446.3	4,015.2	–568.9	2,368.6	2,592.2	–223.6	533.4
2016	5,340.3	6,251.2	–910.9	3,475.5	4,140.6	–665.1	2,421.9	2,667.8	–245.8	557.1
2017	5,483.8	6,438.2	–954.5	3,558.8	4,254.2	–695.4	2,484.2	2,743.3	–259.1	559.3
2018 ᵖ		6,734.7			4,482.3			2,830.5		578.1
2015: I	5,181.1	5,962.5	–781.5	3,388.3	3,939.9	–551.6	2,318.4	2,548.3	–229.8	525.6
II	5,269.9	6,079.2	–809.3	3,446.1	4,017.7	–571.6	2,354.1	2,591.7	–237.7	530.2
III	5,268.7	6,136.2	–867.4	3,446.1	4,057.1	–611.0	2,354.6	2,611.0	–256.4	532.0
IV	5,406.3	6,118.1	–711.8	3,504.9	4,046.1	–541.3	2,447.3	2,617.9	–170.5	545.9
2016: I	5,284.4	6,172.4	–888.0	3,447.2	4,085.2	–638.0	2,376.1	2,626.1	–250.0	539.0
II	5,305.5	6,219.5	–914.0	3,448.4	4,117.3	–668.8	2,411.4	2,656.6	–245.2	554.3
III	5,369.0	6,284.5	–915.4	3,491.8	4,166.7	–674.9	2,442.6	2,683.1	–240.5	565.4
IV	5,402.2	6,328.5	–926.3	3,514.4	4,192.9	–678.6	2,457.5	2,705.2	–247.7	569.7
2017: I	5,465.9	6,387.6	–921.8	3,572.4	4,228.3	–655.9	2,455.0	2,720.8	–265.8	561.6
II	5,443.8	6,376.2	–932.4	3,538.8	4,200.3	–661.5	2,452.0	2,722.9	–270.9	547.0
III	5,524.0	6,439.3	–915.3	3,590.3	4,250.9	–660.5	2,501.0	2,755.7	–254.7	567.3
IV	5,501.4	6,549.9	–1,048.5	3,533.6	4,337.2	–803.6	2,529.0	2,773.9	–244.9	561.2
2018: I	5,413.1	6,613.4	–1,200.2	3,428.3	4,398.2	–969.9	2,564.0	2,794.4	–230.4	579.2
II	5,460.5	6,696.6	–1,236.1	3,456.2	4,449.9	–993.7	2,580.8	2,823.3	–242.4	576.6
III	5,576.8	6,768.8	–1,192.1	3,547.5	4,508.1	–960.6	2,616.3	2,847.8	–231.5	587.0
IV ᵖ		6,860.2			4,573.1			2,856.6		569.6

Note: Federal grants-in-aid to State and local governments are reflected in Federal current expenditures and State and local current receipts. Total government current receipts and expenditures have been adjusted to eliminate this duplication.

Source: Department of Commerce (Bureau of Economic Analysis).

TABLE B–50. State and local government revenues and expenditures, fiscal years 1956–2016

[Millions of dollars]

Fiscal year [1]	General revenues by source [2]							General expenditures by function [2]				
	Total	Property taxes	Sales and gross receipts taxes	Individual income taxes	Corporation net income taxes	Revenue from Federal Government	All other [3]	Total [4]	Education	Highways	Public welfare [4]	All other [4,5]
1956	34,670	11,749	8,691	1,538	890	3,335	8,467	36,715	13,224	6,953	3,139	13,399
1957	38,164	12,864	9,467	1,754	984	3,843	9,252	40,375	14,134	7,816	3,485	14,940
1958	41,219	14,047	9,829	1,759	1,018	4,865	9,701	44,851	15,919	8,567	3,818	16,547
1959	45,306	14,983	10,437	1,994	1,001	6,377	10,514	48,887	17,283	9,592	4,136	17,876
1960	50,505	16,405	11,849	2,463	1,180	6,974	11,634	51,876	18,719	9,428	4,404	19,325
1961	54,037	18,002	12,463	2,613	1,266	7,131	12,562	56,201	20,574	9,844	4,720	21,063
1962	58,252	19,054	13,494	3,037	1,308	7,871	13,488	60,206	22,216	10,357	5,084	22,549
1963	62,891	20,089	14,456	3,269	1,505	8,722	14,850	64,815	23,776	11,135	5,481	24,423
1963–64	68,443	21,241	15,762	3,791	1,695	10,002	15,952	69,302	26,286	11,664	5,766	25,586
1964–65	74,000	22,583	17,118	4,090	1,929	11,029	17,251	74,678	28,563	12,221	6,315	27,579
1965–66	83,036	24,670	19,085	4,760	2,038	13,214	19,269	82,843	33,287	12,770	6,757	30,029
1966–67	91,197	26,047	20,530	5,825	2,227	15,370	21,198	93,350	37,919	13,932	8,218	33,281
1967–68	101,264	27,747	22,911	7,308	2,518	17,181	23,599	102,411	41,158	14,481	9,857	36,915
1968–69	114,550	30,673	26,519	8,908	3,180	19,153	26,117	116,728	47,238	15,417	12,110	41,963
1969–70	130,756	34,054	30,322	10,812	3,738	21,857	29,973	131,332	52,718	16,427	14,679	47,508
1970–71	144,927	37,852	33,233	11,900	3,424	26,146	32,372	150,674	59,413	18,095	18,226	54,940
1971–72	167,535	42,877	37,518	15,227	4,416	31,342	36,156	168,549	65,813	19,021	21,117	62,598
1972–73	190,222	45,283	42,047	17,994	5,425	39,264	40,210	181,357	69,713	18,615	23,582	69,447
1973–74	207,670	47,705	46,098	19,491	6,015	41,820	46,542	199,222	75,833	19,946	25,085	78,358
1974–75	228,171	51,491	49,815	21,454	6,642	47,034	51,735	230,722	87,858	22,528	28,156	92,180
1975–76	256,176	57,001	54,547	24,575	7,273	55,589	57,191	256,731	97,216	23,907	32,604	103,004
1976–77	285,157	62,527	60,641	29,246	9,174	62,444	61,125	274,215	102,780	23,058	35,906	112,472
1977–78	315,960	66,422	67,596	33,176	10,738	69,592	68,435	296,984	110,758	24,609	39,140	122,478
1978–79	343,236	64,944	74,247	36,932	12,128	75,164	79,822	327,517	119,448	28,440	41,898	137,731
1979–80	382,322	68,499	79,927	42,080	13,321	83,029	95,467	369,086	133,211	33,311	47,288	155,276
1980–81	423,404	74,969	85,971	46,426	14,143	90,294	111,599	407,449	145,784	34,603	54,105	172,957
1981–82	457,654	82,067	93,613	50,738	15,028	87,282	128,925	436,733	154,282	34,520	57,996	189,935
1982–83	486,753	89,105	100,247	55,129	14,258	90,007	138,008	466,516	163,876	36,655	60,906	205,080
1983–84	542,730	96,457	114,097	64,871	16,798	96,935	153,571	505,008	176,108	39,419	66,414	223,068
1984–85	598,121	103,757	126,376	70,361	19,152	106,158	172,317	553,899	192,686	44,989	71,479	244,745
1985–86	641,486	111,709	135,005	74,365	19,994	113,099	187,314	605,623	210,819	49,368	75,868	269,568
1986–87	686,860	121,203	144,091	83,935	22,425	114,857	200,350	657,134	226,619	52,355	82,650	295,510
1987–88	726,762	132,212	156,452	88,350	23,663	117,602	208,482	704,921	242,683	55,621	89,090	317,527
1988–89	786,129	142,400	166,336	97,806	25,926	125,824	227,838	762,360	263,898	58,105	97,879	342,479
1989–90	849,502	155,613	177,885	105,640	23,566	136,802	249,996	834,818	288,148	61,057	110,518	375,094
1990–91	902,207	167,999	185,570	109,341	22,242	154,099	262,955	908,108	309,302	64,937	130,402	403,467
1991–92	979,137	180,337	197,731	115,638	23,880	179,174	282,376	981,253	324,652	67,351	158,723	430,526
1992–93	1,041,643	189,744	209,649	123,235	26,417	198,663	293,935	1,030,434	342,287	68,370	170,705	449,072
1993–94	1,100,490	197,141	223,628	128,810	28,320	215,492	307,099	1,077,665	353,287	72,067	183,394	468,916
1994–95	1,169,505	203,451	237,268	137,931	31,406	228,771	330,677	1,149,863	378,273	77,109	196,703	497,779
1995–96	1,222,821	209,440	248,993	146,844	32,009	234,891	350,645	1,193,276	398,859	79,092	197,354	517,971
1996–97	1,289,237	218,877	261,418	159,042	33,820	244,847	371,233	1,249,984	418,416	82,062	203,779	545,727
1997–98	1,365,762	230,150	274,883	175,630	34,412	255,048	395,639	1,318,042	450,365	87,214	208,120	572,343
1998–99	1,434,029	239,672	290,993	189,309	33,922	270,628	409,505	1,402,369	483,259	93,018	218,957	607,134
1999–2000	1,541,322	249,178	309,290	211,661	36,059	291,950	443,186	1,506,797	521,612	101,336	237,336	646,512
2000–01	1,647,161	263,689	320,217	226,334	35,296	324,033	477,592	1,626,063	563,572	107,235	261,622	693,634
2001–02	1,684,879	279,191	324,123	202,832	28,152	360,546	490,035	1,736,866	594,694	115,295	285,464	741,413
2002–03	1,763,212	296,683	337,787	199,407	31,369	389,264	508,702	1,821,917	621,335	117,696	310,783	772,102
2003–04	1,887,397	317,941	361,027	215,215	33,716	423,112	536,386	1,908,543	655,182	117,215	340,523	795,622
2004–05	2,026,034	335,779	384,266	242,273	43,256	438,558	581,902	2,012,110	688,314	126,350	365,295	832,151
2005–06	2,197,475	364,559	417,735	268,667	53,081	452,975	640,458	2,123,663	728,917	136,502	373,846	884,398
2006–07	2,330,611	388,905	440,470	290,278	60,955	464,914	685,089	2,264,035	774,170	145,011	389,259	955,595
2007–08	2,421,977	409,540	449,945	304,902	57,231	477,441	722,919	2,406,183	826,061	153,831	408,920	1,017,372
2008–09	2,429,672	434,818	434,128	270,942	46,280	537,949	705,555	2,500,796	851,689	154,338	437,184	1,057,586
2009–10	2,510,846	443,947	435,571	261,510	44,108	623,801	701,909	2,542,231	860,118	155,912	460,230	1,065,971
2010–11	2,618,037	445,771	463,979	285,293	48,422	647,606	726,966	2,583,805	862,271	153,895	494,682	1,072,957
2011–12	2,598,849	446,101	478,224	307,258	48,934	585,162	733,169	2,592,466	867,508	160,299	489,259	1,075,400
2012–13	2,682,661	453,214	503,486	338,617	52,898	583,545	750,901	2,626,697	877,059	157,627	518,485	1,073,526
2013–14	2,763,644	465,317	522,013	341,357	54,611	602,851	777,496	2,714,357	905,213	161,954	546,735	1,100,455
2014–15	2,915,426	484,351	544,973	367,917	57,235	657,567	803,384	2,842,867	935,754	167,769	617,768	1,121,576
2015–16	3,008,262	503,262	558,871	376,297	54,259	690,209	825,363	2,948,039	972,906	174,990	640,860	1,159,284

[1] Fiscal years not the same for all governments. See Note.
[2] Excludes revenues or expenditures of publicly owned utilities and liquor stores and of insurance-trust activities. Intergovernmental receipts and payments between State and local governments are also excluded.
[3] Includes motor vehicle license taxes, other taxes, and charges and miscellaneous revenues.
[4] Includes intergovernmental payments to the Federal Government.
[5] Includes expenditures for libraries, hospitals, health, employment security administration, veterans' services, air transportation, sea and inland port facilities, parking facilities, police protection, fire protection, correction, protective inspection and regulation, sewerage, natural resources, parks and recreation, housing and community development, solid waste management, financial administration, judicial and legal, general public buildings, other government administration, interest on general debt, and other general expenditures, not elsewhere classified.

Note: Except for States listed, data for fiscal years listed from 1963–64 to 2015–16 are the aggregation of data for government fiscal years that ended in the 12-month period from July 1 to June 30 of those years; Texas used August and Alabama and Michigan used September as end dates. Data for 1963 and earlier years include data for government fiscal years ending during that particular calendar year.

Source: Department of Commerce (Bureau of the Census).

TABLE B-51. U.S. Treasury securities outstanding by kind of obligation, 1980–2018

[Billions of dollars]

End of fiscal year or month	Total Treasury securities outstanding [1]	Marketable							Nonmarketable				
		Total [2]	Treasury bills	Treasury notes	Treasury bonds	Treasury inflation-protected securities			Total	U.S. savings securities [3]	Foreign series [4]	Government account series	Other [5]
						Total	Notes	Bonds					
1980	906.8	594.5	199.8	310.9	83.8	....	....	....	312.3	73.0	25.2	189.8	24.2
1981	996.8	683.2	223.4	363.6	96.2	....	....	....	313.6	68.3	20.5	201.1	23.7
1982	1,141.2	824.4	277.9	442.9	103.6	....	....	....	316.8	67.6	14.6	210.5	24.1
1983	1,376.3	1,024.0	340.7	557.5	125.7	....	....	....	352.3	70.6	11.5	234.7	35.6
1984	1,560.4	1,176.6	356.8	661.7	158.1	....	....	....	383.8	73.7	8.8	259.5	41.8
1985	1,822.3	1,360.2	384.2	776.4	199.5	....	....	....	462.1	78.2	6.6	313.9	63.3
1986	2,124.9	1,564.3	410.7	896.9	241.7	....	....	....	560.5	87.8	4.1	365.9	102.8
1987	2,349.4	1,676.0	378.3	1,005.1	277.6	....	....	....	673.4	98.5	4.4	440.7	129.8
1988	2,601.4	1,802.9	398.5	1,089.6	299.9	....	....	....	798.5	107.8	6.3	536.5	148.0
1989	2,837.9	1,892.8	406.6	1,133.2	338.0	....	....	....	945.2	115.7	6.8	663.7	159.0
1990	3,212.7	2,092.8	482.5	1,218.1	377.2	....	....	....	1,119.9	123.9	36.0	779.4	180.6
1991	3,664.5	2,390.7	564.6	1,387.7	423.4	....	....	....	1,273.9	135.4	41.6	908.4	188.5
1992	4,063.8	2,677.5	634.3	1,566.3	461.8	....	....	....	1,386.3	150.3	37.0	1,011.0	188.0
1993	4,410.7	2,904.9	658.4	1,734.2	497.4	....	....	....	1,505.8	169.1	42.5	1,114.3	179.9
1994	4,691.7	3,091.6	697.3	1,867.5	511.8	....	....	....	1,600.1	178.6	42.0	1,211.7	167.8
1995	4,953.0	3,260.4	742.5	1,980.3	522.6	....	....	....	1,692.6	183.5	41.0	1,324.3	143.8
1996	5,220.8	3,418.4	761.2	2,098.7	543.5	....	....	....	1,802.4	184.1	37.5	1,454.7	126.1
1997	5,407.6	3,439.6	701.9	2,122.2	576.2	24.4	24.4	....	1,968.0	182.7	34.9	1,608.5	141.9
1998	5,518.7	3,331.0	637.6	2,009.1	610.4	58.8	41.9	17.0	2,187.6	180.8	35.1	1,777.3	194.4
1999	5,647.3	3,233.0	653.2	1,828.8	643.7	92.4	67.6	24.8	2,414.3	180.0	31.0	2,005.2	198.1
2000	5,622.1	2,992.8	616.2	1,611.3	635.3	115.0	81.6	33.4	2,629.4	177.7	25.4	2,242.9	183.3
2001 [1]	5,807.5	2,930.7	734.9	1,433.0	613.0	134.9	95.1	39.7	2,876.7	186.5	18.3	2,492.1	179.9
2002	6,228.2	3,136.7	868.3	1,521.6	593.0	138.9	93.7	45.1	3,091.5	193.3	12.5	2,707.3	178.4
2003	6,783.2	3,460.7	918.2	1,799.5	576.9	166.1	120.0	46.1	3,322.5	201.6	11.0	2,912.2	197.7
2004	7,379.1	3,846.1	961.5	2,109.6	552.0	223.0	164.5	58.5	3,533.0	204.2	5.9	3,130.0	192.9
2005	7,932.7	4,084.9	914.3	2,328.8	520.7	307.1	229.1	78.0	3,847.8	203.6	3.1	3,380.6	260.5
2006	8,507.0	4,303.0	911.5	2,447.2	534.7	395.6	293.9	101.7	4,203.9	203.7	3.0	3,722.7	274.5
2007	9,007.7	4,448.1	958.1	2,458.0	561.1	456.9	335.7	121.2	4,559.5	197.1	3.0	4,026.8	332.6
2008	10,024.7	5,236.0	1,489.8	2,624.8	582.9	524.5	380.2	144.3	4,788.7	194.3	3.0	4,297.7	293.8
2009	11,909.8	7,009.7	1,992.5	3,773.8	679.8	551.7	396.2	155.5	4,900.1	192.5	4.9	4,454.3	248.4
2010	13,561.6	8,498.3	1,788.5	5,255.9	849.9	593.8	421.1	172.7	5,063.3	188.7	4.2	4,645.3	225.1
2011	14,790.3	9,624.5	1,477.5	6,412.5	1,020.4	705.7	509.4	196.3	5,165.8	185.1	3.0	4,793.9	183.8
2012	16,066.2	10,749.7	1,616.0	7,120.7	1,198.2	807.7	584.7	223.0	5,316.5	183.8	3.0	4,939.3	190.4
2013	16,738.2	11,596.2	1,530.0	7,758.0	1,366.2	936.4	685.5	250.8	5,142.0	180.0	3.0	4,803.1	156.0
2014	17,824.1	12,294.2	1,411.0	8,167.8	1,534.1	1,044.7	765.2	279.5	5,529.9	176.7	3.0	5,212.5	137.7
2015	18,150.6	12,853.8	1,358.0	8,372.7	1,688.3	1,135.4	832.1	303.3	5,296.9	172.8	.3	5,013.5	110.3
2016	19,573.4	13,660.6	1,647.0	8,631.0	1,825.5	1,210.0	881.6	328.3	5,912.8	167.5	.3	5,604.1	141.0
2017	20,244.9	14,199.8	1,801.9	8,805.5	1,951.7	1,286.5	933.3	353.2	6,045.1	161.7	.3	5,771.1	112.0
2018	21,516.1	15,278.0	2,239.9	9,154.4	2,127.8	1,376.4	993.4	383.0	6,238.0	156.8	.3	5,977.6	103.4
2017: Jan	19,937.3	13,863.8	1,762.0	8,678.5	1,861.7	1,238.6	903.9	334.7	6,073.5	165.1	.3	5,768.7	139.4
Feb	19,959.6	13,898.9	1,753.0	8,684.6	1,878.4	1,246.9	904.1	342.8	6,060.7	164.7	.3	5,758.0	137.7
Mar	19,846.4	13,966.7	1,757.0	8,702.4	1,890.4	1,266.3	921.6	344.7	5,879.7	164.2	.3	5,577.2	138.0
Apr	19,846.3	13,950.5	1,742.0	8,716.7	1,902.5	1,238.7	892.9	345.8	5,895.8	163.8	.3	5,597.2	134.5
May	19,845.9	13,982.7	1,748.0	8,735.9	1,906.9	1,252.3	906.2	346.1	5,863.3	163.3	.3	5,568.5	131.2
June	19,844.6	14,009.4	1,718.0	8,758.3	1,918.9	1,261.6	908.8	352.8	5,835.1	162.8	.3	5,548.8	123.2
July	19,844.9	14,060.2	1,758.0	8,782.3	1,931.2	1,260.6	907.5	353.1	5,784.7	162.6	.3	5,505.4	116.5
Aug	19,844.5	14,093.6	1,747.9	8,788.5	1,939.7	1,276.3	922.8	353.5	5,751.0	162.0	.3	5,476.3	112.5
Sept	20,244.9	14,199.8	1,801.9	8,805.5	1,951.7	1,286.5	933.3	353.2	6,045.1	161.7	.3	5,771.1	112.0
Oct	20,442.5	14,273.7	1,855.9	8,830.1	1,963.7	1,295.4	935.9	359.5	6,168.8	161.1	.3	5,893.5	113.9
Nov	20,590.4	14,437.5	1,970.9	8,830.7	1,980.5	1,313.9	952.5	361.3	6,152.8	160.9	.3	5,875.0	116.7
Dec	20,492.7	14,480.2	1,955.9	8,849.7	1,992.5	1,327.5	966.3	361.2	6,012.5	160.4	.3	5,727.5	124.3
2018: Jan	20,493.7	14,514.5	1,966.9	8,889.2	2,004.9	1,323.1	961.9	361.2	5,979.2	159.9	.3	5,700.7	118.4
Feb	20,855.7	14,677.9	2,078.0	8,899.6	2,024.0	1,331.0	961.3	369.7	6,177.7	159.4	.3	5,902.8	115.2
Mar	21,089.9	14,945.0	2,289.0	8,924.6	2,037.0	1,349.0	977.4	371.6	6,144.9	159.0	.3	5,869.3	116.3
Apr	21,068.2	14,849.9	2,169.0	8,974.2	2,050.0	1,319.4	946.1	373.3	6,218.3	158.6	.3	5,945.6	113.9
May	21,145.2	14,939.4	2,184.0	9,002.2	2,064.4	1,335.6	961.4	374.2	6,205.8	158.2	.3	5,932.1	115.3
June	21,195.3	14,982.6	2,158.0	9,032.2	2,078.4	1,345.9	965.2	380.7	6,212.8	157.8	.3	5,943.9	110.8
July	21,313.1	15,085.3	2,205.9	9,094.9	2,092.4	1,347.8	965.5	382.3	6,227.8	157.5	.3	5,962.2	107.8
Aug	21,458.8	15,301.8	2,340.9	9,120.4	2,112.8	1,365.2	982.3	383.0	6,157.0	157.0	.3	5,895.9	103.8
Sept	21,516.1	15,278.0	2,239.9	9,154.4	2,127.8	1,376.4	993.4	383.0	6,238.0	156.8	.3	5,977.6	103.4
Oct	21,702.4	15,357.9	2,258.0	9,218.2	2,142.8	1,382.3	994.0	388.3	6,344.5	156.4	.3	6,084.1	103.7
Nov	21,850.1	15,560.1	2,389.1	9,240.4	2,158.5	1,395.9	1,007.1	388.8	6,290.0	156.2	.3	6,032.9	100.7
Dec	21,974.1	15,618.3	2,340.0	9,297.0	2,174.5	1,412.6	1,023.2	389.4	6,355.8	155.7	.3	6,101.9	97.9

[1] Data beginning with January 2001 are interest-bearing and non-interest-bearing securities; prior data are interest-bearing securities only.
[2] Data from 1986 to 2002 and 2005 forward include Federal Financing Bank securities, not shown separately. Beginning with data for January 2014, includes Floating Rate Notes, not shown separately.
[3] Through 1996, series is U.S. savings bonds. Beginning 1997, includes U.S. retirement plan bonds, U.S. individual retirement bonds, and U.S. savings notes previously included in "other" nonmarketable securities.
[4] Nonmarketable certificates of indebtedness, notes, bonds, and bills in the Treasury foreign series of dollar-denominated and foreign-currency-denominated issues.
[5] Includes depository bonds; retirement plan bonds through 1996; Rural Electrification Administration bonds; State and local bonds; special issues held only by U.S. Government agencies and trust funds and the Federal home loan banks; for the period July 2003 through February 2004, depositary compensation securities; and for the period August 2008 through April 2016, Hope bonds for the HOPE For Homeowners Program.

Note: The fiscal year is on an October 1–September 30 basis.

Source: Department of the Treasury.

TABLE B–52. Estimated ownership of U.S. Treasury securities, 2005–2018

[Billions of dollars]

End of month	Total public debt [1]	Federal Reserve and Intra-governmental holdings [2]	Held by private investors									
			Total privately held	Depository institutions [3]	U.S. savings bonds [4]	Pension funds		Insurance companies	Mutual funds [6]	State and local governments	Foreign and international [7]	Other investors [8]
						Private [5]	State and local governments					
2005: Mar	7,776.9	3,921.6	3,855.3	149.4	204.2	114.4	157.2	193.3	264.3	429.3	1,952.2	391.0
June	7,836.5	4,033.5	3,803.0	135.9	204.2	115.4	165.9	195.0	248.6	461.1	1,877.5	399.4
Sept	7,932.7	4,067.8	3,864.9	134.0	203.6	116.7	161.1	200.7	246.6	493.6	1,929.6	378.9
Dec	8,170.4	4,199.8	3,970.6	129.4	205.2	116.5	154.2	202.3	254.1	512.2	2,033.9	362.7
2006: Mar	8,371.2	4,257.2	4,114.0	113.0	206.0	116.8	152.9	200.3	254.2	515.7	2,082.1	473.0
June	8,420.0	4,389.2	4,030.8	119.5	205.2	117.7	149.6	196.1	243.4	531.6	1,977.8	490.1
Sept	8,507.0	4,432.8	4,074.2	113.6	203.7	125.8	149.3	196.8	234.2	542.3	2,025.3	483.2
Dec	8,680.2	4,558.1	4,122.1	114.8	202.4	139.8	153.4	197.9	248.2	570.5	2,103.1	392.0
2007: Mar	8,849.7	4,576.6	4,273.1	119.8	200.3	139.7	156.3	185.4	263.2	608.3	2,194.8	405.2
June	8,867.7	4,715.1	4,152.6	110.4	198.6	139.9	162.3	168.9	257.6	637.8	2,192.0	285.1
Sept	9,007.7	4,738.0	4,269.7	119.7	197.1	140.5	153.2	155.1	292.7	643.1	2,235.3	332.9
Dec	9,229.2	4,833.5	4,395.7	129.8	196.5	141.0	144.2	141.9	343.5	647.8	2,353.2	297.8
2008: Mar	9,437.6	4,694.7	4,742.9	125.0	195.4	143.7	135.4	152.1	466.7	646.4	2,506.3	371.9
June	9,492.0	4,685.8	4,806.2	112.7	195.0	145.0	135.5	159.4	440.3	635.1	2,587.4	395.9
Sept	10,024.7	4,692.7	5,332.0	130.0	194.3	147.0	136.7	163.4	631.4	614.0	2,802.4	512.9
Dec	10,699.8	4,806.4	5,893.4	105.0	194.1	147.4	129.9	171.4	758.2	601.4	3,077.2	708.9
2009: Mar	11,126.9	4,785.2	6,341.7	125.7	194.0	155.4	137.0	191.0	721.1	588.2	3,265.7	963.7
June	11,545.3	5,026.8	6,518.5	140.8	193.6	164.1	144.6	200.0	711.8	588.5	3,460.8	914.2
Sept	11,909.8	5,127.1	6,782.7	198.2	192.5	167.2	145.6	210.2	668.5	583.6	3,570.6	1,046.3
Dec	12,311.3	5,276.9	7,034.4	202.5	191.3	175.6	151.4	222.0	668.8	585.6	3,685.1	1,152.1
2010: Mar	12,773.1	5,259.8	7,513.3	269.3	190.2	183.0	153.6	225.7	678.5	585.0	3,877.9	1,350.1
June	13,201.8	5,345.1	7,856.7	266.1	189.6	190.8	150.1	231.8	676.8	584.4	4,070.0	1,497.1
Sept	13,561.6	5,350.5	8,211.1	322.8	188.7	198.2	145.2	240.6	671.0	586.0	4,324.2	1,534.4
Dec	14,025.2	5,656.2	8,368.9	319.3	187.9	206.8	153.7	248.4	721.7	595.7	4,435.6	1,499.9
2011: Mar	14,270.0	5,958.9	8,311.1	321.0	186.7	215.8	157.9	253.5	749.4	585.3	4,481.4	1,360.1
June	14,343.1	6,220.4	8,122.7	279.4	186.0	251.8	158.0	254.8	753.7	572.2	4,690.6	976.1
Sept	14,790.3	6,328.0	8,462.4	293.8	185.1	373.6	155.7	259.6	788.7	557.9	4,912.1	935.8
Dec	15,222.8	6,439.6	8,783.3	279.7	185.2	391.9	160.7	297.3	927.9	562.2	5,006.9	971.4
2012: Mar	15,582.3	6,397.2	9,185.1	317.0	184.8	406.6	169.4	298.1	1,015.4	567.4	5,145.1	1,081.2
June	15,855.5	6,475.8	9,379.7	303.2	184.7	427.4	171.2	293.6	997.8	585.4	5,310.9	1,105.4
Sept	16,066.2	6,446.8	9,619.4	338.2	183.8	453.9	181.7	292.6	1,080.7	596.9	5,476.1	1,015.4
Dec	16,432.7	6,523.7	9,909.1	347.7	182.5	468.0	183.6	292.7	1,031.8	599.6	5,573.8	1,229.4
2013: Mar	16,771.6	6,656.8	10,114.8	338.9	181.7	463.4	193.4	284.3	1,066.7	615.6	5,725.0	1,245.7
June	16,738.2	6,773.3	9,964.9	300.2	180.9	444.5	187.7	276.2	1,000.1	612.6	5,595.0	1,367.8
Sept	16,738.2	6,834.2	9,904.0	293.2	180.0	347.8	187.5	273.2	986.1	624.3	5,652.8	1,359.1
Dec	17,352.0	7,205.3	10,146.6	321.1	179.2	464.9	181.3	271.2	983.3	633.6	5,792.6	1,319.5
2014: Mar	17,601.2	7,301.5	10,299.7	368.3	178.3	474.3	184.3	276.8	1,060.4	632.0	5,948.3	1,177.0
June	17,632.6	7,461.0	10,171.6	407.2	177.6	482.6	198.3	287.7	986.2	638.7	6,018.7	974.5
Sept	17,824.1	7,490.8	10,333.2	469.6	176.7	490.7	198.7	298.1	1,075.8	628.8	6,069.2	925.5
Dec	18,141.4	7,578.9	10,562.6	513.7	175.9	507.1	199.2	307.0	1,121.8	657.3	6,157.7	922.8
2015: Mar	18,152.1	7,521.3	10,630.8	511.7	174.9	447.8	176.7	305.1	1,170.4	676.9	6,172.6	994.7
June	18,152.1	7,536.5	10,615.5	515.4	173.9	373.8	185.7	304.3	1,139.8	658.2	6,163.1	1,101.2
Sept	18,150.6	7,488.7	10,661.9	513.6	172.8	305.3	171.0	306.6	1,195.1	648.4	6,105.9	1,243.3
Dec	18,922.2	7,711.2	11,211.0	546.8	171.6	504.7	174.5	306.7	1,318.3	680.2	6,146.2	1,361.9
2016: Mar	19,264.9	7,801.4	11,463.6	555.3	170.3	524.0	170.4	315.5	1,321.7	691.9	6,284.4	1,430.2
June	19,381.6	7,911.2	11,470.4	570.3	169.0	537.1	185.0	329.8	1,336.0	710.0	6,279.1	1,354.2
Sept	19,573.4	7,863.5	11,709.9	620.4	167.5	544.3	203.3	341.2	1,506.5	721.6	6,155.1	1,449.1
Dec	19,976.9	8,005.6	11,971.3	666.8	165.8	536.4	217.8	330.2	1,593.3	717.9	6,006.3	1,736.7
2017: Mar	19,846.4	7,941.1	11,905.3	660.4	164.2	436.9	238.1	338.4	1,575.0	712.1	6,075.3	1,705.0
June	19,844.6	7,943.4	11,901.1	622.7	162.8	408.5	262.8	348.4	1,438.1	685.4	6,151.9	1,820.5
Sept	20,244.9	8,036.9	12,208.0	604.5	161.7	546.6	261.2	359.7	1,616.4	670.5	6,301.9	1,685.6
Dec	20,492.7	8,132.1	12,360.6	634.4	160.4	404.8	277.3	372.6	1,713.2	687.4	6,211.3	1,899.3
2018: Mar	21,089.9	8,086.6	13,003.3	635.2	159.0	571.4	280.9	360.4	1,880.6	675.2	6,223.2	2,217.4
June	21,195.3	8,106.9	13,088.5	670.0	157.8	593.9	277.3	223.8	1,760.7	699.0	6,214.0	2,491.9
Sept	21,516.1	8,068.1	13,447.9	690.1	156.8	613.6	279.5	223.6	1,795.9	678.8	6,225.6	2,784.1
Dec	21,974.1	8,095.0	13,879.1	....	155.7	....	....	....	....	....	6,265.2	

[1] Face value.
[2] Federal Reserve holdings exclude Treasury securities held under repurchase agreements.
[3] Includes U.S. chartered depository institutions, foreign banking offices in U.S., banks in U.S. affiliated areas, credit unions, and bank holding companies.
[4] Current accrual value includes myRA.
[5] Includes Treasury securities held by the Federal Employees Retirement System Thrift Savings Plan "G Fund."
[6] Includes money market mutual funds, mutual funds, and closed-end investment companies.
[7] Includes nonmarketable foreign series, Treasury securities, and Treasury deposit funds. Excludes Treasury securities held under repurchase agreements in custody accounts at the Federal Reserve Bank of New York. Estimates reflect benchmarks to this series at differing intervals; for further detail, see *Treasury Bulletin* and http://www.treasury.gov/resource-center/data-chart-center/tic/pages/index.aspx.
[8] Includes individuals, Government-sponsored enterprises, brokers and dealers, bank personal trusts and estates, corporate and noncorporate businesses, and other investors.

Source: Department of the Treasury.

Corporate Profits and Finance

TABLE B–53. Corporate profits with inventory valuation and capital consumption adjustments, 1968–2018

[Billions of dollars; quarterly data at seasonally adjusted annual rates]

Year or quarter	Corporate profits with inventory valuation and capital consumption adjustments	Taxes on corporate income	Corporate profits after tax with inventory valuation and capital consumption adjustments		
			Total	Net dividends	Undistributed profits with inventory valuation and capital consumption adjustments
1968	101.7	37.2	64.6	26.0	38.6
1969	98.4	37.0	61.5	27.3	34.2
1970	86.2	31.3	55.0	27.8	27.2
1971	100.6	34.8	65.8	28.4	37.5
1972	117.2	39.1	78.1	30.1	48.0
1973	133.4	45.6	87.8	34.2	53.5
1974	125.7	47.2	78.5	38.8	39.7
1975	138.9	46.3	92.6	38.3	54.3
1976	174.3	59.4	114.9	44.9	70.0
1977	205.8	68.5	137.3	50.7	86.6
1978	238.6	77.9	160.7	57.8	102.9
1979	249.0	80.7	168.2	66.8	101.4
1980	223.6	75.5	148.1	75.8	72.3
1981	247.5	70.3	177.2	87.8	89.4
1982	229.9	51.3	178.6	92.9	85.6
1983	279.8	66.4	213.3	97.7	115.7
1984	337.9	81.5	256.4	106.9	149.5
1985	354.5	81.6	272.9	115.3	157.5
1986	324.4	91.9	232.5	124.0	108.5
1987	366.0	112.7	253.3	130.1	123.2
1988	414.5	124.3	290.2	147.3	142.9
1989	414.3	124.4	289.9	179.6	110.3
1990	417.7	121.8	295.9	192.7	103.2
1991	452.6	117.8	334.8	201.3	133.5
1992	477.2	131.9	345.3	206.3	139.0
1993	524.6	155.0	369.5	221.3	148.2
1994	624.8	172.7	452.1	256.4	195.7
1995	706.2	194.4	511.8	282.3	229.4
1996	789.5	211.4	578.1	323.6	254.5
1997	869.7	224.8	645.0	360.1	284.9
1998	808.5	221.8	586.6	383.6	203.0
1999	834.9	227.4	607.5	373.5	234.1
2000	786.6	233.4	553.2	410.2	142.9
2001	758.7	170.1	588.6	397.9	190.8
2002	911.7	160.6	751.1	424.9	326.2
2003	1,056.3	213.7	842.5	456.0	386.5
2004	1,289.3	278.5	1,010.8	582.2	428.6
2005	1,488.6	379.8	1,108.8	602.0	506.8
2006	1,646.3	430.4	1,215.8	755.1	460.8
2007	1,533.2	392.1	1,141.1	853.5	287.6
2008	1,285.8	256.1	1,029.7	840.3	189.4
2009	1,386.8	204.2	1,182.6	622.1	560.6
2010	1,728.7	272.5	1,456.2	643.2	813.0
2011	1,809.8	281.1	1,528.7	779.1	749.6
2012	1,997.4	334.9	1,662.5	948.7	713.9
2013	2,010.7	362.8	1,647.9	1,009.0	638.9
2014	2,118.8	407.4	1,711.5	1,096.1	615.4
2015	2,057.3	397.2	1,660.1	1,164.9	495.2
2016	2,035.0	392.9	1,642.1	1,187.4	454.7
2017	2,099.3	350.7	1,748.6	1,215.3	533.3
2018 ᵖ				1,241.7	
2015: I	2,133.7	417.5	1,716.3	1,148.0	568.2
II	2,102.5	421.9	1,680.6	1,128.9	551.7
III	2,056.6	391.5	1,665.1	1,157.4	507.7
IV	1,936.2	358.0	1,578.2	1,225.2	353.0
2016: I	1,995.2	384.4	1,610.8	1,180.2	430.6
II	2,017.7	385.5	1,632.2	1,180.9	451.3
III	2,044.6	413.0	1,631.6	1,196.3	435.3
IV	2,082.4	388.5	1,693.9	1,192.4	501.5
2017: I	2,055.9	348.0	1,707.8	1,217.7	490.2
II	2,089.5	355.8	1,733.7	1,233.3	500.4
III	2,101.1	365.2	1,735.9	1,215.5	520.5
IV	2,150.7	333.8	1,816.8	1,194.8	622.0
2018: I	2,177.3	212.0	1,965.3	1,213.2	752.1
II	2,242.3	234.8	2,007.5	1,223.0	784.5
III	2,320.5	243.7	2,076.8	1,250.6	826.2
IV ᵖ				1,279.8	

Source: Department of Commerce (Bureau of Economic Analysis).

TABLE B–54. Corporate profits by industry, 1968–2018

[Billions of dollars; quarterly data at seasonally adjusted annual rates]

Year or quarter	Total	Corporate profits with inventory valuation adjustment and without capital consumption adjustment											Rest of the world
		Domestic industries											
		Total	Financial			Nonfinancial							
			Total	Federal Reserve banks	Other	Total	Manufacturing	Transportation[1]	Utilities	Wholesale trade	Retail trade	Information	Other	
SIC:[2]														
1968	94.3	88.6	12.9	2.5	10.4	75.7	45.9	11.4	....	4.7	6.4	....	7.4	5.6
1969	90.8	84.2	13.6	3.1	10.6	70.6	41.6	11.1	....	4.9	6.4	....	6.5	6.6
1970	79.7	72.6	15.5	3.5	12.0	57.1	32.0	8.8	....	4.6	6.1	....	5.8	7.1
1971	94.7	86.8	17.9	3.3	14.6	68.9	40.0	9.6	....	5.4	7.3	....	6.7	7.9
1972	109.3	99.7	19.5	3.3	16.1	80.3	47.6	10.4	....	7.2	7.5	....	7.6	9.5
1973	126.6	111.7	21.1	4.5	16.6	90.6	55.0	10.2	....	8.8	7.0	....	9.6	14.9
1974	123.3	105.8	20.8	5.7	15.1	85.1	51.0	9.1	....	12.2	2.8	....	10.0	17.5
1975	144.2	129.6	20.4	5.6	14.8	109.2	63.0	11.7	....	14.3	8.4	....	11.8	14.6
1976	182.1	165.6	25.6	5.9	19.7	140.0	82.5	17.5	....	13.7	10.9	....	15.3	16.5
1977	212.8	193.7	32.6	6.1	26.5	161.1	91.5	21.2	....	16.4	12.8	....	19.2	19.1
1978	246.7	223.8	40.8	7.6	33.1	183.1	105.8	25.5	....	16.7	13.1	....	22.0	22.9
1979	261.0	226.4	41.8	9.4	32.3	184.6	107.1	21.6	....	20.0	10.7	....	25.2	34.6
1980	240.6	205.2	35.2	11.8	23.5	169.9	97.6	22.2	....	18.5	7.0	....	24.6	35.5
1981	252.0	222.3	30.3	14.4	15.9	192.0	112.5	25.1	....	23.7	10.7	....	20.1	29.7
1982	224.8	192.2	27.2	15.2	12.0	165.0	89.6	28.1	....	20.7	14.3	....	12.3	32.6
1983	256.4	221.4	36.2	14.6	21.6	185.2	97.3	34.3	....	21.9	19.3	....	12.3	35.1
1984	294.3	257.7	34.7	16.4	18.3	223.0	114.2	44.7	....	30.4	21.5	....	12.1	36.6
1985	289.7	251.6	46.5	16.3	30.2	205.1	107.1	39.1	....	24.6	22.8	....	11.4	38.1
1986	273.3	233.8	56.4	15.5	40.8	177.4	75.6	39.3	....	24.4	23.4	....	14.7	39.5
1987	314.6	266.5	60.3	16.2	44.1	206.2	101.8	42.0	....	18.9	23.3	....	20.3	48.0
1988	366.2	309.2	66.9	18.1	48.8	242.3	132.8	46.8	....	20.4	19.8	....	22.5	57.0
1989	373.1	305.9	78.3	20.6	57.6	227.6	122.3	41.9	....	22.0	20.9	....	20.5	67.1
1990	391.2	315.1	89.6	21.8	67.8	225.5	120.9	43.5	....	19.4	20.3	....	21.3	76.1
1991	434.2	357.8	120.4	20.7	99.7	237.3	109.3	54.5	....	22.3	26.9	....	24.3	76.5
1992	459.7	386.6	132.4	18.3	114.1	254.2	109.8	57.7	....	25.3	28.1	....	33.4	73.1
1993	501.9	425.0	119.9	16.7	103.2	305.1	122.9	70.1	....	26.5	39.7	....	45.8	76.9
1994	589.3	511.3	125.9	18.5	107.4	385.4	162.6	83.9	....	31.4	46.3	....	61.2	78.0
1995	667.0	574.0	140.3	22.9	117.3	433.7	199.8	89.0	....	28.0	43.9	....	73.1	92.9
1996	741.8	639.8	147.9	22.5	125.3	492.0	220.4	91.2	....	39.9	52.0	....	88.5	102.0
1997	811.0	703.4	162.2	24.3	137.9	541.2	248.5	81.0	....	48.1	63.4	....	100.3	107.6
1998	743.8	641.1	138.9	25.6	113.3	502.1	220.4	72.6	....	50.6	72.3	....	86.3	102.8
1999	761.9	640.2	154.6	26.7	127.9	485.6	219.4	49.3	....	46.8	72.5	....	97.6	121.7
2000	729.8	584.1	149.7	31.2	118.5	434.4	205.9	33.8	....	50.4	68.9	....	75.4	145.7
NAICS:[2]														
1998	743.8	641.1	138.9	25.6	113.3	502.1	193.5	12.8	33.3	57.3	62.5	33.1	109.7	102.8
1999	761.9	640.2	154.6	26.7	127.9	485.6	184.5	7.2	34.4	55.6	59.5	20.8	123.5	121.7
2000	729.8	584.1	149.7	31.2	118.5	434.4	175.6	9.5	24.3	59.5	51.3	–11.9	126.1	145.7
2001	697.1	528.3	195.0	28.9	166.1	333.3	75.1	–.7	22.5	51.1	71.3	–26.4	140.2	168.8
2002	797.4	640.6	265.3	23.5	241.9	375.3	78.3	–6.5	10.5	53.5	83.3	5.0	151.2	156.8
2003	955.7	796.7	302.8	20.0	282.7	494.0	123.9	4.4	13.2	56.6	87.9	28.1	179.9	158.9
2004	1,217.5	1,022.4	346.0	20.0	326.0	676.3	186.2	12.0	21.1	72.7	94.0	61.6	228.8	195.1
2005	1,629.2	1,403.4	409.5	26.5	383.0	993.9	279.7	28.4	32.4	96.0	123.3	100.7	333.5	225.7
2006	1,812.2	1,572.5	413.1	33.8	379.3	1,159.4	352.9	40.8	55.2	105.0	133.6	115.2	356.8	239.7
2007	1,708.3	1,370.5	300.2	36.0	264.2	1,070.3	321.1	23.3	49.6	102.8	119.4	120.5	333.6	337.8
2008	1,344.5	954.3	94.6	35.1	59.5	859.7	240.0	29.3	30.4	92.7	82.2	98.8	286.3	390.2
2009	1,470.1	1,121.3	362.7	47.3	315.3	758.7	164.7	21.7	23.4	88.9	107.9	87.0	265.1	348.8
2010	1,786.4	1,400.6	405.8	71.6	334.3	994.8	281.8	44.6	30.6	99.3	115.9	102.3	320.4	385.8
2011	1,750.2	1,337.7	378.4	76.0	302.4	959.3	296.0	30.6	10.2	97.2	115.1	95.7	314.5	412.6
2012	2,144.7	1,739.3	482.4	71.7	410.6	1,256.9	403.0	54.4	13.8	137.9	155.7	112.0	380.1	405.4
2013	2,165.9	1,767.1	430.7	79.7	351.1	1,336.3	446.9	45.2	28.3	146.4	153.3	137.6	378.6	398.8
2014	2,266.1	1,861.2	483.1	103.5	379.6	1,378.1	457.4	55.6	32.7	150.8	158.6	126.3	396.6	404.9
2015	2,187.0	1,784.5	437.6	100.7	336.8	1,346.9	422.5	62.2	20.1	152.1	169.2	140.4	380.4	402.5
2016	2,128.7	1,722.2	468.9	92.0	376.9	1,253.3	322.9	62.9	7.2	127.5	173.5	171.6	387.7	406.5
2017	2,136.4	1,687.5	468.7	78.3	390.4	1,218.9	292.9	59.4	3.8	111.8	162.5	148.6	439.8	448.8
2016: I	2,101.2	1,711.7	377.4	96.4	281.1	1,334.2	395.5	69.0	12.6	151.8	169.6	160.3	375.5	389.5
II	2,114.4	1,714.1	472.1	92.9	379.2	1,241.9	311.1	65.8	10.5	120.6	164.9	186.6	382.4	400.4
III	2,132.3	1,741.9	505.5	90.6	414.9	1,236.4	298.2	61.9	1.2	136.8	179.5	163.3	395.5	390.4
IV	2,166.8	1,721.0	520.4	87.9	432.5	1,200.6	286.6	55.1	4.4	100.7	179.9	176.4	397.6	445.8
2017: I	2,148.0	1,714.8	463.3	89.3	373.9	1,251.5	279.2	61.0	5.9	117.4	171.4	164.1	452.5	433.2
II	2,187.3	1,768.0	468.7	80.1	388.6	1,299.3	306.9	66.4	5.3	128.9	170.7	148.6	472.5	419.3
III	2,199.9	1,740.0	489.0	71.8	417.2	1,251.0	320.8	59.6	2.7	114.7	168.7	157.8	426.6	459.9
IV	2,010.3	1,527.3	453.7	71.9	381.8	1,073.6	264.5	50.6	1.4	86.3	139.2	124.0	407.5	483.0
2018: I	2,036.9	1,550.2	444.5	69.9	374.6	1,105.8	238.5	47.9	–1.1	88.6	155.4	148.9	427.6	486.7
II	2,107.3	1,625.2	461.6	66.6	395.0	1,163.6	267.7	54.0	–.7	83.3	141.1	161.6	456.6	482.1
III	2,189.5	1,706.2	456.3	63.9	392.4	1,249.9	302.9	52.4	–2.2	117.1	164.8	162.6	452.2	483.4

[1] Data on Standard Industrial Classification (SIC) basis include transportation and public utilities. Those on North American Industry Classification System (NAICS) basis include transporation and warehousing. Utilities classified separately in NAICS (as shown beginning 1998).
[2] SIC-based industry data use the 1987 SIC for data beginning in 1987 and the 1972 SIC for prior data. NAICS-based data use 2002 NAICS.

Note: Industry data on SIC basis and NAICS basis are not necessarily the same and are not strictly comparable.

Source: Department of Commerce (Bureau of Economic Analysis).

TABLE B-55.—Historical stock prices and yields, 1949–2003

End of year	Common stock prices (end of period) [1]									Common stock yields (Standard & Poor's) (percent) [5]	
	New York Stock Exchange (NYSE) indexes [2]						Dow Jones industrial average [2]	Standard & Poor's composite index (1941–43=10) [2]	Nasdaq composite index (Feb. 5, 1971=100) [2]	Dividend-price ratio [6]	Earnings-price ratio [7]
	Composite (Dec. 31, 2002= 5,000) [3]	December 31, 1965=50									
		Composite	Industrial	Transpor-tation	Utility [4]	Finance					
1949							200.52	16.76		6.59	15.48
1950							235.42	20.41		6.57	13.99
1951							269.23	23.77		6.13	11.82
1952							291.90	26.57		5.80	9.47
1953		13.60					280.90	24.81		5.80	10.26
1954		19.40					404.39	35.98		4.95	8.57
1955		23.71					488.40	45.48		4.08	7.95
1956		24.35					499.47	46.67		4.09	7.55
1957		21.11					435.69	39.99		4.35	7.89
1958		28.85					583.65	55.21		3.97	6.23
1959		32.15					679.36	59.89		3.23	5.78
1960		30.94					615.89	58.11		3.47	5.90
1961		38.93					731.14	71.55		2.98	4.62
1962		33.81					652.10	63.10		3.37	5.82
1963		39.92					762.95	75.02		3.17	5.50
1964		45.65					874.13	84.75		3.01	5.32
1965	528.69	50.00					969.26	92.43		3.00	5.59
1966	462.28	43.72	43.13	47.56	90.38	44.91	785.69	80.33		3.40	6.63
1967	569.18	53.83	56.59	49.66	86.76	53.80	905.11	96.47		3.20	5.73
1968	622.79	58.90	61.69	56.27	91.64	76.48	943.75	103.86		3.07	5.67
1969	544.86	51.53	54.74	37.85	77.54	67.87	800.36	92.06		3.24	6.08
1970	531.12	50.23	52.91	35.70	81.64	64.34	838.92	92.15		3.83	6.45
1971	596.68	56.43	60.53	49.56	78.78	73.83	890.20	102.09	114.12	3.14	5.41
1972	681.79	64.48	70.33	47.69	84.34	83.34	1,020.02	118.05	133.73	2.84	5.50
1973	547.93	51.82	56.60	37.53	68.66	64.51	850.86	97.55	92.19	3.06	7.12
1974	382.03	36.13	39.15	26.36	53.30	39.84	616.24	68.56	59.82	4.47	11.59
1975	503.73	47.64	52.73	32.98	66.94	45.20	852.41	90.19	77.62	4.31	9.15
1976	612.01	57.88	63.36	42.57	82.54	59.23	1,004.65	107.46	97.88	3.77	8.90
1977	555.12	52.50	56.43	40.50	81.08	53.85	831.17	95.10	105.05	4.62	10.79
1978	566.96	53.62	58.87	41.58	75.38	55.01	805.01	96.11	117.98	5.28	12.03
1979	655.04	61.95	70.24	50.64	73.80	63.45	838.74	107.94	151.14	5.47	13.46
1980	823.27	77.86	91.52	76.19	76.90	70.83	963.99	135.76	202.34	5.26	12.66
1981	751.90	71.11	80.89	66.85	80.10	73.68	875.00	122.55	195.84	5.20	11.96
1982	856.79	81.03	93.02	73.63	86.94	85.00	1,046.54	140.64	232.41	5.81	11.60
1983	1,006.41	95.18	111.35	98.09	92.48	94.32	1,258.64	164.93	278.60	4.40	8.03
1984	1,013.91	96.38	110.58	90.61	103.14	97.63	1,211.57	167.24	247.35	4.64	10.02
1985	1,285.66	121.59	139.27	113.97	126.38	131.29	1,546.67	211.28	324.93	4.25	8.12
1986	1,465.31	138.59	160.11	117.65	147.54	140.05	1,895.95	242.17	348.83	3.49	6.09
1987	1,461.61	138.23	167.04	118.57	134.62	114.57	1,938.83	247.08	330.47	3.08	5.48
1988	1,652.25	156.26	189.42	146.60	149.38	128.19	2,168.57	277.72	381.38	3.64	8.01
1989	2,062.30	195.04	232.76	178.33	204.00	156.15	2,753.20	353.40	454.82	3.45	7.42
1990	1,908.45	180.49	223.60	141.49	182.60	122.06	2,633.66	330.22	373.84	3.61	6.47
1991	2,426.04	229.44	285.82	201.87	204.26	172.68	3,168.83	417.09	586.34	3.24	4.79
1992	2,539.92	240.21	294.39	214.72	209.66	200.83	3,301.11	435.71	676.95	2.99	4.22
1993	2,739.44	259.08	315.26	270.48	229.92	216.82	3,754.09	466.45	776.80	2.78	4.46
1994	2,653.37	250.94	318.10	222.46	198.41	195.80	3,834.44	459.27	751.96	2.82	5.83
1995	3,484.15	329.51	413.29	301.96	252.90	274.25	5,117.12	615.93	1,052.13	2.56	6.09
1996	4,148.07	392.30	494.38	352.30	259.91	351.17	6,448.27	740.74	1,291.03	2.19	5.24
1997	5,405.19	511.19	630.38	466.25	335.19	495.96	7,908.25	970.43	1,570.35	1.77	4.57
1998	6,299.94	595.81	743.65	482.38	445.94	521.42	9,181.43	1,229.23	2,192.69	1.49	3.46
1999	6,876.10	650.30	828.21	466.70	511.15	516.61	11,497.12	1,469.25	4,069.31	1.25	3.17
2000	6,945.57	656.87	803.29	462.76	440.54	646.95	10,786.85	1,320.28	2,470.52	1.15	3.63
2001	6,236.39	589.80	735.71	438.81	329.84	593.69	10,021.50	1,148.08	1,950.40	1.32	2.95
2002	5,000.00	472.87	583.95	395.81	233.08	510.46	8,341.63	879.82	1,335.51	1.61	2.92
2003 [3]	6,440.30	572.56	735.50	519.58	265.58	655.12	10,453.92	1,111.92	2,003.37	1.77	3.84

[1] End of period.
[2] Includes stocks as follows: for NYSE, all stocks listed; for Dow Jones industrial average, 30 stocks; for Standard & Poor's (S&P) composite index, 500 stocks; and for Nasdaq composite index, over 5,000.
[3] The NYSE relaunched the composite index on January 9, 2003, incorporating new definitions, methodology, and base value. (The composite index based on December 31, 1965=50 was discontinued.) Subset indexes on financial, energy, and health care were released by the NYSE on January 8, 2004 (see Table B-56). NYSE indexes shown in this table for industrials, utilities, transportation, and finance were discontinued.
[4] Effective April 1993, the NYSE doubled the value of the utility index to facilitate trading of options and futures on the index. Indexes prior to 1993 reflect the doubling.
[5] Based on 500 stocks in the S&P composite index.
[6] Aggregate cash dividends (based on latest known annual rate) divided by aggregate market value based on Wednesday closing prices. Monthly data are averages of weekly figures; annual data are averages of monthly figures.
[7] Quarterly data are ratio of earnings (after taxes) for four quarters ending with particular quarter-to-price index for last day of that quarter. Annual data are averages of quarterly ratios.

Sources: New York Stock Exchange, Dow Jones & Co., Inc., Standard & Poor's, and Nasdaq Stock Market.

TABLE B-56. Common stock prices and yields, 2000–2018

End of year or month	Common stock prices (end of period) [1]							Common stock yields (Standard & Poor's) (percent) [4]	
	New York Stock Exchange (NYSE) indexes (December 31, 2002=5,000) [2,3]				Dow Jones industrial average [2]	Standard & Poor's composite index (1941–43=10) [2]	Nasdaq composite index (Feb. 5, 1971=100) [2]	Dividend-price ratio [5]	Earnings-price ratio [6]
	Composite	Financial	Energy	Health care					
2000	6,945.57	....	....	....	10,786.85	1,320.28	2,470.52	1.15	3.63
2001	6,236.39	....	....	....	10,021.50	1,148.08	1,950.40	1.32	2.95
2002	5,000.00	5,000.00	5,000.00	5,000.00	8,341.63	879.82	1,335.51	1.61	2.92
2003	6,440.30	6,676.42	6,321.05	5,925.97	10,453.92	1,111.92	2,003.37	1.77	3.84
2004	7,250.06	7,493.92	7,934.49	6,119.07	10,783.01	1,211.92	2,175.44	1.72	4.89
2005	7,753.95	7,996.94	10,109.61	6,458.20	10,717.50	1,248.29	2,205.32	1.83	5.36
2006	9,139.02	9,552.22	11,967.88	6,958.64	12,463.15	1,418.30	2,415.29	1.87	5.78
2007	9,740.32	8,300.68	15,283.81	7,170.42	13,264.82	1,468.36	2,652.28	1.86	5.29
2008	5,757.05	3,848.42	9,434.01	5,340.73	8,776.39	903.25	1,577.03	2.37	3.54
2009	7,184.96	4,721.02	11,415.03	6,427.27	10,428.05	1,115.10	2,269.15	2.40	1.86
2010	7,964.02	4,958.62	12,520.29	6,501.53	11,577.51	1,257.64	2,652.87	1.98	6.04
2011	7,477.03	4,062.88	12,409.61	7,045.61	12,217.56	1,257.60	2,605.15	2.05	6.77
2012	8,443.51	5,114.54	12,606.06	7,904.06	13,104.14	1,426.19	3,019.51	2.24	6.20
2013	10,400.33	6,353.68	14,557.54	10,245.31	16,576.66	1,848.36	4,176.59	2.14	5.57
2014	10,839.24	6,707.16	12,533.54	11,967.04	17,823.07	2,058.90	4,736.05	2.04	5.25
2015	10,143.42	6,305.68	9,343.81	12,385.19	17,425.03	2,043.94	5,007.41	2.10	4.59
2016	11,056.89	6,961.56	11,503.76	11,907.20	19,762.60	2,238.83	5,383.12	2.19	4.17
2017	12,808.84	8,235.89	11,470.58	14,220.58	24,719.22	2,673.61	6,903.39	1.97	4.22
2018	11,374.39	6,969.48	9,341.44	15,158.38	23,327.46	2,506.85	6,635.28	1.90	....
2016: Jan	9,632.70	5,743.94	9,032.22	11,778.53	16,466.30	1,940.24	4,613.95	2.33	....
Feb	9,559.53	5,530.09	8,847.72	11,526.98	16,516.50	1,932.23	4,557.95	2.38	....
Mar	10,207.38	5,931.58	9,681.17	11,795.36	17,685.09	2,059.74	4,869.85	2.23	4.20
Apr	10,436.92	6,120.84	10,601.99	12,213.31	17,773.64	2,065.30	4,775.36	2.18	....
May	10,441.00	6,175.68	10,267.72	12,418.63	17,787.20	2,096.96	4,948.06	2.19	....
June	10,489.76	5,899.18	10,707.35	12,711.06	17,929.99	2,098.86	4,842.67	2.19	4.14
July	10,785.51	6,145.11	10,470.13	13,197.22	18,432.24	2,173.60	5,162.13	2.14	....
Aug	10,764.75	6,363.23	10,480.12	12,595.43	18,400.88	2,170.95	5,213.22	2.12	....
Sept	10,721.74	6,236.63	10,787.85	12,496.06	18,308.15	2,168.27	5,312.00	2.14	4.11
Oct	10,481.89	6,279.55	10,541.10	11,686.99	18,142.42	2,126.15	5,189.14	2.16	....
Nov	10,838.46	6,729.90	11,215.51	11,669.05	19,123.58	2,198.81	5,323.68	2.15	....
Dec	11,056.89	6,961.56	11,503.76	11,907.20	19,762.60	2,238.83	5,383.12	2.08	6.15
2017: Jan	11,222.95	7,064.02	11,202.98	12,061.43	19,864.09	2,278.87	5,614.79	2.08	....
Feb	11,512.39	7,320.48	10,854.83	12,761.57	20,812.24	2,363.64	5,825.44	2.04	....
Mar	11,492.85	7,216.68	10,834.06	12,728.55	20,663.22	2,362.72	5,911.74	2.02	4.24
Apr	11,536.08	7,208.13	10,521.74	13,000.70	20,940.51	2,384.20	6,047.61	2.03	....
May	11,598.03	7,159.54	10,235.99	13,318.92	21,008.65	2,411.80	6,198.52	2.02	....
June	11,761.70	7,468.28	10,083.36	13,732.80	21,349.63	2,423.41	6,140.42	2.01	4.29
July	11,967.67	7,652.38	10,416.42	13,636.10	21,891.12	2,470.30	6,348.12	1.99	....
Aug	11,875.69	7,527.52	9,978.32	13,727.98	21,948.10	2,471.65	6,428.66	2.00	....
Sept	12,209.16	7,780.56	10,911.61	13,959.19	22,405.09	2,519.36	6,495.96	1.99	4.25
Oct	12,341.01	7,921.32	10,889.68	13,971.09	23,377.24	2,575.26	6,727.67	1.94	....
Nov	12,627.80	8,108.70	10,994.32	14,331.40	24,272.35	2,647.58	6,873.97	1.93	....
Dec	12,808.84	8,235.89	11,470.58	14,220.58	24,719.22	2,673.61	6,903.39	1.89	6.91
2018: Jan	13,367.96	8,637.58	11,843.94	15,051.71	26,149.39	2,823.81	7,411.48	1.82	....
Feb	12,652.55	8,246.24	10,625.83	14,357.41	25,029.20	2,713.83	7,273.01	1.89	....
Mar	12,452.06	8,029.25	10,863.28	14,040.86	24,103.11	2,640.87	7,063.45	1.90	4.37
Apr	12,515.36	7,995.25	11,878.26	14,198.80	24,163.15	2,648.05	7,066.27	1.95	....
May	12,527.14	7,877.77	12,056.61	14,292.95	24,415.84	2,705.27	7,442.12	1.92	....
June	12,504.25	7,781.67	12,131.49	14,464.62	24,271.41	2,718.37	7,510.30	1.90	4.51
July	12,963.28	8,097.12	12,282.46	15,409.93	25,415.19	2,816.29	7,671.79	1.85	....
Aug	13,016.89	8,109.69	11,837.21	15,887.99	25,964.82	2,901.52	8,109.54	1.82	....
Sept	13,082.52	7,979.54	12,169.73	16,299.34	26,458.31	2,913.98	8,046.35	1.81	4.47
Oct	12,208.06	7,543.04	10,915.63	15,506.53	25,115.76	2,711.74	7,305.90	1.89	....
Nov	12,457.55	7,713.77	10,478.32	16,505.42	25,538.46	2,760.17	7,330.54	1.95	....
Dec	11,374.39	6,969.48	9,341.44	15,158.38	23,327.46	2,506.85	6,635.28	2.10	....

[1] End of year or month.
[2] Includes stocks as follows: for NYSE, all stocks listed (in 2018, over 2,700); for Dow Jones industrial average, 30 stocks; for Standard & Poor's (S&P) composite index, 500 stocks; and for Nasdaq composite index, in 2018, over 3,000.
[3] The NYSE relaunched the composite index on January 9, 2003, incorporating new definitions, methodology, and base value. Subset indexes on financial, energy, and health care were released by the NYSE on January 8, 2004.
[4] Based on 500 stocks in the S&P composite index.
[5] Aggregate cash dividends (based on latest known annual rate) divided by aggregate market value based on Wednesday closing prices. Monthly data are averages of weekly figures, annual data are averages of monthly figures.
[6] Quarterly data are ratio of earnings (after taxes) for four quarters ending with particular quarter-to-price index for last day of that quarter. Annual data are averages of quarterly ratios.

Sources: New York Stock Exchange, Dow Jones & Co., Inc., Standard & Poor's, and Nasdaq Stock Market.

International Statistics

TABLE B-57. U.S. international transactions, 1968–2018

[Millions of dollars; quarterly data seasonally adjusted]

Year or quarter	Goods [2] Exports	Goods [2] Imports	Goods [2] Balance on goods	Services Exports	Services Imports	Services Balance on services	Balance on goods and services	Primary income receipts and payments Receipts	Primary income receipts and payments Payments	Primary income receipts and payments Balance on primary income	Balance on secondary Income [3]	Balance on current account	Current account balance as a percentage of GDP
1968	33,626	32,991	635	11,918	12,301	–385	250	9,368	3,378	5,990	–5,629	611	0.1
1969	36,414	35,807	607	12,806	13,323	–517	90	10,913	4,869	6,044	–5,735	399	.0
1970	42,469	39,866	2,603	14,171	14,519	–348	2,255	11,748	5,514	6,234	–6,156	2,331	.2
1971	43,319	45,579	–2,260	16,358	15,401	959	–1,301	12,706	5,436	7,270	–7,402	–1,433	–.1
1972	49,381	55,797	–6,416	17,842	16,867	973	–5,443	14,764	6,572	8,192	–8,544	–5,796	–.5
1973	71,410	70,499	911	19,832	18,843	989	1,900	21,809	9,656	12,153	–6,914	7,140	.5
1974	98,306	103,811	–5,505	22,591	21,378	1,212	–4,293	27,587	12,084	15,503	–9,248	1,961	.1
1975	107,088	98,185	8,903	25,497	21,996	3,500	12,403	25,351	12,565	12,786	–7,076	18,117	1.1
1976	114,745	124,228	–9,483	27,971	24,570	3,402	–6,082	29,374	13,312	16,062	–5,686	4,296	.2
1977	120,816	151,907	–31,091	31,486	27,640	3,845	–27,247	32,355	14,218	18,137	–5,227	–14,336	–.7
1978	142,075	176,002	–33,927	36,353	32,189	4,164	–29,763	42,087	21,680	20,407	–5,788	–15,143	–.6
1979	184,439	212,007	–27,568	39,693	36,689	3,003	–24,566	63,835	32,961	30,874	–6,593	–285	.0
1980	224,250	249,750	–25,500	47,585	41,492	6,093	–19,407	72,605	42,533	30,072	–8,349	2,318	.1
1981	237,044	265,067	–28,023	57,355	45,503	11,851	–16,172	86,529	53,626	32,903	–11,702	5,029	.2
1982	211,157	247,642	–36,485	64,078	51,750	12,330	–24,156	96,522	61,359	35,163	–16,545	–5,537	–.2
1983	201,799	268,901	–67,102	64,307	54,973	9,335	–57,767	96,031	59,643	36,388	–17,311	–38,691	–1.1
1984	219,926	332,418	–112,492	71,168	67,748	3,418	–109,074	115,639	80,574	35,065	–20,334	–94,344	–2.3
1985	215,915	338,088	–122,173	73,156	72,863	294	–121,879	105,046	79,324	25,722	–21,999	–118,155	–2.7
1986	223,344	368,425	–145,081	86,690	80,147	6,543	–138,539	102,798	87,304	15,494	–24,131	–147,176	–3.2
1987	250,208	409,765	–159,557	98,661	90,788	7,874	–151,683	113,603	99,309	14,294	–23,265	–160,655	–3.3
1988	320,230	447,189	–126,959	110,920	98,525	12,394	–114,566	141,666	122,981	18,685	–25,274	–121,153	–2.3
1989	359,916	477,665	–117,749	127,087	102,480	24,607	–93,142	166,384	146,560	19,824	–26,169	–99,487	–1.8
1990	387,401	498,438	–111,037	147,833	117,660	30,173	–80,865	176,894	148,345	28,549	–26,654	–78,969	–1.3
1991	414,083	491,020	–76,937	164,260	118,459	45,802	–31,136	155,327	131,198	24,129	9,904	2,897	.0
1992	439,631	536,528	–96,897	177,251	119,566	57,685	–39,212	139,082	114,845	24,237	–36,635	–51,613	–.8
1993	456,943	589,394	–132,451	185,920	123,780	62,141	–70,311	141,606	116,287	25,319	–39,811	–84,805	–1.2
1994	502,859	668,690	–165,831	200,395	133,057	67,338	–98,493	169,447	152,302	17,145	–40,265	–121,612	–1.7
1995	575,204	749,374	–174,170	219,183	141,397	77,786	–96,384	213,661	192,771	20,890	–38,074	–113,567	–1.5
1996	612,113	803,113	–191,000	239,489	152,554	86,935	–104,065	229,530	207,212	22,318	–43,017	–124,764	–1.5
1997	678,366	876,794	–198,428	256,087	165,932	90,155	–108,273	261,357	248,750	12,607	–45,062	–140,726	–1.6
1998	670,416	918,637	–248,221	262,758	180,677	82,081	–166,140	266,244	261,978	4,266	–53,187	–215,062	–2.4
1999	698,524	1,035,592	–337,068	271,343	192,893	78,450	–258,617	299,114	287,981	11,134	–40,881	–288,365	–3.0
2000	784,940	1,231,722	–446,783	290,381	216,115	74,266	–372,517	356,706	338,637	18,069	–49,003	–403,450	–3.9
2001	731,331	1,153,701	–422,370	274,323	213,465	60,858	–361,511	296,977	269,447	27,530	–55,708	–389,689	–3.7
2002	698,036	1,173,281	–475,245	280,670	224,379	56,290	–418,955	286,525	263,860	22,665	–54,507	–450,797	–4.1
2003	730,446	1,272,089	–541,643	289,972	242,219	47,754	–493,890	324,374	289,657	34,716	–59,571	–518,744	–4.5
2004	823,584	1,488,349	–664,766	337,966	283,083	54,882	–609,883	416,085	362,179	53,906	–75,614	–631,591	–5.2
2005	913,016	1,695,820	–782,804	373,006	304,448	68,558	–714,245	534,215	480,317	53,898	–84,887	–745,234	–5.7
2006	1,040,905	1,878,194	–837,289	416,738	341,165	75,573	–761,716	680,830	653,928	26,902	–71,149	–805,964	–5.8
2007	1,165,151	1,986,347	–821,196	488,396	372,575	115,821	–705,375	834,983	749,977	85,005	–90,665	–711,035	–4.9
2008	1,308,795	2,141,287	–832,492	532,817	409,052	123,765	–708,726	815,567	685,918	129,649	–102,312	–681,389	–4.6
2009	1,070,331	1,580,025	–509,694	512,722	386,801	125,920	–383,774	613,249	498,089	115,160	–103,907	–372,521	–2.6
2010	1,290,279	1,938,950	–648,671	562,759	409,313	153,446	–495,225	680,169	511,948	168,221	–104,261	–431,265	–2.9
2011	1,498,887	2,239,886	–740,999	627,061	435,761	191,300	–549,699	755,937	544,853	211,084	–107,047	–445,662	–2.9
2012	1,562,630	2,303,749	–741,119	655,724	452,013	203,711	–537,408	767,972	560,497	207,475	–96,900	–426,832	–2.6
2013	1,593,708	2,294,247	–700,539	700,491	461,087	239,404	–461,135	792,819	586,842	205,977	–93,643	–348,801	–2.1
2014	1,635,563	2,385,480	–749,917	741,094	480,761	260,333	–489,584	824,543	606,152	218,391	–94,006	–365,199	–2.1
2015	1,511,381	2,273,249	–761,868	755,310	491,966	263,343	–498,525	810,073	606,464	203,608	–112,848	–407,764	–2.2
2016	1,456,957	2,208,008	–751,051	758,888	509,838	249,050	–502,001	830,174	637,151	193,023	–123,895	–432,873	–2.3
2017	1,553,383	2,360,878	–807,495	797,690	542,471	255,219	–552,277	928,118	706,386	221,731	–118,597	–449,142	–2.3
2015: I	384,030	577,355	–193,325	189,012	121,395	67,617	–125,708	201,600	149,222	52,378	–28,270	–101,600	–2.3
II	385,894	574,332	–188,438	189,078	122,113	66,965	–121,473	206,389	157,237	49,152	–24,677	–96,999	–2.1
III	377,113	569,157	–192,044	188,535	124,022	64,513	–127,531	206,188	157,172	49,016	–31,035	–109,550	–2.4
IV	364,344	552,406	–188,062	188,685	124,436	64,249	–123,813	195,896	142,834	53,062	–28,865	–99,616	–2.2
2016: I	353,330	539,770	–186,440	186,905	125,727	61,179	–125,261	199,946	154,498	45,447	–32,087	–111,901	–2.4
II	361,159	546,454	–185,295	189,118	125,922	63,196	–122,099	207,929	160,387	47,543	–28,501	–103,057	–2.2
III	371,283	556,600	–185,316	191,760	128,214	63,546	–121,770	206,389	162,480	43,909	–31,465	–109,327	–2.3
IV	371,186	565,185	–194,000	191,104	129,975	61,129	–132,871	215,911	159,787	56,124	–31,842	–108,589	–2.3
2017: I	381,138	579,484	–198,346	195,168	131,781	63,387	–134,959	217,567	164,962	52,604	–25,355	–107,709	–2.2
II	382,492	582,440	–199,948	197,252	134,004	63,248	–136,700	223,979	175,444	48,535	–33,672	–121,837	–2.5
III	387,814	584,637	–196,823	201,293	137,261	64,032	–132,791	237,632	179,410	58,222	–28,878	–103,447	–2.1
IV	401,939	614,317	–212,378	203,977	139,426	64,551	–147,826	248,940	186,569	62,371	–30,692	–116,148	–2.3
2018: I	411,442	632,244	–220,802	205,994	139,182	66,812	–153,989	256,029	194,854	61,175	–28,896	–121,710	–2.4
II	429,431	632,489	–203,058	205,817	137,365	68,452	–134,606	266,274	203,926	62,348	–28,966	–101,224	–2.0
III p	421,762	648,775	–227,012	207,635	139,279	68,356	–158,656	264,523	205,098	59,425	–25,586	–124,817	–2.4

[1] Current and capital account statistics in the international transactions accounts differ slightly from statistics in the National Income and Product Accounts (NIPAs) because of adjustments made to convert the international statistics to national accounting concepts. A reconciliation can be found in NIPA table 4.3B.
[2] Adjusted from Census data to align with concepts and definitions used to prepare the international and national economic accounts. The adjustments are necessary to supplement coverage of Census data, to eliminate duplication of transactions recorded elsewhere in the international accounts, to value transactions according to a standard definition, and for earlier years, to record transactions in the appropriate period.

See next page for continuation of table.

TABLE B-57. U.S. international transactions, 1968-2018—*Continued*

[Millions of dollars; quarterly data seasonally adjusted]

Year or quarter	Balance on capital account [1]	Financial account										Net lending (+) or net borrowing (−) from financial account transactions [5]	Statistical discrepancy
		Net U.S. acquisition of financial assets excluding financial derivatives [net increase in assets / financial outflow (+)]					Net U.S. incurrence of liabilities excluding financial derivatives [net increase in liabilities / financial inflow (+)]				Financial derivatives other than reserves, net transactions		
		Total	Direct investment assets	Portfolio investment assets	Other investment assets	Reserve assets [4]	Total	Direct investment liabilities	Portfolio investment liabilities	Other investment liabilities			
1968		10,977	5,294	1,569	3,244	870	9,928	808	3,780	5,340		1,049	438
1969		11,584	5,960	1,549	2,896	1,179	12,702	1,263	719	10,720		−1,118	−1,517
1970		9,336	7,590	1,076	3,151	−2,481	7,226	1,464	11,710	−5,948		2,110	−219
1971		12,474	7,618	1,113	6,092	−2,349	23,687	368	28,835	−5,516		−11,213	−9,779
1972		14,497	7,747	619	6,127	4	22,171	948	13,123	8,100		−7,674	−1,879
1973		22,874	11,353	672	11,007	−158	18,388	2,800	4,790	10,798		4,486	−2,654
1974		34,745	9,052	1,853	22,373	1,467	35,228	4,761	5,500	24,967		−483	−2,444
1975		39,703	14,244	6,247	18,363	849	16,870	2,603	12,761	1,506		22,833	4,717
1976		51,269	11,949	8,885	27,877	2,558	37,840	4,347	16,165	17,328		13,429	9,134
1977		34,785	11,891	5,459	17,060	375	52,770	3,728	37,615	11,427		−17,985	−3,651
1978		61,130	16,057	3,626	42,179	−732	66,275	7,896	30,083	28,296		−5,145	9,997
1979		66,053	25,223	12,430	27,267	1,133	40,693	11,876	−13,502	42,319		25,360	25,647
1980		86,968	19,222	6,042	53,550	8,154	62,036	16,918	23,825	21,293		24,932	22,614
1981		114,147	9,624	15,650	83,697	5,176	85,684	25,196	17,509	42,979		28,463	23,433
1982		142,722	19,397	12,395	105,965	4,965	109,897	27,475	19,695	62,727		32,825	38,362
1983		74,690	20,844	2,063	50,588	1,195	95,715	18,688	18,382	58,645		−21,025	17,666
1984		50,740	26,770	3,498	17,340	3,132	126,413	34,832	38,695	52,886		−75,673	18,673
1985		47,064	21,241	3,008	18,957	3,858	146,544	22,057	68,004	56,483		−99,480	18,677
1986		107,252	19,524	8,984	79,057	−313	223,854	30,946	104,497	88,411		−116,602	30,570
1987		84,058	39,795	7,903	45,508	−9,148	251,863	63,232	79,631	109,000		−167,805	−7,149
1988		105,747	21,701	4,589	75,544	3,913	244,008	56,910	86,786	100,312		−138,261	−17,108
1989	−207	182,908	50,973	31,166	75,476	25,293	230,302	75,801	74,852	79,649		−47,394	52,299
1990	−7,221	103,985	59,934	30,557	11,336	2,158	162,109	71,247	25,767	65,095		−58,124	28,066
1991	−5,129	75,753	49,253	32,053	210	−5,763	119,586	34,535	72,562	12,489		−43,833	−41,601
1992	1,449	84,899	58,755	50,684	−20,639	−3,901	178,842	30,315	92,199	56,328		−93,943	−43,776
1993	−714	199,399	82,799	137,917	−22,696	1,379	278,607	50,211	174,387	54,009		−79,208	6,313
1994	−1,112	188,758	89,988	54,088	50,028	−5,346	312,995	55,942	131,849	125,204		−124,237	−1,514
1995	−221	363,555	110,041	143,506	100,266	9,742	446,393	69,067	254,431	122,895		−82,838	30,951
1996	−8	424,548	103,024	160,179	168,013	−6,668	559,027	97,644	392,107	69,276		−134,479	−9,706
1997	−256	502,024	121,352	121,036	258,626	1,010	720,999	122,150	311,105	287,744		−218,975	−77,995
1998	−7	385,936	174,751	132,186	72,216	6,783	452,901	211,152	225,878	15,871		−66,965	148,106
1999	−4,176	526,612	247,484	141,007	146,868	−8,747	765,215	312,449	278,697	174,069		−238,603	53,938
2000	−1	587,682	186,371	159,713	241,308	290	1,066,074	349,124	441,966	274,984		−478,392	−74,941
2001	13,198	386,308	146,041	106,919	128,437	4,911	788,345	172,496	431,492	184,357		−402,037	−25,546
2002	−141	319,170	178,984	79,532	56,973	3,681	821,844	111,056	504,155	206,634		−502,673	−51,735
2003	−1,821	371,074	195,218	133,059	44,321	−1,524	911,660	117,107	550,163	244,390		−540,586	−20,021
2004	3,049	1,058,654	374,006	191,956	495,498	−2,806	1,600,881	213,642	867,340	519,899		−542,226	86,316
2005	13,116	562,983	52,591	267,290	257,196	−14,094	1,277,056	142,345	832,037	302,673		−714,073	18,045
2006	−1,788	1,324,607	283,800	493,366	549,814	−2,373	2,120,480	298,464	1,126,735	695,280	−29,710	−825,583	−17,832
2007	384	1,563,459	523,889	380,807	658,641	122	2,190,087	346,615	1,156,612	686,860	−6,222	−632,850	77,801
2008	6,010	−317,607	343,584	−284,269	−381,770	4,848	462,408	341,091	523,683	−402,367	32,947	−747,069	−71,690
2009	−140	131,074	312,597	375,883	−609,662	52,256	325,644	161,082	357,352	−192,789	−44,816	−239,386	133,275
2010	−157	958,703	349,829	199,620	407,420	1,835	1,391,042	264,039	820,434	306,569	−14,076	−446,415	−14,992
2011	−1,186	492,530	436,615	85,365	−45,327	15,877	983,522	263,499	311,626	408,397	−35,006	−525,998	−79,150
2012	6,904	176,764	377,239	248,760	−453,695	4,460	632,034	250,343	747,017	−365,327	7,064	−448,205	−28,277
2013	−412	649,587	392,796	481,298	−221,408	−3,099	1,052,068	288,131	511,987	251,949	2,222	−400,259	−51,046
2014	−45	866,523	387,528	582,676	−100,099	−3,583	1,109,443	251,857	697,607	159,979	−54,335	−297,255	67,989
2015	−42	202,208	307,058	160,410	−258,968	−6,292	501,121	509,087	213,910	−221,876	−27,035	−325,948	81,859
2016	−59	348,625	312,975	36,283	−2,723	2,090	741,529	494,455	231,349	15,725	7,827	−385,078	47,855
2017	24,746	1,182,749	379,222	586,695	218,522	−1,690	1,537,683	354,829	799,182	383,671	23,074	−331,860	92,536
2015: I	−22	348,283	88,547	221,847	42,049	−4,159	429,374	243,726	107,435	78,214	−40,197	−121,288	−19,667
II	−20	46,345	92,779	113,617	−159,175	−877	181,700	116,973	243,152	−178,425	1,701	−133,654	−36,635
III	−1	−74,432	51,137	−97,440	−27,863	−266	−37,175	69,900	−146,760	39,685	722	−36,535	73,016
IV	0	−117,988	74,594	−77,613	−113,979	−990	−72,777	78,489	10,083	−161,350	10,739	−34,471	65,145
2016: I	−58	39,781	76,062	−64,312	29,222	−1,191	152,172	158,914	−52,832	46,089	10,782	−101,609	10,350
II	0	350,387	103,425	147,012	99,761	189	368,537	186,295	4,783	177,458	608	−17,541	85,516
III	−1	40,432	95,894	−33,346	−23,759	1,642	243,723	130,934	217,768	−104,979	3,437	−199,854	−90,527
IV	0	−81,975	37,593	−13,071	−107,947	1,450	−22,901	18,312	61,630	−102,843	−7,000	−66,073	42,515
2017: I	−1	366,101	135,054	141,783	89,505	−241	429,098	112,354	160,111	156,633	−5,609	−68,606	39,104
II	0	315,922	49,976	180,790	85,095	150	445,338	97,118	263,170	85,050	9,306	−120,111	1,727
III	24,787	373,591	102,936	175,910	94,804	−61	504,082	107,107	294,275	102,701	18,600	−111,891	−33,231
IV	−40	127,135	91,256	88,301	−50,883	−1,539	159,164	38,250	81,626	39,288	777	−31,252	84,936
2018: I	−2	251,126	−139,326	304,094	86,365	−7	441,080	57,949	301,503	81,628	29,024	−160,930	−39,218
II	−5	−199,943	−68,060	−14,272	−120,679	3,068	−63,262	16,499	20,596	−100,358	−16,969	−153,650	−52,421
III ᵖ	562	132,689	76,846	72,598	−16,577	−177	151,723	122,336	12,469	16,918	−12,255	−31,289	92,966

[3] Includes U.S. government and private transfers, such as U.S. government grants and pensions, fines and penalties, withholding taxes, personal transfers, insurance-related transfers, and other current transfers.
[4] Consists of monetary gold, special drawing rights (SDRs), the U.S. reserve position in the International Monetary Fund (IMF), and other reserve assets, including foreign currencies.
[5] Net lending means that U.S. residents are net suppliers of funds to foreign residents, and net borrowing means the opposite.

Source: Department of Commerce (Bureau of Economic Analysis).

TABLE B–58. U.S. international trade in goods on balance of payments (BOP) and Census basis, and trade in services on BOP basis, 1990–2018

[Billions of dollars; monthly data seasonally adjusted]

Year or month	Goods: Exports (f.a.s. value)[1,2]							Goods: Imports (customs value)[6]							Services (BOP basis)	
	Total, BOP basis[3,4]	Census basis (by end-use category)						Total, BOP basis[4]	Census basis (by end-use category)						Exports[4]	Imports[4]
		Total, Census basis[3,5]	Foods, feeds, and beverages	Industrial supplies and materials	Capital goods except automotive	Automotive vehicles, parts, and engines	Consumer goods (nonfood) except automotive		Total, Census basis[5]	Foods, feeds, and beverages	Industrial supplies and materials	Capital goods except automotive	Automotive vehicles, parts, and engines	Consumer goods (nonfood) except automotive		
1990	387.4	393.6	35.1	104.4	152.7	37.4	43.3	498.4	495.3	26.6	143.2	116.4	87.3	105.7	147.8	117.7
1991	414.1	421.7	35.7	109.7	166.7	40.0	45.9	491.0	488.5	26.5	131.6	120.7	85.7	108.0	164.3	118.5
1992	439.6	448.2	40.3	109.1	175.9	47.0	51.4	536.5	532.7	27.6	138.6	134.3	91.8	122.7	177.3	119.6
1993	456.9	465.1	40.6	111.8	181.7	52.4	54.7	589.4	580.7	27.9	145.6	152.4	102.4	134.0	185.9	123.8
1994	502.9	512.6	42.0	121.4	205.0	57.8	60.0	668.7	663.3	31.0	162.1	184.4	118.3	146.3	200.4	133.1
1995	575.2	584.7	50.5	146.2	233.0	61.8	64.4	749.4	743.5	33.2	181.8	221.4	123.8	159.9	219.2	141.4
1996	612.1	625.1	55.5	147.7	253.0	65.0	70.1	803.1	795.3	35.7	204.5	228.1	128.9	172.0	239.5	152.6
1997	678.4	689.2	51.5	158.2	294.5	74.0	77.4	876.8	869.7	39.7	213.8	253.3	139.8	193.8	256.1	165.9
1998	670.4	682.1	46.4	148.3	299.4	72.4	80.3	918.6	911.9	41.2	200.1	269.5	148.7	217.0	262.8	180.7
1999	698.5	695.8	46.0	147.5	310.8	75.3	80.9	1,035.6	1,024.6	43.6	221.4	295.7	179.0	241.9	271.3	192.9
2000	784.9	781.9	47.9	172.6	356.9	80.4	89.4	1,231.7	1,218.0	46.0	299.0	347.0	195.9	281.8	290.4	216.1
2001	731.3	729.1	49.4	160.1	321.7	75.4	88.3	1,153.7	1,141.0	46.6	273.9	298.0	189.8	284.3	274.3	213.5
2002	698.0	693.1	49.6	156.8	290.4	78.9	84.4	1,173.3	1,161.4	49.7	267.7	283.3	203.7	307.8	280.7	224.4
2003	730.4	724.8	55.0	173.0	293.7	80.6	89.9	1,272.1	1,257.1	55.8	313.8	295.9	210.1	333.9	290.0	242.2
2004	823.6	814.9	56.6	203.9	327.5	89.2	103.2	1,488.3	1,469.7	62.1	412.8	343.6	228.2	372.9	338.0	283.1
2005	913.0	901.1	59.0	233.0	358.4	98.4	115.3	1,695.8	1,673.5	68.1	523.8	379.3	239.4	407.2	373.0	304.4
2006	1,040.9	1,026.0	66.0	276.0	404.0	107.3	129.1	1,878.2	1,853.9	74.9	602.0	418.3	256.6	442.6	416.7	341.2
2007	1,165.2	1,148.2	84.3	316.4	433.0	121.3	146.0	1,986.3	1,957.0	81.7	634.7	444.5	256.7	474.6	488.4	372.6
2008	1,308.8	1,287.4	108.3	388.0	457.7	121.5	161.3	2,141.3	2,103.6	89.0	779.5	453.7	231.2	481.6	532.8	409.1
2009	1,070.3	1,056.0	93.9	296.5	391.2	81.7	149.5	1,580.0	1,559.6	81.6	462.4	370.5	157.7	427.3	512.7	386.8
2010	1,290.3	1,278.5	107.7	391.7	447.5	112.0	165.2	1,939.0	1,913.9	91.7	603.1	449.4	225.1	483.2	562.8	409.3
2011	1,498.9	1,482.5	126.2	501.1	494.0	133.0	175.3	2,239.9	2,208.0	107.5	755.8	510.8	254.6	514.1	627.1	435.8
2012	1,562.6	1,545.8	133.0	501.2	527.2	146.2	181.7	2,303.7	2,276.3	110.3	730.6	548.7	297.8	516.9	655.7	452.0
2013	1,593.7	1,578.5	136.2	508.2	534.4	152.7	188.8	2,294.2	2,268.0	115.1	681.5	555.7	308.8	531.7	700.5	461.1
2014	1,635.6	1,621.9	143.7	505.8	551.5	159.8	199.0	2,385.5	2,356.4	125.9	667.0	594.1	328.6	557.1	741.1	480.8
2015	1,511.4	1,503.3	127.7	427.0	539.5	151.9	197.7	2,273.2	2,248.8	127.8	486.0	602.5	349.2	594.2	755.3	492.0
2016	1,457.0	1,451.0	130.5	397.0	519.6	150.3	193.7	2,208.0	2,187.6	130.0	443.3	589.9	350.1	583.4	758.9	509.8
2017[p]	1,553.4	1,546.3	132.7	464.7	533.3	157.6	197.7	2,360.9	2,342.0	137.8	507.3	640.6	359.0	601.9	797.7	542.5
2018[p]	....	1,672.9	141.2	538.9	562.0	158.7	206.6	....	2,541.7	147.5	574.9	693.2	372.2	647.8	....	....
2017: Jan	126.7	126.1	10.9	37.3	43.6	13.4	16.4	194.4	192.7	11.1	41.5	50.9	30.9	50.6	64.7	43.9
Feb	127.2	126.6	10.6	38.1	43.1	13.3	16.6	192.6	191.0	11.2	43.3	50.9	29.0	48.9	65.1	43.9
Mar	127.2	126.6	11.2	37.2	43.6	13.0	16.5	192.4	190.7	11.1	42.6	50.8	30.2	48.9	65.4	44.0
Apr	126.8	126.3	11.4	37.6	43.6	12.6	16.6	194.1	192.6	11.4	41.6	51.6	29.8	50.4	65.4	44.1
May	127.1	126.6	11.0	37.6	43.3	12.9	16.8	193.9	192.3	11.4	41.8	52.6	29.3	49.3	65.7	44.7
June	128.6	128.1	11.4	37.7	43.9	13.5	16.5	194.5	192.9	11.4	41.1	52.9	30.2	49.1	66.2	45.1
July	128.5	127.9	11.7	37.6	44.7	12.9	16.6	193.9	192.4	11.6	40.6	53.9	29.5	48.7	66.7	45.5
Aug	128.6	128.1	11.2	36.9	45.2	13.1	16.7	194.1	192.6	11.5	40.4	53.7	30.0	49.2	67.0	45.6
Sept	130.7	130.2	11.3	39.2	44.9	13.1	16.3	196.6	195.1	11.7	41.2	54.8	29.7	49.8	67.7	46.2
Oct	130.9	130.3	10.6	41.5	44.0	12.7	16.4	199.4	198.0	11.7	42.8	55.1	29.5	50.2	67.7	46.2
Nov	134.3	133.5	10.7	41.2	46.2	13.5	16.8	204.8	203.3	11.7	44.9	56.2	30.2	52.0	68.0	46.4
Dec	136.8	136.1	10.9	42.8	47.0	13.5	16.8	210.1	208.5	11.9	45.5	57.1	30.7	55.0	68.2	46.8
2018: Jan	133.8	133.0	10.7	40.9	44.9	13.6	17.9	208.3	206.6	11.8	46.9	55.7	30.7	53.2	68.2	46.0
Feb	136.7	136.0	10.9	43.0	45.7	14.5	16.7	213.5	211.9	12.6	47.1	57.6	31.1	55.7	68.7	46.9
Mar	141.0	140.3	11.8	44.3	47.5	14.1	17.1	210.4	208.9	12.3	46.7	56.5	30.9	54.7	69.0	46.3
Apr	141.3	140.6	12.4	45.7	46.1	13.9	17.2	209.7	208.0	12.3	47.9	56.9	30.0	51.9	68.6	45.9
May	145.0	144.2	14.1	44.4	48.2	13.6	17.8	210.8	208.9	12.4	47.9	59.0	29.7	51.4	68.6	45.6
June	143.1	142.5	14.1	46.3	47.3	12.9	16.4	212.0	210.4	12.2	48.8	57.5	30.2	53.4	68.7	45.9
July	140.8	140.2	13.2	46.5	46.3	13.1	16.0	214.0	212.3	12.4	49.3	58.2	30.7	52.6	69.0	46.2
Aug	139.1	138.5	12.0	44.1	46.4	12.8	17.6	215.7	213.9	12.3	49.7	57.7	31.7	53.5	69.2	46.3
Sept	141.9	141.3	11.0	46.9	47.5	13.0	17.8	219.1	217.6	12.1	49.4	60.1	31.1	55.5	69.5	46.8
Oct	141.5	140.9	10.4	47.2	47.0	12.7	17.9	219.8	218.0	12.3	49.4	56.9	31.8	57.4	69.7	47.1
Nov[p]	140.3	139.7	10.4	45.9	48.4	12.3	17.0	211.9	210.2	12.2	46.0	57.3	32.1	53.1	69.5	47.3
Dec[p]	....	135.7	10.3	43.7	46.7	12.3	17.1	....	215.2	12.6	45.8	59.9	32.1	55.5	....	....

[1] Department of Defense shipments of grant-aid military supplies and equipment under the Military Assistance Program are excluded from total exports through 1985 and included beginning 1986.
[2] F.a.s. (free alongside ship) value basis at U.S. port of exportation for exports.
[3] Beginning with data for 1989, exports have been adjusted for undocumented exports to Canada and are included in the appropriate end-use categories. For prior years, only total exports include this adjustment.
[4] Beginning with data for 1999, exports of goods under the U.S. Foreign Military Sales program and fuel purchases by foreign air and ocean carriers in U.S. ports are included in goods exports (BOP basis) and excluded from services exports. Beginning with data for 1999, imports of petroleum abroad by U.S. military agencies and fuel purchases by U.S. air and ocean carriers in foreign ports are included in goods imports (BOP basis) and excluded from services imports.
[5] Total includes "other" exports or imports, not shown separately.
[6] Total arrivals of imported goods other than in-transit shipments.
[7] Total includes revisions not reflected in detail.
[8] Total exports are on a revised statistical month basis; end-use categories are on a statistical month basis.

Note: Goods on a Census basis are adjusted to a BOP basis by the Bureau of Economic Analysis, in line with concepts and definitions used to prepare international and national accounts. The adjustments are necessary to supplement coverage of Census data, to eliminate duplication of transactions recorded elsewhere in international accounts, to value transactions according to a standard definition, and for earlier years, to record transactions in the appropriate period.
Data include international trade of the U.S. Virgin Islands, Puerto Rico, and U.S. Foreign Trade Zones.

Source: Department of Commerce (Bureau of the Census and Bureau of Economic Analysis).

Table B–59. U.S. international trade in goods and services by area and country, 2000–2017

[Millions of dollars]

Item	2000	2005	2010	2012	2013	2014	2015	2016	2017
EXPORTS									
Total, all countries	1,075,321	1,286,022	1,853,038	2,218,354	2,294,199	2,376,657	2,266,691	2,215,845	2,351,073
Europe	296,284	365,200	503,816	577,786	580,234	606,544	598,616	602,936	632,667
Euro area [1]	173,446	214,355	288,604	319,172	327,600	347,609	346,115	351,059	366,522
France	30,759	35,504	44,114	48,921	50,672	50,989	49,990	51,099	52,980
Germany	45,253	55,247	73,378	76,076	74,644	77,907	80,134	81,283	86,585
Italy	16,761	18,727	22,845	24,930	25,483	26,212	25,453	25,656	27,808
United Kingdom	73,139	83,183	102,648	115,293	108,030	119,074	124,309	122,350	126,192
Canada	203,861	245,134	303,409	356,099	364,968	374,850	336,261	321,595	341,309
Latin America and Other Western Hemisphere	225,116	256,066	409,201	523,576	561,468	585,359	549,554	514,863	548,526
Brazil	21,858	21,230	53,753	68,827	70,900	71,102	59,360	53,917	63,490
Mexico	127,076	142,977	188,371	244,593	256,342	271,635	268,211	261,999	276,701
Venezuela	8,810	9,068	15,784	23,958	20,568	18,045	14,904	11,171	8,788
Asia and Pacific	299,103	341,564	523,131	616,841	634,902	652,735	636,150	639,768	693,496
China	21,464	50,572	115,559	144,894	160,375	169,008	165,526	170,881	188,004
India	6,472	13,232	29,667	34,503	35,231	36,950	40,060	42,296	49,472
Japan	101,247	94,356	104,731	118,044	112,201	114,828	108,417	108,834	114,746
Korea, Republic of	34,744	38,000	55,533	62,336	64,491	66,653	65,327	64,689	73,424
Singapore	24,400	26,482	39,459	44,090	42,025	41,687	42,653	43,387	47,518
Taiwan	30,403	29,232	36,717	37,278	38,317	40,084	38,714	38,193	36,192
Middle East	28,241	48,427	70,094	94,651	100,176	101,881	101,723	98,048	96,338
Africa	17,178	23,003	40,400	46,300	49,212	52,404	41,760	36,052	36,292
Memorandum: Members of OPEC [2]	29,407	49,194	78,985	110,913	117,063	115,626	107,493	106,104	91,962
IMPORTS									
Total, all countries	1,447,837	2,000,268	2,348,263	2,755,762	2,755,334	2,866,241	2,765,215	2,717,846	2,903,349
Europe	359,670	493,933	559,596	651,331	660,838	702,465	703,264	700,730	741,593
Euro area [1]	217,211	303,692	336,152	397,488	407,245	438,198	444,052	442,411	467,402
France	40,829	47,269	54,637	58,937	61,610	64,433	64,666	63,614	66,796
Germany	74,855	109,551	111,902	141,632	147,843	157,554	157,162	148,355	153,314
Italy	31,888	40,719	38,349	48,162	49,464	53,333	55,207	56,851	62,547
United Kingdom	71,400	85,508	93,860	103,222	102,811	108,172	112,216	107,283	110,616
Canada	251,750	316,798	309,173	361,031	369,111	385,992	332,095	314,189	338,548
Latin America and Other Western Hemisphere	249,553	352,076	453,253	547,280	538,026	550,327	519,837	509,002	538,956
Brazil	15,384	26,389	29,343	39,319	34,809	37,851	34,663	32,362	35,011
Mexico	148,258	188,192	246,770	298,599	303,988	322,950	326,244	324,371	345,446
Venezuela	19,291	34,512	33,445	39,630	32,781	31,019	16,470	11,765	13,028
Asia and Pacific	507,225	680,901	836,903	984,908	1,004,303	1,061,705	1,094,871	1,081,812	1,157,557
China	103,433	251,556	376,735	439,832	455,524	483,677	499,058	479,244	523,708
India	12,612	23,648	44,394	59,446	62,368	67,957	69,561	71,937	76,833
Japan	164,213	160,965	147,518	176,439	171,479	168,511	163,659	165,232	171,334
Korea, Republic of	46,203	51,128	59,096	70,226	73,605	81,412	83,579	81,301	82,721
Singapore	21,360	18,799	22,733	26,185	23,539	22,657	25,058	25,004	27,214
Taiwan	44,784	41,661	41,881	46,198	45,194	48,346	48,661	46,988	50,587
Middle East	44,296	81,553	95,077	133,896	124,016	121,193	81,005	75,158	83,070
Africa	31,390	69,921	93,190	75,999	58,784	43,297	33,893	35,512	43,366
Memorandum: Members of OPEC [2]	71,068	139,431	164,837	192,233	163,732	143,029	76,913	89,578	83,012
BALANCE (excess of exports +)									
Total, all countries	−372,517	−714,246	−495,225	−537,408	−461,135	−489,584	−498,525	−502,001	−552,276
Europe	−63,386	−128,733	−55,779	−73,544	−80,604	−95,923	−104,649	−97,795	−108,926
Euro area [1]	−43,765	−89,336	−47,548	−78,316	−79,646	−90,588	−97,938	−91,352	−100,881
France	−10,070	−11,765	−10,524	−10,017	−10,938	−13,444	−14,676	−12,515	−13,816
Germany	−29,603	−54,304	−38,524	−65,557	−73,190	−79,647	−77,029	−67,072	−66,729
Italy	−15,127	−21,991	−15,504	−23,231	−23,980	−27,121	−29,755	−31,196	−34,739
United Kingdom	1,739	−2,324	8,786	12,070	5,219	10,902	12,093	15,065	15,575
Canada	−47,889	−71,663	−5,764	−4,932	−4,144	−11,142	4,165	7,406	2,760
Latin America and Other Western Hemisphere	−24,437	−96,010	−44,052	−23,703	23,442	35,032	29,718	5,861	9,570
Brazil	6,474	−5,158	24,410	29,507	36,091	33,251	24,697	21,556	28,479
Mexico	−21,182	−45,215	−58,399	−54,006	−47,646	−51,317	−58,033	−62,372	−68,745
Venezuela	−10,481	−25,443	−17,662	−15,672	−12,212	−12,974	−1,566	−594	−4,240
Asia and Pacific	−208,122	−339,337	−313,772	−368,067	−369,401	−408,969	−458,722	−442,044	−464,061
China	−81,969	−200,984	−261,176	−294,938	−295,149	−314,669	−333,534	−308,363	−335,704
India	−6,140	−10,416	−14,728	−24,944	−27,136	−31,007	−29,501	−29,641	−27,360
Japan	−62,967	−66,609	−42,787	−58,395	−59,277	−53,683	−55,242	−56,398	−56,588
Korea, Republic of	−11,459	−13,128	−3,564	−7,890	−9,114	−14,759	−18,252	−16,612	−9,297
Singapore	3,041	7,683	16,726	17,904	18,486	19,029	17,595	18,383	20,303
Taiwan	−14,381	−12,428	−5,163	−8,920	−6,878	−8,264	−9,947	−8,794	−14,396
Middle East	−16,054	−33,126	−24,983	−39,245	−23,840	−19,312	20,718	22,890	13,269
Africa	−14,212	−46,917	−52,790	−29,698	−9,571	9,107	7,867	540	−7,074
Memorandum: Members of OPEC [2]	−41,660	−90,237	−85,853	−81,320	−46,669	−27,403	30,580	16,526	8,950

[1] Euro area consists of: Austria, Belgium, Cyprus (beginning in 2008), Estonia (beginning in 2011), Finland, France, Germany, Greece (beginning in 2001), Ireland, Italy, Luxembourg, Malta (beginning in 2008), Netherlands, Portugal, Slovakia (beginning in 2009), Slovenia (beginning in 2007), and Spain.
[2] Organization of Petroleum Exporting Countries, consisting of Algeria, Angola (beginning in 2007), Ecuador (beginning in 2007), Indonesia (ending in 2008), Iran, Iraq, Kuwait, Libya, Nigeria, Qatar, Saudi Arabia, United Arab Emirates, and Venezuela.

Note: Data are on a balance of payments basis. For further details, and additional data by country, see *Survey of Current Business*, February 2019.

Source: Department of Commerce (Bureau of Economic Analysis).

TABLE B-60. Foreign exchange rates, 2000–2018

[Foreign currency units per U.S. dollar, except as noted; certified noon buying rates in New York]

Period	Australia (dollar)[1]	Brazil (real)	Canada (dollar)	China, P.R. (yuan)	EMU Members (euro)[1,2]	India (rupee)	Japan (yen)	Mexico (peso)	South Korea (won)	Sweden (krona)	Switzerland (franc)	United Kingdom (pound)[1]
March 1973	1.4129	...	0.9967	2.2401	...	7.55	261.90	0.013	398.85	4.4294	3.2171	2.4724
2000	.5815	1.8301	1.4855	8.2784	0.9232	45.00	107.80	9.459	1,130.90	9.1735	1.6904	1.5156
2001	.5169	2.3527	1.5487	8.2770	.8952	47.22	121.57	9.337	1,292.01	10.3425	1.6891	1.4396
2002	.5437	2.9213	1.5704	8.2771	.9454	48.63	125.22	9.663	1,250.31	9.7233	1.5567	1.5025
2003	.6524	3.0750	1.4008	8.2772	1.1321	46.59	115.94	10.793	1,192.08	8.0787	1.3450	1.6347
2004	.7365	2.9262	1.3017	8.2768	1.2438	45.26	108.15	11.290	1,145.24	7.3480	1.2428	1.8330
2005	.7627	2.4352	1.2115	8.1936	1.2449	44.00	110.11	10.894	1,023.75	7.4710	1.2459	1.8204
2006	.7535	2.1738	1.1340	7.9723	1.2563	45.19	116.31	10.906	954.32	7.3718	1.2532	1.8434
2007	.8391	1.9461	1.0734	7.6058	1.3711	41.18	117.76	10.928	928.97	6.7550	1.1999	2.0020
2008	.8537	1.8326	1.0660	6.9477	1.4726	43.39	103.39	11.143	1,098.71	6.5846	1.0816	1.8545
2009	.7927	1.9976	1.1412	6.8307	1.3935	48.33	93.68	13.498	1,274.63	7.6539	1.0860	1.5661
2010	.9200	1.7600	1.0298	6.7696	1.3261	45.65	87.78	12.624	1,155.74	7.2053	1.0432	1.5452
2011	1.0332	1.6723	.9887	6.4630	1.3931	46.58	79.70	12.427	1,106.94	6.4878	.8862	1.6043
2012	1.0359	1.9535	.9995	6.3093	1.2859	53.37	79.82	13.154	1,126.16	6.7721	.9377	1.5853
2013	.9683	2.1570	1.0300	6.1478	1.3281	58.51	97.60	12.758	1,094.67	6.5124	.9269	1.5642
2014	.9034	2.3512	1.1043	6.1620	1.3297	61.00	105.74	13.302	1,052.29	6.8576	.9147	1.6484
2015	.7522	3.3360	1.2791	6.2827	1.1096	64.11	121.05	15.874	1,130.96	8.4350	.9628	1.5284
2016	.7445	3.4839	1.3243	6.6400	1.1072	67.16	108.66	18.667	1,159.34	8.5541	.9848	1.3555
2017	.7671	3.1910	1.2984	6.7569	1.1301	65.07	112.10	18.884	1,129.04	8.5430	.9842	1.2890
2018	.7481	3.6513	1.2957	6.6090	1.1817	68.37	110.40	19.218	1,099.29	8.6945	.9784	1.3363
2017: I	.7586	3.1402	1.3237	6.8853	1.0661	66.87	113.52	20.255	1,150.02	8.9198	1.0032	1.2399
II	.7510	3.2152	1.3446	6.8586	1.1008	64.47	111.11	18.548	1,129.92	8.8025	.9847	1.2798
III	.7899	3.1593	1.2530	6.6684	1.1755	64.27	110.95	17.811	1,131.16	8.1329	.9629	1.3089
IV	.7687	3.2491	1.2715	6.6131	1.1778	64.71	112.89	18.974	1,104.96	8.3175	.9868	1.3273
2018: I	.7859	3.2474	1.2656	6.3535	1.2289	64.38	108.27	18.717	1,071.10	8.1182	.9484	1.3920
II	.7568	3.6043	1.2907	6.3772	1.1922	67.00	109.14	19.412	1,079.64	8.6733	.9854	1.3612
III	.7315	3.9492	1.3070	6.8053	1.1629	70.11	111.50	18.945	1,120.84	8.9482	.9843	1.3030
IV	.7174	3.8061	1.3201	6.9143	1.1414	72.13	112.77	19.816	1,126.77	9.0460	.9957	1.2870

	Trade-weighted value of the U.S. dollar					
	Nominal			Real[6]		
	Broad index (January 2006=100)[3]	Advanced foreign economies index (January 2006=100)[4]	Emerging market economies index (January 2006=100)[5]	Broad index (January 2006=100)[3]	Advanced foreign economies index (January 2006=100)[4]	Emerging market economies index (January 2006=100)[5]
2000	...	...	...	...	...	...
2001	...	...	...	...	...	...
2002	...	...	...	...	...	...
2003	...	...	...	...	...	...
2004	...	...	...	...	...	...
2005	...	...	...	...	...	...
2006	98.6180	95.9714	99.8070	98.9402	98.3178	99.7562
2007	93.8431	90.4796	96.1330	94.2867	93.6310	95.1426
2008	90.8882	86.8919	94.1320	90.9832	90.8429	91.2060
2009	96.7742	91.1579	102.0238	95.3306	94.7051	96.1058
2010	93.0696	88.5236	97.2219	90.7766	92.0125	89.5961
2011	88.8310	83.3260	94.0635	86.2804	87.3149	85.2818
2012	91.6426	86.4375	96.5637	88.4827	90.8405	86.1746
2013	92.7779	89.0205	96.1026	88.7777	93.8352	83.9814
2014	95.6108	91.7259	99.0021	90.7991	97.0042	85.0028
2015	108.1046	106.2262	109.4944	101.2526	111.8230	91.7986
2016	113.1535	107.4023	118.2744	105.4676	113.9821	97.6114
2017	112.8357	106.9800	118.1568	104.9129	114.1351	96.4965
2018	112.0443	104.5312	119.1041	104.0657	112.2009	96.5207
2017: I	114.8194	110.7712	120.4457	108.6358	118.0443	100.0331
II	112.2865	109.1314	116.9725	105.7975	116.2253	96.4225
III	108.3938	103.6723	114.6228	102.0967	110.6292	94.2530
IV	109.4182	104.3478	116.0207	103.1217	111.6416	95.2773
2018: I	106.5139	101.1235	113.4157	100.5081	108.3846	93.2050
II	109.0914	103.6642	116.0625	103.0115	111.3112	95.3444
III	112.1177	105.9362	119.9192	105.4847	113.6095	97.9346
IV	114.1331	107.4535	122.4839	107.2587	115.4982	99.5989

[1] U.S. dollars per foreign currency unit.
[2] European Economic and Monetary Union (EMU) members consists of Austria, Belgium, Cyprus (beginning in 2008), Estonia (beginning in 2011), Finland, France, Germany, Greece (beginning in 2001), Ireland, Italy, Luxembourg, Malta (beginning in 2008), Netherlands, Portugal, Slovakia (beginning in 2009), Slovenia (beginning in 2007), and Spain.
[3] Weighted average of the foreign exchange value of the U.S. dollar against the currencies of a broad group of major U.S. trading partners.
[4] Subset of the broad index. Consists of currencies of the Euro area, Australia, Canada, Japan, Sweden, Switzerland, and the United Kingdom.
[5] Subset of the broad index currencies that are emerging market economies. For details, see *Revisions to the Federal Reserve Dollar Indexes*, January 2019.
[6] Adjusted for changes in consumer price indexes for the United States and other countries.

Source: Board of Governors of the Federal Reserve System.

TABLE B-61. Growth rates in real gross domestic product by area and country, 2000-2019

[Percent change]

Area and country	2000-2009 annual average	2010	2011	2012	2013	2014	2015	2016	2017	2018[1]	2019[1]
World	3.9	5.4	4.3	3.5	3.5	3.6	3.5	3.3	3.8	3.7	3.5
Advanced economies	1.8	3.1	1.7	1.2	1.4	2.1	2.3	1.7	2.4	2.3	2.0
Of which:											
United States	1.9	2.6	1.6	2.2	1.8	2.5	2.9	1.6	2.2	2.9	2.5
Euro area[2]	1.4	2.1	1.6	-.9	-.2	1.4	2.1	1.9	2.4	1.8	1.6
Germany	0.8	3.9	3.7	.7	.6	2.2	1.5	2.2	2.5	1.5	1.3
France	1.4	1.9	2.2	.3	.6	1.0	1.0	1.1	2.3	1.5	1.5
Italy	0.5	1.7	.6	-2.8	-1.7	.1	1.0	.9	1.6	1.0	.6
Spain	2.7	.0	-1.0	-2.9	-1.7	1.4	3.6	3.2	3.0	2.5	2.2
Japan	0.5	4.2	-.1	1.5	2.0	.4	1.4	1.0	1.9	.9	1.1
United Kingdom	1.8	1.7	1.6	1.4	2.0	2.9	2.3	1.8	1.8	1.4	1.5
Canada	2.1	3.1	3.1	1.7	2.5	2.9	1.0	1.4	3.0	2.1	1.9
Other advanced economies	3.4	5.9	3.4	2.2	2.4	2.9	2.2	2.3	2.8	2.8	2.5
Emerging market and developing economies	6.1	7.4	6.4	5.3	5.1	4.7	4.3	4.4	4.7	4.6	4.5
Regional groups:											
Commonwealth of Independent States[3]	5.9	4.6	5.3	3.7	2.5	1.1	-1.9	.4	2.1	2.4	2.2
Russia	5.4	4.5	5.1	3.7	1.8	.7	-2.5	-.2	1.5	1.7	1.6
Excluding Russia	7.5	5.0	6.0	3.6	4.2	1.9	-.6	2.0	3.6	3.9	3.7
Emerging and Developing Asia	8.1	9.6	7.9	7.0	6.9	6.8	6.8	6.5	6.5	6.5	6.3
China	10.3	10.6	9.5	7.9	7.8	7.3	6.9	6.7	6.9	6.6	6.2
India[4]	6.9	10.3	6.6	5.5	6.4	7.4	8.2	7.1	6.7	7.3	7.5
ASEAN-5[5]	5.0	6.9	4.7	6.2	5.1	4.6	4.9	4.9	5.3	5.2	5.1
Emerging and Developing Europe	4.0	4.3	6.6	2.5	4.9	3.9	4.7	3.3	6.0	3.8	.7
Latin America and the Caribbean	3.0	6.1	4.6	2.9	2.9	1.3	.3	-.6	1.3	1.1	2.0
Brazil	3.4	7.5	4.0	1.9	3.0	.5	-3.5	-3.5	1.1	1.3	2.5
Mexico	1.4	5.1	3.7	3.6	1.4	2.8	3.3	2.9	2.1	2.1	2.1
Middle East, North Africa, Afghanistan, and Pakistan	5.2	4.6	4.4	4.8	2.6	2.9	2.5	5.1	2.2	2.4	2.4
Saudi Arabia	3.4	5.0	10.0	5.4	2.7	3.7	4.1	1.7	-.9	2.3	1.8
Sub-Saharan Africa	5.6	7.1	5.1	4.6	5.2	5.1	3.3	1.4	2.9	2.9	3.5
Nigeria	8.3	11.3	4.9	4.3	5.4	6.3	2.7	-1.6	.8	1.9	2.0
South Africa	3.6	3.0	3.3	2.2	2.5	1.8	1.3	.6	1.3	.8	1.4

[1] All figures are forecasts as published by the International Monetary Fund. For the United States, initial estimates by the Department of Commerce show that real GDP rose 2.9 percent in 2018.
[2] For 2019, includes data for: Austria, Belgium, Cyprus, Estonia, Finland, France, Germany, Greece, Ireland, Italy, Latvia, Lithuania, Luxembourg, Malta, Netherlands, Portugal, Slovak Republic, Slovenia, and Spain.
[3] Includes Georgia, Turkmenistan, and Ukraine, which are not members of the Commonwealth of Independent States but are included for reasons of geography and similarity in economic structure.
[4] Data and forecasts are presented on a fiscal year basis and output growth is based on GDP at market prices.
[5] Consists of Indonesia, Malaysia, Philippines, Thailand, and Vietnam.

Note: For details on data shown in this table, see *World Economic Outlook*, October 2018, and *World Economic Outlook Update*, January 2019, published by the International Monetary Fund.

Sources: International Monetary Fund and Department of Commerce (Bureau of Economic Analysis).

www.ingramcontent.com/pod-product-compliance
Lightning Source LLC
Chambersburg PA
CBHW080913170526
45158CB00008B/2089